UNION AND LIBERTY

John C. Calhoun

UNION AND LIBERTY

The Political Philosophy of John C. Calhoun

BY JOHN C. CALHOUN

Edited by

ROSS M. LENCE

Liberty Fund
Indianapolis

The cuneiform inscription that serves as our logo and as the design motif for
our endpapers is the earliest-known written appearance of the word
"freedom" (*amagi*), or "liberty." It is taken from a clay document written
about 2300 B.C. in the Sumerian city-state of Lagash.

Frontispiece photo from the Gibbes Museum of Art/Carolina Art
Association, Charleston, South Carolina. Oil on canvas by Rembrandt
Peale. Jacket and cover illustrations: South Carolina State House
(*Harper's Weekly*, August 17, 1861); Capitol, 1839 (P. Lee Phillips,
The Beginnings of Washington, 1917); letter of John C. Calhoun, June 18, 1822
(William M. Meigs, *The Life of John Caldwell Calhoun*, vol. 1, 1917).

Library of Congress Cataloging-in-Publication Data
Calhoun, John C. (John Caldwell), 1782–1850.
Union and liberty : the political philosophy of John C. Calhoun /
by John C. Calhoun : edited by Ross M. Lence.

p.   cm.

Includes bibliographical references and index.
ISBN 0-86597-102-1 (alk. paper).—
ISBN 0-86597-103-X (pbk. : alk. paper)
1. United States—Politics and government—1815–1861.
I. Lence, Ross M., 1943–   .   II. Title.
E337.8.C142   1992   92-10391
320.973—dc20   CIP

C   10   9   8   7   6   5   4   3
P   10   9   8   7   6

CONTENTS

FOREWORD

Much time and energy has been devoted to the rise of American constitutionalism and the nature of the American Union in the eighteenth century. Far less attention has been paid to the interpretation and implementation of the U.S. Constitution during the nineteenth century. Faced with largely unanticipated problems attendant upon economic change, a major influx of new people, and westward expansion, the generation of Daniel Webster, Henry Clay, and John C. Calhoun struggled to sustain what was commonly believed to have been the original intention of the framers. In the absence of an appreciation of the work of those prodigious thinkers of the nineteenth century, no real understanding of the American constitutional tradition is possible.

John C. Calhoun stands out among the leading figures of this era renowned for its great orators and public statesmen. He and the others of this new generation found themselves in a period marked by an increasing degree of uncertainty about the future. Continual controversy over such constitutional issues as executive prerogative, the extent of federal, or state, power, the proper disposition of suffrage, and the need to protect minority rights against the dangers of majority tyranny did little to assuage their apprehension. Added to this uncertainty was the momentous question of defining the nature of the American Union, a seemingly unresolved conundrum exacerbated by repeated congressional

failures after 1819 to administer the admission of new states to the satisfaction of all parties. Thus was there an urgency that suffused Calhoun's
speeches, letters, and philosophical writings. Along with many of his contemporaries, north and south, he realized the fragility of the American
experiment and the importance of his own agency in the development of
constitutional government.

A mere enumeration of his political offices is sufficient to establish his
national stature during this critical early period. After serving briefly in the
South Carolina legislature, Calhoun was elected to the U.S. House of
Representatives in 1810. He served as secretary of war under President
Monroe from 1817 to 1825; as vice-president under John Quincy Adams
and then Andrew Jackson from 1825 to 1832; as senator from South
Carolina from 1832 to 1844; as secretary of state under John Tyler from
1844 to 1845; and again as a member of the Senate from 1845 until his
death in 1850. He was first nominated for president in 1821—at the age
of thirty-nine—and was considered a serious candidate for that office in
every election from 1824 until 1848.

Calhoun's larger substantive and philosophical contributions to American constitutional thought have been in large measure a casualty of history.
The lingering doubts and haunting images of the Civil War, compounded
by Calhoun's defense of slavery and his unwavering commitment to the
doctrine of State Rights, have distracted historians and political scientists
from serious consideration of his ideas.

Calhoun's political and philosophical thought evolved over a forty-
year period of public office. The combination of practical politics and a
noted preference for metaphysical discourse gave his speeches and
writings a distinct tone. In general language he sought political solutions
designed to alleviate the tensions under which the American system
labored. His systematic theory about the nature of man and government, as well as his rigorous analysis of the presumptions and convictions of *The Federalist Papers*, deserves careful attention for his part in
the ongoing discussion of the uneasy, but critical, relationship between
liberty and union.

John Caldwell Calhoun was born to pioneer parents on March 18, 1782. Over a period covering two generations, the family, part of the Scots-Irish immigration into Pennsylvania during the first third of the eighteenth century, was drawn to the western frontier of South Carolina. His father had defended America's decision to renounce the King, fought the local battle to increase the representation of his up-country section of South Carolina against the tidewater minority that controlled the state legislature, and cast a vote against the ratification of the U.S. Constitution. From Calhoun's earliest days, then, he encountered the real-life dynamics of democratic politics—the struggle between the majority and the minority over the distribution of the rewards and burdens of government.

His education in New England provided the intellectual seeds for his subsequent development of a theory of nullification and secession. In 1802, at the age of twenty, Calhoun entered Yale University as a junior. Small-town, localist, antinational sentiment, combined with skepticism of numerical majorities, was then popular in certain parts of New England. Yale University had become the intellectual center for these ideas since the defeat of the Federalists in the election of 1800. Among the most noted of the New England Federalists was Timothy Dwight, the president of Yale College, one of the most influential men in Calhoun's education. After graduating Phi Beta Kappa from Yale in 1804, Calhoun studied law in Litchfield, Connecticut. Among the faculty with whom Calhoun studied at Litchfield were Judge Tapping Reeve (Aaron Burr's brother-in-law) and Judge James Gould. These two staunch Federalists reinforced Timothy Dwight's condemnation of the Jeffersonian majority.

Despite his exposure to these ideas, during his tenure in the House of Representatives from 1811 to 1817 as a representative of South Carolina, Calhoun was an ardent nationalist: He was more concerned about national strength and unity than about curbing majorities to protect intense minority interests. As a member of the Foreign Relations Committee of the House of Representatives, Calhoun was a vocal supporter of the War of 1812. He did not waver in his commitment to a strong foreign policy, even in the

face of bitter protests from the New England states, which claimed that the
Jeffersonian embargo and the War of 1812 were inequitably ruinous to
their commerce and shipping interests. Throughout the early years of his
career, he consistently favored extensive federal assistance for internal
improvements in an effort to encourage domestic commerce and farming.
And most noted of all, he supported the tariff of 1816 as a temporary
measure to raise the money necessary to eliminate the national debt incurred during the War of 1812 and to protect America's fledgling indus-
tries. The issue of the tariff was to become a much more incendiary issue
in the years to come.

Calhoun's views coincided with many opinions prevalent in the nation in
the early 1820s. This harmony combined with his political talents so well
that some people began to advance his name as a possible candidate for
president. In the presidential campaign of 1824, he decided to limit his
obvious ambitions for the time being and settled into the vice-presidency
under the administration of John Quincy Adams. From the very beginning,
their relationship was a troubled one. Personalities were at odds; political
ambitions clashed. When serious wrangling erupted between Adams and
Calhoun (who as vice-president was also the presiding officer of the Senate) over the respective powers of the executive and the legislature, the
controversy spilled over into a series of public letters. In his six letters,
Calhoun argued against the prerogatives claimed by Adams. He declared
that republican government required the diffusion of political power. Liberty would be sacrificed if Americans allowed the abuse of presidential
patronage that was threatening to destroy the delicate balance between
liberty and power established by the Constitution.

At the same time, the tariff issue was looming ever larger in the ongoing
debate in the United States about the locus of political power, significantly
exacerbating smoldering sectional confrontations within the young Union.
Many Southerners, in particular, thought the tariff had stopped being a
means of raising revenue for national defense and was becoming a permanent means of protecting and subsidizing manufacturing interests at the

expense of the South and agricultural interests. The tariff issue strained Calhoun's nationalist sentiments. His own state and southern predilections, the agitation of supporters and friends in the South, as well as his concern about balancing sectional interests, led Calhoun to change his earlier nationalist support for the tariff and embrace the South Carolina position on this matter.

This issue became an important practical and symbolic matter when an exceptionally high tariff was proposed in Congress early in 1828. The proposed tariff was seen by many as a political maneuver by opponents intended to turn popular sentiment against Adams and the tariff. Much to the dismay of the Southern strategists, their schemes to defeat the tariff came to naught. President Adams approved the bill, which became widely known as the Tariff of Abominations. Calhoun found himself in the dilemma of privately opposing a measure supported by the administration he was a part of. Even more troubling to him, opponents in the South, and especially in South Carolina, now began to debate openly the prospect of disunion.

Seeking a means by which such a desperate response could be avoided, Calhoun turned to the doctrine of interposition, which defended the right of a state to interpose its authority and overrule federal legislation. The seeds of this doctrine were introduced by Thomas Jefferson and James Madison in the Kentucky and Virginia Resolutions of 1798 and 1799. Calhoun first advanced it anonymously, in the South Carolina Exposition and Protest, penned during the summer and fall of 1828 for a committee of the South Carolina legislature. It is Calhoun's articulation and development of the doctrine of interposition or nullification for which he was, and is, so well known.

When Andrew Jackson was elected president in November 1828, Calhoun remained as vice-president. He had played an instrumental role in forging the alliance of Westerners, Southerners, and anti-Adams forces in the Northeast to elect the new president. Calhoun was suspicious of the political aspirations of many of the supporters of his new political ally.

Nevertheless, as vice-president in the new administration, he hoped to influence Jackson's policies. His experience with Jackson, however, proved even less successful than his experience with John Quincy Adams had been.

Calhoun's efforts to defuse sectional tension and controversy within a constitutional framework met with little success. The divisions over the tariff and protectionism were intractable. The ultimate logic of his own doctrine of nullification, secession, was taken up as a solution by many in the South. After the election of Jackson and Calhoun, the South Carolina legislature had circulated the Exposition widely. Calhoun's hand in writing the document was widely speculated. In an effort to prevent further alienation of the Northern states and to exhume his possible candidacy for president, Calhoun attempted a public clarification of his position in his 1831 Fort Hill Address. His measured words were noted by virtually everyone. By the closing months of 1832, Calhoun's responsibility for the drafting of the South Carolina Exposition and Protest had become common knowledge. Now it was evident for all to see that the reintroduction of the doctrine of nullification—the right of a single state to negate the laws of the federal government within its jurisdiction—was the work of none other than the Vice-President of the United States.

Throughout this turbulent period, Calhoun was increasingly called upon to defend the South's peculiar institution—slavery—which came progressively to the fore as a defining characteristic of the South and became connected to the debate over states' rights. With one notable exception, Calhoun's remarks concerning this subject were always couched in the general language of history, economics, and philosophy. That one exception is his 1837 address to the Senate in which he goes so far as to declare slavery "a positive good"—a statement which he immediately protested was taken out of context. Calhoun's own inner thoughts on slavery may never be known with certainty, for the ravages of civil war and the fate of the Southern cause have only compounded the engima of how a free people could endorse and defend that pernicious institution.

Calhoun resigned his office as vice-president in December 1832 and took a seat as a senator from South Carolina, which he held until 1844. The brilliance of his mind and the power of his rhetoric made him the natural and unchallenged spokesman for South Carolina and many elements in the South. This was especially apparent in his speech on the Revenue Collection Bill, commonly known as the Force Bill, in February 1833. In this speech, which spanned two days, he argued that recourse to violence to compel obedience to the dictates of the federal government could never be constitutional or legitimate, even if undertaken to preserve the union.

Calhoun's rhetorical strengths in arguing the Southern cause and his opposition to Jackson diminished his national stature. In the succeeding years he gradually regained his standing and was appointed secretary of state by President John Tyler in 1844. He remained firm in his commitment to a national union of states and continued to worry that Southern states would become a minority in the Congress. As secretary of state, he advocated the annexation of Texas as a means of balancing the South and the expanding North. He exerted his efforts on behalf of the Union in its dispute with Great Britain over the territory that later became Oregon.

Upon Polk's election as president in 1845, Calhoun reentered the Senate, where he continued to be active until his death. He used his position as senator to assail the highly popular Mexican-American War. He attempted to develop various public projects in South Carolina and for the South generally, including plans for a railroad connecting the South and the West. Much of his energy in his last years was devoted to writing what was to become the *Disquisition* and the *Discourse*.

On March 4, 1850, a sick and frail Calhoun sat in the Senate and watched as a colleague read what was to be his last major address. He was too weak to deliver it himself. In his prepared text, an obviously despondent Calhoun opposed the admission of California as a free state. Little more could be done, he heard Senator Mason say for him; compromise was no longer possible. This pessimistic speech was his final contribution

to the larger debate on the nature of Union and the relations of the North
and the South. Within the month, on March 31, 1850, Calhoun died in
Washington, D.C.

Although aware of the limited capability of reasoned discourse to resolve
the tensions and centrifugal forces of nineteenth century America, Calhoun
turned increasingly in the last few years of his life to questions of philosophy. He devoted his time and energy to the writing of *A Disquisition on
Government* and *A Discourse on the Constitution and Government of the
United States,* which were completed just before his death.

They are complementary texts: The practical American political experience as advanced in the lengthy *Discourse* makes sense only in the context
of the political theory articulated and developed in the less voluminous
Disquisition. The *Disquisition* expounds his doctrine of the concurrent majority—the right of significant interests to have a veto over either the
enactment or the implementation of a public law—and discusses historical
instances in which it had worked. The *Discourse* traces the constitutional
foundation for the concurrent majority in the American political tradition
and argues for its restoration as the only means to resolve the constitutional and political crisis facing the Union. Both works reveal a philosopher
whose preference for metaphysical discourse is unmistakable. Both works
reveal a seasoned politician who had been an active participant in the
nineteenth century politics of nationalism, sectionalism, and secession.
Reading these two works together, one cannot help but sense that this man
understood the impending crisis all too well.

While Calhoun's *Disquisition* usually is viewed as an elaborate defense
of his doctrine of the concurrent majority, it is also a deep look at the
nature of man and government. It begins with the nature of society and the
nature of the consent of the governed. Calhoun tries to develop a view of
government that avoids the pitfalls he experienced in the U.S. Constitution.
Beneath the surface of his treatise is a systematic analysis and critique of
the founding principles as set forth by Alexander Hamilton, James Madi-

son, and John Jay in *The Federalist Papers*. The *Disquisition* explicitly rejects several of the fundamental maxims advanced by Publius, including the presumption that governmental institutions can be a product of reflection and choice, rather than accident and force (Federalist #1), the theory of the extended, compound republic (Federalist #10), the doctrine of the numerical majority (Federalist #22), and the theory of limiting governmental power through the separation of powers (Federalist #51). In essence, Calhoun suggests that the theory of *The Federalist Papers* makes inadequate safeguards for the maintenance of limited government. In the absence of such provisions, Publius's extended republic not only fails to prevent majority tyranny, but actually encourages it by allowing a numerical majority to make laws on any subject it declares to be the legitimate business of government. Given the nature of man, argues Calhoun, it is not long before such majorities become overbearing: They begin to enact laws to their own advantage and to the disadvantage and abuse of minority interests.

Calhoun's *Discourse* clearly places the arguments of the *Disquisition* within the context of the American political tradition. Calhoun elaborates upon his discussion of the concepts of limited government, separation of powers, judicial review, and the theory of the extended, compound republic. He provides a rigorous analysis of virtually all of the major individuals, events, and documents of the founding and subsequent development of the federal government. He offers a detailed critique of Federalist #39, accusing the celebrated Publius of duplicity and deceit. He challenges the doctrine of judicial review expounded in Federalist #78, arguing that this extra-constitutional practice is incompatible with true federalist principles. He calls for the restoration of the concurrent majority through the operation of the amendment process provided for in the U.S. Constitution. In short, the *Discourse* offers a critique of the major presumptions and convictions upon which the American political order was founded, including consent of the governed, equality, liberty, community, public virtue and private vice, reflection and choice, accident and force. In Calhoun's *Discourse*, each of these receives a bold, precise reformulation.

Calhoun's extended discussion of liberty and union turns on his doctrine of the concurrent majority. Who will be entrusted with the veto power? Who will decide, and on what desiderata, which groups are significant enough to be given a veto or a negative power over the making or executing of the laws? When would this power be exercised? What would prevent these vested groups from favoring the status quo and limiting the progress and development of society? In a Union such as the United States, would the several states exercise the veto power of the concurrent majority? If Calhoun intended the states to exercise such a power, why did he not say so explicitly? On what grounds could one argue that the states constitute organic units, while the federal government does not? How would the rights of a minority within each state be protected against an overbearing majority within that state? Why would a numerical minority in each state not be subject to the whims of an overbearing numerical majority in that state? If the rights of the individual constitute the ultimate test of minority rights, how can a concurrent majority system, which vests power in a few, great interests, be an adequate safeguard for the rights of the individual in society? Questions like these, and many others raised by Calhoun in his *Disquisition* and *Discourse*, represent a legacy of continuing relevance in the ongoing debate in American constitutional thought.

In the present volume, every effort has been made to present as representative a picture of Calhoun's political and philosophical thought as is possible within the confines of a single volume covering Calhoun's some forty years of public service. All selections are complete and unabridged. The reasons for including the *Disquisition* and *Discourse* are obvious. In addition to these larger works, this volume includes twelve speeches, letters, or political essays taken from the literally thousands of pages of Calhoun's speeches and writings. The documents which follow the *Disquisition* and *Discourse* proceed in chronological order. The "Speech on the Resolution of the Committee on Foreign Relations" was Calhoun's first major address to the U.S. House of Representatives and establishes his early credentials as an ardent nationalist. This nationalist theme can also be seen in his 1816 "Speech on the Tariff Bill." For more about the nature and scope of Calhoun's nationalism, the reader may consult his "Speech on United States Bill . . . February 26, 1816" and his "Speech on the Internal Improvement Bill . . . February 4, 1817," not reprinted here.

Following these speeches from Calhoun's days in the House of Representatives, this volume focuses upon three of Calhoun's statements on the great controversy over the tariff, which was triggered by the Tariff of Abominations and culminated in the South Carolina Ordinance of Nullification, the Compromise Tariff of 1833, and President Jackson's Force Bill. The "Exposition and Protest," drafted by Calhoun and promulgated by the South Carolina legislature, articulates the right of the several states to interpose their authority between the federal government and the people of the states. Calhoun's public remarks on the doctrine of interposition are found in his "Address on the Relations of the States and the Federal Government," more commonly known as the "Fort Hill Address." The "Speech on the Revenue Collection [Force] Bill" rigorously applies the principles of the Fort Hill Address to the particular issue of the tariff. Few, if any, of Calhoun's speeches can rival his remarks on the Force Bill for clarity and powers of rhetoric. The language is direct; the style provocative and bold; the analysis rigorous and precise. Those interested in pursuing in greater detail Calhoun's position on interposition, nullification, and the tariff should also consult his rather lengthy letter to General Hamilton not reproduced here.

The next document, Calhoun's 1837 "Speech on the Reception of Abolition Petitions," focuses on one of the most controversial issues of Calhoun's political career, his defense of slavery. Because Calhoun's reputation is so often linked to his remarks on this subject, both the first report and the revised report have been included here.

The highly volatile issue of the national bank is addressed in the "Edgefield Letter." Although this letter is not, strictly speaking, a public address or speech, it received such widespread, public circulation that it seems appropriate to include it in a volume of this nature. This letter offers us the additional advantage of being able to hear, in a very few pages, Calhoun's own justification for his return to the ranks of the Democratic Party and his defense against the charges of political inconsistency on the question of a national bank.

The remaining five speeches in this volume focus on those issues and concerns that came to dominate the conversation between the North and the South in the critical years from 1840 to 1850. All of the elements of that conversation are in place: the tyranny of a numerical majority and the abuse of legislative power ("Speech on the Veto Power"); the nature of compromise in the foundation of constitutional government and in the doctrine of the concurrent majority ("Speech on the Introduction of His Resolutions on the Slave Question"); the need for a Southern party to counteract the corruptive nature of partisan politics ("Speech at the Meeting of the Citizens of Charleston"); the inevitable conflict between liberty and equality ("Speech on the Oregon Bill"); and Calhoun's final assessment of the nature and limits of the Union and the requisites for its preservation ("Speech on the Admission of California—and the General State of the Union"). These five documents also allow us a unique opportunity to see Calhoun's political and philosophical arguments in the years preceding their final articulation in the *Disquisition* and the *Discourse*.

The question arises at this point as to whether it is better to begin one's reading of Calhoun in chronological order, so as to trace the development of his thinking, or whether it is better to begin with the *Disquisition* and *Discourse*, which reveal the philosophical commitments and beliefs on which Calhoun's political discourse and action are founded. Obviously the two approaches are inextricably tied: There can be no real grasp of the development of Calhoun's political philosophy without an understanding of the historical development of nineteenth century America, and no real grasp of Calhoun's political experience in the absence of an understanding of his general theory of government and society. The fact that the *Disquisition* and the *Discourse* are placed at the beginning of this volume is not meant to settle the question of what is the best approach to Calhoun's works.

The noted biographer of Calhoun, Charles M. Wiltse, best summarized the dramatic and controversy-ridden image of John C. Calhoun that prevailed in his time and still does in ours when he observed that the "Senate, the Congress, and the country itself" were "divided over the character and motives of one man."

> There was no middle ground, no compromise, no no-man's land. He attracted, or repelled; he convinced, or he antagonized; he was loved, or he was hated. He was the pure and unsullied patriot, ready to sacrifice position, honors, life itself for the liberties of his country; or he was the very image of Lucifer—the archangel fallen, damned forever to the bottomless pit by his own overmastering ambition. Toward Calhoun indifference was impossible.*

The power of Calhoun's eloquence is undeniable. He had an enormous political influence in the period immediately following the founding of the American system. He understood liberty; he ardently defended it; and he spoke of it in a language and within a culture that are genuinely American. The defense of minority rights against the abuse of an overbearing majority, the cause to which he untiringly devoted himself, has rejoined constitutional discourse as a tenet of contemporary American politics. Rising like a phoenix from the ashes of neglect, John Caldwell Calhoun calls upon us to renew our inquiry into the founding principles of the American system of government.

Ross M. Lence
University of Houston

---

*Charles M. Wiltse, *John C. Calhoun: Nullifier, 1829–1839* (Indianapolis, 1949), p. 178.

EDITOR'S NOTE

Many of the documents reprinted in this volume (including Calhoun's *A Discourse on the Constitution and Government of the United States*) have not been available to the general reader since the initial publication of Richard K. Crallé's six-volume *Works of John C. Calhoun* in 1851–1856. For some fifty years following the publication of Crallé's *Works*, these volumes remained the only source of primary Calhoun materials. In 1900, Calhoun scholarship was renewed when J. Franklin Jameson published a selected edition of Calhoun's correspondence as the fourth annual report of the Historical Manuscripts Commission under the title *Correspondence of John C. Calhoun* (Washington, D.C., 1900). A second volume of Calhoun's correspondence appeared some thirty years later under the editorship of Chauncey S. Boucher and Robert P. Brooks entitled *Correspondence Addressed to John C. Calhoun, 1837–1849: Sixteenth Report of the Historical Manuscripts Commission* (Washington, D.C., 1930). Probably the most circulated of Calhoun's works was his *A Disquisition on Government*, which appeared in two separate editions: John M. Anderson's *Calhoun: Basic Documents* (Bald Eagle Press, 1952) and C. Gordon Post's *A Disquisition on Government and Selections from the Discourse* (Bobbs-Merrill, 1953).

At the present time, the University of South Carolina is engaged in a massive effort to reproduce the entire corpus of Calhoun's works. That collection, entitled *The Papers of John C. Calhoun* (Columbia, S.C., 1959–), under the able editorship of W. Edwin Hemphill, Robert L. Merlwether, and

Clyde Wilson, is expected to take several more years to complete. To date, twenty volumes of Calhoun's works have been published by the University of South Carolina Press, covering the period of Calhoun's political life through December 1844. When that project is completed, it will represent the single most comprehensive source of Calhoun scholarship, bringing together literally thousands of documents and writings of John Calhoun.

NOTE ON SOURCES

The primary source of Calhoun's political essays, speeches, and letters that appear in this volume is the *Works of John C. Calhoun* (New York, 1851–1856), edited by Calhoun's friend and confidant, Richard K. Crallé. Whenever possible, the text of Crallé has been carefully compared to other printed copies of the speeches and writings of Calhoun. The primary bases of comparison were the *Annals of Congress* (a report of the congressional proceedings of the 1st through 12th Congress compiled by Gales and Seaton from newspapers, magazines, and other sources), the *Register of Debates* (a direct report of the congressional proceedings from 1824 to 1837 published by Gales and Seaton), and *The Congressional Globe* (a report of the 23rd through 42nd Congress published by Blair and Rives; F. and J. Rives; F. and J. Rives and George A. Bailey).

There are many reasons for using Crallé's *Works* as the primary text, not the least of which is that Crallé had available to him many manuscripts which are no longer extant. Furthermore, a rigorous comparison of Crallé's text with contemporary reports of Calhoun's remarks seems to confirm Crallé's claim in his advertisement to the first volume of his *Works* that in it is reprinted, with very few exceptions, "the Work . . . as it came from the hands of the author." In those few instances where Crallé seems to alter the text of Calhoun's remarks, for whatever reason, the changes in the text were always minor. Upon reflection, I could find no justification for substituting my own interpretation of the passages in question for those of Crallé, and such a practice would deny Crallé's text its rightful place in the history of Calhoun scholarship.

Those familiar with the *Annals of Congress,* the *Register of Debates,* and *The Congressional Globe* (all forerunners of the *Congressional Record,* which first made its appearance on December 1, 1873) are cognizant of the enormous variance in both the style and language of the speeches reported. Indeed, that variance is evident in the two versions of Calhoun's remarks in his "Speech on the Reception of Abolition Petitions" reprinted in this volume, and in the third-person presentation of some of his speeches. Much of the variance is due to editorial practices of the newspapers of the day, rather than to the vagaries of Calhoun's speech and thought. Calhoun hardly ever reviewed or revised his remarks owing to the press of daily business, and he had almost no concern for questions of style per se.

Again, Crallé's remarks in his advertisement to the first volume of his *Works* are instructive:

> In preparing the manuscripts for the press, the editor has sedulously endeavored to preserve, not only the peculiar modes of expression, but the very words of the author—without regard to ornaments of style or rules of criticism. They who knew him well, need not to be told that, to these, he paid but slight respect. Absorbed by his subject, and earnest in his efforts to present the truth to others, as it appeared to himself, he regarded neither the arts nor the ornaments of meretricious elocution. He wrote as he spoke, sometimes negligently, yet always plainly and forcibly, and it is due to his own character, as well as to the public expectation, that his views should be presented in the plain and simple garb in which he left them.

My general editorial procedure has been, in short, to keep as close as possible to the text of Crallé. Indeed, every effort has been made to be as nonintrusive as possible. Like Crallé, however, I have sometimes found it necessary to correct for minor typographical errors and punctuation, especially where a careful reading of the speeches as reported in other sources suggests that Calhoun intended a different emphasis to these remarks. In no instance have any changes been made without at least one or more primary documents to support such an alteration.

In the few cases where Crallé does not include the entire speech or address, another source was used:

> The first two paragraphs of the Fort Hill Address are taken from *Niles Weekly Register,* Vol. XL, no. 25 (August 20, 1831).

> The First Report of the Speech on the Reception of Abolition Petitions is taken from the *Register of Debates,* 24th Congress, 2nd Sess., Cols. 710–719.

> The Edgefield Letter is taken from the *Niles National Register,* Vol. LIII, no. 14 (December 2, 1837), pp. 217–218.

> The words Calhoun used when introducing Mr. Mason, who read the Speech on the Admission of California and the General State of the Union, are taken from *The Congressional Globe,* Washington, D.C., March 4, 1850, p. 541.

The reader will find within the text occasional commentary describing the reading of resolutions, remarks by other speakers, and other events that occurred during Calhoun's speeches. These explanatory remarks, which often are in brackets, are contained in the version of the speech reproduced in this edition. (The one exception is the First Report on the Reception of Abolition Petitions, as indicated there.)

Acknowledgments

Among the greatest sins in the world must be those of pettiness and ingratitude. I sincerely hope that I am guilty of neither of these in the production of this volume. I would like to thank the late Professor Charles S. Hyneman, Distinguished Service Professor of Indiana University, who first brought John Calhoun to my attention. I still remember his advice to me so many years ago: "Son, if you want to understand America, you don't want to miss this guy Calhoun." I also would like to thank George Carey, Charles McCall, Michael and Caron Jackson, Bill Burrow, Dan Palazzolo, John Leech, and James Gladden, who in one way or another have provided the intellectual stimulation for this project. I am especially appreciative of the research support of Judy Bundy for her work on Calhoun, and of Glenn Gadbois, whose service in the last stages of this manuscript have been invaluable; the patience of countless unnamed students whose long-delayed papers have made it possible for me to find the needed time to work on this project; and last, but by no means least, the moral support of my best friend and mother, whose innumerable hours of cutting and pasting have finally come to fruition.

I hope it will not be thought presumptuous to borrow here the words of Niccolo Machiavelli: *A' quali ordini io al tutto mi rimetto.**

---

*In such methods as theirs I have complete confidence.

UNION AND LIBERTY

A DISQUISITION ON GOVERNMENT

Of all John C. Calhoun's works, none has been more widely read or cited than his Disquisition on Government, *a posthumous work that marked the culmination of Calhoun's political reflections and thought after some forty years of public service. Within the confines of this short, theoretical text, Calhoun offers more than an analysis of the foundation of constitutional government in America: He reveals a bold new understanding of the science of politics. As Calhoun himself noted in his letter of June 15, 1849, from Fort Hill:*

> *I devote all the time left me, to finishing the work I commenced three years ago, or more . . . I finished, yesterday, the preliminary work [A Disquisition], which treats of the elementary principles of the Science of Government. . . . I am pretty well satisfied with its execution. It will be nearly throughout new territory; and, I hope, to lay a solid foundation for political Science. I have written, just as I thought, and told the truth without fear, favor, or affection.* *

In the course of the Disquisition, *Calhoun argues that the principles of government are as certain and as unquestionable as the laws of gravitation or astronomy. Beginning with the two incontestable facts that man is a social animal and that society cannot exist without government, Calhoun*

---

*Annual Report of the American Historical Association for the Year 1899, Vol. II, ed. J. F. Jameson, pp. 766–768, "To Mrs. T. C. Clemson, June 15, 1849."

immediately announces a third fact, that man feels what affects him di-
rectly more intensely than what affects him indirectly through others. From
these three facts, Calhoun then constructs all of his other arguments and
theories, including his doctrine of the concurrent majority, which guaran-
tees every significant interest in the community a concurrent voice either in
the enactment or in the enforcement of public policy. This concurrent ma-
jority not only serves as a necessary check on the dictates of the numerical
majority, but is also the negative principle that distinguishes constitutional
from absolute governments.

In order to have a clear and just conception of the nature and object of government, it is indispensable to understand correctly what that constitution or law of our nature is, in which government originates; or, to express it more fully and accurately—that law, without which government would not, and with which, it must necessarily exist. Without this, it is as impossible to lay any solid foundation for the science of government, as it would be to lay one for that of astronomy, without a like understanding of that constitution or law of the material world, according to which the several bodies composing the solar system mutually act on each other, and by which they are kept in their respective spheres. The first question, accordingly, to be considered is—What is that constitution or law of our nature, without which government would not exist, and with which its existence is necessary?

In considering this, I assume, as an incontestable fact, that man is so constituted as to be a social being. His inclinations and wants, physical and moral, irresistibly impel him to associate with his kind; and he has, accordingly, never been found, in any age or country, in any state other than the social. In no other, indeed, could he exist; and in no other—were it possible for him to exist—could he attain to a full development of his moral and intellectual faculties, or raise himself, in the scale of being, much above the level of the brute creation.

I next assume, also, as a fact not less incontestable, that, while man is so constituted as to make the social state necessary to his existence and the full development of his faculties, this state itself cannot exist without government. The assumption rests on universal experience. In no age or country has any society or community ever been found, whether enlightened or savage, without government of some description.

Having assumed these, as unquestionable phenomena of our nature, I shall, without further remark, proceed to the investigation of the primary and important question—What is that constitution of our nature, which, while it impels man to associate with his kind, renders it impossible for society to exist without government?

The answer will be found in the fact (not less incontestable than either of the others) that, while man is created for the social state, and is accordingly so formed as to feel what affects others, as well as what affects himself, he is, at the same time, so constituted as to feel more intensely what affects him directly, than what affects him indirectly though others; or, to express it differently, he is so constituted, that his direct or individual affections are stronger than his sympathetic or social feelings. I intentionally avoid the expression, *selfish* feelings, as applicable to the former; because, as commonly used, it implies an unusual excess of the individual over the social feelings, in the person to whom it is applied; and, consequently, something depraved and vicious. My object is, to exclude such inference, and to restrict the inquiry exclusively to facts in their bearings on the subject under consideration, viewed as mere phenomena appertaining to our nature—constituted as it is; and which are as unquestionable as is that of gravitation, or any other phenomenon of the material world.

In asserting that our individual are stronger than our social feelings, it is not intended to deny that there are instances, growing out of peculiar relations—as that of a mother and her infant—or resulting from the force of education and habit over peculiar constitutions, in which the latter have overpowered the former; but these instances are few, and always regarded as something extraordinary. The deep impression they make, whenever they occur, is the strongest proof that they are regarded as exceptions to some general and well understood law of our nature; just as some of the minor powers of the material world are apparently to gravitation.

I might go farther, and assert this to be a phenomenon, not of our nature only, but of all animated existence, throughout its entire range, so far as our knowledge extends. It would, indeed, seem to be essentially connected with the great law of self-preservation which pervades all that feels, from man down to the lowest and most insignificant reptile or insect. In none is it stronger than in man. His social feelings may, indeed, in a state of safety and abundance, combined with high intellectual and moral culture, acquire great expansion and force; but not so great as to over-power this all-pervading and essential law of animated existence.

But that constitution of our nature which makes us feel more intensely what affects us directly than what affects us indirectly through others, necessarily leads to conflict between individuals. Each, in consequence, has a greater regard for his own safety or happiness, than for the safety or happiness of others; and, where these come in opposition, is ready to sacrifice the interests of others to his own. And hence, the tendency to a universal state of conflict, between individual and individual; accompanied by the connected passions of suspicion, jealousy, anger and revenge— followed by insolence, fraud and cruelty—and, if not prevented by some controlling power, ending in a state of universal discord and confusion, destructive of the social state and the ends for which it is ordained. This controlling power, wherever vested, or by whomsoever exercised, is GOVERNMENT.

It follows, then, that man is so constituted, that government is necessary to the existence of society, and society to his existence, and the perfection of his faculties. It follows, also, that government has its origin in this twofold constitution of his nature; the sympathetic or social feelings consti-tuting the remote—and the individual or direct, the proximate cause.

If man had been differently constituted in either particular—if, instead of being social in his nature, he had been created without sympathy for his kind, and independent of others for his safety and existence, or if, on the other hand, he had been so created, as to feel more intensely what affected others than what affected himself (if that were possible) or, even, had this supposed interest been equal—it is manifest that, in either case, there would have been no necessity for government, and that none would ever have existed. But, although society and government are thus intimately connected with and dependent on each other—of the two society is the greater. It is the first in the order of things, and in the dignity of its object; that of society being primary—to preserve and perfect our race; and that of government secondary and subordinate, to preserve and perfect society. Both are, however, necessary to the existence and well-being of our race, and equally of Divine ordination.

I have said—if it were possible for man to be so constituted, as to feel what affects others more strongly than what affects himself, or even as strongly—because, it may be well doubted, whether the stronger feeling or affection of individuals for themselves, combined with a feebler and subordinate feeling or affection for others, is not, in beings of limited reason and faculties, a constitution necessary to their preservation and existence. If reversed—if their feelings and affections were stronger for others than for themselves, or even as strong, the necessary result would seem to be, that all individuality would be lost; and boundless and remediless disorder and confusion would ensue. For each, at the same moment, intensely participating in all the conflicting emotions of those around him, would, of course, forget himself and all that concerned him immediately, in his officious intermeddling with the affairs of all others; which, from his limited reason and faculties, he could neither properly understand nor manage. Such a state of things would, as far as we can see, lead to endless disorder and confusion, not less destructive to our race than a state of anarchy. It would, besides, be remediless—for government would be impossible; or, if it could by possibility exist, its object would be reversed. Selfishness would have to be encouraged, and benevolence discouraged. Individuals would have to be encouraged, by rewards, to become more selfish, and deterred, by punishments, from being too benevolent; and this, too, by a government, administered by those who, on the supposition, would have the greatest aversion for selfishness and the highest admiration for benevolence.

To the Infinite Being, the Creator of all, belongs exclusively the care and superintendence of the whole. He, in his infinite wisdom and goodness, has allotted to every class of animated beings its condition and appropriate functions; and has endowed each with feelings, instincts, capacities, and faculties, best adapted to its allotted condition. To man, he has assigned the social and political state, as best adapted to develop the great capacities and faculties, intellectual and moral, with which he has endowed him; and has, accordingly, constituted him so as not only to impel him into the social state, but to make government necessary for his preservation and well-being.

But government, although intended to protect and preserve society, has itself a strong tendency to disorder and abuse of its powers, as all experience and almost every page of history testify. The cause is to be found in the same constitution of our nature which makes government indispensable. The powers which it is necessary for government to possess, in order to repress violence and preserve order, cannot execute themselves. They must be administered by men in whom, like others, the individual are stronger than the social feelings. And hence, the powers vested in them to prevent injustice and oppression on the part of others, will, if left unguarded, be by them converted into instruments to oppress the rest of the community. That, by which this is prevented, by whatever name called, is what is meant by CONSTITUTION, in its most comprehensive sense, when applied to GOVERNMENT.

Having its origin in the same principle of our nature, *constitution* stands to *government,* as *government* stands to *society;* and, as the end for which society is ordained, would be defeated without government, so that for which government is ordained would, in a great measure, be defeated without constitution. But they differ in this striking particular. There is no difficulty in forming government. It is not even a matter of choice, whether there shall be one or not. Like breathing, it is not permitted to depend on our volition. Necessity will force it on all communities in some one form or another. Very different is the case as to constitution. Instead of a matter of necessity, it is one of the most difficult tasks imposed on man to form a constitution worthy of the name; while, to form a perfect one—one that would completely counteract the tendency of government to oppression and abuse, and hold it strictly to the great ends for which it is ordained— has thus far exceeded human wisdom, and possibly ever will. From this, another striking difference results. Constitution is the contrivance of man, while government is of Divine ordination. Man is left to perfect what the wisdom of the Infinite ordained, as necessary to preserve the race.

With these remarks, I proceed to the consideration of the important and difficult question: How is this tendency of government to be counteracted? Or, to express it more fully—How can those who are invested with the powers of government be prevented from employing them, as the means of aggrandizing themselves, instead of using them to protect and preserve society? It cannot be done by instituting a higher power to control the government, and those who administer it. This would be but to change the seat of authority, and to make this bigger power, in reality, the government; with the same tendency, on the part of those who might control its powers, to pervert them into instruments of aggrandizement. Nor can it be done by limiting the powers of government, so as to make it too feeble to be made an instrument of abuse; for, passing by the difficulty of so limiting its powers, without creating a power higher than the government itself to enforce the observance of the limitations, it is a sufficient objection that it would, if practicable, defeat the end for which government is ordained, by making it too feeble to protect and preserve society. The powers necessary for this purpose will ever prove sufficient to aggrandize those who control it, at the expense of the rest of the community.

In estimating what amount of power would be requisite to secure the objects of government, we must take into the reckoning, what would be necessary to defend the community against external, as well as internal dangers. Government must be able to repel assaults from abroad, as well as to repress violence and disorders within. It must not be overlooked, that the human race is not comprehended in a single society or community. The limited reason and faculties of man, the great diversity of language, customs, pursuits, situation and complexion, and the difficulty of intercourse, with various other causes, have, by their operation, formed a great many separate communities, acting independently of each other. Between these there is the same tendency to conflict—and from the same constitution of our nature—as between men individually; and even stronger—because the sympathetic or social feelings are not so strong between different communities, as between individuals of the same community. So powerful, indeed, is this tendency, that it has led to almost incessant wars between contiguous communities for plunder and conquest, or to avenge injuries, real or supposed.

So long as this state of things continues, exigencies will occur, in which the entire powers and resources of the community will be needed to defend its existence. When this is at stake, every other consideration must yield to it. Self-preservation is the supreme law, as well with communities as individuals. And hence the danger of withholding from government the full command of the power and resources of the state; and the great difficulty of limiting its powers consistently with the protection and preservation of the community. And hence the question recurs—By what means can government, without being divested of the full command of the resources of the community, be prevented from abusing its powers?

The question involves difficulties which, from the earliest ages, wise and good men have attempted to overcome—but hitherto with but partial success. For this purpose many devices have been resorted to, suited to the various stages of intelligence and civilization through which our race has passed, and to the different forms of government to which they have been applied. The aid of superstition, ceremonies, education, religion, organic arrangements, both of the government and the community, has been, from time to time, appealed to. Some of the most remarkable of these devices, whether regarded in reference to their wisdom and the skill displayed in their application, or to the permanency of their effects, are to be found in the early dawn of civilization—in the institutions of the Egyptians, the Hindoos, the Chinese, and the Jews. The only materials which that early age afforded for the construction of constitutions, when intelligence was so partially diffused, were applied with consummate wisdom and skill. To their successful application may be fairly traced the subsequent advance of our race in civilization and intelligence, of which we now enjoy the benefits. For, without a constitution—something to counteract the strong tendency of government to disorder and abuse, and to give stability to political institutions—there can be little progress or permanent improvement.

In answering the important question under consideration, it is not necessary to enter into an examination of the various contrivances adopted by these celebrated governments to counteract this tendency to disorder and abuse, nor to undertake to treat of constitution in its most comprehensive sense. What I propose is far more limited—to explain on what principles government must be formed, in order to resist, by its own interior structure—or, to use a single term, *organism*—the tendency to abuse of power. This structure, or organism, is what is meant by constitution, in its strict and more usual sense; and it is this which distinguishes, what are called, constitutional governments from absolute. It is in this strict and more usual sense that I propose to use the term hereafter.

How government, then, must be constructed, in order to counteract, through its organism, this tendency on the part of those who make and execute the laws to oppress those subject to their operation, is the next question which claims attention.

There is but one way in which this can possibly be done; and that is, by such an organism as will furnish the ruled with the means of resisting successfully this tendency on the part of the rulers to oppression and abuse. Power can only be resisted by power—and tendency by tendency. Those who exercise power and those subject to its exercise—the rulers and the ruled—stand in antagonistic relations to each other. The same constitution of our nature which leads rulers to oppress the ruled—regardless of the object for which government is ordained—will, with equal strength, lead the ruled to resist, when possessed of the means of making peaceable and effective resistance. Such an organism, then, as will furnish the means by which resistance may be systematically and peaceably made on the part of the ruled, to oppression and abuse of power on the part of the rulers, is the first and indispensable step towards *forming* a constitutional government. And as this can only be effected by or through the right of suffrage—(the right on the part of the ruled to choose their rulers at proper intervals, and to hold them thereby responsible for their conduct)— the responsibility of the rulers to the ruled, through the right of suffrage, is the indispensable and primary principle in the *foundation* of a constitutional government. When this right is properly guarded, and the people sufficiently enlightened to understand their own rights and the interests of the community, and duly to appreciate the motives and conduct of those appointed to make and execute the laws, it is all-sufficient to give to those who elect, effective control over those they have elected.

I call the right of suffrage the indispensable and primary principle; for it would be a great and dangerous mistake to suppose, as many do, that it is, of itself, sufficient to form constitutional governments. To this erroneous opinion may be traced one of the causes, why so few attempts to form constitutional governments have succeeded; and why, of the few which have, so small a number have had durable existence. It has led, not only to mistakes in the attempts to form such governments, but to their overthrow, when they have, by some good fortune, been correctly formed. So far from being, of itself, sufficient—however well guarded it might be, and however enlightened the people—it would, unaided by other provisions, leave the government as absolute, as it would be in the hands of irresponsible rulers; and with a tendency, at least as strong, towards oppression and abuse of its powers; as I shall next proceed to explain.

The right of suffrage, of itself, can do no more than give complete control to those who elect, over the conduct of those they have elected. In

doing this, it accomplishes all it possibly can accomplish. This is its aim—
and when this is attained, its end is fulfilled. It can do no more, however
enlightened the people, or however widely extended or well guarded the
right may be. The sum total, then, of its effects, when most successful, is,
to make those elected, the true and faithful representatives of those who
elected them—instead of irresponsible rulers—as they would be without
it; and thus, by converting it into an agency, and the rulers into agents, to
divest government of all claims to sovereignty, and to retain it unimpaired
to the community. But it is manifest that the right of suffrage, in making
these changes, transfers, in reality, the actual control over the government,
from those who make and execute the laws, to the body of the community;
and, thereby, places the powers of the government as fully in the mass of
the community, as they would be if they, in fact, had assembled, made,
and executed the laws themselves, without the intervention of representatives or agents. The more perfectly it does this, the more perfectly it
accomplishes its ends; but in doing so, it only changes the seat of authority,
without counteracting, in the least, the tendency of the government to
oppression and abuse of its powers.

If the whole community had the same interests, so that the interests of
each and every portion would be so affected by the action of the government, that the laws which oppressed or impoverished one portion, would
necessarily oppress and impoverish all others—or the reverse—then the
right of suffrage, of itself, would be all-sufficient to counteract the tendency of the government to oppression and abuse of its powers; and, of
course, would form, of itself, a perfect constitutional government. The
interest of all being the same, by supposition, as far as the action of the
government was concerned, all would have like interests as to what laws
should be made, and how they should be executed. All strife and struggle
would cease as to who should be elected to make and execute them. The
only question would be, who was most fit; who the wisest and most capable
of understanding the common interest of the whole. This decided, the
election would pass off quietly, and without party discord; as no one por-

tion could advance its own peculiar interest without regard to the rest, by electing a favorite candidate.

But such is not the case. On the contrary, nothing is more difficult than to equalize the action of the government, in reference to the various and diversified interests of the community; and nothing more easy than to pervert its powers into instruments to aggrandize and enrich one or more interests by oppressing and impoverishing the others; and this too, under the operation of laws, couched in general terms—and which, on their face, appear fair and equal. Nor is this the case in some particular communities only. It is so in all; the small and the great—the poor and the rich— irrespective of pursuits, productions, or degrees of civilization—with, however, this difference, that the more extensive and populous the country, the more diversified the condition and pursuits of its population, and the richer, more luxurious, and dissimilar the people, the more difficult is it to equalize the action of the government—and the more easy for one portion of the community to pervert its powers to oppress, and plunder the other.

Such being the case, it necessarily results, that the right of suffrage, by placing the control of the government in the community must, from the same constitution of our nature which makes government necessary to preserve society, lead to conflict among its different interests—each striving to obtain possession of its powers, as the means of protecting itself against the others—or of advancing its respective interests, regardless of the interests of others. For this purpose, a struggle will take place between the various interests to obtain a majority, in order to control the government. If no one interest be strong enough, of itself, to obtain it, a combination will be formed between those whose interests are most alike—each conceding something to the others, until a sufficient number is obtained to make a majority. The process may be slow, and much time may be required before a compact, organized majority can be thus formed; but formed it will be in time, even without preconcert or design, by the sure workings of that principle or constitution of our nature in which government itself originates. When once formed, the community will be divided into two great parties—a major and minor—between which there will be incessant struggles on the one side to retain, and on the other to obtain the majority—and, thereby, the control of the government and the advantages it confers.

So deeply seated, indeed, is this tendency to conflict between the different interests or portions of the community, that it would result from the action of the government itself, even though it were possible to find a community, where the people were all of the same pursuits, placed in the same condition of life, and in every respect, so situated, as to be without inequality of condition or diversity of interests. The advantages of possessing the control of the powers of the government, and, thereby, of its honors and emoluments, are, of themselves, exclusive of all other considerations, ample to divide even such a community into two great hostile parties.

In order to form a just estimate of the full force of these advantages— without reference to any other consideration—it must be remembered, that government—to fulfill the ends for which it is ordained, and more especially that of protection against external dangers—must, in the present condition of the world, be clothed with powers sufficient to call forth the resources of the community, and be prepared, at all times, to command them promptly in every emergency which may possibly arise. For this purpose large establishments are necessary, both civil and military (including naval, where, from situation, that description of force may be required) with all the means necessary for prompt and effective action—such as fortifications, fleets, armories, arsenals, magazines, arms of all descriptions, with well-trained forces, in sufficient numbers to wield them with skill and energy, whenever the occasion requires it. The administration and management of a government with such vast establishments must necessarily require a host of employees, agents, and officers—of whom many must be vested with high and responsible trusts, and occupy exalted stations, accompanied with much influence and patronage. To meet the necessary expenses, large sums must be collected and disbursed; and, for this purpose, heavy taxes must be imposed, requiring a multitude of officers for their collection and disbursement. The whole united must necessarily place under the control of government an amount of honors and emoluments, sufficient to excite profoundly the ambition of the aspiring and the cupidity of the avaricious; and to lead to the formation of hostile parties, and violent party conflicts and struggles to obtain the control of the government. And what makes this evil remediless, through the right of suffrage of itself, however modified or carefully guarded, or however enlightened the people, is the fact that, as far as the honors and emoluments of the government and its fiscal action are concerned, it is impossible to equalize it. The reason is obvious. Its honors and emoluments, however great, can fall to the lot of but a few, compared to the entire number of the community, and the multitude who will seek to participate in them. But, without this, there is a reason which renders it impossible to equalize the action of the government, so far as its fiscal operation extends—which I shall next explain.

Few, comparatively, as they are, the agents and employees of the government constitute that portion of the community who are the exclusive recipients of the proceeds of the taxes. Whatever amount is taken from the community, in the form of taxes, if not lost, goes to them in the shape of expenditures or disbursements. The two—disbursement and taxation—constitute the fiscal action of the government. They are correlatives. What the one takes from the community, under the name of taxes, is transferred to the portion of the community who are the recipients, under that of disbursements. But, as the recipients constitute only a portion of the community, it follows, taking the two parts of the fiscal process together, that its action must be unequal between the payers of the taxes and the recipients of their proceeds. Nor can it be otherwise, unless what is collected from each individual in the shape of taxes, shall be returned to him, in that of disbursements; which would make the process nugatory and absurd. Taxation may, indeed, be made equal, regarded separately from disbursement. Even this is no easy task; but the two united cannot possibly be made equal.

Such being the case, it must necessarily follow, that some one portion of the community must pay in taxes more than it receives back in disbursements; while another receives in disbursements more than it pays in taxes. It is, then, manifest, taking the whole process together, that taxes must be, in effect, bounties to that portion of the community which receives more in disbursements than it pays in taxes; while, to the other which pays in taxes more than it receives in disbursements, they are taxes in reality—burthens, instead of bounties. This consequence is unavoidable. It results from the nature of the process, be the taxes ever so equally laid, and the disbursements ever so fairly made, in reference to the public service.

It is assumed, in coming to this conclusion, that the disbursements are made within the community. The reasons assigned would not be applicable if the proceeds of the taxes were paid in tribute, or expended in foreign countries. In either of these cases, the burthen would fall on all, in proportion to the amount of taxes they respectively paid.

Nor would it be less a bounty to the portion of the community which received back in disbursements more than it paid in taxes, because received as salaries for official services; or payments to persons employed in executing the works required by the government; or furnishing it with its various supplies; or any other description of public employment—instead of being bestowed gratuitously. It is the disbursements which give additional, and, usually, very profitable and honorable employments to the portion of the community where they are made. But to create such employments, by disbursements, is to bestow on the portion of the community to whose lot the disbursements may fall, a far more durable and lasting benefit—one that would add much more to its wealth and population—than would the bestowal of an equal sum gratuitously: and hence, to the extent that the disbursements exceed the taxes, it may be fairly regarded as a bounty. The very reverse is the case in reference to the portion which pays in taxes more than it receives in disbursements. With them, profitable employments are diminished to the same extent, and population and wealth correspondingly decreased.

The necessary result, then, of the unequal fiscal action of the government is, to divide the community into two great classes; one consisting of those who, in reality, pay the taxes, and, of course, bear exclusively the burthen of supporting the government; and the other, of those who are the recipients of their proceeds, through disbursements, and who are, in fact, supported by the government; or, in fewer words, to divide it into tax-payers and tax-consumers.

But the effect of this is to place them in antagonistic relations, in reference to the fiscal action of the government, and the entire course of policy therewith connected. For, the greater the taxes and disbursements, the greater the gain of the one and the loss of the other—and *vice versa;* and consequently, the more the policy of the government is calculated to increase taxes and disbursements, the more it will be favored by the one and opposed by the other.

The effect, then, of every increase is, to enrich and strengthen the one, and impoverish and weaken the other. This, indeed, may be carried to such an extent, that one class or portion of the community may be elevated to wealth and power, and the other depressed to abject poverty and dependence, simply by the fiscal action of the government; and this too, through disbursements only—even under a system of equal taxes imposed for revenue only. If such may be the effect of taxes and disbursements, when confined to their legitimate objects—that of raising revenue for the public service—some conception may be formed, how one portion of the community may be crushed, and another elevated on its ruins, by systematically perverting the power of taxation and disbursement, for the purpose of aggrandizing and building up one portion of the community at the expense of the other. That it *will* be so used, unless prevented, is, from the constitution of man, just as certain as that it *can* be so used; and that, if not prevented, it must give rise to two parties, and to violent conflicts and struggles between them, to obtain the control of the government, is, for the same reason, not less certain.

Nor is it less certain, from the operation of all these causes, that the dominant majority, for the time, would have the same tendency to oppres sion and abuse of power, which, without the right of suffrage, irresponsible rulers would have. No reason, indeed, can be assigned, why the latter would abuse their power, which would not apply, with equal force, to the former. The dominant majority, for the time, would, in reality, through the right of suffrage, be the rulers—the controlling, governing, and irresponsible power; and those who make and execute the laws would, for the time, be, in reality, but *their* representatives and agents.

Nor would the fact that the former would constitute a majority of the community, counteract a tendency originating in the constitution of man; and which, as such, cannot depend on the number by whom the powers of the government may be wielded. Be it greater or smaller, a majority or minority, it must equally partake of an attribute inherent in each individual composing it; and, as in each the individual is stronger than the social feelings, the one would have the same tendency as the other to oppression and abuse of power. The reason applies to government in all its forms—whether it be that of the one, the few, or the many. In each there must, of necessity, be a governing and governed—a ruling and a subject portion. The one implies the other; and in all, the two bear the same relation to each other—and have, on the part of the governing portion, the same tendency to oppression and abuse of power. Where the majority is that portion, it matters not how its powers may be exercised—whether directly by themselves, or indirectly, through representatives or agents. Be it which it may, the minority, for the time, will be as much the governed or subject portion, as are the people in an aristocracy, or the subjects in a monarchy. The only difference in this respect is, that in the government of a majority, the minority may become the majority, and the majority the minority, through the right of suffrage; and thereby change their relative positions, without the intervention of force and revolution. But the duration, or uncertainty of the tenure, by which power is held, cannot, of itself, counteract the tendency inherent in government to oppression and abuse of power. On the contrary, the very uncertainty of the tenure, combined with the violent party warfare which must ever precede a change of parties under such governments, would rather tend to increase than diminish the tendency to oppression.

As, then, the right of suffrage, without some other provision, cannot counteract this tendency of government, the next question for consideration is—What is that other provision? This demands the most serious consideration; for of all the questions embraced in the science of government, it involves a principle, the most important, and the least understood; and when understood, the most difficult of application in practice. It is, indeed, emphatically, that principle which *makes* the constitution, in its strict and limited sense.

From what has been said, it is manifest, that this provision must be of a character calculated to prevent any one interest, or combination of interests, from using the powers of government to aggrandize itself at the expense of the others. Here lies the evil: and just in proportion as it shall prevent, or fail to prevent it, in the same degree it will effect, or fail to effect the end intended to be accomplished. There is but one certain mode in which this result can be secured; and that is, by the adoption of some restriction or limitation, which shall so effectually prevent any one interest, or combination of interests, from obtaining the exclusive control of the government, as to render hopeless all attempts directed to that end. There is, again, but one mode in which this can be effected; and that is, by taking the sense of each interest or portion of the community, which may be unequally and injuriously affected by the action of the government, separately, through its own majority, or in some other way by which its voice may be fairly expressed; and to require the consent of each interest, either to put or to keep the government in action. This, too, can be accomplished only in one way—and that is, by such an organism of the government— and, if necessary for the purpose, of the community also—as will, by dividing and distributing the powers of government, give to each division or interest, through its appropriate organ, either a concurrent voice in making and executing the laws, or a veto on their execution. It is only by such an organism, that the assent of each can be made necessary to put the govern ment in motion; or the power made effectual to arrest its action, when put in motion—and it is only by the one or the other that the different interests, orders, classes, or portions, into which the community may be divided, can be protected, and all conflict and struggle between them prevented—by rendering it impossible to put or to keep it in action, without the concurrent consent of all.

Such an organism as this, combined with the right of suffrage, constitutes, in fact, the elements of constitutional government. The one, by rendering those who make and execute the laws responsible to those on whom they operate, prevents the rulers from oppressing the ruled; and the other, by making it impossible for any one interest or combination of interests or class, or order, or portion of the community, to obtain exclusive control, prevents any one of them from oppressing the other. It is clear, that oppression and abuse of power must come, if at all, from the one or the other quarter. From no other can they come. It follows, that the two, suffrage and proper organism combined, are sufficient to counteract the tendency of government to oppression and abuse of power; and to restrict it to the fulfilment of the great ends for which it is ordained.

In coming to this conclusion, I have assumed the organism to be perfect, and the different interests, portions, or classes of the community, to be sufficiently enlightened to understand its character and object, and to exercise, with due intelligence, the right of suffrage. To the extent that either may be defective, to the same extent the government would fall short of fulfilling its end. But this does not impeach the truth of the principles on which it rests. In reducing them to proper form, in applying them to practical uses, all elementary principles are liable to difficulties; but they are not, on this account, the less true, or valuable. Where the organism is perfect, every interest will be truly and fully represented, and of course the whole community must be so. It may be difficult, or even impossible, to make a perfect organism—but, although this be true, yet even when, instead of the sense of each and of all, it takes that of a few great and prominent interests only, it would still, in a great measure, if not altogether, fulfil the end intended by a constitution. For, in such case, it would require so large a portion of the community, compared with the whole, to concur, or acquiesce in the action of the government, that the number to be plundered would be too few, and the number to be aggrandized too many, to afford adequate motives to oppression and the abuse of its powers. Indeed, however imperfect the organism, it must have more or less effect in diminishing such tendency.

It may be readily inferred, from what has been stated, that the effect of organism is neither to supersede nor diminish the importance of the right of suffrage; but to aid and perfect it. The object of the latter is, to collect the sense of the community. The more fully and perfectly it accomplishes this, the more fully and perfectly it fulfils its end. But the most it can do, of itself, is to collect the sense of the greater number; that is, of the stronger interests, or combination of interests; and to assume this to be the sense of the community. It is only when aided by a proper organism, that it can collect the sense of the entire community—of each and all its interests; of each, through its appropriate organ, and of the whole, through all of them united. This would truly be the sense of the entire community; for whatever diversity each interest might have within itself—as all would have the same interest in reference to the action of the government, the individuals composing each would be fully and truly represented by its own majority or appropriate organ, regarded in reference to the other interests. In brief, every individual of every interest might trust, with confidence, its majority or appropriate organ, against that of every other interest.

It results, from what has been said, that there are two different modes in which the sense of the community may be taken; one, simply by the right of suffrage, unaided; the other, by the right through a proper organism. Each collects the sense of the majority. But one regards numbers only, and considers the whole community as a unit, having but one common interest throughout; and collects the sense of the greater number of the whole, as that of the community. The other, on the contrary, regards interests as well as numbers—considering the community as made up of different and conflicting interests, as far as the action of the government is concerned; and takes the sense of each, through its majority or appropriate organ, and the united sense of all, as the sense of the entire community. The former of these I shall call the numerical, or absolute majority; and the latter, the concurrent, or constitutional majority. I call it the constitutional majority, because it is an essential element in every constitutional government—be its form what it may. So great is the difference, politically speaking, between the two majorities, that they cannot be confounded, without leading to great and fatal errors; and yet the distinction between them has been so entirely overlooked, that when the term *majority* is used in political discussions, it is applied exclusively to designate the numerical—as if there were no other. Until this distinction is recognized, and better understood, there will continue to be great liability to error in properly constructing constitutional governments, especially of the popular form, and of preserving them when properly constructed. Until then, the latter will have a strong tendency to slide, first, into the government of the numerical majority, and, finally, into absolute government of some other form. To show that such must be the case, and at the same time to mark more strongly the difference between the two, in order to guard against the danger of overlooking it, I propose to consider the subject more at length.

The first and leading error which naturally arises from overlooking the distinction referred to, is, to confound the numerical majority with the people; and this so completely as to regard them as identical. This is a consequence that necessarily results from considering the numerical as the only majority. All admit, that a popular government, or democracy, is the government of the people; for the terms imply this. A perfect government of the kind would be one which would embrace the consent of every citizen or member of the community; but as this is impracticable, in the opinion of those who regard the numerical as the only majority, and who can perceive no other way by which the sense of the people can be taken—they are compelled to adopt this as the only true basis of popular government, in contradistinction to governments of the aristocratical or monarchical form.

Being thus constrained, they are, in the next place, forced to regard the numerical majority, as, in effect, the entire people; that is, the greater part as the whole; and the government of the greater part as the government of the whole. It is thus the two come to be confounded, and a part made identical with the whole. And it is thus, also that all the rights, powers, and immunities of the whole people come to be attributed to the numerical majority; and, among others, the supreme, sovereign authority of establishing and abolishing governments at pleasure.

This radical error, the consequence of confounding the two, and of regarding the numerical as the only majority, has contributed more than any other cause, to prevent the formation of popular constitutional governments—and to destroy them even when they have been formed. It leads to the conclusion that, in their formation and establishment nothing more is necessary than the right of suffrage—and the allotment to each division of the community a representation in the government, in proportion to numbers. If the numerical majority were really the people; and if, to take its sense truly, were to take the sense of the people truly, a government so constituted would be a true and perfect model of a popular constitutional government; and every departure from it would detract from its excellence. But, as such is not the case—as the numerical majority, instead of being the people, is only a portion of them—such a government, instead of being a true and perfect model of the people's government, that is, a people self-governed, is but the government of a part, over a part—the major over the minor portion.

But this misconception of the true elements of constitutional government does not stop here. It leads to others equally false and fatal, in reference to the best means of preserving and perpetuating them, when, from some fortunate combination of circumstances, they are correctly formed. For they who fall into these errors regard the restrictions which organism imposes on the will of the numerical majority as restrictions on the will of the people, and, therefore, as not only useless, but wrongful and mischievous. And hence they endeavor to destroy organism, under the delusive hope of making government more democratic.

Such are some of the consequences of confounding the two, and of regarding the numerical as the only majority. And in this may be found the reason why so few popular governments have been properly constructed, and why, of these few, so small a number have proved durable. Such must continue to be the result, so long as these errors continue to be prevalent.

There is another error, of a kindred character, whose influence contributes much to the same results: I refer to the prevalent opinion, that a written constitution, containing suitable restrictions on the powers of government, is sufficient, of itself, without the aid of any organism—except such as is necessary to separate its several departments, and render them independent of each other—to counteract the tendency of the numerical majority to oppression and the abuse of power.

A written constitution certainly has many and considerable advantages; but it is a great mistake to suppose, that the mere insertion of provisions to restrict and limit the powers of the government, without investing those for whose protection they are inserted with the means of enforcing their observance, will be sufficient to prevent the major and dominant party from abusing its powers. Being the party in possession of the government, they will, from the same constitution of man which makes government necessary to protect society, be in favor of the powers granted by the constitution, and opposed to the restrictions intended to limit them. As the major and dominant party, they will have no need of these restrictions for their protection. The ballot box, of itself, would be ample protection to them. Needing no other, they would come, in time, to regard these limitations as unnecessary and improper restraints—and endeavor to elude them, with the view of increasing their power and influence.

The minor, or weaker party, on the contrary, would take the opposite direction—and regard them as essential to their protection against the dominant party. And, hence, they would endeavor to defend and enlarge the restrictions, and to limit and contract the powers. But where there are no means by which they could compel the major party to observe the restrictions, the only resort left them would be, a strict construction of the constitution, that is, a construction which would confine these powers to the narrowest limits which the meaning of the words used in the grant would admit.

To this the major party would oppose a liberal construction—one which would give to the words of the grant the broadest meaning of which they were susceptible. It would then be construction against construction; the one to contract, and the other to enlarge the powers of the government to the utmost. But of what possible avail could the strict construction of the minor party be, against the liberal interpretation of the major, when the one would have all the powers of the government to carry its construction into effect—and the other be deprived of all means of enforcing its construction? In a contest so unequal, the result would not be doubtful. The party in favor of the restrictions would be overpowered. At first, they might command some respect, and do something to stay the march of encroachment; but they would, in the progress of the contest, be regarded as mere abstractionists; and, indeed, deservedly, if they should indulge the folly of supposing that the party in possession of the ballot box and the physical force of the country, could be successfully resisted by an appeal to reason, truth, justice, or the obligations imposed by the constitution. For when these, of themselves, shall exert sufficient influence to stay the hand of power, then government will be no longer necessary to protect society, nor constitutions needed to prevent government from abusing its powers. The end of the contest would be the subversion of the constitution, either by the undermining process of construction—where its meaning would admit of possible doubt—or by substituting in practice what is called party-usage, in place of its provisions—or, finally, when no other contrivance would subserve the purpose, by openly and boldly setting them aside. By the one or the other, the restrictions would ultimately be annulled, and the government be converted into one of unlimited powers.

Nor would the division of government into separate, and, as it regards each other, independent departments, prevent this result. Such a division may do much to facilitate its operations, and to secure to its administration

greater caution and deliberation; but as each and all the departments—
and, of course, the entire government—would be under the control of the
numerical majority, it is too clear to require explanation, that a mere
distribution of its powers among its agents or representatives, could do
little or nothing to counteract its tendency to oppression and abuse of
power. To effect this, it would be necessary to go one step further, and
make the several departments the organs of the distinct interests or portions of the community; and to clothe each with a negative on the others.
But the effect of this would be to change the government from the numerical into the concurrent majority.

Having now explained the reasons why it is so difficult to form and
preserve popular constitutional government, so long as the distinction between the two majorities is overlooked, and the opinion prevails that a
written constitution, with suitable restrictions and a proper division of its
powers, is sufficient to counteract the tendency of the numerical majority
to the abuse of its power—I shall next proceed to explain, more fully, why
the concurrent majority is an indispensable element in forming constitutional governments; and why the numerical majority, of itself, must, in all
cases, make governments absolute.

The necessary consequence of taking the sense of the community by the
concurrent majority is, as has been explained, to give to each interest or
portion of the community a negative on the others. It is this mutual negative among its various conflicting interests, which invests each with the
power of protecting itself—and places the rights and safety of each, where
only they can be securely placed, under its own guardianship. Without this
there can be no systematic, peaceful, or effective resistance to the natural
tendency of each to come into conflict with the others: and without this
there can be no constitution. It is this negative power—the power of preventing or arresting the action of the government—be it called by what
term it may—veto, interposition, nullification, check, or balance of
power—which, in fact, forms the constitution. They are all but different
names for the negative power. In all its forms, and under all its names, it

results from the concurrent majority. Without this there can be no negative; and, without a negative, no constitution. The assertion is true in
reference to all constitutional governments, be their forms what they may.
It is, indeed, the negative power which makes the constitution—and the
positive which makes the government. The one is the power of acting—
and the other the power of preventing or arresting action. The two, combined, make constitutional governments.

But, as there can be no constitution without the negative power, and no
negative power without the concurrent majority—it follows, necessarily,
that where the numerical majority has the sole control of the government,
there can be no constitution; as constitution implies limitation or restriction—and, of course, is inconsistent with the idea of sole or exclusive
power. And hence, the numerical, unmixed with the concurrent majority,
necessarily forms, in all cases, absolute government.

It is, indeed, the single, or *one power*, which excludes the negative, and
constitutes absolute government; and not the *number* in whom the power is
vested. The numerical majority is as truly a *single power*, and excludes the
negative as completely as the absolute government of one, or of the few.
The former is as much the absolute government of the democratic, or
popular form, as the latter of the monarchical or aristocratical. It has,
accordingly, in common with them, the same tendency to oppression and
abuse of power.

Constitutional governments, of whatever form, are, indeed, much more
similar to each other, in their structure and character, than they are,
respectively, to the absolute governments, even of their own class. All
constitutional governments, of whatever class they may be, take the sense
of the community by its parts—each through its appropriate organ; and
regard the sense of all its parts, as the sense of the whole. They all rest on
the right of suffrage, and the responsibility of rulers, directly or indirectly.
On the contrary, all absolute governments, of whatever form, concentrate
power in one uncontrolled and irresponsible individual or body, whose will
is regarded as the sense of the community. And, hence, the great and

broad distinction between governments is—not that of the one, the few, or the many—but of the constitutional and the absolute.

From this there results another distinction, which, although secondary in its character, very strongly marks the difference between these forms of government. I refer to their respective conservative principle—that is, the principle by which they are upheld and preserved. This principle, in constitutional governments, is *compromise*—and in absolute governments, is *force*—as will be next explained.

It has been already shown, that the same constitution of man which leads those who govern to oppress the governed—if not prevented—will, with equal force and certainty, lead the latter to resist oppression, when possessed of the means of doing so peaceably and successfully. But absolute governments, of all forms, exclude all other means of resistance to their authority, than that of force; and, of course, leave no other alternative to the governed, but to acquiesce in oppression, however great it may be, or to resort to force to put down the government. But the dread of such a resort must necessarily lead the government to prepare to meet force in order to protect itself; and hence, of necessity, force becomes the conservative principle of all such governments.

On the contrary, the government of the concurrent majority, where the organism is perfect, excludes the possibility of oppression, by giving to each interest, or portion, or order—where there are established classes— the means of protecting itself, by its negative, against all measures calculated to advance the peculiar interests of others at its expense. Its effect, then, is, to cause the different interests, portions, or orders—as the case may be—to desist from attempting to adopt any measure calculated to promote the prosperity of one, or more, by sacrificing that of others; and thus to force them to unite in such measures only as would promote the prosperity of all, as the only means to prevent the suspension of the action of the government—and, thereby, to avoid anarchy, the greatest of all evils. It is by means of such authorized and effectual resistance, that oppression is prevented, and the necessity of resorting to force superseded, in governments of the concurrent majority—and, hence, compromise, instead of force, becomes their conservative principle.

It would, perhaps, be more strictly correct to trace the conservative principle of constitutional governments to the necessity which compels the different interests, or portions, or orders, to compromise—as the only way to promote their respective prosperity, and to avoid anarchy—rather than to the compromise itself. No necessity can be more urgent and imperious, than that of avoiding anarchy. It is the same as that which makes government indispensable to preserve society; and is not less imperative than that which compels obedience to superior force. Traced to this source, the voice of a people—uttered under the necessity of avoiding the greatest of calamities, through the organs of a government so constructed as to suppress the expression of all partial and selfish interests, and to give a full and faithful utterance to the sense of the whole community, in reference to its common welfare—may, without impiety, be called *the voice of God*. To call any other so, would be impious.

In stating that force is the conservative principle of absolute, and compromise of constitutional governments, I have assumed both to be perfect in their kind; but not without bearing in mind, that few or none, in fact, have ever been so absolute as not to be under some restraint, and none so perfectly organized as to represent fully and perfectly the voice of the whole community. Such being the case, all must, in practice, depart more or less from the principles by which they are respectively upheld and preserved; and depend more or less for support, on force, or compromise, as the absolute or the constitutional form predominates in their respective organizations.

Nor, in stating that absolute governments exclude all other means of resistance to its authority than that of force, have I overlooked the case of governments of the numerical majority, which form, apparently, an exception. It is true that, in such governments, the minor and subject party, for the time, have the right to oppose and resist the major and dominant party, for the time, through the ballot box; and may turn them out, and take their place, if they can obtain a majority of votes. But, it is no less true, that this would be a mere change in the relations of the two parties. The minor and subject party would become the major and dominant party, with the same absolute authority and tendency to abuse power; and the major and dominant party would become the minor and subject party, with the same right to resist through the ballot box; and, if successful, again to change relations, with like effect. But such a state of things must necessarily be temporary. The conflict between the two parties must be transferred, sooner or later, from an appeal to the ballot-box to an appeal to force—as I shall next proceed to explain.

The conflict between the two parties, in the government of the numerical majority, tends necessarily to settle down into a struggle for the honors and emoluments of the government; and each, in order to obtain an object so ardently desired, will, in the process of the struggle, resort to whatever measure may seem best calculated to effect this purpose. The adoption, by the one, of any measure, however objectionable, which might give it an advantage, would compel the other to follow its example. In such case, it would be indispensable to success to avoid division and keep united—and hence, from a necessity inherent in the nature of such governments, each party must be alternately forced, in order to insure victory, to resort to measures to concentrate the control over its movements in fewer and fewer hands, as the struggle became more and more violent. This, in process of time, must lead to party organization, and party caucuses and discipline; and these, to the conversion of the honors and emoluments of the government into means of rewarding partisan services, in order to secure the fidelity and increase the zeal of the members of the party. The effect of the whole combined, even in the earlier stages of the process, when they exert the least pernicious influence, would be to place the control of the two parties in the hands of their respective majorities; and the government itself, virtually, under the control of the majority of the dominant party, for the time, instead of the majority of the whole community—where the theory of this form of government vests it. Thus, in the very first stage of the process, the government becomes the government of a minority instead of a majority—a minority, usually, and under the most favorable circumstances, of not much more than one-fourth of the whole community.

But the process, as regards the concentration of power, would not stop at this stage. The government would gradually pass from the hands of the majority of the party into those of its leaders; as the struggle became more intense, and the honors and emoluments of the government the all-absorbing objects. At this stage, principles and policy would lose all influence in the elections; and cunning, falsehood, deception, slander, fraud, and gross appeals to the appetites of the lowest and most worthless portions of the community, would take the place of sound reason and wise debate. After these have thoroughly debased and corrupted the community, and all the arts and devices of party have been exhausted, the government would vibrate between the two factions (for such will parties have become) at each successive election. Neither would be able to retain power beyond some fixed term; for those seeking office and patronage would become too numerous to be rewarded by the offices and patronage at the disposal of the government; and these being the sole objects of pursuit, the disappointed would, at the next succeeding election, throw their weight into the opposite scale, in the hope of better success at the next turn of the wheel. These vibrations would continue until confusion, corruption, disorder, and anarchy, would lead to an appeal to force—to be followed by a revolution in the form of the government. Such must be the end of the government of the numerical majority; and such, in brief, the process through which it must pass, in the regular course of events, before it can reach it.

This transition would be more or less rapid, according to circumstances. The more numerous the population, the more extensive the country, the more diversified the climate, productions, pursuits and character of the people, the more wealthy, refined, and artificial their condition— and the greater the amount of revenues and disbursements—the more unsuited would the community be to such a government, and the more rapid would be the passage. On the other hand, it might be slow in its

progress amongst small communities, during the early stages of their
existence, with inconsiderable revenues and disbursements, and a population of simple habits; provided the people are sufficiently intelligent to
exercise properly, the right of suffrage, and sufficiently conversant with
the rules necessary to govern the deliberations of legislative bodies. It is,
perhaps, the only form of popular government suited to a people, while
they remain in such a condition. Any other would be not only too complex
and cumbersome, but unnecessary to guard against oppression, where the
motive to use power for that purpose would be so feeble. And hence,
colonies, from countries having constitutional governments, if left to themselves, usually adopt governments based on the numerical majority. But
as population increases, wealth accumulates, and, above all, the revenues
and expenditures become large—governments of this form must become
less and less suited to the condition of society; until, if not in the mean
time changed into governments of the concurrent majority, they must end
in an appeal to force, to be followed by a radical change in its structure
and character; and, most probably, into monarchy in its absolute form—
as will be next explained.

Such, indeed, is the repugnance between popular governments and
force—or, to be more specific—military power—that the almost necessary consequence of a resort to force, by such governments, in order to
maintain their authority, is, not only a change of their form, but a change
into the most opposite—that of absolute monarchy. The two are the opposites of each other. From the nature of popular governments, the control of
its powers is vested in the many; while military power, to be efficient, must
be vested in a single individual. When, then, the two parties, in governments of the numerical majority, resort to force, in their struggle for
supremacy, he who commands the successful party will have the control of
the government itself. And, hence, in such contests, the party which may
prevail, will usually find, in the commander of its forces, a master, under
whom the great body of the community will be glad to find protection
against the incessant agitation and violent struggles of two corrupt fac-

tions—looking only to power as the means of securing to themselves the honors and emoluments of the government.

From the same cause, there is a like tendency in aristocratical to terminate in absolute governments of the monarchical form; but by no means as strong, because there is less repugnance between military power and aristocratical, than between it and democratical governments.

A broader position may, indeed, be taken; viz., that there is a tendency, in constitutional governments of every form, to degenerate into their respective absolute forms; and, in all absolute governments, into that of the monarchical form. But the tendency is much stronger in constitutional governments of the democratic form to degenerate into their respective absolute forms, than in either of the others; because, among other reasons, the distinction between the constitutional and absolute forms of aristocratical and monarchical governments, is far more strongly marked than in democratic governments. The effect of this is, to make the different orders or classes in an aristocracy, or monarchy, far more jealous and watchful of encroachment on their respective rights; and more resolute and persevering in resisting attempts to concentrate power in any one class or order. On the contrary, the line between the two forms, in popular governments, is so imperfectly understood, that honest and sincere friends of the constitutional form not unfrequently, instead of jealously watching and arresting their tendency to degenerate into their absolute forms, not only regard it with approbation, but employ all their powers to add to its strength and to increase its impetus, in the vain hope of making the government more perfect and popular. The numerical majority, perhaps, should usually be one of the elements of a constitutional democracy; but to make it the sole element, in order to perfect the constitution and make the government more popular, is one of the greatest and most fatal of political errors.

Among the other advantages which governments of the concurrent have over those of the numerical majority—and which strongly illustrates their more popular character, is—that they admit, with safety, a much greater extension of the right of suffrage. It may be safely extended in such

governments to universal suffrage: that is—to every male citizen of mature
age, with few ordinary exceptions; but it cannot be so far extended in those
of the numerical majority, without placing them ultimately under the control of the more ignorant and dependent portions of the community. For, as
the community becomes populous, wealthy, refined, and highly civilized,
the difference between the rich and the poor will become more strongly
marked; and the number of the ignorant and dependent greater in proportion to the rest of the community. With the increase of this difference, the
tendency to conflict between them will become stronger; and, as the poor
and dependent become more numerous in proportion, there will be, in
governments of the numerical majority, no want of leaders among the
wealthy and ambitious, to excite and direct them in their efforts to obtain
the control.

The case is different in governments of the concurrent majority. There,
mere numbers have not the absolute control; and the wealthy and intelligent being identified in interest with the poor and ignorant of their respective portions or interests of the community, become their leaders and
protectors. And hence, as the latter would have neither hope nor inducement to rally the former in order to obtain the control, the right of suffrage,
under such a government, may be safely enlarged to the extent stated,
without incurring the hazard to which such enlargement would expose
governments of the numerical majority.

In another particular, governments of the concurrent majority have
greatly the advantage. I allude to the difference in their respective tendency, in reference to dividing or uniting the community. That of the
concurrent, as has been shown, is to unite the community, let its interests
be ever so diversified or opposed; while that of the numerical is to divide it
into two conflicting portions, let its interests be, naturally, ever so united
and identified.

That the numerical majority will divide the community, let it be ever so
homogeneous, into two great parties, which will be engaged in perpetual
struggles to obtain the control of the government, has already been estab-

lished. The great importance of the object at stake, must necessarily form strong party attachments and party antipathies—attachments on the part of the members of each to their respective parties, through whose efforts they hope to accomplish an object dear to all; and antipathies to the opposite party, as presenting the only obstacle to success.

In order to have a just conception of their force, it must be taken into consideration, that the object to be won or lost appeals to the strongest passions of the human heart—avarice, ambition, and rivalry. It is not then wonderful, that a form of government, which periodically stakes all its honors and emoluments, as prizes to be contended for, should divide the community into two great hostile parties; or that party attachments, in the progress of the strife, should become so strong among the members of each respectively, as to absorb almost every feeling of our nature, both social and individual; or that their mutual antipathies should be carried to such an excess as to destroy, almost entirely, all sympathy between them, and to substitute in its place the strongest aversion. Nor is it surprising, that under their joint influence, the community should cease to be the common centre of attachment, or that each party should find that centre only in itself. It is thus, that, in such governments, devotion to party becomes stronger than devotion to country—the promotion of the interests of party more important than the promotion of the common good of the whole, and its triumph and ascendency, objects of far greater solicitude, than the safety and prosperity of the community. It is thus, also, that the numerical majority, by regarding the community as a unit, and having, as such, the same interests throughout all its parts, must, by its necessary operation, divide it into two hostile parts, waging, under the forms of law, incessant hostilities against each other.

The concurrent majority, on the other hand, tends to unite the most opposite and conflicting interests, and to blend the whole in one common attachment to the country. By giving to each interest, or portion, the power of self-protection, all strife and struggle between them for ascendency, is prevented; and, thereby, not only every feeling calculated to weaken the attachment to the whole is suppressed, but the individual and the social feelings are made to unite in one common devotion to country. Each sees and feels that it can best promote its own prosperity by conciliating the goodwill, and promoting the prosperity of the others. And hence, there will be diffused throughout the whole community kind feelings between its different portions; and, instead of antipathy, a rivalry amongst them to promote the interests of each other, as far as this can be done consistently with the interest of all. Under the combined influence of these causes, the interests of each would be merged in the common interests of the whole; and thus, the community would become a unit, by becoming the common centre of attachment of all its parts. And hence, instead of faction, strife, and struggle for party ascendency, there would be patriotism, nationality, harmony, and a struggle only for supremacy in promoting the common good of the whole.

But the difference in their operation, in this respect, would not end here. Its effects would be as great in a moral, as I have attempted to show they would be in a political point of view. Indeed, public and private morals are so nearly allied, that it would be difficult for it to be otherwise. That which corrupts and debases the community, politically, must also corrupt and debase it morally. The same cause, which, in governments of the numerical majority, gives to party attachments and antipathies such force, as to place party triumph and ascendency above the safety and prosperity of the community, will just as certainly give them sufficient force to overpower all regard for truth, justice, sincerity, and moral obligations of every description. It is, accordingly, found that in the violent strifes between parties for the high and glittering prize of governmental honors and emoluments—falsehood, injustice, fraud, artifice, slander, and breach of faith, are freely resorted to, as legitimate weapons—followed by all their corrupting and debasing influences.

In the government of the concurrent majority, on the contrary, the same cause which prevents such strife, as the means of obtaining power, and which makes it the interest of each portion to conciliate and promote the interests of the others, would exert a powerful influence towards purifying and elevating the character of the government and the people, morally, as well as politically. The means of acquiring power—or, more correctly, influence—in such governments, would be the reverse. Instead of the vices, by which it is acquired in that of the numerical majority, the opposite virtues—truth, justice, integrity, fidelity, and all others, by which respect and confidence are inspired, would be the most certain and effectual means of acquiring it.

Nor would the good effects resulting thence be confined to those who take an active part in political affairs. They would extend to the whole community. For of all the causes which contribute to form the character of a people, those by which power, influence, and standing in the government are most certainly and readily obtained, are, by far, the most powerful. These are the objects most eagerly sought of all others by the talented and aspiring; and the possession of which commands the greatest respect and admiration. But, just in proportion to this respect and admiration will be their appreciation by those, whose energy, intellect, and position in society, are calculated to exert the greatest influence in forming the character of a people. If knowledge, wisdom, patriotism, and virtue, be the most certain means of acquiring them, they will be most highly appreciated and assiduously cultivated; and this would cause them to become prominent traits in the character of the people. But if, on the contrary, cunning, fraud, treachery, and party devotion be the most certain, they will be the most highly prized, and become marked features in their character. So powerful, indeed, is the operation of the concurrent majority, in this respect, that, if it were possible for a corrupt and degenerate community to establish and maintain a well-organized government of the kind, it would of itself purify and regenerate them; while, on the other hand, a government based wholly on the numerical majority, would just as certainly corrupt and debase the most patriotic and virtuous people. So great is their difference in this respect, that, just as the one or the other element predominates in the construction of any government, in the same proportion will the character of the government and the people rise or sink in the scale of patriotism and virtue. Neither religion nor education can counteract the strong tendency of the numerical majority to corrupt and debase the people.

If the two be compared, in reference to the ends for which government is ordained, the superiority of the government of the concurrent majority will not be less striking. These, as has been stated, are twofold; to protect, and to perfect society. But to preserve society, it is necessary to guard the community against injustice, violence, and anarchy within, and against attacks from without. If it fail in either, it would fail in the primary end of government, and would not deserve the name.

To perfect society, it is necessary to develop the faculties, intellectual and moral, with which man is endowed. But the main spring to their development, and, through this, to progress, improvement and civilization, with all their blessings, is the desire of individuals to better their condition. For, this purpose, liberty and security are indispensable. Liberty leaves each free to pursue the course he may deem best to promote his interest and happiness, as far as it may be compatible with the primary end for which government is ordained—while security gives assurance to each, that he shall not be deprived of the fruits of his exertions to better his condition. These combined, give to this desire the strongest impulse of which it is susceptible. For, to extend liberty beyond the limits assigned, would be to weaken the government and to render it incompetent to fulfil its primary end—the protection of society against dangers, internal and external. The effect of this would be, insecurity; and, of insecurity—to weaken the impulse of individuals to better their condition, and thereby retard progress and improvement. On the other hand, to extend the powers of the government, so as to contract the sphere assigned to liberty, would have the same effect, by disabling individuals in their efforts to better their condition.

Herein is to be found the principle which assigns to power and liberty their proper spheres, and reconciles each to the other under all circumstances. For, if power be necessary to secure to liberty the fruits of its exertions, liberty, in turn, repays power with interest, by increased population, wealth, and other advantages, which progress and improvement bestow on the community. By thus assigning to each its appropriate sphere, all conflicts between them cease; and each is made to co-operate with and assist the other, in fulfilling the great ends for which government is ordained.

But the principle, applied to different communities, will assign to them different limits. It will assign a larger sphere to power and a more contracted one to liberty, or the reverse, according to circumstances. To the former, there must ever be allotted, under all circumstances, a sphere sufficiently large to protect the community against danger from without and violence and anarchy within. The residuum belongs to liberty. More cannot be safely or rightly allotted to it.

But some communities require a far greater amount of power than others to protect them against anarchy and external dangers; and, of course, the sphere of liberty in such, must be proportionally contracted. The causes calculated to enlarge the one and contract the other, are numerous and various. Some are physical—such as open and exposed frontiers, surrounded by powerful and hostile neighbors. Others are moral—such as the different degrees of intelligence, patriotism, and virtue among the mass of the community, and their experience and proficiency in the art of self-government. Of these, the moral are, by far, the most influential. A community may possess all the necessary moral qualifications, in so high a degree, as to be capable of self-government under the most adverse circumstances; while, on the other hand, another may be so sunk in ignorance and vice, as to be incapable of forming a conception of liberty, or of living, even when most favored by circumstances, under any other than an absolute and despotic government.

The principle, in all communities, according to these numerous and various causes, assigns to power and liberty their proper spheres. To allow to liberty, in any case, a sphere of action more extended than this assigns, would lead to anarchy, and this, probably, in the end, to a contraction instead of an enlargement of its sphere. Liberty, then, when forced on a people unfit for it, would, instead of a blessing, be a curse; as it would, in its reaction, lead directly to anarchy—the greatest of all curses. No people, indeed, can long enjoy more liberty than that to which their situation and advanced intelligence and morals fairly entitle them. If more than this be allowed, they must soon fall into confusion and disorder—to be followed, if not by anarchy and despotism, by a change to a form of government more simple and absolute; and, therefore, better suited to their condition. And hence, although it may be true, that a people may not have as much liberty as they are fairly entitled to, and are capable of enjoying—yet the reverse is questionably true—that no people can long possess more than they are fairly entitled to.

Liberty, indeed, though among the greatest of blessings, is not so great as that of protection; inasmuch, as the end of the former is the progress and improvement of the race—while that of the latter is its preservation and perpetuation. And hence, when the two come into conflict, liberty must, and ever ought, to yield to protection; as the existence of the race is of greater moment than its improvement.

It follows, from what has been stated, that it is a great and dangerous error to suppose that all people are equally entitled to liberty. It is a reward to be earned, not a blessing to be gratuitously lavished on all alike—a reward reserved for the intelligent, the patriotic, the virtuous and deserving—and not a boon to be bestowed on a people too ignorant, degraded and vicious, to be capable either of appreciating or of enjoying it. Nor is it any disparagement to liberty, that such is, and ought to be the case. On the contrary, its greatest praise—its proudest distinction is, that an all-wise Providence has reserved it, as the noblest and highest reward for the development of our faculties, moral and intellectual. A reward more appropriate than liberty could not be conferred on the deserving—nor a punishment inflicted on the undeserving more just, than to be subject to lawless and despotic rule. This dispensation seems to be the result of some fixed law—and every effort to disturb or defeat it, by attempting to elevate a people in the scale of liberty, above the point to which they are entitled to rise, must ever prove abortive, and end in disappointment. The progress of a people rising from a lower to a higher point in the scale of liberty, is necessarily slow—and by attempting to precipitate, we either retard, or permanently defeat it.

There is another error, not less great and dangerous, usually associated with the one which has just been considered. I refer to the opinion, that liberty and equality are so intimately united, that liberty cannot be perfect without perfect equality.

That they are united to a certain extent—and that equality of citizens, in the eyes of the law, is essential to liberty in a popular government, is conceded. But to go further, and make equality of *condition* essential to liberty, would be to destroy both liberty and progress. The reason is, that inequality of condition, while it is a necessary consequence of liberty, is, at the same time, indispensable to progress. In order to understand why this is so, it is necessary to bear in mind, that the main spring to progress is, the desire of individuals to better their condition; and that the strongest impulse which can be given to it is, to leave individuals free to exert themselves in the manner they may deem best for that purpose, as far at least as it can be done consistently with the ends for which government is ordained—and to secure to all the fruits of their exertions. Now, as individuals differ greatly from each other, in intelligence, sagacity, energy, perseverance, skill, habit of industry and economy, physical power, position and opportunity—the necessary effect of leaving all free to exert themselves to better their condition, must be a corresponding inequality between those who may possess these qualities and advantages in a high degree, and those who may be deficient in them. The only means by which this result can be prevented are, either to impose such restrictions on the exertions of those who may possess them in a high degree, as will place them on a level with those who do not; or to deprive them of the fruits of their exertions. But to impose such restrictions on them would be destructive of liberty—while, to deprive them of the fruits of their exertions, would be to destroy the desire of bettering their condition. It is, indeed, this inequality of condition between the front and rear ranks, in the march of progress, which gives so strong an impulse to the former to maintain their position, and to the latter to press forward into their files. This gives to progress its greatest impulse. To force the front rank back to the rear, or attempt to push forward the rear into line with the front, by the interposition of the government, would put an end to the impulse, and effectually arrest the march of progress.

These great and dangerous errors have their origin in the prevalent opinion that all men are born free and equal—than which nothing can be more unfounded and false. It rests upon the assumption of a fact, which is contrary to universal observation, in whatever light it may be regarded. It is, indeed, difficult to explain how an opinion so destitute of all sound reason, ever could have been so extensively entertained, unless we regard it as being confounded with another, which has some semblance of truth— but which, when properly understood, is not less false and dangerous. I refer to the assertion, that all men are equal in the state of nature; meaning, by a state of nature, a state of individuality, supposed to have existed prior to the social and political state; and in which men lived apart and independent of each other. If such a state ever did exist, all men would have been, indeed, free and equal in it; that is, free to do as they pleased, and exempt from the authority or control of others—as, by supposition, it existed anterior to society and government. But such a state is purely hypothetical. It never did, nor can exist; as it is inconsistent with the preservation and perpetuation of the race. It is, therefore, a great misnomer to call it *the state of nature*. Instead of being the natural state of man, it is, of all conceivable states, the most opposed to his nature—most repugnant to his feelings, and most incompatible with his wants. His natural state is, the social and political—the one for which his Creator made him, and the only one in which he can preserve and perfect his race. As, then, there never was such a state as the, so called, state of nature, and never can be, it follows, that men, instead of being born in it, are born in the social and political state; and of course, instead of being born free and equal, are born subject, not only to parental authority, but to the laws and institutions of the country where born, and under whose protection they draw their first breath. With these remarks, I return from this digression, to resume the thread of the discourse.

It follows, from all that has been said, that the more perfectly a government combines power and liberty—that is, the greater its power and the more enlarged and secure the liberty of individuals, the more perfectly it fulfils the ends for which government is ordained. To show, then, that the government of the concurrent majority is better calculated to fulfil them than that of the numerical, it is only necessary to explain why the former is better suited to combine a higher degree of power and a wider scope of liberty than the latter. I shall begin with the former.

The concurrent majority, then, is better suited to enlarge and secure the bounds of liberty, because it is better suited to prevent government from passing beyond its proper limits, and to restrict it to its primary end—the protection of the community. But in doing this, it leaves, necessarily, all beyond it open and free to individual exertions; and thus enlarges and secures the sphere of liberty to the greatest extent which the condition of the community will admit, as has been explained. The tendency of government to pass beyond its proper limits is what exposes liberty to danger, and renders it insecure; and it is the strong counteraction of governments of the concurrent majority to this tendency which makes them so favorable to liberty. On the contrary, those of the numerical, instead of opposing and counteracting this tendency, add to it increased strength, in consequence of the violent party struggles incident to them, as has been fully explained. And hence their encroachments on liberty, and the danger to which it is exposed under such governments.

So great, indeed, is the difference between the two in this respect, that liberty is little more than a name under all governments of the absolute form, including that of the numerical majority; and can only have a secure and durable existence under those of the concurrent or constitutional form.

The latter, by giving to each portion of the community which may be unequally affected by its action, a negative on the others, prevents all partial or local legislation, and restricts its action to such measures as are designed for the protection and the good of the whole. In doing this, it secures, at the same time, the rights and liberty of the people, regarded individually; as each portion consists of those who, whatever may be the diversity of interests among themselves, have the same interest in reference to the action of the government.

Such being the case, the interest of each individual may be safely confided to the majority, or voice of his portion, against that of all others, and, of course, the government itself. It is only through an organism which vests each with a negative, in some one form or another, that those who have like interests in preventing the government from passing beyond its proper sphere, and encroaching on the rights and liberty of individuals, can co-operate peaceably and effectually in resisting the encroachments of power, and thereby preserve their rights and liberty. Individual resistance is too feeble, and the difficulty of concert and co-operation too great, unaided by such an organism, to oppose, successfully, the organized power of government, with all the means of the community at its disposal; especially in populous countries of great extent, where concert and co-operation are almost impossible. Even when the oppression of the government comes to be too great to be borne, and force is resorted to in order to overthrow it, the result is rarely ever followed by the establishment of liberty. The force sufficient to overthrow an oppressive government is usually sufficient to establish one equally, or more, oppressive in its place. And hence, in no governments, except those that rest on the principle of the concurrent or constitutional majority, can the people guard their liberty against power; and hence, also, when lost, the great difficulty and uncertainty of regaining it by force.

It may be further affirmed, that, being more favorable to the enlargement and security of liberty, governments of the concurrent, must necessarily be more favorable to progress, development, improvement, and civilization—and, of course, to the increase of power which results from, and depends on these, than those of the numerical majority. That it is liberty which gives to them their greatest impulse, has already been shown; and it now remains to show, that these, in turn, contribute greatly to the increase of power.

In the earlier stages of society, numbers and individual prowess constituted the principal elements of power. In a more advanced stage, when communities had passed from the barbarous to the civilized state, discipline, strategy, weapons of increased power, and money—as the means of meeting increased expense—became additional and important elements. In this stage, the effects of progress and improvement on the increase of power, began to be disclosed; but still numbers and personal prowess were sufficient, for a long period, to enable barbarous nations to contend successfully with the civilized—and, in the end, to overpower them—as the pages of history abundantly testify. But a more advanced progress, with its numerous inventions and improvements, has furnished new and far more powerful and destructive implements of offence and defence, and greatly increased the intelligence and wealth, necessary to engage the skill and meet the increased expense required for their construction and application to purposes of war. The discovery of gunpowder, and the use of steam as an impelling force, and their application to military purposes, have for ever settled the question of ascendency between civilized and barbarous communities, in favor of the former. Indeed, these, with other improvements, belonging to the present state of progress, have given to communities the most advanced, a superiority over those the least so, almost as great as that of the latter over the brute creation. And among the civilized, the same causes have decided the question of superiority, where other circumstances are nearly equal, in favor of those whose governments have given the greatest impulse to development, progress, and improvement; that is, to those whose liberty is the largest and best secured. Among these, England and the United States afford striking examples, not only of the effects of liberty in increasing power, but of the more perfect adaptation of govern-

ments founded on the principle of the concurrent, or constitutional majority, to enlarge and secure liberty. They are both governments of this
description, as will be shown hereafter.

But in estimating the power of a community, moral, as well as physical
causes, must be taken into the calculation; and in estimating the effects of
liberty on power, it must not be overlooked, that it is, in itself, an important
agent in augmenting the force of moral, as well as of physical power. It
bestows on a people elevation, self-reliance, energy, and enthusiasm; and
these combined, give to physical power a vastly augmented and almost
irresistible impetus.

These, however, are not the only elements of moral power. There are
others, and among them harmony, unanimity, devotion to country, and a
disposition to elevate to places of trust and power, those who are distinguished for wisdom and experience. These, when the occasion requires it,
will, without compulsion, and from their very nature, unite and put forth
the entire force of the community in the most efficient manner, without
hazard to its institutions or its liberty.

All these causes combined, give to a community its maximum of power.
Either of them, without the other, would leave it comparatively feeble. But
it cannot be necessary, after what has been stated, to enter into any further
explanation or argument in order to establish the superiority of governments of the concurrent majority over the numerical, in developing the
great elements of moral power. So vast is this superiority, that the one, by
its operation, necessarily leads to their development, while the other as
necessarily prevents it—as has been fully shown.

Such are the many and striking advantages of the concurrent over the
numerical majority. Against the former but two objections can be made.
The one is, that it is difficult of construction, which has already been
sufficiently noticed; and the other, that it would be impracticable to obtain
the concurrence of conflicting interests, where they were numerous and
diversified; or, if not, that the process for this purpose, would be too tardy
to meet, with sufficient promptness, the many and dangerous emergencies,

to which all communities are exposed. This objection is plausible; and deserves a fuller notice than it has yet received.

The diversity of opinion is usually so great, on almost all questions of policy, that it is not surprising, on a slight view of the subject, it should be thought impracticable to bring the various conflicting interests of a community to unite on any one line of policy—or, that a government, founded on such a principle, would be too slow in its movements and too weak in its foundation to succeed in practice. But, plausible as it may seem at the first glance, a more deliberate view will show, that this opinion is erroneous. It is true, that, when there is no urgent necessity, it is difficult to bring those who differ, to agree on any one line of action. Each will naturally insist on taking the course he may think best—and, from pride of opinion, will be unwilling to yield to others. But the case is different when there is an urgent necessity to unite on some common course of action, as reason and experience both prove. When something *must* be done—and when it can be done only by the united consent of all—the necessity of the case will force to a compromise—be the cause of that necessity what it may. On all questions of acting, necessity, where it exists, is the overruling motive; and where, in such cases, compromise among the parties is an indispensable condition to acting, it exerts an overruling influence in predisposing them to acquiesce in some one opinion or course of action. Experience furnishes many examples in confirmation of this important truth. Among these, the trial by jury is the most familiar, and on that account, will be selected for illustration.

In these, twelve individuals, selected without discrimination, must unanimously concur in opinion—under the obligations of an oath to find a true verdict, according to law and evidence; and this, too, not unfrequently under such great difficulty and doubt, that the ablest and most experienced judges and advocates differ in opinion, after careful examination. And yet, as impracticable as this mode of trial would seem to a superficial observer, it is found, in practice, not only to succeed, but to be the safest, the wisest and the best that human ingenuity has ever devised. When closely investigated, the cause will be found in the necessity, under which the jury is placed, to agree unanimously, in order to find a verdict. This necessity acts as the predisposing cause of concurrence in some common opinion; and with such efficacy, that a jury rarely fails to find a verdict.

Under its potent influence, the jurors take their seats with the disposition to give a fair and impartial hearing to the arguments on both sides—meet together in the jury-room—not as disputants, but calmly to hear the opinions of each other, and to compare and weigh the arguments on which they are founded—and, finally, to adopt that which, on the whole, is thought to be true. Under the influence of this *disposition to harmonize*, one after another falls into the same opinion, until unanimity is obtained. Hence its practicability—and hence, also, its peculiar excellence. Nothing, indeed, can be more favorable to the success of truth and justice, than this predisposing influence caused by the necessity of being unanimous. It is so much so, as to compensate for the defect of legal knowledge, and a high degree of intelligence on the part of those who usually compose juries. If the necessity of unanimity were dispensed with, and the finding of a jury made to depend on a bare majority, jury trial, instead of being one of the greatest improvements in the judicial department of government, would be one of the greatest evils that could be inflicted on the community. It would be, in such case, the conduit through which all the factious feelings of the day would enter and contaminate justice at its source.

But the same cause would act with still greater force in predisposing the various interests of the community to agree in a well-organized government, founded on the concurrent majority. The necessity for unanimity, in order to keep the government in motion, would be far more urgent, and would act under circumstances still more favorable to secure it. It would be superfluous, after what has been stated, to add other reasons in order to show that no necessity, physical or moral, can be more imperious than that of government. It is so much so that, to suspend its action altogether, even for an inconsiderable period, would subject the community to convulsions and anarchy. But in governments of the concurrent majority such fatal consequences can only be avoided by the unanimous concurrence or acquiescence of the various portions of the community. Such is the imperious character of the necessity which impels to compromise under governments of this description.

But to have a just conception of the overpowering influence it would exert, the circumstances under which it would act must be taken into consideration. These will be found, on comparison, much more favorable than those under which juries act. In the latter case there is nothing besides the necessity of unanimity in finding a verdict, and the inconvenience to which they might be subjected in the event of division, to induce juries to agree, except the love of truth and justice, which, when not counteracted by some improper motive or bias, more or less influences all, not excepting the most depraved. In the case of governments of the concurrent majority, there is, besides these, the love of country, than which, if not counteracted by the unequal and oppressive action of government, or other causes, few motives exert a greater sway. It comprehends, indeed, within itself, a large portion both of our individual and social feelings; and, hence, its almost boundless control when left free to act. But the government of the concurrent majority leaves it free, by preventing abuse and oppression, and, with them, the whole train of feelings and passions which lead to discord and conflict between different portions of the community. Impelled by the imperious necessity of preventing the suspension of the action of government, with the fatal consequences to which it would lead, and by the strong additional impulse derived from an ardent love of country, each portion would regard the sacrifice it might have to make by yielding its peculiar interest to secure the common interest and safety of all, including its own, as nothing compared to the evils that would be inflicted on all, including its own, by pertinaciously adhering to a different line of action. So powerful, indeed, would be the motives for concurring, and, under such circumstances, so weak would be those opposed to it, the wonder would be, not that there should, but that there should not be a compromise.

But to form a juster estimate of the full force of this impulse to compromise, there must be added that, in governments of the concurrent majority, each portion, in order to advance its own peculiar interests, would have to conciliate all others, by showing a disposition to advance theirs; and, for this purpose, each would select those to represent it, whose wisdom, patriotism, and weight of character, would command the confidence of the others. Under its influence—and with representatives so well qualified to accomplish the object for which they were selected—the prevailing desire would be, to promote the common interests of the whole; and, hence, the competition would be, not which should yield the least to promote the common good, but which should yield the most. It is thus, that concession would cease to be considered a sacrifice—would become a free-will offering on the altar of the country, and lose the name of compromise. And herein is to be found the feature, which distinguishes governments of the concurrent majority so strikingly from those of the numerical. In the latter, each faction, in the struggle to obtain the control of the government, elevates to power the designing, the artful, and unscrupulous, who, in their devotion to party—instead of aiming at the good of the whole—aim exclusively at securing the ascendency of party.

When traced to its source, this difference will be found to originate in the fact, that, in governments of the concurrent majority, individual feelings are, from its organism, necessarily enlisted on the side of the social, and made to unite with them in promoting the interests of the whole, as the best way of promoting the separate interests of each; while, in those of the numerical majority, the social are necessarily enlisted on the side of the individual, and made to contribute to the interest of parties, regardless of that of the whole. To effect the former—to enlist the individual on the side of the social feelings to promote the good of the whole, is the greatest possible achievement of the science of government; while, to enlist the social on the side of the individual to promote the interest of parties at the expense of the good of the whole, is the greatest blunder which ignorance can possibly commit.

To this, also, may be referred the greater solidity of foundation on which governments of the concurrent majority repose. Both, ultimately, rest on necessity; for force, by which those of the numerical majority are upheld, is only acquiesced in from necessity; a necessity not more imperious, however, than that which compels the different portions, in governments of the concurrent majority, to acquiesce in compromise. There is, however, a great difference in the motive, the feeling, the aim, which characterize the act in the two cases. In the one, it is done with that reluctance and hostility ever incident to enforced submission to what is regarded as injustice and oppression; accompanied by the desire and purpose to seize on the first favorable opportunity for resistance—but in the other, willingly and cheerfully, under the impulse of an exalted patriotism, impelling all to acquiesce in whatever the common good requires.

It is, then, a great error to suppose that the government of the concurrent majority is impracticable—or that it rests on a feeble foundation. History furnishes many examples of such governments—and among them, one, in which the principle was carried to an extreme that would be thought impracticable, had it never existed. I refer to that of Poland. In this it was carried to such an extreme that, in the election of her kings, the concurrence or acquiescence of every individual of the nobles and gentry present, in an assembly numbering usually from one hundred and fifty to two hundred thousand, was required to make a choice; thus giving to each individual a veto on his election. So, likewise, every member of her Diet (the supreme legislative body) consisting of the king, the senate, bishops and deputies of the nobility and gentry of the palatinates, possessed a veto on all its proceedings—thus making an unanimous vote necessary to enact a law, or to adopt any measure whatever. And, as if to carry the principle to the utmost extent, the veto of a single member not only defeated the particular bill or measure in question, but prevented all others, passed during the session, from taking effect. Further, the principle could not be carried. It, in fact, made every individual of the nobility and gentry, a distinct element in the organism—or, to vary the expression, made him an *Estate of the kingdom*. And yet this government lasted, in this form, more than two centuries; embracing the period of Poland's greatest power and renown. Twice, during its existence, she protected Christendom, when in great danger, by defeating the Turks under the walls of Vienna, and permanently arresting thereby the tide of their conquests westward.

It is true her government was finally subverted, and the people subjugated, in consequence of the extreme to which the principle was carried; not, however, because of its tendency to dissolution *from weakness,* but from the facility it afforded to powerful and unscrupulous neighbors to control, by their intrigues, the election of her kings. But the fact, that a government, in which the principle was carried to the utmost extreme, not only existed, but existed for so long a period, in great power and splendor, is proof conclusive both of its practicability and its compatibility with the power and permanency of government.

Another example, not so striking indeed, but yet deserving notice, is furnished by the government of a portion of the aborigines of our own country. I refer to the Confederacy of the Six Nations, who inhabited what now is called the western portion of the State of New York. One chief delegate, chosen by each nation—associated with six others of his own selection—and making, in all, forty-two members—constituted their federal, or general government. When met, they formed the council of the union—and discussed and decided all questions relating to the common welfare. As in the Polish Diet, each member possessed a veto on its decision; so that nothing could be done without the united consent of all. But this, instead of making the Confederacy weak, or impracticable, had the opposite effect. It secured harmony in council and action, and with them a great increase of power. The Six Nations, in consequence, became the most powerful of all the Indian tribes within the limits of our country. They carried their conquest and authority far beyond the country they originally occupied.

I pass by, for the present, the most distinguished of all these examples—the Roman Republic—where the veto, or negative power, was carried, not indeed to the same extreme as in the Polish government, but very far, and with great increase of power and stability—as I shall show more at large hereafter.

It may be thought—and doubtless many have supposed, that the defects inherent in the government of the numerical majority may be remedied by a free press, as the organ of public opinion—especially in the more advanced stage of society—so as to supersede the necessity of the concurrent majority to counteract its tendency to oppression and abuse of power. It is not my aim to detract from the importance of the press, nor to underestimate the great power and influence which it has given to public opinion. On the contrary, I admit these are so great, as to entitle it to be considered a new and important political element. Its influence is, at the present day, on the increase; and it is highly probable that it may, in combination with the causes which have contributed to raise it to its present importance, effect, in time, great changes—social and political. But, however important its present influence may be, or may hereafter become—or, however great and beneficial the changes to which it may ultimately lead, it can never counteract the tendency of the numerical majority to the abuse of power—nor supersede the necessity of the concurrent, as an essential element in the formation of constitutional governments. These it cannot effect for two reasons, either of which is conclusive.

The one is, that it cannot change that principle of our nature, which makes constitutions necessary to prevent government from abusing its powers—and government necessary to protect and perfect society.

Constituting, as this principle does, an essential part of our nature—no increase of knowledge and intelligence, no enlargement of our sympathetic feelings, no influence of education, or modification of the condition of society can change it. But so long as it shall continue to be an essential part of our nature, so long will government be necessary; and so long as this continues to be necessary, so long will constitutions, also, be necessary to counteract its tendency to the abuse of power—and so long must the concurrent majority remain an essential element in the formation of constitutions. The press may do much—by giving impulse to the progress of knowledge and intelligence, to aid the cause of education, and to bring about salutary changes in the condition of society. These, in turn, may do much to explode political errors—to teach how governments should be constructed in order to fulfil their ends; and by what means they can be best preserved, when so constructed. They may, also, do much to enlarge the social, and to restrain the individual feelings—and thereby to bring about a state of things, when far less power will be required by governments to guard against internal disorder and violence, and external danger; and when, of course, the sphere of power may be greatly contracted and that of liberty proportionally enlarged. But all this would not change the nature of man; nor supersede the necessity of government. For so long as government exists, the possession of its control, as the means of directing its action and dispensing its honors and emoluments, will be an object of desire. While this continues to be the case, it must, in governments of the numerical majority, lead to party struggles; and, as has been shown, to all the consequences, which necessarily follow in their train, and, against which, the only remedy is the concurrent majority.

The other reason is to be found in the nature of the influence, which the press politically exercises.

It is similar, in most respects, to that of suffrage. They are, indeed, both organs of public opinion. The principal difference is, that the one has much more agency in forming public opinion, while the other gives a more authentic and authoritative expression to it. Regarded in either light, the press cannot, of itself, guard any more against the abuse of power, than suffrage; and for the same reason.

If what is called public opinion were always the opinion of the whole community, the press would, as its organ, be an effective guard against the abuse of power, and supersede the necessity of the concurrent majority; just as the right of suffrage would do, where the community, in reference to the action of government, had but one interest. But such is not the case. On the contrary, what is called public opinion, instead of being the united opinion of the whole community, is, usually, nothing more than the opinion or voice of the strongest interest, or combination of interests; and, not unfrequently, of a small, but energetic and active portion of the whole. Public opinion, in relation to government and its policy, is as much divided and diversified, as are the interests of the community; and the press, instead of being the organ of the whole, is usually but the organ of these various and diversified interests respectively; or, rather, of the parties growing out of them. It is used by them as the means of controlling public opinion, and of so moulding it, as to promote their peculiar interests, and to aid in carrying on the warfare of party. But as the organ and instrument of parties, in governments of the numerical majority, it is as incompetent as suffrage itself, to counteract the tendency to oppression and abuse of power—and can, no more than that, supersede the necessity of the concurrent majority. On the contrary, as the instrument of party warfare, it contributes greatly to increase party excitement, and the violence and virulence of party struggles; and, in the same degree, the tendency to oppression and abuse of power. Instead, then, of superseding the necessity of the concurrent majority, it increases it, by increasing the violence and force of party feelings—in like manner as party caucuses and party machinery; of the latter of which, indeed, it forms an important part.

In one respect, and only one, the government of the numerical majority has the advantage over that of the concurrent, if, indeed, it can be called an advantage. I refer to its simplicity and facility of construction. It is simple indeed, wielded, as it is, by a single power—the will of the greater number—and very easy of construction. For this purpose, nothing more is necessary than universal suffrage, and the regulation of the manner of voting, so as to give to the greater number the supreme control over every department of government.

But, whatever advantages simplicity and facility of construction may give it, the other forms of absolute government possess them in a still higher degree. The construction of the government of the numerical majority, simple as it is, requires some preliminary measures and arrangements; while the others, especially the monarchical, will, in its absence, or where it proves incompetent, force themselves on the community. And hence, among other reasons, the tendency of all governments is, from the more complex and difficult of construction, to the more simple and easily constructed; and, finally, to absolute monarchy, as the most simple of all. Complexity and difficulty of construction, as far as they form objections, apply, not only to governments of the concurrent majority of the popular form, but to constitutional governments of every form. The least complex, and the most easily constructed of them, are much more complex and difficult of construction than any one of the absolute forms. Indeed, so great has been this difficulty, that their construction has been the result, not so much of wisdom and patriotism, as of favorable combinations of circumstances. They have, for the most part, grown out of the struggles between conflicting interests, which, from some fortunate turn, have ended in a compromise, by which both parties have been admitted, in some one way or another, to have a separate and distinct voice in the government. Where this has not been the case, they have been the product of fortunate circumstances, acting in conjunction with some pressing danger, which forced their adoption, as the only means by which it could be avoided. It would seem that it has exceeded human sagacity deliberately to plan and construct constitutional governments, with a full knowledge of the principles on which they were formed; or to reduce them to practice without the pressure of some immediate and urgent necessity. Nor is it surprising that such should be the case; for it would seem almost impossible for any man, or body of men, to be so profoundly and thoroughly acquainted with the people of any community which has made any considerable progress in civilization and wealth, with all the diversified interests ever accompanying them, as to be able to organize constitutional governments suited to their condition. But, even were this possible, it would be difficult to find any community sufficiently enlightened and patriotic to adopt such a government, without the compulsion of some pressing necessity. A constitution, to succeed, must spring from the bosom of the community, and be adapted to the intelligence and character of the people, and all the multifarious relations, internal and external, which distinguish one people from another. If it do not, it will prove, in practice, to be, not a constitution, but a cumbrous and useless machine, which must be speedily superseded and laid aside, for some other more simple, and better suited to their condition.

It would thus seem almost necessary that governments should commence in some one of the simple and absolute forms, which, however well suited to the community in its earlier stages, must, in its progress, lead to oppression and abuse of power, and, finally, to an appeal to force—to be succeeded by a military despotism—unless the conflicts to which it leads should be fortunately adjusted by a compromise, which will give to the respective parties a participation in the control of the government; and thereby lay the foundation of a constitutional government, to be afterwards matured and perfected. Such governments have been, emphatically, the product of circumstances. And hence, the difficulty of one people imitating the government of another. And hence, also, the importance of terminating all civil conflicts by a compromise, which shall prevent either party from obtaining complete control, and thus subjecting the other.

Of the different forms of constitutional governments, the popular is the most complex and difficult of construction. It is, indeed, so difficult, that ours, it is believed, may with truth be said to be the only one of a purely popular character, of any considerable importance, that ever existed. The cause is to be found in the fact, that, in the other two forms, society is arranged in artificial orders or classes. Where these exist, the line of distinction between them is so strongly marked as to throw into shade, or, otherwise, to absorb all interests which are foreign to them respectively. Hence, in an aristocracy, all interests are, politically, reduced to two—the nobles and the people; and in a monarchy, with a nobility, into three—the monarch, the nobles, and the people. In either case, they are so few that the sense of each may be taken separately, through its appropriate organ, so as to give to each a concurrent voice, and a negative on the other, through the usual departments of the government, without making it too complex, or too tardy in its movements to perform, with promptness and energy, all the necessary functions of government.

The case is different in constitutional governments of the popular form. In consequence of the absence of these artificial distinctions, the various natural interests, resulting from diversity of pursuits, condition, situation and character of different portions of the people—and from the action of the government itself—rise into prominence, and struggle to obtain the ascendency. They will, it is true, in governments of the numerical majority, ultimately coalesce, and form two great parties; but not so closely as to lose entirely their separate character and existence. These they will ever be ready to re-assume, when the objects for which they coalesced are accomplished. To overcome the difficulties occasioned by so great a diversity of interests, an organism far more complex is necessary.

Another obstacle, difficult to be overcome, opposes the formation of popular constitutional governments. It is much more difficult to terminate the struggles between conflicting interests, by compromise, in absolute popular governments, than in an aristocracy or monarchy.

In an aristocracy, the object of the people, in the ordinary struggle between them and the nobles, is not, at least in its early stages, to overthrow the nobility and revolutionize the government—but to participate in its powers. Notwithstanding the oppression to which they may be subjected, under this form of government, the people commonly feel no small degree of respect for the descendants of a long line of distinguished ancestors; and do not usually aspire to more—in opposing the authority of the nobles—than to obtain such a participation in the powers of the government, as will enable them to correct its abuses and to lighten their burdens. Among the nobility, on the other hand, it sometimes happens that there are individuals of great influence with both sides, who have the good sense and patriotism to interpose, in order to effect a compromise by yielding to the reasonable demands of the people; and, thereby, to avoid the hazard of a final and decisive appeal to force. It is thus, by a judicious and timely compromise, the people, in such governments, may be raised to a participation in the administration sufficient for their protection, without the loss of authority on the part of the nobles.

In the case of a monarchy, the process is somewhat different. Where it is a military despotism, the people rarely have the spirit or intelligence to attempt resistance; or, if otherwise, their resistance must almost necessarily terminate in defeat, or in a mere change of dynasty—by the elevation of their leader to the throne. It is different, where the monarch is surrounded by an hereditary nobility. In a struggle between him and them, both (but especially the monarch) are usually disposed to court the people, in order to enlist them on their respective sides—a state of things highly favorable to their elevation. In this case, the struggle, if it should be long continued without decisive results, would almost necessarily raise them to political importance, and to a participation in the powers of the government.

The case is different in an absolute Democracy. Party conflicts between the majority and minority, in such governments, can hardly ever terminate in compromise—The object of the opposing minority is to expel the majority from power; and of the majority to maintain their hold upon it. It is, on both sides, a struggle for the whole—a struggle that must determine which shall be the governing, and which the subject party—and, in character, object and result, not unlike that between competitors for the sceptre in absolute monarchies. Its regular course, as has been shown, is, excessive violence—an appeal to force—followed by revolution—and terminating at last, in the elevation to supreme power of the general of the successful party. And hence, among other reasons, aristocracies and monarchies more readily assume the constitutional form than absolute popular governments.

Of the three different forms, the monarchical has heretofore been much the most prevalent, and, generally, the most powerful and durable. This result is doubtless to be attributed principally to the fact that, in its absolute form, it is the most simple and easily constructed. And hence, as government is indispensable, communities having too little intelligence to form or preserve the others, naturally fall into this. It may also, in part, be attributed to another cause, already alluded to; that, in its organism and character, it is much more closely assimilated than either of the other two, to military power; on which all absolute governments depend for support. And hence, also, the tendency of the others, and of constitutional governments which have been so badly constructed or become so disorganized as to require force to support them—to pass into military despotism—that is, into monarchy in its most absolute and simple form. And hence, again, the fact, that revolutions in absolute monarchies, end, almost invariably, in a change of dynasty—and not of the forms of the government; as is almost universally the case in the other systems.

But there are, besides these, other causes of a higher character, which contribute much to make monarchies the most prevalent, and, usually, the most durable governments. Among them, the leading one is, they are the most susceptible of improvement—that is, they can be more easily and readily modified, so as to prevent, to a limited extent, oppression and abuse of power, without assuming the constitutional form, in its strict sense. It slides, almost naturally, into one of the most important modifications. I refer to hereditary descent. When this becomes well defined and firmly established, the community or kingdom, comes to be regarded by the sovereign as the hereditary possession of his family—a circumstance which tends strongly to identify his interests with those of his subjects, and thereby, to mitigate the rigor of the government. It gives, besides, great additional security to his person; and prevents, in the same degree, not only the suspicion and hostile feelings incident to insecurity—but invites all those kindly feelings which naturally spring up on both sides, between those whose interests are identified—when there is nothing to prevent it. And hence the strong feelings of paternity on the side of the sovereign— and of loyalty on that of his subjects, which are often exhibited in such governments.

There is another improvement of which it is readily susceptible, nearly allied to the preceding. The hereditary principle not unfrequently extends to other families—especially to those of the distinguished chieftains, by whose aid the monarchy was established, when it originates in conquest. When this is the case—and a powerful body of hereditary nobles surround the sovereign, they oppose a strong resistance to his authority, and he to theirs—tending to the advantage and security of the people. Even when they do not succeed in obtaining a participation in the powers of the government, they usually acquire sufficient weight to be felt and respected. From this state of things, such governments usually, in time, settle down on some fixed rules of action, which the sovereign is compelled to respect, and by which increased protection and security are acquired by all. It was thus the enlightened monarchies of Europe were formed, under which the people of that portion of the globe have made such great advances in power, intelligence, and civilization.

To these may be added the greater capacity, which governments of the monarchical form have exhibited, to hold under subjection a large extent of territory, and a numerous population; and which has made them more powerful than others of a different form, to the extent, that these constitute an element of power. All these causes combined, have given such great and decisive advantages, as to enable them, heretofore, to absorb, in the progress of events, the few governments which have, from time to time, assumed different forms—not excepting even the mighty Roman Republic, which, after attaining the highest point of power, passed, seemingly under the operation of irresistible causes, into a military despotism. I say, heretofore—for it remains to be seen whether they will continue to retain their advantages, in these respects, over the others, under the great and growing influence of public opinion, and the new and imposing form which popular government has assumed with us.

These have already effected great changes, and will probably effect still greater—adverse to the monarchical form; but, as yet, these changes have tended rather to the absolute, than to the constitutional form of popular government—for reasons which have been explained. If this tendency should continue permanently in the same direction, the monarchical form must still retain its advantages, and continue to be the most prevalent. Should this be the case, the alternative will be between monarchy and popular government, in the form of the numerical majority—or absolute democracy; which, as has been shown, is not only the most fugitive of all the forms, but has the strongest tendency of all others to the monarchical. If, on the contrary, this tendency, or the changes referred to, should incline to the constitutional form of popular government—and a proper organism come to be regarded as not less indispensable than the right of suffrage to the establishment of such governments—in such case, it is not improbable that, in the progress of events, the monarchical will cease to be the prevalent form of government. Whether they will take this direction, at least for a long time, will depend on the success of our government—and a correct understanding of the principles on which it is constructed.

To comprehend more fully the force and bearing of public opinion, and to form a just estimate of the changes to which, aided by the press, it will probably lead, politically and socially—it will be necessary to consider it in connection with the causes that have given it an influence so great, as to entitle it to be regarded as a new political element. They will, upon investigation, be found in the many discoveries and inventions made in the last few centuries.

Among the more prominent of those of an earlier date, stand the practical application of the magnetic power to the purposes of navigation, by the invention of the mariner's compass; the discovery of the mode of making gunpowder, and its application to the art of war; and the invention of the art of printing. Among the more recent are, the numerous chemical and mechanical discoveries and inventions, and their application to the various arts of production; the application of steam to machinery of almost every description, especially to such as is designed to facilitate transportation and travel by land and water; and, finally, the invention of the magnetic telegraph.

All these have led to important results. Through the invention of the mariner's compass, the globe has been circumnavigated and explored, and all who inhabit it, with but few exceptions, brought within the sphere of an all-pervading commerce, which is daily diffusing over its surface the light and blessings of civilization. Through that of the art of printing, the fruits of observation and reflection, of discoveries and inventions, with all the accumulated stores of previously acquired knowledge, are preserved and widely diffused. The application of gunpowder to the art of war, has forever settled the long conflict for ascendency between civilization and barbarism, in favor of the former, and thereby guarantied that, whatever knowledge is now accumulated, or may hereafter be added, shall never again be lost. The numerous discoveries and inventions, chemical and mechanical, and the application of steam to machinery, have increased, many-fold, the productive powers of labor and capital; and have, thereby, greatly increased the number, who may devote themselves to study and improvement—and the amount of means necessary for commercial exchanges—especially between the more and the less advanced and civilized portions of the globe— to the great advantage of both, but particularly of the latter. The application of steam to the purposes of travel and transportation, by land and water, has vastly increased the facility, cheapness and rapidity of both—diffusing, with them, information and intelligence almost as quickly and as freely as if borne by the winds; while the electrical wires outstrip them, in velocity— rivalling, in rapidity, even thought itself.

The joint effect of all has been, a great increase and diffusion of knowledge; and, with this, an impulse to progress and civilization heretofore unexampled in the history of the world—accompanied by a mental energy and activity unprecedented.

To all these causes, public opinion, and its organ, the press, owe their origin and great influence. Already they have attained a force in the more civilized portions of the globe sufficient to be felt by all governments, even the most absolute and despotic. But, as great as they now are, they have as yet attained nothing like their maximum force. It is probable, that not one of the causes, which have contributed to their formation and influence, has yet produced its full effect; while several of the most powerful have just begun to operate; and many others, probably of equal or even greater force, yet remain to be brought to light.

When the causes now in operation have produced their full effect, and inventions and discoveries shall have been exhausted—if that may ever be—they will give a force to public opinion, and cause changes, political and social, difficult to be anticipated. What will be their final bearing, time only can decide with any certainty. That they will, however, greatly improve the condition of man ultimately—it would be impious to doubt. It would be to suppose, that the all-wise and beneficent Being—the Creator of all—had so constituted man, as that the employment of the high intellectual faculties, with which He has been pleased to endow him, in order that he might develop the laws that control the great agents of the material world, and make them subservient to his use—would prove to him the cause of permanent evil—and not of permanent good. If, then, such a supposition be inadmissible, they must, in their orderly and full development, end in his permanent good. But this cannot be, unless the ultimate effect of their action, politically, shall be, to give ascendency to that form of government best calculated to fulfil the ends for which government is ordained. For, so completely does the well-being of our race depend on good government, that it is hardly possible any change, the ultimate effect of which should be otherwise, could prove to be a permanent good.

It is, however, not improbable, that many and great, but temporary evils, will follow the changes they have effected, and are destined to effect. It seems to be a law in the political, as well as in the material world, that great changes cannot be made, except very gradually, without convulsions and revolutions; to be followed by calamities, in the beginning, however beneficial they may prove to be in the end. The first effect of such changes, on long established governments, will be, to unsettle the opinions and principles in which they originated—and which have guided their policy—before those, which the changes are calculated to form and establish, are fairly developed and understood. The interval between the decay of the old and the formation and establishment of the new, constitutes a period of transition, which must always necessarily be one of uncertainty, confusion, error, and wild and fierce fanaticism.

The governments of the more advanced and civilized portions of the world are now in the midst of this period. It has proved, and will continue to prove a severe trial to existing political institutions of every form. Those governments which have not the sagacity to perceive what is truly public opinion—to distinguish between it and the mere clamor of faction, or shouts of fanaticism—and the good sense and firmness to yield, timely and cautiously, to the claims of the one—and to resist, promptly and decidedly, the demands of the other—are doomed to fall. Few will be able successfully to pass through this period of transition; and these, not without shocks and modifications, more or less considerable. It will endure until the governing and the governed shall better understand the ends for which government is ordained, and the form best adapted to accomplish them, under all the circumstances in which communities may be respectively placed.

I shall, in conclusion, proceed to exemplify the elementary principles, which have been established, by giving a brief account of the origin and character of the governments of Rome and Great Britain; the two most remarkable and perfect of their respective forms of constitutional governments. The object is to show how these principles were applied, in the more simple forms of such governments; preparatory to an exposition of the mode in which they have been applied in our own more complex system. It will appear that, in each, the principles are the same; and that the difference in their application resulted from the different situation and social condition of the respective communities. They were modified, in each, so as to conform to these; and, hence, their remarkable success. They were applied to communities in which hereditary rank had long prevailed. Their respective constitutions originated in concession to the people; and, through them, they acquired a participation in the powers of government. But with us, they were applied to communities where all political rank and distinction between citizens were excluded; and where government had its origin in the will of the people.

But, however different their origin and character, it will be found that the object in each was the same—to blend and harmonize the conflicting interests of the community; and the means the same—taking the sense of each class or portion through its appropriate organ, and considering the concurrent sense of all as the sense of the whole community. Such being the fact, an accurate and clear conception how this was effected, in their more simple forms, will enable us better to understand how it was accomplished in our far more refined, artificial, and complex form.

It is well known to all, the least conversant with their history, that the Roman people consisted of two distinct orders, or classes—the patricians and the plebeians; and that the line of distinction was so strongly drawn, that, for a long time, the right of intermarriage between them was prohibited. After the overthrow of the monarchy and the expulsion of the Tarquins, the government fell exclusively under the control of the patricians, who, with their clients and dependents, formed, at the time, a very numerous and powerful body. At first, while there was danger of the return of the exiled family, they treated the plebeians with kindness; but, after it had passed away, with oppression and cruelty.

It is not necessary, with the object in view, to enter into a minute account of the various acts of oppression and cruelty to which they were subjected. It is sufficient to state, that, according to the usages of war at the time, the territory of a conquered people became the property of the conquerors; and that the plebeians were harassed and oppressed by incessant wars, in which the danger and toil were theirs, while all the fruits of victory (the lands of the vanquished, and the spoils of war) accrued to the benefit of their oppressors. The result was such as might be expected. They were impoverished, and forced, from necessity, to borrow from the patricians, at usurious and exorbitant interest, funds with which they had been enriched through their blood and toil; and to pledge their all for repayment at stipulated periods. In case of default, the pledge became forfeited; and, under the provisions of law in such cases, the debtors were liable to be seized, and sold or imprisoned by their creditors in private jails prepared and kept for the purpose. These savage provisions were enforced with the utmost rigor against the indebted and impoverished plebeians. They constituted, indeed, an essential part of the system through which they were plundered and oppressed by the patricians.

A system so oppressive could not be endured. The natural consequences followed. Deep hatred was engendered between the orders, accompanied by factions, violence, and corruption, which distracted and weakened the government. At length, an incident occurred which roused the indignation of the plebeians to the utmost pitch, and which ended in a open rupture between the two orders.

An old soldier, who had long served the country, and had fought with bravery in twenty-eight battles, made his escape from the prison of his creditor—squalid, pale, and famished. He implored the protection of the plebeians. A crowd surrounded him; and his tale of service to the country, and the cruelty with which he had been treated by his creditor, kindled a flame, which continued to rage until it extended to the army. It refused to continue any longer in service—crossed the Anio, and took possession of the sacred mount. The patricians divided in opinion as to the course which should be pursued. The more violent insisted on an appeal to arms, but, fortunately, the counsel of the moderate, which recommended concession and compromise, prevailed. Commissioners were appointed to treat with the army; and a formal compact was entered into between the orders, and ratified by the oaths of each, which conceded to the plebeians the right to elect two tribunes, as the protectors of their order, and made their persons sacred. The number was afterwards increased to ten, and their election by centuries changed to election by tribes—a mode by which the plebeians secured a decided preponderance.

Such was the origin of the tribunate—which, in process of time, opened all the honors of the government to the plebeians. They acquired the right, not only of vetoing the passage of all laws, but also their execution; and thus obtained, through their tribunes, a negative on the entire action of the government, without divesting the patricians of their control over the Senate. By this arrangement, the government was placed under the concurrent and joint voice of the two orders, expressed through separate and appropriate organs; the one possessing the positive, and the other the negative powers of the government. This simple change converted it from an absolute, into a constitutional government—from a government of the patricians only, to that of the whole Roman people—and from an aristocracy into a republic. In doing this, it laid the solid foundation of Roman liberty and greatness.

A superficial observer would pronounce a government, so organized, as that one order should have the power of making and executing the laws, and another, or the representatives of another, the unlimited authority of preventing their enactment and execution—if not wholly impracticable, at least, too feeble to stand the shocks to which all governments are subject; and would, therefore, predict its speedy dissolution, after a distracted and inglorious career.

How different from the result! Instead of distraction, it proved to be the bond of concord and harmony; instead of weakness, of unequalled strength—and, instead of a short and inglorious career, one of great length and immortal glory. It moderated the conflicts between the orders; harmonized their interests, and blended them into one; substituted devotion to country in the place of devotion to particular orders; called forth the united strength and energy of the whole, in the hour of danger; raised to power, the wise and patriotic; elevated the Roman name above all others; extended her authority and dominion over the greater part of the then known world, and transmitted the influence of her laws and institutions to the present day. Had the opposite counsel prevailed at this critical juncture; had an appeal been made to arms instead of to concession and compromise, Rome, instead of being what she afterwards became, would, in all probability, have been as inglorious, and as little known to posterity as the insignificant states which surrounded her, whose names and existence would have been long since consigned to oblivion, had they not been preserved in the history of her conquests of them. But for the wise course then adopted, it is not improbable—whichever order might have pre-vailed—that she would have fallen under some cruel and petty tyrant—and, finally, been conquered by some of the neighboring states—or by the Carthaginians, or the Gauls. To the fortunate turn which events then took, she owed her unbounded sway and imperishable renown.

It is true, that the tribunate, after raising her to a height of power and prosperity never before equalled, finally became one of the instruments by which her liberty was overthrown—but it was not until she became ex-posed to new dangers, growing out of increase of wealth and the great extent of her dominions, against which the tribunate furnished no guards. Its original object was the protection of the plebeians against oppression and abuse of power on the part of the patricians. This, it thoroughly accomplished; but it had no power to protect the people of the numerous and wealthy conquered countries from being plundered by consuls and proconsuls. Nor could it prevent the plunderers from using the enormous wealth, which they extorted from the impoverished and ruined provinces, to corrupt and debase the people; nor arrest the formation of parties (irrespective of the old division of patricians and plebeians) having no other object than to obtain the control of the government for the purpose of plunder. Against these formidable evils, her constitution furnished no adequate security. Under their baneful influence, the possession of the government became the object of the most violent conflicts; not between patricians and plebeians—but between profligate and corrupt factions. They continued with increasing violence, until, finally, Rome sunk, as must every community under similar circumstances, beneath the strong grasp, the despotic rule of the chieftain of the successful party—the sad, but only alternative which remained to prevent universal violence, confusion and anarchy. The Republic had, in reality, ceased to exist long before the establishment of the Empire. The interval was filled by the rule of fero-cious, corrupt and bloody factions. There was, indeed, a small but patriotic body of eminent individuals, who struggled, in vain, to correct abuses, and to restore the government to its primitive character and purity—and who sacrificed their lives in their endeavors to accomplish an object so virtuous and noble. But it can be no disparagement to the tribunate, that the great powers conferred on it for wise purposes, and which it had so fully accomplished, should be seized upon, during this violent and corrupt interval, to overthrow the liberty it had established, and so long nourished and supported.

In assigning such consequence to the tribunate, I must not overlook other important provisions of the Constitution of the Roman government. The Senate, as far as we are informed, seems to have been admirably constituted to secure consistency and steadiness of action. The power—when the Republic was exposed to imminent danger—to appoint a dictator—vested, for a limited period, with almost boundless authority; the two consuls, and the manner of electing them; the auguries; the sibylline books; the priesthood, and the censorship—all of which appertained to the patricians—were, perhaps indispensable to withstand the vast and apparently irregular power of the tribunate—while the possession of such great powers by the patricians, made it necessary to give proportionate strength to the only organ through which the plebeians could act on the government with effect. The government was, indeed, powerfully constituted; and, apparently, well proportioned both in its positive and negative organs. It was truly an iron government. Without the tribunate, it proved to be one of the most oppressive and cruel that ever existed; but with it, one of the strongest and best.

The origin and character of the British government are so well known, that a very brief sketch, with the object in view, will suffice.

The causes which ultimately moulded it into its present form, commenced with the Norman Conquest. This introduced the feudal system, with its necessary appendages, a hereditary monarchy and nobility; the former in the line of the chief, who led the invading army—and the latter in that of his distinguished followers. They became his feudatories. The country—both land and people (the latter as serfs)—was divided between them. Conflicts soon followed between the monarch and the nobles—as must ever be the case under such systems. They were followed, in the progress of events, by efforts, on the part both of monarchs and nobles, to conciliate the favor of the people. They, in consequence, gradually rose to power. At every step of their ascent, they became more important—and were more and more courted—until at length their influence was so sensibly felt, that they were summoned to attend the meeting of parliament by delegates; not, however, as an estate of the realm, or constituent member of the body politic. The first summons came from the nobles; and was designed to conciliate their good feelings and secure their cooperation in the war against the king. This was followed by one from him; but his object was simply to have them present at the meeting of parliament, in order to be *consulted* by the crown, on questions relating to taxes and supplies; not, indeed, to discuss the right to lay the one, and to raise the other—for the King claimed the arbitrary authority to do both—but with a view to facilitate their collection, and to reconcile them to their imposition.

From this humble beginning, they, after a long struggle, accompanied by many vicissitudes, raised themselves to be considered one of the estates of the realm; and, finally, in their efforts to enlarge and secure what they had gained, overpowered, for a time, the other two estates; and thus concentrated all power in a single estate or body. This, in effect, made the government absolute, and led to consequences which, as by a fixed law, must ever result in popular governments of this form—namely—to organized parties, or, rather, factions, contending violently to obtain or retain the control of the government; and this, again, by laws almost as uniform, to the concentration of all the powers of government in the hands of the military commander of the successful party.

His heir was too feeble to hold the sceptre he had grasped; and the general discontent with the result of the revolution, led to the restoration of the old dynasty; without defining the limits between the powers of the respective estates.

After a short interval, another revolution followed, in which the lords and commons united against the king. This terminated in his overthrow;

and the transfer of the crown to a collateral branch of the family, accompanied by a declaration of rights, which defined the powers of the several estates of the realm; and, finally, perfected and established the constitution. Thus, a feudal monarchy was converted, through a slow but steady process of many centuries, into a highly refined constitutional monarchy, without changing the basis of the original government.

As it now stands, the realm consists of three estates; the king; the lords temporal and spiritual; and the commons. The parliament is the grand council. It possesses the supreme power. It enacts laws, by the concurring assent of the lords and commons—subject to the approval of the king. The executive power is vested in the monarch, who is regarded as constituting the first estate. Although irresponsible himself, he can only act through responsible ministers and agents. They are responsible to the other estates; to the lords, as constituting the high court before whom all the servants of the crown may be tried for malpractices, and crimes against the realm, or official delinquencies—and to the commons, as possessing the impeaching power, and constituting the grand inquest of the kingdom. These provisions, with their legislative powers—especially that of withholding supplies—give them a controlling influence on the executive department, and, virtually, a participation in its powers—so that the acts of the government, throughout its entire range, may be fairly considered as the result of the concurrent and joint action of the three estates—and, as these embrace all the orders—of the concurrent and joint action of the estates of the realm.

He would take an imperfect and false view of the subject who should consider the king, in his mere individual character, or even as the head of the royal family—as constituting an estate. Regarded in either light, so far from deserving to be considered as the First Estate—and the head of the realm, as he is—he would represent an interest too inconsiderable to be an object of special protection. Instead of this, he represents what in reality is, habitually and naturally, the most powerful interest, all things considered, under every form of government in all civilized communities—*the tax-consuming interest;* or, more broadly, the great interest which necessarily grows out of the action of the government, be its form what it may—the interest that *lives by the government*. It is composed of the recipients of its honors and emoluments; and may be properly called, the government interest, or party—in contradistinction to the rest of the community—or (as they may be properly called) the people or commons. The one comprehends all who are supported by the government—and the other all who support the government—and it is only because the former are strongest, all things being considered, that they are enabled to retain, for any considerable time, advantages so great and commanding.

This great and predominant interest is naturally represented by a single head. For it is impossible, without being so represented, to distribute the honors and emoluments of the government among those who compose it, without producing discord and conflict—and it is only by preventing these, that advantages so tempting can be long retained. And, hence, the strong tendency of this great interest to the monarchical form—that is, to be represented by a single individual. On the contrary, the antagonistic interest—that which supports the government, has the opposite tendency—a tendency to be represented by many; because a large assembly can better judge, than one individual or a few, what burdens the community can bear—and how it can be most equally distributed, and easily collected.

In the British government, the king constitutes an Estate, because he is the head and representative of this great interest. He is the conduit through which, all the honors and emoluments of the government flow—while the House of Commons, according to the theory of the government, is the head and representative of the opposite—the great tax-paying interest, by which the government is supported.

Between these great interests, there is necessarily a constant and strong tendency to conflict; which, if not counteracted, must end in violence and an appeal to force—to be followed by revolution, as has been explained. To prevent this, the House of Lords, as one of the estates of the realm, is interposed; and constitutes the conservative power of the government. It consists, in fact, of that portion of the community who are the principal recipients of the honors, emoluments, and other advantages derived from the government; and whose condition cannot be improved, but must be made worse by the triumph of either of the conflicting estates over the other; and, hence, it is opposed to the ascendency of either—and in favor of preserving the equilibrium between them.

This sketch, brief as it is, is sufficient to show, that these two constitutional governments—by far the most illustrious of their respective kinds— conform to the principles that have been established, alike in their origin and in their construction. The constitutions of both originated in a pressure, occasioned by conflicts of interests between hostile classes or orders, and were intended to meet the pressing exigencies of the occasion; neither party, it would seem, having any conception of the principles involved, or the consequences to follow, beyond the immediate objects in contemplation. It would, indeed, seem almost impossible for constitutional governments, founded on orders or classes, to originate in any other manner. It is difficult to conceive that any people, among whom they did not exist, would, or could voluntarily institute them, in order to establish such governments; while it is not at all wonderful, that they should grow out of conflicts between different orders or classes when aided by a favorable combination of circumstances.

The constitutions of both rest on the same principle—an organism by which the voice of each order or class is taken through its appropriate organ; and which requires the concurring voice of all to constitute that of the whole community. The effects, too, were the same in both—to unite and harmonize conflicting interests—to strengthen attachments to the whole community, and to moderate that to the respective orders or classes; to rally all, in the hour of danger, around the standard of their country; to elevate the feeling of nationality, and to develop power, moral and physical, to an extraordinary extent. Yet each has its distinguishing features, resulting from the difference of their organisms, and the circumstances in which they respectively originated.

In the government of Great Britain, the three orders are blended in the legislative department; so that the separate and concurring act of each is necessary to make laws; while, on the contrary, in the Roman, one order had the power of making laws, and another of annulling them, or arresting their execution. Each had its peculiar advantages. The Roman developed more fully the love of country and the feelings of nationality. *"I am a Roman citizen,"* was pronounced with a pride and elevation of sentiment, never, perhaps, felt before or since, by any citizen or subject of any community, in announcing the country to which he belonged.

It also developed more fully the power of the community. Taking into consideration their respective population, and the state of the arts at the different periods, Rome developed more power, comparatively, than Great Britain ever has—vast as that is, and has been—or, perhaps, than any other community ever did. Hence, the mighty control she acquired from a beginning so humble. But the British government is far superior to that of Rome, in its adaptation and capacity to embrace under its control extensive dominions, without subverting its constitution. In this respect, the Roman constitution was defective—and, in consequence, soon began to exhibit marks of decay, after Rome had extended her dominions beyond Italy; while the British holds under its sway, without apparently impairing either, an empire equal to that, under the weight of which the constitution and liberty of Rome were crushed. This great advantage it derives from its different structure, especially that of the executive department; and the character of its conservative principle. The former is so constructed as to prevent, in consequence of its unity and hereditary character, the violent and factious struggles to obtain the control of the government—and, with it, the vast patronage which distracted, corrupted, and finally subverted the Roman Republic. Against this fatal disease, the latter had no security whatever; while the British government—besides the advantages it possesses, in this respect, from the structure of its executive department— has, in the character of its conservative principle, another and powerful security against it. Its character is such, that patronage, instead of weakening, strengthens it—for, the greater the patronage of the government, the greater will be the share which falls to the estate constituting the conserva-tive department of the government; and the more eligible its condition, the greater its opposition to any radical change in its form. The two causes combined, give to the government a greater capacity of holding under subjection extensive dominions, without subverting the constitution or de-stroying liberty, than has ever been possessed by any other. It is difficult, indeed, to assign any limit to its capacity in this respect. The most probable which can be assigned is, its ability to bear increased burdens—the taxa-tion necessary to meet the expenses incident to the acquisition and govern-ment of such vast dominions, may prove, in the end, so heavy as to crush, under its weight, the laboring and productive portions of the population.

I have now finished the brief sketch I proposed, of the origin and character of these two renowned governments; and shall next proceed to consider the character, origin and structure of the Government of the United States. It differs from the Roman and British, more than they differ from each other; and, although an existing government of recent origin, its character and structure are perhaps less understood than those of either.

A DISCOURSE ON THE CONSTITUTION AND GOVERNMENT OF THE UNITED STATES

———•◆•———

Immediately following the completion of his Disquisition, *Calhoun turned his attention to a second major work, a project that he anticipated would "be more than twice as voluminous as the elementary work, but not near so difficult of execution."* * *That extended essay is in his* Discourse on the Constitution and Government of the United States, *an essay which offers a detailed and practical application of his theory of the concurrent majority to the government and constitution of the United States. Although Calhoun's* Discourse *follows an elaborate outline, the subject matter can be divided into three general categories: (1) the original intentions of the founders concerning the formation and ratification of the Constitution; (2) the dangers inherent in the encroachment of the federal government upon the reserved powers of the states; and (3) the call for the restoration of the doctrine of the concurrent majority, if consolidation and disunion are to be avoided. Within this general framework, Calhoun provides a critical analysis of each of the articles of the Constitution, as well as all of the major agencies of the general government. Also included is an analysis and critical reading of many of the founding documents, especially* Federalist #10, #39, #51, *and* #78.

---

*Annual Report of the American Historical Association for the Year 1899, Vol. II, ed. J. F. Jameson, p. 768, "To Mrs. T. C. Clemson, June 15, 1849."

OURS is a system of governments, compounded of the separate governments of the several States composing the Union, and of one common government of all its members, called the Government of the United States. The former preceded the latter, which was created by their agency. Each was framed by written constitutions; those of the several States by the people of each, acting separately, and in their sovereign character; and that of the United States, by the same, acting in the same character—but jointly instead of separately. All were formed on the same model. They all divide the powers of government into legislative, executive, and judicial; and are founded on the great principle of the responsibility of the rulers to the ruled. The entire powers of government are divided between the two; those of a more general character being specifically delegated to the United States; and all others not delegated, being reserved to the several States in their separate character. Each, within its appropriate sphere, possesses all the attributes, and performs all the functions of government. Neither is perfect without the other. The two combined, form one entire and perfect government. With these preliminary remarks, I shall proceed to the consideration of the immediate subject of this discourse.

The Government of the United States was formed by the Constitution of the United States—and ours is a democratic, federal republic.

It is democratic, in contradistinction to aristocracy and monarchy. It excludes classes, orders, and all artificial distinctions. To guard against their introduction, the constitution prohibits the granting of any title of nobility by the United States, or by any State.[1] The whole system is, indeed, democratic throughout. It has for its fundamental principle, the great cardinal maxim, that the people are the source of all power; that the governments of the several States and of the United States were created by them, and for them; that the powers conferred on them are not surrendered, but delegated; and, as such, are held in trust, and not absolutely; and can be rightfully exercised only in furtherance of the objects for which they were delegated.

It is federal as well as democratic. *Federal,* on the one hand, in contradistinction to *national,* and, on the other, to a *confederacy.* In showing this, I shall begin with the former.

It is federal, because it is the government of States united in political union, in contradistinction to a government of individuals socially united; that is, by what is usually called, a social compact. To express it more concisely, it is federal and not national, because it is the government of a community of States, and not the government of a single State or nation.

That it is federal and not national, we have the high authority of the convention which framed it. General Washington, as its organ, in his letter submitting the plan to the consideration of the Congress of the then confederacy, calls it, in one place—"the general government of the Union"—and in another—"the federal government of these States." Taken together, the plain meaning is, that the government proposed would be, if adopted, the government of the States adopting it, in their united character as members of a common Union; and, as such, would be a federal government. These expressions were not used without due consideration, and an accurate and full knowledge of their true import. The subject was not a novel one. The convention was familiar with it. It was much agitated in their deliberations. They divided, in reference to it, in the early stages of their proceedings. At first, one party was in favor of a national and the

[1] 1st Article 9 and 10 Section.

other of a federal government. The former, in the beginning, prevailed; and in the plans which they proposed, the constitution and government are styled "National." But, finally, the latter gained the ascendency, when the term "National" was superseded, and *United States* substituted in its place. The constitution was accordingly styled—*"The constitution of the United States of America"*—and the government—*"The government of the United States"* leaving out "America," for the sake of brevity. It cannot admit of a doubt, that the Convention, by the expression "United States," meant the States united in a federal Union; for in no other sense could they, with propriety, call the government, *"the federal government of these States"*—and *"the general government of the Union"*—as they did in the letter referred to. It is thus clear, that the Convention regarded the different expressions—"the federal government of the United States"—"the general government of the Union"—and—"government of the United States"—as meaning the same thing—a federal, in contradistinction to a national government.

Assuming it then, as established, that they are the same, it is only necessary, in order to ascertain with precision, what they meant by "federal government"—to ascertain what they meant by "the government of the United States." For this purpose it will be necessary to trace the expression to its origin.

It was, at that time, as our history shows, an old and familiar phrase—having a known and well-defined meaning. Its use commenced with the political birth of these States; and it has been applied to them, in all the forms of government through which they have passed, without alteration. The style of the present constitution and government is precisely the style by which the confederacy that existed when it was adopted, and which it superseded, was designated. The instrument that formed the latter was called—"Articles of Confederation and Perpetual Union." Its first article declares that the style of this confederacy shall be, "The United States of America;" and the second, in order to leave no doubt as to the relation in which the States should stand to each other in the confederacy about to be

formed, declared—"Each State retains its sovereignty, freedom and independence; and every power, jurisdiction, and right, which is not, by this
confederation, expressly delegated to the United States in Congress assembled." If we go one step further back, the style of the confederacy will be
found to be the same with that of the revolutionary government, which
existed when it was adopted, and which it superseded. It dates its origin
with the Declaration of Independence. That act is styled—"The unanimous Declaration of the thirteen United States of America." And here
again, that there might be no doubt how these States would stand to each
other in the new condition in which they were about to be placed, it
concluded by declaring—"that these United Colonies are, and of right
ought to be, free and independent States;" "and that, as free and independent States, they have full power to levy war, conclude peace, contract
alliances, and to do all other acts and things which independent States may
of right do." The "United States" is, then, the baptismal name of these
States—received at their birth—by which they have ever since continued
to call themselves; by which they have characterized their constitution,
government and laws—and by which they are known to the rest of the
world.

The retention of the same style, throughout every stage of their existence, affords strong, if not conclusive evidence that the political relation
between these States, under their present constitution and government, is
substantially the same as under the confederacy and revolutionary government; and what that relation was, we are not left to doubt; as they are
declared expressly to be *"free, independent* and *sovereign* States."* They,
then, are now united, and have been, throughout, simply as 'confederated
States. If it had been intended by the members of the convention which
framed the present constitution and government, to make any essential
change, either in the relation of the States to each other, or the basis of
their union, they would, by retaining the style which designated them under
the preceding governments, have practised a deception, utterly unworthy
of their character, as sincere and honest men and patriots. It may, there-

fore, be fairly inferred, that, retaining the same style, they intended to attach to the expression—"the United States," the same meaning, substantially, which it previously had; and, of course, in calling the present government—"the federal government of these States," they meant by "federal," that they stood in the same relation to each other—that their union rested, without material change, on the same basis—as under the confederacy and the revolutionary government; and that federal, and confederated States, meant substantially the same thing. It follows, also, that the changes made by the present constitution were not in the foundation, but in the superstructure of the system. We accordingly find, in confirmation of this conclusion, that the convention, in their letter to Congress, stating the reasons for the changes that had been made, refer only to the necessity which required a different *"organization"* of the government, without making any allusion whatever to any change in the relations of the States towards each other—or the basis of the system. They state that, "the friends of our country have long seen and desired, that the power of making war, peace, and treaties; that of levying money and regulating commerce, and the correspondent executive and judicial authorities, should be fully and effectually vested in the Government of the Union: but the impropriety of delegating such extensive trusts to one body of men is evident; hence results the necessity of a *different organization*." Comment is unnecessary.

We thus have the authority of the convention itself for asserting that the expression, "United States," has essentially the same meaning, when applied to the present constitution and government, as it had previously; and, of course, that the States have retained their separate existence, as independent and sovereign communities, in all the forms of political existence, through which they have passed. Such, indeed, is the literal import of the expression—"the United States"—and the sense in which it is ever used, when it is applied politically—I say, *politically*—because it is often applied, *geographically*, to designate the portion of this continent occupied by the States composing the Union, including territories belonging to them.

This application arose from the fact, that there was no appropriate term for that portion of this continent; and thus, not unnaturally, the name by which these States are politically designated, was employed to designate the region they occupy and possess. The distinction is important, and cannot be overlooked in discussing questions involving the character and nature of the government, without causing great confusion and dangerous misconceptions.

But as conclusive as these reasons are to prove that the government of the United States is federal, in contradistinction to national, it would seem, that they have not been sufficient to prevent the opposite opinion from being entertained. Indeed, this last seems to have become the prevailing one; if we may judge from the general use of the term "national," and the almost entire disuse of that of "federal." National, is now commonly applied to "the general government of the Union"—and "the federal government of these States"—and all that appertains to them or to the Union. It seems to be forgotten that the term was repudiated by the convention, after full consideration; and that it was carefully excluded from the constitution, and the letter laying it before Congress. Even those who know all this— and, of course, how falsely the term is applied—have, for the most part, slided into its use without reflection. But there are not a few who so apply it, because they believe it to be a national government in fact; and among these are men of distinguished talents and standing, who have put forth all their powers of reason and eloquence, in support of the theory. The question involved is one of the first magnitude, and deserves to be investigated thoroughly in all its aspects. With this impression, I deem it proper—clear and conclusive as I regard the reasons already assigned to prove its federal character—to confirm them by historical references; and to repel the arguments adduced to prove it to be a national government. I shall begin with the formation and ratification of the constitution.

That the States, when they formed and ratified the constitution, were distinct, independent, and sovereign communities, has already been established. That the people of the several States, acting in their separate,

independent, and sovereign character, adopted their separate State constitutions, is a fact uncontested and incontestable; but it is not more certain
than that, acting in the same character, they ratified and adopted the
constitution of the United States; with this difference only, that in making
and adopting the one, they acted without concert or agreement; but, in the
other, with concert in making, and mutual agreement in adopting it. That
the delegates who constituted the convention which framed the constitution, were appointed by the several States, each on its own authority; that
they voted in the convention by States; and that their votes were counted
by States—are recorded and unquestionable facts. So, also, the facts that
the constitution, when framed, was submitted to the people of the several
States for their respective ratification; that it was ratified by them, each for
itself; and that it was binding on each, only in consequence of its being so
ratified by it. Until then, it was but the plan of a constitution, without any
binding force. It was the act of ratification which established it as a constitution between the States ratifying it; and only between *them*, on the condition that not less than nine of the then thirteen States should concur in the
ratification—as is expressly provided by its seventh and last article. It is in
the following words: "The ratification of the conventions of nine States
shall be sufficient for the establishment of this constitution between the
States so ratifying the same." If additional proof be needed to show that it
was only binding between the States that ratified it, it may be found in the
fact, that two States, North Carolina and Rhode Island, refused, at first, to
ratify; and were, in consequence, regarded in the interval as foreign States,
without obligation, on their parts, to respect it, or, on the part of their
citizens, to obey it. Thus far, there can be no difference of opinion. The
facts are too recent and too well established—and the provision of the
constitution too explicit, to admit of doubt.

That the States, then, retained, after the ratification of the constitution,
the distinct, independent, and sovereign character in which they formed and
ratified it, is certain; unless they divested themselves of it by the act of
ratification, or by some provision of the constitution. If they have not, the

constitution must be federal, and not national; for it would have, in that case, every attribute necessary to constitute it federal, and not one to make it national. On the other hand, if they have divested themselves, then it would necessarily lose its federal character, and become national. Whether, then, the government is federal or national, is reduced to a single question; whether the act of ratification, of itself, or the constitution, by some one, or all of its provisions, did, or did not, divest the several States of their character of separate, independent, and sovereign communities, and merge them all in one great community or nation, called the American people?

Before entering on the consideration of this important question, it is proper to remark, that, on its decision, the character of the government, as well as the constitution, depends. The former must, necessarily, partake of the character of the latter, as it is but its agent, created by it, to carry its powers into effect. Accordingly, then, as the constitution is federal or national, so must the government be; and I shall, therefore, use them indiscriminately in discussing the subject.

Of all the questions which can arise under our system of government, this is by far the most important. It involves many others of great magnitude; and among them, that of the allegiance of the citizen; or, in other words, the question to whom allegiance and obedience are ultimately due. What is the true relation between the two governments—that of the United States and those of the several States? and what is the relation between the individuals respectively composing them? For it is clear, if the States still retain their sovereignty as separate and independent communities, the allegiance and obedience of the citizens of each would be due to their respective States; and that the government of the United States and those of the several States would stand as equals and co-ordinates in their respective spheres; and, instead of being united socially, their citizens would be politically connected through their respective States. On the contrary, if they have, by ratifying the constitution, divested themselves of their individuality and sovereignty, and merged themselves into one great community or nation, it is equally clear, that the sovereignty would reside in the whole—or what is called the American people; and that allegiance and obedience would be due to them. Nor is it less so, that the government of the several States would, in such case, stand to that of the United States, in the relation of inferior and subordinate, to superior and paramount; and that the individuals of the several States, thus fused, as it were, into one general mass, would be united *socially*, and not *politically*. So great a change of condition would have involved a thorough and radical revolution, both socially and politically—a revolution much more radical, indeed, than that which followed the Declaration of Independence.

They who maintain that the ratification of the constitution effected so mighty a change, are bound to establish it by the most demonstrative proof. The presumption is strongly opposed to it. It has already been shown, that the authority of the convention which formed the constitution is clearly against it; and that the history of its ratification, instead of supplying evidence in its favor, furnishes strong testimony in opposition to it. To these, others may be added; and, among them, the presumption drawn from the history of these States, in all the stages of their existence down to the time of the ratification of the constitution. In all, they formed separate, and, as it respects each other, independent communities; and were ever remarkable for the tenacity with which they adhered to their rights as such. It constituted, during the whole period, one of the most striking traits in their character—as a very brief sketch will show.

During their colonial condition, they formed distinct communities— each with its separate charter and government—and in no way connected with each other, except as dependent members of a common empire. Their first union amongst themselves was, in resistance to the encroachments of the parent country on their chartered rights—when they adopted the title of—"the United Colonies." Under that name they acted, until they declared their independence—always, in their joint councils, voting and acting as separate and distinct communities—and not in the aggregate, as composing one community or nation. They acted in the same character in declaring independence; by which act they passed from their dependent, colonial condition, into that of free and sovereign States. The declaration was made by delegates appointed by the several colonies, each for itself, and on its own authority. The vote making the declaration was taken by delegations, each counting one. The declaration was announced to be unanimous, not because every delegate voted for it, but because the majority of each delegation did; showing clearly, that the body itself, regarded it as the united act of the several colonies, and not the act of the whole as one community. To leave no doubt on a point so important, and in reference to which the several colonies were so tenacious, the declaration was made in the name, and by the authority of the people of the colonies, represented in Congress; and that was followed by declaring them to be—"free and independent States." The act was, in fact, but a formal and solemn annunciation to the world, that the colonies had ceased to be dependent communities, and had become free and independent States; without involving any other change in their relations with each other, than those necessarily incident to a separation from the parent country. So far were they from supposing, or intending that it should have the effect of merging their existence, as separate communities, into one nation, that they had appointed a committee—which was actually sitting, while the declaration was under discussion—to prepare a plan of a confederacy of the States, preparatory to entering into their new condition. In fulfilment of their appointment, this committee prepared the draft of the articles of confederation and perpetual union, which afterwards was adopted by the governments of the several States. That it instituted a mere confederacy and union of the States has already been shown. That, in forming and assenting to it, the States were exceedingly jealous and watchful in delegating power, even to a confederacy; that they granted the powers delegated most reluctantly and sparingly; that several of them long stood out, under all the pressure of the revolutionary war, before they acceded to it; and that, during the interval which elapsed between its adoption and that of the present constitution, they evinced, under the most urgent necessity, the same reluctance and jealousy, in delegating power—are facts which cannot be disputed.

To this may be added another circumstance of no little weight, drawn from the preliminary steps taken for the ratification of the constitution. The plan was laid, by the convention, before the Congress of the confederacy, for its consideration and action, as has been stated. It was the sole organ and representative of these States in their confederated character. By submitting it, the convention recognized and acknowledged its authority over it, as the organ of distinct, independent, and sovereign States. It had the right to dispose of it as it pleased; and, if it had thought proper, it might have defeated the plan by simply omitting to act on it. But it thought proper to act, and to adopt the course recommended by the convention— which was, to submit it—"to a convention of delegates, chosen in each State, by the people thereof, for their assent and adoption." All this was in strict accord with the federal character of the constitution, but wholly repugnant to the idea of its being national. It received the assent of the States in all the possible modes in which it could be obtained: first—in their confederated character, through its only appropriate organ, the Congress; next, in their individual character, as separate States, through their respective State governments, to which the Congress referred it; and finally, in their high character of independent and sovereign communities, through a convention of the people, called in each State, by the authority of its government. The States acting in these various capacities, might, at every stage, have defeated it or not, at their option, by giving or withholding their consent.

With this weight of presumptive evidence, to use no stronger expression, in favor of its federal, in contradistinction to its national character, I shall next proceed to show, that the ratification of the constitution, instead of furnishing proof against, contains additional and conclusive evidence in its favor.

We are not left to conjecture, as to what was meant by the ratification of the constitution, or its effects. The expressions used by the conventions of the States, in ratifying it, and those used by the constitution in connection with it, afford ample means of ascertaining with accuracy, both its meaning and effect. The usual form of expression used by the former is: "We, the delegates of the State," (naming the State) "do, in behalf of the people of the State, assent to, and ratify the said constitution." All use, "ratify"—and all, except North Carolina, use, "assent to." The delegates of that State use, "adopt," instead of "assent to;" a variance merely in the form of expression, without, in any degree, affecting the meaning. Ratification was, then, the act of the several States in their separate capacity. It was performed by delegates appointed expressly for the purpose. Each appointed its own delegates; and the delegates of each, acted in the name of, and for the State appointing them. Their act consisted in, "assenting to," or, what is the same thing, "adopting and ratifying" the constitution.

By turning to the seventh article of the constitution, and to the preamble, it will be found what was the effect of ratifying. The article expressly provides, that, "the ratification of the conventions of nine States, shall be sufficient for the establishment of this constitution, between the States so ratifying the same." The preamble of the constitution is in the following words—"We, the people of the United States, in order to form a more perfect union, establish justice, insure domestic tranquillity, provide for the common defence, promote the general welfare, and secure the blessings of liberty to ourselves and our posterity, do ordain and establish this constitution for the United States of America." The effect, then, of its ratification was, to ordain and establish the constitution—and, thereby, to make, what was before but a plan—"The constitution of the United States of America." All this is clear.

It remains now to show, *by whom*, it was ordained and established; *for whom*, it was ordained and established; *for what*, it was ordained and established; and *over whom*, it was ordained and established. These will be considered in the order in which they stand.

Nothing more is necessary, in order to show by whom it was ordained and established, than to ascertain who are meant by—"We, the people of the United States;" for, by their authority, it was done. To this there can be but one answer—it meant the people who ratified the instrument; for it was the act of ratification which ordained and established it. Who they were, admits of no doubt. The process preparatory to ratification, and the acts by which it was done, prove, beyond the possibility of a doubt, that it was ratified by the several States, through conventions of delegates, chosen in each State by the people thereof; and acting, each in the name and by the authority of its State: and, as all the States ratified it—"We, the people of the United States"—mean,—We, the people of the several States of the Union. The inference is irresistible. And when it is considered that the States of the Union were then members of the confederacy—and that, by the express provision of one of its articles, "each State retains its sovereignty, freedom, and independence," the proof is demonstrative, that— "We, the people of the United States of America," mean the people of the several States of the Union, acting as free, independent, and sovereign States. This strikingly confirms what has been already stated; to wit, that the convention which formed the constitution, meant the same thing by the terms—"United States"—and, "federal"—when applied to the constitution or government—and that the former, when used politically, always mean—these States united as independent and sovereign communities.

Having shown, by *whom*, it was ordained, there will be no difficulty in determining, *for whom,* it was ordained. The preamble is explicit—it was ordained and established for—"The United States of America;" adding, "America," in conformity to the style of the then confederacy, and the Declaration of Independence. Assuming, then, that the "United States" bears the same meaning in the conclusion of the preamble, as it does in its commencement (and no reason can be assigned why it should not) it follows, necessarily, that the constitution was ordained and established *for* the people of the several States, *by* whom it was ordained and established.

Nor will there be any difficulty in showing, *for what,* it was ordained and established. The preamble enumerates the objects. They are—"to form a more perfect union, to establish justice, insure domestic tranquillity, provide for the common defence, promote the general welfare, and secure the blessings of liberty to ourselves and our posterity." To effect these objects, they ordained and established, to use their own language—"the constitution for the United States of America"—clearly meaning by "for," that it was intended to be *their* constitution; and that the objects of ordaining and establishing it were, to perfect *their* union, to establish justice among *them*—to insure *their* domestic tranquillity, to provide for *their* common defense and general welfare, and to secure the blessings of liberty to *them* and *their* posterity. Taken all together, it follows, from what has been stated, that the constitution was ordained and established *by* the several States, as *distinct, sovereign communities;* and that it was ordained and established by them for *themselves*—for their common welfare and safety, as *distinct and sovereign communities.*

It remains to be shown, *over whom,* it was ordained and established. That it was not over *the several States,* is settled by the seventh article beyond controversy. It declares, that the ratification by nine States shall be sufficient to establish the constitution between the States so ratifying. "Between," necessarily excludes "over"—as that which is *between* States cannot be *over* them. Reason itself, if the constitution had been silent, would have led, with equal certainty, to the same conclusion. For it was the several States, or, what is the same thing, their people, in their sovereign capacity, who ordained and established the constitution. But the authority which ordains and establishes, is higher than that which is ordained and established; and, of course, the latter must be subordinate to the former— and cannot, therefore, be *over* it. "Between," always means more than "over"—and implies in this case, that the authority which ordained and established the constitution, was the joint and united authority of the States ratifying it; and that, among the effects of their ratification, it became a contract between them; and, *as a compact,* binding on them—but only as such. In that sense the term, "between," is appropriately applied. In no other, can it be. It was, doubtless, used in that sense in this instance; but the question still remains, *over whom,* was it ordained and established? After what has been stated, the answer may be readily given. It was *over the government* which it created, and all its functionaries in their official character—and the individuals composing and inhabiting the several States, as far as they might come within the sphere of the powers delegated to the United States.

I have now shown, conclusively, by arguments drawn from the act of ratification, and the constitution itself, that the several States of the Union, acting in their confederated character, ordained and established the constitution; that they ordained and established it for themselves, in the same character; that they ordained and established it for their welfare and safety, in the like character; that they established it as a compact *between* them, and not as a constitution *over* them; and that, as a compact, they are parties to it, in the same character. I have thus established, conclusively, that these States, in ratifying the constitution, did not lose the confederated character which they possessed when they ratified it, as well as in all the preceding stages of their existence; but, on the contrary, still retained it to the full.

Those who oppose this conclusion, and maintain the national character of the government, rely, in support of their views, mainly on the expressions, "we, the people of the United States," used in the first part of the preamble; and, "do ordain and establish this constitution for the United States of America," used in its conclusion. Taken together, they insist, in the first place, that, "we, the people," mean, the people in their individual character, as forming a single community; and that, "the United States of America," designates them in their aggregate character, as the American people. In maintaining this construction, they rely on the omission to enumerate the States by name, after the word "people," (so as to make it read, "We, the people of New Hampshire, Massachusetts, &c.," as was done in the articles of the confederation, and, also, in signing the Declaration of Independence)—and, instead of this, the simple use of the general term "United States."

However plausible this may appear, an explanation perfectly satisfactory may be given, why the expression, as it now stands, was used by the framers of the constitution; and why it should not receive the meaning

attempted to be placed upon it. It is conceded that, if the enumeration of
the States after the word, "people," had been made, the expression would
have been freed from all ambiguity; and the inference and argument
founded on the failure to do so, left without pretext or support. The omission is certainly striking, but it can be readily explained. It was made
intentionally, and solely from the necessity of the case. The first draft of
the constitution contained an enumeration of the States, by name, after the
word "people;" but it became impossible to retain it after the adoption of
the seventh and last article, which provided, that the ratification by nine
States should be sufficient to establish the constitution as between *them;*
and for the plain reason, that it was impossible to determine, whether all
the States would ratify—or, if any failed, which, and how many of the
number; or, if nine should ratify, how to designate them. No alternative
was thus left but to omit the enumeration, and to insert the "United States
of America," in its place. And yet, an omission, so readily and so satisfactorily explained, has been seized on, as furnishing strong proof that the
government was ordained and established by the American people, in the
aggregate—and is therefore national.

But the omission, of itself, would have caused no difficulty, had there
not been connected with it a two-fold ambiguity in the expression as it now
stands. The term "United States," which always means, in constitutional
language, the several States in their confederated character, means also, as
has been shown, when applied geographically, the country occupied and
possessed by them. While the term "people," has, in the English language,
no plural, and is necessarily used in the singular number, even when
applied to many communities or states confederated in a common union—
as is the case with the United States. Availing themselves of this double
ambiguity, and the omission to enumerate the States by name, the advocates of the national theory of the government, assuming that, "we, the
people, meant individuals generally, and not people as forming States; and
that "United States" was used in a geographical and not a political sense,
made out an argument of some plausibility, in favor of the conclusion that,

"we, the people of the United States of America," meant the aggregate population of the States regarded *en masse,* and not in their distinctive character as forming separate political communities. But in this gratuitous assumption, and the conclusion drawn from it, they overlooked the stubborn fact, that the very people who ordained and established the constitution, are identically the same who ratified it; for it was by the act of ratification alone, that it was ordained and established—as has been conclusively shown. This fact, of itself, sweeps away every vestige of the argument drawn from the ambiguity of those terms, as used in the preamble.

They next rely, in support of their theory, on the expression—"ordained and established this constitution." They admit that the constitution, in its incipient state, assumed the form of a compact; but contend that, "ordained and established," as applied to the constitution and government, are incompatible with the idea of compact; that, consequently, the instrument or plan lost its federative character when it was ordained and established as a constitution; and, thus, the States ceased to be parties to a compact, and members of a confederated union, and became fused into one common community, or nation, as subordinate and dependent divisions or corporations.

I do not deem it necessary to discuss the question whether there is any incompatibility between the terms—"ordained and established"—and that of "compact," on which the whole argument rests; although it would be no difficult task to show that it is a gratuitous assumption, without any foundation whatever for its support. It is sufficient for my purpose, to show, that the assumption is wholly inconsistent with the constitution itself—as much so, as the conclusion drawn from it has been shown to be inconsistent with the opinion of the convention which formed it. Very little will be required, after what has been already stated, to establish what I propose.

That the constitution regards itself in the light of a compact, still existing between the States, after it was ordained and established; that it regards the union, then existing, as still existing; and the several States, of course, still members of it, in their original character of confederated States, is

clear. Its seventh article, so often referred to, in connection with the arguments drawn from the preamble, sufficiently establishes all these points,
without adducing others; except that which relates to the continuance of the
union. To establish this, it will not be necessary to travel out of the preamble and the letter of the convention, laying the plan of the constitution
before the Congress of the confederation. In enumerating the objects for
which the constitution was ordained and established, the preamble places
at the head of the rest, as its leading object—"to form a more perfect
union." So far, then, are the terms—"ordained and established," from
being incompatible with the union, or having the effect of destroying it, the
constitution itself declares that it was intended, "to form a more perfect
union." This, of itself, is sufficient to refute the assertion of their incompatibility. But it is proper here to remark, that it could not have been intended, by the expression in the preamble—"to form a more perfect
union"—to declare, that the old was abolished, and a new and more
perfect union established in its place: for we have the authority of the
convention which formed the constitution, to prove that their object was to
continue the then existing union. In their letter, laying it before Congress,
they say—"In all our deliberations on this subject, we kept steadily in our
view, that which appears to us, the greatest interest of every true American, the consolidation of our union." "Our union," can refer to no other
than the then existing union—the old union of the confederacy, and of the
revolutionary government which preceded it—of which these States were
confederated members. This must, of course, have been the union to which
the framers referred in the preamble. It was this, accordingly, which the
constitution intended to make more perfect; just as the confederacy made
more perfect, that of the revolutionary government. Nor is there any thing
in the term, "consolidation," used by the convention, calculated to weaken
the conclusion. It is a strong expression; but as strong as it is, it certainly
was not intended to imply the destruction of the union, as it is supposed to
do by the advocates of a national government; for that would have been
incompatible with the context, as well as with the continuance of the

union—which the sentence and the entire letter imply. Interpreted, then, in conjunction with the expression used in the preamble—"to form a more perfect union"—although it may more strongly intimate closeness of connection; it can imply nothing incompatible with the professed object of perfecting the union—still less a meaning and effect wholly inconsistent with the nature of a confederated community. For to adopt the interpretation contended for, to its full extent, would be to *destroy* the union, and not to consolidate and perfect it.

If we turn from the preamble and the ratifications, to the body of the constitution, we shall find that it furnishes most conclusive proof that the government is federal, and not national. I can discover nothing, in any portion of it, which gives the least countenance to the opposite conclusion. On the contrary, the instrument, in all its parts, repels it. It is, throughout, federal. It every where recognizes the existence of the States, and invokes their aid to carry its powers into execution. In one of the two houses of Congress, the members are elected by the legislatures of their respective States; and in the other, by the people of the several States, not as composing mere districts of one great community, but as distinct and independent communities. General Washington vetoed the first act apportioning the members of the House of Representatives among the several States, under the first census, expressly on the ground, that the act assumed as its basis, the former, and not the latter construction. The President and Vice-President are chosen by electors, appointed by their respective States; and, finally, the Judges are appointed by the President and the Senate; and, of course, as these are elected by the States, they are appointed through their agency.

But, however strong be the proofs of its federal character derived from this source, that portion which provides for the amendment of the constitution, furnishes, if possible, still stronger. It shows, conclusively, that the people of the several States still retain that supreme ultimate power, called sovereignty—the power by which they ordained and established the constitution; and which can rightfully create, modify, amend, or abolish it, at its pleasure. Wherever this power resides, there the sovereignty is to be found. That it still continues to exist in the several States, in a modified form, is clearly shown by the fifth article of the constitution, which provides for its amendment. By its provisions, Congress may propose amendments, on its own authority, by the vote of two-thirds of both houses; or it may be compelled to call a convention to propose them, by two-thirds of the legislatures of the several States: but, in either case, they remain, when thus made, mere proposals of no validity, until adopted by three-fourths of the States, through their respective legislatures; or by conventions, called by them, for the purpose. Thus far, the several States, in ordaining and establishing the constitution, agreed, for their mutual convenience and advantage, to modify, by compact, their high sovereign power of creating and establishing constitutions, as far as it related to the constitution and government of the United States. I say, for their mutual convenience and advantage; for without the modification, it would have required the separate consent of all the States of the Union to alter or amend their constitutional compact; in like manner as it required the consent of all to establish it between them; and to obviate the almost insuperable difficulty of making such amendments as time and experience might prove to be necessary, by the unanimous consent of all, they agreed to make the modification. But that they did not intend, by this, to divest themselves of the high sovereign right (a right which they still retain, notwithstanding the modification) to change or abolish the present constitution and government at their pleasure, cannot be doubted. It is an acknowledged principle, that sovereigns may, by compact, modify or qualify the exercise of their power, without impairing their sovereignty; of which, the confederacy existing at the time, furnishes a striking illustration. It must reside, unimpaired and in its plenitude, somewhere. And if it do not reside in the people of the several States, in their confederated character, where—so far as it relates to the constitution and government of the United States—can it be found? Not, certainly, in the government; for, according to our theory, sovereignty resides in the people, and not in the government. That it cannot be found in the people, taken in the aggregate, as forming one community or nation, is equally certain. But as certain as it cannot, just so certain is it, that it must reside in the people of the several States: and if it reside in them at all, it must reside in them as separate and distinct communities; for it has been shown, that it does not reside in them in the aggregate, as forming one community or nation. These are the only aspects under which it is possible to regard the people; and, just as certain as it resides in them, in that character, so certain is it that ours is a federal, and not a national government.

The theory of the nationality of the government, is, in fact, founded on fiction. It is of recent origin. Few, even yet, venture to avow it to its full extent; while they entertain doctrines, which spring from, and must necessarily terminate in it. They admit that the people of the several States form separate, independent, and sovereign communities—and that, to this extent, the constitution is federal; but beyond this, and to the extent of the delegated powers—regarding them as forming one people or nation, they maintain that the constitution is national.

Now, unreasonable as is the theory that it is wholly national, this, if possible, is still more so; for the one, although against reason and recorded evidence, is possible; but the other, while equally against both, is absolutely impossible. It involves the absurdity of making the constitution federal in reference to a class of powers, which are expressly excluded from it; and, by consequence, from the compact itself, into which the several States entered when they established it. The term, "federal," implies a league—and this, a compact between sovereign communities; and, of course, it is impossible for the States to be federal, in reference to powers expressly reserved to them in their character of separate States, and not included in the compact. If the States are national at all—or, to express it more definitely—if they form a NATION at all, it must be in reference to the delegated, and not the reserved powers. But it has already been established that, as to these, they have no such character—no such existence. It is, however, proper to remark, that while it is impossible for them to be federal, as to their reserved powers, they could not be federal without them. For had all the powers of government been delegated, the separate constitutions and governments of the several States would have been superseded and destroyed; and what is now called the constitution and government of the United States, would have become the sole constitution and government of the whole—the effect of which, would have been to supersede and destroy the States themselves. The people respectively composing them, instead of constituting political communities, having appropriate organs to will and to act—which is indispensable to the existence of a State—would, in such case, be divested of all such organs; and, by consequence, reduced into an unorganized mass of individuals—as far as related to the respective States—and merged into one community or nation, having but one constitution and government as the organ, through which to will and to act. The idea, indeed, of a federal constitution and government, necessarily implies reserved and delegated powers—powers reserved in part, to be exercised exclusively by the States in their original separate character—and powers delegated, by mutual agreement, to be exercised jointly by a common council or government. And hence, consolidation and disunion are, equally, destructive of such government—one by merging the States composing the Union into one community or nation; and the other, by resolving them into their original elements, as separate and disconnected States.

It is difficult to imagine how a doctrine so perfectly absurd, as that the States are federal as to the reserved, and national as to the delegated powers, could have originated; except through a misconception of the meaning of certain terms, sometimes used to designate the latter. They are sometimes called *granted* powers; and at others, are said to be powers *surrendered* by the States. When these expressions are used without reference to the fact, that all powers, under our system of government, are trust powers, they imply that the States have parted with such as are said to be granted or surrendered, absolutely and irrecoverably. The case is different when applied to them as trust powers. They then become identical, in their meaning, with delegated powers; for to grant a power in trust, is what is meant by delegating it. It is not, therefore, surprising, that they who do not bear in mind that all powers of government are, with us, trust powers, should conclude that the powers said to be granted and surrendered by the States, are absolutely transferred from them to the government of the United States—as is sometimes alleged—or to the people as constituting one nation, as is more usually understood—and, thence, to infer that the government is national to the extent of the granted powers.

But that such inference and conclusion are utterly unwarrantable—that the powers in the constitution called granted powers, are, in fact, delegated powers—powers granted in trust—and not absolutely transferred—we have, in addition to the reasons just stated, the clear and decisive authority of the constitution itself. Its tenth amended article provides that "the powers not delegated to the United States by the constitution, nor prohibited by it to the States, are reserved to the States respectively, or to the people."

In order to understand the full force of this provision, it is necessary to state that this is one of the amended articles, adopted at the recommendation of several of the conventions of the States, contemporaneously with the ratification of the constitution—in order to supply what were thought to be its defects—and to guard against misconceptions of its meaning. It is admitted, that its principal object was to prevent the reserved from being drawn within the sphere of the granted powers, by the force of construction—a danger, which, at the time, excited great, and, as experience has proved, just apprehension. But in guarding against this danger, care was also taken to guard against others—and among them, against mistakes, as to whom powers were granted, and to whom they were reserved. The former was done by using the expression, "the powers not delegated to the United States," which, by necessary implication means, that the powers granted are delegated to them in their confederated character—and the latter, by the remaining portion of the article, which provides that such powers "are reserved to the States respectively, or to the people"—meaning clearly by, "respectively," that the reservation was to the several States and people in their separate character, and not to the whole, as forming one people or nation. They thus repudiate nationality, applied either to the delegated or to reserved powers.

But it may be asked—why was the reservation made both to the States and to the people? The answer is to be found in the fact, that, what are called, "reserved powers," in the constitution of the United States, include all powers not delegated to Congress by it—or prohibited by it to the States. The powers thus designated are divided into two distinct classes— those delegated by the people of the several States to their separate State governments, and those which they still retain—not having delegated them to either government. Among them is included the high sovereign power, by which they ordained and established both; and by which they can modify, change or abolish them at pleasure. This, with others not delegated, are those which are reserved to the people of the several States respectively.

But the article in its precaution, goes further—and takes care to guard against the term, "granted," used in the first article and first section of the constitution, which provides that, "all legislative powers herein *granted,* shall be vested in a Congress of the United States"—as well as against other terms of like import used in other parts of the instrument. It guarded against it, indirectly, by substituting, "delegated," in the place of "granted"—and instead of declaring that the powers not "granted," are reserved, it declares that the powers not "delegated," are reserved. Both terms—"granted," used in the constitution as it came from its framers, and "delegated," used in the amendments—evidently refer to the same class of powers; and no reason can be assigned, why the amendment substituted "delegated," in the place of "granted," but to free it from its ambiguity, and to provide against misconstruction.

It is only by considering the granted powers, in their true character of trust or delegated powers, that all the various parts of our complicated system of government can be harmonized and explained. Thus regarded, it will be easy to perceive how the people of the several States could grant certain powers to a joint—or, as its framers called it—a general govern-

ment, in trust, to be exercised for their common benefit, without an absolute surrender of them—or without impairing their independence and
sovereignty. Regarding them in the opposite light, as powers absolutely
surrendered and irrevocably transferred, inexplicable difficulties present
themselves. Among the first, is that which springs from the idea of divided
sovereignty; involving the perplexing question—how the people of the several States can be partly sovereign, and partly, *not* sovereign—sovereign
as to the reserved—and not sovereign, as to the delegated powers? There
is no difficulty in understanding how powers, appertaining to sovereignty,
may be divided; and *the exercise* of one portion delegated to one set of
agents, and another portion to another: or how sovereignty may be vested
in one man, or in a few, or in many. But how sovereignty itself—the
supreme power—can be divided—how the people of the several States
can be partly sovereign, and partly *not* sovereign—partly supreme, and
partly *not* supreme, it is impossible to conceive. Sovereignty is an entire
thing—to divide, is—to destroy it.

But suppose this difficulty surmounted—another not less perplexing
remains. If sovereignty be surrendered and transferred, in part or entirely,
by the several States, it must be transferred to somebody; and the question
is, to whom? Not, certainly, to the government—as has been thoughtlessly
asserted by some; for that would subvert the fundamental principle of our
system—that sovereignty resides in the people. But if not to the government, it must be transferred—if at all—to the people, regarded in the
aggregate, as a nation. But this is opposed, not only by a force of reason
which cannot be resisted, but by the preamble and tenth amended article
of the constitution, as has just been shown. If then it be transferred neither
to the one nor the other, it cannot be transferred at all; as it is impossible
to conceive to whom else the transfer could have been made. It must,
therefore, and of course, remain unsurrendered and unimpaired in the
people of the several States—to whom, it is admitted, it appertained when
the constitution was adopted.

Having now established that the powers delegated to the United States, were delegated to them in their confederated character, it remains to be explained in what sense they were thus delegated. The constitution here, as in almost all cases, where it is fairly interpreted, furnishes the explanation necessary to expel doubt. Its first article, already cited, affords it in this case. It declares that "all legislative power herein granted (delegated), shall be vested in the Congress of the United States;" that is, in the Congress for the time being. It also declares, that "the executive power shall be vested in the President of the United States"—and that "the judicial power shall be vested in a Supreme Court, and such inferior courts, as Congress may, from time to time, ordain and establish." They are then delegated to the United States, by vesting them in the respective departments of the government, to which they appropriately belong; to be exercised by the government of the United States, as their joint agent and representative, in their confederated character. It is, indeed, difficult to conceive how else it could be delegated to them—or in what other way they could mutually participate in the exercise of the powers delegated. It has, indeed, been construed by some to mean, that each State, reciprocally and mutually, delegated to each other, the portion of its sovereignty embracing the delegated powers. But besides the difficulty of a divided sovereignty, which it would involve, the expression, "delegated powers," repels that construction. If, however, there should still remain a doubt, the articles of confederation would furnish conclusive proof of the truth of that construction which I have placed upon the constitution; and, also, that not a particle of sovereignty was intended to be transferred, by delegating the powers conferred on the different departments of the government of the United States. I refer to its second article—so often referred to already. It declares, as will be remembered, that—"each State retains its sovereignty, freedom, and independence; and every power, jurisdiction, and right, which is not, by this confederation, expressly delegated to the United States in Congress assembled." The powers delegated by it were, therefore, delegated, like those of the present constitution, to the *United States.* The only difference is, that "the United States," is followed, in the articles of confederation, by the words—"in Congress assembled"—which are omitted in the parallel expression in the amended article of the constitution. But this omission is supplied in it, by the first article, and by others of a similar character, already referred to; and by vesting the powers delegated to the United States, in the respective appropriate departments of the government. The reason of the difference is plain. The constitution could not vest them in Congress alone—because there were portions of the delegated powers vested also in the other departments of the government: while the articles of confederation could, with propriety, vest them in Congress—as it was the sole representative of the confederacy. Nor could it vest them in the government of the United States; for that would imply that the powers were vested in the whole, as a unit—and not, as the fact is, in its separate departments. The constitution, therefore, in borrowing this provision from the articles of confederation, adopted the mode best calculated to express the same thing that was expressed in the latter, by the words—"in Congress assembled." That the articles of confederation, in delegating powers to the United States, did not intend to declare that the several States had parted with any portion of their sovereignty, is placed beyond doubt by the declaration contained in them, that—"each State retains its sovereignty, freedom, and independence;" and it may be fairly inferred, that the framers of the constitution, in borrowing this expression, did not design that it should bear a different interpretation.

If it be possible still to doubt that the several States retained their sovereignty and independence unimpaired, strong additional arguments might be drawn from various other portions of the instrument—especially from the third article, section third, which declares, that—"treason against the United States, shall consist only in levying war against them or in adhering to their enemies, giving them aid and comfort." It might be easily shown that—"the United States"—mean here—as they do everywhere in the constitution—the several States in their confederated character—that treason against them, is treason against their joint sovereignty—and, of course, as much treason against each State, as the act would be against any one of them, in its individual and separate character. But I forbear. Enough has already been said to place the question beyond controversy.

Having now established that the constitution is federal throughout, in contradistinction to national; and that the several States still retain their sovereignty and independence unimpaired, one would suppose that the conclusion would follow, irresistibly, in the judgment of all, that the government is also federal. But such is not the case. There are those, who admit the *constitution* to be entirely federal, but insist that the *government* is partly federal, and partly national. They rest their opinion on the authority of the "Federalist." That celebrated work comes to this conclusion, after explicitly admitting that the constitution was ratified and adopted by the people of the several States, and not by them as individuals composing one entire nation—that the act establishing the constitution is, itself, a federal, and not a national act—that it resulted neither from the act of a majority of the people of the Union, nor from a majority of the States; but from the unanimous assent of the several States—differing no otherwise from their ordinary assent than as being given, not by their legislatures, but by the people themselves—that they are parties to it—that each State, in ratifying it, was considered as a sovereign body, independent of all others, and is bound only by its own voluntary act—that, in consequence, the constitution itself is federal and not national—that, if it had been formed by the people as one nation or community, the will of the majority of the whole people of the Union would have bound the minority—that the idea of a national government involves in it, not only authority over individual citizens, but an indefinite supremacy over all persons and things, so far as they are objects of lawful government—that among the people consolidated into one nation, this supremacy is completely vested in the government; that State governments, and all local authorities, are subordinate to it, and may be controlled, directed, or abolished by it at pleasure—and, finally, that the States are regarded, by the constitution, as distinct, independent, and sovereign.[2]

[2]See Federalist, Nos. 39 and 40.

How strange, after all these admission, is the conclusion that the government is partly federal and partly national! It is the constitution which determines the character of the government. It is impossible to conceive how the constitution can be *exclusively* federal (as it is admitted, and has been clearly proved to be) and the government *partly* federal and *partly* national. It would be just as easy to conceive how a constitution can be exclusively monarchical, and the government partly monarchical, and partly aristocratic or popular; and *vice versa*. Monarchy is not more strongly distinguished from either, than a *federal* is from a *national* government. Indeed, these are even more adverse to each other; for the other forms may be blended in the constitution and the government; while, as has been shown, and as is indirectly admitted by the work referred to, the one of these so excludes the other, that it is impossible to blend them in the same constitution, and, of course, in the same government. I say, indirectly admitted, for it admits, that a federal government is one to which States are parties, in their distinct, independent, and sovereign character; and that—"the idea of a national government involves in it, not only an authority over individual citizens, but an indefinite supremacy over all persons and things, so far as they are objects of lawful government"—and, "that it is one, in which all local authorities are subordinate to the supreme, and may be controlled, directed, and abolished by it at pleasure." How, then, is it possible for institutions, admitted to be so utterly repugnant in their nature as to be directly destructive of each other, to be so blended as to form a government partly federal and partly national? What can be more contradictious? This, of itself, is sufficient to destroy the authority of the work on this point—as celebrated as it is—without showing, as might be done, that the admissions it makes throughout, are, in like manner, in direct contradiction to the conclusions, to which it comes.

But, strange as such a conclusion is, after such admissions, it is not more strange than the reasons assigned for it. The first, and leading one—that on which it mainly relies—is drawn from the source whence, as it alleges, the powers of the government are derived. It states, that the House of Represen tatives will derive its powers from the people of "America;" and adds, by way of confirmation, "The people will be represented in the same proportion, and on the same principle, as they are in the legislatures of each particular State"—and hence concludes that it would be national and not federal. Is the fact so? Does the House of Representatives really derive its powers from the people of America?—that is, from the people in the aggregate, as forming one nation; for such must be the meaning—to give the least force, or even plausibility, to the assertion. Is it not a fundamental principle, and universally admitted—admitted even by the authors themselves—that all the powers of the government are derived from the constitution—including those of the House of Representatives, as well as others? And does not this celebrated work admit—most explicitly, and in the fullest manner—that the constitution derives all its powers and authority from the people of the several States, acting, each for itself, in their independent and sovereign character as States? that they still retain the same character, and, as such, are parties to it? and that it is a federal, and not a national, constitution? How, then, can it assert, in the face of such admissions, that the House of Representatives derives its authority from the American people, in the aggregate, as forming one people or nation? To give color to the assertion, it affirms, that the people will be represented on the same principle, and in the same proportion, as they are in the legislature of each particular State. Are either of these propositions true? On the contrary, is it not universally known and admitted, that they are represented in the legislature of every State of the Union, as mere individuals—and, by election districts, entirely subordinate to the government of the State—while the members of the House of Representatives are elected—be the mode of election what it may—as delegates of the several States, in their distinct, independent, and sovereign character, as members of the Union—and not as delegates from the States, considered as mere election districts? It was on this ground, as has been stated, that President Washington vetoed the act to apportion the members, under the first census, among the several States; and his opinion has, ever since, been acquiesced in.

Neither is it true that the people of each State are represented in the House of Representatives in the same proportion as in their respective legislatures. On the contrary, they are represented in the former according to one uniform ratio proportion among the several States, fixed by the constitution itself;[3] while in each State legislature, the ratio, fixed by its separate State constitution, is different in different States—and in scarcely any are they represented in the same proportion in the legislature, as in the House of Representatives. The only point of uniformity in this respect is, that "the electors of the House of Representatives shall have the qualifications requisite for electors of the most numerous branch of the State legislatures;"[4] a rule which favors the federal, and not the national character of the government.

The authors of the work conclude, on the same affirmation—and by a similar course of reasoning—that the executive department of the government is partly national, and partly federal—*federal*, so far as the number of electors of each State, in the election of President, depends on its Senatorial representation—and so far as the final election (when no choice is made by the electoral college) depends on the House of Representatives—because they vote and count by the States—and *national*, so far as the number of its electors depends on its representation in the Lower House. As the argument in support of this proposition is the same as that relied on to prove that the House of Representatives is national, I shall pass it by with a single remark. It overlooks the fact that the electors, by an express provision of the constitution, are appointed by the several States;[5] and, of course, derive their powers from them. It would, therefore, seem, according to their course of reasoning, that the executive department, when the election is made by the colleges, ought to be regarded as *federal*—while, on the other hand, when it is made by the House of Repre-

[3] 1st ART. 2d SEC. of the Constitution.
[4] 1st ART. 2d SEC. of the Constitution.
[5] 2d ART. 1st SEC. of the Constitution.

sentatives, in the event of a failure on the part of the electors to make a choice, it ought to be regarded as *national*, and not federal, as they contend. It would, indeed, seem to involve a strange confusion of ideas to make the same department partly federal and partly national, on such a process of reasoning. It indicates a deep and radical error somewhere in the conception of the able authors of the work, in reference to a question the most vital that can arise under our system of government.

The next reason assigned is, that the government will operate on individuals composing the several States, and not on the States themselves. This, however, is very little relied on. It admits that even a confederacy may operate on individuals without losing its character as such—and cites the articles of confederation in illustration; and it might have added, that mere treaties, in some instances, operate in the same way. It is readily conceded that one of the strongest characteristics of a confederacy is, that it usually operates on the states or communities which compose it, in their corporate capacity. When it operates on individuals, it departs, to that extent, from its appropriate sphere. But this is not the case with a federal government— as will be shown when I come to draw the line of distinction between it and a confederacy. The argument, then, might be appropriate to prove that the government is not a confederacy—but not that it is a national government.

It next relies on the amending power to prove that it is partly national and partly federal. It states that—"were it wholly national, the supreme and ultimate authority would reside in a majority of the people of the whole Union; and this authority would be competent, at all times, like that of a majority of every national society, to alter or abolish its established government. Were it wholly federal, on the other hand, the concurrence of each State in the Union would be essential to any alteration, that would be binding on all." It is remarkable how often this celebrated work changes its ground, as to what constitutes a national, and what a federal government— and this, too, after defining them in the clearest and most precise manner. It tells us, in this instance, that were the government wholly national—the supreme and ultimate authority would reside in the people of the Union;

and, of course, such a government must derive its authority from that source. It tells us, elsewhere, that a federal government is one, to which the States, in their distinct, independent and sovereign character, are parties—and, of course, such a government must derive its authority from them as its source. A government, then, to be partly one, and partly the other, ought, accordingly, to derive its authority partly from the one, and partly from the other; and no government could be so, which did not—and yet we are told, at one time, that the constitution is federal, because it derived its authority, neither from the majority of the people of the Union, nor a majority of the States—implying, of course, that a government, which derived its authority from a majority of the States, would be national; as well as that which derived it from a majority of the people—and, at another, that the election of the President by the House of Representatives would be a federal act—although the House, itself, is national, because it derived its authority from the American people. And now we are told, that the amending power is partly national, because three-fourths of the States, voting as States, without regard to population, can, instead of the whole, amend the constitution; although the vote of a majority of the House of Representatives, taken by States, made the election of the President, to that extent, federal. If we turn from this confusion of ideas, to its own clear conceptions of what makes a federal, and what a national government, nothing is more evident than that the amending power is not derived from, nor exercised under the authority of the people of the Union, regarded in the aggregate—but from the several States, in their original, distinct and sovereign character; and that it is but a modification of the original creating power, by which the constitution was ordained and established—and which required the consent of each State to make it a party to it—and not a negation or inhibition of that power—as has been shown. In support of these views, it endeavors to show, by reasons equally unsatisfactory and inconclusive, that the object of the convention which framed the constitution was, to establish, "a firm *national* government." To ascertain the powers and objects of the convention, reference ought to be made, one would suppose, to the commissions given to their respective delegates, by the several States, which were represented in it. If that had been done, it would have been found that no State gave the slightest authority to its delegates to form a national government, or made the least allusion to such government as one of its objects. The word, *National*, is not even used in any one of the commissions. On the contrary, they designate the objects to be, to revise the federal constitution, and to make it adequate to the exigencies of the Union. But, instead of to these, the authors of this work resort to the act of Congress referring the proposition for calling a convention, to the several States, in conformity with the recommendation of the Annapolis convention—which, of itself, could give no authority. And further—even in this reference, they obviously rely, rather on the preamble of the act, than on the resolution adopted by Congress, submitting the proposition to the State governments. The preamble and resolution are in the following words—"Whereas, there is a provision, in the articles of confederation and perpetual union, for making alterations therein, by the assent of a Congress of the United States and of the legislatures of the several States—and, whereas, experience has evinced that there are defects in the present confederation—as a mean to the remedy of which, several of the States, and particularly the State of New York, by express instruction to their delegates in Congress, have suggested a convention for the purpose expressed in the following resolution, and such convention appearing to be the most probable mean of establishing, in the States, a firm National Government,

Resolved, That, in the opinion of Congress, it is expedient that, on the second Monday of May next, a convention of delegates, who shall have been appointed by the several States, be held in Philadelphia, for the *sole* and *express* purpose of *revising the articles of confederation;* and reporting to Congress and the several legislatures, such *alterations* and *provisions therein* as shall render the *federal constitution* adequate to the exigencies of the government and the preservation of THE UNION."

Now, assuming that the mere opinion of Congress, and not the commissions of the delegates from the several States, ought to determine the object of the convention—is it not manifest, that it is clearly in favor, not of establishing a firm national government, but of simply revising the articles of confederation for the purposes specified? Can any expression be more explicit than the declaration contained in the resolution, that the convention shall be held, "for the sole and express purpose of revising the articles of confederation?" If to this it be added, that the commissions of the delegates of the several States, accord with the resolution, there can be no doubt that the real object of the convention was—(to use the language of the resolution)—"to render the federal constitution adequate to the exigencies of the government and the preservation of the Union;" and not to establish a national constitution and government in its place—and, that such was the impression of the convention itself, the fact (admitted by the work) that they did establish a federal, and not a national constitution, conclusively proves.

How the distinguished and patriotic authors of this celebrated work fell—against their own clear and explicit admissions—into an error so radical and dangerous—one which has contributed, more than all others combined, to cast a mist over our system of government, and to confound and lead astray the minds of the community as to a true conception of its real character, cannot be accounted for, without adverting to their history and opinions as connected with the formation of the constitution. The two principal writers were prominent members of the convention; and leaders, in that body, of the party, which supported the plan for a national government. The other, although not a member, is known to have belonged to the same party. They all acquiesced in the decision, which overruled their favorite plan, and determined, patriotically, to give that adopted by the convention, a fair trial; without, however, surrendering their preference for their own scheme of a national government. It was in this state of mind, which could not fail to exercise a strong influence over their judgments, that they wrote the Federalist: and, on all questions connected with the character of the government, due allowance should be made for the force of the bias, under which their opinions were formed.

From all that has been stated, the inference follows, irresistibly, that the government is a federal, in contradistinction to a national government—a government formed by the States; ordained and established by the States, and for the States—without any participation or agency whatever, on the part of the people, regarded in the aggregate as forming a nation; that it is throughout, in whole, and in every part, simply and purely federal—"the federal government of these States"—as is accurately and concisely expressed by General Washington, the organ of the convention, in his letter laying it before the old Congress—words carefully selected, and with a full and accurate knowledge of their import. There is, indeed, no such community, *politically* speaking, as the people of the United States, regarded in the light of, and as constituting one people or nation. There never has been any such, in any stage of their existence; and, of course, they neither could, nor ever can exercise any agency—or have any participation, in the formation of our system of government, or its administration. In all its parts—including the federal as well as the separate State governments, it emanated from the same source—the people of the several States. The whole, taken together, form a federal community—a community composed of States united by a political compact—and not a nation composed of individuals united by, what is called, a social compact.

I shall next proceed to show that it is federal, in contradistinction to a confederacy.

It differs and agrees, but in opposite respects, with a national government, and a confederacy. It differs from the former, inasmuch as it has, for its basis, a confederacy, and not a nation; and agrees with it in being a government: while it agrees with the latter, to the extent of having a confederacy for its basis, and differs from it, inasmuch as the powers delegated to it are carried into execution by a government—and not by a mere congress of delegates, as is the case in a confederacy. To be more full and explicit—a federal government, though based on a confederacy, is, to the extent of the powers delegated, as much a government as a national government itself. It possesses, to this extent, all the authorities possessed by the latter, and as fully and perfectly. The case is different with a confederacy; for, although it is sometimes called a *government*—its Congress, or Council, or the body representing it, by whatever name it may be called, is much more nearly allied to an assembly of diplomatists, convened to deliberate and determine how a league or treaty between their several sovereigns, for certain defined purposes, shall be carried into execution; leaving to the parties themselves, to furnish their quota of means, and to cooperate in carrying out what may have been determined on. Such was the character of the Congress of our confederacy; and such, substantially, was that of similar bodies in all confederated communities, which preceded our present government. Our system is the first that ever substituted a *government* in lieu of such bodies. This, in fact, constitutes its peculiar characteristic. It is new, peculiar, and unprecedented.

In asserting that such is the difference between our present government and the confederacy, which it superseded, I am supported by the authority of the convention which framed the constitution. It is to be found in the second paragraph of their letter, already cited. After stating the great extent of powers, which it was deemed necessary to delegate to the United States—or as they expressed it—"the general government of the Union"—the paragraph concludes in the following words: "But the impropriety of delegating such extensive trusts to one body of men (the Congress of the confederacy) is evident; and hence results the necessity of a different organization." This "different organization," consisted in substituting a *government* in place of the Congress of the confederation; and was, in fact, the great and essential change made by the convention. All others were, relatively, of little importance—consisting rather in the modification of its language, and the mode of executing its powers, made necessary by it—than in the powers themselves. The restrictions and limitations imposed on the powers delegated, and on the several States, are much the same in both. The change, though the only essential one, was, of itself, important, viewed in relation to the structure of the system; but it was much more so, when considered in its consequences as necessarily implying and involving others of great magnitude; as I shall next proceed to show.

It involved, in the first place, an important change in the source whence it became necessary to derive the delegated powers, and the authority by which the instrument delegating them should be ratified. Those of the confederacy were derived from the governments of the several States. They delegated them, and ratified the instrument by which they were delegated, through their representatives in Congress assembled, and duly authorized for the purpose. It was, then, their work throughout; and their powers were fully competent to it. They possessed, as a confederate council, the power of making compacts and treaties, and of constituting the necessary agency to superintend their execution. The articles of confederation and union constituted, indeed, a solemn league or compact, entered into for the purposes specified; and Congress was but the joint agent or representative appointed to superintend its execution. But the governments of the several States could go no further, and were wholly deficient in the requisite power to form a constitution and government in their stead. That could only be done by the sovereign power; and that power, according to the fundamental principles of our system, resides, not in the government, but exclusively in the people—who, with us, mean the people of the several States—and hence, the powers delegated to the government had to be derived from them—and the constitution to be ratified, and ordained and established by them. How this was done has already been fully explained.

It involved, in the next place, an important change in the character of the system. It had previously been, in reality, a league between the governments of the several States; or to express it more fully and accurately, between the States, *through the organs of their respective governments;* but it became a union, in consequence of being ordained and established between the people of the several States, by themselves, and for themselves, in their character of sovereign and independent communities. It was this important change which (to use the language of the preamble of the constitution) "formed a more perfect union." It, in fact, perfected it. It could not be extended further, or be made more intimate. To have gone a step beyond, would have been to consolidate the *States*, and not the Union—and thereby to have destroyed the latter.

It involved another change, growing out of the division of the powers of government, between the United States and the separate States—requiring that those delegated to the former should be carefully enumerated and specified, in order to prevent collision between them and the powers reserved to the several States respectively. There was no necessity for such great caution under the confederacy, as its Congress could exercise little power, except through the States, and with their co-operation. Hence the care, circumspection and precision, with which the grants of powers are made in the one, and the comparatively loose, general, and more indefinite manner in which they are made in the other.

It involved another, intimately connected with the preceding, and of great importance. It entirely changed the relation which the separate governments of the States sustained to the body, which represented them in their confederated character, under the confederacy; for this was essentially different from that which they now sustain to the government of the United States, their present representative. The governments of the States sustained, to the former, the relation of superior to subordinate—of the creator to the creature; while they now sustain, to the latter, the relation of equals and co-ordinates. Both governments—that of the United States and those of the separate States, derive their powers from the same source, and were ordained and established by the same authority—the only difference being, that in ordaining and establishing the one, the people of several States acted with concert or mutual understanding—while, in ordaining and establishing the others, the people of each State acted separately, and without concert or mutual understanding—as has been fully explained. Deriving their respective powers, then, from the same source, and being ordained and established by the same authority—the two governments, State and Federal, must, of necessity, be equal in their respective spheres; and both being ordained and established by the people of the States,

respectively—each for itself, and by its own separate authority—the constitution and government of the United States must, of necessity, be the
constitution and government of each—as much so as its own separate and
individual constitution and government; and, therefore, they must stand, in
each State, in the relation of co-ordinate constitutions and governments. It
is on this ground only, that the former is the constitution and government
of all the States—not because it is the constitution and government of the
whole, considered in the aggregate as constituting one nation, but because
it is the constitution and government of each respectively: for to suppose
that they are the constitution and government of *each*, because of the
whole, would be to assume, what is not true, that they were ordained and
established by the American people in the aggregate, as forming one nation. This would be to reduce the several States to subordinate and local
divisions; and to convert their separate constitutions and governments into
mere charters and subordinate corporations: when, in truth and fact, they
are equals and co-ordinates.

It, finally, involved a great change in the manner of carrying into execution the delegated powers. As a government, it was necessary to clothe it
with the attribute of deciding, in the first instance, on the extent of its
powers—and of acting on individuals, directly, in carrying them into execution; instead of appealing to the agency of the governments of the
States—as was the case with the Congress of the confederacy.

Such are the essential distinctions between a federal government and a
confederacy—and such, in part, the important changes necessarily involved, in substituting a government, in the place of the Congress of the
confederacy.

It now remains to be shown, that the government is a republic—a
republic—or (if the expression be preferred) a constitutional democracy,
in contradistinction to an absolute democracy.

It is not an uncommon impression, that the government of the United
States is a government based simply on population; that numbers are its
only element, and a numerical majority its only controlling power. In brief,

that it is an absolute democracy. No opinion can be more erroneous. So far from being true, it is, in all the aspects in which it can be regarded, pre-eminently a government of the concurrent majority: with an organization, more complex and refined, indeed, but far better calculated to express the sense of the whole (in the only mode by which this can be fully and truly done—to wit, by ascertaining the sense of all its parts) than any government ever formed, ancient or modern. Instead of population, mere numbers, being the sole element, the numerical majority is, strictly speaking, excluded, even as one of its elements; as I shall proceed to establish, by an appeal to figures; beginning with the formation of the constitution, regarded as the fundamental law which ordained and established the government; and closing with the organization of the government itself, regarded as the agent or trustee to carry its powers into effect.

I shall pass by the Annapolis convention, on whose application, the convention which framed the constitution, was called; because it was a partial and informal meeting of delegates from a few States; and commence with the Congress of the confederation, by whom it was authoritatively called. That Congress derived its authority from the articles of confederation; and these, from the unanimous agreement of all the States—and not from the numerical majority, either of the several States, or of their population. It voted, as has been stated, by delegations; each counting one. A majority of each delegation, with a few important exceptions, decided the vote of its respective State. Each State, without regard to population, had thus an equal vote. The confederacy consisted of thirteen States; and, of course, it was in the power of any seven of the smallest, as well as the largest, to defeat the call of the convention; and, by consequence, the formation of the constitution.

By the first census, taken in 1790—three years after the call—the population of the United States amounted to 3,394,563, estimated in federal numbers. Assuming this to have been the whole amount of its population at the time of the call (which can cause no material error) the population of the seven smallest States was 959,801; or less than one third of the whole: so that, less than one-third of the population could have defeated the call of the convention.

The convention voted, in like manner, by States; and it required the votes of a majority of the delegations present, to adopt the measure. There were twelve States represented—Rhode Island being absent—so that the votes of seven delegations were required; and, of course, less than one-third of the population of the whole, could have defeated the formation of the constitution.

The plan, when adopted by the convention, had again to be submitted to Congress—and to receive its sanction, before it could be submitted to the several States for their approval—a necessary preliminary to its final reference to the conventions of the people of the several States for their ratification. It had thus, of course, to pass again the ordeal of Congress; when the delegations of seven of the smallest States, representing less than one-third of the population, could again have defeated, by refusing to submit it for their consideration. And, stronger still—when submitted, it required, by an express provision, the concurrence of nine of the thirteen, to establish it, between the States ratifying it; which put it in the power of any four States, the smallest as well as the largest, to reject it. The four smallest, to wit: Delaware, Rhode Island, Georgia, and New Hampshire, contained, by the census of 1790, a federal population of only 336,948—but a little more than one-eleventh of the whole: but, as inconsiderable as was their population, they could have defeated it, by preventing its ratification. It thus appears, that the numerical majority of the population, had no agency whatever in the process of forming and adopting the constitution; and that neither this, nor a majority of the States, constituted an element in its ratification and adoption.

In the provision for its amendment, it prescribes, as has been stated, two modes—one, by two-thirds of both houses of Congress; and the other, by a convention of delegates from the States, called by Congress, on the application of two-thirds of their respective legislatures. But, in neither case can the proposed amendment become a part of the constitution, unless ratified by the legislatures of three-fourths of the States, or by conventions of the people of three-fourths—as Congress may prescribe; so that, in the one, it requires the consent of two-thirds of the States to propose amendments— and, in both cases, of three-fourths to adopt and ratify them, before they can become a part of the constitution. As there are, at present, thirty States in the Union, it will take twenty to propose, and, of course, would require but eleven to defeat, a proposition to amend the constitution; or, nineteen votes in the Senate—if it should originate in Congress—and the votes of eleven legislatures, if it should be to call a convention. By the census of 1840, the federal population of all the States—including the three, which were then territories, but which have since become States—was 16,077,604. To this add Texas, since admitted, say 110,000—making the aggregate, 16,187,604. Of this amount, the eleven smallest States (Vermont being the largest of the number) contained a federal population of but 1,638,521: and yet they can prevent the other nineteen States, with a federal population of 14,549,082, from even proposing amendments to the constitution: while the twenty smallest (of which Maine is the largest) with a federal population of 3,526,811, can compel Congress to call a convention to propose amendments, against the united votes of the other ten, with a federal population of 12,660,793. Thus, while less than one-eighth of the population, may, in the one case, prevent the adoption of a proposition to amend the constitution—less than one-fourth can, in the other, adopt it.

But, striking as are these results, the process, when examined with reference to the ratification of proposals to amend, will present others still more so. Here the consent of three-fourths of the States is required; which, with the present number, would make the concurrence of twenty-three States necessary to give effect to the act of ratification; and, of course, puts it in the power of any eight States to defeat a proposal to amend. The federal population of the eight smallest is but 776,969; and yet, small as this is, they can prevent amendments, against the united votes of the other twenty two, with a federal population of 15,410,635; or nearly twenty times their number. But while so small a portion of the entire population can prevent an amendment, twenty-three of the smallest States—with a federal population of only 7,254,400—can amend the constitution, against the united votes of the other seven, with a federal population of 8,933,204. So that a numerical minority of the population can amend the constitution, against a decided numerical majority; when, at the same time, one-nineteenth of the population can prevent the other eighteen-nineteenths from amending it. And more than this: any one State—Delaware, for instance, with a federal population of only 77,043—can prevent the other twenty-nine States, with a federal population of 16,110,561, from so amending the constitution as to deprive the States of an equality of representation in the Senate. To complete the picture: Sixteen of the smallest States—that is, a majority of them, with a population of only 3,411,672—a little more than one-fifth of the whole—can, in effect, destroy the government and dissolve the Union, by simply declining to appoint Senators; against the united voice of the other fourteen States, with a population of 12,775,932—being but little less than four-fifths of the whole.

These results, resting on calculations, which exclude doubt, incontestably prove—not only that the authority which formed, ratified, and even amended the constitution, regulates entirely the numerical majority, as one of its elements—but furnish additional and conclusive proof, if additional were needed, that ours is a federal government—a government made by the several States; and that States, and not individuals, are its constituents. The States, throughout, in forming, ratifying and amending the constitution, act as equals, without reference to population.

Regarding the Government, apart from the Constitution, and simply as the trustee or agent to carry its powers into execution, the case is somewhat different. It is composed of two elements: One, the States, regarded in their corporate character—and the other, their representative population—estimated in, what is called, "federal numbers"—which is ascertained, "by adding to the whole number of free persons, including those bound to service for a term of years—and excluding Indians not taxed—three-fifths of all others."[6] These elements, in different proportions, enter into, and constitute all the departments of the government; as will be made apparent by a brief sketch of its organization.

The government is divided into three separate departments, the legislative, the executive, and the judicial. The legislative consists of two bodies—the Senate, and the House of Representatives. The two are called the Congress of the United States: and all the legislative powers delegated to the government, are vested in it. The Senate is composed of two members from each State, elected by the legislature thereof, for the term of six years; and the whole number is divided into three classes; of which one goes out at the expiration of every two years. It is the representative of the States, in their corporate character. The members vote *per capita*, and a majority decides all questions of a legislative character. It has equal power with the House, on all such questions—except that it cannot originate "bills for raising revenue." In addition to its legislative powers, it participates in the powers of the other two departments. Its advice and consent are necessary to make treaties and appointments; and it constitutes the high tribunal, before which impeachments are tried. In advising and consenting to treaties, and in trials of impeachments, two-thirds are necessary to decide. In case the electoral college fails to choose a Vice-President, the power devolves on the Senate to make the selection from the two candidates having the highest number of votes. In selecting, the members vote by States, and a majority of the States decide. In such cases, two-thirds of the whole number of Senators are necessary to form a quorum.

The House of Representatives is composed of members elected by the people of the several States, for the term of two years. The right of voting for them, in each State, is confined to those who are qualified to vote for the members of the most numerous branch of its own legislature. The number of members is fixed by law, under each census—which is taken

[6] 1st ART. 2d SEC. of Constitution.

every ten years. They are apportioned among the several States, according
to their population, estimated in federal numbers; but each State is entitled
to have one. The House, in addition to its legislative powers, has the sole
power of impeachment; as well as of choosing the President (in case of a
failure to elect by the electoral college) from the three candidates, having
the greatest number of votes. The members, in such case, vote by States—
the vote of each delegation, if not equally divided, counts one, and a
majority decides. In all other cases they vote *per capita*, and the majority
decides; except only on a proposition to amend the constitution.

The executive powers are vested in the President of United States. He
and the Vice-President, are chosen for the term of four years, by electors,
appointed in such manner as the several States may direct. Each State is
entitled to a number, equal to the whole number of its Senators and
Representatives for the time. The electors vote *per capita*, in their respective States, on the same day throughout the Union; and a majority of the
votes of all the electors is requisite to a choice. In case of a failure to elect,
either in reference to the President or Vice-President, the House or the
Senate, as the case may be, make the choice, in the manner before stated.
If the House fail to choose before the fourth day of March next ensuing—
or in case of the removal from office, death, resignation, or inability of the
President—the Vice-President acts as President. In addition to the ordinary executive powers, the President has the authority to make treaties and
appointments, by, and with the advice and consent of the Senate; and to
approve or disapprove all bills before they become laws; as well as all
orders, resolutions or votes, to which the concurrence of both houses of
Congress is necessary—except on questions of adjournment—before they
can take effect. In case of his disapproval, the votes of two-thirds of both
houses are necessary to pass them. He is allowed ten days (Sundays not
counted) to approve or disapprove; and if he fail to act within that period,
the bill, order, resolution or vote (as the case may be) becomes as valid, to
all intents and purposes, as if he had signed it; unless Congress, by its
adjournment, prevent its return.

The judicial power is vested in one Supreme Court, and such inferior courts, as Congress may establish. The Judges of both are appointed by the President in the manner above stated; and hold their office during good behavior.

The President, Vice-President, Judges, and all the civil officers, are liable to be impeached for treason, bribery, and other high crimes and misdemeanors.

From this brief sketch, it is apparent that the States, regarded in their corporate character, and the population of the States, estimated in federal numbers, are the two elements, of which the government is exclusively composed; and that they enter, in different proportions, into the formation of all its departments. In the legislative they enter in equal proportions, and in their most distinct and simple form. Each, in that department, has its appropriate organ; and each acts by its respective majorities—as far as legislation is concerned. No bill, resolution, order, or vote, partaking of the nature of a law, can be adopted without their concurring assent: so that each house has a veto on the other, in all matters of legislation. In the executive they are differently blended. The powers of this department are vested in a single functionary; which made it impossible to give to them separate organs, and concurrent action. In lieu of this, the two elements are blended in the constitution of the college of electors, which chooses the President: but as this gave a decided preponderance to the element of population—because of the greater number of which it was composed—in order to combat and to compensate this advantage—and to preserve, as far as possible, the equipoise between the two, the power was vested in the House, voting by States, to choose him from the three candidates, having the largest number of votes, in case of a failure of choice by the college; and in case of a failure to select by the House, or of removal, death, resignation, or inability, the Vice-President was authorized to act as President. These provisions gave a preponderance, even more decided, to the other element, in the eventual choice. This was still more striking as the constitution stood at its adoption. It originally provided that each elector should vote for two candidates, without designating which should be the President, or which the Vice-President; the person having the highest number of votes to be the President, if it should be a majority of the whole number given. If there should be more than one having such majority—and an equal number of votes—the House, voting by States, should choose between them, which should be President—but if none should have a majority, the House, voting in the same way, should choose the President from the five having the greatest number of votes; the person having the greatest number of votes, after the choice of the President, to be the Vice-President. But in case of two or more having an equal number, the Senate should elect from among them the Vice-President.

Had these provisions been left unaltered, and not superseded, in practice, by caucuses and party conventions, their effect would have been to give to the majority of the people of the several States, the right of nominating five candidates; and to the majority of the States, acting in their corporate character, the right of choosing from them, which should be President, and which Vice-President. The President and Vice-President would, virtually, have been elected by the concurrent majority of the several States, and of their population, estimated in federal numbers; and, in this important respect, the executive would have been assimilated to the legislative department. But the Senate, in addition to its legislative, is vested also with supervisory powers in respect to treaties and appointments, which give it a participation in executive powers, to that extent; and a corresponding weight in the exercise of two of its most important functions. The treaty-making power is, in reality, a branch of the law-making power; and we accordingly find that treaties as well as the constitution itself, and the acts of Congress, are declared to be the supreme law of the land. This important branch of the law-making power includes all questions between the United States and foreign nations, which may become the subjects of negotiation and treaty; while the appointing power is intimately connected with the performance of all its functions.

In the Judiciary the two elements are blended, in proportions different from either of the others. The President, in the election of whom they are both united, nominates the judges; and the Senate, which consists exclusively of one of the elements, confirms or rejects: so that they are, to a certain extent, concurrent in this department; though the States, considered in their corporate capacity, may be said to be its predominant element.

In the impeaching power, by which it was intended to make the executive and judiciary responsible, the two elements exist and act separately, as in the legislative department—the one, constituting the impeaching power, resides in the House of Representatives; and the other, the power that tries and pronounces judgment, in the Senate: and thus, although existing separately in their respective bodies, their joint and concurrent action is necessary to give effect to the power.

It thus appears, on a view of the whole, that it was the object of the framers of the constitution, in organizing the government, to give to the two elements, of which it is composed, separate, but concurrent action; and, consequently, a veto on each other, whenever the organization of the department, or the nature of the power would admit: and when this could not be done, so to blend the two, as to make as near an approach to it, in effect, as possible. It is, also, apparent, that the government, regarded apart from the constitution, is the government of the concurrent, and not of the numerical majority. But to have an accurate conception how it is calculated to act in practice; and to establish, beyond doubt, that it was neither intended to be, nor is, in fact, the government of the numerical majority, it will be necessary again to appeal to figures.

That, in organizing a government with different departments, in each of which the States are represented in a twofold aspect, in the manner stated, it was the object of the framers of the constitution, to make it more, instead of less popular than it would have been as a government of the mere numerical majority—that is, as requiring a more numerous, instead of a less numerous constituency to carry its powers into execution—may be inferred from the fact, that such actually is the effect. Indeed, the necessary effect of the concurrent majority is, to make the government more popular—that is, to require more wills to put it in action, than if any one of the majorities, of which it is composed, were its sole element—as will be apparent by reference to figures.

If the House, which represents population, estimated in federal numbers, had been invested with the sole power of legislation, then six of the larger States, to wit, New York, Pennsylvania, Virginia, Ohio, Massachusetts and Tennessee, with a federal population of 8,216,279, would have had the power of making laws for the other twenty-four, with a federal population of 7,971,325. On the other hand, if the Senate had been invested with the sole power, sixteen of the smallest States—embracing Maryland as the largest—with a federal population of 3,411,672, would have had the power of legislating for the other fourteen, with a population of 12,775,932. But the constitution, in giving each body a negative on the other, in all matters of legislation, makes it necessary that a majority of each should concur to pass a bill, before it becomes an act; and the smallest number of States and population, by which this can be effected, is six of the larger voting for it in the House of Representatives—and ten of the smaller, uniting with them in their vote, in the Senate. The ten smaller, including New Hampshire as the largest, have a federal population of 1,346,575; which, added to that of the six larger, would make 9,572,852. So that no bill can become a law, with less than the united vote of sixteen States, representing a constituency containing a federal population of 9,572,852, against fourteen States, representing a like population of 6,614,752.

But, when passed, the bill is subject to the President's approval or disapproval. If he disapprove, or, as it is usually termed, vetoes it, it cannot become a law unless passed by two-thirds of the members of both bodies. The House of Representatives consists of 228—two-thirds of which is 152—which, therefore, is the smallest number that can overcome his veto. It would take ten of the larger States, of which Georgia is the smallest, to make up that number—the federal population of which is 10,853,175: and, in the Senate, it would require the votes of twenty States to overrule it—and, of course, ten of the larger united with ten of the smaller. But the ten smaller States have a federal population of only 1,346,575—as has been stated—which added to that of the ten larger, would give 12,199,748, as the smallest population by which his veto can be overruled, and the act become a law. Even then, it is liable to be pronounced unconstitutional by the judges, should it, in any case before them, come in conflict with their views of the constitution—a decision which, in respect to individuals, operates as an absolute veto, which can only be overruled by an amendment of the constitution. In all these calculations, I assume a full House, and full votes—and that members vote according to the will of their constituents.

If the election of the President, by the electoral college, be compared with the passage of a bill by Congress, it will be found that it requires a smaller federal number to elect, than to pass a bill—resulting from the fact that the two majorities, in the one case, are united and blended together, instead of acting concurrently, as in the other. There are, at present, 288 members of Congress, of which 60 are Senators, and the others, members of the House of Representatives; and, as each State is entitled to appoint as many electors as it has members of Congress, there is, of course, the same number of electors. One hundred and forty-five constitute a majority of the whole; and, of course, are necessary to a choice. Seven of the States of the largest class, say, New York, Pennsylvania, Virginia, Ohio, Tennessee, Kentucky and Indiana, combined with one of a medium size, say, New Hampshire, are entitled to that number—and, with a federal population of 9,125,936, may overrule the vote of the other twenty-two, with a population of 7,061,668: so that a small minority of States, with not a large majority of population, can elect a President by the electoral college—against a very large majority of the States, with a population not greatly under a majority. It follows, therefore, that the choice of a President, when made by the electoral college, may be less popular in its character than when made by Congress—which cannot elect without a concurrence of a federal population of upwards of nine and a half millions.

But to compensate this great preponderance of the majority based on population, over that based on the States, regarded in their corporate character, in an election by the college of electors, the provision giving to the House of Representatives, voting by States, the eventual choice, in case the college fail to elect, was adopted. Under its operation, sixteen of the smallest States, with a federal population of 3,411,672, may elect the President, against the remaining fourteen, with a federal population of 12,775,932—which gives a preponderance equally great to the States, without reference to population, in the contingency mentioned.

From what has been stated, the conclusion follows, irresistibly, that the constitution and the government, regarding the latter apart from the former, rest, throughout, on the principle of the concurrent majority; and that it is, of course, a Republic—a constitutional democracy, in contradistinction to an absolute democracy; and that, the theory which regards it as a government of the mere numerical majority, rests on a gross and groundless misconception. So far is this from being the case, the numerical majority was entirely excluded as an element, throughout the whole process of forming and ratifying the constitution: and, although admitted as one of the two elements, in the organization of the government, it was with the important qualification, that it should be the numerical majority of the population of the *several States*, regarded in their corporate character, and not of the whole Union, regarded as one community. And further than this—it was to be the numerical majority, not of their entire population, but of their federal population; which, as has been shown, is estimated artificially—by excluding two-fifths of a large portion of the population of many of the States of the Union. Even with these important qualifications, it was admitted as the less prominent of the two. With the exception of the impeaching power, it has no direct participation in the functions of any department of the government, except the legislative; while the other element participates in some of the most important functions of the executive; and, in the constitution of the Senate, as a court to try impeachments, in the highest of the judicial functions. It was, in fact, admitted, not because it was the numerical majority, nor on the ground, that, as such, it ought, of right, to constitute one of its elements—much less the only one—but for a very different reason. In the federal constitution, the equality of the States, without regard to population, size, wealth, institutions, or any other consideration, is a fundamental principle; as much so as is the equality of their citizens, in the governments of the several States, without regard to property, influence, or superiority of any description. As, in the one, the citizens form the constituent body—so, in the other, the States. But the latter, in forming a government for their mutual protection and welfare, deemed it proper, as a matter of fairness and sound policy, and not of right, to assign to it an increased weight, bearing some reasonable proportion to the different amount of means which the several States might, respectively, contribute to the accomplishment of the ends, for which they were about to enter into a federal union. For this purpose they admitted, what is called federal numbers, as one of the elements of the government about to be established; while they were, at the same time, so jealous of the effects of admitting it, with all its restrictions—that, in order to guard effectually the other element, they provided that no State, without its consent, should be deprived of its equal suffrage in the Senate; so as to place their equality, in that important body, beyond the reach even of the amending power.

I have now established, as proposed at the outset, that the government of the United States is a democratic federal Republic—democratic in contradistinction to aristocratic, and monarchical—federal, in contradistinction to national, on the one hand—and to a confederacy, on the other; and a Republic—a government of the concurrent majority, in contradistinction to an absolute democracy—or a government of the numerical majority.

But the government of the United States, with all its complication and refinement of organization, is but a part of a system of governments. It is the representative and organ of the States, only to the extent of the powers delegated to it. Beyond this, each State has its own separate government, which is its exclusive representative and organ, as to all the other powers of government—or, as they are usually called, the reserved powers. However correct, then, our conception of the character of the government of the United States viewed by itself, may be, it must be very imperfect, unless viewed at the same time, in connection with the complicated system, of which it forms but a part. In order to present this more perfect view, it will be essential, first, to present the outlines of the entire system, so far as it may be necessary to show the nature and character of the relation between the two—the government of the United States and the separate State governments. For this purpose, it will be expedient to trace, historically, the origin and formation of the system itself, of which they constitute the parts.

I have already shown, that the present government of the United States was reared on the foundation of the articles of confederation and perpetual union; that these last did but little more than define the powers and the extent of the government and the union, which had grown out of the exigencies of the revolution; and that these, again, had but enlarged and strengthened the powers and the union which the exigencies of a common defence against the aggression of the parent country, had forced the colonies to assume and form. What I now propose is, to trace briefly downwards, from the beginning, the causes and circumstances which led to the formation, in all its parts, of our present peculiar, complicated, and remarkable system of governments. This may be readily done—for we have the advantage (possessed by few people, who, in past times, have formed and flourished under remarkable political institutions) of historical accounts, so full and accurate, of the origin, rise, and formation of our institutions, throughout all their stages—as to leave nothing relating to either, to vague and uncertain conjecture.

It is known to all, in any degree familiar with our history, that the region embraced by the original States of the Union appertained to the crown of Great Britain, at the time of its colonization; and that different portions of it were granted to certain companies or individuals, for the purpose of settlement and colonization. It is also known, that the thirteen colonies, which afterwards declared their independence, were established under charters which, while they left the sovereignty in the crown, and reserved the general power of supervision to the parent country, secured to the several colonies popular representation in their respective governments, or in one branch, at least, of their legislatures—with the general rights of British subjects. Although the colonies had no political connection with each other, except as dependent provinces of the same crown—they were closely bound together by the ties of a common origin, identity of language, similarity of religion, laws, customs, manners, commercial and social intercourse—and by a sense of common danger—exposed, as they were, to the incursions of a savage foe, acting under the influence of a powerful and hostile nation.

In this embryo state of our political existence, are to be found all the elements which subsequently led to the formation of our peculiar system of governments. The revolution, as it is called, produced no other changes than those which were necessarily caused by the declaration of independence. These were, indeed, very important. Its first and necessary effect was, to cut the cord which had bound the colonies to the parent country— to extinguish all the authority of the latter—and, by consequence, to convert them into thirteen independent and sovereign States. I say, "independent and sovereign," because, as the colonies were, politically and in respect to each other, wholly independent—the sovereignty of each, regarded as distinct and separate communities, being vested in the British crown—the necessary effect of severing the tie which bound them to it was, to devolve the sovereignty on each respectively, and, thereby, to convert them from dependent colonies, into independent and sovereign States. Thus, the region occupied by them, came to be divided into as many States as there were colonies, each independent of the others—as they were expressly declared to be; and only united to the extent necessary to defend their independence, and meet the exigencies of the occasion— and hence that great and, I might say, providential territorial division of the country, into independent and sovereign States, on which our entire system of government rests.

Its next effect was, to transfer the sovereignty which had, heretofore, resided in the British crown, not to the *governments* of, but to the *people* composing the *several* States. It could only devolve on them. The declaration of independence, by extinguishing the British authority in the several colonies, necessarily destroyed every department of their governments, except such as derived their authority from, and represented their respective people. Nothing, then, remained of their several governments, but the popular and representative branches of them. But a representative government, even when entire, cannot possibly be the seat of sovereignty—the supreme and ultimate power of a State. The very term, "representative," implies a superior in the individual or body represented. Fortunately for us, the people of the several colonies constituted, not a mere mass of individuals, without any organic arrangements to express their sovereign will, or carry it into effect. On the contrary, they constituted organized communities—in the full possession and constant exercise of the right of suffrage, under their colonial governments. Had they constituted a mere mass of individuals—without organization, and unaccustomed to the exercise of the right of suffrage, it would have been impossible to have prevented those internal convulsions, which almost ever attend the change of the seat of sovereignty—and which so frequently render the change rather a curse than a blessing. But in their situation, and under its circumstances, the change was made without the least convulsion, or the slightest disturbance. The mere will of the sovereign communities, aided by the remaining fragments—the popular branches of their several colonial governments, speedily ordained and established governments, each for itself; and thus passed, without anarchy—without a shock, from their dependent condition under the colonial governments, to that of independence under those established by their own authority.

Thus commenced the division between the constitution-making and the law-making powers—between the power which ordains and establishes the fundamental laws—which creates, organizes and invests government with its authority, and subjects it to restrictions—and the power that passes acts to carry into execution, the powers thus delegated to government. The one, emanating from the people, as forming a *sovereign community*, creates the government—the other, as a representative appointed to execute its powers, enacts laws to regulate and control the conduct of the people, regarded as *individuals*. This division between the two powers—thus necessarily incident to the separation from the parent country—constitutes an element in our political system as essential to its formation, as the great and primary territorial division of independent and sovereign States. Between them, it was our good fortune never to have been left, for a moment, in doubt, as to where the sovereign authority was to be found; or how, and by whom it should be exercised: and, hence, the facility, the promptitude and safety, with which we passed from one state to the other, as far as internal causes were concerned. Our only difficulty and danger lay in the effort to resist the immense power of the parent country.

The governments of the several States were thus rightfully and regularly constituted. They, in the course of a few years, by entering into articles of confederation and perpetual union, established and made more perfect the union which had been informally constituted, in consequence of the exigencies growing out of the contest with a powerful enemy. But experience soon proved that the confederacy was wholly inadequate to effect the objects for which it was formed. It was then, and not until then, that the causes which had their origin in our embryo state, and which had, thus far, led to such happy results, fully developed themselves. The failure of the confederacy was so glaring, as to make it appear to all, that something must be done to meet the exigencies of the occasion—and the great question which presented itself to all was—what should, or could be done?

To dissolve the Union was too abhorrent to be named. In addition to the causes which had connected them by such strong cords of affection while colonies, there were superadded others, still more powerful—resulting from the common dangers to which they had been exposed, and the common glory they had acquired, in passing successfully through the war of the revolution. Besides, all saw that the hope of reaping the rich rewards of their successful resistance to the encroachment of the parent country, depended on preserving the Union.

But, if disunion was out of the question, consolidation was not less repugnant to their feelings and opinions. The attachments of all to their respective States and institutions, were strong, and of long standing—since they were identified with their respective colonies; and, for the most part, had survived the separation from the parent country. Nor were they unaware of the danger to their liberty and property, to be apprehended from a surrender of their sovereignty and existence, as separate and independent States, and a consolidation of the whole into one nation. They regarded disunion and consolidation as equally dangerous; and were, therefore, equally opposed to both.

To change the form of government to an aristocracy or monarchy, was not to be thought of. The deepest feelings of the common heart were in opposition to them, and in favor of popular government.

These changes or alterations being out of the question, what other remained to be considered? Men of the greatest talents and experience were at a loss for an answer. To meet the exigencies of the occasion, a convention of the States was called. When it met, the only alternative, in the opinion of the larger portion of its most distinguished members, was, the establishment of a *national* government; which was but another name, in reality, for *consolidation*. But where wisdom and experience proved incompetent to provide a remedy, the necessity of doing something, combined with the force of those causes, which had thus far shaped our destiny, carried us successfully through the perilous juncture. In the hour of trial, we realized the precious advantages we possessed in the two great and prime elements that distinguish our system of governments—the division of the country, territorially, into independent and sovereign States—and the division of the powers of government into *constitution-* and *law*-making powers. Of the materials which they jointly furnished, the convention was enabled to construct the present system—the only alternative left, by which we could escape the dire consequences attendant on the others; and which has so long preserved peace among ourselves, and protected us against danger from abroad. Each contributed essential aid towards the accomplishment of this great work.

To the former, we owe the mode of constituting the convention—as well as that of voting, in the formation and adoption of the constitution—and, finally, in the ratification of it by the States: and to them, jointly, are we exclusively indebted for that peculiar form which the constitution and government finally assumed. It is impossible to read the proceedings of the convention, without perceiving that, if the delegates had been appointed by the people at large, and in proportion to population, nothing like the present constitution could have been adopted. It would have assumed the form best suited to the views and interests of the more populous and wealthy portions; and, for that purpose, been made paramount to the existing State governments: in brief, a consolidated, *national* government would have been formed. But as the convention was composed of delegates from separate independent and sovereign States, it involved the necessity of voting by States, in framing and adopting the constitution; and—what is of far more importance—the necessity of submitting it to the States for their respective ratifications; so that each should be bound by its own act, and not by that of a majority of the States, nor of their united population. It was this necessity of obtaining the consent of a majority of the States in convention, as, also, in the intermediate process—and, finally, the unanimous approval of all, in order to make it obligatory on all, which rendered it indispensable for the convention to consult the feelings and interests of all. This, united with the absolute necessity of doing something, in order to avert impending calamities of the most fearful character, impressed all with feelings of moderation, forbearance, mutual respect, concession, and compromise, as indispensable to secure the adoption of some measure of security. It was the prevalence of these impressions, that stamped their work with so much fairness, equity, and justice—as to receive, finally, the unanimous ratification of the States; and which has caused it to continue ever since, the object of the admiration and attachment of the reflecting and patriotic.

But the moderation, forbearance, mutual respect, concession, and compromise, superinduced by the causes referred to, could, of themselves, have effected nothing, without the aid of the division between the constitution- and the law-making powers. Feebleness and a tendency to disorder are inherent in confederacies; and cannot be remedied, simply by the employment or modification of their powers. But as governments, according to our conceptions, cannot ordain and establish constitutions—and as those of the States had already gone as far as they rightfully could, in framing and adopting the articles of confederation and perpetual union, it would have been impossible to have called the present constitution and government into being, without invoking the high creating power, which ordained and established those of the several States. There was none other competent to the task. It was, therefore, invoked; and formed a constitution and government for the United States, as it had formed and modelled those of the several States. The first step was—the division of the powers of government—which was effected, by leaving subject to the exclusive control of the several States in their separate and individual character, all powers which, it was believed, they could advantageously exercise for themselves respectively—without incurring the hazard of bringing them in conflict with each other—and by delegating, specifically, others to the United States, in the manner explained. It is this division of the powers of the government into such as are delegated, specifically, to the common and joint government of all the States—to be exercised for the benefit and safety of each and all—and the reservation of all others to the States respectively—to be exercised through the separate government of each, which makes ours, *a system of governments*, as has been stated.

It is obvious, from this sketch, brief as it is—taken in connection with what has been previously established—that the two governments, General and State, stand to each other, in the first place, in the relation of parts to the whole; not, indeed, in reference to their organization or functions—for in this respect both are perfect—but in reference to their *powers*. As they divide between them the delegated powers appertaining to government—

and as, of course, each is divested of what the other possesses—it necessarily requires the two united to constitute one entire government. That
they are both paramount and supreme within the sphere of their respective
powers—that they stand, within these limits, as equals—and sustain the
relation of co-ordinate governments, has already been fully established. As
co-ordinates, they sustain to each other the same relation which subsists
between the different departments of the government—the executive, the
legislative, and the judicial—and for the same reason. These are co-
ordinates; because each, in the sphere of its powers, is equal to, and
independent of the others; and because the three united make the government. The only difference is that, in the illustration, each department, by
itself, is not a government—since it takes the whole in connection to form
one; while the governments of the several States respectively, and that of
the United States, although perfect governments in themselves, and in their
respective spheres, require to be united in order to constitute one entire
government. They, in this respect, stand as principal and supplemental—
while the co-departments of each stand in the relation of parts to the whole.
The opposite theory, which would make the constitution and government of
the United States the government of the whole—and the government of
each, *because* the government of the whole—and not that of *all*, because of
each—besides the objection already stated, would involve the absurdity of
each State having only half a constitution, and half a government; and this,
too, while possessed of the supreme sovereign power. Taking all the parts
together, the people of thirty independent and sovereign States, confederated by a solemn constitutional compact into one great federal community,
with a system of government, in all of which, powers are separated into the
great primary divisions of the *constitution*-making and the *law*-making
powers; those of the latter class being divided between the common and
joint government of all the States, and the separate and local governments
of each State respectively—and, finally, the powers of both distributed
among three separate and independent departments, legislative, executive,
and judicial—presents, in the whole, a political system as remarkable for

its grandeur as it is for its novelty and refinement of organization. For the structure of such a system—so wise, just, and beneficent—we are far more indebted to a superintending Providence, that so disposed events as to lead, as if by an invisible hand, to its formation, than to those who erected it. Intelligent, experienced, and patriotic as they were, they were but builders under its superintending direction.

Having shown in what relation the government of the United States and those of the separate States stand to each other, I shall next proceed to trace the line which divides their respective powers; or, to express it in constitutional language—which distinguishes between the powers delegated to the United States, and those reserved to the States respectively— with the restrictions imposed on each. In doing this, I propose to group the former under general heads, accompanied by such remarks as may be deemed necessary, in reference to the object in view.

In deciding what powers ought, and what ought not to be granted, the leading principle undoubtedly was, to delegate those only which could be more safely, or effectually, or beneficially exercised for the common good of all the States, by the joint or general government of all, than by the separate government of each State; leaving all others to the several States respectively. The object was, not to supersede the separate governments of the States—but to establish a joint supplemental government; in order to do that, which either could not be done at all, or as safely and well done by them, as by a joint government of all. This leading principle embraced two great divisions of power, which may be said to comprehend all, or nearly all the delegated powers; either directly, or as a means to carry them into execution. One of them embraces all the powers appertaining to the relations of the States with the rest of the world, called their foreign relations; and the other, of an internal character, embraces such as appertain to the exterior relations of the States with each other. It is clear that both come within the leading principle; as each is of a description which the States, in their separate character, are either incompetent to exercise at all, or if competent, to exercise consistently with their mutual peace, safety, and prosperity. Indeed, so strong and universal has this opinion been, in reference to the powers appertaining to their foreign relations, that, from the Declaration of Independence to the present time, in all the changes through which they have passed, the Union has had exclusive charge of this great division of powers. To the rest of the world, the States composing this Union are now, and ever have been known in no other than their united, confederated character. Abroad—to the rest of the world—they are but *one*. It is only at home, in their interior relations, that they are *many*; and it is to this twofold aspect that their motto, "E pluribus unum," appropriately and emphatically applies. So imperious was the necessity of union, and a common government to take charge of their foreign relations, that it may be safely affirmed, not only that it led to their formation, but that, without it, the States never would have been united. The same necessity still continues to be one of the strongest bonds of their union. But, strong as was, and still is, the inducement to union, in order to preserve their mutual peace and safety *within*, it was not, of itself, sufficiently strong to unite the parts composing this vast federal fabric; nor, probably, is it, of itself, sufficiently strong to hold them together.

This great division of authority appertains to the treaty-making power; and is vested in the President and Senate. The power of negotiating treaties belongs exclusively to the former; but he cannot make them without the advice and consent of the latter. When made, they are declared to be the supreme law of the land. The reason for vesting this branch of the law-making power exclusively in the President and Senate, to the exclusion of the House of Representatives, is to be traced to the necessity of secrecy in conducting negotiations and making treaties—as they often involve considerations calculated to have great weight—but which cannot be disclosed without hazarding their success. Hence the objection to so numerous a body as the House of Representatives participating in the exercise of the power. But to guard against the dangers which might result from confiding the power to so small a body, the advice and consent of *two-thirds* of the Senators present was required.

There is a very striking difference between the manner in which the treaty-making and the law-making power, in its strict sense, are delegated, which deserves notice. The former is vested in the President and Senate by a few general words, without enumerating or specifying, particularly, the power delegated. The constitution simply provides that, "he shall have power, by and with the advice and consent of the Senate, to make treaties; provided two-thirds of the Senators present concur"—while the legislative powers vested in Congress, are, one by one, carefully enumerated and specified. The reason is to be found in the fact, that the treaty-making power is vested, *exclusively*, in the government of the United States; and, therefore, nothing more was necessary in delegating it, than to specify, as is done, the portion or department of the government in which it is vested. It was, then, not only unnecessary, but it would have been absurd to enumerate, specially, the powers embraced in the grant. Very different is the case in regard to legislative powers. They are divided between the Federal government and the State governments; which made it absolutely necessary, in order to draw the line between the delegated and reserved powers, that the one or the other should be carefully enumerated and specified; and, as the former was intended to be but supplemental to the latter—and to embrace the comparatively few powers which could not be either exercised at all—or, if at all, could not be so well and safely exercised by the separate governments of the several States—it was proper that the former, and not the latter, should be enumerated and specified. But, although the treaty-making power is exclusively vested, and without enumeration or specification, in the government of the United States, it is nevertheless subject to several important limitations.

It is, in the first place, strictly limited to questions *inter alios;* that is, to questions between us and foreign powers which require negotiation to adjust them. All such clearly appertain to it. But to extend the power beyond these, be the pretext what it may, would be to extend it beyond its allotted sphere; and, thus, a palpable violation of the constitution. It is, in the next place, limited by all the provisions of the constitution which inhibit

certain acts from being done by the government, or any of its departments—of which description there are many. It is also limited by such
provisions of the constitution as direct certain acts to be done in a particular way, and which prohibit the contrary; of which a striking example is to
be found in that which declares that, "no money shall be drawn from the
treasury but in consequence of appropriations to be made by law." This
not only imposes an important restriction on the power, but gives to Congress, as the law-making power, and to the House of Representatives as a
portion of Congress, the right to withhold appropriations; and, thereby, an
important control over the treaty-making power, whenever money is required to carry a treaty into effect—which is usually the case, especially in
reference to those of much importance. There still remains another, and
more important limitation; but of a more general and indefinite character.
It can enter into no stipulation calculated to change the character of the
government; or to do that which can only be done by the constitution-
making power; or which is inconsistent with the nature and structure of the
government—or the objects for which it was formed. Among which, it
seems to be settled, that it cannot change or alter the boundary of a
State—or cede any portion of its territory without its consent. Within these
limits, all questions which may arise between us and other powers, be the
subject matter what it may, fall within the limits of the treaty-making
power, and may be adjusted by it.

The greater part of the powers delegated to Congress, relate, directly or
indirectly, to one or the other of these two great divisions; that is, to those
appertaining to the foreign relations of the States, or their exterior relations
with each other. The former embraces the power to declare war; grant
letters of marque and reprisals; make rules concerning captures on land
and water; to raise and support armies; to provide and maintain a navy; to
make rules for the government and regulation of the land and naval forces;
to regulate commerce with foreign nations and the Indian tribes; and to
exercise exclusive jurisdiction over all places purchased, with the consent
of the States, for forts, magazines, dockyards, &c.

There are only two which apply directly to the exterior relations of the States with each other; the power to regulate commerce between them—and to establish post offices and post roads. But there are two others intimately connected with these relations—the one, to establish uniform rules of naturalization, and uniform laws on the subject of bankruptcies, throughout the United States—and the other, to secure, for a limited time, to authors and inventors, the exclusive right to their respective writings and discoveries.

In addition, there is a class which relates to both. They consist of "the power to coin money, regulate the value thereof, and of foreign coins, and to fix the standard of weights and measures—to provide for the punishment of counterfeiting the securities and current coin of the United States; to provide for calling forth the militia, to suppress insurrections and repel invasions; to provide for organizing, arming and disciplining the militia, and for governing such parts of them as may be employed in the service of the United States; reserving to the States, respectively, the appointment of the officers, and the authority of training the militia according to the discipline prescribed by Congress." The two first relate to the power of regulating commerce; and the others, principally, to the war power. Indeed, far the greater part of the powers vested in Congress relate to them.

These embrace all the powers expressly delegated to Congress—except, "the power to lay and collect taxes, duties, imposts and excises, to pay the debts and provide for the common defence and general welfare of the United States—to establish tribunals inferior to the Supreme Court; to provide for calling forth the militia to execute the laws of the Union; to exercise exclusive jurisdiction over such district—not exceeding ten miles square, as may, by cession of particular States, and the acceptance of Congress, become the seat of government of the United States; and to make all laws necessary and proper for carrying into execution the foregoing powers, and all other powers vested in the government of the United States, or in any department or officer thereof." It is apparent, that all these powers relate to the other powers, and are intended to aid in carrying them into execution; and as the others are embraced in the two great divisions of powers, of which the one relates to their foreign relations, and the other to their exterior relations with each other, it may be clearly inferred that the regulation of these relations constituted the great, if not the exclusive objects for which the government was ordained and established.

If additional proof be required to sustain this inference, it may be found in the prohibitory and miscellaneous provisions of the constitution. A large portion of them are intended, directly, to regulate the exterior relations of the States with each other, which would have required treaty stipulations between them, had they been separate communities, instead of being united in a federal union. They are, indeed, treaty stipulations of the most solemn character, inserted in the compact of union. And here it is proper to remark, that there is a material difference between the modes in which these two great divisions of power are regulated. The powers embraced by, or appertaining to foreign relations, are left to be regulated by the treaty-making power, or by Congress; and, if by the latter, are enumerated and specifically delegated. They embrace a large portion of its powers. But those relating to the exterior relations of the States among themselves, with few exceptions, are regulated by provisions inserted in the constitution itself. To this extent, it is, in fact, a treaty—under the form of a constitutional compact—of the highest and most sacred character. It provides that no tax or duty shall be laid on articles exported from any State; that no preference shall be given, by any regulation of commerce or of revenue, to the ports of one State over those of another; nor shall any vessel bound to, or from one State, be obliged to enter, clear, or pay duties in another; that no State shall enter into any treaty, alliance, or confederation, grant letters of marque and reprisal; coin money; emit bills of credit; make any thing but gold or silver a tender in payment of debts, or pass any law impairing the obligation of contracts—that no State shall, without the consent of Congress, lay any import or export duties, except what may be absolutely necessary for the execution of its inspection laws, and that the net proceeds of all duties and imposts, laid by any State on imports or exports, shall be for the use of the treasury of the United States; and all such laws shall be subject to the revision and control of Congress; no State shall, without the consent of Congress, lay any duty on tonnage; keep troops, or ships of war, in time of peace; enter into any agreement or compact with another State or with a foreign power, or engage in war, unless actually invaded, or in such imminent danger as will not admit of delay; that full faith and credit shall be given, in each State, to the public acts, records, and judicial proceedings of any other State; that the citizens of each State shall be entitled to all the privileges and immunities of citizens of the several States; that a person charged in any State, with treason, felony, or other crime, who shall flee from justice, and be found in another State, shall, on demand of the executive authority of the State from which he fled, be delivered up to be removed to the State having jurisdiction of the crime; that no person held to service or labor in one State, under the laws thereof, escaping into another, shall, in consequence of any law or regulation thereof, be discharged from such service or labor; but shall be delivered up on claim of the party to whom such labor may be due; that the United States shall guarantee to each State in this Union a republican form of government, and shall protect each of them against invasion—and, on application of the legislature, or of the executive, when the legislature cannot be convened, against domestic violence.

The other prohibitory provisions, and those of a miscellaneous character, contained in the constitution as ratified, provide against Congress prohibiting the emigration or importation of such persons as any of the States may choose to admit, prior to the year 1808; against the suspension of the writ of *Habeas Corpus;* against passing bills of attainder, and *ex post facto* laws; against laying a capitation or other direct tax, unless in proportion to population, to be ascertained by the census; against drawing money out of the treasury, except in consequence of appropriations made by law; against granting titles of nobility; against persons holding office under the United States, accepting any present or emolument, office or title, from any foreign power, without the consent of Congress; for defining and punishing treason against the United States; for the admission of new States into the Union; for disposing of, and making rules and regulations respecting the territory and other property of the United States; for the amendment of the constitution; for the validity of existing debts and engagements against the United States under the constitution; for the supremacy of the constitution, and the laws of the United States which shall be made in pursuance thereof, and all treaties made, or which shall be made under the authority of the United States; that the Judges in every State shall be bound thereby, any thing in the constitution or laws of any State to the contrary notwithstanding; and that members of Congress and of the State legislatures, and the executive and judicial officers of the United States, and of the several States, shall be bound by oath, or affirmation, to support the constitution; but that no religious test shall be required to hold office under the United States.

Twelve amendments, or, as they are commonly called, amended articles, have been added since its adoption. They provide against passing laws respecting the establishment of religion, or abridging its free exercise; for the freedom of speech and of the press; for the right of petition; for the right of the people to bear arms; and against quartering soldiers in any house against the consent of the owner; against unreasonable searches, or seizures of persons, papers, and effects; against issuing warrants, but on oath or affirmation; against holding persons to answer for a capital, or other infamous crime, except on presentment or indictment of a grand jury; for a public and speedy trial in all criminal prosecutions, by an impartial jury of the State and district where the offence is charged to have been committed; for the right of jury trial in controversies exceeding twenty dollars; against excessive bail and fines, and against cruel and unusual punishments; against so construing the constitution as that the enumeration of certain powers should be made to disparage or deny those not enumerated; against extending the judicial power of the United States to any suit, in law or equity, against one of the United States, by citizens of another State, or citizens or subjects of a foreign state; and for the amendment of the constitution in reference to the election of the President and Vice-President. In addition, the amended article, already cited, provides that the powers not delegated to the United States, nor prohibited to the States, are reserved to the States respectively or to the people.

It will be manifest, on a review of all the provisions, including those embraced by the amendments, that none of them have any *direct* relation to the immediate objects for which the union was formed; and that, with few exceptions, they are intended to guard against improper constructions of the constitution, or the abuse of the delegated powers by the government—or, to protect the government itself in the exercise of its proper functions.

In delegating power to the other two departments, the same general principle prevails. Indeed, in their very nature they are restricted, in a great measure, to the execution, each in its appropriate sphere, of the acts, and, of course, the powers vested in the legislative department; and, in this respect, their powers are consequently limited to the two great divisions which appertain to this department. But where either of them have other vested powers, beyond what is necessary for this purpose, it will be found, when I come to enumerate them, that, if they have any reference at all to the division of power between the general government and those of the several States, they directly relate to those appertaining to one or the other of these divisions.

The executive powers are vested in the President. They embrace the powers belonging to him, as commander in chief of the army and navy of the United States, and the militia of the several States, when called into the actual service of the United States—the right of requiring the opinion, in writing, of the principal officers in each of the executive departments, upon any subject relating to the duties of their respective offices; of granting reprieves and pardons for offences against the United States—except in cases of impeachment; of making treaties, by and with the advice and consent of the Senate—provided two-thirds of the Senators present concur; of nominating and, by and with the advice and consent of the Senate, appointing ambassadors, other public ministers and consuls, judges of the Supreme Court, and all other officers of the United States, whose appointments have not been otherwise provided for, and which shall be established by law—reserving to Congress the right to invest, by law, the appointment of such inferior officers as they may think proper—in the President alone, in the courts of law, or in the heads of departments; of receiving ambassadors and other public ministers; of convening, on extraordinary occasions, both houses of Congress, or either of them; and, in case of disagreement between them, with respect to the time of adjournment, of adjourning them to such time as he may think proper; of commissioning all the officers of the United States. In addition, it is made his duty to give to Congress information of the state of the Union; and to recommend to their consideration, such measures as he may deem necessary and expedient; to take care that the laws are faithfully executed; and, finally, he is vested with the power of approving or disapproving bills passed by Congress, before they become laws—which is called his veto. By far the greater part of these powers and duties appertain to him as chief of the executive department. The principal exception is, the treaty-making power; which appertains exclusively to the foreign relations of the States—and, consequently, is embraced in that division of the delegated powers; as does, also, the appointment of ambassadors, other ministers and consuls, and the reception of the two former. The other exceptions are merely organic, without reference to any one class or division of powers between the two co-ordinate governments.

The judicial power of the United States is vested in the Supreme Court, and such inferior courts as Congress may, from time to time, ordain and establish. The judges hold their offices during good behavior; and have a fixed salary which can neither be increased nor diminished during their continuance in office. Their power extends to all cases in law or equity, arising under the constitution, the laws of the United States, and treaties made, or which shall be made under their authority; to all cases affecting ambassadors, other public ministers and consuls; to all cases of admiralty and marine jurisdiction; to controversies to which the United States shall be a party; to those between two or more States; between citizens of different States; between citizens of the same State, claiming lands under grants of different States; and between a State and the citizens thereof, and foreign states, citizens or subjects. The fact that, in all cases, where the judicial power is extended beyond what may be regarded its appropriate sphere, it contemplates matters connected directly with the foreign or external relations of the States, rather than those connected with their exterior relations with each other—strikingly illustrates the position—that the powers appertaining to the one or the other of these relations, and those necessary to carry them into execution, embrace almost all that have been delegated to the United States. Indeed, on a review of the whole, it may be safely asserted, not only that they embrace almost all of the powers delegated, but that all of the general and miscellaneous provisions (excluding those, of course, belonging to the organism of government, whether they prohibit certain acts, or impose certain duties—as well as those intended to protect the government, and guard against its abuse of power) appertain, with few exceptions, to the one or the other of these divisions. For, if the principle which governed in the original division or distribution of powers between the two co-ordinate governments, be that already stated; that is, to delegate such powers only as could not be exercised at all, or as well, or safely exercised by the governments of the States acting separately, and to reserve the residue—it would be difficult to conceive what others could be embraced in them; since there are none delegated to either, which do not appertain to the States in their relations with each other, or in their relations with the rest of the world. As to all other purposes, the separate governments of the several States were far more competent and safe, than the general government of all the States. Their knowledge of the local interests and domestic institutions of these respectively, must be much more accurate, and the responsibility of each to their respective people much more perfect. This is so obvious, as to render it incredible, that they would have admitted the interference of a general government in their interior and local concerns, farther than was absolutely necessary to the regulation of their exterior relations with each other and the rest of the world—or that a general government should have been adopted for any other purpose. To this extent, it was manifestly necessary—but beyond this, it was not only not necessary, but clearly calculated to jeopard, in part, the ends for which the constitution was adopted—"to establish justice, insure domestic tranquillity, and secure the blessings of liberty."

Having, now, enumerated the delegated powers, and laid down the principle which guided in drawing the line between them and the reserved powers, the next question which offers itself for consideration is; what provisions does the constitution of the United States, or the system itself, furnish, to preserve this, and its other divisions of power? and whether they are sufficient for the purpose?

The great, original, and primary division, as has been stated, is that of distinct, independent, and sovereign States. It is the basis of the whole system. The next in order is, the division into the constitution-making and the law-making powers. The next separates the delegated and the reserved powers, by vesting the one in the government of the United States, and the other in the separate governments of the respective States, as co-ordinate governments; and the last, distributes the powers of government between the several departments of each. These divisions constitute the elements of which the organism of the whole system is formed. On their preservation depend its duration and success, and the mighty interests involved in both. I propose to take the divisions in the reverse order to that stated, by beginning with the last, and ending with the first.

The question, then, is—what provision has the constitution of the United States made to preserve the division of powers among the several departments of the government? And this involves another; whether the departments are so constituted, that each has, within itself, the power of self-protection; the power, by which, it may prevent the others from encroaching on, and absorbing the portion vested in it, by the constitution?

Without such power, the strongest would, in the end, inevitably absorb and concentrate the powers of the others in itself, as has been fully shown in the preliminary discourse—where, also, it is shown that there is but one mode in which this can be prevented; and that is, by investing each division of power, or the representative and organ of each, with a veto, or something tantamount, in some one form or another. To answer, then, the question proposed, it is necessary to ascertain what provisions the constitution, or the system itself, has made for the exercise of this important power. I shall begin with the legislative department, which, in all popular governments, must be the most prominent, and, at least in theory, the strongest.

Its powers are vested in Congress. To it, all the functionaries of the other two departments are responsible, through the impeaching power; while its members are responsible only to the people of their respective States—those of the Senate to them in their corporate character as States; and those of the House of Representatives, in their individual character as citizens of the several States. To guard its members more effectually against the control of the other two departments, they are privileged from arrest in all cases, except for treason, felony, and breach of the peace—during their attendance on the session of their respective houses—and in going to and returning from the same; and from being questioned, in any other place, for any speech or debate in either house. It possesses besides, by an express provision of the constitution, all the discretionary powers vested in the government, whether the same appertain to the legislative, executive, or judicial departments. It is to be found in the 1st ART., 8th SEC., 18th clause; which declares that Congress shall have power "to make all laws necessary and proper for carrying into execution the foregoing powers" (those vested in Congress), "and all other powers vested, by the constitution, in the government of the United States, or in any department or officer thereof." This clause is explicit. It includes all that are usually called "implied powers;" that is—powers to carry into effect those expressly delegated; and vests them expressly in Congress, so

clearly, as to exclude the possibility of doubt. Neither the judicial department, nor any officer of the government can exercise any power not
expressly, and by name, vested in them, either by the constitution, or by
an act of Congress: nor can they exercise any implied power, in carrying
them into execution, without the express sanction of law. The effect of this
is, to place the powers vested in the legislative department, beyond the
reach of the undermining process of insidious construction, on the part of
any of the other departments, or of any of the officers of government.
With all these provisions, backed by its widely extended and appropriate
powers—its security, resulting from freedom of speech in debate—and
its close connection and immediate intercourse with its constituents, the
legislative department is possessed of ample means to protect itself
against the encroachment on, and absorption of its powers, by the other
two departments. It remains to be seen, whether these, in their turn, have
adequate means of protecting themselves, respectively, against the encroachments of each other—as well as of the legislative department. I
shall begin with the executive.

Its powers are vested in the President. To protect them, the constitution,
in the first place, makes him independent of Congress, by providing, that
he "shall, at stated times, receive for his services, a compensation, which
shall be neither increased nor diminished during the period for which he
shall have been elected; and that he shall not receive, within that period,
any other emolument from the United States, or any one of them."[7]

He is, in the next place, vested with the power to veto, not only all acts
of Congress—but it is also expressly provided that, "every order, resolution, or vote, to which the concurrence of the Senate and House of Representatives may be necessary (except on a question of adjournment), shall
be presented to the President of the United States; and, before the same
shall take effect, shall be approved by him; or being disapproved by him,
shall be repassed by two-thirds of the Senate and House of Representa-

[7] 2d Art. 1st Sec. 6th clause of the Constitution.

tives, according to the rules and limitations prescribed in the case of a bill."[8]

He is vested, in the next place, with the power of nominating and appointing, with the advice and consent of the Senate, all the officers of the government whose appointments are not otherwise provided for by the constitution; except such inferior officers as may be authorized, by Congress, to be appointed by the President alone, or by the courts of law, or heads of departments. I do not add the power of removing officers, the tenure of whose office is not fixed by the constitution, which has grown into practice; because it is not a power vested in the President by the constitution, but belongs to the class of implied powers; and as such, can only be rightfully exercised and carried into effect by the authority of Congress.

He has, in the next place, the exclusive control of the administration of the government, with the vast patronage and influence appertaining to the distribution of its honors and emoluments; a patronage so great as to make the election of the President the rallying point of the two great parties that divide the country; and the successful candidate, the leader of the dominant party in power, for the time.

He is, besides, commander in chief of the army and navy; and of the militia, when called into the service of the United States. These, combined with his extensive powers, make his veto (which requires the concurrence of two-thirds of both houses to overrule it) almost as absolute as it would be without any qualification—during the term for which he is elected. The whole combined, vests the executive with ample means to protect its powers from being encroached on, or absorbed by the other departments.

Nor are those of the judiciary less ample, for the same purpose, against the two other departments. Its powers are vested in the courts of the United States. To secure the independence of the judges, they are appointed to hold their offices during good behavior; and to receive for their services, a compensation which cannot be diminished during their continu-

[8] 1st Art. 7th Sec. 7th clause of the Constitution.

ance in office. Besides these means for securing their independence, they have, virtually, a negative on the acts of the other departments—resulting from the nature of our system of government. This requires particular explanation. According to it, constitutions are of paramount authority to laws or acts of the government, or of any of its departments; so that, when the latter come in conflict with the former, they are null and void, and of no binding effect whatever. From this fact it results, that, when a case comes before the courts of the United States, in which a question of conflict between the acts of Congress or any department may arise, the judges are bound, from the necessity of the case, to determine whether, in fact, there is any conflict or not; and if, in their opinion, there be such conflict, to decide in favor of the constitution; and thereby, virtually, to annul or veto the act, as far as it relates to the department or government, and the parties to the suit or controversy. This, with the provisions to secure their independence, gives, not only means of self-protection, but a weight and dignity to the judicial department never before possessed by the judges in any other government of which we have any certain knowledge.

But, however ample may be the means possessed by the several departments to protect themselves against the encroachments of each other, regarded as independent and irresponsible bodies, it by no means follows, that the equilibrium of power, established between them by the constitution, will, necessarily, remain undisturbed. For they are, in fact, neither independent nor irresponsible bodies. They are all representatives of the several States, either in their organized character of governments, or of their people, estimated in federal numbers; and are under the control of their joint majority—blended, however, in unequal proportions, in the several departments. In order, then, to preserve the equilibrium between the departments, it is indispensable to preserve that between the two majorities which have the power to control them, and to which they are all responsible, directly or indirectly. For it is manifest that if this equilibrium, established by the constitution, be so disturbed, as to give the ascendency to either, it must disturb, or would be calculated to disturb, in turn, the equilibrium between the departments themselves; inasmuch as the weight of the majority which might gain it, would be thrown in favor of the one or the other, as the means of increasing its influence over the government. In order, then, to determine whether the equilibrium between the departments is liable to be disturbed, it is necessary to ascertain what provisions the constitution has made to preserve it between the two majorities, in reference to the several departments; and to determine whether they are sufficient for the purpose intended. I shall, again, commence with the legislative.

In this department the two majorities or elements, of which the government is composed, act separately. Each has its own organ; one the Senate, and the other the House of Representatives: and each has, through its respective organ, a negative on the other, in all acts of legislation, which require their joint action. This gives to each complete and perfect means to guard against the encroachments of the other. The same is the case in the judiciary. There, the judges, in whom the powers of the department are vested, are nominated by the President, and, by and with the advice and consent of the Senate, appointed by him; which gives each element also a negative on the other; and, of course, like means of preserving the equilibrium established by the constitution between them. But the case is different in reference to the executive department.

The two elements in this department are blended into one, when the choice of a President is made by the electoral college—which, as has been stated, gives a great preponderance to the element representing the federal population of the several States, over that which represents them in their organized character as governments. To compensate this, a still greater preponderance is given to the latter, in the eventual choice by the House of Representatives. But they have, in neither case, a veto upon the acts of each other; nor any equivalent means to prevent encroachments, in choosing the individual to be vested, for the time, with the powers of the department; and, hence, no means of preserving the equilibrium, as established between them by the constitution. The result has been—as it ever must be in such cases—the ascendency of the stronger element over the weaker. The incipient measure to effect this was adopted at an early period. The first step was, to diminish the number of candidates, from which the selection should be made, from the five, to the three highest on the list; and—in order to lessen the chances of a failure to choose by the electoral college—to provide that the electors, instead of voting for two, without discriminating the offices, should designate which was for the President, and which for the Vice-President. This was effected in the regular way, by an amendment of the constitution. Since then, the constitution, as amended, has been, in practice, superseded, by what is called, *the usage of parties;* that is, by each selecting, informally, persons to meet at some central point, to nominate candidates for the Presidency and Vice-Presidency— with the avowed object of preventing the election from going into the House of Representatives; and, of course, by superseding the eventual choice on the part of this body, to abolish, in effect, one of the two elements of which the government is constituted, so far, at least, as the executive department is concerned. As it now stands, the complex and refined machinery provided by the constitution for the election of the President and Vice-President, is virtually superseded. The nomination of the successful party, by irresponsible individuals makes, in reality, the choice. It is in this way that the provisions of the constitution, which intended to give equal weight to the two elements in the executive department of the government, have been defeated; and an overwhelming preponderance given to that which is represented in the House of Representatives, over that which is represented in the Senate.

But the decided preponderance of this element in the executive department, cannot fail greatly to disturb the equilibrium between it and the other two departments, as established by the constitution. It cannot but throw the weight of the more populous States and sections on the side of that department, over which their control is the most decisive; and place the President, in whom its powers are vested for the time, more completely under their control. This, in turn, must place the honors and emoluments of the government, also, more under their control; and, of course, give a corresponding influence over all who aspire to participate in them; and especially over the members, for the time, of the legislative department. Even those, composing the judiciary, for the time, will not be unaffected by an influence so great and pervading.

I come now to examine, what means the constitution of the United States, or the system itself provides, for preserving the division between the delegated and reserved powers. The former are vested in the government of the United States; and the latter, where they have not been reserved to the people of the several States respectively, are vested in their respective State governments. The two, as has been established, stand in the relation of co-ordinate governments; that is, the government of the United States is, in each State, the co-ordinate of its separate government; and taken together, the two make the entire government of each, and of all the States. On the preservation of this peculiar and important division of power, depend the preservation of all the others, and the equilibrium of the entire system. It cannot be disturbed, without, at the same time, disturbing the whole, with all its parts.

The only means which the constitution of the United States contains or provides for its preservation, consists, in the first place, in the enumeration and specification of the powers delegated to the United States, and the express reservation to the States of all powers not delegated; in the next, in imposing such limitations on both governments, and on the States themselves, in their separate character, as were thought best calculated to prevent the abuse of power, or the disturbance of the equilibrium between the two co-ordinate governments; and, finally, in prescribing that the members of Congress, and of the legislatures of the several States, and all executive and judicial officers of the United States, and of the several States, shall be bound, by oath or affirmation, to support the constitution of the United States. These were, undoubtedly, proper and indispensable means; but that they were, of themselves, deemed insufficient to preserve, undisturbed, this new and important partition of power between co-ordinate governments, is clearly inferrible from the proceedings of the convention, and the writings and speeches of eminent individuals, pending the ratification of the constitution. No question connected with the formation and adoption of the constitution of the United States, excited deeper solicitude—or caused more discussion, than this important partition of power. The ablest men divided in reference to it, during these discussions. One side maintained that the danger was, that the delegated would absorb the reserved; while the other not less strenuously contended, that the reserved would absorb the delegated powers. So widely extended was this diversity of opinion, and so deep the excitement it produced, that it contributed more than all other questions combined, to the organization of the two great parties, which arose with the formation of the constitution; and which, finally, assumed the names of "Federal" and "Republican." In all these discussions, neither side relied on the provisions of the constitution of the United States, just referred to, as the means of preserving the partition of power between the co-ordinate governments; and thereby, of preventing either from encroaching on, and absorbing the powers of the other. Both looked to the co-ordinate governments, to control each other; and by their mutual action and reaction, to keep each other in their proper spheres. The doubt, on one side, was, whether the delegated, were not too strong for the reserved powers; and, on the other, whether the latter were not too strong for the former. One apprehended that the end would be, *consolidation;* and the other, *dissolution.* Both parties, to make out their case, appealed to the respective powers of the two; compared their relative force, and decided accordingly, as the one or the other appeared the stronger. Both, in the discussion, assumed, that those who might administer the two co-ordinate governments, for the time, would stand in antagonistic relations to each other, and be ready to seize every opportunity to enlarge their own at the expense of the powers of the other; and rather hoped than believed, that this reciprocal action and reaction would prove so well balanced as to be sufficient to preserve the equilibrium, and keep each in its respective sphere.

Such were the views taken, and the apprehensions felt, on both sides, at the time. They were both right, in looking to the co-ordinate governments for the means of preserving the equilibrium between these two important classes of powers; but time and experience have proved, that both mistook the source and the character of the danger to be apprehended, and the means of counteracting it; and, thereby, of preserving the equilibrium, which both believed to be essential to the preservation of the complex system of government about to be established. Nor is it a subject of wonder, that statesmen, as able and experienced as the leaders of the two sides were, should both fall into error, as to what would be the working of political elements, wholly untried; and which made so great an innovation in governments of the class to which ours belonged. It is clear, from the references so frequently made to previous confederacies, in order to determine how the government about to be established, would operate, that the framers of the constitution themselves, as well as those who took an active part in discussing the question of its adoption, were far from realizing the magnitude of the change which was made by it in governments of that form. Had this been fully realized, they would never have assumed that those who administered the government of the United States, and those of the separate States, would stand in hostile relations to each other; or have believed that it would depend on the relative force of the powers delegated and the powers reserved, whether either would encroach on, and absorb the other—an assumption and belief which experience has proved to be utterly unfounded. The conflict took, from the first, and has continued ever since to move in, a very different direction. Instead of a contest for power between the government of the United States, on the one side, and the separate governments of the several States, on the other—the real struggle has been to obtain the control of the former—a struggle in which both States and people have united: And the result has shown that, instead of

depending on the relative force of the delegated and reserved powers, the
latter, in all contests, have been brought in aid of the former, by the States
on the side of the party in the possession and control of the government of
the United States—and by the States on the side of the party in the
opposition, in their efforts to expel those in possession, and to take their
place. There must then be at all times—except in a state of transition of
parties, or from some accidental cause—a majority of the several States,
and of their people, estimated in federal numbers, on the side of those in
power; and, of course, on the side of the delegated powers and the government of the United States. Its real authority, therefore, instead of being
limited to the delegated powers alone, must, habitually, consist of these,
united with the reserved powers of the joint majority of the States, and of
their population, estimated in federal numbers. Their united strength must
necessarily give to the government of the United States, a power vastly
greater than that of all the co-ordinate governments of the States on the
side of the party in opposition. It is their united strength, which makes it
one of the strongest ever established; greatly stronger than it could possibly be as a national government. And, hence, all conclusions, drawn from
a supposed antagonism between the delegated powers, on the one hand,
and the reserved powers, on the other, have proved, and must ever prove
utterly fallacious. Had it, in fact, existed, there can now be no doubt, that
the apprehensions of those, who feared that the reserved powers would
encroach on and absorb the delegated, would have been realized, and
dissolution, long since, been the fate of the system: for it was this very
antagonism which caused the weakness of the confederation, and threatened the dissolution of the Union. The difference between it and the
present government, in this respect, results from the fact, that the States,
in the confederation, had but few and feeble motives to form combinations,
in order to obtain the control of its powers; because neither the State
governments, nor the citizens of the several States were subject to its
control. Hence, they were more disposed to elude its requisitions, and
reserve their means for their own control and use, than to enter into

combinations to control its councils. But very different is the case in their existing confederated character. The present government possesses extensive and important powers; among others, that of carrying its acts into execution by its own authority, without the intermediate agency of the States. And, hence, the principal motives to get the control of the government, with all its powers and vast patronage; and for this purpose, to form combinations as the only means by which it can be accomplished. Hence, also, the fact, that the present danger is directly the reverse of that of the confederacy. The one tended to dissolution—the other tends to consolidation. But there is this difference between these tendencies. In the former, they were far more rapid—not because they were stronger, but because there were few or no impediments in their way; while in the latter, many and powerful obstacles are presented. In the case of the confederacy, the antagonistic position which the States occupied in respect to it—and their indifference to its acts, after the acknowledgment of their independence, led to a non-compliance with its requisitions—and this, without any active measure on their parts, was sufficient, if left to itself, to have brought about a dissolution of the Union, from its weakness, at no distant day. But such is not the case under the present system of government. To form combinations in order to get the control of the government, in a country of such vast extent—and consisting of so many States, having so great a variety of interests, must necessarily be a slow process, and require much time, before they can be firmly united, and settle down into two organized and compact parties. But the motives to obtain this control are sufficiently powerful to overcome all these impediments; and the formation of such parties is just as certain to result from the action of political affinities and antipathies, as the formation of bodies, where different elements in the material world, having mutual attraction and repulsion, are brought in contact. Nor is the organization of the government of the United States, which requires the concurrence of the two majorities to control it—though intended for the purpose—sufficient, of itself, to prevent it. The same constitution of man, which would, in time, lead to the organization of a party, consisting of a simple majority—if such had the power of control—will, just as certainly, in time, form one, consisting of the two combined. The only difference is, that the one would be formed more easily, and in a shorter time than the other. The motives are sufficiently strong to overcome the impediments in either case.

In forming these combinations, which, in fact, constitute the two parties, circumstances must, of course, exert a powerful influence. Similarity of origin, language, institutions, political principles, customs, pursuits, interests, color, and contiguity of situations—all contribute to facilitate them: while their opposites necessarily tend to repel them, and, thus, to form an antagonistic combination and party. In a community of so great an extent as ours, contiguity becomes one of the strongest elements in forming party combinations, and distance one of the strongest elements in repelling them. The reason is, that nothing tends more powerfully to weaken the social or sympathetic feelings, than remoteness; and, in the absence of causes calculated to create aversion, nothing to strengthen them more, than contiguity. We feel intensely the sufferings endured under our immediate observation—when we would be almost indifferent, were they removed to a great distance from us. Besides, contiguity of situation usually involves a similarity of interests—especially, when considered in reference to those more remote—which greatly facilitates the formation of local combinations and parties in a country of extensive limits. If to this, we add other diversities—of pursuits, of institutions, origin, and the like, which not unusually exist in such cases, parties must almost necessarily partake, from the first, more or less, of a local character: and, by an almost necessary operation, growing out of the unequal fiscal action of the government, as explained in the preliminary discourse, must become entirely so, in the end, if not prevented by the resistance of powerful causes. We accordingly find, that such has been the case with us, under the operation of the present government. From the first, they assumed, in some degree, this character; and have since been gradually tending more and more to this form, until they have become, almost entirely, sectional. When they shall

have become so entirely—(which must inevitably be the case, if not prevented)—when the stronger shall concentrate in itself both the majorities
which form the elements of the government of the United States—(and
this, it must shortly do)—every barrier, which the constitution, and the
organism of the government oppose to one overruling combination of interests, will have been broken down, and the government become as absolute,
as would be that of the mere numerical majority; unless, indeed, the
system itself, shall be found to furnish some means sufficiently powerful to
resist this strong tendency, inherent in governments like ours, to absorb
and consolidate all power in its own hands.

What has been stated is sufficient to show, that no such means are to be
found in the constitution of the United States, or in the organism of the
government. Nor can they be found in the right of suffrage; for it is
through its instrumentality that the party combinations are formed. Neither
can they be found in the fact, that the constitution of the United States is a
written instrument; for this, of itself, cannot possibly enforce the limitations
and restrictions which it imposes, as has been fully shown in the preliminary discourse. Nor can they be enforced, and the government held strictly
to the sphere assigned, by resorting to a strict construction of the constitution—for the plain reason, that the stronger party will be in favor of a
liberal construction; and the strict construction of the minority can be of no
avail against the liberal construction of the majority—as has also been
shown in the same discourse. Nor can they be found in the force of public
opinion—operating through the Press; for it has been, therein, also shown,
that its operation is similar to that of the right of suffrage; and that its
tendency, with all its good effects in other respects, is to increase party
excitement, and to strengthen the force of party attachments and party
combinations, in consequence of its having become a party organ and the
instrument of party warfare. Nor can the veto power of the President, or
the power of the Judges to decide on the constitutionality of the acts of the
other departments, furnish adequate means to resist it—however important they may be, in other respects, and in particular instances—for the

plain reason, that the party combinations which are sufficient to control the two majorities constituting the elements of the government of the United States, must, habitually, control all the departments—and make them all, in the end, the instruments of encroaching on, and absorbing the reserved powers; especially the executive department—since the provisions of the constitution, in reference to the election of the President and Vice-President, have been superseded, and their election placed, substantially, under the control of the single element of federal numbers. But if none of these can furnish the means of effective resistance, it would be a waste of time to undertake to show, that freedom of speech, or the trial by jury, or any guards of the kind, however indispensable as auxiliary means, can, of themselves, furnish them.

If, then, neither the constitution, nor any thing appertaining to it, furnishes means adequate to prevent the encroachment of the delegated on the reserved powers, they must be found in some other part of the system, if they are to be found in it at all. And, further—if they are to be found there, it must be in the powers not delegated; since it has been shown that they are not to be found in those delegated, nor in any thing appertaining to them—and the two necessarily embrace all the powers of the whole system. But, if they are to be found in the reserved powers, it must be in those vested in the separate governments of the several States, or in those retained by the people of the several States, in their sovereign character—that character in which they ordained and established the constitution and government; and, in which, they can amend or abolish it—since all the powers, not delegated, are expressly reserved, by the 10th Article of Amendments, to the one or the other. In one, then, or the other of these, or in both, the means of resisting the encroachments of the powers delegated to the United States, on those reserved to the States respectively, or to the people thereof—and thereby to preserve the equilibrium between them, must be found, if found in the system at all. Indeed, in one constituted as ours, it would seem neither reasonable nor philosophical to look to the government of the United States, in which the delegated powers are vested, for the means of resisting encroachments on the reserved powers. It would not be reasonable; because it would be to look for protection against danger, to the quarter from which it was apprehended, and from which only it could possibly come. It would not be philosophical; because it would be against universal analogy. All organic action, as far as our knowledge extends—whether it appertain to the material or political world, or be of human or divine mechanism—is the result of the reciprocal action and reaction of the parts of which it consists. It is this which confines the parts to their appropriate spheres, and compels them to perform their proper functions. Indeed, it would seem impossible to produce organic action by a single power—and that it must ever be the result of two or more powers, mutually acting and reacting on each other. And hence the political axiom—that there can be no constitution, without a division of power, and no liberty without a constitution. To this a kindred axiom may be added—that there can be no division of power, without a self-protecting power in each of the parts into which it may be divided; or in a superior power to protect each against the others. Without a division of power there can be no organism; and without the power of self-protection, or a superior power to restrict each to its appropriate sphere, the stronger will absorb the weaker, and concentrate all power in itself.

The members, then, of the convention, which framed the constitution, and those who took an active part in the question of its adoption, were not wrong in looking to this reciprocal action and reaction, between the delegated and the reserved powers—between the government of the United States and the separate governments of the several States—as furnishing the means of resisting the encroachments of the one or the other—however much they may have erred as to the *mode* in which they would mutually act. No one, indeed, seems, at the time, to have formed any clear or definite conception of the manner in which, a division so novel, would act, when put into operation. All seem to have agreed that there would be conflict between the two governments. They differed only as to which would prove the stronger; yet indulging the hope that their respective powers were so well adjusted, that neither would be able to prevail over the other. Under the influence of this hope, and the diversity of opinion entertained, the framers of the constitution contented themselves with drawing, as strongly as possible, the line of separation between the two powers—leaving it to time and experience to determine where the danger lay; to develop whatever remedy the system might furnish to guard against it—and, if it furnished none, they left it to those, who should come after them, to supply the defect. We now have the benefit of these: Time and Experience have shown fully, where the danger lies, and what is its nature and character. They have established, beyond all doubt, that the antagonism relied on—as existing in theory, between the government of the United States, on the one hand, and all the separate State governments, on the other, has proved to be, in practice, between the former, supported by a majority of the latter, and of their population, estimated in federal numbers—and a minority of the States and of their population, estimated in the same manner. And, consequently, that the government of the United States, instead of being the weaker, as was believed by many, has proved to be immeasurably the stronger; especially, since the two majorities constituting the elements of which it is composed, have centred in one of the two great sections which divide the Union. The effect has been, to give to this section entire and absolute control over the government of the United States; and through it, over the other section, on all questions, in which their interests or views of policy may come in conflict. The system, in consequence of this, instead of tending towards dissolution from weakness, tends strongly towards consolidation from exuberance of strength—so strongly, that, if not opposed by a resistance proportionally powerful, the end must be its destruction—either by the bursting asunder of its parts, in consequence of the intense conflict of interest, produced by being too closely pressed together, or by consolidating all the powers of the system in the government of the United States, or in some one of its departments—to be wielded with despotic force and oppression. The present system must be preserved in its integrity and full vigor; for there can be no other means—no other form of government, save that of absolute power, which can govern and keep the whole together. Disregarding this, the only alternatives are—a government in form and in action, absolute and irresponsible—a consolidation of the system under the existing form, with powers equally despotic and oppressive—or a dissolution.

With these preliminary remarks, I shall next proceed to consider the question—whether the reserved powers, if fully developed and brought into action, are sufficient to resist this powerful and dangerous tendency of the delegated, to encroach on them? or, to express the same thing in a different form—whether the separate government of a State, and its people in their sovereign character, to whom all powers, not delegated to the United States, appertain, can—one or both—rightfully oppose sufficient resistance to the strong tendency on the part of the government of the latter, to prevent its encroachment. I use the expression—"a State and its people"—because the powers not delegated to the United States, are reserved to each State respectively, or to its people; and, of course, it results that, whatever resistance the reserved powers can oppose to the delegated, must, to be within constitutional limits, proceed from the government and the people of the several States, in their separate and individual character.

The question is one of the first magnitude—and deserves the most serious and deliberate consideration. I shall begin with considering—what means the government of a State possesses, to prevent the government of the United States from encroaching on its reserved powers? I shall, however, pass over the right of remonstrating against its encroachments; of adopting resolutions against them, as unconstitutional; of addressing the governments of its co-States, and calling on them to unite and co-operate in opposition to them; and of instructing its Senators in Congress, and requesting its members of the House of Representatives, to oppose them—and other means of a like character; not because they are of no avail, but because they are utterly impotent to arrest the strong and steady tendency of the government of the United States to encroach on the reserved powers; however much they may avail, in particular instances. To rely on them to counteract a tendency so strong and steady, would be as idle as to rely on reason and justice, as the means to prevent oppression and abuse of power on the part of government, without the aid of constitutional provisions. Nothing short of a negative, absolute or in effect, on the part of the government of a State, can possibly protect it against the encroachments of the government of the United States, whenever their powers come in conflict That there is, in effect, a mutual negative on the part of each, in such cases, is what I next propose to show.

It results from their nature; from the relations which subsist between them; and from a law universally applicable to a division of power. I will consider each in the order stated.

That they are both governments, and, as such, possess all the powers appertaining to government, within the sphere of their respective powers— the one as fully as the other—cannot be denied. Nor can it be denied that, among the other attributes of government, they possess the right to judge of the extent of their respective powers, as it regards each other. In addition to this, it may be affirmed as true, that governments, in full possession of all the powers appertaining to government, have the right to enforce their decisions as to the extent of their powers, against all opposition. But the case is different in a system of governments like ours—where the powers appertaining to government are divided—a portion being delegated to one government, and a portion to another—and the residue retained by those who ordained and established both. In such case, neither can have the right to enforce its decisions, as to the extent of its powers, when a conflict occurs between them in reference to it; because it would be, in the first place, inconsistent with the relation in which they stand to each other as co-ordinates. The idea of co-ordinates, excludes that of superior and subordinate, and, necessarily, implies that of equality. But to give either the right, not only to judge of the extent of its own powers, but, also, of that of its co-ordinate, and to enforce its decision against it, would be, not only to destroy the equality between them, but to deprive one of an attribute—appertaining to all governments   to judge, in the first instance, of the extent of its powers. The effect would be to raise one from an equal to a superior—and to reduce the other from an equal to a subordinate; and, by divesting it of an attribute appertaining to government, to sink it into a dependent corporation. In the next place, it would be inconsistent with what is meant by a division of power; as this necessarily implies, that each of the parties, among whom it may be partitioned, has an equal right to its respective share, be it greater or smaller; and to judge as to its extent, and to maintain its decision against its copartners. This is what constitutes, and what is meant by, a division of power. Without it, there could be no division. To allot a portion of power to one, and another portion to another, and to give either the exclusive right to say, how much was allotted to each, would be no division at all. The one would hold as a mere tenant at will—to be deprived of its portion whenever the other should choose to assume the whole. And, finally, because, no reason can be assigned, why one should possess the right to judge of the extent of its powers, and to enforce its decision, which would not equally apply to the other co-ordinate government. If one, then, possess the right to enforce its decision, so, also, must the other. But to assume that both possess it, would be to leave the umpirage, in case of conflict, to mere brute force; and thus to destroy the equality, clearly implied by the relation of co-ordinates, and the division between the two governments. In such case, force alone would determine which should be the superior, and which the subordinate; which should have the exclusive right of judging, both as to the extent of its own powers and that of its co-ordinates—and which should be deprived of the right of judging as to the extent of those of either—which should, and which should not possess any other power than that which its co-ordinate—now raised to its superior—might choose to permit it to exercise. As the one or the other might prove the stronger, consolidation or disunion would, inevitably, be the consequence; and which of the twain, no one who has paid any attention to the working of our system, can doubt. An assumption, therefore, which would necessarily lead to the destruction of the whole system in the end, and the substitution of another, of an entirely different character, in its place—must be false.

But, if neither has the exclusive right, the effect, where they disagree as to the extent of their respective powers, would be, a mutual negative on the acts of each, when they come into conflict. And the effect of this again, would be, to vest in each the power to protect the portion of authority allotted to it, against the encroachment of its co-ordinate government. Nothing short of this can possibly preserve this important division of power, on which rests the equilibrium of the entire system.

The party, in the convention, which favored a national government, clearly saw that the separate governments of the several States would have the right of judging of the extent of their powers, as between the two governments, unless some provision should be adopted to prevent it. This is manifest from the many and strenuous efforts which they made to deprive them of the right, by vesting the government of the United States with the power to veto or overrule their acts, when they might be thought to come in conflict with its powers. These efforts were made in every stage of the proceedings of the convention, and in every conceivable form—as its journals will show.

The very first project of a constitution submitted to the convention, (Gov. Randolph's) contained a provision, "to grant power to negative all acts contrary, in the opinion of the national legislature, to the articles—or any treaty, subsisting under the power of the Union; and to call forth the force of the Union, against any member of the Union, failing to fulfill its duties, under the articles thereof."

The next plan submitted (Mr. Charles Pinckney's) contained a provision that—"the legislature of the United States shall have power to revise the laws that may be supposed to impinge the powers exclusively delegated, by this constitution, to Congress; and to negative and annul such as do." The next submitted (Mr. Paterson's) provided that, "if any State, or body of men in any State, shall oppose, or prevent the carrying into execution, such acts, or treaties" (of the Union), "the federal executive shall be authorized to call forth the forces of the confederated States, or so much thereof, as shall be necessary, to enforce or compel obedience to such acts, or the observance of such treaties." The committee of the whole, to whom was referred Mr. Randolph's project, reported a provision, that the jurisdiction of the national judiciary should extend to all "questions, which involved the national peace and harmony." The next project, (Mr. Hamilton's)—after declaring all the laws of the several States, which were contrary to the constitution and the laws of the United States, to be null and void—provides, that, "the better to prevent such laws from being passed, the Governor, or President of each State, shall be appointed by the general government; and shall have a negative upon the laws, about to be passed in the State of which he is Governor or President." This was followed by a motion, made by Mr. C. Pinckney, to vest in the legislature of the United States the power, "to negative all laws, passed by the several States, interfering, in the opinion of the legislature, with the general interest and harmony of the Union; provided that two thirds of each house assent to the same."

It is not deemed necessary to trace, through the journals of the convention, the history and the fate of these various propositions. It is sufficient to say—that they were all made, and not one adopted; although perseveringly urged by some of the most talented and influential members of the body, as indispensable to protect the government of the United States, against the apprehended encroachments of the governments of the several States. The fact that they were proposed and so urged, proves, conclusively, that it was believed, even by the most distinguished members of the national party, that the former had no right to enforce its measures against the latter, where they disagreed as to the extent of their respective powers—without some express provision to that effect; while the refusal of the convention to adopt any such provision, under such circumstances, proves, equally conclusively, that it was opposed to the delegation of such powers to the government, or any of its departments, legislative, executive, or judicial, in any form whatever.

But, if it be possible for doubt still to remain, the ratification of the constitution by the convention of Virginia, and the 10th amended article, furnish proofs in confirmation so strong, that the most skeptical will find it difficult to resist them.

It is well known, that there was a powerful opposition to the adoption of the constitution of the United States. It originated in the apprehension, that it would lead to the consolidation of all power in the government of the United States—notwithstanding the defeat of the national party, in the convention—and the refusal to adopt any of the proposals to vest it with the power to negative the acts of the governments of the separate States. This apprehension excited a wide and deep distrust, lest the scheme of the national party might ultimately prevail, through the influence of its leaders, over the government about to be established. The alarm became so great as to threaten the defeat of the ratification by nine States—the number necessary to make the constitution binding between the States ratifying it. It was particularly great in Virginia—on whose act, all sides believed the fate of the instrument depended. Before the meeting of her convention, seven States had ratified. It was generally believed that, of the remaining States, North Carolina and Rhode Island would not ratify; and New York was regarded so doubtful, that her course would, in all probability, depend on the action of Virginia. Her refusal, together with that of Virginia, would have defeated the adoption of the constitution. The struggle, accordingly, between the two parties in her convention, was long and ardent. The magnitude of the question at issue, called out the ablest and most influential of her citizens on both sides; and elicited the highest efforts of their talents. The discussion turned, mainly, on the danger of consolidation from construction; and was conducted with such ability and force of argument, by the opponents of ratification, that it became necessary, in order to obtain a majority for it, to guard against such construction, by incorporating in the act of ratification itself, provisions to prevent it. The act is in the following words: "We, the delegates of the people of Virginia, duly elected in pursuance of a recommendation from the general assembly, and now met in convention, having fully and freely investigated and discussed the proceedings of the federal convention, and being prepared as well as the most mature deliberation hath enabled us to decide thereon, do, in the name and in behalf of the people of Virginia, declare and make known, that the powers granted under the constitution, being derived from the people of the United States, may be resumed by them, whensoever the same shall be perverted to their injury or oppression; and that every power not granted thereby, remains with them and at their will: that, therefore, no right, of any denomination, can be cancelled, abridged, restrained, or modified, by the Congress, by the Senate, or House of Representatives, acting in any capacity, by the President or any department, or officer of the United States, except in those instances in which power is given by the constitution for those purposes; and that among other essential rights, the liberty of conscience and of the press cannot be cancelled, abridged, restrained or modified by any authority of the United States.

"With these impressions—with a solemn appeal to the Searcher of hearts for the purity of our intentions, and under the conviction, that, whatsoever imperfections may exist in the constitution ought rather to be examined in the mode prescribed therein, than to bring the Union into danger by delay, with the hope of obtaining amendments, previous to the ratification: We, the said delegates, in the name and behalf of the people of Virginia, do by these presents, assent to and ratify the constitution, &c."—concluding in the usual form.

Such is the recorded construction, which that great and leading State placed on the constitution, in her act of ratification. That her object was to guard against the abuse of construction, the act itself, on its face, and the discussions in her convention abundantly prove. It was done effectually, as far as it depended on words. It declares that all powers granted by the constitution, are derived from the people of the United States; and may be *resumed* by them when *perverted* to their injury or oppression; and, that every power *not granted*, remains with them, and at their will; and that no right of any description can be cancelled, abridged, restrained or modified by Congress, the Senate, the House of Representatives, the President, or any department, or officer of the United States. Language cannot be stronger. It guards the reserved powers against the government as a whole, and against all its departments and officers; and in every mode by which they might be impaired; showing, clearly, that the intention was to place the reserved powers beyond the possible interference and control of the government of the United States. Now, when it is taken into consideration, that the right of the separate governments of the several States is as full and perfect to protect their own powers, as is that of the government of the United States to protect those which are delegated to it; and, of course, that it belongs to their reserved powers; that all the attempts made in the convention which framed the constitution, to deprive them of it, by vesting the latter with the power to overrule the right, equally failed; that Virginia could not be induced to ratify without incorporating the true construction she placed on it in her act of ratification; that, without her ratification, it would not, in all probability, have been adopted; and that it was accepted by the other States, subject to this avowed construction, without objection on their part—it is difficult to resist the inference, that their acceptance, under all these circumstances, was an implied admission of the truth of her construction; and that it makes it as binding on them as if it had been inserted in the constitution itself.

But her convention took the further precaution of having it inserted, in substance, in that instrument. Those who composed it were wise, experienced, and patriotic men; and knew full well, how difficult it is to guard against the abuses of construction. They accordingly proposed, as an amendment of the constitution, the substance of her construction. It is in the following words: "That each State in the Union shall respectively retain every power, jurisdiction, and right, which is not, by the constitution, delegated to the Congress of the United States, or to the departments of the federal government." This was modified and proposed, as an amendment, in the regular constitutional form; and was ratified by the States. It constitutes the 10th amendment article, which has already been quoted at length. It is worthy of note, that Massachusetts, New Hampshire, and South Carolina, proposed, when they ratified the constitution, amendments similar in substance, and with the same object—clearly showing how extensively the alarm felt by Virginia, had extended; and how strong the desire was to guard against the evil apprehended.

Such, and so convincing are the arguments going to show, that the government of the United States has no more right to enforce its decisions against those of the separate governments of the several States, where they disagree as to the extent of their respective powers, than the latter have of enforcing their decisions in like cases. They both stand on equal grounds, in this respect. But as convincing as are these arguments, there are many, who entertain a different opinion—and still affirm that the government of the United States possesses the right, fully, absolutely, and exclusively.

In support of this opinion, they rely, in the first place, on the second section of the sixth article, which provides that—"This constitution, and the laws of the United States, which shall be made in pursuance thereof, and all treaties made, or which shall be made, under the authority of the United States, shall be the supreme law of the land: and the judges in every State shall be bound thereby, any thing in the constitution or laws of any State to the contrary notwithstanding."

It is sufficient, in reply, to state, that the clause is declaratory; that it vests no new power whatever in the government, or in any of its departments. Without it, the constitution and the laws made in pursuance of it, and the treaties made under its authority, would have been the supreme law of the land, as fully and perfectly as they now are; and the judges in every State would have been bound thereby, any thing in the constitution or laws of a State, to the contrary notwithstanding. Their supremacy results from the nature of the relation between the federal government, and those of the several States, and their respective constitutions and laws. Where two or more States form a common constitution and government, the authority of these, within the limits of the delegated powers, must, of necessity, be supreme, in reference to their respective separate constitutions and governments. Without this, there would be neither a common constitution and government, nor even a confederacy. The whole would be, in fact, a mere nullity. But this supremacy is not an absolute supremacy. It is limited in extent and degree. It does not extend beyond the delegated powers—all others being reserved to the States and the people of the States. Beyond these the constitution is as destitute of authority, and as powerless as a blank piece of paper; and the measures of the government mere acts of assumption. And, hence, the supremacy of laws and treaties is expressly restricted to such as are made in pursuance of the constitution, or under the authority of the United States; which can, in no case, extend beyond the delegated powers. There is, indeed, no power of the government without restriction; not even that, which is called the discretionary power of Congress. I refer to the grant which authorizes it to pass laws to carry into effect the powers expressly vested in it—or in the government of the United States—or in any of its departments, or officers. This power, comprehensive as it is, is, nevertheless, subject to two important restrictions; one, that the law must be necessary—and the other, that it must be proper.

To understand the import of the former, it must be borne in mind, that no power can execute itself. They all require means, and the agency of government, to apply them. The means themselves may, indeed, be regarded as auxiliary powers. Of these, some are so intimately connected with the principal power, that, without the aid of one, or all of them, it could not be carried into execution—and, of course, without them, the power itself would be nugatory. Hence, they are called implied powers; and it is to this description of incidental or auxiliary powers, that Congress is restricted, in passing laws, necessary to carry into execution the powers expressly delegated.

But the law must, also, be proper as well as necessary, in order to bring it within its competency. To understand the true import of the term in this connection, it is necessary to bear in mind, that even the implied powers themselves are subject to important conditions, when used as means to carry powers or rights into execution. Among these the most prominent and important is, that they must be so carried into execution as not to injure others; and, as connected with, and subordinate to this—that, where the implied powers, or means used, come in conflict with the implied powers, or means used by another, in the execution of the powers or rights vested in it, the less important should yield to the more important—the convenient, to the useful; and both to health and safety—because it is *proper they should do so*. Both rules are universal, and rest on the fundamental principles of morals.

Such is the true import of the term "proper," superadded to "necessary," when applied to this important question. And hence, when a law of Congress, carrying into execution one of the delegated powers, comes into conflict with a law of one of the States, carrying its reserved powers into execution, it does not necessarily follow that the latter must yield to the former, because the laws made in pursuance of the constitution, are declared to be the supreme law of the land: for the restriction imposed by the term "proper," takes it out of the power of Congress, even where the implied power is necessary, and brings it under the operation of those fundamental rules of universal acceptation, to determine which shall yield. Without this restriction, most of the reserved powers of the States—and, among them, those relating to their internal police, including the health, tranquillity, and safety of their people—might be made abortive, by the laws passed by Congress, to carry into effect the delegated powers; especially in regard to those regulating commerce, and establishing post offices and post roads.

The alterations finally made in this clause of the constitution, compared with it as originally reported by the committee on detail, deserve notice— as shedding considerable light on its phraseology and objects. As reported by that committee, it was in the following words: "The acts of the legislature of the United States, made in pursuance of this constitution, and all treaties made under the authority of the United States, shall be the supreme law of the several States, and of their citizens and inhabitants; and the Judges of the several States shall be bound thereby, in their decisions; any thing in the constitutions or laws of the several States to the contrary notwithstanding." After a long discussion of the plan of the constitution, as reported by this committee; and after many alterations were made, the whole, as amended, was referred to the committee of revision, or "style," as it was also called. This particular clause had received no amendment; and, of course, was referred as reported by the committee on detail. The committee of revision, or style, reported it back as it now stands. On comparing the two, it will be found, that the word "constitution," which was omitted in the plan of the committee on detail, is added, as a part of the supreme law of the land; that the expression, "the acts of the legislature of the United States," is changed into "laws of Congress," and "land" substituted in lieu of, "several States and of their citizens and inhabitants." These modifications of phraseology were, doubtless, introduced to make the clause conform to what was believed to be the views of the convention, as disclosed in the discussion on the plan reported by the committee on detail, and to improve the manner of expression; for such were plainly the objects of referring the plan, as amended, to the committee of revision and style. "Constitution" was doubtless added, because, although a compact as between the States, it is a law—and the highest law—in reference to the citizens and inhabitants of the several States, regarded individually. The substitution of "Congress" for "the legislature of the United States," requires no explanation. It is a mere change of phraseology. For the substitution of "land," in place of the "several States and their citizens and inhabitants," no reason is assigned, so far as I can discover; but one will readily suggest itself on a little reflection. As the expression stood in the plan reported by the committee on detail, the supremacy of the acts of the legislature of the United States, and of treaties made under their authority, was limited to the "several States, and their citizens and inhabitants;" and, of course, would not have extended over the *territorial possessions* of the United States; or, as far as their authority might otherwise extend. It became necessary, therefore, to give them a wider scope; especially after the word, "constitution," was introduced in connection with, "laws of the United States;" as their authority never can extend beyond the limits, to which it is carried by the constitution. As far as this extends, their authority extends; but no further. To give to the constitution and the laws and treaties made in pursuance thereof, a supremacy coextensive with these limits, it became necessary to adopt a more comprehensive expression than that reported by the committee on detail; and, hence, in all probability, the adoption of that substituted by the committee of revision and style—"the supreme law of the land," being deemed the more appropriate.

Such are the limitations imposed on the authority of the constitution, and laws of the United States, and treaties made under their authority, regarded as the supreme law of the land. To carry their supremacy beyond this—and to extend it over the reserved powers, in any form or shape, or through any channel—be it the government itself or any of its departments—would finally destroy the system by consolidating all its powers in the hands of the one or the other.

The limitation of their supremacy, *in degree*, is not less strongly marked, than it is *in extent*. While they are supreme, within their sphere, over the constitutions and laws of the several States—the constitution of the United States, and all that appertains to it, are subordinate to the power which ordained and established it—as much so, as are the constitutions of the several States, and all which appertains to them, to the same creative power. In this respect, as well as their supremacy in regard to each other, in their respective spheres, they stand on the same level. Neither has any advantage, in either particular, over the other.

Those who maintain that the government of the United States has the right to enforce its decisions as to the extent of the powers delegated to it, against the decisions of the separate governments of the several States as to the extent of the reserved powers, in case of conflict between the two— next rely, in support of their opinion, on the 2d Sec. 3d Art. of the constitution—which is in the following words: "The judicial power shall extend to all cases, in law and equity, arising under this constitution, the laws of the United States, and treaties made, or which shall be made, under their authority—to all cases affecting ambassadors, other public ministers and consuls—to all cases of admiralty and maritime jurisdiction—to controversies, to which the United States shall be a party—to controversies between two or more States—between a State and the citizens of another State—between citizens of different States—between citizens of the same State claiming lands under grants of different States, and between a State or the citizens thereof, and foreign states, citizens or subjects."

It will be sufficient, in reply, to show, that this section contains no provisions whatever, which would authorize the judiciary to enforce the determination of the government, against that of the government of a State, in such cases.

It may be divided into two parts; that which gives jurisdiction to the judicial power, in reference to the *subject matter*, and that which gives it jurisdiction, in reference to the *parties litigant*. The first clause, which extends it, "to all cases in law and equity, arising under this constitution, the laws of the United States, and treaties made, or which shall be made under their authority," embraces the former; and the residue of the section, the latter.

It is clear on its face, that the object of the clause was, to make the jurisdiction of the judicial power, commensurate with the authority of the constitution and the several departments of the government, as far as it related to cases arising under them—and no further. Nor is it less manifest that the word "cases," being a well-defined technical term, is used in its proper legal sense—and embraces only such questions as are of a judicial character—that is, questions in which the parties litigant are amenable to the process of the courts. Now, as there is nothing in the constitution which vests authority in the government of the United States, or any of its departments, to enforce its decision against that of the separate government of a State; and nothing in this clause which makes the several States amenable to its process, it is manifest that there is nothing in it, which can possibly give the judicial power authority to enforce the decision of the government of the United States, against that of a separate State, where their respective decisions come into conflict. If, then, there be any thing that authorizes it, it must be contained in the remainder of the section, which vests jurisdiction with reference to the parties litigant. But this contains no provision which extends the jurisdiction of the judicial power to questions involving such conflict between the two co-ordinate governments—either express or implied—as I shall next proceed to show.

It will not be contended that either the government of the United States, or those of the separate States are amenable to the process of the courts; unless made so by their consent respectively; for no legal principle is better established than that, a government, though it may be plaintiff in a case, or controversy, cannot be made defendant, or, in any way, amenable to the process of the courts, without its consent. That there is no *express* provision in the section, by which, either of the co-ordinate governments can be made defendants, or amenable to the process of the courts, in a question between them, is manifest.

If, then, there be any, it must be *implied* in some one of its provisions: and it is, accordingly, contended, that it is *implied* in the clause, which provides that the judicial power shall extend, "to controversies to which the United States shall be a party." This clause, it is admitted, clearly extends the jurisdiction of the judiciary to all controversies to which the United States are a party, as plaintiff or defendant, by their consent. So far, it is not a matter of implication, but of express provision. But the inquiry is, does it go further, and, by implication, authorize them to make a State a defendant without its consent, in a question or controversy between it and them? It contains not a word or syllable that would warrant such an implication; and any construction which could warrant it, would authorize a State, or an individual, to make the United States a party defendant, in a controversy between them, without their consent.

There is, not only nothing to warrant such construction, but much to show that it is utterly unwarrantable. Nothing, in the first place, short of the strongest implication, is sufficient to authorize a construction, that would deprive a State of a right so important to its sovereignty, as that of not being held amenable to the process of the courts; or to be made a defendant, in any case or controversy whatever, without its consent—more especially, in one between it and a coequal government, where the effect would necessarily be, to reduce it from an equal to a subordinate station.

It would, in the next place, be contrary to the construction placed on a similar clause in the same section, by an authority higher than that of the judicial, or of any other, or of all the departments of the government taken together. I refer to the last clause, which provides that the judicial power shall extend to controversies, "between a State or citizens thereof, and foreign states, citizens or subjects." It would be much more easy to make out something like a plausible argument in support of the position, that a State might be made defendant and amenable to the process of the courts of the United States, under this clause, than under that in question. In the former, the States are not even named. They can be brought in only by implication, and then, by another implication, divested of a high sovereign right: and this, too, without any assignable reason for either. Here they are not only named, but the other parties to the controversies are also named; without stating which shall be plaintiff, or which defendant. This was left undefined; and, of course, the question, whether the several States might not be made defendants as well as plaintiffs, in controversies between the parties, left open to construction—and in favor of the implication, a very plausible reason may be assigned. The clause puts a State and its citizens on the same ground. In the controversies, to which it extends the judicial power, the State and its citizens stand on one side, and foreign states, citizens and subjects, on the other. Now as foreign states, citizens, or subjects may, under its provisions, make the citizens of a State defendants, in a controversy between them, it would not be an unnatural inference, that the State might also be included. Under this construction, an action was, in fact, commenced in the courts of the United States, against one of the States. The States took the alarm; and, in the high sovereign character, in which they ordained and established the constitution, declared that it should "not be so construed, as to extend to any suit in law or equity, commenced or prosecuted against one of the United States, by citizens of another State, or by citizens or subjects of any foreign state.''[9]

If additional reasons could be thought necessary to sustain a conclusion supported by arguments so convincing, they might be found in the fact, that as long as the government has existed—and as numerous as have been the questions between the United States and many of the several States—the former never have attempted, in any of them, to bring the latter into the courts of the United States. If to this it be added, that all attempts made in the convention, to extend the judicial power, "to all questions, which involved the national peace and harmony"—or which might have the effect of subjecting the several States to its jurisdiction, failed—the conclusion against all constructive efforts, having the same objects in view, and based on any one of the clauses of this section, is irresistible.

It is, in the last place, contended—that the Supreme Court of the United States has the right to decide on the constitutionality of all laws; and, in virtue of this, to decide, in the last resort, all questions involving a conflict between the constitution of the United States and laws and treaties made in pursuance thereof, on the one side, and the constitutions and laws of the several States, on the other.

It is admitted, that the court has the right, in all questions of a judicial character which may come before it, where the laws and treaties of the United States, and the constitution and laws of a State are in conflict or brought in question, to decide which is, or is not consistent with the constitution of the United States. But it is denied that this power is peculiar to it; or that its decision, in the last resort, is binding on any but the parties to it, and its co-departments. So far from being peculiar to it, the right appertains, not only to the Supreme Court of the United States, but to all the courts of the several States, superior and inferior; and even to foreign courts—should a question be brought before them involving such conflict.

[9]Amendments, Art. XI.

It results, necessarily, from our system of government; where power is not only divided, but where constitutions and laws emanate from different authorities. Where this is the fact, it is the duty of the court to pronounce what is the law in the case before it—and, of course—where there is conflict between different laws—to pronounce which is paramount. Now, as the constitution of the United States is, within its sphere, supreme over all others appertaining to the system, it necessarily results, that where any law conflicts with it, it is the duty of the court, before which the question arises, to pronounce the constitution to be paramount. If it be the Supreme Court of the United States, its decision—being that of the highest judicial tribunal, in the last resort, of the parties to the case or controversy—is, of course, final as it respects them—but only as it respects them. It results, that its decision is not binding as between the United States and the several States, as neither can make the other defendant in any controversy between them.

Others, who are forced by the strength of the argument to admit, that the judicial power does not extend to them, contend that Congress, the great organ of the government, has the right to decide, in the last resort, in all such controversies—or in all questions involving the extent of their respective powers. They do not pretend to derive this high power from any specific provision of the constitution; they claim it to be a right incident to all governments, to decide as to the extent of its powers; and to enforce its decision by its own proper authority.

It is manifest, that they who contend for this right to its full extent, overlook the distinction, in this respect, between *single* governments, vested with all the powers appertaining to government, and *co-ordinate* governments, in a system where the powers of government are divided between two or more, as is the case with us. If it be admitted that the right belongs to both, and that co-ordinate governments, in this respect, stand on the same ground as single governments—whatever right or power in such case, belongs to the one, must necessarily belong to the other: and, if so, the result must be, where they differ as to the extent of their respective powers, either a mutual negative on the acts of each other—or the right of each to enforce its decision on the other. But it has already been established, that they have not the latter; and hence, under any aspect in which the question can be viewed, the same conclusion follows—that where the two governments differ as to the extent of their respective powers, a mutual negative is the consequence.

The effect of this is, to make each, as against the other, the guardian and protector of the powers allotted to it, and of which it is the organ and representative. By no other device, could the separate governments of the several States, as the weaker of the two, prevent the government of the United States, as the stronger, from encroaching on that portion of the reserved powers allotted to them, and finally absorbing the whole; except, indeed, by so organizing the former, as to give to each of the States a concurrent voice in making and administering the laws; and, of course, a veto on its action. The powers not delegated are expressly reserved to the respective States or the people; that is, to the governments of the respective States and the people thereof; and by them only can they be protected and preserved. The reason has been fully explained in the discourse on the elementary principles of government. But the several States, as weaker parties, can protect the portion not delegated, only in one of two ways; either by having a concurrent voice in the action of the government of the United States; or a negative on its acts, when they disagree as to the extent of their respective powers. One or the other is indispensable to the preservation of the reserved rights—and to prevent the consolidation of all power in the government of the United States, as the stronger. Why the latter was preferred by the convention which formed the constitution, may, probably, be attributed to the great number of States, and the belief that it was impossible so to organize the government, as to give to each a concurrent voice in its action, without rendering it too feeble and tardy to fulfil the ends for which it was intended. But, be this as it may, not having adopted it, no device remained, by which the reserved powers could be protected and preserved, but the one which they, in effect, did adopt—by refusing to vest the government of the United States with a veto on the acts of the separate governments of the several States, in any form or manner whatever.

But it may be alleged, that the effect of a mutual negative on the part of the two co-ordinate governments, where they disagree as to the extent of their respective powers, will, while it guards against consolidation on one side—lead to collision and conflict between them on the other—and, finally, to disunion.

That the division of the powers of government between the two, without some means to prevent such result, would necessarily lead to collision and conflict, will not be denied. They are incident to every division of powers, of every description; whether it be that of co-ordinate departments, co-ordinate estates or classes, co-ordinate governments, or any other division of power appertaining to our system, or to that of any other constitutional government. It is impossible to construct one without dividing the powers of government. But wherever, and however power may be divided, collision and conflict are necessary consequences, if not prevented. The more numerous and complex the divisions, the stronger the tendency to both, and the greater the necessity for powerful and effectual guards to prevent them. It is one of the evils incident to constitutional governments of every form. But we must take things as they are, with all their incidents, bad or good. The choice between constitutional and absolute governments, lies between the good and evil, incident to each. If the former be exposed to collision and conflict between its various parts, the latter is exposed to all the oppressions and abuses, ever incident to uncontrolled and irresponsible power, in all its forms. With us the choice lies between a national, consolidated and irresponsible government of a dominant portion, or section of the country—and a federal, constitutional and responsible government, with all the divisions of powers indispensable to form and preserve such a government, in a country of such vast extent, and so great a diversity of interest and institutions as ours. The advantages of both, without the evils incident to either, we cannot have. Their nature and character are too opposite and hostile to be blended in the same system.

But while it is admitted that collision and conflict may be necessarily incident to a division of powers, it is utterly denied, that the effects of the mutual negative between the two co-ordinate governments would contribute to either, or necessarily lead to disunion. On the contrary, its effects would be the very reverse. Instead of leading to either, it is an indispensable means to prevent the collision and conflict, which must necessarily arise between the delegated and reserved powers; and which, if not prevented, would, in the end, destroy the system, either by consolidation or dissolution. Its aim and end is to prevent the encroachment of either of the co-ordinate governments on the other. For this purpose it is the effectual, and the only effectual means that can be devised. By preventing such encroachments, it prevents collision and conflict between them. These are their natural offspring: collision follows encroachment—and conflict, collision, in the order of events—unless encroachment be acquiesced in. In that case, the weaker would be absorbed, and all power concentrated in the stronger.

But it may be alleged, that, in preventing these, it would lead to consequences not less to be dreaded—that a negative on the part of the governments of so many States, where either might disagree with that of the United States, as to the extent of their respective powers, would lead to such embarrassment and confusion, and interpose so many impediments in its way, as to render it incompetent to fulfil the ends for which it was established. The objection is plausible; but it will be found, on investigation, that strong as the remedy is, it is not stronger than is required by the disease; and that the system furnishes ample means to correct whatever disorder it may occasion.

It may be laid down as a fundamental principle in constructing constitutional governments, that a strong government requires a negative proportionally strong, to restrict it to its appropriate sphere; and that, the stronger the government—if the negative be proportionally strong, the better the government. It is only by making it proportionally strong, than an equilibrium can be established between the positive and negative powers—the power of acting, and the power of restricting action to its assigned limits. It is difficult to form a conception of a constitutional government stronger than that of the United States; and, consequently, of one requiring a stronger negative to keep it within its appropriate sphere. Combining, habitually, as it necessarily does, the united power and patronage of a majority of the States and of their population estimated in federal numbers, in opposition to a minority of each, with nothing but their separate and divided power and patronage, it is, to the full as strong, if not stronger, than was the government of Rome—with its powerfully constituted Senate, including its control of the auspices, the censorship, and the dictatorship. It will, of course, require, in order to keep it within its proper bounds, a negative fully as strong in proportion, as the tribuneship; which, in its prime, consisted of ten members, elected by the Plebeians, each of whom (as has been supposed by some—but a majority of whom, all admit) had a negative, not only on the acts of the Senate, but on their execution. As powerful as was this negative, experiment proved that it was not too strong for the positive power of the government. If the circumstances be considered, under which the negative of the several States will be brought into action, it will be found, on comparison, to be weaker in proportion, than the negative possessed by the tribuneship; and far more effectually guarded in its possible tendencies to disorder, or the derangement of the system.

In the first place, the negative of the tribunes extended to all the acts of the Senate, and to their execution; and—as it was a single government without limitation on its authority—to all the acts of government. On the other hand, the negative of the governments of the several States extends only to the *execution* of such acts of the government of the United States, as may present a question involving their respective powers; which, relatively, are very few, compared to the whole. In the next place, every tribune, or, at least, the majority of the college, possessed the power; and was ordinarily disposed to exercise it, as they all represented the portion of the Roman people, which their veto was intended to protect against oppression and abuse of power on the part of the Senate. On the contrary, the habitual relation between the governments of the several States and the government of the United States for the time, is such, as to identify the majority of them, in power and interest, with the latter; and to dispose them rather to enlarge and sustain its authority, than to resist its encroachments—which, from their position, they regard as extending—and not as contracting their powers. This limits the negative power of the governments of the several States to the minority, for the time: and even that minority will have, as experience proves, a minority in its own limits, almost always opposed to its will, and nearly of equal numbers with itself, identified in views and party feelings, with the majority in possession of the control of the government of the United States; and ever ready to counteract any opposition to its encroachments on the reserved powers. To this it may be added, that even the majority in this minority of the States, will, for the most part, be averse to making a stand against its encroachments; as they, themselves, hope, in their turn, to gain the ascendency; and are, therefore, naturally disinclined to weaken their party connections with the minority in the States possessing, for the time, the control of the government—and whose interest and feelings, aside from party ties, would be with the majority of their respective States. Such being the case, it is apparent that there will be far less disposition on the part of the governments of the several States to resist the encroachments of the government of the United States on their reserved rights—or to make an issue with it, when they disagree as to the extent of their respective powers—than there was in the tribunate of the Roman republic to oppose acts, or the execution of acts, calculated to oppress, or deprive their order of its rights.

If to this it be further added, that the federal constitution provides—not only that all the functionaries of the United States, but also those of the several States, including, expressly, the members of their legislatures, and all their executive and judicial officers—shall be bound, by oath or affirmation, to support the constitution—and that the decision of the highest tribunal of the judicial power is final, as between the parties to a case or controversy—the danger of any serious derangement or disorder from the effects of the negative on the parts of the separate governments of the several States, must appear, not only much less than that from the Roman tribunate, but very inconsiderable. The danger is, indeed, the other way— that the disposition on the part of the governments of the several States, to acquiesce in the encroachments of the government of the United States, will prove stronger than the disposition to resist; and the negative, compared with the positive power, will be found to be too feeble to preserve the equilibrium between them. But if it should prove otherwise—and if, in consequence, any serious derangement of the system should ensue, there will be found, in the earliest and highest division of power, which I shall next proceed to consider, ample and safe means of correcting them.

I refer to that resulting from, and inseparably connected with the primitive territorial division of the country itself—coeval with its settlement into separate and distinct communities; and which, though dependent at the first on the parent country, became, by a successful resistance to its encroachments on their chartered rights, independent and sovereign States. In them severally—or to express it more precisely, in the people composing them, regarded as independent and sovereign communities, the ultimate power of the whole system resided, and from them the whole system emanated. Their first act was, to ordain and establish their respective separate constitutions and governments—each by itself, and for itself— without concert or agreement with the others; and their next, after the failure of the confederacy, was to ordain and establish the constitution and government of the United States, in the same way in every respect, as has been shown; except that it was done by concert and agreement with each other. That this high, this supreme power, has never been either delegated to, or vested in the separate governments of the States, or the federal government—and that it is, therefore, one of the powers declared, by the 10th Art. of amendments, to be reserved to the people of the respective States; and that, of course, it still resides with them, will hardly be questioned. It must reside somewhere. No one will assert that it is extinguished.

But, according to the fundamental principles of our system, sovereignty resides in the people, and not in the government; and if in them, it must be in them, as the people of the several States; for, politically speaking, there is no other known to the system. It not only resides in them, but resides in its plenitude, unexhausted and unimpaired. If proof be required, it will be found in the fact—which cannot be controverted, so far as the United States are concerned—that the people of the several States, acting in the same capacity and in the same way, in which they ordained and established the federal constitution, can, by their concurrent and united voice, change or abolish it, and establish another in its place; or dissolve the Union, and resolve themselves into separate and disconnected States. A power which can rightfully do all this, must exist in full plenitude, unexhausted and unimpaired; for no higher act of sovereignty can be conceived.

But it does not follow from this, that the people of the several States, in ordaining and establishing the constitution of the United States, imposed no restriction on the exercise of sovereign power; for a sovereign may voluntarily impose restrictions on his acts, without, in any degree, exhausting or impairing his sovereignty; as is admitted by all writers on the subject. In the act of ordaining and establishing it, they have, accordingly, imposed several important restrictions on the exercise of their sovereign power. In order to ascertain what these are, and how far they extend, it will be necessary to ascertain, in what relation they stand to the constitution; and to each other in reference to it.

They stand then, as to the one, in the relation of superior to subordinate—the creator to the created. The people of the several States called it into existence, and conferred, by it, on the government, whatever power or authority it possesses. Regarded simply as a constitution, it is as subordinate to them, as are their respective State constitutions; and it imposes no more restrictions on the exercise of any of their sovereign rights, than they do. The case however is different as to the relations which the people of the several States bear to each other, in reference to it. Having ratified and adopted it, by mutual agreement, they stand to it in the relation of parties to a constitutional compact; and, of course, it is binding between them as a *compact*, and not on, or over them, as a *constitution*. Of all compacts that can exist between independent and sovereign communities, it is the most intimate, solemn, and sacred—whether regarded in reference to the closeness of connection, the importance of the objects to be effected, or to the obligations imposed. Laying aside all intermediate agencies, the people of the several States, in their sovereign capacity, agreed to unite themselves together, in the closest possible connection that could be formed, without merging their respective sovereignties into one common sovereignty—to establish one common government, for certain specific objects, which, regarding the mutual interest and security of each, and of all, they supposed could be more certainly, safely, and effectually promoted by it, than by their several separate governments; pledging their faith, in the most solemn manner possible, to support the compact thus formed, by respecting its provisions, obeying all acts of the government made in conformity with them, and preserving it, as far as in them lay, against all infractions. But, as solemn and sacred as it is, and as high as the obligations may be which it imposes—still it is but a *compact* and not a *constitution—regarded in reference to the people of the several States, in their sovereign capacity.* To use the language of the constitution itself, it was ordained as a "constitution *for* the United States"—not *over* them; and established, not *over,* but "*between* the States ratifying it:" and hence, a State, acting in its sovereign capacity, and in the same manner in which it ratified and adopted the constitution, may be guilty of violating it *as a compact,* but cannot be guilty of violating it as a *law.* The case is the reverse, as to the action of its citizens, regarding them in their individual capacity. To them it is a law—the supreme law within its sphere. They may be guilty of violating it *as a law,* or of violating the laws and treaties made in pursuance of, or under its authority, regarded as laws or treaties; but cannot be guilty of violating it as a *compact.* The constitution was ordained and established *over them* by their respective States, to whom they owed allegiance; and they are under the same obligation to respect and obey its authority, within its proper sphere, as they are to respect and obey their respective State constitutions; and for the same reason, viz.: that the State to which they owe allegiance, commanded it in both cases.

It follows, from what has been stated, that the people of the several States, regarded as parties to the constitutional compact, have imposed restrictions on the exercise of their sovereign power, by entering into a solemn obligation to do no act inconsistent with its provisions, and to uphold and support it within their respective limits. To this extent the restrictions go—but no further. As parties to the constitutional compact, they retain the right, unrestricted, which appertains to such a relation in all cases where it is not surrendered, to judge as to the extent of the obligation imposed by the agreement or compact—in the first instance, where there is a higher authority; and, in the last resort, where there is none. The principle on which this assertion rests, is essential to the nature of contracts; and is in accord with universal practice. But the right to judge as to the extent of the obligation imposed, necessarily involves the right of pronouncing whether an act of the federal government, or any of its departments, be, or be not, in conformity to the provisions of the constitutional compact; and, if decided to be inconsistent, of pronouncing it to be unauthorized by the constitution, and, therefore, null, void, and of no effect. If the constitution be a compact, and the several States, regarded in their sovereign character, be parties to it, all the rest follow as necessary consequences. It would be puerile to suppose the right of judging existed, without the right of pronouncing whether an act of the government violated the provisions of the constitution or not; and equally so to suppose, that the right of judging existed, without the authority of declaring the consequence, to wit; that, as such, it is null, void, and of no effect. And hence, those who are unwilling to admit the consequences, have been found to deny that the constitution is a compact; in the face of facts as well established as any in our political history, and in utter disregard of that provision of the constitution, which expressly declares, that the ratification of nine States shall be sufficient to establish it "between the States so ratifying the same."

But the right, with all these consequences, is not more certain than that possessed by the several States, as parties to the compact, of interposing for the purpose of arresting, within their respective limits, an act of the federal government in violation of the constitution; and thereby of preventing the delegated from encroaching on the reserved powers. Without such right, all the others would be barren and useless abstractions—and just as puerile as the right of judging, without the right of pronouncing an act to be unconstitutional, and, as such, null and void. Nor is this right more certain, than that of the States, in the same character and capacity, to decide on the mode and measure to be adopted to arrest the act, and prevent the encroachment on the reserved powers. It is a right indispensable to all the others, and, without which, they would be valueless.

These conclusions follow irresistibly from incontestable facts and well-established principles. But the possession of a right is one thing, and the exercise of it another. Rights, themselves, must be exercised with prudence and propriety: when otherwise exercised, they often cease to be rights, and become wrongs. The more important the right, and the more delicate its character, the higher the obligation to observe, strictly, the rules of prudence and propriety. But, of all the rights appertaining to the people of the several States, as members of a common Union, the one in question, is by far the most important and delicate; and, of course, requires, in its exercise, the greatest caution and forbearance. As parties to the compact which constitutes the Union, they are under obligations to observe its provisions, and prevent their infraction. In exercising the right in question, they are bound to take special care that they do not themselves, violate this, the most sacred of obligations. To avoid this, prudence and propriety require that they should abstain from interposing their authority, to arrest an act of their common government, unless the case, in their opinion, involve a clear and palpable infraction of the instrument. They are bound to go further— and to forbear from interposing, even when it is clear and palpable, unless it be, at the same time, highly dangerous in its character, and apparently admitting of no other remedy; and for the plain reason, that prudence and propriety require, that a right so high and delicate should be called into exercise, only in cases of great magnitude and extreme urgency. But even when, in the opinion of the people of a State, such a case has occurred—that nothing, short of the interposition of their authority, can arrest the danger and preserve the constitution, they ought to interpose in good faith—not to weaken or destroy the Union, but to uphold and preserve it, by causing the instrument on which it rests, to be observed and respected; and to this end, the mode and measure of redress ought to be exclusively directed and limited. In such a case, a State not only has the right, but is, in duty to itself and the Union, bound to interpose—as the last resort, to arrest the dangerous infraction of the constitution—and to prevent the powers reserved to itself, from being absorbed by those delegated to the United States.

That the right, so exercised, would be, in itself, a safe and effectual security against so great an evil, few will doubt. But the question arises—Will prudence and propriety be sufficient to prevent the wanton abuse of a right, so high and delicate, by the thirty parties to the compact—and the many others hereafter to be added to the number?

I answer, no. Nor can any one, in the least acquainted with that constitution of our nature which makes governments necessary, give any other answer. The highest moral obligations—truth, justice, and plighted faith—much less, prudence and propriety—oppose, of themselves, but feeble resistance to the abuse of power. But what they, of themselves, cannot effect, may be effected by other influences of a far less elevated character. Of these, many are powerful, and well calculated to prevent the abuse of this high and delicate right. Among them may be ranked, as most prominent and powerful, that which springs from the habitual action of a majority of the States and of their population, estimated in federal numbers, on the side of the federal government—a majority naturally prone, and ever ready—in all questions between it and a State, involving an infraction of the constitution, to throw its weight in the scale of the former. To this, may be added another, of no small force. I refer to that of party ties. Experience, as well as reason shows, that a government, operating as ours does, must give rise to two great political parties—which, although partaking, from the first, more or less of a sectional character, extend themselves, in unequal proportions, over the whole Union—carrying with them, notwithstanding their sectional tendency, party sympathy and party attachment of such strength, that few are willing to break or weaken them, by resisting, even an acknowledged infraction of the constitution, of a nature alike oppressive and dangerous to their section. Both of these tend powerfully to resist the abuse of the right, by preventing it from being exercised imprudently and improperly. But I will not dwell on them, as they have been already considered in another connection. There are others, more especially connected with the subject at present before us, which I shall next consider.

The first may be traced to a fact, disclosed by experience, that, in most of the States, the preponderance of neither party is so decisive, that the minority may not hope to become the majority; and that, with this hope, it stands always ready to seize on any act of the majority, of doubtful propriety, as the means of turning it out of power and taking its place. Should the majority in any State, where the balance thus vibrates, venture to take a stand, and to interpose its authority, against the encroachment of the federal government on its reserved powers, it would be difficult to conceive a case, however clear and palpable the encroachment, or dangerous its character, in which the minority would not resist its action, and array itself on the side of the federal government. And there are very few, in which, with the aid of its power and patronage, backed by the numerous presses in its support, the minority would not succeed in overcoming the majority—taking their place, and, thereby, placing the State at the foot of the federal government. To this, another of great force may be added. The dominant party of the State, for the time, although it may be in a minority in the Union for the time, looks forward, of course, to the period when it will be in a majority of the Union; and have at its disposal all the honors and emoluments of the federal government. The leaders of such party, therefore, would not be insensible to the advantage, which their position, as such, would give them, to share largely in the distribution. This advantage they would not readily jeopard, by taking a stand which would render them, not only odious to the majority of the Union, at the time, but unpopular with their own party in the other States—as putting in hazard their chance to become the majority. Under such circumstances, it would require, not only a clear and palpable case of infraction, and one of urgent necessity, but high virtue, patriotism and courage to exercise the right of interposition—even if it were admitted to be clear and unquestionable. And hence, it is to be feared that, even this high right, combined with the mutual negative of the two co-ordinate governments, will be scarcely sufficient to counteract the vast and preponderating power of the federal government, and to prevent the absorption of the reserved by the delegated powers.

Indeed the negative power is always far weaker, in proportion to its appearance, than the positive. The latter having the control of the government, with all its honors and emoluments, has the means of acting on and influencing those who exercise the negative power, and of enlisting them on its side, unless it be effectually guarded: while, on the other hand, those who exercise the negative, have nothing but the simple power, and possess no means of influencing those who exercise the positive power.

But, suppose it should prove otherwise; and that the negative power should become so strong as to cause dangerous derangements and disorders in the system—the constitution makes ample provisions for their correction—whether produced by the interposition of a State, or the mutual negative, or conflict of power between the two co-ordinate governments. I refer to the amending power. Why it was necessary to provide for such a power—what is its nature and character—why it was modified as it is—and whether it be safe, and sufficient to effect the objects intended—are the questions, which I propose next to consider.

It is, as has already been explained, a fundamental principle, in forming such a federal community of States, and establishing such a federal constitution and government as ours, that no State could be bound but by its separate ratification and adoption. The principle is essentially connected with the independence and sovereignty of the several States. As the several States, in such a community, with such a constitution and government, still retained their separate independence and sovereignty, it followed, that the compact into which they entered, could not be altered or changed, in any way, but by the unanimous assent of all the parties, without some express provision authorizing it. But there were strong objections to requiring the consent of all to make alterations or changes in the constitution. Those who formed it were not so vain as to suppose that they had made a perfect instrument; nor so ignorant as not to see, however perfect it might be, that derangements and disorders, resulting from time, circumstances, and the conflicting elements of the system itself, would make amendments necessary. But to leave it, without making some special provision for the purpose, would have been, in effect, to leave it to any one of the States to prevent amendments; which, in practice, would have been almost tantamount to leaving it without any power to amend—notwithstanding its necessity. And, hence, the subject of making some special provision for amending the constitution, was forced on the attention of the convention.

There was diversity of opinion as to what the nature and character of the amending power should be. All agreed that it should be a modification of the original creative power, which ordained and established the separate constitutions and governments of the several States; and, by which alone, the proposed constitution and government could be ordained and established: or, to express it differently and more explicitly—that amendments should be the acts of the several States, voting as States—each counting one—and not the act of the government. But there was great diversity of opinion as to what *number* of States should be required to concur, or agree, in order to make an amendment. It was first moved to require the consent of all the States. This was followed by a motion to amend, requiring *two-thirds;* which was overruled by a considerable majority. It was then moved to require the concurrence of *three-fourths*, which was agreed to, and finally adopted without dissent.

To understand fully the reasons for so modifying the original creative power, as to require the concurrence of three-fourths to make an amendment, it will be necessary to advert to another portion of the proceedings of the convention, intimately connected with the present question. I refer to that which contains a history of its action in regard to the number of States required to ratify the constitution, before it should become binding between those so ratifying it. It is material to state, that although the article in respect to ratifications, which grew out of these proceedings, stands last in the constitution, it was finally agreed on and adopted before the article in regard to amendments—and had, doubtless, no inconsiderable influence in determining the number of States required for that purpose.

There was, in reference to both, great diversity of opinion as to the requisite number of States. With the exception of one State, all agreed that entire unanimity should not be required; but the majority divided as to the number which should be required. One of the most prominent leaders of the party, originally in favor of a national government, was in favor of requiring only a bare majority of the States. Another, not less distinguished, was in favor of the same proposition; but so modified as to require such majority to contain, also, a majority of the entire population of all the States; and, in default of this, as many additional States as would be necessary to supply the deficiency. On the other hand, the more prominent members of the party in favor of a federal government, inclined to a larger number. One of the most influential of these, moved to require ten States; on which motion the convention was nearly equally divided. Finally, the number nine was agreed on—constituting *three-fourths* of all the States represented in the convention—and, as nearly as might be, of all the States at that time in the Union.

Why the first propositions were rejected, and the last finally agreed on, requires explanation. The first proposition, requiring the ratification of all the States, before the constitution should become binding between those so ratifying the same, was rejected, doubtless, because it was deemed unreasonable that the fate of the others should be made dependent on the will of a single State. The convention acted under the pressure of very trying exigencies. The confederacy had failed; and it was absolutely necessary that something should be done to save the credit of the Union, and to guard against confusion and anarchy. The plan of the constitution and government adopted, was the only one that could be agreed on; and the fate of the country apparently rested on its ratification by the States. In such a state of things, it seemed to be too hazardous to put it in the power of a single State to defeat it. Nothing short of so great a pressure could justify an act which made so great a change in the articles of confederation—which expressly provided that no alteration should be made in any of them, "unless such alteration be agreed to in a Congress of the United States, and be afterwards confirmed by the legislatures of every State."

The rejection of the other proposition, which required a mere majority of the States to make it binding as between the States so ratifying it, will scarcely require explanation. It exposed the States to the hazard of forming, not one, but two Unions; or, if this should be avoided—by forcing the other States to come in reluctantly, under the force of circumstances, it endangered the harmony and duration of the Union, and the proposed constitution and government. It would, besides, have evinced too great an indifference to the stipulation contained in the articles of the confederation just cited.

It remains now to be explained why the particular number, between these two extremes, was finally agreed on. Among other reasons, one, doubtless, is to be found in the fact, that the articles of the then existing confederation, required the consent of nine States to give validity to many of the acts of their Congress—among which, were the acts declaring war—granting letters of marque and reprisal in time of peace, and emitting bills, or borrowing money on the credit of the United States. The object of requiring so great a number was, to guard against the abuses of these and the other great and delicate powers contained in the provision. A mere majority of the States, was too few to be intrusted with such powers; and, to make the trust more safe, the consent of nine States was required; which was within a small fraction of *three-fourths* of the whole number at the time. The precedent—and the same consideration which induced the legislatures of all the States to assent to it, in adopting the articles of confederation, must have had, undoubtedly, much weight in determining what number of States should ratify the constitution, before it should become binding between them. If the legislatures of all the States should have unanimously deemed it not unreasonable, that the highest and most delicate acts of the old Congress, when agreed to by nine or more States, should be acquiesced in by the others, it was very natural that the members of the convention should think it not unreasonable to require an equal number to give validity to the constitution, as between them—leaving it to the others to say whether they would ratify or not. Nine, or *three-fourths* of the whole, were, unquestionably, regarded as a safe and sufficient guaranty against oppression and abuse, both in the highest acts of the confederacy, and in establishing the constitution between the States ratifying it. And it is equally certain that a smaller number was not regarded either as safe, or sufficient.

The force of these precedents, combined with the reasons for adopting them, must have had great weight in determining the proportional number which should be required to amend the constitution. Indeed, after determining the proportion in the provision for the ratification of the constitution, it would seem to follow, as a matter of course, that the same proportion should be required in the provision for amending it. It would be difficult to assign a reason, why the proportion should be different in the two cases; and why, if *three-fourths* should be required in the one, it should not also be required in the other. If it would have been unreasonable and improper in the one, that a few States in proportion should, by their obstinacy, prevent the others from forming a constitution—it would have been equally so, and for the same reason, that the like proportion should have the power to prevent amendments, however necessary they might be to the well working and safety of the system. So, again, if it would have been dangerous and improper, to permit a bare majority of the States, or any proportion less than that required to make the constitution binding as between the States ratifying—it would have been no less so to permit such number or proportion to amend it. The two are, indeed, nearly allied, and involve, throughout, the same principle—and hence, the same diversity of opinion between the two parties in the convention, in reference to both, and the adoption of the same proportion of States in each. I say the same proportion—for although nine States were rather less than *three-fourths* of the whole number when the constitution was ratified—this proportion of the States was required in order to amend it (without regard to an inconsiderable fraction) because of the facility of its application.

But independently of these considerations, there were strong reasons for adopting that proportion in providing a power to amend. It was, at least, as necessary to guard against too much facility as too much difficulty, in amending it. If, to require the consent of all the States for that purpose would be, in effect, to prevent amendments which time should disclose to be—or change of circumstances make necessary—so, on the other hand, to require a bare majority only, or but a small number in proportion to the whole, would expose the constitution to hasty, inconsiderate, and even sinister amendments, on the part of the party dominant for the time. If the one would give it too much fixedness, the other would deprive it of all stability. Of the two, the latter would be more dangerous than the former. It would defeat the very ends of a constitution, regarded as a fundamental law. Indeed, it would involve a glaring absurdity to require the separate ratification of nine States to make the constitution binding as between them—and to provide that a mere majority of States, or even a small one, when compared with the whole number, should have the power, as soon as it went into operation, to amend it as they pleased. It would be difficult to find any other proportion better calculated to avoid this absurdity, and, at the same time, the difficulties attending the other extreme, than that adopted by the convention. While it affords sufficient facility, it guards against too much, in amending the constitution—and thereby unites stability with the capacity of adjusting itself to all such changes as may become necessary; and thus combines all the requisites that are necessary in the amending power. It hardly admits of a doubt, that these combined reasons—the conviction that it possessed all the requisites for such a power, in a higher degree than any other proportion—with the force of the two precedents above explained, induced the convention to adopt it.

Possessing these, it possesses all the requisites, of course, to render the power at once safe in itself, and sufficient to effect the objects for which it was intended. It is safe; because the proportion is sufficiently large to prevent a dominant portion of the Union, or combination of the States, from using the amending power as an instrument to make changes in the constitution, adverse to the interests and rights of the weaker portion of the Union, or a minority of the States. It may not, in this respect, be as perfectly safe as it would be in the unmodified state in which it ordained and established the constitution; but, for all practical purposes, it is believed to be safe as an *amending* power. It is difficult to conceive a case, where so large a portion as *three-fourths* of the States would undertake to insert a power, by way of amendment, which, instead of improving and perfecting the constitution, would deprive the remaining *fourth* of any right, essentially belonging to them as members of the Union, or clearly intended to oppress them. There are many powers, which a dominant combination of States would assume by *construction*, and use for the purpose of aggrandizement, which they would not dare to propose to insert as amendments. But should an attempt be successfully made to engraft an amendment for such a purpose, the case would not be without remedy, as will be shown in the proper place.

I say, as large a proportion as *three-fourths*—for the larger the proportion required to do an act, the less is the danger of the power being used for the purpose of oppression and aggrandizement. The reason is plain. With the increase of the proportion, the difficulty of so using it, is increased—while the inducement is diminished in the same proportion. The former is increased—because the difficulty of forming combinations for such purpose is increased with the increase of the number required to combine; and the latter decreased, because the greater the number to be aggrandized, and the less the number, by whose oppression this can be effected, the less the inducement to oppression. And hence, by increasing the proportion, the number to be aggrandized may be made so large, and the number to be oppressed so small, as to make the effort bootless— when the motive to oppress, as well as to abuse power will, of course, cease.

But, while *three-fourths* furnish a safe proportion against making changes in the constitution, under the color of amendments, by the dominant portion of the Union, with a view to oppress the weaker for its aggrandizement, the proportion is equally safe, in view of the opposite danger—as it furnishes a sufficient protection against the combination of a few States to prevent the rest from making such amendments as may become necessary to preserve or perfect it. It thus guards against the dangers, to which a less, or greater proportion might expose the system.

It is not less sufficient than safe to effect the object intended. As a modification of the power which ordained and established the system, its authority is above all others, except itself in its simple and absolute form. Within its appropriate sphere—that of *amending* the constitution—all others are subject to its control, and may be modified, changed and altered at its pleasure. Within that sphere it truly represents the intention of the power, of which it is a modification, when it ordained and established the constitution—as to the limits to which the system might be safely and properly extended, and beyond which it could not. The same wisdom, which saw the necessity of having as much harmony as possible, in ratifying the constitution, saw, also, the necessity of preserving it, after it went into operation; and therefore required the same proportion of States to make an amendment, as to ratify the instrument, before it could become binding between the States ratifying. It saw, that, if there was danger from *too little*, there was also danger from *too much* union (if I may be allowed so to express myself)—and that, while one led to weakness, the other led to discord and alienation. To guard against each, it so modified the amending power as to avoid both extremes—and thus to preserve the equilibrium of the powers of the system as originally established, so far as human contrivance could.

Thus the power which, in its simple and absolute form, was the creator, becomes, in its modified form, the preserver of the system. By no other device, nor in any other form, could the high functions appertaining to this character, be safely and efficiently discharged—and by none other could the system be preserved. It is, when properly understood, the *vis medicatrix* of the system—its great repairing, healing, and conservative power—intended to remedy its disorders, in whatever cause or causes originating; whether in the original errors or defects of the constitution itself—or the operation of time and change of circumstances, or in conflicts between its parts—including those between the co-ordinate governments. By it alone, can the equilibrium of the various powers and divisions of the system be preserved; as by it alone, can the stronger be prevented from encroaching on, and finally absorbing the weaker. For this purpose, it is, as has been shown, entirely safe and all-sufficient. In performing its high functions, it acts, not as a judicial power, but in the far more elevated and authoritative character of an *amending* power—the only one in which it can be called into action at all. In this character, it can amend the constitution, by modifying its existing provisions—or, in case of a disputed power, whether it be between the federal government and one of its co-ordinates—or between the former and an interposing State—by declaring, authoritatively, what is the constitution.

Having now explained the nature and object of the amending power, and shown its safety and sufficiency, in respect to the object for which it was provided—I shall next proceed to show, that it is the duty of the federal government to invoke its aid, should any dangerous derangement or disorder result from the mutual negative of the two co-ordinate governments, or from the interposition of a State, in its sovereign character, to arrest one of its acts—in case all other remedies should fail to adjust the difficulty.

In order to form a clear conception of the true ground and reason of this duty, it is necessary to premise, that it is difficult to conceive of a case, where a conflict of power could take place between the government of a State, or the State itself in its sovereign character, and the federal government, in which the former would not be in a minority of the States and of their population, estimated in federal numbers; and, of course, the latter in a majority of both. The reason is obvious. If it were otherwise, the remedy would at once be applied through the federal government—by a repeal of the act asserting the power—and the question settled by yielding it to the State. Such being the case, the conflict, whenever it takes place, must be between the reserved and delegated powers; the latter, supported by a majority both of the States and of their population, claiming the right to exercise the power—and the former, by a State constituting one of the minority—(at least as far as it relates to the power in controversy)—denying the claim.

Now it is a clear and well-established principle, that the party who claims the right to exercise a power, is bound to make it good, against the party denying the right; and that, if there should be an authority higher than either provided, by which the question between them can be adjusted, he, in such case, has no right to assert his claim on his own authority—but is bound to appeal to the tribunal appointed, according to the forms prescribed, and to establish and assert his right through its authority.

If a principle, so clear and well established, should, in a case like the one supposed, require confirmation—it may be found in the fact, that the powers of the federal government are all enumerated and specified in the constitution—while those belonging to the States embrace the whole residuary mass of powers, not enumerated and specified. Hence, in a conflict of power between the two, the presumption is in favor of the latter, and against the former; and, therefore, it is doubly bound to establish the power in controversy, through the appointed authority, before it can rightfully undertake to exercise it.

But as conclusive as these reasons are, there are others not less so. Among these, it may be stated, that the federal government, being of the party of the majority in such conflicts, may, at pleasure, make the appeal to the amending power; while the State, being of the party of the minority, cannot possibly do so. The reason is plain. To make it, requires, on the part of the State, more than a bare majority. It would then be absurd, to transfer the duty from the party of the majority, which has the power, to that of the minority, which has it not—and this, too, when, with such a majority, the question of power could be settled in its favor, more easily and promptly, through the federal government itself.

There is also another reason—if not more conclusive, yet of deeper import. The federal government never will make an appeal to the amending power, in case of conflict, unless compelled—nor, indeed, willingly in any case, except with a view to enlarge the powers it has usurped by construction. The only means, by which it can be compelled to make an appeal, are the negative powers of the constitution—and especially, so far as the reserved powers are concerned—by that of its co-ordinates—and State interposition. But to transfer the duty from itself to the States, would, necessarily, have the effect, so far as they are concerned, of leaving it in the full and quiet exercise of the contested power, until the appeal was made and finally acted on—instead of suspending the exercise of the power, until the decision was pronounced—as would be the case, if the duty were not transferred. In the latter case, it would have every motive to exert itself to make the appeal, and to obtain a speedy and final action in its favor, if possible; but in the former, it would be the reverse. The motive would be to use every effort to prevent a successful appeal, and to defeat action on it; as, in the mean time, it would be left in full possession of the power in question. Nor would it have any difficulty in effecting what it desired; as it would be impossible for the State, even without opposition, to succeed in making an appeal, for the reason already assigned.

Its effect would be a revolution in the character of the system. It would virtually destroy the relation of co-ordinates between the federal government and those of the several States, by rendering the negative of the latter, in case of conflict with it, of no effect. It would supersede and render substantially obsolete, not only the amending power, but the original sovereign power of the several States, as parties to the constitutional compact— by making them, also, of no effect; and, thereby, elevate the federal government to the absolute and supreme authority of the system, with liberty to assume, by construction, whatever power the cupidity or ambition of a dominant party or section might crave.

It would, in a word, practically transform the federal, into a consolidated national government, against the avowed intention of its framers—the plain meaning of the constitution itself—and the understanding of the people of the States, when they ratified and adopted it. Such a result is, itself, the strongest, the most conclusive argument against the position. If there were none other, this, of itself, would be ample to prove, that it is the duty of the federal government to invoke the action of the amending power, by proposing a declaratory amendment affirming the power it claims, according to the forms prescribed in the constitution; and, if it fail, to abandon the power.

On the other hand, should it succeed in obtaining the amendment, the act of the government of the separate State which caused the conflict, and operated as a negative on the act of the federal government, would, in all cases, be overruled; and the latter become operative within its limits. But the result is, in some respects, different—where a State, acting in her sovereign character, and as a party to the constitutional compact, has interposed, and declared an act of the federal government to be unauthorized by the constitution—and, therefore, null and void. In this case, if the act of the latter be predicated on a power consistent with the character of the constitution, the ends for which it was established, and the nature of our system of government—or, more briefly, if it come fairly within the scope of the amending power, the State is bound to acquiesce, by the solemn obligation which it contracted, in ratifying the constitution. But if it transcends the limits of the amending power—be inconsistent with the character of the constitution and the ends for which it was established—or with the nature of the system—the result is different. In such case, the State is not bound to acquiesce. It may choose whether it will, or whether it will not secede from the Union. One or the other course it must take. To refuse acquiescence, would be tantamount to secession; and place it as entirely in the relation of a foreign State to the other States, as would a positive act of secession. That a State, as a party to the constitutional compact, has the right to secede—acting in the same capacity in which it ratified the constitution—cannot, with any show of reason, be denied by any one who regards the constitution as a compact—if a power should be inserted by the amending power, which would radically change the character of the constitution, or the nature of the system; or if the former should fail to fulfil the ends for which it was established. This results, necessarily, from the nature of a compact—where the parties to it are sovereign; and, of course, have no higher authority to which to appeal. That the effect of secession would be to place her in the relation of a foreign State to the others, is equally clear. Nor is it less so, that it would make her (not her citizens *individually*) responsible to them, in that character. All this results, necessarily, from the nature of a compact between sovereign parties.

In case the State acquiesces, whether it be where the power claimed is within or beyond the scope of the amending power, it must be done, by rescinding the act, by which, she interposed her authority and declared the act of the federal government to be unauthorized by the constitution—and, therefore, null and void; and this too by the same authority which passed it. The reason is, that, until this is done, the act making the declaration continues binding on her citizens. As far as they are concerned, the State, as a party to the constitutional compact, has the right to decide, in the last resort—and, acting in the same character in which it ratified the constitution, to determine to what limits its powers extend, and how far they are bound to respect and obey it, and the acts made under its authority. They are bound to obey them, only, because the State, to which they owe allegiance, by ratifying, ordained and established it as its own constitution and government; just in the same way, in which it ordained and established its own separate constitution and government—and by precisely the same authority. They owe *obedience* to both; because their State commanded them to obey; but they owe *allegiance* to neither; since sovereignty, by a fundamental principle of our system, resides in the *people*, and not in the *government.* The same authority which commanded *obedience,* has the right, in both cases, to determine, as far as they are concerned, the extent to which they were bound to obey; and this determination remains binding until rescinded by the authority which pronounced and declared it.

I have now finished the discussion of the question—What means does the constitution, or the system itself furnish, to preserve the division between the delegated and reserved powers? In its progress, I have shown, that the federal government contains, within itself, or in its organization, no provisions, by which, the powers delegated could be prevented from encroaching on the powers reserved to the several States; and that, the only means furnished by the system itself, to resist encroachments, are, the mutual negative between the two co-ordinate governments, where their acts come into conflict as to the extent of their respective powers; and the interposition of a State in its sovereign character, as a party to the constitutional compact, against an unconstitutional act of the federal government. It has also been shown, that these are sufficient to restrict the action of the federal government to its appropriate sphere; and that, if they should lead to any dangerous derangements or disorders, the amending power makes ample and safe provision for their correction. It now remains to be considered, what must be the result, if the federal government is left to operate without these exterior means of restraint.

That the federal government, as the representative of the delegated powers, supported, as it must habitually be, by a majority of the States and of their population, estimated in federal numbers, is vastly stronger than the opposing States and their population, has been shown. But the fact of its greater strength is not more certain than the consequence—that it will encroach, if left to decide in the last resort, on the extent of its own powers, and to enforce its own decisions, without some adequate means to restrict it to its allotted sphere. It would encroach; because the dominant combination of States and population, which, for the time, may control it, would have every inducement to do so; since it would increase their power and the means of aggrandizement. Nor would their encroachments cease until all the reserved powers—those reserved to the people of the several States in their sovereign character, as well as those delegated to their respective separate governments, should be absorbed: because, the same powerful motives which induced the first step towards it, would continue, until the whole was concentrated in the federal government. The written restrictions and limitations of the constitution, would oppose no effectual resistance. They would all be gradually undermined by the slow and certain process of construction; which would be continued until the instrument itself, would be of no more force or validity than an ordinary act of Congress—nor would it be more respected. The opposing construction of the minority would become the subject of ridicule and scorn—as mere abstractions—until all encroachments would cease to be opposed. Nor would the effects end with the absorption of the reserved powers.

While the process was going on, it would react on the division of the powers of the federal government itself, and disturb its own equilibrium. The legislative department would be the first to feel its influence, and to cumulate authority, by encroachments; since Congress, as the organ of the delegated powers, possesses, by an express provision of the constitution, all the discretionary powers of the government. Neither of the other two can constitutionally exercise any power, which is not either expressly delegated by the constitution, or provided for by law. So long, then, as Congress remained faithful to its trust, neither of the others could encroach; since the officers of both are responsible to it, through the impeaching power; and hence the work of aggression must commence with it, or by its permission. But whatever encroachments it might make, the benefit, in the end, would accrue, not to itself, but to the President—as the head of the executive department. Every enlargement of the powers of the government which may be made, every measure which may be adopted to aggrandize the dominant combination which may control the government for the time, must necessarily enlarge, in a greater or less degree, his patronage and influence. With their enlargement, his power to control the other departments of the government, and the organs of public opinion, and through them, the community at large, must increase, and in the same degree. With their increase, the motive to obtain possession of the control of the government, in order to enjoy its honors and emoluments, regardless of all considerations of principle or policy, would become stronger and stronger, until it would stand alone, the paramount and all-absorbing motive. And— to trace further the fatal progress—just in proportion as this motive should become stronger, the election of the President would be, more and more, the all-important question—until every other would be regarded as subordinate to it. But as this became more and more paramount to all others, party combinations, and party organization and discipline, would become more concentrated and stringent—their control over individual opinion and action more and more decisive; and, with it, the control of the President, as the head of the dominant party. When this should be increased to such a degree, that he, as its head, could, through party organs and party machinery, wield sufficient influence over the constituents of the members of Congress, belonging to his party, as to make their election dependent, not on their fidelity to the constitution or to the country, but on their devotion and submission to party and party interest—his power would become absolute. They then would cease, virtually, to represent the people. Their responsibility would be, not to them, but to him; or to those who might control and use him as an instrument. The Executive, at this stage, would become absolute, so far as the party in power was concerned. It would control the action of the dominant party as effectually as would an hereditary chief-magistrate, if in possession of its powers—if not more so; and the time would not be distant, when the President would cease to be elective; when a contested election, or the paid corruption and violence attending an election, would be made a pretext, by the occupant, or his party, for holding over after the expiration of his term.

Such must be the result, if the process of absorption should be permitted to progress regularly, through all its stages. The causes which would control the event, are as fixed and certain as any in the physical world. But it is not probable that they would be permitted to take their regular course, undisturbed. In a country of such vast extent and diversity of interests as ours, parties, in all their stages, must partake, as I have already shown, more or less of a sectional character. The laws which control their formation, necessarily lead to this. Distance, as has been stated, always weakens, and proximity—where there is no counteracting cause—always strengthens the social and sympathetic feelings. Sameness of interests and similarity of habits and character, make it more easy for those who are contiguous, to associate together and form a party than for those who are remote. In the early stages of the government, when principles bore a stronger sway, the effects of these causes were not so perceptible, or their influence so great. But as party violence increases, and party efforts sink down into a mere struggle to obtain the honors and emoluments of government, the tendency to appeal to local feelings, local interests, and local prejudices will become stronger and stronger—until, ultimately, parties must assume a decidedly sectional character. When it comes to this—and when the two majorities which control the federal government, come to centre in the same section, and all the powers of the entire system, virtually to unite in the executive department, the dominant section will become the governing, and the other the subordinate section; as much so as if it were a dependent province, without any real participation in the government. Its condition will be even worse; for its nominal participation in the acts of government would afford it no means of protecting itself, where the interests of the dominant and governing section should come into conflict with its own—whilst it would serve as a covering to disguise its subjection, and, thereby, induce it to bear wrongs, which it would not otherwise tolerate. In this state of things, discontent, alienation, and hostility of feelings would be engendered between the sections; to be followed by discord, disorder, convulsions, and, not improbably, a disruption of the system.

In one or the other of these results, it must terminate, if the federal government be left to decide, definitively and in the last resort, as to the extent of its powers. Having no sufficient counteraction, exterior to itself, it must necessarily move in the direction marked out by the inherent tendency belonging to its character and position. As a constitutional, popular government, its tendency will be, in the first place, to an absolute form, under the control of the numerical majority; and, finally, to the most simple of these forms, that of a single, irresponsible individual. As a federal government, extending over a vast territory, the tendency will be, in the first place, to the formation of sectional parties, and the concentration of all power in the stronger section; and, in the next, to conflict between the sections, and disrupture of the whole system. One or the other must be the end, in the case supposed. The laws that would govern are fixed and certain. The only question would be, as to *which end,* and at *what time.* All the rest is as certain as the future, if not disturbed by causes exterior to the system.

So strong indeed is the tendency of the government in the direction assigned—if left to itself—that nothing short of the most powerful negatives, exterior to itself, can effectually counteract and arrest it. These, from the nature of the system, can only be found in the mutual negative of the two co-ordinate governments, and the interposition of a State, as has been explained—the one to protect the powers which the people of the several States delegated to their respective separate State governments—and the other, to protect the powers which the people of the several States, in delegating powers to both of their co-ordinate governments, expressly reserved to themselves respectively. The object of the negative power is, to protect the several portions or interests of the community against each other. Ours is a federal community, of which States form the constituent parts. They reserved the powers not delegated to the federal or common government to themselves individually—but in a twofold character, as embracing separate governments, and as a several people in their sovereign capacity. But where the powers of government are divided, nothing short of a negative—either positive, or in effect—can protect those allotted to the weaker, against the stronger—or the parts of the community against each other. The party to whom the power belongs, is the only party interested in protecting it; and to such party only, can its defence be safely trusted. To intrust it, in this case, to the party interested in absorbing it, and possessed of ample power to do so, is, as has been shown, to trust the lamb to the custody of the wolf.

Nor can any other, so appropriate, so safe or efficient, be devised, as the twofold negative provided by the system. They are appropriate to the twofold character of the State, to which, the powers not delegated, are reserved. That they are safe and sufficient, if called into action, has been shown. All other provisions, without them, would be of little avail—such as the right of suffrage—written constitutions—the division of the powers of the government into three separate and independent departments—the formation of the people into individual and independent States, and the freedom of the press and of speech. These all have their value. They may retard the progress of the government towards its final termination—but without the two negative powers, cannot arrest it—nor can any thing, short of these, preserve the equilibrium of the system. Without them, every other power would be gradually absorbed by the federal government, or be superseded or rendered obsolete. It would remain the only vital power, and the sole organ of a consolidated community.

If we turn now from this to the other aspect of the subject, where these negative powers are brought into full action in order to counteract the tendency of the federal government to supersede and absorb the powers of the system, the contrast will be striking. Instead of weakening the government by counteracting its tendencies, and restricting it to its proper sphere, they would render it far more powerful. A strong government, instead of being weakened, is greatly strengthened, by a correspondingly strong negative. It may lose something in promptitude of action, in calling out the physical force of the country, but would gain vastly in moral power. The security it would afford to all the different parts and interests of the country—the assurance that the powers confided to it, would not be abused—and the harmony and unanimity resulting from the conviction that no one section or interest could oppress another, would, in an emergency, put the whole resources of the Union, moral and physical, at the disposal of the government—and give it a strength which never could be acquired by the enlargement of its powers beyond the limits assigned to it. It is, indeed, only by such confidence and unanimity, that a government can, with certainty, breast the billows and ride through the storms which the vessel of State must often encounter in its progress. The stronger the pressure of the steam, if the boiler be but proportionally strong, the more securely the bark buffets the wave, and defies the tempest.

Nor is there any just ground to apprehend that the federal government would lose any power which properly belongs to it, or which it should desire to retain, by being compelled to resort to the amending power, when this becomes necessary in consequence of a conflict between itself and one of its co-ordinates; or, in case of the interposition of a State. There can certainly be no danger of this, so long as the same feelings and motives which induced them voluntarily to ratify and adopt the constitution unanimously, shall continue to actuate them. While these remain, there can be no hazard in placing what all freely and unanimously adopted, in the charge of three-fourths of the States to protect and preserve. Nor can there be any just ground to apprehend that these feelings and motives will undergo any change, so long as the constitution shall fulfil the ends for which it was ordained and established; to wit: that each and all might enjoy, more perfectly and securely, liberty, peace, tranquillity, security from danger, both internal and external, and all other blessings connected with their respective rights and advantages. It was a great mistake to suppose that the States would naturally stand in antagonistic relations to the federal government; or that there would be any disposition, on their part, to diminish its

power or to weaken its influence. They naturally stand in a reverse relation—pledged to cherish, uphold, and support it. They freely and voluntarily created it, for the common good of each and of all—and will cherish
and defend it so long as it fulfills these objects. If its safe-keeping cannot
be intrusted to its creators, it can be safely placed in the custody of no
other hands.

But it cannot be confined to its proper sphere, and its various powers
kept in a state of equilibrium, as originally established, but by the counteracting resistance of the States, acting in their twofold character, as has
been explained and established. Nor can it fulfil its end without confining it
to its proper sphere, and preserving the equilibrium of its various powers.
Without this, the federal government would concentrate all the powers of
the system in itself, and become an instrument in the hands of the dominant portion of the States, to aggrandize itself at the expense of the rest—
as has also been fully explained and established. With the defeat of the
ends for which it was established, the feelings and motives which induced
the States to establish it, would gradually change; and, finally, give place to
others of a very different character. The weaker and oppressed portion
would regard it with distrust, jealousy, and, in the end, aversion and hostility; while the stronger and more favored, would look upon it, not as the
means of promoting the common good and safety of each and all, but as an
instrument to control the weaker, and to aggrandize itself at its expense.

As nothing but the counteracting resistance of the States can prevent
this result, so nothing short of a full recognition of this, the only means, by
which they can make such resistance, and call it freely into action—can
correct the disorders, and avert the dangers which must ensue from an
opposite and false conception of the system; and thus restore the feelings
and motives which led to the free and unanimous adoption of the federal
constitution and government. With their restoration, the amending power
may be safely trusted, as the preserving, repairing, and protecting power.
There would be no danger whatever, that the government, under its action,
would lose any power which properly belonged to it, and which it ought to

retain; for there would be no motive or interest, on any side, to divest it of any power necessary to enable it to fulfil the ends for which it was established; or to impair, unduly, the strength of the Union. Indeed, it is so modified as to afford an ample guaranty that the Union would be safe in its custody—since it was designedly so constructed as to represent, at all times, the extent to which it might be safely carried, and beyond which it ought not to go. It may, indeed, in case of conflict between it and one of its co-ordinate governments, or an interposing state, modify and restrict the power in contest, in strict conformity with the design and the spirit of the constitution. For it may be laid down as a principle, that the power and action of the Union, instead of being increased, ought to be diminished, with the increase of its extent and population. The reason is, that the greater its extent, and the more numerous and populous the members composing it, the greater will be the diversity of interests, the less the sympathy between the remote parts, the less the knowledge and regard of each, for the interests of the others, and, of course, the less *closeness of union* (so to speak), consistently with its safety. The same principle, according to which it was provided that there should not be more closeness of union than three-fourths should agree to, equally applies in all stages of the growth and progress of the country; to wit: that there should not be, at any time, more than the same proportion would agree to. It ought ever to be borne in mind that the Union may have too much power, and be too intimate and close; as well as too little power, intimacy, and closeness. Either is dangerous. If the latter, from weakness, exposes it to dissolution, the former, from exuberance of strength, and from the parts being too closely compressed together, exposes it, at least equally, either to consolidation and despotism, on the one hand—or to rupture and destruction, by the repulsion of its parts, on the other. The amending power, if duly called into action, would protect the Union against either extreme; and thereby guard against the dangers to which it is on either hand exposed.

It is by thus bringing all the powers of the system into active operation and only by this means, that its equilibrium can be preserved, and adjusted to the changes, which the enlargement of the Union, and its increase of population, or other causes, may require. Thus only, can the Union be preserved; the government made permanent; the limits of the country be enlarged; the anticipations of the founders of the system, as to its future prosperity and greatness—be realized; and the revolutions and calamities, necessarily incident to the theory which would make the federal government the sole and exclusive judge of its powers, be averted.

I have now finished the portion of this discourse which relates to the character and structure of the government of the United States—its various divisions of power, as well as those of the system of which it is a part—and the means which they furnish to protect each division against the encroachment of the others. The government has now been in operation for more than sixty years; and it remains to be considered, whether it has conformed, in practice, with its true theory; and, if not, what has caused its departure; and what must be the consequence, should its aberrations remain uncorrected. I propose to consider these in the order stated.

There are few who will not admit, that the government has, in practice, departed, more or less, from its original character and structure—however great may be the diversity of opinion, as to what constitutes a departure— a diversity caused by the different views entertained in reference to its character and structure. They who believe that the government of the United States is a national, and not a federal government—or who believe that it is partly national and partly federal—will, of course, on the question—whether it has conformed to, or departed from its true theory—form very different opinions from those who believe that it is federal throughout. They who believe that it is exclusively national, very logically conclude, according to their theory, that the government has the exclusive right, in the last resort, to decide as to the extent of its powers, and to enforce its decisions against all opposition, through some one or all of its departments—while they who believe it to be exclusively federal, cannot consistently come to any other conclusion, than that the two governments— federal and State—are coequal and co-ordinate governments; and, as such, neither can possess the right to decide as to the extent of its own powers, or to enforce its own decision against that of the other. The case is different with those who believe it to be partly national, and partly federal. They seem incapable of forming any definite or distinct opinion on the subject— vital and important as it is. Indeed, it is difficult to conceive how, with their views, any rational and fixed opinion can be formed on the subject: for, according to their theory, as far as it is national, it must possess the right contended for by those who believe it to be altogether national; and, on the other hand, as far as it is federal, it must possess the right, which those who believe it to be wholly federal contend for. But how the two can coexist, so that the government shall have the final right to decide on the extent of its powers, and to enforce its decisions as to one portion of its powers, and not as to the other, it is difficult to imagine. Indeed, the difficulty of realizing their views extends to the whole theory. Entertaining these different opinions, as to the true theory of the government, it follows, of course, that there must be an equal diversity of opinion, as to what constitutes a departure from it; and, that, what one considers a departure, the other must, almost necessarily, consider a conformity—and, *vice versa*. When compared with these different views, the course of the government will be found to have conformed, much more closely, to the *national*, than to the *federal* theory.

At its outset, during the first Congress, it received an impulse in that direction, from which it has never yet recovered. Congress, among its earliest measures, adopted one, which, in effect, destroyed the relation of coequals and co-ordinates between the federal government and the govern- ments of the individual States; without which, it is impossible to preserve its federal character. Indeed, I might go further, and assert with truth, that without it, the former would, in effect, cease to be federal, and become national. It would be superior—and the individual governments of the several States, would become subordinate to it—a relation inconsistent with the federal, but in strict conformity to the national theory of the government.

I refer to the 25th section of the Judiciary Act, approved the 24th Sept., 1789. It provides for an appeal from, and revisal of a "final judgment or decree in any suit, in the highest courts of law or equity of a State, in which a decision in the suit could be had, where is drawn in question the validity of a treaty or statute of, or an authority exercised under, the United States, and the decision is against their validity; or where is drawn in question the validity of a statute of, or an authority exercised under, any State, on the ground of their being repugnant to the constitution, treaties, or laws of the United States—and the decision is in favor of their validity; or where is drawn in question the construction of any clause of the constitution, or of a treaty—or statute of, or commission held under, the United States, and the decision is against such title, &c., specially set up by either, &c." The effect, so far as these cases extend, is to place the highest tribunal of the States, both of law and equity, in the same relation to the Supreme Court of the United States, which the circuit and inferior courts of the United States bear to it. To this extent, they are made equally subordinate and subject to its control; and, of course, the judicial departments of the separate governments of the several States, to the same extent, cease to stand, under these provisions, in the relation of coequal and co-ordinate departments with the federal judiciary. Nor does the effect stop here. Their other departments, the legislative and executive—to the same extent, through their respective State judiciaries, no longer continue to stand in the relation of coequals and co-ordinates with the corresponding departments of the federal government. The reason is obvious. As the laws and the acts of the government and its departments, can, if opposed, reach the people individually only through the courts—to whatever extent the judiciary of the United States is made paramount to that of the individual States, to the same extent will the legislative and executive departments of the federal government—and, thus, the entire government itself, be made paramount to the legislative and executive departments—and the entire governments of the individual States. It results, of course, that if the right of appeal from the State courts to those of the United States, should be extended as far as

the government of the United States may claim that its powers and authority extend, the government of the several States would cease, in effect, to
be its coequals and co-ordinates; and become, in fact, dependent upon,
and subordinate to it. Such being the case, the important question presents
itself for consideration—does the constitution vest Congress with the
power to pass an act authorizing such appeals?

It is certain, that no such power is expressly delegated to it: and equally
so, that there is none vested in it which would make such a power, as an
incident, necessary and proper to carry it into execution. It would be vain
to attempt to find either in the constitution. If, then, it be vested in Congress at all, it must be as a power necessary and proper to carry into
execution some power vested in one of the two other departments—or in
the government of the United States, or some officer thereof: for Congress,
by an express provision of the constitution, is limited, in the exercise of
implied powers, to the passage of such laws only, as are necessary and
proper to carry into effect, the powers vested in itself, or in some other
department, or in the government of the United States, or some officer
thereof. But it would be vain to look for a power, either in the executive
department, or in the government of the United States or any of its officers,
which would make a law, containing the provisions of the section in question, necessary and proper to carry it into execution. No one has ever
pretended to find, or can find any such power in either, all, or any one of
them. If, then, it exist at all, it must be among the powers of the department of the judiciary itself. But there is only one of its powers which has
ever been claimed, or can be claimed, as affording even a pretext for
making a law, containing such provisions, necessary and proper to carry it
into effect. I refer to the second and third clauses of the third article of the
constitution, heretofore cited. The second extends the judicial power "to
all cases in law and equity, arising under this constitution, the laws of the
United States, and treaties made, or which shall be made under their
authority"—and to all cases between parties therein enumerated, without
reference to the nature of the question in litigation. The third enumerates

certain cases, in which the Supreme Court shall have original jurisdiction, and then provides, that "in all others before mentioned, it shall have appellate jurisdiction, both as to law and fact, with such exceptions and under such regulations as the Congress shall make."

The question is thus narrowed down to a single point—Has Congress the authority, in carrying this power into execution, to make a law providing for an appeal from the courts of the several States, to the Supreme Court of the United States?

There is, on the face of the two clauses, nothing whatever to authorize the making of such a law. Neither of them names or refers, in the slightest manner to the States, or to the courts of the States; or gives the least authority, apparently, to legislate over or concerning either. The object of the former of these two clauses, is simply to extend the judicial power, so as to make it commensurate with the other powers of the government; and to confer jurisdiction over certain cases, not arising under the constitution, and laws of the United States, or treaties made under their authority. While the latter simply provides, in what cases the Supreme Court of the United States shall have original, and in what, appellate jurisdiction. Appellate stands in contradistinction to original jurisdiction, and as the latter implies that the case must commence in the Supreme Court, so the former implies that the case must commence in an inferior court, not having final jurisdiction; and, therefore, liable to be carried up to a higher, for final decision. Now, as the constitution vests the judicial power of the United States, "in one Supreme Court, and such inferior courts, as Congress may, from time to time ordain," the natural and plain meaning of the clause is, that, in the cases enumerated, the Supreme Court should have original jurisdiction; and in all others, originating in the inferior courts of the United States, it should have jurisdiction only on an appeal from their decisions.

Such being the plain meaning and intent of these clauses—the question is—How can Congress derive from them, authority to make a law providing for an appeal from the highest courts of the several States, in the cases specified in the 25th section of the Judiciary Act, to the Supreme Court of the United States?

To this question no answer can be given, without assuming that the State Courts—even the highest—stand in the relation of the inferior courts to the Supreme Court of the United States, wherever a question touching their authority comes before them. Without such an assumption, there is not, and cannot be, a shadow of authority to warrant an appeal from the former to the latter. But does the fact sustain the assumption? Do the courts of the States stand, as to such questions, in the relation of the inferior to the Supreme Court of the United States? If so, it must, be by some provision of the constitution of the United States. It cannot be a matter of course. How can it be reconciled with the admitted principle, that the federal government and those of the several States, are each supreme in their respective spheres? Each, it is admitted, is supreme, as it regards the other, in its proper sphere; and, of course, as has been shown, coequal, and co-ordinate.[10]

---

[10]Reference is here made to various pencil notes in the margin of the manuscript, which, from the contractions used and the illegible manner in which they are written, I have not been able satisfactorily to decipher; and have, therefore, not incorporated with the text. They indicate that the author designed to have elaborated more fully this part of the subject—and, as far as I can gather the meaning, to have shown that the State courts, in taking cognizance of cases in which the constitution, treaties, and laws of the United States are drawn in question, act, not in virtue of any provision of the constitution or laws of the United States, but by an authority independent of both. That this authority is the constitution-making power—the people of the States respectively. That, according to a principle of jurisprudence, universally admitted, courts of justice must look to the *whole* law, by which their decisions are to be guided and governed. That this principle is eminently applicable in the cases mentioned. That, as the constitution and laws of the United States are the constitution and laws of each State, the State courts must have the right—and are in duty bound to decide on the validity of such laws as may be drawn in question, in all cases rightfully before them. And that the principle which would authorize an appeal from the decision of the highest judicial tribunal of a State to the Supreme Court of the United States, in cases where the constitution, treaties, and laws of the

If this be true, then the respective departments of each must be necessarily and equally so—as the whole includes the parts. The State courts are the representatives of the reserved rights, vested in the governments of the several States, as far as it relates to the judicial power. Now as these are reserved *against* the federal government—as the very object and intent of the reservation, was to place them beyond the reach of its control—how can the courts of the States be inferior to the Supreme Court of the United States; and, of course, subject to have their decisions re-examined and reversed by it, without, at the same time, subjecting the portion of the reserved rights of the governments of the several States, vested in it, to the control of the federal government? Still higher ground may be taken. If the State courts stand in the relation of inferiors to the Supreme Court of the United States—what reason can possibly be assigned, why the other departments of the State governments—the legislative and executive, should not stand in the same relation to the corresponding departments of the federal government? Where is there to be found any provision of the constitution which makes, in this respect, any distinction between the judiciary and the other departments? Or, on what principle can such a distinction be made? There is no such distinction; and, it must follow, that if the judicial department, or the courts of the governments of the individual States, stand in the relation of inferior courts to the Supreme Court of the United States, the other departments must stand in the same relation to the corresponding departments of the federal government. It must also follow, that the governments of the several States, instead of being coequal and co-ordinate with the federal government, are inferior and subordinate. All these are necessary consequences.

United States are drawn in question, would equally authorize an appeal from the latter to the former, in cases where the constitution and laws of the State have been drawn in question, and the decision has been adverse to them.—*Cralle.*

But it may be alleged that the section in question does not assume the broad principle, that the State courts stand, in all cases, in the relation of the inferior courts to the Supreme Court of the United States; that it is restricted to appeals from the final judgments of the highest courts of the several States; to suits in law and equity (excluding criminal cases) and, in such cases, to those only, where the validity of a treaty, statute of, or an authority exercised under the United States; or the construction of the constitution, or of a treaty, or law of, or commission held under the United States, are drawn in question, and the decision is adverse to the right claimed under the United States; or, where the validity of any law of, or authority exercised under a State are involved, on the ground that they are repugnant to the constitution, treaties or laws of the United States—and the decision is in favor of the law or the authority of the State. It may, also, be alleged that, to this extent, it was necessary to regard the courts of the States as inferior courts; and, as such, to provide for an appeal from them to the Supreme Court of the United States, in order to preserve uniformity in decisions; and to avoid collision and conflict between the federal government and those of the several States.

If uniformity of decision be one of the objects of the section, its provisions are very illy calculated to accomplish it. They are far better suited to enlarge the powers of the government of the United States, and to contract, to the same degree, those of the governments of the individual States, than to secure uniformity of decision. They provide for appeals only in cases where the decision is *adverse* to the power claimed for the former, or in *favor* of that of the latter. They assume that the courts of the States are always *right* when they decide in *favor* of the government of the United States, and always *wrong,* when they decide in *favor* of the power of their respective States; and, hence, they provide for an appeal in the latter case, but for none in the former. The result is, that if the courts of a State should commit an error, in deciding *against* the State, or in favor of the United States, and the Supreme Court of the latter should, in like cases, make the reverse decisions, the want of uniformity would remain uncorrected. Uniformity, then, would seem to be of no importance, when the decision was calculated to impair the reserved powers; and only so, when calculated to impair the delegated.

But it might have been thought, that, so strong would be the leaning of the State courts towards their respective States, there would be no danger of a decision against them, and in favor of the United States; except in cases, so clear as not to admit of a doubt. This might be the case, if all the State governments stood in antagonistic relations to the federal government. But it has been established that such is not the case; and that, on the contrary, a majority of them must be, habitually, arrayed on its side; and their courts as much inclined to sustain its powers as its own courts. But if the State courts should have a strong leaning in favor of the powers of their respective States, what reason can be assigned, why the Supreme Court of the United States should not have a leaning, equally strong, in favor of the federal government? If one, in consequence, cannot be trusted in making a decision adverse to the delegated powers, on what principle can the other be trusted in making a decision adverse to the reserved powers? Is it to be supposed, that the judges of the courts of the States, who *are sworn to support the constitution of the United States*, are less to be trusted, in cases where the *delegated* powers are involved, than the federal judges, who *are not bound by oath to support the constitutions of the States*, are, in cases, where the *reserved* powers are concerned? Are not the two powers equally independent of each other? And is it not as important to protect the reserved against the encroachments of the delegated, as the delegated against those of the reserved powers? And are not the latter, being much the weaker, more in need of protection than the former? Why, then, not leave the courts of each, without the right of appeal, on either side, to guard and protect the powers confided to them respectively?

As far as uniformity of decision is concerned—the appeal was little needed; and well might the author of the section in question be so indifferent about securing it. The extension of the judicial power of the United

States, so as to make it commensurate with the government itself, is suffi-cient, without the aid of an appeal from the courts of the States, to secure all the uniformity consistent with a federal government like ours. It gives choice to the plaintiff to institute his suit, either in the federal or State courts, at his option. If he select the latter, and its decision be adverse to him, he has no right to complain; nor has he a right to a new trial in the former court, as it would, in reality be, under the cover of an appeal. He selected his tribunal, and ought to abide the consequences. But his fate would be a warning to all other plaintiffs in similar cases. It would show that the State courts were adverse—and admonish them to commence their suits in the federal courts; and, thereby, uniformity of decision, in such cases, would be secured. Nor would the defendant, in such cases, have a right to complain, and have a new trial in the courts of the United States, if the decision of the State courts should be adverse to him. If he be a citizen of the State, he would have no right to do either, if the courts of his own State should decide against him; nor could a resident of the State or sojourner in it—since both, by voluntarily putting themselves under the protection of its laws, are bound to acquiesce in the decisions of its tribunals.

But there is another object which the appeal is well calculated to effect—and for the accomplishment of which, its provisions are aptly drawn up, as far as they go—that is—to decide all conflicts between the delegated and reserved powers, as to the extent of their respective limits, in favor of the former. For this purpose, it was necessary to provide for an appeal from the State courts, whenever their decisions were *in favor* of the power of the States, or *adverse* to the power of the United States. In no other cases was it necessary; and, hence, probably, the reason why it was limited to these, notwithstanding the alleged object. Uniformity of decision required it to embrace, not only these, but the reverse cases. As it stands, it enables the Supreme Court of the United States, in all cases of conflict between the two powers, coming within the provisions of the section, to overrule the decisions of the courts of the States, and to

decide, exclusively, and in the last resort, as to the extent of the delegated powers.

The object of the section was, doubtless, to prevent collision between
the federal and State governments—the delegated and reserved powers—
by giving to the former (and by far the stronger), through the Supreme
Court—the right, under the color of an appeal, to decide as to the extent of
the former—and to enforce its decisions against the resistance of a State.
The expedient may, for a time, be effectual; but must, in the end, lead to
collisions of the most dangerous character. It should ever be borne in
mind, that collisions are incident to a division of power—but that without
division of power, there can be no organization; and without organization,
no constitution; and without this no liberty. To prevent collision, then, by
destroying the division of power, is, in effect, to substitute an absolute for a
constitutional government, and despotism in the place of liberty—evils far
greater than those intended to be remedied. It is the part of wisdom and
patriotism, then, not to destroy the divisions of power in order to prevent
collisions, but devise means, by which they may be prevented from leading
to an appeal to force. This, as has been shown, the constitution, in a
manner most safe and expedient, has provided through the amending
power—a power, so constituted as to preserve in all time, and under all
circumstances, an equilibrium between the various divisions of power of
which the system is composed.

It is true, as has been alleged, that the provisions of the section are
restricted—that they are limited to civil cases, and to appeals from the
highest State courts to the Supreme Court of the United States. Thus
restricted, they would not be sufficient to subject the reserved powers
completely to the delegated, and to lead, at least—speedily—to all the
consequences stated. But what assurance can there be, that the right, if
admitted, will not be carried much further? The right of appeal itself, can
only be maintained, as has been shown, on the assumption that the courts
of the States stand in the relation of inferior courts to the Supreme Court of
the United States. Resting on this broad assumption, no definite limits can

be assigned to the right, if it exists at all. It may be extended to criminal as well as civil cases—to the circuit courts of the United States as well as to the Supreme Court; to the transfer of a case, civil or criminal, at any stage, before as well as after final decision, from the State courts to either the circuit or Supreme Court of the United States; to the exemption of all the employees and officers of the United States, when acting under the color of their authority, from civil and criminal proceedings in the courts of the State, and subjecting those of the States, acting under their respective laws, to the civil and criminal process of the United States; to authorize the judges of the United States court to grant writs of habeas corpus to persons confined under the authority of the States, on the allegation that the acts for which they were confined, were done under color of the authority of the United States; and, finally, to authorize the President to use the entire force of the Union—the militia, the army and navy—to enforce, in all such cases, the claim of power on the part of the United States. If the courts of the States, be, indeed, inferior courts—if an appeal from them to the Supreme Court of the United States can be rightfully authorized by Congress, all this may be done. May! It has already been done. All that has been stated as possible, is but a transcript of the provisions of the act approved 3d March, 1833, entitled "An act to provide for the collection of duties on imports"—as far as it relates to the matter in question.

But if such powers can be rightfully vested in the courts of the United States by Congress, for the collection of the revenue, no reason can be assigned why it may not vest like powers in them to carry into execution any power which it may choose to claim, or exercise. Take, for illustration, what is called the "guaranty section" of the constitution, which, among other things, provides that, "the United States shall guarantee to each State in this Union a republican form of government; and protect each of them, on application of the legislature, or of the executive (when the legislature cannot be convened) against domestic violence." Congress, of course, as the representative of the United States, in their legislative capacity, has the right to make laws to carry these guaranties into execution. This involves the right, in reference to the first, to determine what form of government is republican. To decide this important question, the government of the United States and the several State governments, at the time the constitution of the United States was adopted and the States became members of the federal Union, furnished a plain and safe standard, as they were, of course, all deemed republican. But suppose Congress, instead of being regulated by it, should undertake to fix a standard, without regard to that fixed by those who framed, or those who adopted the constitution of the United States; and suppose it should adopt, what now, it is to be feared, is the sentiment of the dominant portion of the Union, that no government is republican where universal suffrage does not prevail—where the numerical majority of the whole population is not recognized as the supreme governing power: And, suppose, acting on this false standard, that Congress should declare that the governments of certain States of the Union, a large portion of whose population are not permitted to exercise the right of suffrage, were not republican; and should undertake, in execution of its declaration, to make laws to compel all such States to adopt governments conforming to its views, by extending the right of suffrage to every description of its population, and placing the power in the hands of the mere numerical majority. What, in such case, would there be to prevent Congress from adopting the provisions of the act of 3d March, 1833, to carry such laws into execution? If it had the right to adopt them, in that case, it would have an equal right to adopt them in the case supposed, or in any other that might be. No distinction can possibly be made between them, or between it and any other case, where Congress may claim to exercise a power. If it has the right to regard the courts of the States as standing in the relation of inferiors to the courts of the United States, *in any case*, it has a right to consider them so *in every case;* and, as such, subject to the authority of the latter, whenever, and to whatever extent it may think proper. What, then, would be the effect of extending the provisions of the act to the case supposed? The officers of the State, and all in authority under her, and all her citizens, who might stand up in defence of her government and institutions, would be regarded as insurgents, for resisting the act of Congress; and, as such, liable to be arrested, tried and punished by the courts of the United States; while those who might desert the State, and join in overthrowing her government and institutions, would be protected by them against her laws and her courts. To be true to the State, would come to be regarded as treason to the United States, and punishable as the highest crime; whilst to be false to her, would come to be regarded as fidelity to them, and be a passport to the honors of the Union. More briefly, fidelity to her, would be treason to the United States, and treason to her, fidelity to them.

But the clause in question embraces the protection of the government of each State against domestic violence, as well as the guaranty of a republican form of government to each. Suppose, then, a party should be formed in any State to overthrow its government, on the ground that it was not republican—because its constitution restricted the right of suffrage, and did not recognize the right of the numerical majority to govern absolutely. Suppose that this party should apply to Congress to enforce the pledge of the United States to guarantee a republican form of government—and the State should apply to enforce the guaranty of protection against domestic violence—and Congress should side with the former and pass laws to aid them: what reason can be assigned, why the provisions of the act of the 3d March, 1833, could not be extended to such a case—and the government of the State, with all its functionaries, and all their aiders and abettors, be arrested, tried, convicted and punished as traitors, by the courts of the United States? And all, who combined to overthrow the government of the State, protected against the laws and courts of the State?

It may be objected that the supposition, in both cases, is imaginary and never can occur—that it is not even to be supposed that Congress ever will so far forget its duty, as to pervert guaranties, solemnly entered into by the States, in forming a federal Union to protect each other in their republican forms of government—and the separate government of each against domestic violence—into means of effecting ends the very opposite of those intended. The objection, if it should ever be made, would indicate very little knowledge of the barriers which constitutions and plighted faith oppose to governments, when they can be transcended with impunity. They may not be openly assailed at first. They are usually sapped and undermined by construction, preparatory to their entire demolition. But what construction may fail to accomplish, the open assaults of fanaticism, or the lust of power, or the violence of party, will, in the end, prostrate. Of the truth of this, history, both political and religious, affords abundant proofs. Already our own furnishes many examples, of which, not a few, much to the point, might be cited. The very act, which the statute of the 3d March, 1833, was intended to enforce, was a gross and palpable perversion of the taxing power; and the movement to subvert the government of Rhode Island, a few years since, threatened, at one time, to furnish, by a like perversion of the guarantee to protect its government against domestic violence, the means of subverting it.

But it may be alleged that, if Congress should so far forget its duty as to make the gross and dangerous perversion supposed, the State would find security in the independent tenure, by which the judges of the United States courts hold their office. As highly important as this tenure is to protect the judiciary against the encroachments of the other departments of the government, and to insure an upright administration of the laws, as between individuals, it would be greatly to overestimate its importance to suppose, that it secures an efficient resistance against Congress, in the case supposed; or, more generally, against the encroachment of the federal government on the reserved powers. There are many and strong reasons why it cannot.

In the first place, all cases like those supposed, where the power is perverted from the object intended to be effected by it, and made the means of effecting another of an entirely different character—are beyond the cognizance of the courts. The reason is plain. If the act be constitutional on its face; if its title be such as to indicate that the power exercised, is one which Congress is authorized by the constitution to exercise—and there be nothing on the face of the act calculated, beyond dispute, to show it did not correspond with the purpose professed—the courts cannot look beyond to ascertain the real object intended, however different it may be. It has (to illustrate by the case in question) the right to make laws to carry into execution the guaranty of a republican form of government to the several States of the Union; and, for this purpose, to determine whether the form of the government of a certain State be republican or not. But if, under the pretext of exercising this power, it should use it for the purpose of subjecting to its control any obnoxious member, or members of the Union—be it for the impulse of fanaticism, lust of power, party resentment, or any other motive, it would not be within the competency of the courts to inquire into the objects intended.

But, if it were otherwise—if the judiciary could take cognizance of this, and any other description of perversion or infraction by the other departments, it could oppose no permanent resistance to them. The reason is to be found in the fact, that, like the others, it emanates from, and is under the control of the two combined majorities—that of the States, and that of their populations, estimated in federal numbers. The independent tenure, by which the judges hold their office, may render the judiciary less easily and readily acted on by these united majorities; but as they become permanently concentrated in one of the sections of the Union, and as that section becomes permanently the dominant one, the judiciary must yield, ultimately, to its control. It would possess all the means of acting on the hopes and fears of the judges. As high as their office—or independent as their tenure of office is, it does not place them above the influences which control the other members of government. They may aspire higher. The other judges of the Supreme Court, may, will, and honorably aspire to the place of the Chief Justice—and he and all of his associates, to the highest post under the government. As far as these influences extend, they must give a leaning to the side which can control the elections, and, through them, the department which has at its disposal the patronage of the government. Nor does their office place them beyond the reach of fear. As independent as it is, they are, like all the other officers of government, liable to be impeached: and the powers of impeaching and of trying impeachments, are vested, respectively, in the House of Representatives and the Senate—both of which emanate directly from the combined majorities which control the government. But, if both hope and fear should be insufficient to overcome the independence of the judges, the appointing power, which emanates from the same source, would, in time, fill the bench with those only whose opinions and principles accord with the other departments. And hence, all reliance on the judiciary for protection, under the most favorable view that can be taken, must, in the end, prove vain and illusory.

I have now shown that the 25th section of the judiciary act is unauthorized by the constitution; and that it rests on an assumption which would give to Congress the right to enforce, through the judiciary department, whatever measures it might think proper to adopt; and to put down all resistance by force. The effect of this is to make the government of the United States the sole judge, in the last resort, as to the extent of its powers, and to place the States and their separate governments and institutions at its mercy. It would be a waste of time to undertake to show that an assumption, which would destroy the relation of co-ordinates between the government of the United States and those of the several States—which would enable the former, at pleasure, to absorb the reserved powers and to destroy the institutions, social and political, which the constitution was ordained and established to protect, is wholly inconsistent with the federal theory of the government, though in perfect accordance with the national theory. Indeed, I might go further, and assert, that it is, of itself, all sufficient to convert it into a national, consolidated government—and thus to consummate, what many of the most prominent members of the convention so long, and so perseveringly contended for. Admit the right of Congress to regard the courts of the States as inferior to those of the United States, and every other act of assumption is made easy. It is the great enforcing power to compel a State to submit to all acts, however unconstitutional, oppressive or outrageous—or to oppose them at its peril. This one departure, of which the 25th section of the judiciary act was the entering wedge, and the act of the 3d March, 1833, the consummation, may be fairly regarded as the salient point of all others—for without it, they either would not have occurred, or if they had, might have been readily remedied. Or, rather, without it, the whole course of the government would have been different—the conflict between the co-ordinate governments, in reference to the extent of their respective powers, would have been subject to the action of the amending power; and thereby the equilibrium of the system been preserved, and the practice of the government made to conform to its federal character.

It remains to be explained how, at its very outset, the government received a direction so false and dangerous. For this purpose it will be necessary to recur to the history of the formation and adoption of the constitution.

The convention which framed it, was divided, as has been stated, into two parties—one in favor of a *national,* and the other of a *federal* government. The former, consisting, for the most part, of the younger and more talented members of the body—but of the less experienced—prevailed in the early stages of its proceedings. A negative on the action of the governments of the several States, in some form or other, without a corresponding one, on their part, on the acts of the government about to be formed, was indispensable to the consummation of their plan. They, accordingly, as has been shown, attempted, at every stage of the proceedings of the convention, and in all possible forms, to insert some provision in the constitution, which would, in effect, vest it with a negative—but failed in all. The party in favor of a *federal* form, subsequently gained the ascendency—the national party acquiesced, but without surrendering their preference for their own favorite plan—or yielding, entirely, their confidence in the plan adopted—or the necessity of a negative on the action of the separate governments of the States. They regarded the plan as but an experiment; and determined, as honest men and good patriots, to give it a fair trial.

They even assumed the name of federalists; and two of their most talented leaders, Mr. Hamilton and Mr. Madison, after the adjournment of the convention, and while the ratification of the constitution was pending, wrote the major part of that celebrated work, "The Federalist;" the object of which was to secure its adoption. It did much to explain and define it, and to secure the object intended; but it shows, at the same time, that its authors had not abandoned their predilection in favor of the national plan.

When the government went into operation, they both filled prominent places under it: Mr. Hamilton, that of secretary of the treasury—then, by far the most influential post belonging to the executive department—if we except its head; and Mr. Madison, that of a member of the House of Representatives—at the time, a much more influential body than the Senate, which sat with closed doors, on legislative, as well as executive business. No position could be assigned, better calculated to give them control over the action of the government, or to facilitate their efforts to carry out their predilections in favor of a national form of government, as far as, in their opinion, fidelity to the constitution would permit. How far this was, may be inferred from the fact, that their joint work, THE FEDERALIST, maintained that the government was partly federal and partly national, notwithstanding it calls itself "the government of the United States"—and notwithstanding the convention repudiated the word "national," and designated it by the name of "federal," in their letter laying the plan before the old Congress, as has been shown. When to this it is added, that the party, originally in favor of a national plan of government, was strongly represented, and that the President and Vice-President had, as was supposed, a leaning that way, it is not surprising that it should receive from the first, an impulse in that direction much stronger than was consistent with its federal character; and that some measure should be adopted calculated to have the effect of giving it, what was universally desired by that party in the convention, a negative on the action of the separate governments of the several States. Indeed, believing as they did, that they would prove too strong for the government of the United States, and that such a negative was indispensable to secure harmony, and to avoid conflict between them, it was their duty to use their best efforts to adopt some such measure—provided that, in their opinion, there should be no constitutional objection in the way. Nor would it be difficult, under such impressions, to be satisfied with reasons in favor of the constitutionality of some such measure which, under a different, or neutral state of mind, would be rejected as having little or no weight. But there was none other, except that embraced in the 25th section of the judiciary act, which had the least show, even of plausibility in its favor—and it is even probable that it was adopted without a clear conception of the principle on which it rested, or the extent to which it might be carried.

Many are disposed to attribute a higher authority to the early acts of the government, than they are justly entitled to—not only because factions and selfish feelings had less influence at the time, but because many, who had been members of the convention, and engaged in forming the constitution, were members of Congress, or engaged in administering the government—circumstances, which were supposed to exempt them from improper influence, and to give them better means of understanding the instrument, than could be possessed by those who had not the same advantages. The purity of their motives is admitted to be above suspicion; but it is a great error to suppose that they could better understand the system they had constructed, and the dangers incident to its operation, than those who came after them. It required time and experience to make them fully known—as is admitted by Mr. Madison himself. After stating the difficulties to be encountered in forming a constitution, he asks; "Is it unreasonable to conjecture, that the errors which may be contained in the plan of the convention, are such as have resulted, rather from defect of antecedent experience on this complicated and difficult subject, than from the want of accuracy or care in the investigation of it, and, consequently, that they are such as will not be ascertained, until an actual trial will point them out? This conjecture is rendered probable, not only by many considerations of a general nature, but by the particular case of the articles of confederation.

It is observable, that, among the numerous objections and amendments suggested by the several States, when these articles were under consideration, not one is found which alludes to the great and radical error, which, on trial, has discovered itself.'"[11] If this was true in reference to the confederacy—an old and well known form of government—how much more was actual trial necessary to point out the dangers to which the present system was exposed—a system, so novel in its character, and so vastly more complicated than the confederacy? The very opinion, so confidently entertained by Mr. Madison, Gen. Hamilton, and the national party generally (and which, in all probability led to the insertion of the 25th section of the judiciary bill), that the federal government would prove too weak to resist the State governments—strongly illustrates the truth of Mr. Madison's remarks. No one can now doubt, that the danger is on the other side. Indeed, the public man, who has had much experience of the working of the system, and does not more clearly perceive where the danger lies, than the ablest and most sagacious member of the convention, must be a dull observer.

But this is not the only instance of a great departure, during the same session, from the principles of the constitution. Among others, a question was decided in discussing the bill to organize the treasury department, which strikingly illustrates how imperfectly, even the framers of so complex a system as ours, understood it; and how necessary time and experience were to a full knowledge of it. During the pendency of the bill, a question arose, whether the President, without the sanction of an act of Congress, had the power to remove an officer of the government, the tenure of whose office was not fixed by the constitution? It was elaborately discussed. Most of the prominent members took part in the debate. Mr. Madison, and others who agreed with him, insisted that he had the power. They rested their argument mainly on the ground, that it belonged to the class of executive powers; and that it was indispensable to the performance

[11]38th No. of the Federalist.

of the duty, "to take care that the laws be faithfully executed." Both parties agreed that the power was not expressly vested in him. It was, finally, decided that he had the power—both sides overlooking a portion of the constitution which expressly provides for the case. I refer to a clause, already cited, and more than once alluded to, which empowers Congress to make all laws necessary and proper to carry its own powers into execution; and, also, whatever power is vested in the government, or any of its departments, or officers. And what makes the fact more striking, the very argument used by those, who contended that he had the power, independently of Congress, conclusively showed that it could not be exercised without its authority, and that the latter department had the right to determine the mode and manner in which it should be executed. For, if it be not expressly vested in the President, and only results as necessary and proper to carry into execution a power vested in him, it irresistibly follows, under the provisions of the clause referred to, that it cannot be exercised without the authority of Congress. But while it effected this important object, the constitution provided means to secure the independence of the other departments; that of the executive, by requiring the approval of the President of all the acts of Congress—and that of the judiciary, by its right to decide definitively, as far as the other departments are concerned, the constitutionality of all laws involved in cases brought before it.

No decision ever made, or measure ever adopted, except the 25th section of the judiciary act, has produced so great a change in the practical operation of the government, as this. It remains, in the face of this express and important provision of the constitution, unreversed. One of its effects has been, to change, entirely, the intent of the clause, in a most important particular. Its main object, doubtless, was, to prevent collision in the action of the government, without impairing the independence of the departments, by vesting *all discretionary power* in the Legislature. Without this, each department would have had equal right to determine what powers were necessary and proper to carry into execution the powers vested in it; which could not fail to bring them into dangerous conflicts, and to increase the hazard of multiplying unconstitutional acts. Indeed, instead of a government, it would have been little less than the *regime* of three separate and conflicting departments—ultimately to be controlled by the executive; in consequence of its having the command of the patronage and forces of the Union. This is avoided, and unity of object and action is secured by vesting all its discretionary power in Congress; so that no department or officer of the government, can exercise any power not expressly authorized by the constitution or the laws. It is thus made a legal, as well as a constitutional government; and if there be any departure from the former, it must be either with the sanction or the permission of Congress. Such was the intent of the constitution; but it has been defeated, in practice, by the decision in question.

Another of its effects has been to engender the most corrupting, loathsome and dangerous disease, that can infect a popular government—I mean that, known by the name of "the Spoils." It is a disease easily contracted under all forms of government—hard to prevent, and most difficult to cure, when contracted; but of all the forms of governments, it is, by far, the most fatal of those of a popular character. The decision, which left the President free to exercise this mighty power, according to his will and pleasure—uncontrolled and unregulated by Congress, scattered, broadcast, the seeds of this dangerous disease, throughout the whole system. It might be long before they would germinate—but that they would spring up in time; and, if not eradicated, that they would spread over the whole body politic a corrupting and loathsome distemper, was just as certain as any thing in the future. To expect, with its growing influence and patronage, that the honors and emoluments of the government if left to the free and unchecked will of the Executive, would not be brought, in time, to bear on the presidential election, implies profound ignorance of that constitution of our nature, which renders governments necessary, to preserve society, and constitutions, to prevent the abuses of governments.

There was another departure during the same Congress, which was followed by important consequences; and which strikingly illustrates how dangerous it is for it to permit either of the other departments to exercise any power not expressly vested in it by the constitution, or authorized by law. I refer to the order issued by the, then, Secretary of the Treasury, Gen. Hamilton, authorizing, under certain restrictions, bank notes to be received in payment of the dues of the government.

To understand the full extent of the evils consequent on this measure, it is necessary to premise, that, during the revolution, the country had been inundated by an issue of paper, on the part of the confederacy and the governments of the several States; and at the time the constitution was adopted, was suffering severely under its effects. To put an end to the evil, and to guard against its recurrence, the constitution vested Congress with the power, "to coin money, regulate the value thereof, and of foreign coins," and prohibited the States from "coining money, emitting bills of credit, and making any thing but gold and silver coin a tender in payment of debts." With the intent of carrying out the object of these provisions, Congress provided, in the act laying duties upon imports, that they should be received in gold and silver coin only. And yet, the Secretary, in the face of this provision, issued an order, authorizing the collectors to receive bank notes; and thus identified them, as far as the fiscal action of the government was concerned, with gold and silver coin, against the express provision of the act, and the intent of the constitution.

This departure led, almost necessarily, to another, which followed shortly after—the incorporation of, what was called, in the report of the Secretary recommending its establishment, A NATIONAL BANK—a report strongly indicating the continuance of his predilections in favor of a national government. I say, *almost necessarily;* for if the government has the right to receive, and actually receives and treats bank notes as money, in its receipts and payments, it would seem to follow that it had the right, and was in duty bound, to adopt all means necessary and proper to give them uniformity and stability of value, as far as practicable. Thus the one departure led to the other, and the two combined, to great and important changes in the character and the course of the government.

During the same Congress, a foundation was laid for other and great departures; the results of which, although not immediately developed, have since led to the most serious evils. I refer to the report of the Secretary of the Treasury on the subject of manufactures. He contended, not only that duties might be imposed to encourage manufactures, but that it belonged (to use his own language) "to the discretion of the national Legislature to pronounce upon the objects which concern the general welfare, and for which, under that description, an appropriation of money is requisite and proper. And there seems to be no doubt, that whatever concerns the general interests of agriculture, of manufactures and of commerce, is within the sphere of the national councils, as far as regards an application of money." It is a bold and an unauthorized assumption, that Congress has the power to pronounce what objects belong, and what do not belong to the general welfare; and to appropriate money, at its discretion, to such as it may deem to belong to it. No such power is delegated to it—nor is any such necessary and proper to carry into execution those which are delegated. On the contrary, to pronounce on the general welfare of the States is a high constitutional power, appertaining not to Congress, but to the people of the several States, acting in their sovereign capacity. That duty they performed in ordaining and establishing the constitution. This pronounced to what limits the general welfare extended, and beyond which it did not extend. All within them, appertained to the general welfare, and all without them, to the particular welfare of the respective States. The money power, including both the taxing and appropriating powers, and all other powers of the federal government are restricted to these limits. To prove, then, that any particular object belongs to the *general* welfare of the States of the Union, it is necessary to show that it is included in some one of the delegated powers, or is necessary and proper to carry some one of them into effect—before a tax can be laid or money appropriated to effect it. For Congress, then, to undertake to pronounce what does, or what does not belong to the general welfare—without regard to the extent of the delegated powers—is to usurp the highest authority—one belonging exclusively to the people of the several States in their sovereign capacity. And yet, on this assumption, thus boldly put forth, in defiance of a fundamental principle of a federal system of government, most onerous duties have been laid on imports—and vast amounts of money appropriated to objects not named among the delegated powers, and not necessary or proper to carry any one of them into execution; to the great impoverishment of one portion of the country, and the corresponding aggrandizement of the other.

Such are some of the leading measures, which were adopted, or had their origin during the first Congress that assembled under the constitution. They all evince a strong predilection for a national government; so strong, indeed, that very feeble arguments were sufficient to satisfy those, who had the control of affairs at the time; provided the measure tended to give the government an impulse in that direction. Not that it was intended to change its character from a *federal* to a *national* government (for that would involve a want of good faith)—but that it was thought to be necessary to strengthen it on, what was sincerely believed to be, its weak side. But, be this as it may, the government then received an impulse adverse to its federal, and in favor of a national, consolidated character, from which it has never recovered—and which, with slight interruption and resistance, has been constantly on the increase. Indeed, to the measures then adopted and projected, almost all subsequent departures from the federal character of the government, and all encroachments on the reserved powers may be fairly traced, numerous and great as they have been.

So many measures, following in rapid succession, and strongly tending to concentrate all power in the government of the United States, could not fail to excite much alarm among those who were in favor of preserving the reserved rights; and, with them, the federal character of the government. They, accordingly, soon began to rally in opposition to the Secretary of the Treasury and his policy, under Mr. Jefferson—then Secretary of State—and in favor of the reserved powers—or, as they were called, "reserved rights," of the States. They assumed the name of the Republican party. Its great object was to protect the reserved, against the encroachments of the delegated powers; and, with this view, to give a direction to the government of the United States, favorable to the preservation of the one, and calculated to prevent the encroachment of the other. And hence they were often called, "the State Rights party."

Things remained in this state during the administration of General Washington—but shortly after the accession of his successor—the elder Adams, the advocates of the reserved powers, became a regularly organized party in opposition to his administration. The introduction of, what are well known as, the Alien and Sedition laws, was the immediate cause of systematic and determined resistance. The former was fiercely assailed, as wholly unauthorized by the constitution; and as vesting arbitrary and despotic power in the President, over alien friends as well as alien enemies—and the latter, not only as unauthorized, but in direct violation of the provision of the constitution, which prohibits Congress from making any law "abridging the freedom of speech or of the press." The passage of these acts, especially the latter—caused deep and general excitement and opposition throughout the Union; being intended, as was supposed, to protect the government in its encroachment on the reserved powers.

Virginia, seconded by Kentucky, took the lead in opposition to these measures. At the meeting of her legislature, ensuing their passage, a series of resolutions were introduced and passed, early in the session, declaratory of the principles of State rights, and condemnatory of the Alien and Sedition acts, and other measures of the government having a tendency to change its character from a federal to a national government. Among other things, these resolutions affirm that, "it (the General Assembly) views the powers of the federal government, as resulting from the compact, to which the States are parties, as limited by the plain sense and intention of the instrument constituting that compact; as no further valid than they are authorized by the grants enumerated in that compact—and that in case of a deliberate, palpable, and dangerous exercise of other powers, not granted by said compact, the States who are parties thereto, have the right and are in duty bound to interpose for arresting the progress of the evil, and for maintaining within their respective limits the authorities, rights and liberties appertaining to them. That the general assembly doth also express its deep regret, that a spirit has, in sundry instances, been manifested by the federal government to enlarge its powers by a forced construction of the constitutional charter, which defines them; and that indications have appeared of a design to expound certain general phrases—(which having been copied from the very limited grant of powers, in the former articles of confederation, were the less liable to be misconstrued)—so as to destroy the meaning and effect of the particular enumeration, which, necessarily, explains and limits the general phrases; so as to consolidate the States by degrees into one sovereignty, the obvious tendency and inevitable result of which would be, to transform the present republican system of the United States into an absolute, or, at least, mixed monarchy."

The Kentucky resolutions, which are now known to have emanated from the pen of Mr. Jefferson—then the Vice-President, and the acknowledged head of the party—are similar in objects and substance with those of Virginia; but as they are differently expressed, and, in some respects, fuller than the latter, it is proper to give the two corresponding resolutions. The former is in the following words: "That the several States, composing the United States of America, are not united on the principle of unlimited submission to the general government; but that, by a compact under the style and title of a constitution of the United States, and of amendments thereto, they constituted a general government for special purposes— delegated to that government, certain definite powers; reserving, each State to itself, the residuary mass of right to their own self-government; that whensoever the general government assumes undelegated powers, its acts are unauthoritative, void, and of no force; that to this compact each State acceded as a State, and is an integral party—its co-States forming, as to itself, the other party; that the government created by this compact, was not made the exclusive or final judge of the extent of the powers delegated to it—since that would have made its discretion, and not the constitution, the measure of its powers, but that, as in all other cases of compact among parties, having no common judge, each party has an equal right to judge for itself, as well of infractions as of the mode and measure of redress." The other is in the following words: "That the construction applied by the general government (as evinced by sundry of their proceedings), to those parts of the constitution of the United States, which delegate to Congress a power to lay and collect taxes, duties, imposts and excises; to pay the debts, and provide for the common defence and general welfare of the United States; and to make all laws necessary and proper for carrying into execution the powers vested by the constitution in the government of the United States, or any department thereof, goes to the destruction of all the limits prescribed to their power by the constitution. That words, meant by that instrument to be subsidiary only to the execution of the limited powers, ought not to be so construed, as themselves to give unlimited powers, nor a part so to be taken, as to destroy the whole residue of the instrument."

The resolutions adopted by both States were sent, by the governor of each, at the request of the general assembly of each, to the governors of the other States, to be laid before their respective legislatures.

In the mean time, Mr. Madison had retired from Congress and was elected a member of the legislature of his own State. As thoroughly in favor of a national government, as he had been in the convention; and as strong as his predilections in its favor continued to be, after the adoption of the federal plan of government, he could not, with the views he entertained of the present government, as being partly national and partly federal, go the whole length of the policy recommended and supported by General Hamilton—and, accordingly, had separated from him and allied himself with Mr. Jefferson.

All the legislatures of the New England States, and that of New York, responded unfavorably to the principles and views set forth in the Virginia and Kentucky resolutions, and in approbation of the course of the federal government. At the next session of the General Assembly of Virginia, these resolutions were referred to a committee, of which Mr. Madison was the chairman. The result was a report from his pen, which triumphantly vindicated and established the positions taken in the resolutions. It successfully maintained, among other things, that the people of the States—acting in their sovereign capacity, have the right "to decide, in the last resort, whether the compact made by them be violated;" and shows, conclusively, that, without it, and the right of the States to interfere to protect themselves and the constitution, "there would be an end to all relief from usurped powers, and a direct subversion of the rights specified or recognized under all the State constitutions, as well as a plain denial of the fundamental principle, on which our independence itself was declared." It also successfully maintained "that the ultimate right of the parties to the constitution, to judge whether the compact has been dangerously violated, must extend to the violation by one delegated authority as well as another, by the judiciary, as well as by the executive or the legislative." And that, "however true, therefore, it may be, that the judicial department is, in all questions submitted to it by the forms of the constitution, to decide, in the last resort, this resort must necessarily be deemed the last in relation to the authority of the other departments of the government; not in relation to the rights of the parties to the constitutional compact, from which the judicial as well as the other departments hold their delegated trust." It conclusively refutes the position, taken by Gen. Hamilton, that it belongs to the discretion of the national legislature to pronounce upon objects, which concern the general welfare, as far as it regards the application of money, already quoted; denies the right of Congress to use the fiscal power, either in imposing taxes, or appropriating money, to promote any objects but those specified in the constitution—shows that the effect of the right, for which he contends, would necessarily be consolidation—by superseding the sovereignty of the States, and extending the power of the federal government to all cases whatsoever; and that, the effect of consolidation would be to transform our federal system into a monarchy.

The unfavorable responses of the other States were, by the House of Representatives of the Kentucky legislature, referred to the committee of the whole—which reported a resolution containing a summary of their former resolutions, which was unanimously adopted. Among other things, it asserts, "that the several States, which formed that instrument (the constitution), being sovereign and independent, have the unquestionable right to judge of its infraction; and that a nullification, by those sovereignties, of all unconstitutional acts, done under color of that instrument, is the rightful remedy."

The report of Mr. Madison, and the Virginia and Kentucky resolutions, constituted the political creed of the State rights republican party. They were understood as being in full accord with Mr. Jefferson's opinion, who was its acknowledged head. They made a plain and direct issue with the principles and policy maintained by Gen. Hamilton—who, although not nominally the head of the federal party, as they called themselves, was its soul and spirit. The ensuing presidential election was contested on this issue, and terminated in the defeat of Mr. Adams, the election of Mr. Jefferson as President, and the elevation of the republican party into power. To the principles and doctrines, so plainly and ably set forth in their creed, they owed their elevation, and the long retention of power under many and severe trials. They secured the confidence of the people, because they were in accord with what they believed to be the true character of the constitution, and of our federal system of government.

Mr. Jefferson came into power with an earnest desire to reform the government. He certainly did a good deal in undoing what had been done; and in arresting the progress of the government towards consolidation. His election caused the repeal, in effect, of the alien and sedition laws, and a permanent acquiescence in their unconstitutionality. They constituted the prominent questions in the issue between the parties in the contest. He did much to reduce the expenses of the government, and made ample provisions for the payment of the public debt. He took strong positions against the bank of the United States, and laid the foundation for its final overthrow. Amidst great difficulties, he preserved the peace of the country during the period of his administration. But he did nothing to arrest many great and radical evils—nothing towards elevating the judicial departments of the governments of the several States, from a state of subordination to the judicial department of the government of the United States, to their rightful, constitutional position, as co-ordinates; nothing towards maintaining the rights of the States as parties to the constitutional compact, to judge, in the last resort, as to the extent of the delegated powers; nothing towards restoring to Congress the exclusive right to adopt measures necessary and proper to carry into execution, its own, as well as all other powers vested in the government, or in any of its departments; nothing towards reversing the order of Gen. Hamilton which united the government with the banks; and nothing effectual towards restricting the money power to objects specifically enumerated and delegated by the constitution.

Why Mr. Jefferson should have failed to undo, effectually, the consolidating, national policy of Gen. Hamilton, and to restore the government to its federal character, many reasons may be assigned. In the first place, the struggle which brought him into power, was too short to make any deep and lasting impression on the great body of the community. It lasted but two or three years, and the principal excitement, as far as constitutional questions were concerned, turned on the two laws which were the immediate cause of opposition. In the next, the state of the world was such as to turn the attention of the government, mainly, to what concerned the foreign relations of the Union, and to party contests growing out of them. To these it may be added, that Gen. Hamilton had laid the foundation of his policy so deep, and with so much skill, that it was difficult, if not impossible, to reverse it; at least, until time and experience should prove it to be destructive to the federal character of the government—inconsistent with the harmony and union of the States, and fatal to the liberty of the people. It is, indeed, even possible that, not even he—much less his cabinet and party generally—had a just and full conception of the danger, and the utter impracticability of some of the leading measures of his policy.

Not longer after the expiration of his term, his successor in the presidency, Mr. Madison, was forced into a war with Great Britain, after making

every effort to avoid it. This, of course, absorbed the attention of the
government and the country for the time, and arrested all efforts to carry
out the doctrines and policy which brought the party into power. It did
more; for the war, however just and necessary, gave a strong impulse
adverse to the federal, and favorable to the national line of policy. This is,
indeed, one of the unavoidable consequences of war; and can be counteracted, only by bringing into full action the negatives necessary to the
protection of the reserved powers. These would, of themselves, have the
effect of preventing wars, so long as they could be honorably and safely
avoided—and, when necessary, of arresting, to a great extent, the tendency of the government to transcend the limits of the constitution, during
its prosecution; and of correcting all departures, after its termination. It
was by force of the tribunitial power, that the plebeians retained, for so
long a period, their liberty, in the midst of so many wars.

How strong this impulse was, was not fully realized until after its termination. It left the country nearly without any currency, except irredeemable
bank notes—greatly depreciated, and of very different value in the different sections of the Union—which forced on the government the establishment of another national bank—the charter of the first having expired
without a renewal. This, and the embargo, with the other restrictive measures, which preceded it, had diverted a large portion of the capital of the
country from commerce and other pursuits to manufactures; which, in
time, produced a strong pressure in favor of a protective tariff. The great
increase, too, of the public expenditures of the government—in consequence of the war—required a corresponding increase of income; and this,
of course, increased, in the same proportion, its patronage and influence.
All these causes combined, could not fail to give a direction to the course
of government, adverse to the federal and favorable to the national policy—or, in other words, adverse to the principles and policy which brought
Mr. Jefferson and the republican party into power, and favorable to those
for which Mr. Adams and the federal party had contended.

In the mean time, the latter party was steadily undergoing the process of dissolution. It never recovered from the false step it took and the unwise course it pursued, during the war. It gradually lost its party organization; and even its name became extinct. But while this process was going on, the republican party, also, was undergoing a great change. It was gradually resolving itself into two parties; one of which was gradually departing from the State rights creed, and adopting the national. It rose into power, by electing the younger Adams, as the successor of Mr. Monroe, and took the name of the "National Republican party." It differed little, in doctrine or policy, from the old federal party; but, in tone and character, was much more popular—and much more disposed to court the favor of the people.

At the same time, the other portion of the party was undergoing a mutation, not less remarkable—and which finally led to a change of name. It took the title of the "Democratic party;" or—more emphatically—"the Democracy." The causes, which led to this change of name, began to operate before Mr. Monroe's administration expired. Indeed, with the end of his administration—the last of the line of Virginia Presidents—the old State rights party, ceased to exist as a party, after having held power for twenty-four years. The Democracy, certainly had much more affinity with it in feelings—but, as a party—especially its northern wing—had much less devotion to the reserved powers; and was much more inclined to regard mere numbers as the sole political element—and the numerical majority as entitled to the absolute right to govern. It was, also, much more inclined to adopt the national than the republican creed—as far as the money power of the government was concerned; and, to this extent, much more disposed to act with the advocates of the former, than the latter.

No state of things could be more adverse to carrying out the principles and policy which brought the old republican party into power, or to restoring those of the party, which they expelled from power—as events have proved. One of its first fruits was the passage of the act of 19th May, 1828, entitled, "An act in alteration of the several acts imposing duties on imports"—called, at the time, the "Bill of Abominations"—as it truly proved to be. It was passed by the joint support and vote of both parties—

National Republicans, and those who, afterwards, assumed the name of "the Democracy"—the southern wing of each excepted. The latter, indeed, took the lead both in its introduction and support.

All preceding acts imposing duties, which this purported to alter, had some reference to, and regard for revenue; however much the rate of duties might have been controlled by the desire to afford protection. But such was not the case with this. It was passed under such circumstances as conclusively proved that it was intended, wholly and exclusively for protection; without any view, whatever, to revenue. The public debt, including the remnant of that contracted in the war of the Revolution, and the whole of that incurred in the war of 1812, was on the eve of being finally discharged, under the operation of the effective sinking fund, established at the close of the latter. And so ample was the revenue, at the time, that fully one-half of the whole, was annually applied to the discharge of the principal and interest of the public debt—leaving an ample surplus, to meet the current expenses of the government on a liberal scale. It was clear, that under such circumstances, no increase of duties was required for revenue—so clear, indeed, that the advocates of the bill openly avowed that its object was protection, not revenue; although they refused to adopt an amendment, which proposed to declare its real object, in order that its constitutionality might be decided by the judicial department.

It was under such circumstances that this act was passed; which, instead of reducing the duties one-half (to take effect after the final discharge of the public debt) as, on every principle of revenue and justice—of fairness and of good faith, it ought to have done, doubled them. I say of justice, fairness, and good faith—because the duties were originally raised to meet the expenses of the war, and to discharge the public debt—with the understanding, that when these objects were effected, they would be reduced—and the burden they imposed on the tax-payers be lightened. Without this understanding, they could not have been raised.

As, then, the duties imposed by the act, were not intended for revenue—and as there is no power, specifically delegated to Congress, to lay duties except for revenue; it is obvious that it had no right to pass the bill, unless upon the principle contended for by General Hamilton—of applying the money power to accomplish whatever it might pronounce to be for the general welfare—not only by the direct appropriation of money, but by the imposition of duties and taxes. Indeed, there is no substantial difference between the two; for if Congress have the right to appropriate money, in the shape of bounties, to encourage manufactures—it may, for the same purpose, lay protective duties, to give the manufacturer a monopoly of the home market, and *vice versa*—and such, accordingly, was the opinion of General Hamilton.

But, although the authors of this act aimed at transferring the bounty it conferred, directly into the pockets of the manufacturers, without passing through the treasury, yet they contemplated, and were prepared to meet the contingency of its bringing into the treasury a sum beyond the wants of the government, when the public debt should be extinguished. Their scheme was, to distribute the surplus among the States—that is, to appropriate to the government of each State, a sum proportioned to its representation in Congress, as an addition to its annual revenue. They thus assumed, not only, that Congress had a right to impose duties to provide, for what it might deem the *general welfare*—but also, and at the same time, to appropriate the receipts derived from them to the States, respectively—to be applied to their *individual* and *local welfare*. This last measure was urged, again and again, on Congress, and would, in all probability have been adopted, had not the act, of which it was intended to have been a supplement, been arrested. A more extravagant and gross abuse of the money power can scarcely be conceived. Its consequences were as fatal as its violation of the constitution was outrageous and palpable. The vast surplus revenue, which it threw into the treasury notwithstanding its arrest, did much to corrupt both government and people; and was the principal cause of the explosion of the banking system in 1837; and the overthrow of the party in 1840, which took the lead in introducing and supporting it.

But these were not its only evil consequences. It led to another, and, if

possible, a deeper and more dangerous inroad on the principles and policy
which brought Mr. Jefferson and the old State rights party into power. The
act of the 3d March, 1833, already referred to—thoroughly subjecting the
judicial departments of the governments of the several States to the federal
judiciary, was introduced, expressly, to enforce this grossly unconstitutional and outrageous act. It received the support and votes—as did the
original act—both of the national and the democratic parties (a few excepted, who still adhered to the creed of the old State rights party), the
latter taking the lead and direction in both instances.

It was thus, from the identity of doctrine and of policy which distinguished both parties, in reference to the money power, that two of the most
prominent articles in the creed of the republican party, by force of which
Mr. Jefferson, as its leader, came into power, were set aside; and their
dangerous opposites, on account of which, Mr. Adams, as the head of the
federal party, was expelled, were brought into full and active operation—
namely—the right claimed by the latter for Congress, to pronounce upon
what appertains to the general welfare—and which is so forcibly condemned in the Virginia and Kentucky resolutions, and the report of Mr.
Madison—and the right of the federal judiciary to decide, in the last
resort, as to the extent of the reserved as well as of the delegated powers.
The one authorizes Congress to do as it pleases—and the other endows the
court with the power to enforce whatever it may do—if its authority should
be adequate—and if not, to call in the aid of the Executive with the entire
force of the country. Their joint effect is to give unlimited control to the
government of the United States, not only over those of the several States,
but over the States themselves; in utter subversion of the relation of co-
ordinates, and in total disregard of the rights of the several States, as
parties to the constitutional compact, to judge, in the last resort, as to the
extent of the powers delegated—a right so conclusively established by Mr.
Madison, in his report.

These measures greatly increased the power and patronage of the federal government; and with them, the desire to obtain its control; especially

of the executive department—which is invested mainly with the power of disposing of its honors and emoluments. As a necessary consequence of this, the presidential election became of more absorbing interest—the struggle between the two parties more and more intense—and every means which promised success was readily resorted to, without the least regard to their bearing, morally or politically. To secure the desired object, the concentration of party action and the stringency of party discipline were deemed indispensable. And hence, contemporaneously with these measures, party conventions were, for the first time, called to nominate the candidates for the presidency and vice-presidency—and party organization established all over the Union. And hence, also, for the first time, the power of removing from office, at the discretion of the President, so unconstitutionally conceded to him by the first Congress, was brought into active and systematic operation, as the means of rewarding partisan services, and of punishing party opposition or party delinquencies. In these measures the democratic party took the lead—but were soon followed by their opponents. There is, at present, no distinction between them in this respect. The effects of the whole have been, to supersede the provision of the constitution, as far as it relates to the election of President and Vice-President, as has been shown; to give a decided control over these elections to those who hold or seek office; to stake all the powers and emoluments of the government as prizes, to be won or lost by victory or defeat; and to make success in the election paramount to every other consideration.

But there is another cause that has greatly contributed to place the control of the presidential elections in the hands of those who hold or seek office. I allude, to what is called, the general ticket system; which has become, with the exception of a single State, the universal mode of appointing electors to choose the President and Vice-President. It was adopted to prevent a division of the vote of the several States, in the choice of their highest officers; and to make the election more popular, by giving it, as was professed to be its object, to the people. The former of these ends it has effected, but It has utterly failed as to the latter. It professes to give the people, individually, a right which it was impossible to exercise, except in the very smallest class of States, and even in these, very imperfectly. To call on a hundred thousand voters, scattered over fifty or sixty thousand square miles, to make out a ticket of a dozen or more electors, is to ask them to do that which, individually, they cannot properly or successfully do. Very few would have the information necessary to make a proper selection; and even if every voter had such information, the diversity of opinion and the want of concentration on the same persons, would be so great, that it would be a matter of mere accident, who would have the majority. To avoid this, a ticket must be formed by each party. But the few of each, who form the ticket, actually make the appointment of the electors; for the people individually, have no choice, but to vote for the one or the other ticket—or otherwise, virtually, to throw away their vote—for there would be no chance of success against the concentrated votes of the two parties. Never was there a scheme better contrived to transfer power from the body of the community, to those whose occupation is to get or hold offices, and to merge the contests of party into a mere struggle for the spoils.

It is due to the Democratic party to state that, while they took the lead, and are principally responsible for bringing about this state of things, they are entitled to the credit of putting down the Bank of the United States; of checking extravagant expenditures on internal improvements; of separating the government from the banks; and, more recently, of opposing protective tariffs; and of adopting the ad valorem principle in imposing duties on imports. These are all important measures; and indicate a disposition to take a stand against the perversion of the money power. But, until the measures which led to these mischiefs—and in the adoption of which they bore so prominent a part—are entirely reversed, nothing permanent will be gained.

In the meanwhile the sectional tendency of parties has been increasing with the central tendency of the government. They are, indeed, intimately connected. The more the powers of the system are centralized in the

federal government, the greater will be its power and patronage; proportionate with these, and increasing with their increase, will be the desire to
possess the control over them, for the purpose of aggrandizement; and the
stronger this desire, the less will be the regard for principles, and the
greater the tendency to unite for sectional objects—the stronger section
with a view to power and aggrandizement—the weaker, for defence and
safety. Any strongly marked diversity will be sufficient to draw the line; be
it diversity of pursuit, of origin, of character, of habits, or of local institutions. The latter, being more deeply and distinctly marked than any other
existing in the several States composing the Union, has, at all times, been
considered by the wise and patriotic, as a delicate point—and to be, with
great caution, touched. The dangers connected with this, began to exhibit
themselves in the old Congress of the confederation, in respect to the
North-Western Territory; and continued down to the time of the formation
of the present constitution. They constituted the principal difficulty in
forming it; but it was fortunately overcome, and adjusted to the satisfaction
of both parties.

For a long period, nothing occurred to disturb this happy state of things.
But in the session of 1819–20, a question arose that exposed the latent
danger. The admission of the territory of Missouri, as a State of the Union,
was resisted on the ground that its constitution did not prohibit slavery.
The contest, after a long and angry discussion, was finally adjusted by a
compromise, which admitted her as a slaveholding State, on condition that
slavery should be prohibited in all the territories belonging then to the
United States, lying north of 36°30′. This compromise was acquiesced in
by the people of the South; and the danger, apparently, and, as every one
supposed, permanently removed. Experience, however, has proved how
erroneous were their calculations. The disease lay deep. It touched a fanatical as well as a political cord. There were not a few in the northern portion
of the Union, who believed that slavery was a sin, as well as a great
political evil; and who remained quiet in reference to it, only because they
believed that it was beyond their control—and that they were in no way

responsible for it. So long as the government was regarded as a federal government with limited powers, this belief of the sinfulness of slavery remained in a dormant state—as it still does in reference to the institution in foreign countries; but when it was openly proclaimed, as it was by the passage of the act of 1833, that the government had the right to judge, in the last resort, of the extent of its powers; and to use the military and naval forces of the Union to carry its decisions into execution; and when its passage by the joint votes of both parties furnished a practical assertion of the right claimed in an outrageous case, the cord was touched which roused it into action. The effects were soon made visible. In two years thereafter, in 1835, a systematic movement was, for the first time, commenced to agitate the question of abolition, by flooding the southern States with documents calculated to produce discontent among the slaves—and Congress, with petitions to abolish slavery in the District of Columbia.

The agitation was, however, at first, confined comparatively to a few; and they obscure individuals without influence. The great mass of the people viewed it with aversion. But here again, the same measure which roused it into action, mainly contributed to keep alive the agitation, and ultimately to raise a party (consisting, at first, of a few fanatics) sufficiently numerous and powerful to exercise a controlling influence over the entire northern section of the Union. By the great increase of power and patronage which it conferred on the government, it contributed vastly to increase the concentration and intensity of party struggles, and to make the election of President the all absorbing question. The effect of this was, to induce both parties to seek the votes of every faction or combination by whose aid they might hope to succeed—flattering them in return, with the prospect of establishing the doctrines they professed, or of accomplishing the objects they desired. This state of things could not fail to give importance to any fanatical party, however small, which cared more for the object that united them, than for the success of either party; especially if it should be of a character to accord, in the abstract, with the feeling of that portion of the community generally. Each of the great parties, in order to secure their support, would, in turn, endeavor to conciliate them, by professing a great respect for them, and a disposition to aid in accomplishing the objects they wished to effect. This dangerous system of electioneering could not fail to increase the party, and to give it great additional strength; to be followed, of course, by an increased anxiety on the part of those who desired its aid, to conciliate its favor; thus keeping up the action and reaction of those fatal elements, from day to day—the one, rising in importance, as its influence extended over the section—the other sinking in subserviency to its principles and purposes.

In the mean time, the same causes must needs contribute, in the other section, to a state of things well calculated to aid this process. In proportion to the power and patronage of the government, would be the importance, to party success, of concentration and intensity in party struggles: and in proportion to these, the attachment and devotion to party, where the spoils are the paramount object. In the same proportion also, would be the unwillingness of the two wings of the respective parties, in the different sections, to separate, and their desire to hold together; and, of course, the disposition on the part of that in the weaker, to excuse and palliate the steps taken by their political associates in the stronger section, to conciliate the abolition party, in order to obtain its votes. Thus the section assaulted would be prevented from taking any decided stand to arrest the danger, while it might be safely and easily done—and seduced to postpone it, until it shall have acquired—as it already has done—a magnitude, almost, if not altogether, beyond the reach of means within the constitution. The difficulty and danger have been greatly increased, since the Missouri compromise; and the other sectional measures, in reference to the recently acquired territories, now in contemplation (should they succeed), will centralize the two majorities that constitute the elements of which the government of the United States is composed, permanently in the northern section; and thereby subject the southern, on this, and on all other questions, in which their feelings or interest may come in conflict, to its control.

Such has been the practical operation of the government, and such its effects. It remains to be considered, what will be the consequence? to what will the government of the numerical majority probably lead?

On this point, we are not without some experience. The present disturbed and dangerous state of things are its first fruits. It is the legitimate result of that long series of measures (of which the acts of the 19th of May, 1828, and the 3d of March, 1833, are the most prominent), by which the powers of the whole system have been concentrated, virtually, in the government of the United States; and thereby transformed it from its original federal character, into the government of the numerical majority. To these fatal measures are to be attributed the violence of party struggles—the total disregard of the provisions of the constitution in respect to the election of the President; the predominance of the honors and emoluments of the government over every other consideration; the rise and growth of the abolition agitation; the formation of geographical parties; and the alienation and hostile feelings between the two great sections of the Union. These are all the unavoidable consequences of the government of the numerical majority, in a country of such great extent, and with such diversity of institutions and interests as distinguish ours. They will continue, with increased and increasing aggregation, until the end comes. In a country of moderate extent, and with an executive department less powerfully constituted than in ours, this termination would be in appeal to force, to decide the contest between the two hostile parties; and in a monarchy, by the commander of the successful party becoming master of both, and of the whole community, as has been stated. But there is more uncertainty in a country of such extent as ours, and where the executive department is so powerfully constituted. The only thing that is certain is, that it cannot last. But whether it will end in a monarchy, or in disunion, is uncertain. In the one or the other it will, in all probability, terminate if not prevented; but in which, time alone can decide. There are powerful influences in operation—a part impelling it towards the one, and a part towards the other.

Among those impelling it towards monarchy, the two most prominent are, the national tendency of the numerical majority to terminate in that form of government; and the structure of the executive department of the government of the United States. The former has been fully explained in the preliminary discourse, and will be passed over with the single remark— that it will add great force to the impulse of the latter in the same direction. To understand the extent of this force will require some explanation.

The vast power and patronage of the department are vested in a single officer, the President of the United States. Among these powers, the most prominent, as far as it relates to the present subject, are those which appertain to the administration of the government; to the office of commander-in-chief of the army and navy of the United States; to the appointment of the officers of the government, with few exceptions; and to the removal of them at his pleasure—as his authority has been interpreted by Congress. These, and especially the latter, have made his election the great and absorbing object of party struggles; and on this the appeal to force will be made, whenever the violence of the struggle and the corruption of parties will no longer submit to the decision of the ballot box. To this end it must come, if the force impelling it in the other direction should not previously prevail. If it comes to this, it will be, in all probability, in a contested election; when the question will be, Which is the President? The incumbent—if he should be one of the candidates—or, if not, the candidate of the party in possession of power? or of the party endeavoring to obtain possession? On such an issue, the appeal to force would make the *candidate* of the successful party, master of the whole—and not the *commander*, as would be the case under different circumstances.

The contest would put an end, virtually, to the elective character of the department. The form of election might, for a time, be preserved; but the ballot box would be much less relied on for the decision, than the sword and bayonet. In time, even the form would cease, and the successor be appointed by the incumbent—and thus the absolute form of a popular, would end in the absolute form of a monarchical government. Scarcely a possibility would exist of forming a constitutional monarchy. There would be no material out of which it could be formed; and if formed, it would be too feeble, with such material as would constitute it, to hold in subjection a country of such great extent and population as ours must be.

Such will be the end to which the government, as it is now operating, must, in all probability, come, should the other alternative not occur, and nothing, in the mean time, be done to prevent it. It is idle to suppose that, operating as the system now does—with the increase of the country in extent, population and wealth, and the consequent increase of the power and patronage of the government, the head of the executive department can remain elective. The future is indeed, for the most part, uncertain; but there are causes in the political world as steady and fixed in their operation, as any in the physical; and among them are those, which, *subject to the above conditions,* will lead to the result stated.

Those impelling the government towards disunion are, also, very powerful. They consist chiefly of two; the one, arising from the great extent of the country—the other, from its division into separate States, having local institutions and interests. The former, under the operation of the numerical majority, has necessarily given to the two great parties, in their contest for the honors and emoluments of the government, a geographical character; for reasons which have been fully stated. This contest must finally settle down in a struggle on the part of the stronger section to obtain the permanent control; and on the part of the weaker to preserve its independence and equality as members of the Union. The conflict will thus become one between the States, occupying the different sections—that is, between organized bodies on both sides; each, in the event of separation, having the means of avoiding the confusion and anarchy, to which the parts would be subject without such organization. This would contribute much to increase the power of resistance on the part of the weaker section against the stronger, in possession of the government. With these great advantages and resources, it is hardly possible that the parties occupying the weaker section, would consent, quietly, under any circumstances, to sink down from independent and equal sovereignties, into a dependent and colonial condition—and still less so, under circumstances that would revolutionize them *internally*, and put their very existence, as a people, at stake. Never was there an issue between independent States that involved greater calamity to the conquered, than is involved in that between the States which compose the two sections of this Union. The condition of the weaker, should it sink from a state of independence and equality to one of dependence and subjection, would be more calamitous than ever before befell a civilized people. It is vain to think that, with such consequences before them, they will not resist; especially when resistance *may* save them, and cannot render their condition worse. That this will take place, unless the stronger section desists from its course, may be assumed as certain: and that—if forced to resist, the weaker section would prove successful, and the system end in disunion, is, to say the least, highly probable. But if it should fail, the great increase of power and patronage which must, in consequence, accrue to the government of the United States, would but render certain, and hasten the termination in the other alternative. So that, at all events, to the one, or to the other—to monarchy, or disunion it must come, if not prevented by strenuous and timely efforts. And this brings up the question—How is it to be prevented? How can these sad alternatives be averted?

For this purpose, it is indispensable that the government of the United States should be restored to its federal character. Nothing short of a perfect restoration, as it came from the hands of its framers, can avert them. It is folly to suppose that any popular government, except one strictly federal, in *practice*, as well as in *theory*, can last, over a country of such vast extent and diversity of interests and institutions. It would not be more irrational to suppose, that it could last, without the responsibility of the rulers to the ruled. The tendency of the former to oppress the latter, is not stronger than is the tendency of the more powerful section, to oppress the weaker. Nor is the right of suffrage more indispensable to enforce the responsibility of the rulers to the ruled, than a *federal organization*, to compel the parts to respect the rights of each other. It requires the united action of both to prevent the abuse of power and oppression, and to constitute, really and truly, a constitutional government. To supersede either, is to convert it *in fact*, whatever may be its *theory*, into an absolute government.

But it cannot be restored to its federal character without restoring the separate governments of the several States, and the States themselves, to their true position. From the latter the whole system emanated. They ordained and established all the parts; first, by their separate action, their respective State governments; and next, by their concurrent action, with the indispensable co-operation of their respective governments, they ordained and established a common government, as a supplement to their separate governments. The object was, to do that, by a *common agent*, which could not be as well done, or done at all, by their separate agencies. The relation, then, in which the States stand to the system, is that of the creator to the creature; and that, in which the two governments stand to each other, is of coequals and co-ordinates—as has been fully established—with the important difference, in this last respect, that the separate governments of the States were the first in the order of time, and that they exercised an active and indispensable agency in the creation of the common government of all the States; or, as it is styled, the government of the United States.

Such is their true position—a position, not only essential in *theory*, in the *formation* of a federal government—but to its *preservation* in *practice*. Without it, the system could not have been formed—and without it, it cannot be preserved. The supervision of the creating power is indispensable to the preservation of the created. But they no longer retain their true position. In the practical operation of the system, they have both been superseded and reduced to subordinate and dependent positions: and this, too, by the power last in the order of formation, and which was brought into existence, as auxiliary to the first—and through the aid of its active co-operation. It has assumed control over the whole—and thus a thorough revolution has been effected, the creature taking the place of the creator.

This must be reversed, and each restored to its true position, before the federal character of the government can be perfectly restored.

For this purpose the first and indispensable step is to repeal the 25th section of the Judiciary Act—the whole of the act of the 3d of March, 1833, and all other acts containing like provisions. These, by subjecting the judiciary of the States to the control of the federal judiciary, have subjected the separate governments of the several States, including all their departments and functionaries—and, thereby, the States themselves, to a subordinate and dependent condition. It is only by their repeal, that the former can be raised to their true relation as coequals and co-ordinates—and the latter can retain their high sovereign power of deciding, in the last resort, on the extent of the delegated powers, or of interposing to prevent their encroachment on the reserved powers. It is only by restoring these to their true position, that the government of the United States can be reduced to its true position, as the coequal and co-ordinate of the separate governments of the several States, and restricted to the discharge of those auxiliary functions assigned to it by the constitution.

But this indispensable and important step will have to be followed by several others, before the work of restoration will have been completed. One of the most important will be, the repeal of all acts by which the money power is carried beyond its constitutional limits, either in laying duties, or in making appropriations. The federal character of the government may be as effectually destroyed by encroaching on, and absorbing all the reserved powers, as by subjecting the governments of the several States themselves directly to its control. Either would make it, in fact, the sole and absolute power, and virtually, the government of the numerical majority. But of all the powers ever claimed for the government of the United States, that which invests Congress with the right to determine what objects belong to the general welfare—to use the money power in the form of laying duties and taxes, and to make appropriations for the purpose of promoting such as it may deem to be of this character, is the most encroaching and comprehensive. In civilized communities, money may be said to be the universal means, by which all the operations of governments are carried on. If, then, it be admitted, that the government of the United States has the right to decide, at its discretion, what is, and what is not for the common good of the country, and to lay duties and taxes, and to appropriate their proceeds to effect whatever it may determine to be for the common good, it would be difficult to assign any limits to its authority, or to prevent it from absorbing, finally, all the reserved powers, and thereby, destroying its federal character.

But still more must be done to complete the work of restoration. The executive department must be rigidly restricted within its assigned limits, by divesting the President of all discretionary powers, and confining him strictly to those expressly conferred on him by the constitution and the acts of Congress. According to the express provisions of the former, he cannot rightfully exercise any other. Nor can he be permitted to go beyond, and to assume the exercise of whatever power he may deem necessary to carry those vested in him into execution, without finally absorbing all the powers vested in the other departments and making himself absolute. Having the disposal of the patronage of the government, and the command of all its forces, and standing at the head of the dominant party for the time, he will be able, in the event of a contest between him and either of the other departments, as to the extent of their respective powers, to make good his own, against its construction.

There is still another step, connected with this, which will be necessary to complete the work of restoration. The provisions of the constitution in reference to the election of the President and Vice-President, which has been superseded in *practice*, must be restored. The virtual repeal of this provision, as already stated, has resulted in placing the control of their election in the hands of the leaders of the office-seekers and office-holders; and this, with the unrestricted power of removal from office, and the vast patronage of the government, has made their election the all absorbing question; and the possession of the honors and emoluments of the government, the paramount objects in the Presidential contest. The effect has been, to increase vastly the authority of the President, and to enable him to extend his powers with impunity, under color of the right conceded him, against the express provision of the constitution, of deciding what means are necessary to carry into execution the powers vested in him. The first step in the enlargement of his authority, was to pervert the power of removal (the intent of which was, to enable him to supply the place of an incompetent or an unworthy officer, with the view of better administering the laws) into an instrument for punishing opponents and rewarding partisans. This has been followed up by other acts, which have greatly changed the relative powers of the departments, by increasing those of the executive. Even the power of making war—and the unlimited control over all conquests, during its continuance, have, it is to be apprehended, passed from Congress into the hands of the President. His powers, in consequence of all this, have accumulated to a degree little consistent with those of a chief magistrate of a federal republic; and hence, the necessity for reducing them within their strict constitutional limits, and restoring the provisions of the constitution in reference to his election, in order to restore the government completely to its federal character. Experience may, perhaps, prove, that the provisions of the constitution in this respect are imperfect—that they are too complicated and refined for practice; and that a radical change is necessary in the organization of the executive department. If such should prove to be the case, the proper remedy would be, not to supersede them in practice, as has been done, but to apply to the power which has been provided to correct all its defects and disorders.

But the restoration of the government to its federal character, however entire and perfect it may be—will not, of itself, be sufficient to avert the evil alternatives—to the one or the other of which it must tend, as it is now operating. Had its federal character been rigidly maintained in practice from the first, it would have been all sufficient, in itself, to have secured the country against the dangerous condition in which it is now placed, in consequence of a departure from it. But the means which may be sufficient to *prevent* diseases, are not usually sufficient to *remedy* them. In slight cases of recent date, they may be—but additional means are necessary to restore health, when the system has been long and deeply disordered. Such, at present, is the condition of our political system. The very causes which have occasioned its disorders, have, at the same time, led to consequences, not to be removed by the means which would have prevented them. They have destroyed the equilibrium between the two great sections, and alienated that mutual attachment between them, which led to the formation of the Union, and the establishment of a common government for the promotion of the welfare of all.

When the government of the United States was established, the two sections were nearly equal in respect to the two elements of which it is composed; a fact which, doubtless, had much influence, in determining the convention to select them as the basis of its construction. Since then, their equality in reference to both, has been destroyed, mainly through the action of the government established for their mutual benefit. The first step towards it occurred under the old Congress of the confederation. It was among its last acts. It took place while the convention, which formed the present constitution and government, was in session, and may be regarded as contemporaneous with it. I refer to the ordinance of 1787; which, among other things, contained a provision excluding slavery from the North-Western Territory; that is, from the whole region lying between the Ohio and Mississippi rivers. The effect of this was, to restrict the Southern States, in that quarter, to the country lying south of it; and to extend the Northern over the whole of that great and fertile region. It was literally to restrict the one and extend the other; for the whole territory belonged to Virginia, the leading State of the former section. She, with a disinterested patriotism rarely equalled, ceded the whole, gratuitously, to the Union— with the exception of a very limited portion, reserved for the payment of her officers and soldiers, for services rendered in the war of the revolution. The South received no equivalent for this magnificent cession, except a pledge inserted in the ordinance, similar to that contained in the constitution of the United States, to deliver up fugitive slaves. It is probable that there was an understanding among the parties, that it should be inserted in both instruments—as the old Congress and the convention were then in session in the same place; and that it contributed much to induce the southern members of the former to agree to the ordinance. But be this as it may, both, in practice, have turned out equally worthless. Neither have, for many years, been respected. Indeed, the act itself was unauthorized. The articles of confederation conferred not a shadow of authority on Congress to pass the ordinance—as is admitted by Mr. Madison; and yet this unauthorized, one-sided act (as it has turned out to be), passed in the last moments of the old confederacy, was relied on, as a precedent, for excluding the South from two-thirds of the territory acquired from France by the Louisiana treaty, and the whole of the Oregon territory; and is now relied on to justify her exclusion from all the territory acquired by the Mexican war—and all that may be acquired—in any manner, hereafter. The territory from which she has already been excluded, has had the effect to destroy the equilibrium between the sections as it originally stood; and to concentrate, permanently, in the northern section the two majorities of which the government of the United States is composed. Should she be excluded from the territory acquired from Mexico, it will give to the Northern States an overwhelming preponderance in the government.

In the mean time the spirit of fanaticism, which had been long lying dormant, was roused into action by the course of the government—as has been explained. It aims, openly and directly, at destroying the existing relations between the races in the southern section; on which depend its peace, prosperity and safety. To effect this, exclusion from the territories is an important step; and, hence, the union between the abolitionists and the advocates of exclusion, to effect objects so intimately connected.

All this has brought about a state of things hostile to the continuance of the Union, and the duration of the government. Alienation is succeeding to attachment, and hostile feelings to alienation; and these, in turn, will be followed by revolution, or a disruption of the Union, unless timely prevented. But this cannot be done by restoring the government to its federal character—however necessary that may be as a first step. What has been done cannot be undone. The equilibrium between the two sections has been permanently destroyed by the measures above stated. The northern section, in consequence, will ever concentrate within itself the two majorities of which the government is composed; and should the southern be excluded from all territories, now acquired, or to be hereafter acquired, it will soon have so decided a preponderance in the government and the Union, as to be able to mould the constitution to its pleasure. Against this, the restoration of the federal character of the government can furnish no remedy. So long as it continues, there can be no safety for the weaker section. It places in the hands of the stronger and hostile section, the power to crush her and her institutions; and leaves her no alternative, but to resist, or sink down into a colonial condition. This must be the consequence, if some effectual and appropriate remedy be not applied.

The nature of the disease is such, that nothing can reach it, short of some organic change—a change which shall so modify the constitution, as to give to the weaker section, in some form or another, a negative on the action of the government. Nothing short of this can protect the weaker, and restore harmony and tranquillity to the Union, by arresting, effectually, the tendency of the dominant and stronger section to oppress the weaker. When the constitution was formed, the impression was strong, that the tendency to conflict would be between the larger and smaller States; and effectual provisions were, accordingly, made to guard against it. But experience has proved this to have been a mistake; and that, instead of being, as was then supposed, the conflict is between the two great sections, which are so strongly distinguished by their institutions, geographical character, productions and pursuits. Had this been then as clearly perceived as it now is, the same jealousy which so vigilantly watched and guarded against the danger of the larger States oppressing the smaller, would have taken equal precaution to guard against the same danger between the two sections. It is for us, who see and feel it, to do, what the framers of the constitution would have done, had they possessed the knowledge, in this respect, which experience has given to us—that is—provide against the dangers which the system has practically developed; and which, had they been foreseen at the time, and left without guard, would undoubtedly have prevented the States, forming the southern section of the confederacy, from ever agreeing to the constitution; and which, under like circumstances, were they now out of, would forever prevent them from entering into, the Union.

How the constitution could best be modified, so as to effect the object, can only be authoritatively determined by the amending power. It may be done in various ways. Among others, it might be effected through a reorganization of the executive department; so that its powers, instead of being vested, as they now are, in a single officer, should be vested in two—to be so elected, as that the two should be constituted the special organs and representatives of the respective sections, in the executive department of the government; and requiring each to approve all the acts of Congress before they shall become laws. One might be charged with the administration of matters connected with the foreign relations of the country—and the other, of such as were connected with its domestic institutions; the selection to be decided by lot. It would thus effect, more simply, what was intended by the original provisions of the constitution, in giving to one of the majorities composing the government, a decided preponderance in the electoral college—and to the other majority a still more decided influence in the eventual choice—in case the college failed to elect a President. It was intended to effect an equilibrium between the larger and smaller States in this department—but which, in practice, has entirely failed; and, by its failure, done much to disturb the whole system, and to bring about the present dangerous state of things.

Indeed, it may be doubted, whether the framers of the constitution did not commit a great mistake, in constituting a single, instead of a plural executive. Nay, it may even be doubted whether a single chief magistrate—invested with all the powers properly appertaining to the executive department of the government, as is the President—is compatible with the

permanence of a popular government; especially in a wealthy and populous community, with a large revenue and a numerous body of officers and
employees. Certain it is, that there is no instance of a popular government
so constituted, which has long endured. Even ours, thus far, furnishes no
evidence in its favor, and not a little against it; for, to it, the present
disturbed and dangerous state of things, which threatens the country with
monarchy, or disunion, may be justly attributed. On the other hand, the
two most distinguished constitutional governments of antiquity, both in
respect to permanence and power, had a dual executive. I refer to those of
Sparta and of Rome. The former had two hereditary, and the latter two
elective chief magistrates. It is true, that England, from which ours, in this
respect, is copied, has a single hereditary head of the executive department
of her government—but it is not less true, that she has had many and
arduous struggles, to prevent her chief magistrate from becoming absolute;
and that, to guard against it effectually, she was finally compelled to divest
him, substantially, of the power of administering the government, by transferring it, practically, to a cabinet of responsible ministers, who, by established custom, cannot hold office, unless supported by a majority of the
two houses of Parliament. She has thus avoided the danger of the chief
magistrate becoming absolute; and contrived to unite, substantially, a single with a plural executive, in constituting that department of her government. We have no such guard, and can have none such, without an entire
change in the character of our government; and her example, of course,
furnishes no evidence in favor of a single chief magistrate in a popular
form of government like ours—while the examples of former times, and
our own thus far, furnish strong evidence against it.

But it is objected that a plural executive necessarily leads to intrigue and
discord among its members; and that it is inconsistent with prompt and
efficient action. This may be true, when they are all elected by the same
constituency; and may be a good reason, where this is the case, for prefer-
ring a single executive, with all its objections, to a plural executive. But the
case is very different where they are elected by different constituencies—

having conflicting and hostile interests; as would be the fact in the case under consideration. Here the two would have to act, concurringly, in approving the acts of Congress—and, separately, in the sphere of their respective departments. The effect, in the latter case, would be, to retain all the advantages of a single executive, as far as the administration of the laws were concerned; and, in the former, to insure harmony and concord between the two sections, and, through them, in the government. For as no act of Congress could become a law without the assent of the chief magistrates representing both sections, each, in the elections, would choose the candidate, who, in addition to being faithful to its interests, would best command the esteem and confidence of the other section. And thus, the presidential election, instead of dividing the Union into hostile geographical parties, the stronger struggling to enlarge its powers, and the weaker to defend its rights—as is now the case—would become the means of restoring harmony and concord to the country and the government. It would make the Union a union in truth—a bond of mutual affection and brotherhood—and not a mere connection used by the stronger as the instrument of dominion and aggrandizement—and submitted to by the weaker only from the lingering remains of former attachment, and the fading hope of being able to restore the government to what it was originally intended to be, a blessing to all.

Such is the disease—and such the character of the only remedy which can reach it. In conclusion, there remains to be considered, the practical question—Shall it be applied? Shall the only power which can apply it be invoked for the purpose?

The responsibility of answering this solemn question, rests on the States composing the stronger section. Those of the weaker are in a minority, both of the States and of population; and, of consequence, in every department of the government. They, then, cannot be responsible for an act which requires the concurrence of two-thirds of both houses of Congress, or two-thirds of the States to originate, and three-fourths of the latter to consummate. With such difficulties in their way, the States of the weaker section can do nothing, however disposed, to save the Union and the government, without the aid and co-operation of the States composing the stronger section: but with their aid and co-operation both may be saved. On the latter, therefore, rests the responsibility of invoking the high power, which alone can apply the remedy—and, if they fail to do so, of all the consequences which may follow.

Having now finished what I proposed to say on the constitution and government of the United States, I shall conclude with a few remarks relative to the constitution and governments of the individual States. Standing, as they do, in the relation of co-ordinates with the constitution and government of the United States, whatever may contribute to derange and disorder the one, must, necessarily contribute, more or less, to derange and disorder the other; and, thus, the whole system. And hence the importance—viewed simply in reference to the government of the United States, without taking into consideration those of the several States—that the individual governments of each, as well as the united government of all, should assume and preserve the constitutional, instead of the absolute form of popular government—that of the concurrent, instead of the numerical majority.

It is much more difficult to give to the government of the States, this constitutional form, than to the government of the United States; for the same reason that it is more easy to form a constitutional government for a community divided into classes or orders, than for one purely popular. Artificial distinctions of every description, be they of States or Estates, are more simple and strongly marked than the numerous and blended natural distinctions of a community purely popular. But difficult as it is to form such constitutional governments for the separate States, it may be affected by making the several departments, as far as it may be necessary, the organs of the more strongly marked interests of the State, from whatever causes they may have been produced—and by such other devices, whereby the sense of the State may be taken by its parts, and not as a whole—by the concurrent, and not by the numerical majority. It is only by the former that it can be truly taken. Indeed, the numerical majority often fails to accomplish that at which it professes to aim—to take truly the sense of the majority. It assumes, that by assigning to every part of the State a representative in every department of its government, in proportion to its population, it secures to each a weight in the government, in exact proportion to its population, under all circumstances. But such is not the fact. The relative weight of population depends as much on circumstances, as on numbers. The concentrated population of cities, for example, would ever have, under such a distribution, far more weight in the government, than the same number in the scattered and sparse population of the country. One hundred thousand individuals concentrated in a city two miles square, would have much more influence than the same number scattered over two hundred miles square. Concert of action and combination of means would be easy in the one, and almost impossible in the other; not to take into the estimate, the great control that cities have over the press, the great organ of public opinion. To distribute power, then, in proportion to population, would be, in fact, to give the control of the government, in the end, to the cities; and to subject the rural and agricultural population to that description of population which usually congregate in them—and ultimately, to the dregs of their population. This can only be counteracted by such a distribution of power as would give to the rural and agricultural population, in some one of the two legislative bodies or departments of the government, a decided preponderance. And this may be done, in most cases, by allotting an equal number of members in one of the legislative bodies to each election district; as a majority of the counties or election districts will usually have a decided majority of its population engaged in agricultural or other rural pursuits. If this should not be sufficient, in itself, to establish an equilibrium—a maximum of representation might be established, beyond which the number allotted to each election district or city should never extend.

Other means of a similar character might be adopted, by which, the different and strongly marked interests of the States—especially those resulting from geographical features, or the diversity of pursuits, might be prevented from coming into conflict, and the one secured against the control of the other. By these, and other contrivances suited to the peculiar condition of a State, its government might be made to assume the character of that of a concurrent majority, and have all the tranquillity and stability belonging to such a form of government; and thereby avoid the disorder and anarchy in which the government of the numerical majority must ever end. While the government of the United States continues, it will, indeed, require a much less perfect government on the part of a State, to protect it from the evils to which an imperfectly organized government would expose it, than if it formed a separate and independent community. The reason is, that the States, as members of a Union, bound to defend each other against all external dangers and domestic violence, are relieved from the necessity of collecting and disbursing large amounts of revenue, which otherwise would be required; and are, thereby, relieved from that increased tendency to conflict and disorder which ever accompanies an increase of revenue and expenditures. In order to give a practical illustration of the mode in which a State government may be organized, on the principle of the concurrent majority, I shall, in concluding this discourse, give a brief account of the constitution and government of the State of South Carolina.

Its government, like that of all the other States, is divided into three departments—the Legislative, Executive, and Judicial. Its executive powers, as in all the others, are vested in a single chief magistrate. He is elected by the legislature, holds his office for two years, and is not again eligible for two years after the expiration of the term for which he was elected. His powers and patronage are very limited. The judges are, also, appointed by the legislature. They hold their office during good behavior. The legislative department is, like that of all the other States, divided into two bodies, the Senate and the House of Representatives. The members of the former are divided into two classes, of which the term of one expires every other year. The members of the House are elected for two years. The two are called, when convened, the General Assembly. In addition to the usual and appropriate power of legislative bodies, it appoints all the important officers of the State. The local officers are elected by the people of the respective districts (counties) to which they belong. The right of suffrage, with few and inconsiderable exceptions, is universal. No convention of the people can be called, but by the concurrence of two-thirds of both houses—that is—two-thirds, respectively, of the entire representative body. Nor can the constitution be amended, except by an act of the General Assembly, passed by two-thirds of both bodies of the whole representation; and passed again, in like manner, at the first session of the assembly immediately following the next election of the members of the House of Representatives. But that which is peculiar to its constitution, and which distinguishes it from those of all the other States, is, the principle on which power is distributed among the different portions of the State. It is this, indeed, which makes the constitution, in contradistinction to the government. The elements, according to which power is distributed, are taxation, property, and election districts. In order to understand why they were adopted, and how the distribution has affected the operations of government, it will be necessary to give a brief sketch of the political history of the State.

The State was first settled, on the coast, by emigrants from England and France. Charleston became the principal town; and to it the whole political power of the colony, was exclusively confined, during the government of the Lords Proprietors—although its population was spread over the whole length of its coast, and to a considerable distance inland, and the region occupied by the settlements, organized into parishes. The government of these was overthrown by the people, and the colony became a dependent on the Crown. The right of electing members to the popular branch of the legislature, was extended to the parishes. Under the more powerful protection of the Crown, the colony greatly increased, and extended still further inland, towards the falls of the great rivers—carrying with them the same organization.

About the middle of the last century, a current of population flowed in from New Jersey, Pennsylvania, Maryland, Virginia, and North Carolina, to the region extending from the falls of the rivers to the mountains—now known as the upper country, in contradistinction to the section lying below. Between the two settlements there was a wide unsettled space; and for a considerable length of time no political connection, and little intercourse existed between them. The upper country had no representation in the government, and no political existence as a constituent portion of the State, until a period near the commencement of the revolution. Indeed during the revolution, and until the formation of the present constitution, in 1790, its political weight was scarcely felt in the government. Even then, although it had become the most populous section, power was so distributed under the new constitution, as to leave it in a minority in every department of the government.

Such a state of things could not long continue without leading to discontent. Accordingly, a spirited movement or agitation commenced openly in 1794, the object of which was to secure a weight in the government, proportional to its population. Once commenced, it continued to increase with the growing population of that section, until its violence, and the distraction and disorder which it occasioned, convinced the reflecting portion of both sections, that the time had arrived when a vigorous effort should be made to bring it to a close. For this purpose, a successful attempt was made in the session of 1807. The lower section was wise and patriotic enough to propose an adjustment of the controversy, by giving to each an equal participation in the government; and the upper section, as wisely and patriotically, waived its claims, and accepted the compromise. To carry it into execution, an act was passed during the session to amend the constitution, according to the form it prescribes; and again passed, in like manner, during the ensuing session— an intervening election of the members of the House of Representatives having taken place—and, thereby, became a part of the constitution as it now stands. The object intended to be effected will explain the provisions of the amendment; and why it was necessary to incorporate in the constitution the three elements above stated.

To effect this, the Senate, which consists of one member from each election district, except Charleston, which has two (one for each of its two parishes), remained unchanged. This, in consequence of the organization of the lower district into parishes, and these again into election districts, gave the lower section a decided preponderance in that branch of the legislature. To give the upper section a like preponderance in the House of Representatives, it became necessary to remodel it. For this purpose, there were assigned to this branch of the legislature, one hundred and twenty-four members—of which sixty-two were allotted to white population, and sixty-two to taxation; to be distributed according to the election districts—giving to each the number it would be entitled to under the combined ratios of the two elements. To ascertain this proportion, from time to time, a census of the population was ordered to be taken every ten years, and a calculation made, at the same time, of the amount of the tax paid by each election district during the last ten years; in order to furnish the data on which to make the distribution. These gave to the upper section a preponderance, equally decisive, in the House of Representatives. And thus an equilibrium was established between the two sections in the legislative department of the government; and, as the governor, judges, and all the important officers under the government are appointed by the legislature—an equilibrium in every department of the government. By making the election districts the element of which one branch of the legislature is constituted, it protects the agricultural and rural interests against the preponderance, which, in time, the concentrated city population might otherwise acquire—and by making taxation one of the elements of which the other branch is composed, it guards effectually against the abuse of the taxing power. The effect of such abuse would be, to give to the portion of the State which might be overtaxed, an increased weight in the government proportional to the excess—and to diminish, in the same proportion, the weight of the section which might exempt itself from an equal share of the burden of taxation.

The results which followed the introduction of these elements into the

constitution, in the manner stated, were most happy. The government—
instead of being, as it was under the constitution of 1790, the government
of the lower section—or becoming, subsequently, as it must have become,
the government of the upper section, had numbers constituted the only
element—was converted into that of the concurrent majority, and made,
emphatically, the government of the entire population—of the whole people of South Carolina—and not of one portion of its people over another
portion. The consequence was, the almost instantaneous restoration of
harmony and concord between the two sections. Party division and party
violence, with the distraction and disorder attendant upon them, soon dis-
appeared. Kind feelings, and mutual attachment between the two sections,
took their place—and have continued uninterrupted for more than forty
years. The State, as far as its internal affairs are concerned, may be
literally said to have been, during the whole period, without a party. Party
organization, party discipline, party proscription—and their offspring, *the
spoils principle*, have been unknown to the State. Nothing of the kind is
necessary to produce concentration; as our happy constitution makes an
united people—with the exception of occasional, but short local dissen-
sions, in reference to the action of the federal government—and even the
most violent of these ceased, almost instantly, with the occasion which
produced it.

Such are the happy fruits of a wisely constituted Republic—and such
are some of the means by which it may be organized and established.
Ours, like all other well-constituted constitutional governments, is the offspring of a conflict, timely and wisely compromised. May its success, as an
example, lead to its imitation by others—until our whole system—the
united government of all the States, as well as the individual governments
of each—shall settle down in like concord and harmony.

THE END

SPEECH ON THE RESOLUTION
OF THE COMMITTEE ON
FOREIGN RELATIONS

[December 12, 1811]

———•———

On November 29, 1811, the Committee on Foreign Relations submitted its report on the deteriorating relations between Britain and the United States and recommended several resolutions relating to American foreign policy. Much of the House debate focused upon the second of these resolutions:

> *2. Resolved, That an additional force of ten thousand regular troops ought to be immediately raised to serve for three years; and that a bounty in lands ought to be given to encourage enlistments.* *

John Randolph of Virginia, an established member of the House and well known for his scintillating and discursive eloquence, had condemned the report on a number of grounds, including the dangers of a standing army and the impropriety of aiding the despotism of Napoleon Bonaparte. In his first major speech as a member of Congress, Calhoun took upon himself the task of responding to the arguments of the gentleman from Roanoke—the first of many disagreements with an opponent for whom Calhoun would come to develop the most intense admiration. In spite of his protestations about the embarrassment of a young man addressing such an audience for the first time and his wish that the task of defending this important task

---

Annals of the Congress of the United States, First Session, 1853, Washington: Gales and Seaton, p. 377.

had fallen to abler hands, Calhoun's address not only established his repu-
tation as an ardent nationalist, but also adumbrated the extraordinary
powers of rhetoric and analysis that would mark his later public career.

MR. SPEAKER: I understood the opinion of the Committee on Foreign Relations differently from what the gentleman from Virginia (Mr. Randolph) has stated to be his impression. I certainly understood that the committee recommended the measures now before the House, as a preparation for war; and such, in fact, was its express resolve, agreed to, I believe, by every member, except that gentleman. I do not attribute any wilful misstatement to him, but consider it the effect of inadvertency or mistake. Indeed, the Report could mean nothing but war or empty menace. I hope no member of this House is in favor of the latter. A bullying, menacing system, has everything to condemn and nothing to recommend it. In expense, it almost rivals war. It excites contempt abroad, and destroys confidence at home. Menaces are serious things; and ought to be resorted to with as much caution and seriousness as war itself; and should, if not successful, be invariably followed by it. It was not the gentleman from Tennessee (Mr. Grundy) who made this a war question. The resolve contemplates an additional regular force; a measure confessedly improper but as a preparation for war, but undoubtedly necessary in that event.

Sir, I am not insensible to the weighty importance of the proposition, for the first time submitted to this House, to compel a redress of our long list of complaints against one of the belligerents. According to my mode of thinking on this subject, the more serious the question, the stronger and more unalterable ought to be our convictions before we give it our support.

War, in our country, ought never to be resorted to but when it is clearly justifiable and necessary; so much so, as not to require the aid of logic to convince our understandings, nor the ardor of eloquence to inflame our passions. There are many reasons why this country should never resort to war but for causes the most urgent and necessary. It is sufficient that, under a government like ours, none but such will justify it in the eyes of the people; and were I not satisfied that such is the present case, I certainly would be no advocate of the proposition now before the House.

Sir, I might prove the war, should it ensue, justifiable, by the express admission of the gentleman from Virginia—and necessary, by facts undoubted, and universally admitted; such as he did not pretend to controvert. The extent, duration, and character of the injuries received; the failure of those peaceful means heretofore resorted to for the redress of our wrongs, my proof that it is necessary. Why should I mention the impressment of our seamen; depredations on every branch of our commerce, including the direct export trade, continued for years, and made under laws which professedly undertake to regulate our trade with other nations; negotiation resorted to, again and again, till it is become hopeless; the restrictive system persisted in to avoid war, and in the vain expectation of returning justice? The evil still grows, and, in each succeeding year, swells in extent and pretension beyond the preceding. The question, even in the opinion and by the admission of our opponents is reduced to this single point—Which shall we do, abandon or defend our own commercial and maritime rights, and the personal liberties of our citizens employed in exercising them? These rights are vitally attacked, and war is the only means of redress. The gentleman from Virginia has suggested none—unless we consider the whole of his speech as recommending patient and resigned submission as the best remedy. Sir, which alternative this House will embrace, it is not for me to say. I hope the decision is made already, by a higher authority than the voice of any man. It is not for the human tongue to instil the sense of independence and honor. This is the work of nature; a generous nature that disdains tame submission to wrongs.

This part of the subject is so imposing as to enforce silence even on the gentleman from Virginia. He dared not deny his country's wrongs, or vindicate the conduct of her enemy.

Only one part of that gentleman's argument had any, the most remote relation to this point. He would not say, we had not a good cause for war; but insisted, that it was our duty to define that cause. If he means that this House ought, at this stage of its proceedings, or any other, to specify any particular violation of our rights to the exclusion of all others, he prescribes a course, which neither good sense nor the usage of nations warrants. When we contend, let us contend for all our rights; the doubtful and the certain; the unimportant and essential. It is as easy to struggle, or even more so, for the whole as for a part. At the termination of the contest, secure all that our wisdom and valor and the fortune of the war will permit. This is the dictate of common sense; such also is the usage of nations. The single instance alluded to, the endeavor of Mr. Fox to compel Mr. Pitt to define the object of the war against France, will not support the gentleman from Virginia in his position. That was an extraordinary war for an extraordinary purpose, and could not be governed by the usual rules. It was not for conquest, or for redress of injury, but to impose a government on France, which she refused to receive; an object so detestable that an avowal dared not be made.

Sir, I might here rest the question. The affirmative of the proposition is established. I cannot but advert, however, to the complaint of the gentleman from Virginia when he was first up on this question. He said he found himself reduced to the necessity of supporting the negative side of the question, before the affirmative was established. Let me tell the gentleman, that there is no hardship in his case. It is not every affirmative that ought to be proved. Were I to affirm, that the House is now in session, would it be reasonable to ask for proof? He who would deny its truth, on him would be the proof of so extraordinary a negative. How then could the gentleman, after his admissions, with the facts before him and the country, complain? The causes are such as to warrant, or rather make it indispensable, in any nation not absolutely dependent, to defend its rights by force. Let him, then, show the reasons why we ought not so to defend ourselves. On him lies the burden of proof. This he has attempted; he has endeavored to support his negative. Before I proceed to answer him particularly, let me call the attention of the House to one circumstance; that is—that almost the whole of his arguments consisted of an enumeration of evils always incident to war, however just and necessary; and which, if they have any force, are calculated to produce unqualified submission to every species of insult and injury. I do not feel myself bound to answer arguments of this description; and if I should touch on them, it will be only incidentally, and not for the purpose of serious refutation.

The first argument of the gentleman which I shall notice, is the unprepared state of the country. Whatever weight this argument might have in a question of immediate war, it surely has little in that of preparation for it. If our country is unprepared, let us remedy the evil as soon as possible. Let the gentleman submit his plan; and if a reasonable one, I doubt not it will be supported by the House. But, Sir, let us admit the fact and the whole force of the argument. I ask whose is the fault? Who has been a member, for many years past, and seen the defenceless state of his country even near home, under his own eyes, without a single endeavor to remedy so serious an evil? Let him not say, "I have acted in a minority." It is no less the duty of the minority than a majority to endeavor to defend the country. For that purpose we are sent here, and not for that of opposition.

We are next told of the expenses of the war; and that the people will not pay taxes. Why not? Is it from want of means? What, with 1,000,000, tons of shipping; a commerce of $100,000,000 annually; manufactures yielding a yearly product of $150,000,000; and agriculture of thrice that amount, shall we be told the country wants capacity to raise and support ten thousand or fifteen thousand additional regulars? No; it has the ability; that is admitted; and will it not have the disposition? Is not the cause a just and necessary one? Shall we then utter this libel on the people? Where will proof be found of a fact so disgraceful? It is answered—in the history of the country twelve or fifteen years ago. The case is not parallel. The ability of the country is greatly increased since. The whiskey-tax was unpopular. But on this, as well as my memory serves me—the objection was not to the tax or its amount, but the mode of collection. The people were startled by the number of officers; their love of liberty shocked with the multiplicity of regulations. We, in the vile spirit of imitation, copied from the most oppressive part of European laws on the subject of taxes, and imposed on a young and virtuous people all the severe provisions made necessary by corruption and long-practised evasions. If taxes should become necessary, I do not hesitate to say the people will pay cheerfully. It is for their government and their cause, and it would be their interest and their duty to pay. But it may be, and I believe was said, that the people will not pay taxes, because the rights violated are not worth defending; or that the defence will cost more than the gain. Sir, I here enter my solemn protest against this low and "calculating avarice" entering this hall of legislation. It is only fit for shops and counting-houses; and ought not to disgrace the seat of sovereignty by its squalid and vile appearance. Whenever it touches sovereign power, the nation is ruined. It is too short-sighted to defend itself. It is a compromising spirit, always ready to yield a part to save the residue. It is too timid to have in itself the laws of self-preservation. It is never safe but under the shield of honor. There is, Sir, one principle necessary to make us a great people—to produce not the form, but real spirit of union—and that is, to protect every citizen in the lawful pursuit of his business. He will then feel that he is backed by the government—that its arm is his arms; and will rejoice in its increased strength and prosperity. Protection and patriotism are reciprocal. This is the way which has led nations to greatness. Sir, I am not versed in this calculating policy; and will not, therefore, pretend to estimate in dollars and cents the value of national independence, or national affection. I cannot measure in shillings and pence the misery, the stripes, and the slavery of our impressed seamen; nor even the value of our shipping, commercial and agricultural losses, under the orders in council, and the British system of blockade. In thus expressing myself, I do not intend to condemn any prudent estimate of the means of a country, before it enters on a war. This is wisdom—the other folly.

The gentleman from Virginia has not failed to touch on the calamity of war, that fruitful source of declamation by which humanity is made the advocate of submission. If he desires to repress the gallant ardor of our countrymen by such topics, let me inform him, that true courage regards only the cause, that it is just and necessary; and that it contemns the sufferings and dangers of war. If he really wishes to promote the cause of humanity, let his eloquence be addressed to Lord Wellesley or Mr. Percival, and not the American Congress. Tell them if they persist in such daring insult and injury to a neutral nation, that, however inclined to peace, it will be bound in honor and safety to resist; that their patience and endurance, however great, will be exhausted; that the calamity of war will ensue, and that they, in the opinion of the world, will be answerable for all its devastation and misery. Let a regard to the interests of humanity stay the hand of injustice, and my life on it, the gentleman will not find it difficult to dissuade his country from rushing into the bloody scenes of war.

We are next told of the dangers of war. I believe we are all ready to acknowledge its hazards and misfortunes; but I cannot think we have any extraordinary danger to apprehend, at least none to warrant an acquiescence in the injuries we have received. On the contrary, I believe, no war can be less dangerous to the internal peace, or safety of the country. But we are told of the black population of the Southern States. As far as the gentleman from Virginia speaks of his own personal knowledge, I shall not question the correctness of his statement. I only regret that such is the state of apprehension in his particular part of the country. Of the Southern section, I, too, have some personal knowledge; and can say, that in South Carolina no such fears in any part are felt. But, Sir, admit the gentleman's statement; will a war with Great Britain increase the danger? Will the country be less able to suppress insurrection? Had we anything to fear from that quarter (which I do not believe), in my opinion, the period of the greatest safety is during a war; unless, indeed, the enemy should make a lodgment in the country. Then the country is most on its guard; our militia the best prepared; and our standing army the greatest. Even in our revolution no attempts at insurrection were made by that portion of our population; and however the gentleman may alarm himself with the disorganizing effects of French principles, I cannot think our ignorant blacks have felt much of their baneful influence. I dare say more than one-half of them never heard of the French revolution.

But as great as he regards the danger from our slaves, the gentleman's fears end not there—the standing army is not less terrible to him. Sir, I think a regular force raised for a period of actual hostilities cannot properly be called a standing army. There is a just distinction between such a force, and one raised as a permanent peace establishment. Whatever would be the composition of the latter, I hope the former will consist of some of the best materials of the country. The ardent patriotism of our young men, and the reasonable bounty in land which is proposed to be given, will impel them to join their country's standard and to fight her battles; they will not forget the citizen in the soldier, and in obeying their officers, learn to contemn their government and constitution. In our officers and soldiers we will find patriotism no less pure and ardent than in the private citizen; but if they should be depraved as represented, what have we to fear from twenty-five thousand or thirty thousand regulars? Where will be the boasted militia of the gentleman? Can one million of militia be overpowered by thirty thousand regulars? If so, how can we rely on them against a foe invading our country? Sir, I have no such contemptuous idea of our militia—their untaught bravery is sufficient to crush all foreign and internal attempts on their country's liberties.

But we have not yet come to the end of the chapter of dangers. The gentleman's imagination, so fruitful on this subject, conceives that our constitution is not calculated for war, and that it cannot stand its rude shock. This is rather extraordinary. If true, we must then depend upon the commiseration or contempt of other nations for our existence. The constitution, then, it seems, has failed in an essential object, ''to provide for the common defence." No, says the gentleman from Virginia, it is competent for a defensive, but not for an offensive war. It is not necessary for me to expose the error of this opinion. Why make the distinction in this instance? Will he pretend to say that this is an offensive war; a war of conquest? Yes, the gentleman has dared to make this assertion; and for reasons no less extraordinary than the assertion itself. He says our rights are violated on the ocean, and that these violations affect our shipping, and commercial rights, to which the Canadas have no relation. The doctrine of retaliation has been much abused of late by an unreasonable extension; we have now to witness a new abuse. The gentleman from Virginia has limited it down to a point. By his rule if you receive a blow on the breast, you dare not return it on the head; you are obliged to measure and return it on the precise point on which it was received. If you do not proceed with this mathematical accuracy, it ceases to be just self-defence; it becomes an unprovoked attack.

In speaking of Canada the gentleman from Virginia introduced the name of Montgomery with much feeling and interest. Sir, there is danger in that name to the gentleman's argument. It is sacred to heroism. It is indignant of submission! It calls our memory back to the time of our revolution, to the Congress of '74 and '75. Suppose a member of that day had risen and urged all the arguments which we have heard on this subject; had told that Congress—your contest is about the right of laying a tax; and that the attempt on Canada had nothing to do with it; that the war would be expensive; that danger and devastation would overspread our country; and that the power of Great Britain was irresistible. With what sentiment, think you, would such doctrines have been then received? Happy for us, they had no force at that period of our country's glory. Had such been then acted on, this hall would never have witnessed a great people convened to deliberate for the general good; a mighty empire, with prouder prospects than any nation the sun ever shone on, would not have risen in the west. No; we would have been base subjected colonies; governed by that imperious rod which Britain holds over her distant provinces.

The gentleman from Virginia attributes the preparation for war to everything but its true cause. He endeavored to find it in the probable rise in the price of hemp. He represents the people of the Western States as willing to plunge our country into war from such interested and base motives. I will not reason on this point. I see the cause of their ardor, not in such unworthy motives, but in their known patriotism and disinterestedness.

No less mercenary is the reason which he attributes to the Southern States. He says that the Non-Importation Act has reduced cotton to nothing, which has produced a feverish impatience. Sir, I acknowledge the cotton of our plantations is worth but little; but not for the cause assigned by the gentleman from Virginia. The people of that section do not reason as he does; they do not attribute it to the efforts of their government to maintain the peace and independence of their country. They see, in the low price of their produce, the hand of foreign injustice; they know well without the market to the continent, the deep and steady current of supply will glut that of Great Britain; they are not prepared for the colonial state to which again that power is endeavoring to reduce us, and the manly spirit of that section of our country will not submit to be regulated by any foreign power.

The love of France and the hatred of England have also been assigned as the cause of the present measures. France has not done us justice, says the gentleman from Virginia, and how can we, without partiality, resist the aggressions of England. I know, Sir, we have still causes of complaint against France; but they are of a different character from those against England. She professes now to respect our rights, and there cannot be a reasonable doubt but that the most objectionable parts of her decrees, as far as they respect us, are repealed. We have already formally acknowledged this to be a fact. But I protest against the principle from which his conclusion is drawn. It is a novel doctrine, and nowhere avowed out of this House, that you cannot select your antagonist without being guilty of partiality. Sir, when two invade your rights, you may resist both or either at your pleasure. It is regulated by prudence and not by right. The stale imputation of partiality for France is better calculated for the columns of a newspaper, than for the walls of this House.

The gentleman from Virginia is at a loss to account for what he calls our hatred to England. He asks how can we hate the country of Locke, of Newton, Hampden, and Chatham; a country having the same language and customs with ourselves, and descending from a common ancestry. Sir, the laws of human affections are steady and uniform. If we have so much to attach us to that country, potent indeed must be the cause which has overpowered it.

Yes, there is a cause strong enough; not in that occult courtly affection which he has supposed to be entertained for France; but it is to be found in continued and unprovoked insult and injury—a cause so manifest, that the gentleman from Virginia had to exert much ingenuity to overlook it. But, the gentleman, in his eager admiration of that country, has not been sufficiently guarded in his argument. Has he reflected on the cause of that admiration? Has he examined the reasons of our high regard for her Chatham? It is his ardent patriotism, the heroic courage of his mind, that could not brook the least insult or injury offered to his country, but thought that her interest and honor ought to be vindicated at every hazard and expense. I hope, when we are called upon to admire, we shall also be asked to imitate. I hope the gentleman does not wish a monopoly of those great virtues for England.

The balance of power has also been introduced, as an argument for submission. England is said to be a barrier against the military despotism of France. There is, Sir, one great error in our legislation. We are ready, it would seem from this argument, to watch over the interests of foreign nations, while we grossly neglect our own immediate concerns. This argument of the balance of power is well calculated for the British Parliament, but not at all suited to the American Congress. Tell the former that they have to contend with a mighty power, and that if they persist in insult and injury to the American people, they will compel them to throw their whole weight into the scale of their enemy. Paint the danger to them, and if they will desist from injuring us, we, I answer for it, will not disturb the balance of power. But it is absurd for us to talk about the balance of power, while they, by their conduct, smile with contempt at what they regard our simple, good-natured policy. If, however, in the contest, it should be found that they underrate us—which I hope and believe—and that we can affect the balance of power, it will not be difficult for us to obtain such terms as our rights demand.

I, Sir, will now conclude by adverting to an argument of the gentleman from Virginia, used in debate on a preceding day. He asked, why not declare war immediately? The answer is obvious: because we are not yet prepared. But, says the gentleman, such language as is here held, will provoke Great Britain to commence hostilities. I have no such fears. She knows well that such a course would unite all parties here—a thing which, above all others, she most dreads. Besides, such has been our past conduct, that she will still calculate on our patience and submission, until war is actually commenced.

SPEECH ON
THE TARIFF BILL

[April 4, 1816]

————————•◆•————————

*With the exception of the controversy over the national bank, no other issue
proved as controversial or as divisive during the formative years of the American republic as did the tariff. The debate on the tariff of 1816 again found
Calhoun and Randolph on opposite sides of an issue. Randolph argued that
the proposed tariff was in fact little more than "an immense tax on one
portion of the community to put money into the pockets of another." Calhoun, on the other hand, argued that while manufacturing interests were not
without moral difficulties or objections, agriculture and commerce alone were
not sufficient to produce the wealth necessary to make the new nation secure.
The encouragement of the manufacturing element would form a new and
most powerful cement for union; and a strong union would be the greatest
defense of liberty. The greatest threat to liberty, argued Calhoun, was not the
tariff, but a new and pressing danger—disunion.*

*This speech, like many of the speeches Calhoun delivered during his early
years in the U.S. House of Representatives on the tariff, national bank, and
internal improvements, argues for a strong federal government. In the South
Carolina Exposition (1828), however, Calhoun was among those who denounced the Tariff of Abominations as an unconstitutional and tyrannical
act of an overbearing, numerical majority. Calhoun addresses the question
of the consistency of his position on the floor of the Senate in his remarks on
the Force Bill (1833). Both the Exposition and the speech on the Force Bill
are reproduced in this volume.*

THE debate heretofore on this subject has been on the degree of protection which ought to be afforded to our cotton and woollen manufactures: all professing to be friendly to those infant establishments, and to be willing to extend to them adequate encouragement. The present motion assumes a new aspect. It is introduced professedly on the ground that manufactures ought not to receive any encouragement; and will, in its operation, leave our cotton establishments exposed to the competition of the cotton goods of the East Indies, which, it is acknowledged on all sides, they are not capable of meeting with success, without the proviso proposed to be stricken out by the motion now under discussion. Till the debate assumed this new form, he had determined to be silent; participating, as he largely did, in that general anxiety which is felt, after so long and laborious a session, to return to the bosom of our families. But, on a subject of such vital importance, touching, as it does, the security and permanent prosperity of our country, he hoped that the House would indulge him in a few observations. He regretted much his want of preparation; he meant not a verbal preparation, for he had ever despised such, but that due and mature meditation and arrangement of thought which the House is entitled to on the part of those who occupy any portion of their time. But, whatever his arguments might want on that account in weight, he hoped might be made up in the disinterestedness of his situation. He was no manufacturer; he was not from that portion of our country supposed to be peculiarly interested.

Coming, as he did, from the South; having, in common with his immediate constituents, no interest, but in the cultivation of the soil, in selling its products high, and buying cheap the wants and conveniences of life, no motives could be attributed to him but such as were disinterested.

He had asserted that the subject before them was connected with the security of the country. It would, doubtless, by some be considered a rash assertion; but he conceived it to be susceptible of the clearest proof; and he hoped, with due attention, to establish it to the satisfaction of the House.

The security of a country mainly depends on its spirit and its means; and the latter principally on its moneyed resources. Modified as the industry of this country now is, combined with our peculiar situation and want of a naval ascendency, whenever we have the misfortune to be involved in a war with a nation dominant on the ocean—and it is almost only with such we can at present be—the moneyed resources of the country to a great extent must fail. He took it for granted that it was the duty of this body to adopt those measures of prudent foresight which the event of war made necessary. We cannot, he presumed, be indifferent to dangers from abroad, unless, indeed, the House is prepared to indulge in the phantom of eternal peace, which seems to possess the dream of some of its members. Could such a state exist, no foresight or fortitude would be necessary to conduct the affairs of the republic; but as it is the mere illusion of the imagination, as every people that ever has or ever will exist, are subjected to the vicissitudes of peace and war, it must ever be considered as the plain dictate of wisdom, in peace to prepare for war. What, then, let us consider, constitute the resources of this country, and what are the effects of war on them? Commerce and agriculture, till lately almost the only, still constitute the principal sources of our wealth. So long as these remain uninterrupted, the country prospers; but war, as we are now circumstanced, is equally destructive to both. They both depend on foreign markets; and our country is placed, as it regards them, in a situation strictly insular; a wide ocean rolls between. Our commerce neither is nor can be protected by the present means of the country. What, then, are the effects of a war with a

maritime power—with England? Our commerce annihilated, spreading individual misery and producing national poverty; our agriculture cut off
from its accustomed markets, the surplus product of the farmer perishes
on his hands, and he ceases to produce, because he cannot sell. His
resources are dried up, while his expenses are greatly increased; as all
manufactured articles, the necessaries as well as the conveniences of life,
rise to an extravagant price. The recent war fell with peculiar pressure on
the growers of cotton and tobacco, and other great staples of the country;
and the same state of things will recur in the event of another, unless
prevented by the foresight of this body.

If the mere statement of facts did not carry conviction to every mind, as
he conceives it is calculated to do, additional arguments might be drawn
from the general nature of wealth. Neither agriculture, manufactures, nor
commerce, taken separately, is the cause of wealth; it flows from the three
combined, and cannot exist without each. The wealth of any single nation
or an individual, it is true, may not immediately depend on the three, but
such wealth always presupposes their existence. He viewed the words in
the most enlarged sense. Without commerce, industry would have no stimulus; without manufactures, it would be without the means of production;
and without agriculture neither of the others can subsist. When separated
entirely and permanently, they perish. War in this country produces, to a
great extent, that effect; and hence the great embarrassment which follows
in its train. The failure of the wealth and resources of the nation necessarily involved the ruin of its finances and its currency. It is admitted by the
most strenuous advocates, on the other side, that no country ought to be
dependent on another for its means of defence; that, at least, our musket
and bayonet, our cannon and ball, ought to be of domestic manufacture.
But what, he asked, is more necessary to the defence of a country than its
currency and finance? Circumstanced as our country is, can these stand
the shock of war? Behold the effect of the late war on them. When our
manufactures are grown to a certain perfection, as they soon will under the
fostering care of Government, we will no longer experience these evils.

The farmer will find a ready market for his surplus produce; and, what is almost of equal consequence, a certain and cheap supply of all his wants. His prosperity will diffuse itself to every class in the community; and, instead of that languor of industry and individual distress now incident to a state of war and suspended commerce, the wealth and vigor of the community will not be materially impaired. The arm of Government will be nerved; and taxes in the hour of danger, when essential to the independence of the nation, may be greatly increased; loans, so uncertain and hazardous, may be less relied on; thus situated, the storm may beat without, but within all will be quiet and safe.

To give perfection to this state of things, it will be necessary to add, as soon as possible, a system of internal improvements, and at least such an extension of our navy as will prevent the cutting off our coasting trade. The advantage of each is so striking as not to require illustration, especially after the experience of the recent war. It is thus the resources of this Government and people would be placed beyond the power of a foreign war materially to impair. But it may be said that the derangement then experienced, resulted, not from the cause assigned, but from the errors of the weakness of the Government. He admitted that many financial blunders were committed, for the subject was new to us; that the taxes were not laid sufficiently early, or to as great an extent as they ought to have been; and that the loans were in some instances injudiciously made; but he ventured to affirm that, had the greatest foresight and fortitude been exerted, the embarrassment would have been still very great; and that even under the best management, the total derangement which was actually felt would not have been postponed eighteen months, had the war so long continued. How could it be otherwise? A war, such as this country was then involved in, in a great measure dries up the resources of individuals, as he had already proved; and the resources of the Government are no more than the aggregate of the surplus incomes of individuals called into action by a system of taxation. It is certainly a great political evil, incident to the character of the industry of this country, that, however prosperous our situation when at peace, with an uninterrupted commerce—and nothing then could exceed it—the moment that we were involved in war the whole is reversed. When resources are most needed; when indispensable to maintain the honor; yes, the very existence of the nation, then they desert us. Our currency is also sure to experience the shock, and become so deranged as to prevent us from calling out fairly whatever of means is left to the country. The result of a war in the present state of our naval power, is the blockade of our coast, and consequent destruction of our trade. The wants and habits of the country, founded on the use of foreign articles, must be gratified; importation to a certain extent continues, through the policy of the enemy, or unlawful traffic; the exportation of our bulky articles is prevented, too; the specie of the country is drawn to pay the balance perpetually accumulating against us; and the final result is, a total derangement of our currency.

To this distressing state of things there were two remedies—and only two; one in our power immediately, the other requiring much time and exertion; but both constituting, in his opinion, the essential policy of this country: he meant the navy and domestic manufactures. By the former, we could open the way to our markets; by the latter, we bring them from beyond the ocean, and naturalize them. Had we the means of attaining an immediate naval ascendency, he acknowledged that the policy recommended by this bill would be very questionable; but as that is not the fact—as it is a period remote, with any exertion, and will be probably more so from that relaxation of exertion so natural in peace, when necessity is not felt, it becomes the duty of this House to resort, to a considerable extent, at least as far as is proposed, to the only remaining remedy.

But to this it has been objected that the country is not prepared, and that the result of our premature exertion would be to bring distress on it without effecting the intended object. Were it so, however urgent the reasons in its favor, we ought to desist, as it is folly to oppose the laws of necessity. But he could not for a moment yield to the assertion; on the contrary, he firmly believed that the country is prepared, even to maturity, for the introduction of manufactures. We have abundance of resources, and things naturally tend at this moment in that direction. A prosperous commerce has poured an immense amount of commercial capital into this country. This capital has, till lately, found occupation in commerce; but that state of the world which transferred it to this country, and gave it active employment, has passed away, never to return. Where shall we now find full employment for our prodigious amount of tonnage; where markets for the numerous and abundant products of our country? This great body of active capital, which for the moment has found sufficient employment in supplying our markets, exhausted by the war and measures preceding it, must find a new direction; it will not be idle. What channel can it take but that of manufactures? This, if things continue as they are, will be its direction. It will introduce a new era in our affairs, in many respects highly advantageous, and ought to be countenanced by the Government. Besides, we have already surmounted the greatest difficulty that has ever been found in undertakings of this kind. The cotton and woollen manufactures are not to be introduced— they are already introduced to a great extent; freeing us entirely from the hazards, and, in a great measure, the sacrifices experienced in giving the capital of the country a new direction. The restrictive measures and the war, though not intended for that purpose, have, by the necessary operation of things, turned a large amount of capital to this new branch of industry. He had often heard it said, both in and out of Congress, that this effect alone would indemnify the country for all of its losses. So high was this tone of feeling when the want of these establishments was practically felt, that he remembered, during the war, when some question was agitated respecting the introduction of foreign goods, that many then opposed it on the grounds of injuring our manufactures. He then said that war alone furnished sufficient stimulus, and perhaps too much, as it would make their growth unnaturally rapid; but that, on the return of peace, it would then be time for us to show our affection for them. He at that time did not expect an apathy and aversion to the extent which is now seen. But it will no doubt be said, if they are so far established, and if the situation of the country is so favorable to their growth, where is the necessity of affording them protection? It is to put them beyond the reach of contingency. Besides, capital is not yet, and cannot for some time be, adjusted to the new state of things. There is, in fact, from the operation of temporary causes, a great pressure on these establishments. They had extended so rapidly during the late war, that many, he feared, were without the requisite surplus capital or skill to meet the present crisis. Should such prove to be the fact, it would give a back set, and might, to a great extent, endanger their ultimate success. Should the present owners be ruined, and the workmen dispersed and turned to other pursuits, the country would sustain a great loss. Such would, no doubt, be the fact to a considerable extent, if not protected. Besides, circumstances, if we act with wisdom, are favorable to attract to our country much skill and industry. The country in Europe having the most skilful workmen is broken up. It is to us, if wisely used, more valuable than the repeal of the Edict of Nantz was to England. She had the prudence to profit by it: let us not discover less political sagacity. Afford to ingenuity and industry immediate and ample protection, and they will not fail to give a preference to this free and happy country.

It has been objected to this bill, that it will injure our marine, and consequently impair our naval strength. How far it is fairly liable to this charge, he was not prepared to say. He hoped and believed it would not, at least to any alarming extent, have that effect immediately; and he firmly believed that its lasting operation would be highly beneficial to our commerce. The trade to the East Indies would certainly be much affected; but it was stated in debate that the whole of that trade employed but six hundred sailors. But, whatever might be the loss in this, or other branches of our foreign commerce, he trusted it would be amply compensated in our coasting trade, a branch of navigation wholly in our own hands. It has at all times employed a great amount of tonnage; something more, he believed, than one-third of the whole: nor is it liable to the imputation thrown out by a member from North Carolina (Mr. Gaston), that it produced inferior sailors. It required long and dangerous voyages; and, if his information was correct, no branch of trade made better or more skilful seamen. The fact that it is wholly in our own hands is a very important one, while every branch of our foreign trade must suffer from competition with other nations.

Other objections of a political character were made to the encouragement of manufactures. It is said they destroy the moral and physical power of the people. This might formerly have been true, to a considerable extent, before the perfection of machinery, and when the success of the manufactures depended on the minute subdivision of labor. At that time it required a large portion of the population of a country to be engaged in them; and every minute subdivision of labor is undoubtedly unfavorable to the intellect; but the great perfection of machinery has in a considerable degree obviated these objections. In fact, it has been stated that the manufacturing districts in England furnish the greatest number of recruits to her army; and that, as soldiers, they are not materially inferior to the rest of her population. It has been further asserted that manufactures are the fruitful cause of pauperism; and England has been referred to as furnishing conclusive evidence of its truth. For his part, he could perceive no such tendency in them, but the exact contrary, as they furnished new stimulus and means of subsistence to the laboring classes of the community. We ought not to look to the cotton and woollen establishments of Great Britain for the prodigious numbers of poor with which her population was disgraced. Causes much more efficient exist. Her poor laws, and statutes regulating the price of labor, with heavy taxes, were the real causes. But, if it must be so—if the mere fact that England manufactured more than any other country, explained the cause of her having more beggars, it is just as reasonable to refer to it her courage, spirit, and all her masculine virtues, in which she excels all other nations, with a single exception—he meant our own—in which we might, without vanity, challenge a pre-eminence.

Another objection had been made, which, he must acknowledge, was better founded: that capital employed in manufacturing produced a greater dependence on the part of the employed, than in commerce, navigation, or agriculture. It is certainly an evil, and to be regretted; but he did not think it a decisive objection to the system; especially when it had incidental political advantages which, in his opinion, more than counterpoised it. It produced an interest strictly American—as much so as agriculture; in which it had the decided advantage of commerce or navigation. The country will from this derive much advantage. Again, it is calculated to bind together more closely our widely spread republic. It will greatly increase our mutual dependence and intercourse; and will, as a necessary consequence, excite an increased attention to Internal Improvements, a subject every way so intimately connected with the ultimate attainment of national strength and the perfection of our political institutions. He regarded the fact that it would make the parts adhere more closely; that it would form a new and most powerful cement, far outweighing any political objections that might be urged against the system. In his opinion the liberty and the union of this country were inseparably united. That, as the destruction of the latter would most certainly involve the former, so its maintenance will, with equal certainty, preserve it. He did not speak lightly. He had often and long revolved it in his mind, and he had critically examined into the causes that destroyed the liberty of other states. There are none that apply to us, or apply with a force to alarm. The basis of our republic is too broad, and its structure too strong, to be shaken by them. Its extension and organization will be found to afford effectual security against their operation; but let it be deeply impressed on the heart of this House and country, that, while they guarded against the old, they exposed us to a new and terrible danger—disunion. This single word comprehended almost the sum of our political dangers; and against it we ought to be perpetually guarded.

EXPOSITION AND PROTEST

[December 19, 1828]

———◆———

Although it is common to refer to the "Exposition and Protest" as two parts of a single document, such is not the case. The "Exposition" is an essay enumerating South Carolina's grievances against the "American System" of protective tariffs and calling for constitutional safeguards to protect the states from the abuse of federal power. The "Protest" consists of the actual formal resolutions adopted by the General Assembly of South Carolina. Both appeared anonymously.

Returning to the language of the Virginia and Kentucky Resolutions of 1798, the "Exposition" reiterates the doctrine of interposition, which recognizes a state's right to interpose state authority between the citizens of that state and the laws of the United States, declaring such laws null and void. This right of interposition, argues the "Exposition," is the only possible constitutional remedy for settling disputes between the states and the federal government.

Many of the elements of Calhoun's theories about majority tyranny, which later appear in his Disquisition *and* Discourse, *are already evident in the pages of the "Exposition." Concurring with Publius, Calhoun identifies this tyranny as the problem of democratic governments, but he explicitly rejects Publius's claim that extensiveness of the republic offers a cure to the mischiefs of faction. Only through a judicious exercise of the reserved powers of the states and the amending process of the U.S. Constitution can liberty in America be preserved.*

Calhoun's draft bore the title, "Rough Draft of What Is Called the South Carolina Exposition." When he compiled his 1851–1856 edition of Calhoun's Works, *editor Richard K. Crallé used Calhoun's original title, as does this volume (see page 313). While the draft of the "Exposition" is in Calhoun's own hand, there is no such extant copy of the "Protest" that would confirm Calhoun's contributions to that document. Following the precedent found in the sixth volume of Crallé's edition of Calhoun's* Works, *however, both documents have been reprinted here.*

ROUGH DRAFT OF WHAT IS CALLED THE
SOUTH CAROLINA EXPOSITION

The committee have bestowed on the subjects referred to them the deliberate attention which their importance demands; and the result, on full investigation, is a unanimous opinion that the act of Congress of the last session, with the whole system of legislation imposing duties on imports—not for revenue, but the protection of one branch of industry at the expense of others—is unconstitutional, unequal, and oppressive, and calculated to corrupt the public virtue and destroy the liberty of the country; which propositions they propose to consider in the order stated, and then to conclude their report with the consideration of the important question of the remedy.

The committee do not propose to enter into an elaborate or refined argument on the question of the constitutionality of the Tariff system. The General Government is one of specific powers, and it can rightfully exercise only the powers expressly granted, and those that may be necessary and proper to carry them into effect, all others being reserved expressly to the States or the people. It results, necessarily, that those who claim to exercise power under the Constitution, are bound to show that it is expressly granted, or that it is necessary and proper as a means to some of the granted powers. The advocates of the Tariff have offered no such proof. It is true that the third section of the first article of the Constitution authorizes Congress to lay and collect an impost duty, but it is granted as a tax power for the sole purpose of revenue—a power in its nature essentially different from that of imposing protective or prohibitory duties. Their objects are incompatible. The prohibitory system must end in destroying the revenue from imports. It has been said that the system is a violation of the spirit, and not the letter of the Constitution. The distinction is not material. The Constitution may be as grossly violated by acting against its meaning as against its letter; but it may be proper to dwell a moment on the point in order to understand more fully the real character of the acts under which the interest of this, and other States similarly situated, has been sacrificed. The facts are few and simple. The Constitution grants to Congress the power of imposing a duty on imports for revenue, which power is abused by being converted into an instrument of rearing up the industry of one section of the country on the ruins of another. The violation, then, consists in using a power granted for one object to advance another, and that by the sacrifice of the original object. It is, in a word, a violation by perversion—the most dangerous of all, because the most insidious, and difficult to resist. Others cannot be perpetrated without the aid of the judiciary—this may be by the Executive and Legislative departments alone. The courts cannot look into the motives of legislators. They are obliged to take acts by their titles and professed objects, and if these be constitutional, they cannot interpose their power, however grossly the acts may, in reality, violate the Constitution. The proceedings of the last session sufficiently prove that the House of Representatives are aware of the distinction, and determined to avail themselves of its advantage.

In the absence of arguments, drawn from the Constitution itself, the advocates of the power have attempted to call in the aid of precedent. The committee will not waste their time in examining the instances quoted. If they were strictly in point, they would be entitled to little weight. Ours is not a Government of precedents, nor can they be admitted, except to a very limited extent, and with great caution, in the interpretation of the Constitution, without changing, in time, the entire character of the instrument. The only safe rule is the Constitution itself—or, if that be doubtful, the history of the times. In this case, if doubts existed, the journals of the Convention itself would remove them. It was moved in that body to confer on Congress the very power in question to encourage manufactures, but it was deliberately withheld, except to the extent of granting patent rights for new and useful inventions. Instead of granting the power, permission was given to the States to impose duties, with the consent of Congress, to encourage their own manufactures; and thus, in the true spirit of justice, imposing the burden on those who were to be benefited. But, giving the precedents every weight that may be claimed for them, the committee feel confident that, in this case, there are none in point previous to the adoption of the present Tariff system. Every instance which has been quoted, may fairly be referred to the legitimate power of Congress, to impose duties on imports for revenue. It is a necessary incident of such duties to act as an encouragement to manufactures, whenever imposed on articles which may be manufactured in our country. In this incidental manner, Congress has the power of encouraging manufactures; and the committee readily concede that, in the passage of an impost bill, that body may, in modifying the details, so arrange the provisions of the bill, as far as it may be done consistently with its proper object, as to aid manufactures. To this extent Congress may constitutionally go, and has gone from the commencement of the Government, which will fully explain the precedents cited from the early stages of its operation. Beyond this they never proceeded till the commencement of the present system, the inequality and oppression of which they will next proceed to consider.

On entering on this branch of the subject, the committee feel the painful character of the duty which they must perform. They would desire never to speak of our country, as far as the action of the General Government is concerned, but as one great whole, having a common interest, which all the parts ought zealously to promote. Previously to the adoption of the Tariff system, such was the unanimous feeling of this State; but in speaking of its operation, it will be impossible to avoid the discussion of sectional interest, and the use of sectional language. On its authors, and not on us, who are compelled to adopt this course in self-defence, by injustice and oppression, be the censure.

So partial are the effects of the system, that its burdens are exclusively on one side and its benefits on the other. It imposes on the agricultural interest of the South, including the South-west, and that portion of the country particularly engaged in commerce and navigation, the burden not only of sustaining the system itself, but that also of the Government. In stating the case thus strongly, it is not the intention of the committee to exaggerate. If exaggeration were not unworthy of the gravity of the subject, the reality is such as to make it unnecessary.

That the manufacturing States, even in their own opinion, bear no share of the burden of the Tariff in reality, we may infer with the greatest certainty from their conduct. The fact that they urgently demand an increase, and consider every addition as a blessing, and a failure to obtain one as a curse, is the strongest confession that, whatever burden it imposes, in reality falls, not on them, but on others. Men ask not for burdens, but benefits. The tax paid by the duties on imports, by which, with the exception of the receipts from the sale of the public lands, and a few incidental items, the Government is wholly supported, and which, in its gross amount, annually equals about $23,000,000, is then, in truth, no tax on them. Whatever portion of it they advance as consumers of the articles on which it is imposed, returns to them with usurious interest through an artfully contrived system. That such are the facts, the committee will proceed to demonstrate by other arguments besides the confession of the parties interested in these acts, as conclusive as that ought to be considered. If the duties were imposed on the exports instead of the imports, no one would doubt their partial operation, or that the duties, in that form, would fall on those engaged in producing articles for the foreign market; and as rice, tobacco, and cotton, constitute the great mass of our exports, such duties would, of necessity, mainly fall on the Southern States, where they are exclusively cultivated. To prove, then, that the burden of the Tariff falls also on them almost exclusively, it is only necessary to show that, as far as their interest is concerned, there is little or no difference between an export and an import duty. We export to import. The object is an exchange of the fruits of our labor for those of other countries. We have, from soil and climate, a facility in rearing certain great agricultural staples, while other and older countries, with dense population and capital greatly accumulated, have equal facility in manufacturing various articles suited to our use; and thus a foundation is laid for an exchange of the products of labor mutually advantageous. A duty, whether it be on the imports or exports, must fall on this exchange; and, however laid, must, in reality, be paid by the producer of the articles exchanged. Such must be the operation of all taxes on sales or exchanges. The producer, in reality, pays it, whether laid on the vendor or purchaser. It matters not in the sale of a tract of land, or any other article, if a tax be imposed, whether it be paid by him who sells or him who buys. The amount must, in both cases, be deducted from the price. Nor can it alter, in this particular, the operation of such a tax, by being imposed on the exchanges of different countries. Such exchanges are but the aggregate of sales of the individuals of the respective countries; and must, if taxed, be governed by the same rules. Nor is it material whether the exchange be barter or sale, direct or circuitous. In any case it must fall on the producer. To the growers of cotton, rice, and tobacco, it is the same, whether the Government takes one-third of what they raise, for the liberty of sending the other two-thirds abroad, or one-third of the iron, salt, sugar, coffee, cloth, and other articles they may need in exchange, for the liberty of bringing them home. In both cases he gets a third less than he ought. A third of his labor is taken; yet the one is an import duty, and the other an export. It is true that a tax on the imports, by raising the price of the articles imported, may in time produce the supply at home, and thus give a new direction to the exchanges of the country; but it is also true that a tax on the exports, by diminishing at home the price of the same material, may have the same effect, and with no greater burden to the grower. Whether the situation of the South will be materially benefited by this new direction given to its exchanges, will be considered hereafter; but whatever portion of her foreign exchanges may, in fact, remain, in any stage of this process of changing her market, must be governed by the rule laid down. Whatever duty may be imposed to bring it about, must fall on the foreign trade which remains, and be paid by the South almost exclusively—as much so, as an equal amount of duty on their exports.

Let us now trace the operation of the system in some of its prominent details, in order to understand, with greater precision, the extent of the burden it imposes on us, and the benefits which it confers, at our expense, on the manufacturing States. The committee, in the discussion of this point, will not aim at minute accuracy. They have neither the means nor the time requisite for that purpose, nor do they deem it necessary, if they had, to estimate the fractions of loss or gain on either side on subjects of such great magnitude.

The exports of domestic produce, in round numbers, may be estimated as averaging $53,000,000 annually; of which the States growing cotton, rice, and tobacco, produce about $37,000,000. In the last four years the average amount of the export of cotton, rice, and tobacco, exceeded $35,500,000; to which, if we add flour, corn, lumber, and other articles exported from the States producing the former, their exports cannot be estimated at a less sum than that stated. Taking it at that sum, the exports of the Southern or staple States, and other States, will stand as $37,000,000 to $16,000,000—or considerably more than the proportion of two to one; while their population, estimated in federal numbers, is the reverse; the former sending to the House of Representatives but 76 members, and the latter 137. It follows that about one-third of the Union exports more than two-thirds of the domestic products. Such, then, is the amount of labor which our country annually exchanges with the rest of the world—and such our proportion. The Government is supported almost exclusively by a tax on this exchange, in the shape of an impost duty, and which amounts annually to about $23,000,000, as has already been stated. Previous to the passage of the act of the last session, this tax averaged about 37½ per cent on the value of imports. What addition that has made, it is difficult, with the present data, to estimate with precision; but it may be assumed, on a very moderate calculation, to be 7½ per cent—thus making the present duty to average at least 45 per cent, which, on $37,000,000, the amount of our share of the exports, will give the sum of $16,650,000, as our share of the contribution to the general Treasury.

Let us take another, and perhaps more simple and striking view of this important point. Exports and imports, allowing for the profit and loss of trade, must be equal in a series of years. This is a principle universally conceded. Let it then be supposed, for the purpose of illustration, that the United States were organized into two separate and distinct custom-house establishments—one for the staple States, and the other for the rest of the Union; and that all commercial intercourse between the two sections were taxed in the same manner and to the same extent with the commerce of the rest of the world. The foreign commerce, under such circumstances, would be carried on from each section, direct with the rest of the world; and the imports of the Southern Custom-House, on the principle that exports and imports must be equal, would amount annually to $37,000,000; on which 45 per cent, the average amount of the impost duty, would give an annual revenue of $16,650,000, without increasing the burden already imposed on the people of those States one cent. This would be the amount of revenue on the exchanges of that portion of their products which go abroad; but if we take into the estimate the duty which would accrue on the exchange of their products with the manufacturing States, which now, in reality, is paid by the Southern States in the shape of increased prices, as a bounty to manufactures, but which, on the supposition, would constitute a part of their revenue, many millions more would have to be added.

But, it is contended, that the consumers really pay the impost—and that, as the manufacturing States consume a full share, in proportion to their population, of the articles imported, they must also contribute their full share to the Treasury of the Union. The committee will not deny the position that their consumption is in proportion to their population—nor that the consumers pay, provided they be mere consumers, without the means, through the Tariff, of indemnifying themselves in some other character. Without the qualification, no proposition can be more fallacious than that the consumers pay. That the manufacturing States do, in fact, indemnify themselves, and more than indemnify themselves for the increased price they pay on the articles they consume, we have, as has already been stated, their confession in a form which cannot deceive—we mean their own acts. Nor is it difficult to trace the operation by which this is effected. The very acts of Congress, imposing the burdens on them, as consumers, give them the means, through the monopoly which it affords their manufactures in the home market, not only of indemnifying themselves for the increased price on the imported articles which they may consume, but, in a great measure, to command the industry of the rest of the Union. The argument urged by them for the adoption of the system (and with so much success), that the price of property and products in those States must be thereby increased, clearly proves that the facts are as stated by your committee. It is by this very increased price, which must be paid by their fellow-citizens of the South, that their industry is affected, and the fruits of our toil and labor, which, on any principle of justice, ought to belong to ourselves, are transferred from us to them. The maxim, that the consumers pay, strictly applies to us. We are mere consumers, and destitute of all means of transferring the burden from ours to the shoulders of others. We may be assured that the large amount paid into the Treasury under the duties on imports, is really derived from the labor of some portion of our citizens. The Government has no mines. Someone must bear the burden of its support. This unequal lot is ours. We are the serfs of the system—out of whose labor is raised, not only the money paid into the Treasury, but the funds out of which are drawn the rich rewards of the manufacturer and his associates in interest. Their encouragement is our discouragement. The duty on imports, which is mainly paid out of our labor, gives them the means of selling to us at a higher price; while we cannot, to compensate the loss, dispose of our products at the least advance. It is then, indeed, not a subject of wonder, when understood, that our section of the country, though helped by a kind Providence with a genial sun and prolific soil, from which spring the richest products, should languish in poverty and sink into decay, while the rest of the Union, though less fortunate in natural advantages, are flourishing in unexampled prosperity.

The assertion, that the encouragement of the industry of the manufacturing States is, in fact, discouragement to ours, was not made without due deliberation. It is susceptible of the clearest proof. We cultivate certain great staples for the supply of the general market of the world: They manufacture almost exclusively for the home market. Their object in the Tariff is to keep down foreign competition, in order to obtain a monopoly of the domestic market. The effect on us is, to compel us to purchase at a higher price, both what we obtain from them and from others, without receiving a correspondent increase in the price of what we sell. The price at which we can afford to cultivate must depend on the price at which we receive our supplies. The lower the latter, the lower we may dispose of our products with profit—and the same degree our capacity of meeting competition is increased; and, on the contrary, the higher the price of our supplies, the less the profit, and the less, consequently, the capacity for meeting competition. If, for instance, cotton can be cultivated at 10 cents the pound, under an increase price of forty-five per cent on what we purchase, in return, it is clear, if the prices of what we consume were reduced forty-five per cent (the amount of the duty), we could, under such reduced prices, afford to raise the article at 5½ cents per pound, with a profit, as great as what we now obtain at 10 cents; and that our capacity of meeting the competition of foreigners in the general market of the world, would be increased in the same proportion. If we can now, with the increased price from the Tariff, contend with success, under a reduction of 45 per cent in the prices of our products, we could drive out all competition; and thus add annually to the consumption of our cotton, three or four hundred thousand bales, with a corresponding increase of profit. The case, then, fairly stated between us and the manufacturing States is, that the Tariff gives them a protection against foreign competition in our own market, by diminishing, in the same proportion, our capacity to compete with our rivals, in the general market of the world. They who say that they cannot compete with foreigners at their own doors, without an advantage of 45 per cent, expect us to meet them abroad under disadvantage equal to their encouragement.

But this oppression, as great as it is, will not stop at this point. The trade between us and Europe has, heretofore, been a mutual exchange of products. Under the existing duties, the consumption of European fabrics must, in a great measure, cease in our country; and the trade must become, on their part, a cash transaction. He must be ignorant of the principles of commerce, and the policy of Europe, particularly England, who does not see that it is impossible to carry on a trade of such vast extent on any other basis than barter; and that, if it were not so carried on, it would not long be tolerated. We already see indications of the commencement of a commercial warfare, the termination of which no one can conjecture—though our fate may easily be. The last remains of our great and once flourishing agriculture must be annihilated in the conflict. In the first instance, we will be thrown on the home market, which cannot consume a fourth of our products; and instead of supplying the world, as we would with a free trade, we would be compelled to abandon the cultivation of three-fourths of what we now raise, and receive for the residue, whatever the manufacturers, who would then have their policy consummated by the entire possession of our market, might choose to give. Forced to abandon our ancient and favorite pursuit, to which our soil, climate, habits, and peculiar labor are adapted, at an immense sacrifice of property, we would be compelled, without capital, experience, or skill, and with a population untried in such pursuits, to attempt to become the rivals, instead of the customers of the manufacturing States. The result is not doubtful. If they, by superior capital and skill, should keep down successful competition on our part, we would be doomed to toil at our unprofitable agriculture—selling at the prices which a single and very limited market might give. But, on the contrary, if our necessity should triumph over their capital and skill—if, instead of raw cotton, we should ship to the manufacturing States cotton yarn and cotton goods, the thoughtful must see that it would inevitably bring about a state of things which could not long continue. Those who now make war on our gains, would then make it on our labor. They would not tolerate, that those, who now cultivate our plantations, and furnish them with the material, and the market for the products of their arts, should, by becoming their rivals, take bread out of the mouths of their wives and children. The committee will not pursue this painful subject; but, as they clearly see that the system, if not arrested, must bring the country to this hazardous extremity, neither prudence nor patriotism would permit them to pass it by without raising a warning voice against a danger of such menacing character.

It was conceded, in the course of the discussion, that the consumption of the manufacturing States, in proportion to population, was as great as ours. How they, with their limited means of payment, if estimated by the exports of their own products, could consume as much as we do with our ample exports, has been partially explained; but it demands a fuller consideration. Their population, in round numbers, may be estimated at about eight, and ours at four millions; while the value of their products exported, compared with ours, is as sixteen to thirty-seven millions of dollars. If to the aggregate of these sums be added the profits of our foreign trade and navigation, it will give the amount of the fund out of which is annually paid the price of foreign articles consumed in our country. This profit, at least so far as it constitutes a portion of the fund out of which the price of the foreign articles is paid, is represented by the difference between the value of the exports and imports—that of both being estimated at our own ports—and which, taking the average of the last five years, amount to about $4,000,000—and which, as the foreign trade of the country is principally in the hands of the manufacturing States, we will add to their means of consumption; which will raise theirs to $20,000,000, and will place the relative means of the consumption of the two sections, as twenty to thirty-seven millions of dollars; while, on the supposition of equal consumption in proportion to population, their consumption would amount to thirty-eight millions of dollars, and ours to nineteen millions. Their consumption would thus exceed their capacity to consume, if judged by the value of their exports, and the profits of their foreign commerce, by eighteen millions; while ours, judged the same way, would fall short by the same sum. The inquiry which naturally presents itself is, how is this great change in the relative condition of the parties, to our disadvantage, affected?—which the committee will now proceed to explain.

It obviously grows out of our connections. If we were entirely separated, without political or commercial connection, it is manifest that the consumption of the manufacturing States, of foreign articles, could not exceed twenty-two millions—the sum at which the value of their exports and profit of their foreign trade is estimated. It would, in fact, be much less; as the profits of foreign navigation and trade, which have been added to their means, depend almost exclusively on the great staples of the South, and would have to be deducted, if no connection existed, as supposed. On the contrary, it is equally manifest, that the means of the South to consume the products of other countries, would not be so materially affected in the state supposed. Let us, then, examine what are the causes growing out of this connection, by which so great a change is effected. They may be comprehended under three heads—the Custom-House, the appropriations, and the monopoly of the manufacturers; all of which are so intimately blended as to constitute one system, which its advocates, by a perversion of all that is associated with the name, call the "AMERICAN SYSTEM." The Tariff is the soul of this system.

It has already been proved that our contribution, through the Custom-House, to the Treasury of the Union, amounts annually to $16,650,000, which leads to the inquiry—What becomes of so large an amount of the products of our labor, placed, by the operation of the system, at the disposal of Congress? One point is certain—a very small share returns to us, out of whose labor it is extracted. It would require much investigation to state, with precision, the proportion of the public revenue disbursed annually in the Southern, and other States respectively; but the committee feel a thorough conviction, on examination of the annual appropriation acts, that a sum much less than two millions of dollars falls to our share of the disbursements; and that it would be a moderate estimate to place our contribution, above what we receive back, through all of the appropriations, at $15,000,000; constituting, to that great amount, an annual, continued, and uncompensated draft on the industry of the Southern States, through the Custom-House alone. This sum, deducted from the $37,000,000—the amount of our products annually exported, and added to the $20,000,000, the amount of the exports of the other States, with the profits of foreign trade and navigation, would reduce our means of consumption to $22,000,000, and raise theirs to $35,000,000—still leaving $3,000,000 to be accounted for; and which may be readily explained, through the operation of the remaining branch of the system—the monopoly which it affords the manufacturers in our market; and which empowers them to force their goods on us at a price equal to the foreign article of the same description, with the addition of the duty—thus receiving, in exchange, our products, to be shipped, on their account—and thereby increasing their means, and diminishing ours in the same proportion. But this constitutes a part only of our loss under this branch. In addition to the thirty-five millions of our products which are shipped to foreign countries, a very large amount is annually sent to the other States, for their own use and consumption. The article of cotton alone, is estimated at 150,000 bales—which, valued at thirty dollars the bale, would amount to $4,500,000, and constitutes a part of this forced exchange.

Such is the process, and the amount, in part, of the transfer of our property annually to other sections of the country, estimated on the supposition that each section consumes of imported articles, an amount equal in proportion to its population. But the committee are aware that they have rated our share of the consumption far higher than the advocates of the

system place it. Some of them rate it as low as five millions of dollars
annually; not perceiving that, by thus reducing ours, and raising that of the
manufacturing States, in the same proportion, they demonstratively prove
how oppressive the system is to us, and how gainful to them; instead of
showing, as they suppose, how little we are affected by its operation. Our
complaint is, that we are not permitted to consume the fruits of our labor;
but that, through an artful and complex system, in violation of every principle of justice, they are transferred from us to others. It is, indeed, wonderful that those who profit by our loss, blinded as they are by self-interest,
when reducing our consumption as low as they have, never thought to
inquire what became of the immense amount of the products of our industry, which are annually sent out in exchange with the rest of the world; and
if we did not consume its proceeds, who did—and by what means. If, in
the ardent pursuit of gain, such a thought had occurred, it would seem
impossible, that all the sophistry of self-interest, deceiving as it is, could
have disguised from their view our deep oppression, under the operation of
the system.

Your committee do not intend to represent, that the commercial connection between us and the manufacturing States is wholly sustained by the
Tariff system. A great, natural, and profitable commercial communication
would exist between us, without the aid of monopoly on their part; which,
with mutual advantage, would transfer a large amount of their products to
us, and an equal amount of ours to them, as the means of carrying on their
commercial operations with other countries, But even this legitimate commerce is greatly affected, to our disadvantage, through the Tariff system;
the very object of which is, to raise the price of labor, and the profits of
capital, in the manufacturing States—which, from the nature of things,
cannot be done, without raising, correspondingly, the price of all products,
in the same quarter, as well those protected, as those not protected. That
such would be the effect, we know has been urged in argument mainly to
reconcile all classes in those States to the system; and with such success,
as to leave us no room to doubt its correctness; and yet, such are the

strange contradictions, in which the advocates of an unjust cause must ever involve themselves, when they attempt to sustain it, that the very persons, who urge the adoption of the system in one quarter, by holding out the temptation of high prices for all they make, turn round and gravely inform us, that its tendency is to depress, and not to advance prices. The capitalist, the farmer, the wool-grower, the merchant and laborer, in the manufacturing States, are all to receive higher rates of wages and profits—while we, who consume, are to pay less for the products of their labor and capital. As contradictory and absurd as are their arguments, they, at least, conclusively establish the important fact, that those who advance them are conscious that the proof of the partial and oppressive operation of the system, is unanswerable if it be conceded that we, in consequence, pay higher prices for what we consume. Were it possible to meet this conclusion on other grounds, it could not be, that men of sense would venture to encounter such palpable contradictions. So long as the wages of labor, and the profits of capital, constitute the principal elements of price, as they ever must, the one or the other argument—that addressed to us, or that to the manufacturing States—must be false. But, in order to have a clear conception of this important point, the committee propose to consider more fully the assertion, that it is the tendency of high duties, by affording protection, to reduce, instead of to increase prices; and if they are not greatly mistaken, it will prove, on examination, to be utterly erroneous.

Before entering on the discussion, and in order to avoid misapprehension, the committee will admit, that there is a single exception. When a country is fully prepared to manufacture, that is, when wages and interest are as low, and natural advantages as great, as in the countries from which it draws its supplies, it may happen, that high duties, by starting manufactories, under such circumstances, may be followed by a permanent reduction in prices; and which, if the Government had the power, and the people possessed sufficient guarantees against abuse, might render it wise and just, in reference to the general interest, in many instances to afford protection to infant manufacturing establishments. But, where permanent support is required—which must ever be the case when a country is not ripe—such duties must ever be followed by increased prices. The temporary effect may be different, from various causes. Against this position, it is urged, that the price depends on the proportion between the supply and demand—that protection, by converting mere consumers into rival manufacturers, must increase the supply without raising the demand—and, consequently, must tend to reduce prices. If it were necessary, it might be conclusively shown, that this tendency must be more than countervailed, by subtracting, as must ever be the case when the system is forced, capital and labor from more profitable, and turning them to less profitable pursuit, by an expensive bounty, paid out of the labor of the country. But, admitting the argument to be true, the reduction of price must be in proportion to the addition made to the general supply of the commercial world, which is so great that, if we were to suppose our share of the demand to be wholly withdrawn, its tendency to reduce the general price would be small compared to the tendency to high prices, in consequence of the high duties. But the argument rests on an assumption wholly false. It proceeds on the supposition that, without the Tariff, the manufacturing States would not have become such—than which nothing can be more erroneous. They had no alternative, but to emigrate, or to manufacture. How could they otherwise obtain clothing or other articles necessary for their supply? How could they pay for them? To Europe they could ship almost nothing. Their agricultural products are nearly the same with those of that portion of the globe; and the only two articles, grain and lumber, in the production of which they have advantages, are, in that quarter, either prohibited, or subject to high duties. From us, who are purely an agricultural people, they could draw nothing but the products of the soil. The question, then, is not, whether those States should or should not manufacture—for necessity, and the policy of other nations had decided that question—but whether they should, with or without a bounty. It was our interest that they should without. It would compel them to contend with the rest of the world in our market, in free and open competition; the effects of which would have been, a reduction of prices to the lowest point; thereby enabling us to exchange the products of our labor most advantageously—giving little, and receiving much; while, on the other hand, in order to meet European competition, they would have been compelled to work at the lowest wages and profits. To avoid this, it was their interest to manufacture with a bounty; by which our situation was completely reversed. They were relieved by our depression. Thus, through our political connection, by a perversion of the powers of the Constitution, which was intended to protect the States of the Union in the enjoyment of their natural advantages, they have stripped us of the blessings bestowed by nature, and converted them to their own advantage. Restore our advantages, by giving us free trade with the world, and we would become, what they now are by our means, the most flourishing people on the globe. But these are withheld from us under the fear that, with their restoration, they would become, what we are by their loss, among the most depressed.

Having answered the argument in the abstract, the committee will not swell their report by considering the various instances which have been quoted, to show that prices have not advanced since the commencement of the system. We know that they would instantly fall nearly fifty per cent, if its burdens were removed; and that is sufficient for us to know. Many and conclusive reasons might be urged, to show why, from other causes, prices have declined since that period. The fall in the price of raw materials—the effects of the return of peace—the immense reduction in the amount of the circulating medium of the world, by the withdrawal from circulation of a vast amount of paper, both in this country and in Europe—the important improvements in the mechanical and chemical arts—and, finally, the still progressive depression arising from the great improvements which preceded that period a short time, particularly in the use of steam and the art of spinning and weaving—have all contributed to this result. The final reduction of prices, which must take place in the articles whose production is affected by such improvements, cannot be suddenly realized. Another generation will probably pass away, before they will reach that point of depression which must follow their universal introduction.

We are told, by those who pretend to understand our interest better than we do, that the excess of production, and not the Tariff, is the evil which afflicts us; and that our true remedy is, a reduction of the quantity of cotton, rice, and tobacco, which we raise, and not a repeal of the Tariff. They assert, that low prices are the necessary consequence of excess of supply, and that the only proper correction is in diminishing the quantity. We would feel more disposed to respect the spirit in which the advice is offered, if those from whom it comes accompanied it with the weight of their example. *They* also, occasionally, complain of low prices; but instead of diminishing the supply, as a remedy for the evil, demand an enlargement of the market, by the exclusion of all competition. *Our market is the world;* and as we cannot imitate their example by enlarging it for our products, through the exclusion of others, we must decline their advice— which, instead of alleviating, would increase our embarrassments. We have no monopoly in the supply of our products; one-half of the globe may produce them. Should we reduce our production, others stand ready, by increasing theirs, to take our place; and, instead of raising prices, we would only diminish our share of the supply. We are thus compelled to produce, on the penalty of losing our hold on the general market. Once lost, it may be lost forever—and lose it we must, if we continue to be constrained, as we now are, on the one hand, by the general competition of the world, to sell *low;* and, on the other, by the Tariff to buy *high.* We cannot withstand this double action. Our ruin must follow. In fact, our only permanent and safe remedy is, not from the rise in the price of what we *sell,* in which we can receive but little aid from our Government, but a reduction in the price of what we *buy;* which is prevented by the interference of the Government. Give us a free and open competition in our own market, and we fear not to encounter like competition in the general market of the world. If, under all our discouragement by the acts of our Government, we are still able to contend there against the world, can it be doubted, if this impediment were removed, we would force out all competition; and thus, also enlarge our market—not by the oppression of our fellow-citizens of other States, but by our industry, enterprise, and natural advantages. But while the system prevents this great enlargement of our foreign market, and endangers what remains to us, its advocates attempt to console us by the growth of the home market for our products, which, according to their calculation, is to compensate us amply for all our losses; though, in the leading article of our products, cotton, the home market now consumes but a sixth; and if the prohibitory system as to cotton goods were perfected by the exclusion of all importations, the entire consumption of cotton goods would not raise the home consumption of cotton above a fifth of what we raise.

In the other articles, rice and tobacco, it is much less. But brilliant prospects are held out, of our immense export trade in cotton goods, which is to consume an immense amount of the raw material—without reflecting to what countries they are to be shipped. Not to Europe, for there we will meet prohibition for prohibition—not to the Southern portions of this continent, for already they have been taught to imitate our prohibitory policy. The most sanguine will not expect extensive or profitable markets in the other portions of the globe. But, admitting that no other impediment existed, the system itself is an effectual barrier against extensive exports. The very means which secures the domestic market must lose the foreign. High wages and profits are an effectual stimulus when enforced by monopoly, as in our market, but they must be fatal to competition in the open and free market of the world. Besides, when manufactured articles are exported, they must follow the same law to which the products of the soil are subject when exported. They will be sent out in order to be exchanged for the products of other countries; and if these products be taxed on their introduction, as a back return, it has been demonstrated that, like all other taxes on exchange, it must be paid by the producer of the articles. The nature of the operation will be seen, if it be supposed, in their exchange with us, instead of receiving our products free of duty, the manufacturer had to pay forty-five per cent in the back return, on the cotton and other products which they may receive from us in exchange. If to these insuperable impediments to a large export trade it be added, that our country rears the products of almost every soil and climate, and that scarcely an article can be imported, but what may come in competition with some of the products of our arts or our soil, and consequently ought to be excluded on the principles of the system, it must be apparent, when perfected, the system itself must essentially exclude exports; unless we should charitably export for the supply of the wants of others, without expecting a return trade. The loss of the exports, and with it the imports also, must, in truth, be the end of the system. If we export, we must import; and if we exclude all imported products which come in competition with ours, unless we can invent new articles of exchange, or enlarge, tenfold, the consumption of the few which we cannot produce, with the ceasing of importation, exportation must also cease. If it did not, then neither would importation cease; and the continuance of imports must be followed, as stated, by that of exports—and this again would require—in order to complete the system by excluding competition in our own markets—new duties; and thus, an incessant and unlimited increase of duties would be the result of the competition, of which the manufacturing States complain. The evil is in the exports—and the most simple and efficient system to secure the home market, would, in fact, be, to prohibit exports; and as the Constitution only prohibits duties on exports, and as duties are not prohibitions, we may yet witness this addition to the system—the same construction of the instrument which justifies the system itself, would equally justify this, as a necessary means to perfect it.

The committee deemed it more satisfactory to present the operation of the system on the staple States generally, than its peculiar operation on this. In fact, they had not the data, had they felt the inclination, to distinguish the oppression under which this State labors, from that of the other staple States. The fate of the one must be that of the others. It may, however, be truly said, that we are among the greatest sufferers. No portion of the world, in proportion to population and wealth, ever exchanged with other countries a greater amount of its products. With the proceeds of the sales of a few great staples we purchase almost all our supplies; and that system must, indeed, act with the desolation of a famine on such a people, where the Government exacts a tax of nearly fifty per cent on so large a proportion of their exchanges, in order that a portion of their fellow citizens might, in effect, lay one as high on the residue.

The committee have, thus far, considered the question in its relative effects on the staple and manufacturing States—comprehending, under the latter, all those that support the Tariff system. It is not for them to determine whether all those States have an equal interest in its continuance. It is manifest that their situation, in respect to its operation, is very different. While, in some, the manufacturing interest wholly prevails—in others, the commercial and navigating interests—and in a third, the agricultural interest greatly predominates—as is the case in all the Western States. It is difficult to conceive what real interest the last can have in the system. They manufacture but little, and must consequently draw their supplies, principally, either from abroad, or from the real manufacturing States; and, in either case, must pay the increased price in consequence of the high duties, which, at the same time, must diminish their means with ours, from whom they are principally derived, through an extensive interior commercial intercourse. From the nature of our commercial connections, our loss must precede theirs; but theirs will with certainty follow, unless compensation for the loss of our trade can be found somewhere in the system. Its authors have informed us that it consists of two parts—of which *protection* is the essence of one, and *appropriation* of the other. In both capacities it impoverishes us—and in both it enriches the real manufacturing States. The agricultural States of the West are differently affected. As a *protective* system, they lose in common with us—and it will remain with them to determine, whether an adequate compensation can be found, in appropriations for internal improvements, or any other purpose, for the steady and rich returns which a free exchange of the produce of their fertile soil with the staple States must give, provided the latter be left in full possession of their natural advantages.

The question, in what manner the loss and gain of the system distribute themselves among the several classes of society, is intimately connected with that of their distribution among the several sections. Few subjects present more important points for consideration; but as it is not possible for the committee to enter fully into the discussion of them, without swelling their report beyond all reasonable bounds, they will pass them over with a few brief and general remarks.

The system has not been sufficiently long in operation with us, to display its real character in reference to the point now under discussion. To understand its ultimate tendency, in distributing the wealth of society among the several classes, we must turn our eyes to Europe, where it has been in action for centuries—and operated as one among the efficient causes of that great inequality of property which prevails in most European countries. No system can be more efficient to rear up a moneyed aristocracy. Its tendency is, to make the poor poorer, and the rich richer. Heretofore, in our country, this tendency has displayed itself principally in its effects, as regards the different sections—but the time will come when it will produce the same results between the several classes in the manufacturing States. After we are exhausted, the contest will be between the capitalists and operatives; for into these two classes it must, ultimately, divide society. The issue of the struggle here must be the same as it has been in Europe. Under the operation of the system, wages must sink more rapidly than the prices of the necessaries of life, till the operatives will be reduced to the lowest point—when the portion of the products of their labor left to them, will be barely sufficient to preserve existence. For the present, the pressure of the system is on our section. Its effects on the staple States produce almost universal suffering. In the mean time, an opposite state of things exists in the manufacturing States. For the present, every interest among them—except that of foreign trade and navigation, flourishes. Such must be the effect of a monopoly of so rich and extensive a market as that of the Southern States, till it is impoverished—as ours rapidly must be, by the operation of the system, when its natural tendencies, and effects on the several classes of the community, will unfold themselves, as has been described by the committee.

It remains to be considered, in tracing the effects of the system, whether the gain of one section of the country be equal to the loss of the other. If such were the fact—if all we lose be gained by the citizens of the other sections, we would, at least, have the satisfaction of thinking that, however unjust and oppressive, it was but a transfer of property, without diminishing the wealth of the community. Such, however, is not the fact; and to its other mischievous consequences we must add, that it destroys much more than it transfers. Industry cannot be forced out of its natural channel without loss; and this, with the injustice, constitutes the objection to the improper intermeddling of the Government with the private pursuits of individuals, who must understand their own interests better than the Government. The exact loss from such intermeddling, it may be difficult to ascertain, but it is not, therefore, the less certain. The committee will not undertake to estimate the millions, which are annually lost to our country, under the existing system; but some idea may be formed of its magnitude, by stating, that it is, at least, equal to the difference between the profits of our manufacturers, and the duties imposed for their protection, where these are not prohibitory. The lower the profit, and the higher the duty (if not, as stated, prohibitory)—the greater the loss. If, with these certain data, the evidence reported by the Committee on Manufactures at the last session of Congress, be examined, a pretty correct opinion may be formed of the extent of the loss of the country—provided the manufacturers have fairly stated their case. With a duty of about forty per cent on the leading articles of consumption (if we are to credit the testimony reported), the manufacturers did not realize, generally, a profit equal to the legal rate of interest; which would give a loss of largely upwards of thirty per cent to the country on its products. It is different with the foreign articles of the same description. On them, the country, at least, loses nothing. There, the duty passes into the Treasury—lost, indeed, to the Southern States, out of whose labor, directly or indirectly, it must, for the most part, be paid—but transferred, through appropriations in a hundred forms, to the pockets of others. It is thus the system is cherished by appropriators; and well may its advocates affirm, that *they* constitute an essential portion of the American System. Let this conduit, through which it is so profusely supplied, be closed, and we feel confident that scarcely a State, except a real manufacturing one, would tolerate its burden. A total prohibition of importations, by cutting off the revenue, and thereby the means of making appropriations, would, in a short period, destroy it. But the excess of its loss over its gains, leads to the consoling reflection, that its abolition would relieve us, much more than it would embarrass the manufacturing States. We have suffered too much to desire to see others afflicted, even for our relief, when it can be possibly avoided. We would rejoice to see our manufactures flourish on any constitutional principle, consistent with justice and the public liberty. It is not against them, but the means by which they have been forced, to our ruin, that we object. As far as a moderate system, founded on imposts for revenue, goes, we are willing to afford protection, though we clearly see that, even under such a system, the national revenue would be based on our labor, and be paid by our industry. With such constitutional and moderate protection, the manufacturer ought to be satisfied. His loss would not be so great as might be supposed. If low duties would be followed by low prices, they would also diminish the costs of manufacturing; and thus the reduction of profit would be less in proportion than the reduction of the prices of the manufactured article. Be this, however, as it may, the General Government cannot proceed beyond this point of protection, consistently with its powers, and justice to the whole. If the manufacturing States deem further protection necessary, it is in their power to afford it to their citizens, within their own limits, against foreign competition, to any extent they may judge expedient. The Constitution authorizes them to lay an impost duty, with the assent of Congress, which, doubtless, would be given; and if that be not sufficient, they have the additional and efficient power of giving a direct bounty for their encouragement—which the ablest writers on the subject concede to be the least burdensome and most effectual mode of encouragement. Thus, they who are to be benefited, will bear the burden, as they ought; and those who believe it is wise and just to protect manufactures, may have the satisfaction of doing it at their expense, and not at that of their fellow-citizens of the other States, who entertain precisely the opposite opinion.

The committee having presented its views on the partial and oppressive operation of the system, will proceed to discuss the next position which they proposed—its tendency to corrupt the Government, and to destroy the liberty of the country.

If there be a political proposition universally true—one which springs directly from the nature of man, and is independent of circumstances—it is, that irresponsible power is inconsistent with liberty, and must corrupt those who exercise it. On this great principle our political system rests. We consider all powers as delegated by the people, and to be controlled by them, who are interested in their just and proper exercise; and our Governments, both State and General, are but a system of judicious contrivances to bring this fundamental principle into fair, practical operation. Among the most prominent of these is, the responsibility of representatives to their constituents, through frequent periodical elections, in order to enforce a faithful performance of their delegated trust. Without such a check on their powers, however clearly they may be defined, and distinctly prescribed, our liberty would be but a mockery. The Government, instead of being directed to the general good, would speedily become but the instrument to aggrandize those who might be intrusted with its administration. On the other hand, if laws were uniform in their operation—if that which imposed a burden on one, imposed it likewise on all—or that which acted beneficially for one, acted also, in the same manner, for all—the responsibility of representatives to their constituents would alone be sufficient to guard against abuse and tyranny—provided the people be sufficiently intelligent to understand their interest, and the motives and conduct of their public agents. But, if it be supposed that, from diversity of interests in the several classes and sections of the country, the laws act differently, so that the same law, though couched in general terms and apparently fair, shall, in reality, transfer the power and property of one class or section to another—in such case, responsibility to constituents, which is but the means of enforcing fidelity of representatives to them, must prove wholly insufficient to preserve the purity of public agents, or the liberty of the country. It would, in fact, fall short of the evil. The disease would be in the community itself—in the constituents, and not their representatives. The opposing interests of the community would engender, necessarily, opposing, hostile parties—organized on this very diversity of interests—the stronger of which, if the Government provided no efficient check, would exercise unlimited and unrestrained power over the weaker. The relation of equality between the parts of the community, established by the Constitution, would be destroyed, and in its place there would be substituted the relation of sovereign and subject, between the stronger and weaker interests, in its most odious and oppressive form. That this is a possible state of society, even where the representative system prevails, we have high authority. Mr. Hamilton, in the 51st number of the Federalist, says, "It is of the greatest importance in a republic, not only to guard society against the oppression of its rulers, but to guard one part of society against the injustice of the other part. Different interests necessarily exist in different classes of citizens. If a majority be united by a common interest, the rights of the minority will be insecure." Again—"In a society, under the forms of which the stronger faction can readily unite and oppress the weaker, anarchy may be said as truly to reign, as in a state of nature, where the weaker individual is not secured against the violence of the stronger." We have still higher authority—the unhappy existing example, of which we are the victims. The committee has labored to little purpose, if they have not demonstrated that the very case, which Mr. Hamilton so forcibly describes, does not now exist in our country, under the name of the AMERICAN SYSTEM—and which, if not timely arrested, must be followed by all the consequences which never fail to spring from the exercise of irresponsible power. On the great and vital point, the industry of the country—which comprehends almost every interest, the interest of the two great sections is opposed. We want free trade—they restrictions; we want moderate taxes, frugality in the Government, economy, accountability, and a rigid application of the public money to the payment of the debt, and to the objects authorized by the Constitution. In all these particulars, if we may judge by experience, their views of their interest are precisely the opposite. They feel and act, on all questions connected with the American System, as sovereigns—as men invariably do who impose burdens on others for their own benefit; and we, on the other hand, like those on whom such burdens are imposed. In a word, to the extent stated, the country is divided and organized into two great parties—the one sovereign and the other subject—bearing towards each other all the attributes which must ever accompany that relation, under whatever form it may exist. That our industry is controlled by many, instead of one—by a majority in Congress, *elected* by a majority in the community having a opposing interest, instead of by *hereditary* rulers— forms not the slightest mitigation of the evil. In fact, instead of mitigating, it aggravates. In our case, one opposing branch of industry cannot prevail without associating others; and thus, instead of a single act of oppression, we must bear many. The history of the Woollens Bill will illustrate the truth of this position. The woollen manufacturers found they were too feeble to enforce their exactions alone, and, of necessity, resorted to the expedient, which will ever be adopted in such cases, of associating other interests, till a majority be formed—and the result of which, in this case, was, that instead of increased duties on woollens alone—which would have been the fact if that interest alone governed, we have to bear equally increased duties on more than a dozen other of the leading articles of consumption. It would be weakness to attempt to disguise the fact—on a full knowledge of which, and of the danger it threatens, the hope of devising some means of security depends—that different and opposing interests do, and must ever exist in all societies, against the evil of which representation opposes not the slightest resistance. Laws, so far from being uniform in their operation, are scarcely ever so. It requires the greatest wisdom and moderation to extend over any country a system of equal laws; and it is this very diversity of interests, which is found in all associations of men for common purposes, be they private or public, that constitutes the main difficulty in forming and administering free and just governments. It is the door through which despotic power has, heretofore, ever entered, and must ever continue to enter, till some effectual barrier be provided. Without some such, it would be folly to hope for the duration of liberty—as much so as to expect it without representation itself—and for the same reason. The essence of liberty comprehends the idea of responsible power—that those who make and execute the laws should be controlled by those on whom they operate—that the *governed* should *govern*. To prevent rulers from abusing their trusts, constituents must control them through elections; and to prevent the major from oppressing the minor interests of society, the Constitution must provide (as the committee hope to prove it does) a check, founded on the same principle and equally efficacious. In fact, the abuse of delegated power, and the tyranny of the stronger over the weaker interests, are the two dangers, and the only two to be guarded against; and if this be done effectually, liberty must be eternal. Of the two, the latter is the greater and most difficult to resist. It is less perceptible. Every circumstance of life teaches us the liability of delegated power to abuse. We cannot appoint an agent without being admonished of the fact; and, therefore, it has become well understood, and is effectually guarded against in our political institutions. Not so as to the other and greater danger. Though it in fact exists in all associations, yet the law, the courts, and the Government itself, act as a check to its extreme abuse in most cases of private and subordinate companies, which prevents the full display of its real tendency. But let it be supposed that there was no paramount authority—no court, no government to control, what sober individual, who expected himself to act honestly, would place his property in joint-stock with any number of individuals, however respectable, to be disposed of by the unchecked will of the majority, whether acting in a body as stockholders, or through representation, by a direction? Who does not see that a major and a minor interest would, sooner or later, spring up, and that the result would be that, after the stronger had divested the feebler of all interest in the concern, they would, in turn, divide until the whole would centre in a single interest? It is the principle which must ever govern such associations; and what is government itself, but a great joint-stock company, which comprehends every interest, and which, as there can be no higher power to restrain its natural operation, must, if not checked within itself, follow the same law? The actual condition of our race in every country, at this and all preceding periods, attests the truth of the remark. No government, based on the naked principle that the majority ought to govern, however true the maxim in its proper sense, and under proper restrictions, can preserve its liberty even for a single generation. The history of all has been the same— violence, injustice, and anarchy—succeeded by the government of one, or a few, under which the people seek refuge from the more oppressive despotism of the many. Those governments only which provide checks— which limit and restrain within proper bounds the power of the majority, have had a prolonged existence, and been distinguished for virtue, patriotism, power, and happiness; and, what is strikingly true, they have been thus distinguished almost in exact proportion to the number and efficacy of their checks. If arranged in relation to these, we would place them in the order of the Roman, English, Spartan, the United Provinces, the Athenian, and several of the small confederacies of antiquity; and if arranged according to the higher attributes which have been enumerated, they would stand almost precisely in the same order. That this coincidence is not accidental, we may be fully assured. The latest and most profound investigator of the Roman History and Constitution (Niebuhr) has conclusively shown that, after the expulsion of the kings, this great commonwealth continued to decline in power, and was the victim of the most violent domestic struggles, which tainted both public and private morals, till the passage of the Licinian law, which gave to the people an efficient veto through their tribunes, as a check on the predominant power of the Patricians. From that period she began to rise superior to all other States in virtue, patriotism, and power. May we profit by the example, and restore the almost lost virtue and patriotism of the Republic, by giving due efficiency, in practice, to the check which our Constitution has provided against a danger so threatening—and which constitutes the only efficient remedy against that unconstitutional and dangerous system which the committee have been considering—as they will now proceed to show.

The committee has demonstrated that the present disordered state of our political system originated in the diversity of interests which exists in the country—a diversity recognized by the Constitution itself, and to which it owes one of its most distinguished and peculiar features—the division of the delegated powers between the State and General Governments. Our short experience, before the formation of the present Government, had conclusively shown that, while there were powers which in their nature were local and peculiar, and which could not be exercised by all, without oppression to some of the parts—so, also, there were those which, in their operation, necessarily affected the whole, and could not, therefore, be exercised by any of the parts, without affecting injuriously the others. On this different character, by which powers are distinguished in their geographical operation, our political system was constructed. Viewed in relation to them, to a certain extent we have a community of interests, which can only be justly and fairly supervised by concentrating the will and authority of the several States in the General Government; while, at the same time, the States have distinct and separate interests, over which no supervision can be exercised by the general power without injustice and oppression. Hence the division in the exercise of sovereign powers. In drawing the line between the powers of the two—the General and State Governments—the great difficulty consisted in determining correctly to which of the two the various political powers ought to belong. This difficult task was, however, performed with so much success that, to this day, there is an almost entire acquiescence in the correctness with which the line was drawn. It would be extraordinary if a system, thus resting with such profound wisdom on the diversity of geographical interests among the States, should make no provision against the dangers to which its very basis might be exposed. The framers of our Constitution have not exposed themselves to the imputation of such weakness. When their work is fairly examined, it will be found that they have provided, with admirable skill, the most effective remedy; and that, if it has not prevented the danger with which the system is now threatened, the fault is not theirs, but ours, in neglecting to make its proper application. In the primary division of the sovereign powers, and in their exact and just classification, as stated, are to be found the first provisions or checks against the abuse of authority on the part of the absolute majority. The powers of the General Government are particularly enumerated and specifically delegated; and all powers not expressly delegated, or which are not necessary and proper to carry into effect those that are so granted, are reserved expressly to the States or the people. The Government is thus positively restricted to the exercise of those general powers that were supposed to act uniformly on all the parts—leaving the residue to the people of the States, by whom alone, from the very nature of these powers, they can be justly and fairly exercised, as has been stated.

Our system, then, consists of two distinct and independent Governments. The general powers, expressly delegated to the General Government, are subject to its sole and separate control; and the States cannot, without violating the constitutional compact, interpose their authority to check, or in any manner to counteract its movements, so long as they are confined to the proper sphere. So, also, the peculiar and local powers reserved to the States are subject to their exclusive control; nor can the General Government interfere, in any manner, with them, without violating the Constitution.

In order to have a full and clear conception of our institutions, it will be proper to remark that there is, in our system, a striking distinction between *Government* and *Sovereignty*. The separate governments of the several States are vested in their Legislative, Executive, and Judicial Departments;

while the sovereignty resides in the people of the States respectively. The powers of the General Government are also vested in its Legislative, Executive, and Judicial Departments, while the sovereignty resides in the people of the several States who created it. But, by an express provision of the Constitution, it may be amended or changed by three-fourths of the States; and thus each State, by assenting to the Constitution with this provision, has modified its original right as a sovereign, of making its individual consent necessary to any change in its political condition; and, by becoming a member of the Union, has placed this important power in the hands of three-fourths of the States—in whom the highest power known to the Constitution actually resides. Not the least portion of this high sovereign authority resides in Congress, or any of the departments of the General Government. They are but the creatures of the Constitution, and are appointed but to execute its provisions; and, therefore, any attempt by all, or any of these departments, to exercise any power which, in its consequences, may alter the nature of the instrument, or change the condition of the parties to it, would be an act of usurpation.

It is thus that our political system, resting on the great principle involved in the recognized diversity of geographical interests in the community, has, in theory, with admirable sagacity, provided the most efficient check against their dangers. Looking to facts, the Constitution has formed the States into a community only to the extent of their common interests; leaving them distinct and independent communities as to all other interests, and drawing the line of separation with consummate skill, as before stated. It is manifest that, so long as this beautiful theory is adhered to in practice, the system, like the atmosphere, will press equally on all the parts. But reason and experience teach us that theory of itself, however excellent, is nugatory, unless there be means of efficiently enforcing it in practice—which brings under consideration the highly important question—What means are provided by the system for enforcing this fundamental provision?

If we look to the history and practical operation of the system, we shall find, on the side of the States, no means resorted to in order to protect their reserved rights against the encroachments of the General Government; while the latter has, from the beginning, adopted the most efficient to prevent the States from encroaching on those delegated to them. The 25th section of the Judiciary Act, passed in 1789—immediately after the Constitution went into operation—provides for an appeal from the State courts to the Supreme Court of the United States in all cases, in the decision of which, the construction of the Constitution—the laws of Congress, or treaties of the United States may be involved; thus giving to that high tribunal the right of final interpretation, and the power, in reality, of nullifying the acts of the State Legislatures whenever, in their opinion, they may conflict with the powers delegated to the General Government. A more ample and complete protection against the encroachments of the governments of the several States cannot be imagined; and to this extent the power may be considered as indispensable and constitutional. But, by a strange misconception of the nature of our system—and, in fact, of the nature of government—it has been regarded as the ultimate power, not only of protecting the General Government against the encroachments of the governments of the States, but also of the encroachments of the former on the latter—and as being, in fact, the only means provided by the Constitution of confining all the powers of the system to their proper constitutional spheres; and, consequently, of determining the limits assigned to each. Such a construction of its powers would, in fact, raise one of the departments of the General Government above the parties who created the constitutional compact, and virtually invest it with the authority to alter, at its pleasure, the relative powers of the General and State Governments, on the distribution of which, as established by the Constitution, our whole system rests—and which, by an express provision of the instrument, can only be altered by three-fourths of the States, as has already been shown. It would go farther. Fairly considered, it would, in effect, divest the people of the States of the sovereign authority, and clothe that department with the robe of supreme power. A position more false and fatal cannot be conceived. Fortunately, it has been so ably refuted by Mr. Madison, in his Report to the Virginia Legislature in 1800, on the Alien and Sedition Acts, as to supersede the necessity of further comments on the part of the committee. Speaking of the right of the State to interpret the Constitution for itself, in the last resort, he remarks: "It has been objected that the Judicial Authority is to be regarded as the sole expositor of the Constitution. On this objection, it might be observed—*first*—that there may be instances of usurped power" (the case of the Tariff is a striking illustration of the truth), "which the forms of the Constitution could never draw within the control of the Judicial Department—*secondly*—that if the decision of the Judiciary be raised above the authority of the sovereign parties to the Constitution, the decision of the other departments, not carried by the forms of the Constitution before the Judiciary, must be equally authoritative and final with the decision of that department. But the proper answer to the objection is, that the resolution of the General Assembly relates to those great and extraordinary cases in which the forms of the Constitution may prove ineffectual against infractions dangerous to the essential rights of the parties to it. The resolution supposes that dangerous powers not delegated, may not only be usurped and exercised by the other departments, but that the Judicial Department also may exercise or sanction dangerous powers beyond the grant of the Constitution; and consequently, that the ultimate right of the parties to the Constitution to judge whether the compact has been dangerously violated, must extend to violations by one delegated authority as well as by another; by the Judiciary as well as by the Executive or the Legislative. However true, therefore, it may be that the Judicial Department is, in all questions submitted to it by the forms of the Constitution, to decide in the last resort, this resort must necessarily be considered the last in relation to the authorities of the other departments of the Government; not in relation to the rights of the parties to the constitutional compact, from which the Judicial and all other departments hold their delegated trusts. On any other hypothesis the delegation of judicial power would annul the authority delegating it; and the concurrence of this department with others in usurped powers might subvert for ever, and beyond the possible reach of any rightful remedy, the very Constitution which all were instituted to preserve."

As a substitute for the rightful remedy, in the last resort, against the encroachments of the General Government on the reserved powers, resort has been had to a rigid construction of the Constitution. A system like ours, of divided powers, must necessarily give great importance to a proper system of construction; but it is perfectly clear that no rule of construction, however perfect, can, in fact, prescribe bounds to the operation of power. All such rules constitute, in fact, but an appeal from the minority to the justice and reason of the majority; and if such appeals were sufficient of themselves to restrain the avarice or ambition of those vested with power, then may a system of technical construction be sufficient to protect against the encroachment of power; but, on such supposition, reason and justice might alone be relied on, without the aid of any constitutional or artificial restraint whatever. Universal experience, in all ages and countries, however, teaches that power can only be restrained by power, and not by reason and justice; and that all restrictions on authority, unsustained by an equal antagonist power, must forever prove wholly inefficient in practice. Such, also, has been the decisive proof of our own short experience. From the beginning, a great and powerful minority gave every force of which it was susceptible to construction, as a means of restraining the majority of Congress to the exercise of its proper powers; and though that original minority, through the force of circumstances, has had the advantage of becoming a majority, and to possess, in consequence, the administration of the General Government during the greater portion of its existence, yet we this day witness, under these most favorable circumstances, such an extension of its powers as to leave to the States scarcely a right worth the possessing. In fact, the power of construction, on which its advocates relied to preserve the rights of the States, has been wielded, as it ever must be, if not checked, to destroy those rights. If the minority has a right to prescribe its rule of construction, a majority, on its part, will exercise a similar right;

but with this striking difference—that the right of the former will be a mere nullity against that of the latter. But that protection, which the minor interests must ever fail to find in any technical system of construction, may be found in the reserved rights of the States themselves, if they be properly called into action; and there only will they ever be found of sufficient efficacy. The right of protecting their powers results, necessarily, by the most simple and demonstrative arguments, from the very nature of the relation subsisting between the States and General Government.

If it be conceded, as it must be by every one who is the least conversant with our institutions, that the sovereign powers delegated are divided between the General and State Governments, and that the latter hold their portion by the same tenure as the former, it would seem impossible to deny to the States the right of deciding on the infractions of their powers, and the proper remedy to be applied for their correction. The right of judging, in such cases, is an essential attribute of sovereignty—of which the States cannot be divested without losing their sovereignty itself—and being reduced to a subordinate corporate condition. In fact, to divide power, and to give to one of the parties the exclusive right of judging of the portion allotted to each, is, in reality, not to divide it at all; and to reserve such exclusive right to the General Government (it matters not by what department to be exercised), is to convert it, in fact, into a great consolidated government, with unlimited powers, and to divest the States, in reality, of all their rights. It is impossible to understand the force of terms, and to deny so plain a conclusion. The opposite opinion can be embraced only on hasty and imperfect views of the relation existing between the States and the General Government. But the existence of the right of judging of their powers, so clearly established from the sovereignty of States, as clearly implies a veto or control, within its limits, on the action of the General Government, on contested points of authority; and this very control is the remedy which the Constitution has provided to prevent the encroachments of the General Government on the reserved rights of the States; and by which the distribution of power, between the General and

State Governments, may be preserved forever inviolable, on the basis established by the Constitution. It is thus effectual protection is afforded to the minority, against the oppression of the majority. Nor does this important conclusion stand on the deduction of reason alone. It is sustained by the highest contemporary authority. Mr. Hamilton, in the number of the Federalist already cited, remarks that, "in a single republic, all the power surrendered by the people is submitted to the administration of a single government; and usurpations are guarded against, by a division of the government into distinct and separate departments. In the compound republic of America, the power surrendered by the people is first divided between two distinct governments, and then the portion allotted to each subdivided among distinct and separate departments. Hence a double security arises to the rights of the people. The different governments will control each other; at the same time that each will be controlled by itself." He thus clearly affirms the control of the States over the General Government, which he traces to the division in the exercise of the sovereign powers under our political system; and by comparing this control to the veto, which the departments in most of our constitutions respectively exercise over the acts of each other, clearly indicates it as his opinion, that the control between the General and State Governments is of the same character. Mr. Madison is still more explicit. In his report, already alluded to, in speaking on this subject, he remarks: "The resolutions, having taken this view of the Federal compact, proceed to infer that, in cases of a deliberate, palpable, and dangerous exercise of other powers, not granted by the said compact, the States, who are parties thereto, have the right, and are in duty bound to interpose to arrest the evil, and for maintaining, within their respective limits, the authorities, rights, and liberties appertaining to them. It appears to your committee to be a plain principle, founded in common sense, illustrated by common practice, and essential to the nature of compacts, that where resort can be had to no tribunal superior to the rights of the parties, the parties themselves must be the rightful judges, in the last resort, whether the bargain made has been pursued or violated. The Constitution of the United States was formed by the sanction of the States, given by each in its sovereign capacity. It adds to the stability and dignity, as well as to the authority of the Constitution, that it rests on this solid foundation. The States, then, being parties to the constitutional compact, and in their sovereign capacity, it follows of necessity that there can be no tribunal above their authority to decide, in the last resort, whether the compact made by them be violated; and, consequently, as parties to it, they must themselves decide, in the last resort, such questions as may be of sufficient magnitude to require their interposition." To these, the no less explicit opinions of Mr. Jefferson may be added; who, in the Kentucky resolutions on the same subject, which have always been attributed to him,[1] states that—"The Government, created by this compact, was not made the exclusive or final judge of the extent of the powers delegated to itself; since that would have made its discretion, and not the Constitution, the measure of its powers—but, as in all other cases of compact between parties having no common judge, each party has an equal right to judge for itself, as well of infractions as of the mode and measure of redress."

To these authorities, which so explicitly affirm the right of the States, in their sovereign capacity, to decide, in the last resort, on the infraction of their rights and the remedy, there may be added the solemn decisions of the Legislatures of two leading States—Virginia and Kentucky—that the power in question rightfully belongs to the States—and the implied sanction which a majority of the States gave, in the important political revolution which shortly followed, and brought Mr. Jefferson into power. It is scarcely possible to add to the weight of authority by which this fundamental principle in our system is sustained.

The committee have thus arrived, by what they deem conclusive reasoning, and the highest authority, at the constitutional and appropriate remedy against the unconstitutional oppression under which this, in common with

[1]Not now a matter of doubt. The manuscript, in his own handwriting, has since been published.—*Crallé.*

the other staple States, labors—and the menacing danger which now hangs over the liberty and happiness of our country—and this brings them to the inquiry—How is the remedy to be applied by the States? In this inquiry a question may be made—whether a State can interpose its sovereignty through the ordinary Legislature, but which the committee do not deem it necessary to investigate. It is sufficient that plausible reasons may be assigned against this mode of action, if there be one (and there is one) free from all objections. Whatever doubts may be raised as to the question— whether the respective Legislatures fully represent the sovereignty of the States for this high purpose, there can be none as to the fact that a Convention fully represents them for all purposes whatever. Its authority, therefore, must remove every objection as to form, and leave the question on the single point of the right of the States to interpose at all. When convened, it will belong to the Convention itself to determine, authoritatively, whether the acts of which we complain be unconstitutional; and, if so, whether they constitute a violation so deliberate, palpable, and dangerous, as to justify the interposition of the State to protect its rights. If this question be decided in the affirmative, the Convention will then determine in what manner they ought to be declared null and void within the limits of the State; which solemn declaration, based on her rights as a member of the Union, would be obligatory, not only on her own citizens, but on the General Government itself; and thus place the violated rights of the State under the shield of the Constitution.

The committee, having thus established the constitutional right of the States to interpose, in order to protect their reserved powers, it cannot be necessary to bestow much time or attention, in order to meet possible objections—particularly as they must be raised, not against the soundness of the arguments, by which the position is sustained, and which they deem unanswerable—but against apprehended consequences, which, even if well founded, would be an objection, not so much to the conclusions of the committee, as to the Constitution itself. They are persuaded that, whatever objection may be suggested, it will be found, on investigation, to be destitute of solidity. Under these impressions, the committee propose to discuss such as they suppose may be urged, with all possible brevity.

It may be objected, then—in the first place, that the right of the States to interpose rests on mere inference, without any express provision in the Constitution; and that it is not to be supposed—if the Constitution contemplated the exercise of powers of such high importance—that it would have been left to inference alone. In answer, the committee would ask, whether the power of the Supreme Court to declare a law unconstitutional is not among the very highest and most important that can be exercised by any department of the Government—and if any express provision can be found to justify its exercise? Like the power in question, it also rests on mere inference—but an inference so clear, that no express provision could render it more certain. The simple fact, that the Judges must decide according to law, and that the Constitution is paramount to the acts of Congress, imposes a necessity on the court to declare the latter void whenever, in its opinion, they come in conflict, in any particular case, with the former. So, also, in the question under consideration. The right of the States— even supposing it to rest on inference, stands on clearer and stronger grounds than that of the Court. In the distribution of powers between the General and State Governments, the Constitution professes to *enumerate* those assigned to the former, in whatever department they may be vested; while the powers of the latter are reserved in general terms, without attempt at enumeration. It may, therefore, constitute a presumption against the former—that the Court has no right to declare a law unconstitutional, because the power is not enumerated among those belonging to the Judiciary—while the omission to enumerate the power of the States to interpose in order to protect their rights—being strictly in accord with the principles on which its framers formed the Constitution, raises not the slightest presumption against its existence. Like all other *reserved* rights, it is to be inferred from the simple fact that it is *not delegated*—as is clearly the case in this instance.

Again—it may be objected to the power, that it is inconsistent with the necessary authority of the General Government—and, in its consequences, must lead to feebleness, anarchy, and finally disunion.

It is impossible to propose any limitation on the authority of governments, without encountering, from the supporters of power, this very objection of feebleness and anarchy: and we accordingly find, that the history of every country which has attempted to establish free institutions, proves that, on this point, the opposing parties—the advocates of power and of freedom—have ever separated. It constituted the essence of the controversy between the Patricians and Plebeians in the Roman Republic—the Tories and Whigs in England—the Ultras and Liberals in France—and, finally, the Federalists and Republicans in our own country—as illustrated by Mr. Madison's Report—and if it were proposed to give to Russia or Austria a representation of the people, it would form the point of controversy between the Imperial and Popular parties. It is, in fact, not at all surprising that, to a people unacquainted with the nature of liberty, and inexperienced in its blessings, all limitations on supreme power should appear incompatible with its nature, and as tending to feebleness and anarchy. Nature has not permitted us to doubt the necessity of a paramount power in all institutions. All see and feel it; but it requires some effort of reason to perceive that, if not controlled, such power must necessarily lead to abuse—and still higher efforts to understand that it may be checked without destroying its efficiency. With us, however, who know from our own experience, and that of other free nations, the truth of these positions, and that power can only be rendered useful and secure by being properly checked—it is, indeed, strange that any intelligent citizen should consider limitations on the authority of government incompatible with its nature—or should fear danger from any check properly lodged, which may be necessary to guard against usurpation or abuse, and protect the great and distinct interests of the country. That there are such interests represented by the States, and that the States are the only competent powers to protect them, has been sufficiently established; and it only remains, in order to meet the objection, to prove that, for this purpose, the States may be safely vested with the right of interposition.

If the committee do not greatly mistake, the checking or veto power never has, in any country, or under any institutions, been lodged where it was less liable to abuse. The great number, by whom it must be exercised, of the people of a State—the solemnity of the mode—a Convention specially called for the purpose, and representing the State in her highest capacity—the delay—the deliberation—are all calculated to allay excitement—to impress on the people a deep and solemn tone, highly favorable to calm investigation and decision. Under such circumstances, it would be impossible for a mere party to maintain itself in the State, unless the violation of its rights be palpable, deliberate, and dangerous. The attitude in which the State would be placed in relation to the other States—the force of public opinion which would be brought to bear on her—the deep reverence for the General Government—the strong influence of all public men who aspire to office or distinction in the Union—and, above all, the local parties which must ever exist in the State, and which, in this case, must ever throw the powerful influence of the minority on the side of the General Government—constitute impediments to the exercise of this high protective right of the State, which must render it safe. So powerful, in fact, are these difficulties, that nothing but truth and a deep sense of oppression on the part of the people of the State, will ever sustain the exercise of the power—and if it should be attempted under other circumstances, it must speedily terminate in the expulsion of those in power, to be replaced by others who would make a merit of closing the controversy, by yielding the point in dispute.

But, in order to understand more fully what its operation really would be in practice, we must take into the estimate the effect which a recognition of the power would have on the tone of feeling, both of the General and State Governments. On the part of the former, it would necessarily produce, in the exercise of doubtful powers, the most marked moderation. In the discussion of measures involving such powers, the argument would be felt with decisive weight, that the State, also, had the right of judging of the constitutionality of the power; which would cause an abandonment of the measure—or, at least, lead to such modifications as would make it acceptable. On the part of the State, a feeling of conscious security, depending on herself—with the effect of moderation and kindness on the part of the General Government, would effectually put down jealousy, hatred, and animosity—and thus give scope to the natural attachment to our institutions, to expand and grow into the full maturity of patriotism. But withhold this protective power from the State, and the reverse of all these happy consequences must follow—which the committee will not undertake to describe, as the living example of discord, hatred, and jealousy—threatening anarchy and dissolution, must impress on every beholder a more vivid picture than any they could possibly draw. The continuance of this unhappy state must lead to the loss of all affection—when the Government must be sustained by *force* instead of *patriotism*. In fact, to him who will duly reflect, it must be apparent that, where there are important separate interests, there is no alternative but a veto to protect them, or the military to enforce the claims of the majority interests.

If these deductions be correct—as can scarcely be doubted—under that state of moderation and security, followed by mutual kindness, which must accompany the acknowledgment of the right, the necessity of exercising the veto would rarely exist, and the possibility of its abuse, on the part of the State, would be almost wholly removed. Its acknowledged existence would thus supersede its exercise. But suppose in this the committee should be mistaken—still there exists a sufficient security. As high as this right of interposition on the part of a State may be regarded in relation to the General Government, the constitutional compact provides a remedy against its abuse. There is a higher power—placed above all by the consent of all—the creating and preserving power of the system—to be exercised by three-fourths of the States—and which, under the character of the amending power, can modify the whole system at pleasure—and to the acts of

which none can object. Admit, then, the power in question to belong to the
States—and admit its liability to abuse—and what are the utmost consequences, but to create a presumption against the constitutionality of the
power exercised by the General Government—which, if it be well founded,
must compel them to abandon it—or, if not, to remove the difficulty by
obtaining the contested power in the form of an amendment to the Constitution. If, on an appeal for this purpose, the decision be favorable to the
General Government, a disputed power will be converted into an expressly
granted power—but, on the other hand, if it be adverse, the refusal to
grant will be tantamount to an inhibition of its exercise: and thus, in either
case, the controversy will be determined. And ought not a sovereign State,
as a party to the constitutional compact, and as the guardian of her citizens
and her peculiar interests, to have the power in question? Without it, the
amending power must become obsolete, and the Constitution, through the
exercise of construction, in the end utterly subverted. Let us examine the
case. The disease is, that a majority of the States, through the General
Government, by construction, usurp powers not delegated, and by their
exercise, increase their wealth and authority at the expense of the minority.
How absurd, then, to expect the injured States to attempt a remedy by
proposing an amendment to be ratified by three-fourths of the States,
when, by supposition, there is a majority opposed to them? Nor would it be
less absurd to expect the General Government to propose amendments,
unless compelled to that course by the acts of a State. The Government
can have no inducement. It has a more summary mode—the assumption
of power by construction. The consequence is clear—neither would resort
to the amending power—the one, because it would be useless—and the
other, because it could effect its purpose without it—and thus the highest
power known to the Constitution—on the salutary influence of which, on
the operations of our political institutions, so much was calculated, would
become, in practice, obsolete, as stated; and in lieu of it, the will of the
majority, under the agency of construction, would be substituted, with
unlimited and supreme power. On the contrary, giving the right to a State

to compel the General Government to abandon its pretensions to a constructive power, or to obtain a positive grant of it, by an amendment to the Constitution, would call efficiently into action, on all important disputed questions, this highest power of the system—to whose controlling authority no one can object, and under whose operation all controversies between the States and General Government would be adjusted, and the Constitution gradually acquire all the perfection of which it is susceptible. It is thus that the *creating* becomes the *preserving* power; and we may rest assured it is no less true in politics than in theology, that the power which creates can alone preserve—and that preservation is perpetual creation. Such will be the operation and effect of State interposition.

But it may be objected, that the exercise of the power would have the effect of placing the majority under the control of the minority. If the objection were well founded, it would be fatal. If the majority cannot be trusted, neither can the minority: and to transfer power from the former to the latter, would be but the repetition of the old error, in taking shelter under monarchy or aristocracy, against the more oppressive tyranny of an illy constructed republic. But it is not the consequence of proper checks to change places between the majority and minority. It leaves the power controlled still independent; as is exemplified in our political institutions, by the operation of acknowledged checks. The power of the Judiciary to declare an act of Congress, or of a State Legislature, unconstitutional, is, for its appropriate purpose, a most efficient check; but who that is acquainted with the nature of our Government ever supposed that it ever really vested (when confined to its proper object) a supreme power in the Court over Congress or the State Legislatures? Such was neither the intention, nor is it the effect.

The Constitution has provided another check, which will still further illustrate the nature of their operation. Among the various interests which exist under our complex system, that of large and small States is, perhaps, the most prominent, and among the most carefully guarded in the organization of our Government. To settle the relative weight of the States in the system, and to secure to each the means of maintaining its proper political consequence in its operation, formed one of the most difficult duties in framing the Constitution. No one subject occupied greater space in the proceedings of the Convention. In its final adjustment, the large States had assigned to them a preponderating influence in the House of Representatives, by having therein a weight proportioned to their numbers; but to compensate which, and to secure their political rights against this preponderance, the small States had an equality assigned them in the Senate; while, in the constitution of the Executive branch, the two were blended. To secure the consequence allotted to each, as well as to insure due deliberation in legislating, a veto is allowed to each in the passage of bills; but it would be absurd to suppose that this veto placed either above the other: or was incompatible with the portion of the sovereign power intrusted to the House, the Senate, or the President.

It is thus that our system has provided appropriate checks between the Departments—a veto to guard the supremacy of the Constitution over the laws, and to preserve the due importance of the States, considered in reference to large and small, without creating discord or weakening the beneficent energy of the Government. And so, also, in the division of the sovereign authority between the General and State Governments—by leaving to the States an efficient power to protect, by a veto, the minor against the major interests of the community, the framers of the Constitution acted in strict conformity with the principle which invariably prevails throughout the whole system, where separate interests exist. They were, in truth, no ordinary men. They were wise and practical statesmen, enlightened by history and their own enlarged experience, acquired in conducting our country through a most important revolution—and understood profoundly the nature of man and of government. They saw and felt that there existed in our nature the necessity of government, and government of adequate powers—that the selfish predominate over the social feelings; and that, without a government of such powers, universal conflict and anarchy must prevail among the component parts of society; but they also clearly saw that, our nature remaining unchanged by change of condition, unchecked power, from this very predominance of the selfish over the social feelings, which rendered government necessary, would, of necessity, lead to corruption and oppression on the part of those vested with its exercise. Thus the necessity of government and of checks originates in the same great principle of our nature; and thus the very selfishness which impels those who have power to desire more, will also, with equal force, impel those on whom power operates to resist aggression; and on the balance of these opposing tendencies, liberty and happiness must forever depend. This great principle guided in the formation of every part of our political system. There is not one opposing interest throughout the whole that is not counterpoised. Have the rulers a separate interest from the people? To check its abuse, the relation of representative and constituent is created between them, through periodical elections, by which the fidelity of the representative to the constituent is secured. Have the States, as members of the Union, distinct political interests in reference to their magnitude? Their relative weight is carefully settled, and each has its appropriate agent, with a veto on each other, to protect its political consequence. May there be a conflict between the Constitution and the laws, whereby the rights of citizens may be affected? A remedy may be found in the power of the courts to declare the law unconstitutional in such cases as may be brought before them. Are there, among the several States, separate and peculiar geographical interests? To meet this, a particular organization is provided in the division of the sovereign powers between the State and General Governments. Is there danger, growing out of this division, that the State Legislatures may encroach on the powers of the General Government? The authority of the Supreme Court is adequate to check such encroachments. May the General Government, on the other hand, encroach on the rights reserved to the States respectively? To the States respectively—each in its sovereign capacity—is reserved the power, by its veto, or right of interposition, to arrest the encroachment. And, finally, may this power be abused by a State, so as to interfere improperly with the powers delegated to the General Government? There is provided a power, even over the Constitution itself, vested in three-fourths of the States, which Congress has the authority to invoke, and may terminate all controversies in reference to the subject, by granting or withholding the right in contest. Its authority is acknowledged by all; and to deny or resist it, would be, on the part of the State, a violation of the constitutional compact, and a dissolution of the political association, as far as it is concerned. This is the ultimate and highest power—and the basis on which the whole system rests.

That there exists a case which would justify the interposition of this State, in order to compel the General Government to abandon an unconstitutional power, or to appeal to this high authority to confer it by express grant, the committee do not in the least doubt; and they are equally clear in the necessity of its exercise, if the General Government should continue to persist in its improper assumption of powers belonging to the State— which brings them to the last point they propose to consider—viz.: When would it be proper to exercise this high power?

If the committee were to judge only by the magnitude of the interests at stake, they would, without hesitation, recommend the call of a Convention without delay. But they deeply feel the obligation of respect for the other members of the confederacy, and the necessity of great moderation and forbearance in the exercise even of the most unquestionable right, between parties who stand connected by the closest and most sacred political compact. With these sentiments, they deem it advisable, after presenting the views of the Legislature in this solemn manner (if the body concur with the committee), to allow time for further consideration and reflection, in the hope that a returning sense of justice on the part of the majority, when they come to reflect on the wrongs which this and the other staple States have suffered, and are suffering, may repeal the obnoxious and unconstitutional acts—and thereby prevent the necessity of interposing the veto of the State.

The committee are further induced, at this time, to recommend this course, under the hope that the great political revolution, which will displace from power, on the 4th of March next, those who have acquired authority by setting the will of the people at defiance—and which will bring in an eminent citizen, distinguished for his services to his country, and his justice and patriotism, may be followed up, under his influence, with a complete restoration of the pure principles of our Government. But, in thus recommending delay, the committee wish it to be distinctly understood, that neither doubts of the rightful power of the State, nor apprehension of consequences, constitute the smallest part of their motives. They would be unworthy of the name of freemen—of Americans—of Carolinians, if danger, however great, could cause them to shrink from the maintenance of their constitutional rights. But they deem it preposterous to anticipate danger under a system of laws, where a sovereign party to the compact, which formed the Government, exercises a power which, after the fullest investigation, she conscientiously believes to belong to her under the guarantee of the Constitution itself—and which is essential to the preservation of her sovereignty. The committee deem it not only the right of the State, but her duty, under the solemn sanction of an oath, to interpose, if no other remedy be applied. They interpret the oath to defend the Constitution, not simply as imposing an obligation to abstain from violation, but to prevent it on the part of others. In their opinion, he is as guilty of violating that sacred instrument, who permits an infraction, when it is in his power to prevent it, as he who actually perpetrates the violation. The one may be bolder, and the other more timid—but the sense of duty must be weak in both.

With these views the committee are solemnly of the impression—if the present usurpations and the professed doctrines of the existing system be persevered in—after due forbearance on the part of the State—that it will be her sacred duty to interpose—a duty to herself—to the Union—to the present, and to future generations—and to the cause of liberty over the world, to arrest the progress of a usurpation which, if not arrested, must, in its consequences, corrupt the public morals and destroy the liberty of the country.

[*Note:*—The above is indorsed, in the handwriting of the author— "Rough draft of what is called the South Carolina Exposition." On the concluding page is written in the same hand:

"Concluded by a few remarks on the proposition for the State to impose an excise duty on protected articles, and on her consumption of the same. The first disapproved, and the last approved.

"And, finally, with sundry resolutions."

These "remarks" are not preserved; nor the resolutions that accompanied the report. The committee, to whom the subject was referred, reported a series of resolutions, which the reader will find below. Whether they be identical with those referred to is a matter of conjecture. Those reported and adopted are in the following words]:

PROTEST

The Senate and House of Representatives of South Carolina, now met and sitting in General Assembly, through the Hon. William Smith and the Hon. Robert Y. Hayne, their Representatives in the Senate of the United States, do, in the name and on behalf of the good people of the said Commonwealth, solemnly protest against the system of protecting duties, lately adopted by the Federal Government, for the following reasons:

1st. Because the good people of this commonwealth believe, that the powers of Congress were delegated to it, in trust for the accomplishment of certain specified objects which limit and control them, and that every exercise of them, for any other purposes, is a violation of the Constitution as unwarrantable as the undisguised assumption of substantive, independent powers not granted, or expressly withheld.

2d. Because the power to lay duties on imports is, and in its very nature can be, only a means of effecting objects specified by the Constitution; since no free government, and least of all a government of enumerated powers, can, of right, impose any tax, any more than a penalty, which is not at once justified by public necessity and clearly within the scope and purview of the social compact; and since the right of confining appropriations of the public money to such legitimate and constitutional objects is as essential to the liberties of the people, as their unquestionable privilege to be taxed only by their own consent.

3d. Because they believe that the Tariff Law passed by Congress at its last session, and all other acts of which the principal object is the protection of manufactures, or any other branch of domestic industry, if they be considered as the exercise of a supposed power in Congress to tax the people at its own good will and pleasure, and to apply the money raised to objects not specified in the Constitution, is a violation of these fundamental principles, a breach of a well-defined trust, and a perversion of the high powers vested in the Federal Government for federal purposes only.

4th. Because such acts, considered in the light of a regulation of commerce, are equally liable to objection—since, although the power to regulate commerce, may like other powers be exercised so as to protect domestic manufactures, yet it is clearly distinguishable from a power to do so, *eo nomine*, both in the nature of the thing and in the common acceptation of the terms; and because the confounding of them would lead to the most extravagant results, since the encouragement of domestic industry implies an absolute control over all the interests, resources, and pursuits of a people, and is inconsistent with the idea of any other than a simple, consolidated government.

5th. Because, from the contemporaneous exposition of the Constitution in the numbers of the Federalist (which is cited only because the Supreme Court has recognized its authority), it is clear that the power to regulate commerce was considered by the Convention as only incidentally connected with the encouragement of agriculture and manufactures; and because the power of laying imposts and duties on imports, was not understood to justify, in any case, a prohibition of foreign commodities, except as a means of extending commerce, by coercing foreign nations to a fair reciprocity in their intercourse with us, or for some other bona fide commercial purpose.

6th. Because, whilst the power to protect manufactures is nowhere expressly granted to Congress, nor can be considered as necessary and proper to carry into effect any specified power, it seems to be expressly reserved to the States, by the tenth section of the first article of the Constitution.

7th. Because, even admitting Congress to have a constitutional right to protect manufactures by the imposition of duties or by regulations of commerce, designed principally for that purpose, yet a Tariff, of which the operation is grossly unequal and oppressive, is such an abuse of power, as is incompatible with the principles of a free government and the great ends of civil society—justice, and equality of rights and protection.

8th. Finally, because South Carolina, from her climate, situation, and peculiar institutions, is, and must ever continue to be, wholly dependent upon agriculture and commerce, not only for her prosperity, but for her very existence as a State—because the valuable products of her soil—the blessings by which Divine Providence seems to have designed to compensate for the great disadvantages under which she suffers in other respects—are among the very few that can be cultivated with any profit by slave labor—and if, by the loss of her foreign commerce, these products should be confined to an inadequate market, the fate of this fertile State would be poverty and utter desolation; her citizens, in despair, would emigrate to more fortunate regions, and the whole frame and constitution of her civil polity, be impaired and deranged, if not dissolved entirely.

Deeply impressed with these considerations, the representatives of the good people of this commonwealth, anxiously desiring to live in peace with their fellow-citizens and to do all that in them lies to preserve and perpetuate the union of the States and the liberties of which it is the surest pledge—but feeling it to be their bounden duty to expose and resist all encroachments upon the true spirit of the Constitution, lest an apparent acquiescence in the system of protecting duties should be drawn into precedent—do, in the name of the commonwealth of South Carolina, claim to enter upon the journals of the Senate, their protest against it as unconstitutional, oppressive, and unjust.

Which Exposition and Protest are respectfully submitted.

J. GREGG, *Chairman.*

THE FORT HILL ADDRESS: ON THE RELATIONS OF THE STATES AND FEDERAL GOVERNMENT

[July 26, 1831]

———

By 1831, Calhoun's role in the "Exposition and Protest" had become a matter of common knowledge. As Calhoun himself notes in his introductory remarks to the editor of the Pendleton Messenger, *his official role as president of the Senate had afforded him no opportunity to express his own position on the matter of the proper relation between the states and the general government. Calhoun, clarifying his own position, declares: "Stripped of all its covering, the naked question is, whether ours is a federal or a consolidated government; a constitutional or absolute one; a government resting ultimately on the solid basis of the sovereignty of the States, or on the unrestrained will of a majority; a form of government, as in all other unlimited ones, in which injustice, violence, and force must ultimately prevail." Calhoun leaves no doubt that an improper answer to the question will mean nothing less than the total destruction of liberty.*

While the Fort Hill Address is a forceful articulation of the states rights position on the federal-state question, its endorsement of the natural right of interposition is much more guarded. Calhoun's sense of propriety as vice-president of the United States, as well as his hope of forging a new national coalition, prevented a more radical statement. Calhoun himself admits the cautious nature of his remarks when he notes in his letter to General Hamilton in August 1832 that his initial discussion in the Fort Hill Address "fell far short of exhausting the subject." Still, the Fort Hill Address remains a critical document in American history, for it is Mr. Calhoun's first public effort to generalize the controversy between South Carolina and the federal government.

MR. SYMMES: I must request you to permit me to use your columns, as the medium to make known my sentiments on the deeply important question, of the relation, which the states and general government bear to each other, and which is at this time a subject of so much agitation.

It is one of the peculiarities of the station I occupy, that while it necessarily connects its incumbent with the politics of the day, it affords him no opportunity officially to express his sentiments, except accidentally on an equal division of the body, over which he presides. He is thus exposed, as I have often experienced, to have his opinions erroneously and variously represented. In ordinary cases I conceive the correct course to be to remain silent, leaving to time and circumstances the correction of misrepresentations; but there are occasions so vitally important, that a regard both to duty and character would seem to forbid such a course; and such I conceive, to be the present. The frequent allusion to my sentiments, will not permit me to doubt, that such also is the public conception, and that it claims the right to know, in relation to the question referred to, the opinions of those, who hold important official stations; while on my part desiring to receive neither unmerited praise, nor blame, I feel, I trust the solicitude, which every honest and independent man ought, that my sentiments should be truly known whether they be such, as may be calculated to recommend them to public favor, or not. Entertaining these impressions, I have concluded that it is my duty to make known my sentiments: and I have adopted the mode, which on reflection seemed to be the most simple, and best calculated to effect the object in view.

The question of the relation which the States and General Government bear to each other is not one of recent origin. From the commencement of our system, it has divided public sentiment. Even in the Convention, while the Constitution was struggling into existence, there were two parties as to what this relation should be, whose different sentiments constituted no small impediment in forming that instrument. After the General Government went into operation, experience soon proved that the question had not terminated with the labors of the Convention. The great struggle that preceded the political revolution of 1801, which brought Mr. Jefferson into power, turned essentially on it; and the doctrines and arguments on both sides were embodied and ably sustained—on the one, in the Virginia and Kentucky Resolutions, and the Report to the Virginia Legislature—and on the other, in the replies of the Legislature of Massachusetts and some of the other States. These Resolutions and this Report, with the decision of the Supreme Court of Pennsylvania about the same time (particularly in the case of Cobbett, delivered by Chief Justice M'Kean, and concurred in by the whole bench), contain what I believe to be the true doctrine on this important subject. I refer to them in order to avoid the necessity of presenting my views, with the reasons in support of them, in detail.

As my object is simply to state my opinions, I might pause with this reference to documents that so fully and ably state all the points immediately connected with this deeply important subject; but as there are many who may not have the opportunity or leisure to refer to them, and, as it is possible, however clear they may be, that different persons may place different interpretations on their meaning, I will, in order that my sentiments may be fully known, and to avoid all ambiguity, proceed to state, summarily, the doctrines which I conceive they embrace.

The great and leading principle is, that the General Government emanated from the people of the several States, forming distinct political communities, and acting in their separate and sovereign capacity, and not from all of the people forming one aggregate political community; that the Constitution of the United States is, in fact, a compact, to which each State is a party, in the character already described; and that the several States, or parties, have a right to judge of its infractions; and in case of a deliberate, palpable, and dangerous exercise of power not delegated, they have the right, in the last resort, to use the language of the Virginia Resolutions, "to interpose for arresting the progress of the evil, and for maintaining, within their respective limits, the authorities, rights, and liberties appertaining to them." This right of interposition, thus solemnly asserted by the State of Virginia, be it called what it may—State-right, veto, nullification, or by any other name—I conceive to be the fundamental principle of our system, resting on facts historically as certain as our revolution itself, and deductions as simple and demonstrative as that of any political, or moral truth whatever; and I firmly believe that on its recognition depend the stability and safety of our political institutions.

I am not ignorant, that those opposed to the doctrine have always, now and formerly, regarded it in a very different light, as anarchical and revolutionary. Could I believe such, in fact, to be its tendency, to me it would be no recommendation. I yield to none, I trust, in a deep and sincere attachment to our political institutions and the union of these States. I never breathed an opposite sentiment; but, on the contrary, I have ever considered them the great instruments of preserving our liberty, and promoting the happiness of ourselves and our posterity; and next to these I have ever held them most dear. Nearly half my life has been passed in the service of the Union, and whatever public reputation I have acquired is indissolubly identified with it. To be too national has, indeed, been considered by many, even of my friends, to be my greatest political fault. With these strong feelings of attachment, I have examined, with the utmost care, the bearing of the doctrine in question; and, so far from anarchical or revolutionary, I solemnly believe it to be the only solid foundation of our system, and of the Union itself, and that the opposite doctrine, which denies to the States the right of protecting their reserved powers, and which would vest in the General Government (it matters not through what department), the right of determining, exclusively and finally, the powers delegated to it, is incompatible with the sovereignty of the States, and of the Constitution itself, considered as the basis of a Federal Union. As strong as this language is, it is not stronger than that used by the illustrious Jefferson, who said, to give to the General Government the final and exclusive right to judge of its powers, is to make "its discretion, and not the Constitution, the measure of its powers;" and that, "in all cases of compact between parties having no common judge, each party has an equal right to judge for itself, as well of the infraction as of the mode and measure of redress." Language cannot be more explicit; nor can higher authority be adduced.

That different opinions are entertained on this subject, I consider, but as an additional evidence of the great diversity of the human intellect. Had not able, experienced, and patriotic individuals, for whom I have the highest respect, taken different views, I would have thought the right too clear to admit of doubt; but I am taught by this, as well as by many similar instances, to treat with deference opinions differing from my own. The error may, possibly, be with me; but if so, I can only say that, after the most mature and conscientious examination, I have not been able to detect it. But, with all proper deference, I must think that theirs is the error, who deny, what seems to be an essential attribute of the conceded sovereignty of the States; and who attribute to the General Government a right utterly incompatible with what all acknowledge to be its limited and restricted character; an error originating principally, as I must think, in not duly reflecting on the nature of our institutions, and on what constitutes the only rational object of all political constitutions.

It has been well said by one of the most sagacious men of antiquity, that the object of a constitution is, to *restrain the government, as that of laws* is to restrain *individuals*. The remark is correct; nor is it less true, where the government is vested in a majority, than where it is in a single or a few individuals—in a republic, than a monarchy or aristocracy. No one can have a higher respect for the maxim that the majority ought to govern than I have, taken in its proper sense, subject to the restrictions imposed by the Constitution, and confined to objects in which every portion of the community have similar interests; but it is a great error to suppose, as many do, that the right of a majority to govern is a natural and not a conventional right; and, therefore absolute and unlimited. By nature, every individual has the right to govern himself; and governments, whether founded on majorities or minorities, must derive their right from the assent, expressed or implied, of the governed, and be subject to such limitations as they may impose. Where the interests are the same, that is, where the laws that may benefit one, will benefit all, or the reverse, it is just and proper to place them under the control of the majority; but where they are dissimilar, so that the law that may benefit one portion may be ruinous to another, it would be, on the contrary, unjust and absurd to subject them to its will; and such, I conceive to be the theory on which our Constitution rests.

That such dissimilarity of interests may exist, it is impossible to doubt. They are to be found in every community, in a greater or less degree, however small or homogeneous; and they constitute, everywhere, the great difficulty of forming and preserving free institutions. To guard against the unequal action of the laws, when applied to dissimilar and opposing interests, is, in fact, what mainly renders a constitution indispensable; to overlook which, in reasoning on our Constitution, would be to omit the principal element by which to determine its character. Were there no contrariety of interests, nothing would be more simple and easy than to form and preserve free institutions. The right of suffrage alone would be a sufficient guarantee. It is the conflict of opposing interests which renders it the most difficult work of man.

Where the diversity of interests exists in separate and distinct classes of the community, as is the case in England, and was formerly the case in Sparta, Rome, and most of the free States of antiquity, the rational constitutional provision is, that each should be represented in the government, as a separate estate, with a distinct voice, and a negative on the acts of its co-estates, in order to check their encroachments. In England, the Constitution has assumed expressly this form; while in the governments of Sparta and Rome, the same thing was effected under different, but not much less efficacious forms. The perfection of their organization, in this particular, was that which gave to the constitutions of these renowned States all their celebrity, which secured their liberty for so many centuries, and raised them to so great a height of power and prosperity. Indeed, a constitutional provision giving to the great and separate interests of the community the right of self-protection, must appear, to those who will duly reflect on the subject, not less essential to the preservation of liberty than the right of suffrage itself. They, in fact, have a common object, to effect which the one is as necessary as the other to secure *responsibility*; that is, *that those who make and execute the laws should be accountable to those on whom the laws in reality operate—the only solid and durable foundation of liberty*. If, without the right of suffrage, our rulers would oppress us, so, without the right of self-protection, the major would equally oppress the minor interests of the community. The absence of the former would make the governed the slaves of the rulers; and of the latter, the feebler interests, the victim of the stronger.

Happily for us, we have no artificial and separate classes of society. We have wisely exploded all such distinctions; but we are not, on that account, exempt from all contrariety of interests, as the present distracted and dangerous condition of our country, unfortunately, but too clearly proves. With us they are almost exclusively geographical, resulting mainly from difference of climate, soil, situation, industry, and production; but are not, therefore, less necessary to be protected by an adequate constitutional provision, than where the distinct interests exist in separate classes. The necessity is, in truth, greater, as such separate and dissimilar geographical interests are more liable to come into conflict, and more dangerous, when in that state, than those of any other description; so much so, that *ours is the first instance on record where they have not formed, in an extensive territory, separate and independent* communities, *or subjected the whole to despotic sway.* That such may not be our unhappy fate also, must be the sincere prayer of every lover of his country.

So numerous and diversified are the interests of our country, that they could not be fairly represented in a single government, organized so as to give to each great and leading interest, a separate and distinct voice, as in governments to which I have referred. A plan was adopted better suited to our situation, but perfectly novel in its character. The powers of government were divided, not, as heretofore, in reference to classes, but geographically. One General Government was formed for the whole, to which were delegated all the powers supposed to be necessary to regulate the interests common to all the States, leaving others subject to the separate control of the States, being, from their local and peculiar character, such, that they could not be subject to the will of a majority of the whole Union, without the certain hazard of injustice and oppression. It was thus that the interests of the whole were subjected, as they ought to be, to the will of the whole, while the peculiar and local interests were left under the control of the States separately, to whose custody only, they could be safely confided. This distribution of power, settled solemnly by a constitutional compact, to which all the States are parties, constitutes the peculiar character and excellence of our political system. It is truly and emphatically *American, without example or parallel.*

To realize its perfection, we must view the General Government and those of the States as a whole, each in its proper sphere, sovereign and independent; each perfectly adapted to its respective objects; the States acting separately, representing and protecting the local and peculiar interests; and acting jointly through one General Government, with the weight respectively assigned to each by the Constitution, representing and protecting the interest of the whole; and thus perfecting, by an admirable but simple arrangement, the great principle of representation and responsibility, without which no government can be free or just. To preserve this sacred distribution, as originally settled, by coercing each to move in its proscribed orbit, is the great and difficult problem, on the solution of which, the duration of our Constitution, of our Union, and, in all probability, our liberty depends. How is this to be effected?

The question is new, when applied to our peculiar political organization, where the separate and conflicting interests of society are represented by distinct, but connected governments; but it is, in reality, an old question under a new form, long since perfectly solved. Whenever separate and dissimilar interests have been separately represented in any government; whenever the sovereign power has been divided in its exercise, the experience and wisdom of ages have devised but one mode by which such political organization can be preserved—the mode adopted in England, and by all governments, ancient and modern, blessed with constitutions deserving to be called free—to give to each co-estate the right to judge of its powers, with a negative or veto on the acts of the others, in order to protect against encroachments, the interests it particularly represents: a principle which all of our constitutions recognize in the distribution of power among their respective departments, as essential to maintain the independence of each; but which, to all who will duly reflect on the subject, must appear far more essential, for the same object, in that great and fundamental distribution of powers between the states and General Government. So essential is the principle, that, to withhold the right from either, where the sovereign power is divided, is, in fact, *to annul the division* itself, and to *consolidate*, in the one left in the exclusive possession of the right, *all* powers of government; for it is not possible to distinguish, practically, between a government having all power, and one having the right to take what powers it pleases. Nor does it in the least vary the principle, whether the distribution of power be between co-estates, as in England, or between distinctly organized, but connected governments, as with us. The reason is the same in both cases, while the necessity is greater in our case, as the danger of conflict is greater where the interests of a society are divided geographically than in any other, as has already been shown.

These truths do seem to me to be incontrovertible; and I am at a loss to understand how any one, who has maturely reflected on the nature of our institutions, or who has read history, or studied the principles of free governments to any purpose, can call them in question. The explanation must, it appears to me, be sought in the fact that, in every free State there are those who look more to the necessity of maintaining power than guarding against its abuses. I do not intend reproach, but simply to state a fact apparently necessary to explain the contrariety of opinions among the intelligent, where the abstract consideration of the subject would seem scarcely to admit of doubt. If such be the true cause, I must think the fear of weakening the government too much, in this case, to be in a great measure unfounded, or, at least, that the danger is much less from that than the opposite side. I do not deny that a power of so high a nature may be abused by a State; but when I reflect that the States unanimously called the General Government into existence with all of its powers, which they freely delegated on their part, under the conviction that their common peace, safety, and prosperity required it; that they are bound together by a common origin, and the recollection of common suffering and common triumph in the great and splendid achievement of their independence; and that the strongest feelings of our nature, and among them the love of national power and distinction, are on the side of the Union; it does seem to me that the fear which would strip the States of their sovereignty, and degrade them, in fact, to mere dependent corporations, lest they should abuse a right indispensable to the peaceable protection of those interests which they reserved under their own peculiar guardianship when they created the General Government, is unnatural and unreasonable. If those who voluntarily created the system cannot be trusted to preserve it, what power can?

So, far from extreme danger, I hold that there never was a free State in which this great conservative principle, indispensable to all, was ever so safely lodged. In others, when the co-estates representing the dissimilar and conflicting interests of the community came into contact, the only alternative was compromise, submission, or force. Not so in ours. Should the General Government and a State come into conflict, we have a higher remedy: the power which called the General Government into existence, which gave it all of its authority, and can enlarge, contract, or abolish its powers at its pleasure, may be invoked. The States themselves may be appealed to—three-fourths of which, in fact, form a power, whose decrees are the Constitution itself, and whose voice can silence all discontent. The utmost extent, then, of the power is, that a State, acting in its sovereign capacity, as one of the parties to the constitutional compact, may compel the Government, created by that compact, to submit a question touching its infraction, to the parties who created it; to avoid the supposed dangers of which, it is proposed to resort to the novel, the hazardous, and, I must add, fatal project of giving to the General Government the sole and final right of interpreting the Constitution—thereby reversing the whole system, making that instrument the creature of its will, instead of a rule of action impressed on it at its creation, and annihilating, in fact, the authority which imposed it, and from which the Government itself derives its existence.

That such would be the result, were the right in question vested in the Legislative or Executive branch of the Government, is conceded by all. No one has been so hardy as to assert that Congress or the President ought to have the right, or to deny that, if vested finally and exclusively in either, the consequences which I have stated would necessarily follow; but its advocates have been reconciled to the doctrine, on the supposition that there is one department of the General Government which, from its peculiar organization, affords an independent tribunal, through which the Government may exercise the high authority, which is the subject of consideration, with perfect safety to all.

I yield, I trust, to few in my attachment to the Judiciary Department. I am fully sensible of its importance, and would maintain it, to the fullest extent, in its constitutional powers and independence; but it is impossible for me to believe, that it was ever intended by the Constitution, that it should exercise the power in question, or that it is competent to do so; and, if it were, that it would be a safe depository of the power.

Its powers are judicial, and not political; and are expressly confined by the Constitution "to all *cases* in law and equality arising under this Constitution, the laws of the United States, and the treaties made, or which shall be made, under its authority;" and which I have high authority in asserting, excludes political questions, and comprehends those only where there are parties amenable to the process of the court.[1] Nor is its incompetency less clear than its want of constitutional authority. There may be many, and the most dangerous infractions on the part of Congress, of which, it is conceded by all, the court, as a judicial tribunal, cannot, from its nature, take cognizance. The Tariff itself is a strong case in point; and the reason applies equally *to all others where Congress perverts a power from an object intended, to one not intended, the most insidious and dangerous of all infractions; and which may be extended to all of its powers, more especially to the taxing and appropriating.* But, supposing it competent to take cognizance of all infractions of every description, the insuperable objection still remains, that it would not be a safe tribunal to exercise the power in question.

It is a universal and fundamental political principle, that the power to protect can safely be confided only to those interested in protecting, or their responsible agents—a maxim not less true in private than in public

---

[1] I refer to the authority of Chief Justice Marshall, in the case of Jonathon Robbins. I have not been able to refer to the speech, and speak from memory.*

    * The following are the remarks referred to by Mr. Calhoun:

    "By extending the judicial power to all cases in law and equity, the Constitution *had never been understood* to confer on that department any *political power whatever*. To come within this description, a question must assume a *legal* form, for forensic litigation and judicial decision. There must be parties to come into court who can be reached by its process and bound by its power; whose rights admit of ultimate decision by a tribunal, to which they are bound to submit. A 'case in Law and Equity,' proper for judicial decision, may arise under a treaty, where the *rights of individuals*, acquired or secured by a treaty, are to be asserted or defended in court—as under the fourth and sixth articles of the treaty of peace with Great Britain; or under those articles of our late treaties with France, Prussia, and other nations, which secure to *the subjects* of these nations *their property* within the United States; but the *judicial power cannot extend to political compacts.*" Speech in the House of Representatives, in the case of Thomas Nash, alias Jonathan Robbins, Sept. 1797.—*Crallé.*

affairs. The danger in our system is, that the General Government, which represents the interests of the whole, may encroach on the States, which represent the peculiar and local interests, or that the latter may encroach on the former.

In examining this point, we ought not to forget that the Government, through all its departments, judicial as well as others, is administered by delegated and responsible agents; and that *the power which really controls, ultimately, all the movements is not in the agents, but those who elect or appoint them.* To understand, then, its real character, and what would be the action of the system in any supposable case, we must raise our view from the mere agents to this high controlling power, which finally impels every movement of the machine. By doing so, we shall find all under the control of the will of a majority, compounded of the majority of the States, taken as corporate bodies, and the majority of the people of the States, estimated in federal numbers. These, united, constitute the real and final power which impels and directs the movements of the General Government. The majority of the States elect the majority of the Senate; of the people of the States, that of the House of Representatives; the two united, the President; and the President and a majority of the Senate appoint the judges; a majority of whom, and a majority of the Senate and House, with the President, really exercise all of the powers of the Government, with the exception of the cases where the Constitution requires a greater number than a majority. The judges are, in fact, as truly the judicial representatives of this united majority, as the majority of Congress itself, or the President, is its legislative or executive representative; and to confide "the power to the Judiciary to determine finally and conclusively, what powers are delegated, and what reserved, would be, in reality, to confide it to the majority, whose agents they are, and by whom they can be controlled in various ways; and, of course, to subject (against the fundamental principle of our system and all sound political reasoning) the reserved powers of the States, with all of the local and peculiar interests they were intended to protect, to the will of the very majority against which the protection was intended. Nor will the tenure by which the judges hold their office, however valuable the provision in many other respects, materially vary the case. Its highest possible effect would be to *retard*, and not *finally* to *resist*, the will of a dominant majority.

But it is useless to multiply arguments. Were it possible that reason could settle a question where the passions and interests of men are concerned, this point would have been long since settled forever by the State of Virginia. The report of her Legislature, to which I have already referred, has really, in my opinion, placed it beyond controversy. Speaking in reference to this subject, it says: "It has been objected" (to the right of a State to interpose for the protection of her reserved rights) "that the judicial authority is to be regarded as the sole expositor of the Constitution. On this objection it might be observed, first, that there may be instances of usurped powers which the forms of the Constitution could never draw within the control of the Judicial Department; secondly, that, if the decision of the judiciary be raised above the sovereign parties to the Constitution, the decisions of the other departments, not carried by the forms of the Constitution before the Judiciary, must be equally authoritative and final with the decision of that department. But the proper answer to the objection is, that the resolution of the General Assembly relates to those great and extraordinary cases, in which all the forms of the Constitution may prove ineffectual against infractions dangerous to the essential rights of the parties to it. The resolution supposes that dangerous powers, not delegated, may not only be usurped and executed by the other departments, but that the Judicial Department may also exercise or sanction dangerous powers, beyond the grant of the Constitution, and, consequently, that the ultimate right of the parties to the Constitution to judge whether the compact has been dangerously violated, must extend to violations by one delegated authority, as well as by another—by the judiciary, as well as by the executive or legislative."

Against these conclusive arguments, as they seem to me, it is objected, that, if one of the parties has the right to judge of infractions of the

Constitution, so has the other; and that, consequently, in cases of contested powers between a State and the General Government, each would have a right to maintain its opinion, as is the case when sovereign powers differ in the construction of treaties or compacts; and that, of course, it would come to be a mere question of force. The error is in the assumption that the General Government is a party to the constitutional compact. The States, as has been shown, formed the compact, acting as Sovereign and independent communities. The General Government is but its creature; and though, in reality, a government, with all the rights and authority which belong to any other government, within the orbit of its powers, it is, nevertheless, a government emanating from a compact between sovereigns, and partaking, in its nature and object, of the character of a joint commission, appointed to superintend and administer the interests in which all are jointly concerned; but having, beyond its proper sphere, no more power than if it did not exist. To deny this would be to deny the most incontestable facts, and the clearest conclusions; while to acknowledge its truth is, to destroy utterly the objection that the appeal would be to force, in the case supposed. For if each party has a right to judge, then, under our system of government, the final cognizance of a question of contested power would be in the States, and not in the General Government. It would be the duty of the latter, as in all similar cases of a contest between one or more of the principals and a joint commission or agency, to refer the contest to the principals themselves. Such are the plain dictates of both reason and analogy. On no sound principle can the agents have a right to final cognizance, as against the principals, much less to use force against them to maintain their construction of their powers. Such a right would be monstrous; and has never, heretofore, been claimed in similar cases.

That the doctrine is applicable to the case of a contested power between the States and the General Government, we have the authority, not only of reason and analogy, but of the distinguished statesman already referred to. Mr. Jefferson, at a late period of his life, after long experience and mature reflection, says, "With respect to our State and Federal Governments, I do not think their relations are correctly understood by foreigners. They suppose the former are subordinate to the latter. This is not the case. They are co-ordinate departments of one simple and integral whole. But you may ask, If the two departments should claim each the same subject of power, where is the umpire to decide between them? In cases of little urgency or importance, the prudence of both parties will keep them aloof from the questionable ground; but, if it can neither be avoided nor compromised, a convention of the States must be called to ascribe the doubtful power to that department which they may think best."

It is thus that our Constitution, by authorizing amendments, and by prescribing the authority and mode of making them, has, by a simple contrivance, with its characteristic wisdom, provided a power which, in the last resort, supersedes effectually the necessity, and even the pretext for force: a power to which none can fairly object; with which the interests of all are safe; which can definitively close all controversies in the only effectual mode, by freeing the compact of every defect and uncertainty, by an amendment of the instrument itself. It is impossible for human wisdom, in a system like ours, to devise another mode which shall be safe and effectual, and, at the same time, consistent with what are the relations and acknowledged powers of the two great departments of our Government. It gives a beauty and security peculiar to our system, which, if duly appreciated, will transmit its blessings to the remotest generations; but, if not, our splendid anticipations of the future will prove but an empty dream. Stripped of all its covering, the naked question is, whether ours is a federal or a consolidated government; a constitutional or absolute one; a government resting ultimately on the solid basis of the sovereignty of the States, or on the unrestrained will of a majority; a form of government, as in all other unlimited ones, in which injustice, and violence, and force must finally prevail. *Let it never be forgotten that, where the majority rules, the minority is the subject*; and that, if we should absurdly attribute to the former, the exclusive right of construing the Constitution, there would be, in fact, between the sovereign and subject, under such a government, no

Constitution; or, at least, nothing deserving the name, or serving the legitimate object of so sacred an instrument.

How the States are to exercise this high power of interposition, which constitutes so essential a portion of their reserved rights that it *cannot be delegated without an entire surrender of their sovereignty*, and converting our system from a *federal* into a *consolidated* Government, is a question that the States only are competent to determine. The arguments which prove that they possess the power, equally prove that they are, in the language of Jefferson, "the rightful judges of the mode and measure of redress." But the spirit of forbearance, as well as the nature of the right itself, forbids a recourse to it, except in cases of dangerous infractions of the Constitution; and then only in the last resort, when all reasonable hope of relief from the ordinary action of the Government has failed; when, if the right to interpose did not exist, the alternative would be submission and oppression on one side, or resistance by force on the other. That our system should afford, in such extreme cases, an intermediate point between these dire alternatives, by which the Government may be brought to a pause, and thereby an interval obtained to compromise differences, or, if impracticable, be compelled to submit the question to a constitutional adjustment, through an appeal to the States themselves, is an evidence of its high wisdom: an element not, as is supposed by some, of weakness, but of strength; not of anarchy or revolution, but of peace and safety. *Its general recognition would of itself, in a great measure, if not altogether, supersede the necessity of its exercise, by impressing on the movements of the Government that moderation and justice so essential to harmony and peace, in a country of such vast extent and diversity of interests as ours*; and would, if controversy should come, turn the resentment of the aggrieved from the system to those who had abused its powers (a point all-important), and cause them to seek redress, *not in revolution or overthrow, but in reformation*. It is, in fact, properly understood, *a substitute—where the alternative would be force—tending to prevent, and, if that fails, to correct peaceably the aberrations to which all political systems are liable, and*

which, if permitted to accumulate without correction, must finally end in a
general catastrophe.

I have now said what I intended in reference to the abstract question of
the relation of the States to the General Government, and would here
conclude, did I not believe that a mere general statement on an abstract
question, without including that which may have caused its agitation, would
be considered by many imperfect and unsatisfactory. Feeling that such
would be justly the case, I am compelled, reluctantly, to touch on the
Tariff, so far, at least, as may be necessary to illustrate the opinions which
I have already advanced. Anxious, however, to intrude as little as possible
on the public attention, I will be as brief as possible; and with that view,
will, as far as may be consistent with my object, avoid all debatable topics.

Whatever diversity of opinion may exist in relation to the principle, or
the effect on the productive industry of the country, of the present, or any
other Tariff of protection, there are certain political consequences flowing
from the present which none can doubt, and all must deplore. It would be
in vain to attempt to conceal that it has divided the country into two great
geographical divisions, and arrayed them against each other, in opinion at
least, if not interests also, on some of the most vital of political subjects—
on its finance, its commerce, and its industry—subjects calculated, above
all others, in time of peace, to produce excitement, and in relation to which
the Tariff has placed the sections in question in deep and dangerous conflict. If there be any point on which the (I was going to say, southern
section, but to avoid, as far as possible, the painful feelings such discussions are calculated to excite, I shall say) weaker of the two sections is
unanimous, it is, that its prosperity depends, in a great measure, on free
trade, light taxes, economical, and, as far as possible, equal disbursements
of the public revenue, and unshackled industry—leaving them to pursue
whatever may appear most advantageous to their interests. From the Potomac to the Mississippi, there are few, indeed, however divided on other
points, who would not, if dependent on their volition, and if they regarded
the interest of their particular section only, remove from commerce and

industry every shackle, reduce the revenue to the lowest point that the wants of the Government fairly required, and restrict the appropriations to the most moderate scale consistent with the peace, the security, and the engagements of the public; and who do not believe that the opposite system is calculated to throw on them an unequal burden, to repress their prosperity, and to encroach on their enjoyment.

On all these deeply important measures, the opposite opinion prevails, if not with equal unanimity, with at least a greatly preponderating majority, in the other and stronger section; so much so, that no two distinct nations ever entertained more opposite views of policy than these two sections do, on all the important points to which I have referred. Nor is it less certain that this unhappy conflict, flowing directly from the Tariff, has extended itself to the halls of legislation, and has converted the deliberations of Congress into an annual struggle between the two sections; the stronger to maintain and increase the superiority it has already acquired, and the other to throw off or diminish its burdens: a struggle in which all the noble and generous feelings of patriotism are gradually subsiding into sectional and selfish attachments.[2] Nor has the effect of this dangerous conflict ended here. It has not only divided the two sections on the important point already stated, but on the deeper and more dangerous questions, the constitutionality of a protective Tariff, and the general principles and theory of the Constitution itself: the stronger, in order to maintain their superiority, giving a construction to the instrument which the other believes would convert the General Government into a consolidated, irresponsible government, with the total destruction of liberty; and the weaker, seeing no hope of relief with such assumption of powers, turning its eye to the reserved sovereignty of the States, as the only refuge from oppression. I

[2]The system, if continued, must end, not only in subjecting the industry and property of the weaker section to the control of the stronger, but in proscription and political disfranchisement. It must finally control elections and appointments to offices, as well as acts of legislation, to the great increase of the feelings of animosity, and of the fatal tendency to a complete alienation between the sections.

shall not extend these remarks, as I might, by showing that, while the effect of the system of protection was rapidly alienating one section, it was not less rapidly, by its necessary operation, distracting and corrupting the other; and, between the two, subjecting the administration to violent and sudden changes, totally inconsistent with all stability and wisdom in the management of the affairs of the nation, of which we already see fearful symptoms. Nor do I deem it necessary to inquire whether this unhappy conflict grows out of true or mistaken views of interest on either or both sides. Regarded in either light, it ought to admonish us of the extreme danger to which our system is exposed, and the great moderation and wisdom necessary to preserve it. If it comes from mistaken views—if the interests of the two sections, as affected by the Tariff, be really the same, and the system, instead of acting unequally, in reality diffuses equal blessings, and imposes equal burdens on every part—it ought to teach us how liable those who are differently situated, and who view their interests under different aspects, are to come to different conclusions, even when their interests are strictly the same; and, consequently, with what extreme caution any system of policy ought to be adopted, and with what a spirit of moderation pursued, in a country of such great extent and diversity as ours. But if, on the contrary, the conflict springs really from contrariety of interests—if the burden be on one side, and the benefit on the other— then are we taught a lesson not less important, how little regard we have for the interests of others while in pursuit of our own; or, at least, how apt we are to consider our own interest the interest of all others; and, of course, how great the danger, in a country of such acknowledged diversity of interests, of the oppression of the feebler by the stronger interest, and, in consequence of it, of the most fatal sectional conflicts. But whichever may be the cause, the real or supposed diversity of interest, it cannot be doubted that the political consequences of the prohibitory system, be its effects in other respects beneficial or otherwise, are really such as I have stated; nor can it be doubted that a conflict between the great sections, on questions so vitally important, indicates a condition of the country so distempered and dangerous, as to demand the most serious and prompt attention. It is only when we come to consider of the remedy, that, under the aspect I am viewing the subject, there can be, among the informed and considerate, any diversity of opinion.

Those who have not duly reflected on its dangerous and inveterate character, suppose that the disease will cure itself; that events ought to be left to take their own course; and that experience, in a short time, will prove that the interest of the whole community is the same in reference to the Tariff, or, at least, whatever diversity there may now be, time will assimilate. Such has been their language from the beginning, but, unfortunately, the progress of events has been the reverse. The country is now more divided than in 1824, and then more than in 1816. The majority may have increased, but the opposite sides are, beyond dispute, more determined and excited than at any preceding period. Formerly, the system was resisted mainly as inexpedient; but now, as unconstitutional, unequal, unjust, and oppressive. Then, relief was sought exclusively from the General Government; but now, many, driven to despair, are raising their eyes to the reserved sovereignty of the States as the only refuge. If we turn from the past and present to the future, we shall find nothing to lessen, but much to aggravate the danger. The increasing embarrassment and distress of the staple States, the growing conviction, from experience, that they are caused by the prohibitory system principally, and that, under its continued operation, their present pursuits must become profitless, and with a conviction that their great and peculiar agricultural capital cannot be diverted from its ancient and hereditary channels without ruinous losses—all concur to increase, instead of dispelling, the gloom that hangs over the future. In fact, to those who will duly reflect on the subject, the hope that the disease will cure itself must appear perfectly illusory. The question is, in reality, one between the exporting and non-exporting interests of the country. *Were there no exports, there would be no tariff.* It would be perfectly useless. On the contrary, so long as there are States which raise the great agricultural staples, with the view of obtaining their supplies, and which must depend on the general market of the world for their sales, the conflict must remain, if the system should continue, and the disease become more and more inveterate. Their interest, and that of those who, by high duties, would confine the purchase of their supplies to the home market, must, from the nature of things, in reference to the Tariff, be in conflict. Till, then, we cease to raise the great staples, cotton, rice, and tobacco, for the general market, and till we can find some other profitable investment for the immense amount of capital and labor now employed in their production, the present unhappy and dangerous conflict cannot terminate, unless with the prohibitory system itself.

In the mean time, while idly waiting for its termination through its own action, the progress of events in another quarter is rapidly bringing the contest to an immediate and decisive issue. We are fast approaching a period very novel in the history of nations, and bearing directly and powerfully on the point under consideration—the final payment of a long-standing funded debt—a period that cannot be sensibly retarded, or its natural consequences eluded, without proving disastrous to those who attempt either, if not to the country itself. When it arrives, the Government will find itself in possession of a surplus revenue of $10,000,000 or $12,000,000, if not previously disposed of, which presents the important question, What previous disposition ought to be made?—a question which must press urgently for decision at the very next session of Congress. It cannot be delayed longer without the most distracting and dangerous consequences.

The honest and obvious course is, to prevent the accumulation of the surplus in the Treasury, by a timely and judicious reduction of the imposts; and thereby to leave the money in the pockets of those who made it, and from whom it cannot be honestly nor constitutionally taken, unless required by the fair and legitimate wants of the Government. If, neglecting a disposition so obvious and just, the Government should attempt to keep up the present high duties, when the money is no longer wanted, or to dispose of this immense surplus by enlarging the old, or devising new schemes of appropriations; or, finding that to be impossible, it should adopt the most dangerous, unconstitutional, and absurd project ever devised by any government, of dividing the surplus among the States—a project which, if carried into execution, would not fail to create an antagonist interest between the States and General Government on all questions of appropriations, which would certainly end in reducing the latter to a mere office of collection and distribution—either of these modes would be considered, by the section suffering under the present high duties, as a fixed determination to perpetuate forever what it considers the present unequal, unconstitutional, and oppressive burden; and from that moment it would cease to look to the General Government for relief. This deeply interesting period, which must prove so disastrous should a wrong direction be given, but so fortunate and glorious, should a right one, is just at hand. The work must commence at the next session, as I have stated, or be left undone, or, at least, be badly done. The succeeding session would be too short, and too much agitated by the presidential contest, to afford the requisite leisure and calmness; and the one succeeding would find the country in the midst of the crisis, when it would be too late to prevent an accumulation of the surplus; which I hazard nothing in saying, judging from the nature of men and government, if once permitted to accumulate, would create an interest strong enough to perpetuate itself; supported, as it would be, by others so numerous and powerful; and thus would pass away a moment, never to be quietly recalled, so precious, if properly used, to lighten the public burden; to equalize the action of the Government; to restore harmony and peace; and to present to the world the illustrious example, which could not fail to prove most favorable to the great cause of liberty everywhere, of a nation the freest, and, at the same time, the best and most cheaply governed; of the highest earthly blessing at the least possible sacrifice.

As the disease will not, then, heal itself, we are brought to the question, Can a remedy be applied? and if so, what ought it to be?

To answer in the negative would be to assert that our Union has utterly failed; and that the opinion, so common before the adoption of our Constitution, that a free government could not be practically extended over a large country, was correct; and that ours had been destroyed by giving it limits so great as to comprehend, not only dissimilar, but irreconcilable interests. I am not prepared to admit a conclusion that would cast so deep a shade on the future; and that would falsify all the glorious anticipations of our ancestors, while it would so greatly lessen their high reputation for wisdom. Nothing but the clearest demonstration, founded on actual experience, will ever force me to a conclusion so abhorrent to all my feelings. As strongly as I am impressed with the great dissimilarity, and, as I must add, as truth compels me to do, contrariety of interests in our country, resulting from the causes already indicated, and which are so great that they cannot be subjected to the unchecked will of a majority of the whole without defeating the great end of government—and without which it is a curse— justice: yet I see in the Union, as ordained by the Constitution, the means, if wisely used, not only of reconciling all diversities, but also the means, and the only effectual one, of securing to us justice, peace, and security, at home and abroad, and with them that national power and renown, the love of which Providence has implanted, for wise purposes, so deeply in the human heart; in all of which great objects every portion of our country, widely extended and diversified as it is, has a common and identical interest. If we have the wisdom to place a proper relative estimate on these more elevated and durable blessings, the present and every other conflict of like character may be readily terminated; but if, reversing the scale, each section should put a higher estimate on its immediate and peculiar gains, and, acting in that spirit, should push favorite measures of mere policy, without some regard to peace, harmony, or justice, our sectional conflicts would then, indeed, without some constitutional check, become interminable, except by the dissolution of the Union itself. That we have, in fact, so reversed the estimate, is too certain to be doubted, and the result is our present distempered and dangerous condition. The cure must commence in the correction of the error; and not to admit that we have erred would be the worst possible symptom. It would prove the disease to be incurable, through the regular and ordinary process of legislation; and would compel, finally, a resort to extraordinary, but I still trust, not only constitutional, but safe remedies.

No one would more sincerely rejoice than myself to see the remedy applied from the quarter where it could be most easily and regularly done. It is the only way by which those, who think that it is the only quarter from which it may constitutionally come, can possibly sustain their opinion. To omit the application by the General Government, would compel even them to admit the truth of the opposite opinion, or force them to abandon our political system in despair; while, on the other hand, all their enlightened and patriotic opponents would rejoice at such evidence of moderation and wisdom, on the part of the General Government, as would supersede a resort to what they believe to be the higher powers of our political system, as indicating a sounder state of public sentiment than has ever heretofore existed in any country; and thus affording the highest possible assurance of the perpetuation of our glorious institutions to the latest generation. For, as a people advance in knowledge, in the same degree they may dispense with mere artificial restrictions in their government; and we may imagine (but dare not expect to see) a state of intelligence so universal and high, that all the guards of liberty may be dispensed with, except an enlightened public opinion, acting through the right of suffrage; but it presupposes a state where every class and every section of the community are capable of estimating the effects of every measure, not only as it may affect itself, but every other class and section; and of fully realizing the sublime truth that the highest and wisest policy consists in maintaining justice, and promoting peace and harmony; and that, compared to these, schemes of mere gain are but trash and dross. I fear experience has already proved that we are far removed from such a state; and that we must, consequently, rely on the old and clumsy, but approved mode of checking power, in order to prevent or correct abuses; but I do trust that, though far from perfect, we are, at least, so much so as to be capable of remedying the present disorder in the ordinary way; and thus to prove that, with us, public opinion is so enlightened, and our political machine so perfect, as rarely to require for its preservation the intervention of the power that created it. How is this to be effected?

The application may be painful, but the remedy, I conceive, is certain and simple. There is but one effectual cure—an honest reduction of the duties to a fair system of revenue, adapted to the just and constitutional wants of the Government. Nothing short of this will restore the country to peace, harmony, and mutual affection. There is already a deep and growing conviction in a large section of the country, that the impost, even as a revenue system, is extremely unequal, and that it is mainly paid by those who furnish the means of paying the foreign exchanges of the country on which it is laid; and that the ease would not be varied, taking into the estimate the entire action of the system, whether the producer or consumer pays in the first instance.

I do not propose to enter formally into the discussion of a point so complex and contested; but, as it has necessarily a strong practical bearing on the subject under consideration in all its relations, I cannot pass it without a few general and brief remarks.

If the producer, in reality, pays, none will doubt but the burden would mainly fall on the section it is supposed to do. The theory that the consumer pays, in the first instance, renders the proposition more complex, and will require, in order to understand where the burden, in reality, ultimately falls, on that supposition, to consider the protective, or, as its friends call it, the American System, under its threefold aspect of taxation, of protection, and of distribution—or as performing, at the same time, the several functions of giving a revenue to the Government, of affording protection to certain branches of domestic industry, and furnishing means to Congress of distributing large sums through its appropriations; all of which are so blended in their effects, that it is impossible to understand its true operation without taking the whole into the estimate.

Admitting, then, as supposed, that he who consumes the article pays the tax in the increased price, and that the burden falls wholly on the consumers, without affecting the producers as a class (which, by the by, is far from being true, except in the single case, if there be such a one, where the producers have a monopoly of an article, so indispensable to life, that the quantity consumed cannot be affected by any increase of price), and that, considered in the light of a tax, merely, the impost duties fall equally on every section in proportion to its population, still, when combined with its other effects, the burden it imposes as a tax may be so transferred from one section to the other as to take it from one and place it wholly on the other. Let us apply the remark first to its operation as a system of protection:

The tendency of the tax or duty on the imported article is, not only to raise its price, but also, in the same proportion, that of the domestic article of the same kind, for which purpose, when intended for protection, it is, in fact, laid; and, of course, in determining where the system ultimately places the burden in reality, this effect, also, must be taken into the estimate. If one of the sections exclusively produces such domestic articles and the other purchases them from it, then it is clear that, to the amount of such increased prices, the tax or duty on the consumption of foreign articles would be transferred from the section producing the domestic articles to the one that purchased and consumed them—unless the latter, in turn, be indemnified by the increased price of the objects of its industry, which none will venture to assert to be the case with the great staples of the country, which form the basis of our exports, the price of which is regulated by the foreign, and not the domestic market. To those who grow them, the increased price of the foreign and domestic articles both, in consequence of the duty on the former, is in reality, and in the strictest sense, a tax, while it is clear that the increased price of the latter acts as a bounty to the section producing them; and that, as the amount of such increased prices on what it sells to the other section is greater or less than the duty it pays on the imported articles, the system will, in fact, operate as a bounty or tax: if greater, the difference would be a bounty; if less, a tax.

Again, the operation may be equal in every other respect, and yet the pressure of the system, relatively, on the two sections, be rendered very unequal by the appropriations or distribution. If each section receives back what it paid into the treasury, the equality, if it previously existed, will continue; but if one receives back less, and the other proportionably more than is paid, then the difference in relation to the sections will be to the former a loss, and to the latter a gain; and the system, in this aspect, would operate to the amount of the difference, as a contribution from the one receiving less than it paid, to the other that receives more. Such would be incontestably its general effects, taken in all its different aspects, even on the theory supposed to be most favorable to prove the equal action of the system, that the consumer pays, in the first instance, the whole amount of the tax.

To show how, on this supposition, the burden and advantages of the system would actually distribute themselves between the sections, would carry me too far into details; but I feel assured, after full and careful examination, that they are such as to explain, what otherwise would seem inexplicable, that one section should consider its repeal a calamity, and the other a blessing; and that such opposite views should be taken by them as to place them in a state of determined conflict in relation to the great fiscal and commercial interest of the country. Indeed, were there no satisfactory explanation, the opposite views that prevail in the two sections, as to the effects of the system, ought to satisfy all of its unequal action. There can be no safer, or more certain rule, than to suppose each portion of the country equally capable of understanding their respective interests, and that each is a much better judge of the effects of any system or measures on its peculiar interests than the other can possibly be.

But, whether the opinion of its unequal action be correct or erroneous, nothing can be more certain than that the impression is widely extending itself, that the system, under all its modifications, is essentially unequal; and if to this be added, a conviction still deeper and more universal, that every duty imposed *for the purpose of protection is not only unequal, but also unconstitutional*, it would be a fatal error to suppose that any remedy, short of that which I have stated, can heal our political disorders.

In order to understand more fully the difficulty of adjusting this unhappy contest on any other ground, it may not be improper to present a general view of the constitutional objection, that it may be clearly seen how hopeless it is to expect that it can be yielded by those who have embraced it.

They believe that all the powers vested by the Constitution in Congress are, not only restricted by the limitations expressly imposed, but also by the nature and object of the powers themselves. Thus, though the power to impose duties on imports be granted in general terms, without any other express limitations, but that they shall be equal, and no preference shall be given to the ports of one State over those of another, yet, as being a portion of the taxing power, given with the view of raising revenue, it is, from its nature, restricted to that object, as much so as if the Convention had expressly so limited it; and that to use it to effect any other purpose, not specified in the Constitution, is an infraction of the instrument in its most dangerous form—an infraction by perversion, more easily made, and more difficult to resist, than any other. The same view is believed to be applicable to the power of regulating commerce, as well as all the other powers. To surrender this important principle, it is conceived, would be to surrender all power, and to render the Government unlimited and despotic; and to yield it up, in relation to the particular power in question, would be, in fact, to surrender the control of the whole industry and capital of the country to the General Government, and would end in placing the weaker section in a colonial relation towards the stronger. For nothing are more dissimilar in their nature, or may be more unequally affected by the same laws, than different descriptions of labor and property; and if taxes, by increasing the amount and changing the intent only, may be perverted, in fact, into a system of penalties and rewards, it would give all the power that could be desired to subject the labor and property of the minority to the will of the majority, to be regulated without regarding the interest of the former in subserviency to the will of the latter. Thus thinking, it would seem unreasonable to expect, that any adjustment, based on the recognition of the correctness of a construction of the Constitution which would admit the exercise of such a power, would satisfy the weaker of two sections, particularly with its peculiar industry and property, which experience has shown may be so injuriously affected by its exercise. Thus much for one side.

The just claim of the other ought to be equally respected. Whatever excitement the system has justly caused in certain portions of our country, I hope and believe all will conceive that the change should be made with the least possible detriment to the interests of those who may be liable to be affected by it; consistently, with what is justly due to others, and the principles of the Constitution. To effect this will require the kindest spirit of conciliation and the utmost skill; but, even with these, it will be impossible to make the transition without a shock, greater or less; though I trust, if judiciously effected, it will not be without many compensating advantages. That there will be some such, cannot be doubted. It will, at least, be followed by greater stability, and will tend to harmonize the manufacturing with all the other great interests of the country, and bind the whole in mutual affection. But these are not all. Another advantage of essential importance to the ultimate prosperity of our manufacturing industry will follow. *It will cheapen production*; and, in that view, the loss of any one branch will be nothing like in proportion to the reduction of duty on that particular branch. Every reduction will, in fact, operate as a bounty to every other branch except the one reduced; and thus the effect of a general reduction will be to cheapen, universally, the price of production, by cheapening living, wages, and material, so as to give, if not equal profits after the reduction—profits by no means reduced proportionally to the duties—an effect which, as it regards the foreign markets, is of the utmost importance. It must be apparent, on reflection, that the means adopted to secure the home market for our manufactures are precisely the opposite of those necessary to obtain the foreign. In the former, the increased expense of production, in consequence of a system of protection, may be more than compensated by the increased price at home of the article protected; but in the latter, this advantage is lost; and, as there is no other corresponding compensation, the increased cost of production must be a dead loss in the foreign market. But whether these advantages, and many others that might be mentioned, will ultimately compensate to the full extent or not the loss to the manufacturers, on the reduction of the duties, certain it is, that we have approached a point at which a great change cannot be much longer delayed; and that the more promptly it may be met, the less excitement there will be, and the greater leisure and calmness for a cautious and skilful operation in making the transition; and which it becomes those more immediately interested duly to consider. Nor ought they to overlook, in considering the question, the different character of the claims of the two sides. The one asks from Government no advantage, but simply to be let alone in the undisturbed possession of their natural advantages, and to secure which, as far as was consistent with the other objects of the Constitution, was one of their leading motives in entering into the Union; while the other side claims, for the advancement of their prosperity, the positive interference of the Government. In such cases, on every principle of fairness and justice, such interference ought to be restrained within limits strictly compatible with the natural advantages of the other. He who looks to all the causes in operation—the near approach of the final payment of the public debt—the growing disaffection and resistance to the system in so large a section of the country—the deeper principles on which opposition to it is gradually turning—must be, indeed, infatuated not to see a great change is unavoidable; and that the attempt to elude or much longer delay it must, finally, but increase the shock and disastrous consequences which may follow.

In forming the opinions I have expressed, I have not been actuated by an unkind feeling towards our manufacturing interest. I now am, and ever have been, decidedly friendly to them, though I cannot concur in all of the measures which have been adopted to advance them. I believe considerations higher than any question of mere pecuniary interest forbade their use. But subordinate to these higher views of policy, I regard the advancement of mechanical and chemical improvements in the arts with feelings little short of enthusiasm; not only as the prolific source of national and individual wealth, but as the great means of enlarging the domain of man over the material world, and thereby of laying the solid foundation of a highly improved condition of society, morally and politically. I fear not that we shall extend our power too far over the great agents of nature; but, on the contrary, I consider such enlargement of our power as tending more certainly and powerfully to better the condition of our race, than any one of the many powerful causes now operating to that result. With these impressions, I not only rejoice at the general progress of the arts in the world, but in their advancement in our own country; and as far as protection may be incidentally afforded, in the fair and honest exercise of our constitutional powers, I think now, as I have always thought, that sound policy connected with the security, independence, and peace of the country, requires it should be done; but that we cannot go a single step beyond without jeopardizing our peace, our harmony and our liberty—considerations of infinitely more importance to us than any measure of mere policy can possibly be.

In thus placing my opinions before the public, I have not been actuated by the expectation of changing the public sentiment. Such a motive, on a question so long agitated, and so beset with feelings of prejudice and interest, would argue, on my part, an insufferable vanity, and a profound ignorance of the human heart. To avoid, as far as possible, the imputation of either, I have confined my statement, on the many and important points on which I have been compelled to touch, to a simple declaration of my opinion, without advancing any other reasons to sustain them than what appeared to me to be indispensable to the full understanding of my views; and if they should, on any point, be thought to be not clearly and explicitly developed, it will, I trust, be attributed to my solicitude to avoid the imputations to which I have alluded, and not from any desire to disguise my sentiments, nor the want of arguments and illustrations to maintain positions, which so abound in both, that it would require a volume to do them any thing like justice. I can only hope the truths which, I feel assured, are essentially connected with all that we ought to hold most dear, may not be weakened in the public estimation by the imperfect manner in which I have been, by the object in view, compelled to present them.

With every caution on my part, I dare not hope, in taking the step I have, to escape the imputation of improper motives; though I have, without reserve, freely expressed my opinions, not regarding whether they might or might not be popular. I have no reason to believe that they are such as will conciliate public favor, but the opposite; which I greatly regret, as I have ever placed a high estimate on the good opinion of my fellow-citizens. But, be that as it may, I shall, at least, be sustained by feelings of conscious rectitude. I have formed my opinions after the most careful and deliberate examination, with all the aids which my reason and experience could furnish; I have expressed them honestly and fearlessly, regardless of their effects personally, which, however interesting to me individually, are of too little importance to be taken into the estimate, where the liberty and happiness of our country are so vitally involved.

JOHN C. CALHOUN.

SPEECH ON THE REVENUE COLLECTION [FORCE] BILL

[February 15–16, 1833]

———————

In December 1832, Calhoun resigned his position as vice-president of the United States to begin his new career as U.S. senator from South Carolina. Although there was some fear that if Calhoun arrived in Washington, D.C., to assume his duties in the Senate, President Jackson planned to have him arrested and tried for treason, Calhoun assumed his seat on January 4, 1833, without incident. Much to the dismay of his critics, Calhoun was credited with the modification of the tariff through the passage of legislation already being considered when he arrived in the Senate.

Beginning on February 15, Calhoun delivered over a two-day period what is probably the most stunning and powerful address of his entire career. Freed from the confines of his position as president of the Senate, he applied here the principles of the Fort Hill Address to the particular issue of the tariff. He condemned both the logic and intentions of the Force Bill that would have given President Jackson the authority to coerce South Carolina into obeying the tariff measures at hand, and he addressed directly those who charged him with having reversed his stand on the question of the tariff—a reversal they claimed was motivated by the bitterness of disappointed ambition. Undaunted by the personal assault on his character, Calhoun boldly proclaimed that "Death is not the greatest calamity . . . [but] loss of liberty and honor." The Union may indeed be preserved through force, "but such a union would be the bond between master and slave—a union of exaction on one side and of unqualified obedience *on the other.*"

While Calhoun's arguments were not compelling enough to convince his contemporaries to defeat the Force Bill, from that day until the outbreak of the Civil War, Calhoun was the foremost intellectual spokesman of the South.

MR. PRESIDENT: I know not which is most objectionable, the provisions of the bill, or the temper in which its adoption has been urged. If the extraordinary powers with which the bill proposes to clothe the Executive, to the utter prostration of the constitution and the rights of the States, be calculated to impress our minds with alarm at the rapid progress of despotism in our country, the zeal with which every circumstance calculated to misrepresent or exaggerate the conduct of Carolina in the controversy is seized on, with a view to excite hostility against her, but too plainly indicates the deep decay of that brotherly feeling which once existed between these States, and to which we are indebted for our beautiful federal system, and by the continuance of which alone it can be preserved. It is not my intention to advert to all these misrepresentations; but there are some so well calculated to mislead the mind as to the real character of the controversy, and to hold up the State in a light so odious, that I do not feel myself justified in permitting them to pass unnoticed.

Among them, one of the most prominent is the false statement that the object of South Carolina is to exempt herself from her share of the public burdens, while she participates in the advantages of the Government. If the charge were true—if the State were capable of being actuated by such low and unworthy motives, mother as I consider her, I would not stand up on this floor to vindicate her conduct. Among her faults—and faults I will not deny she has no one has ever yet charged her with that low and most sordid of vices—avarice. Her conduct, on all occasions, has been marked with the very opposite quality. From the commencement of the Revolution—from its first breaking out at Boston till this hour, no State has been more profuse of its blood in the cause of the country; nor has any contributed so largely to the common treasury in proportion to her wealth and population. She has, in that proportion, contributed more to the exports of the Union—on the exchange of which with the rest of the world the greater portion of the public burden has been levied—than any other State. No: the controversy is not such as has been stated; the State does not seek to participate in the advantages of the Government without contributing her full share to the public treasury. Her object is far different. A deep constitutional question lies at the bottom of the controversy. The real question at issue is: Has this Government a right to impose burdens on the capital and industry of one portion of the country, not with a view to revenue, but to benefit another? And I must be permitted to say that, after the long and deep agitation of this controversy, it is with surprise that I perceive so strong a disposition to misrepresent its real character. To correct the impression which those misrepresentations are calculated to make, I will dwell on the point under consideration for a few moments longer.

The Federal Government has, by an express provision of the constitution, the right to lay duties on imports. The State has never denied or resisted this right, nor even thought of so doing. The Government has, however, not been contented with exercising this power as she had a right to do, but has gone a step beyond it, by laying imposts, not for revenue, but for protection. This the State considers as an unconstitutional exercise of power—highly injurious and oppressive to her and the other staple States, and has, accordingly, met it with the most determined resistance. I do not intend to enter, at this time, into the argument as to the unconstitutionality of the protective system. It is not necessary. It is sufficient that the power is nowhere granted; and that, from the journals of the Convention which formed the constitution, it would seem that it was refused. In support of the journals, I might cite the statement of Luther Martin, which has

already been referred to, to show that the Convention, so far from conferring the power on the Federal Government, left to the State the right to
impose duties on imports, with the express view of enabling the several
States to protect their own manufactures. Notwithstanding this, Congress
has assumed, without any warrant from the constitution, the right of exercising this most important power, and has so exercised it as to impose a
ruinous burden on the labor and capital of the State, by which her resources are exhausted—the enjoyments of her citizens curtailed—the
means of education contracted—and all her interests essentially and injuriously affected. We have been sneeringly told that she is a small State;
that her population does not much exceed half a million of souls; and that
more than one-half are not of the European race. The facts are so. I know
she never can be a great State, and that the only distinction to which she
can aspire must be based on the moral and intellectual acquirements of her
sons. To the development of these much of her attention has been directed;
but this restrictive system, which has so unjustly exacted the proceeds of
her labor, to be bestowed on other sections, has so impaired the resources
of the State, that, if not speedily arrested, it will dry up the means of
education, and with it, deprive her of the only source through which she
can aspire to distinction.

There is another misstatement, as to the nature of the controversy, so
frequently made in debate, and so well calculated to mislead, that I feel
bound to notice it. It has been said that South Carolina claims the right to
annul the constitution and laws of the United States; and to rebut this
supposed claim, the gentleman from Virginia (Mr. Rives) has gravely
quoted the constitution, to prove that the constitution, and the laws made in
pursuance thereof, are the supreme laws of the land—as if the State
claimed the right to act contrary to this provision of the constitution. Nothing can be more erroneous: her object is not to resist laws made in pursuance of the constitution, but those made without its authority, and which
encroach on her reserved powers. She claims not even the right of judging
of the delegated powers, but of those that are reserved, and to resist the

former, when they encroach upon the latter. I will pause to illustrate this important point.

All must admit that there are delegated and reserved powers, and that the powers reserved are reserved to the States respectively. The powers, then, of the system are divided between the General and the State Governments; and the point immediately under consideration is, whether a State has any right to judge as to the extent of its reserved powers, and to defend them against the encroachments of the General Government. Without going deeply into this point at this stage of the argument, or looking into the nature and origin of the Government, there is a simple view of the subject which I consider as conclusive. The very idea of a divided power implies the right on the part of the State for which I contend. The expression is metaphorical when applied to power. Every one readily understands that the division of matter consists in the separation of the parts. But in this sense it is not applicable to power. What, then, is meant by a division of power? I cannot conceive of a division, without giving an equal right to each to judge of the extent of the power allotted to each. Such right I hold to be essential to the existence of a division; and that to give to either party the conclusive right of judging, not only of the share allotted to it, but of that allotted to the other, is to annul the division, and to confer the whole power on the party vested with such right.

But it is contended that the constitution has conferred on the Supreme Court the right of judging between the States and the General Government. Those who make this objection, overlook, I conceive, an important provision of the constitution. By turning to the tenth amended article of the constitution, it will be seen that the reservation of power to the States is not only against the powers delegated to Congress, but against the United States themselves; and extends, of course, as well to the judiciary as to the other departments of the Government. The article provides, that all powers not delegated to the United States, or prohibited by it to the States, are reserved to the States respectively, or to the people. This presents the inquiry, What powers are delegated to the United States? They may be classed under four divisions: first, those that are delegated by the States to each other, by virtue of which the constitution may be altered or amended by three-fourths of the States, when, without which, it would have required the unanimous vote of all; next, the powers conferred on Congress; then those on the President; and finally, those on the judicial department—all of which are particularly enumerated in the parts of the constitution which organize the respective departments. The reservation of powers to the States is, as I have said, against the whole; and is as full against the judicial as it is against the executive and legislative departments of the Government. It cannot be claimed for the one without claiming it for the whole, and without, in fact, annulling this important provision of the constitution.

Against this, as it appears to me, conclusive view of the subject, it has been urged that this power is expressly conferred on the Supreme Court by that portion of the constitution which provides that the judicial power shall extend to all cases in law and equity arising under the constitution, the laws of the United States, and treaties made under their authority. I believe the assertion to be utterly destitute of any foundation. It obviously is the intention of the constitution simply to make the judicial power commensurate with the law-making and treaty-making powers; and to vest it with the right of applying the constitution, the laws, and the treaties, to the cases which might arise under them; and not to make it the judge of the constitution, the laws, and the treaties themselves. In fact, the power of applying the laws to the facts of the case, and deciding upon such application, constitutes, in truth, the judicial power. The distinction between such power, and that of judging of the laws, will be perfectly apparent when we advert to what is the acknowledged power of the court in reference to treaties or compacts between sovereigns. It is perfectly established, that the courts have no right to judge of the violation of treaties; and that, in reference to them, their power is limited to the right of judging simply of the violation of rights under them; and that the right of judging of infractions belongs exclusively to the parties themselves, and not to the courts: of which we have an example in the French treaty, which was declared by

Congress null and void, in consequence of its violation by the Government
of France. Without such declaration, had a French citizen sued a citizen of
this country under the treaty, the court could have taken no cognizance of
its infraction; nor, after such a declaration, would it have heard any argument or proof going to show that the treaty had not been violated.

The declaration, of itself, is conclusive on the court. But it will be asked
how the court obtained the power to pronounce a law or treaty unconstitutional, when they come in conflict with that instrument. I do not deny that it
possesses the right; but I can by no means concede that it was derived
from the constitution. It had its origin in the necessity of the case. Where
there are two or more rules established, one from a higher, the other from
a lower authority, which may come into conflict, in applying them to a
particular case, the judge cannot avoid pronouncing in favor of the superior against the inferior. It is from this necessity, and this alone, that the
power which is now set up to overrule the rights of the States, against an
express provision of the constitution, was derived. It had no other origin.
That I have traced it to its true source, will be manifest from the fact that it
is a power which, so far from being conferred exclusively on the Supreme
Court, as is insisted, belongs to every court—inferior and superior—State
and General—and even to foreign courts.

But the senator from Delaware (Mr. Clayton) relies on the journals of
the Convention to prove that it was the intention of that body to confer on
the Supreme Court the right of deciding, in the last resort, between a State
and the General Government. I will not follow him through the journals, as
I do not deem that to be necessary to refute his argument. It is sufficient
for this purpose to state, that Mr. Rutledge reported a resolution, providing
expressly that the United States and the States might be parties before the
Supreme Court. If this proposition had been adopted, I would ask the
senator whether this very controversy between the United States and South
Carolina might not have been brought before the court? I would also ask
him whether it can be brought before the court as the constitution now
stands? If he answers the former in the affirmative, and the latter in the

negative, as he must, then it is clear, his elaborate argument to the contrary notwithstanding, that the report of Mr. Rutledge was not, in substance, adopted as he contended; and that the journals, so far from supporting, are in direct opposition to the position which he attempts to maintain. I might push the argument much farther against the power of the court, but I do not deem it necessary, at least in this stage of the discussion. If the views which have already been presented be correct, and I do not see how they can be resisted, the conclusion is inevitable, that the reserved powers were reserved equally against every department of the Government, and as strongly against the judicial as against the other departments; and, of course, were left under the exclusive will of the States.

There still remains another misrepresentation of the conduct of the State, which has been made with the view of exciting odium. I allude to the charge, that South Carolina supported the tariff of 1816, and is, therefore, responsible for the protective system. To determine the truth of this charge, it becomes necessary to ascertain the real character of that law—whether it was a tariff for revenue or for protection—and, as involved in this, to inquire, What was the condition of the country at the period? The late war with Great Britain had just terminated, which, with the restrictive system that preceded it, had diverted a large amount of capital and industry from commerce to manufacturers, particularly to the cotton and woollen branches. There was a debt, at the same time, of one hundred and thirty millions of dollars hanging over the country, and the heavy war duties were still in existence. Under these circumstances, the question was presented, as to what point the duties ought to be reduced? This question involved another—at what time the debt ought to be paid?—which was a question of policy, involving in its consideration all the circumstances connected with the then condition of the country. Among the most prominent arguments in favor of an early discharge of the debt was, that the high duties which it would require to effect it would have, at the same time, the effect of sustaining the infant manufactures, which had been forced up under the circumstances to which I have adverted. This view of the subject had a decided influence in determining in favor of an early payment of the debt. The sinking fund was, accordingly, raised from seven to ten millions of dollars, with the provision to apply the surplus which might remain in the treasury as a contingent appropriation to that fund; and the duties were graduated to meet this increased expenditure. It was thus that the policy and justice of protecting the large amount of capital and industry which had been diverted by the measures of the Government into new channels, as I have stated, was combined with the fiscal action of the Government, and which, while it secured a prompt payment of the debt, prevented the immense losses to the manufacturers which would have followed a sudden and great reduction. Still, revenue was the main object, and protection but the incidental. The bill to reduce the duties was reported by the Committee of Ways and Means, and not of Manufactures, and it proposed a heavy reduction on the then existing rate of duties. But what of itself, without other evidence, is decisive as to the character of the bill, is the fact that it fixed a much higher rate of duties on the unprotected than on the protected articles. I will enumerate a few leading articles only. Woollen and cotton above the value of twenty-five cents on the square yard, though they were the leading objects of protection, were subject to a permanent duty of only twenty per cent. Iron, another leading article among the protected, had a protection of not more than nine per cent as fixed by the act, and of but fifteen as reported in the bill. These rates were all below the average duties as fixed in the act, including the protected, the unprotected, and even the free articles. I have entered into some calculation, in order to ascertain the average rate of duties under the act. There is some uncertainty in the data, but I feel assured that it is not less than thirty per cent *ad valorem:* showing an excess of the average duties above that imposed on the pro-tected articles enumerated of more than ten per cent, and thus clearly establishing the character of the measure—that it was for revenue, and not protection.

Looking back, even at this distant period, with all our experience, I perceive but two errors in the act: the one in reference to iron, and the other the minimum duty on coarse cottons. As to the former, I conceive that the bill, as reported, proposed a duty relatively too low, which was still farther reduced in its passage through Congress. The duty, at first, was fixed at seventy-five cents the hundredweight; but, in the last stage of its passage, it was reduced, by a sort of caprice, occasioned by an unfortunate motion, to forty-five cents. This injustice was severely felt in Pennsylvania, the State, above all others, most productive of iron; and was the principal cause of that great reaction which has since thrown her so decidedly on the side of the protective policy. The other error was that as to coarse cottons, on which the duty was as much too high as that on iron was too low. It introduced, besides, the obnoxious minimum principle, which has since been so mischievously extended; and to that extent, I am constrained in candor to acknowledge, as I wish to disguise nothing, the protective principle was recognized by the act of 1816. How this was overlooked at the time, it is not in my power to say. It escaped my observation, which I can account for only on the ground that the principle was then new, and that my attention was engaged by another important subject—the question of the currency, then so urgent, and with which, as chairman of the committee, I was particularly charged. With these exceptions, I again repeat, I see nothing in the bill to condemn; yet it is on the ground that the members from the State voted for the bill, that the attempt is now made to hold up South Carolina as responsible for the whole system of protection which has since followed, though she has resisted its progress in every stage. Was there ever greater injustice? And how is it to be accounted for, but as forming a part of that systematic misrepresentation and calumny which has been directed for so many years, without interruption, against that gallant and generous State? And why has she thus been assailed? Merely because she abstained from taking any part in the Presidential canvass—believing that it had degenerated into a mere system of imposition on the people—controlled, almost exclusively, by those whose object it is to obtain the patronage of the Government, and that without regard to principle or policy. Standing apart from what she considered a contest in which the public had no interest, she has been assailed by both parties with a fury altogether unparalleled; but which, pursuing the course which she believed liberty and duty required, she has met with a firmness equal to the fierceness of the assault. In the midst of this attack, I have not escaped. With a view of inflicting a wound on the State through me, I have been held up as the author of the protective system, and one of its most strenuous advocates. It is with pain that I allude to myself on so deep and grave a subject as that now under discussion, and which, I sincerely believe, involves the liberty of the country. I now regret that, under the sense of injustice, which the remarks of a senator from Pennsylvania (Mr. Wilkins) excited for the moment, I hastily gave my pledge to defend myself against the charge which has been made in reference to my course in 1816: not that there will be any difficulty in repelling the charge, but because I feel a deep reluctance in turning the discussion, in any degree, from a subject of so much magnitude to one of so little importance as the consistency or inconsistency of myself, or any other individual, particularly in connection with an event so long since passed. But for this hasty pledge, I would have remained silent as to my own course on this occasion; and would have borne, with patience and calmness, this, with the many other misrepresentations with which I have been so incessantly assailed for so many years.

The charge that I was the author of the protective system has no other foundation but that I, in common with the almost entire South, gave my support to the tariff of 1816. It is true that I advocated that measure, for which I may rest my defence, without taking any other, on the ground that it was a tariff for revenue, and not for protection; which I have established beyond the power of controversy. But my speech on the occasion has been brought in judgment against me by the senator from Pennsylvania. I have since cast my eyes over the speech; and I will surprise, I have no doubt, the senator, by telling him that, with the exception of some hasty and unguarded expressions, I retract nothing I uttered on that occasion. I only ask that I may be judged in reference to it, in that spirit of fairness and justice which is due to the occasion: taking into consideration the circumstances under which it was delivered, and bearing in mind that the subject was a tariff for revenue, and not for protection; for reducing, and not raising the duties. But, before I explain the then condition of the country, from which my main arguments in favor of the measure were drawn, it is nothing but an act of justice to myself that I should state a fact in connection with my speech, that is necessary to explain what I have called hasty and unguarded expressions. My speech was an *impromptu;* and, as such, I apologized to the House, as appears from the speech as printed, for offering my sentiments on the question without having duly reflected on the subject. It was delivered at the request of a friend, when I had not previously the least intention of addressing the House. I allude to Samuel D. Ingham, then, and now, as I am proud to say, a personal and political friend—a man of talents and integrity—with a clear head, and firm and patriotic heart; then among the leading members of the House; in the palmy state of his political glory, though now for a moment depressed— depressed, did I say? no! it is his State which is depressed—Pennsylvania, and not Samuel D. Ingham! Pennsylvania, which has deserted him under circumstances which, instead of depressing, ought to have elevated him in her estimation. He came to me, when sitting at my desk writing, and said that the House was falling into some confusion, accompanying it with a remark, that I knew how difficult it was to rally so large a body when once broken on a tax bill, as had been experienced during the late war. Having a higher opinion of my influence than it deserved, he requested me to say something to prevent the confusion. I replied that I was at a loss what to say; that I had been busily engaged on the currency, which was then in great confusion, and which, as I have stated, had been placed particularly under my charge, as the chairman of the committee on that subject. He repeated his request; and the speech which the senator from Pennsylvania has complimented so highly was the result.

I will ask whether the facts stated ought not, in justice, to be borne in mind by those who would hold me accountable, not only for the general scope of the speech, but for every word and sentence which it contains?

But, in asking this question, it is not my intention to repudiate the speech. All I ask is, that I may be judged by the rules which, in justice, belong to the case. Let it be recollected that the bill was a revenue bill; and, of course, that it was constitutional. I need not remind the Senate that, when the measure is constitutional, all arguments calculated to show its beneficial operation may be legitimately pressed into service, without taking into consideration whether the subject to which the arguments refer be within the sphere of the constitution or not. If, for instance, a question were before this body to lay a duty on Bibles, and a motion were made to reduce the duty, or admit Bibles duty free; who could doubt that the argument in favor of the motion that the increased circulation of the Bible would be in favor of the morality and religion of the country would be strictly proper? Or, who would suppose that he who adduced it had committed himself on the constitutionality of taking the religion or morals of the country under the charge of the Federal Government? Again: suppose the question to be, to raise the duty on silk, or any other article of luxury; and that it should be supported on the ground that it was an article mainly consumed by the rich and extravagant—could it be fairly inferred that in the opinion of the speaker, Congress had a right to pass sumptuary laws? I only ask that these plain rules may be applied to my argument on the tariff of 1816. They turn almost entirely on the benefits which manufactures conferred on the country in time of war, and which no one could doubt. The country had recently passed through such a state. The world was at that time deeply agitated by the effects of the great conflict which had so long raged in Europe, and which no one could tell how soon again might return. Bonaparte had but recently been overthrown; the whole southern part of this continent was in a state of revolution, and threatened with the interference of the Holy Alliance, which, had it occurred, must almost necessarily have involved this country in a most dangerous conflict. It was under these circumstances that I delivered the speech, in which I urged the House that, in the adjustment of the tariff, reference ought to be had to a state of war as well as peace; and that its provisions ought to be fixed on the compound views of the two periods—making some sacrifice in peace, in order that less might be made in war. Was this principle false? and, in urging it, did I commit myself to that system of oppression since grown up, and which has for its object the enriching of one portion of the country at the expense of the other?

The plain rule in all such cases is, that when a measure is proposed, the first thing is to ascertain its constitutionality; and, that being ascertained, the next is its expediency; which last opens the whole field of argument for and against. Every topic may be urged calculated to prove it wise or unwise: so in a bill to raise imposts. It must first be ascertained that the bill is based on the principles of revenue, and that the money raised is necessary for the wants of the country. These being ascertained, every argument, direct and indirect, may be fairly offered, which may go to show that, under all the circumstances, the provisions of the bill are proper or improper. Had this plain and simple rule been adhered to, we should never have heard of the complaint of Carolina. Her objection is not against the improper modification of a bill acknowledged to be for revenue, but that, under the name of imposts, a power essentially different from the taxing power is exercised—partaking much more of the character of a penalty than a tax. Nothing is more common than that things closely resembling in appearance should widely and essentially differ in their character. Arsenic, for instance, resembles flour, yet one is a deadly poison, and the other that which constitutes the staff of life. So duties imposed, whether for revenue or protection, may be called imposts; though nominally and apparently the same, yet they differ essentially in their real character.

I shall now return to my speech on the tariff of 1816. To determine what my opinions really were on the subject of protection at that time, it will be proper to advert to my sentiments before and after that period. My sentiments preceding 1816, on this subject, are a matter of record. I came into Congress in 1812, a devoted friend and supporter of the then administration; yet one of my first efforts was to brave the administration, by opposing its favorite measure, the restrictive system—embargo, non-intercourse, and all—and that upon the principle of free trade. The system remained in fashion for a time; but, after the overthrow of Bonaparte, I reported a bill from the Committee on Foreign Relations, to repeal the whole system of restrictive measures. While the bill was under consideration, a worthy man, then a member of the House (Mr. McKim of Baltimore), moved to except the Non-Importation Act, which he supported on the ground of encouragement to manufactures. I resisted the motion on the very grounds on which Mr. McKim supported it. I maintained that the manufacturers were then receiving too much protection, and warned its friends that the withdrawal of the protection which the war and the high duties then afforded would cause great embarrassment; and that the true policy, in the mean time, was to admit foreign goods as freely as possible, in order to diminish the anticipated embarrassment on the return of peace; intimating, at the same time, my desire to see the tariff revised, with a view of affording a moderate and permanent protection.

Such was my conduct before 1816. Shortly after that period I left Congress, and had no opportunity of making known my sentiments in reference to the protective system, which shortly after began to be agitated. But I have the most conclusive evidence that I considered the arrangement of the revenue, in 1816, as growing out of the necessity of the case, and due to the consideration of justice. But, even at that early period, I was not without my fears that even that arrangement would lead to abuse and future difficulties. I regret that I have been compelled to dwell so long on myself; but trust that, whatever censure may be incurred, will not be directed against me, but against those who have drawn my conduct into the controversy; and who may hope, by assailing my motives, to wound the cause with which I am proud to be identified.

I may add, that all the Southern States voted with South Carolina in support of the bill: not that they had any interest in manufactures, but on the ground that they had supported the war, and, of course, felt a corresponding obligation to sustain those establishments which had grown up under the encouragement it had incidentally afforded; while most of the

New England members were opposed to the measure principally, as I believe, on opposite principles.

I have now, I trust, satisfactorily repelled the charge against the State, and myself personally, in reference to the tariff of 1816. Whatever support the State has given the bill, originated in the most disinterested motives. There was not within the limits of the State, so far as my memory serves me, a single cotton or woollen establishment. Her whole dependence was on agriculture, and the cultivation of two great staples, rice and cotton. Her obvious policy was to keep open the market of the world unchecked and unrestricted; to buy cheap, and to sell high; but, from a feeling of kindness, combined with a sense of justice, she added her support to the bill. We had been told by the agents of the manufacturers, that the protection which the measure afforded would be sufficient; to which we the more readily conceded, as it was considered a final adjustment of the question.

Let us now turn our eyes forward, and see what has been the conduct of the parties to this arrangement. Have Carolina and the South disturbed this adjustment? No; they have never raised their voice in a single instance against it, even though this measure, moderate comparatively as it is, was felt with no inconsiderable pressure on their interests. Was this example imitated on the opposite side? Far otherwise. Scarcely had the President signed his name, before application was made for an increase of duties, which was repeated, with demands continually growing, till the passage of the act of 1828. What course now, I would ask, did it become Carolina to pursue in reference to these demands? Instead of acquiescing in them, because she had acted generously in adjusting the tariff of 1816, she saw, in her generosity on that occasion, additional motives for that firm and decided resistance which she has since made against the system of protection. She accordingly commenced a systematic opposition to all further encroachments, which continued from 1818 till 1828—by discussions and by resolutions, by remonstrances and by protests, through her legislature. These all proved insufficient to stem the current of encroachment: but, notwithstanding the heavy pressure on her industry, she never despaired of relief till the passage of the act of 1828—that bill of abominations—engendered by avarice and political intrigue. Its adoption opened the eyes of the State, and gave a new character to the controversy. Till then, the question had been, whether the protective system was constitutional and expedient; but, after that, she no longer considered the question whether the right of regulating the industry of the States was a reserved or delegated power, but what right a State possesses to defend her reserved powers against the encroachments of the Federal Government: a question, on the decision of which, the value of all the reserved powers depends. The passage of the act of 1828, with all its objectionable features, and with the odious circumstances under which it was adopted, had almost, if not entirely, closed the door of hope through the General Government. It afforded conclusive evidence that no reasonable prospect of relief from Congress could be entertained; yet, the near approach of the period of the payment of the public debt, and the elevation of General Jackson to the Presidency, still afforded a ray of hope—not so strong, however, as to prevent the State from turning her eyes, for final relief, to her reserved powers.

Under these circumstances commenced that inquiry into the nature and extent of the reserved powers of a State, and the means which they afford of resistance against the encroachments of the General Government, which has been pursued with so much zeal and energy, and, I may add, intelligence. Never was there a political discussion carried on with greater activity, and which appealed more directly to the intelligence of a community. Throughout the whole, no address has been made to the low and vulgar passions; but, on the contrary, the discussion has turned upon the higher principles of political economy, connected with the operations of the tariff system, calculated to show its real bearing on the interests of the State, and on the structure of our political system; and to show the true character of the relationship between the States and the General Government; and the means which the States possess of defending those powers which they reserved in forming the Federal Government.

In this great canvass, men of the most commanding talents and acquirements have engaged with the greatest ardor; and the people have been addressed through every channel—by essays in the public press, and by speeches in their public assemblies—until they have become thoroughly instructed on the nature of the oppression, and on the rights which they possess, under the constitution, to throw it off.

If gentlemen suppose that the stand taken by the people of Carolina rests on passion and delusion, they are wholly mistaken. The case is far otherwise. No community, from the legislator to the ploughman, were ever better instructed in the rights; and the resistance on which the State has resolved, is the result of mature reflection, accompanied with a deep conviction that their rights have been violated, and that the means of redress which they have adopted are consistent with the principles of the constitution.

But while this active canvass was carried on, which looked to the reserved powers as the final means of redress if all others failed, the State at the same time cherished a hope, as I have already stated, that the election of General Jackson to the presidency would prevent the necessity of a resort to extremities. He was identified with the interests of the staple States; and, having the same interest, it was believed that his great popularity—a popularity of the strongest character, as it rested on military services—would enable him, as they hoped, gradually to bring down the system of protection, without shock or injury to any interest. Under these views, the canvass in favor of General Jackson's election to the Presidency was carried on with great zeal, in conjunction with that active inquiry into the reserved powers of the States on which final reliance was placed. But little did the people of Carolina dream that the man whom they were thus striving to elevate to the highest seat of power would prove so utterly false to all their hopes. Man is, indeed, ignorant of the future; nor was there ever a stronger illustration of the observation than is afforded by the result of that election! The very event on which they had built their hopes has been turned against them, and the very individual to whom they looked as a deliverer, and whom, under that impression, they strove for so many years to elevate to power, is now the most powerful instrument in the hands of his and their bitterest opponents to put down them and their cause!

Scarcely had he been elected, when it became apparent, from the organization of his cabinet and other indications, that all their hopes of relief through him were blasted. The admission of a single individual into the cabinet, under the circumstances which accompanied that admission, threw all into confusion. The mischievous influence over the President, through which this individual was admitted into the cabinet, soon became apparent. Instead of turning his eyes forward to the period of the payment of the public debt, which was then near at hand, and to the present dangerous political crisis, which was inevitable unless averted by a timely and wise system of measures, the attention of the President was absorbed by mere party arrangements, and circumstances too disreputable to be mentioned here, except by the most distant allusion.

Here I must pause for a moment to repel a charge which has been so often made, and which even the President has reiterated in his proclamation—the charge that I have been actuated, in the part which I have taken, by feelings of disappointed ambition. I again repeat, that I deeply regret the necessity of noticing myself in so important a discussion; and that nothing can induce me to advert to my own course but the conviction that it is due to the cause, at which a blow is aimed through me. It is only in this view that I notice it.

It illy became the chief magistrate to make this charge. The course which the State took, and which led to the present controversy between her and the General Government, was taken as far back as 1828—in the very midst of that severe canvass which placed him in power—and in that very canvass Carolina openly avowed and zealously maintained those very principles which he, the chief magistrate, now officially pronounces to be treason and rebellion. That was the period at which he ought to have spoken. Having remained silent then, and having, under his approval, implied by that silence, received the support and the vote of the State, I, if a sense of decorum did not prevent it, might recriminate with the double charge of deception and ingratitude. My object, however, is not to assail the President, but to defend myself against a most unfounded charge. The time alone, when he pursued the course upon which this charge of *disappointed ambition* is founded, will, of itself, repel it in the eye of every unprejudiced and honest man. The doctrine which I now sustain, under the present difficulties, I openly avowed and maintained immediately after the act of 1828, that "bill of abominations," as it has been so often and properly termed. Was I at that period disappointed in any views of ambition I might be supposed to entertain? I was Vice-President of the United States, elected by an overwhelming majority. I was a candidate for re-election on the ticket with General Jackson himself, with a certain prospect of the triumphant success of that ticket, and with a fair prospect of the highest office to which an American citizen can aspire. What was my course under these prospects? Did I look to my own advancement, or to an honest and faithful discharge of my duty? Let facts speak for themselves. When the bill to which I have referred came from the other House to the Senate, the almost universal impression was, that its fate would depend upon my casting vote. It was known that, as the bill then stood, the Senate was nearly equally divided; and as it was a combined measure, originating with the politicians and manufacturers, and intended as much to bear upon the Presidential election as to protect manufactures, it was believed that, as a stroke of political policy, its fate would be made to depend on my vote, in order to defeat General Jackson's election, as well as my own. The friends of General Jackson were alarmed, and I was earnestly entreated to leave the chair in order to avoid the responsibility, under the plausible argument that, if the Senate should be equally divided, the bill would be lost without the aid of my casting vote. The reply to this entreaty was, that no consideration personal to myself could induce me to take such a course; that I considered the measure as of the most dangerous character, and calculated to produce the most fearful crisis; that the payment of the public debt was just at hand; and that the great increase of revenue which it would pour into the treasury would accelerate the approach of that period, and that the country would be placed in the most trying of situations—with an immense revenue without the means of absorption upon any legitimate or constitutional object of appropriation, and compelled to submit to all the corrupting consequences of a large surplus, or to make a sudden reduction of the rates of duties, which would prove ruinous to the very interests which were then forcing the passage of the bill. Under these views I determined to remain in the chair, and if the bill came to me, to give my casting vote against it, and in doing so, to give my reasons at large; but at the same time I informed my friends that I would retire from the ticket, so that the election of General Jackson might not be embarrassed by any act of mine. Sir, I was amazed at the folly and infatuation of that period. So completely absorbed was Congress in the game of ambition and avarice—from the double impulse of the manufacturers and politicians—that none but a few appeared to anticipate the present crisis, at which all are now alarmed, but which is the inevitable result of what was then done. As to myself, I clearly foresaw what has since followed. The road of ambition lay open before me—I had but to follow the corrupt tendency of the times—but I chose to tread the rugged path of duty.

It was thus that the reasonable hope of relief through the election of General Jackson was blasted; but still one other hope remained—that the final discharge of the public debt, an event near at hand, would remove our burden. That event would leave in the treasury a large surplus: a surplus that could not be expended under the most extravagant schemes of appropriation, having the least color of decency or constitutionality. That event at last arrived. At the last session of Congress, it was avowed on all sides that the public debt, for all practical purposes, was in fact paid, the small surplus remaining being nearly covered by the money in the treasury and the bonds for duties which had already accrued; but with the arrival of this event our last hope was doomed to be disappointed. After a long session of many months, and the most earnest effort on the part of South Carolina and the other Southern States to obtain relief, all that could be effected was a small reduction in the amount of the duties; but a reduction of such a character, that, while it diminished the amount of burden, distributed that burden more unequally than even the obnoxious act of 1828: reversing the principle adopted by the bill of 1816, of laying higher duties on the unprotected than the protected articles, by repealing almost entirely the duties laid upon the former, and imposing the burden almost entirely on the latter. It was thus that, instead of relief—instead of an equal distribution of the burdens and benefits of the Government, on the payment of the debt, as had been fondly anticipated—the duties were so arranged as to be, in fact, bounties on one side, and taxation on the other; thus placing the two great sections of the country in direct conflict in reference to its fiscal action, and thereby letting in that flood of political corruption which threatens to sweep away our constitution and our liberty.

This unequal and unjust arrangement was pronounced, both by the administration, through its proper organ, the Secretary of the Treasury, and by the opposition, to be a *permanent* adjustment; and it was thus that all hope of relief through the action of the General Government terminated; and the crisis so long apprehended at length arrived, at which the State was compelled to choose between absolute acquiescence in a ruinous system of oppression, or a resort to her reserved powers—powers of which she alone was the rightful judge, and which alone, in this momentous juncture, could save her. She determined on the latter.

The consent of two-thirds of her legislature was necessary for the call of a convention, which was considered the only legitimate organ through which the people, in their sovereignty, could speak. After an arduous struggle, the State Rights party succeeded: more than two-thirds of both branches of the legislature favorable to a convention were elected; a convention was called—the ordinance adopted. The convention was succeeded by a meeting of the legislature, when the laws to carry the ordinance into execution were enacted: all of which have been communicated by the President, have been referred to the Committee on the Judiciary, and this bill is the result of their labor.

Having now corrected some of the prominent misrepresentations as to the nature of this controversy, and given a rapid sketch of the movement of the State in reference to it, I will next proceed to notice some objections connected with the ordinance and the proceedings under it.

The first and most prominent of these is directed against what is called the test oath, which an effort has been made to render odious. So far from deserving the denunciation which has been levelled against it, I view this provision of the ordinance as but the natural result of the doctrines entertained by the State, and the position which she occupies. The people of Carolina believe that the Union is a union of States, and not of individuals; that it was formed by the States, and that the citizens of the several States were bound to it through the acts of their several States; that each State ratified the constitution for itself, and that it was only by such ratification of a State that any obligation was imposed upon its citizens. Thus believing, it is the opinion of the people of Carolina that it belongs to the State which has imposed the obligation to declare, in the last resort, the extent of this obligation, as far as her citizens are concerned; and this upon the plain principles which exist in all analogous cases of compact between sovereign bodies. On this principle, the people of the State, acting in their sovereign capacity in convention, precisely as they had adopted their own and the federal constitutions, have declared, by the ordinance, that the acts of Congress which imposed duties under the authority to lay imposts, are acts, not for revenue, as intended by the constitution, but for protection, and therefore null and void. The ordinance thus enacted by the people of the State themselves, acting as a sovereign community, is, to all intents and purposes, a part of the constitution of the State; and though of a peculiar character, is as obligatory on the citizens of the State as any portion of the constitution. In prescribing, then, the oath to obey the ordinance, no more was done than to prescribe an oath to obey the constitution. It is, in fact, but a particular oath of allegiance, and in every respect similar to that which is prescribed, under the constitution of the United States, to be administered to all the officers of the State and Federal Governments; and is no more deserving the harsh and bitter epithets which have been heaped upon it, than that, or any similar oath.

It ought to be borne in mind, that, according to the opinion which prevails in Carolina, the right of resistance to the unconstitutional acts of Congress belongs to the State, and not to her individual citizens; and that, though the latter may, in a mere question of *meum* and *tuum*, resist, through the courts, an unconstitutional encroachment upon their rights, yet the final stand against usurpation rests not with them, but with the State of which they are members; and such act of resistance by a State binds the conscience and allegiance of the citizen. But there appears to be a general misapprehension as to the extent to which the State has acted under this part of the ordinance. Instead of sweeping every officer by a general proscription of the minority, as has been represented in debate, as far as my knowledge extends, not a single individual has been removed. The State has, in fact, acted with the greatest tenderness, all circumstances considered, towards citizens who differed from the majority; and, in that spirit, has directed the oath to be administered only in case of some official act directed to be performed, in which obedience to the ordinance is involved.

It has been further objected, that the State has acted precipitately. What! precipitately! after making a strenuous resistance for twelve years—by discussion here and in the other House of Congress—by essays in all forms—by resolutions, remonstrances, and protests on the part of her legislature—and, finally, by attempting an appeal to the judicial power of the United States? I say attempting, for they have been prevented from bringing the question fairly before the court, and that by an act of that very majority in Congress who now upbraid them for not making that appeal; of that majority who, on a motion of one of the members in the other House from South Carolina, refused to give to the act of 1828 its true title—that it was a *protective,* and not a *revenue* act. The State has never, it is true, relied upon that tribunal, the Supreme Court, to vindicate its reserved rights; yet they have always considered it as an auxiliary means of defence, of which they would gladly have availed themselves to test the constitutionality of protection, had they not been deprived of the means of doing so by the act of the majority.

Notwithstanding this long delay of more than ten years, under this continued encroachment of the Government, we now hear it on all sides, by friends and foes, gravely pronounced that the State has acted precipitately—that her conduct has been rash! That such should be the language of an interested majority, who, by means of this unconstitutional and oppressive system, are annually extorting millions from the South, to be bestowed upon other sections, is not at all surprising. Whatever impedes the course of avarice and ambition, will ever be denounced as rash and precipitate; and had South Carolina delayed her resistance fifty instead of twelve years, she would have heard from the same quarter the same language; but it is really surprising, that those who are suffering in common with herself, and who have complained equally loud of their grievances; who have pronounced the very acts which she has asserted within *her* limits to be oppressive, unconstitutional, and ruinous, after so long a struggle—a struggle longer than that which preceded the separation of these States from the mother-country—longer than the period of the Trojan war— should now complain of precipitancy! No, it is not Carolina which has acted precipitately; but her sister States, who have suffered in common with her, have acted tardily. Had they acted as she has done, had they performed their duty with equal energy and promptness, our situation this day would be very different from what we now find it. Delays are said to be dangerous; and never was the maxim more true than in the present case, a case of monopoly. It is the very nature of monopolies to grow. If we take from one side a large portion of the proceeds of its labor, and give it to the other, the side from which we take must constantly decay, and that to which we give must prosper and increase. Such is the action of the protective system. It exacts from the South a large portion of the proceeds of its industry, which it bestows upon the other sections, in the shape of bounties to manufactures, and appropriations in a thousand forms; pensions, improvement of

rivers and harbors, roads and canals, and in every shape that wit or ingenuity can devise. Can we, then, be surprised that the principle of monopoly
grows, when it is so amply remunerated at the expense of those who
support it? And this is the real reason of the fact which we witness, that all
acts for protection pass with small minorities, but soon come to be sustained by great and overwhelming majorities. Those who seek the monopoly endeavor to obtain it in the most exclusive shape; and they take care,
accordingly, to associate only a sufficient number of interests barely to
pass it through the two Houses of Congress, on the plain principle, that the
greater the number from whom the monopoly takes, and the fewer on
whom it bestows, the greater is the advantage to the monopolists. Acting in
this spirit, we have often seen with what exact precision they count: adding
wool to woollens, associating lead and iron, feeling their way, until a bare
majority is obtained, when the bill passes, connecting just as many interests as are sufficient to ensure its success, and no more. In a short time,
however, we have invariably found that this *lean* becomes a decided majority, under the certain operation which compels individuals to desert the
pursuits which the monopoly has rendered unprofitable, that they may
participate in those which it has rendered profitable. It is against this
dangerous and growing disease that South Carolina has acted—a disease,
whose cancerous action would soon have spread to every part of the system, if not arrested.

There is another powerful reason why the action of the State could not
have been safely delayed. The public debt, as I have already stated, for all
practical purposes, has already been paid; and, under the existing duties, a
large annual surplus of many millions must come into the treasury. It is
impossible to look at this state of things without seeing the most mischievous consequences; and, among others, if not speedily corrected, it would
interpose powerful and almost insuperable obstacles to throwing off the
burden under which the South has been so long laboring. The disposition
of the surplus would become a subject of violent and corrupt struggle, and
could not fail to rear up new and powerful interests in support of the

existing system, not only in those sections which have been heretofore benefited by it, but even in the South itself. I cannot but trace to the anticipation of this state of the treasury the sudden and extraordinary movements which took place at the last session in the Virginia Legislature, in which the whole South is vitally interested.[1] It is impossible for any rational man to believe that that State could seriously have thought of effecting the scheme to which I allude by her own resources, without powerful aid from the General Government.

It is next objected, that the enforcing acts have legislated the United States out of South Carolina. I have already replied to this objection on another occasion, and will now but repeat what I then said: that they have been legislated out only to the extent that they had no right to enter. The constitution has admitted the jurisdiction of the United States within the limits of the several States only so far as the delegated powers authorize; beyond that they are intruders, and may rightfully be expelled; and that they have been efficiently expelled by the legislation of the State, through her civil process, as has been acknowledged on all sides in the debate, is only a confirmation of the truth of the doctrine for which the majority in Carolina have contended.

The very point at issue between the two parties there is, whether nullification is a peaceable and a efficient remedy against an unconstitutional act of the General Government, and may be asserted, as such, through the State tribunals. Both parties agree that the acts against which it is directed are unconstitutional and oppressive. The controversy is only as to the means by which our citizens may be protected against the acknowledged encroachments on their rights. This being the point at issue between the parties, and the very object of the majority being an efficient protection of the citizens through the State tribunals, the measures adopted to enforce the ordinance of course received the most decisive character. We were not children, to act by halves. Yet for acting thus efficiently the State is de-

[1] Having for their object the emancipation and colonization of slaves.

nounced, and this bill reported, to overrule, by military force, the civil tribunals and civil process of the State! Sir, I consider this bill, and the arguments which have been urged on this floor in its support, as the most triumphant acknowledgment that nullification is peaceful and efficient, and so deeply intrenched in the principles of our system, that it cannot be assailed but by prostrating the constitution, and substituting the supremacy of military force in lieu of the supremacy of the laws. In fact, the advocates of this bill refute their own argument. They tell us that the ordinance is unconstitutional; that it infracts the constitution of South Carolina; although, to me, the objection appears absurd, as it was adopted by the very authority which adopted the constitution itself. They also tell us that the Supreme Court is the appointed arbiter of all controversies between a State and the General Government. Why, then, do they not leave this controversy to that tribunal? Why do they not confide to them the abrogation of the ordinance, and the laws made in pursuance of it, and the assertion of that supremacy which they claim for the laws of Congress? The State stands pledged to resist no process of the court. Why, then, confer on the President the extensive and unlimited powers provided in this bill? Why authorize him to use military force to arrest the civil process of the State? But one answer can be given: That, in a contest between the State and the General Government, if the resistance be limited on both sides to the civil process, the State, by its inherent sovereignty, standing upon its reserved powers, will prove too powerful in such a controversy, and must triumph over the Federal Government, sustained by its delegated and limited authority; and in this answer we have an acknowledgment of the truth of those great principles for which the State has so firmly and nobly contended.

Having made these remarks, the great question is now presented, Has Congress the right to pass this bill? which I will next proceed to consider. The decision of this question involves an inquiry into the provisions of the bill. What are they? It puts at the disposal of the President the army and navy, and the entire militia of the country; it enables him, at his pleasure, to subject every man in the United States, not exempt from militia duty, to martial law; to call him from his ordinary occupation to the field, and under the penalty of fine and imprisonment, inflicted by a court martial, to imbrue his hand in his brother's blood. There is no limitation on the power of the sword—and that over the purse is equally without restraint; for among the extraordinary features of the bill, it contains no appropriation; which, under existing circumstances, is tantamount to an unlimited appropriation. The President may, under its authority, incur any expenditure, and pledge the national faith to meet it. He may create a new national debt, at the very moment of the termination of the former—a debt of millions, to be paid out of the proceeds of the labor of that section of the country whose dearest constitutional rights this bill prostrates! Thus exhibiting the extraordinary spectacle, that the very section of the country which is urging this measure, and carrying the sword of devastation against us, is, at the same time, incurring a new debt, to be paid by those whose rights are violated; while those who violate them are to receive the benefits, in the shape of bounties and expenditures.

And for what purpose is the unlimited control of the purse and of the sword thus placed at the disposition of the Executive? To make war against one of the free and sovereign members of this confederation, which the bill proposes to deal with, not as a State, but as a collection of banditti or outlaws. Thus exhibiting the impious spectacle of this Government, the creature of the States, making war against the power to which it owes its existence.

The bill violates the constitution, plainly and palpably, in many of its provisions, by authorizing the President, at his pleasure, to place the different ports of this Union on an unequal footing, contrary to that provision of the constitution which declares that no preference shall be given to one port over another. It also violates the constitution by authorizing him, at his discretion, to impose cash duties on one port, while credit is allowed in others; by enabling the President to regulate commerce, a power vested in Congress alone; and by drawing within the jurisdiction of the United States

Courts, powers never intended to be conferred on them. As great as these objections are, they become insignificant in the provisions of a bill which, by a single blow—by treating the States as a mere lawless mass of individuals—prostrates all the barriers of the constitution. I will pass over the minor considerations, and proceed directly to the great point. This bill proceeds on the ground that the entire sovereignty of this country belongs to the American people, as forming one great community, and regards the States as mere fractions or counties, and not as integral parts of the Union; having no more right to resist the encroachments of the Government than a county has to resist the authority of a State; and treating such resistance as the lawless acts of so many individuals, without possessing sovereignty or political rights. It has been said that the bill declares war against South Carolina. No. It decrees a massacre of her citizens! War has something ennobling about it, and, with all its horrors, brings into action the highest qualities, intellectual and moral. It was, perhaps, in the order of Providence that it should be permitted for that very purpose. But this bill declares no war, except, indeed, it be that which savages wage—a war, not against the community, but the citizens of whom that community is composed. But I regard it as worse then *savage* warfare—as an attempt to take away life under the color of law, without the trial by jury, or any other safeguard which the constitution has thrown around the life of the citizen! It authorizes the President, or even his deputies, when they may suppose the law to be violated, without the intervention of a court or jury, to kill without mercy or discrimination!

It has been said by the senator from Tennessee (Mr. Grundy) to be a measure of peace! Yes, such peace as the wolf gives to the lamb—the kite to the dove! Such peace as Russia gives to Poland, or death to its victim! A peace, by extinguishing the political existence of the State, by awing her into an abandonment of the exercise of every power which constitutes her a sovereign community. It is to South Carolina a question of self-preservation: and I proclaim it, that, should this bill pass, and an attempt be made to enforce it, it will be resisted, at every hazard—even that of death itself.

Death is not the greatest calamity: there are others still more terrible to the free and brave, and among them may be placed the loss of liberty and honor. There are thousands of her brave sons who, if need be, are prepared cheerfully to lay down their lives in defence of the State, and the great principles of constitutional liberty for which she is contending. God forbid, that this should become necessary! It never can be, unless this Government is resolved to bring the question to extremity, when her gallant sons will stand prepared to perform the last duty—to die nobly.

I go on the ground that this constitution was made by the States; that it is a federal union of the States, in which the several States still retain their sovereignty. If these views be correct, I have not characterized the bill too strongly; and the question is, whether they be or be not. I will not enter into the discussion of this question now. I will rest it, for the present, on what I have said on the introduction of the resolutions now on the table, under a hope that another opportunity will be afforded for more ample discussion. I will, for the present, confine my remarks to the objections which have been raised to the views which I presented when I introduced them. The authority of Luther Martin has been adduced by the Senator from Delaware, to prove that the citizens of a State, acting under the authority of a State, are liable to be punished as traitors by this government. Eminent as Mr. Martin was as a lawyer, and high as his authority may be considered on a legal point, I cannot accept it in determining the point at issue. The attitude which he occupied, if taken into view, would lessen, if not destroy, the weight of his authority. He had been violently opposed in convention to the constitution, and the very letter from which the Senator has quoted was intended to dissuade Maryland from its adoption. With this view, it was to be expected that every consideration calculated to effect that object should be urged; that real objections should be exaggerated; and that those having no foundation, except mere plausible deductions, should be presented. It is to this spirit that I attribute the opinion of Mr. Martin in reference to the point under consideration. But if his authority be good on one point, it must be admitted to be equally so on another. If his opinion be sufficient to prove that a citizen of a State may be punished as a traitor when acting under allegiance to the State, it is also sufficient to show that no authority was intended to be given in the constitution for the protection of manufactures by the General Government, and that the provision in the constitution permitting a State to lay an impost duty, with the consent of Congress, was intended to reserve the right of protection to the States themselves, and that each State should protect its own industry. Assuming his opinion to be of equal authority on both points, how embarrassing would be the attitude in which it would place the Senator from Delaware, and those with whom he is acting—that of using the sword and bayonet to enforce the execution of an unconstitutional act of Congress. I must express my surprise that the slightest authority in favor of *power* should be received as the most conclusive evidence, while that which is, at least, equally strong in favor of right and *liberty,* is wholly overlooked or rejected.

Notwithstanding all that has been said, I may say that neither the Senator from Delaware (Mr. Clayton), nor any other who has spoken on the same side, has directly and fairly met the great question at issue: Is this a federal union? a union of States, as distinct from that of individuals? Is the sovereignty in the several States, or in the American people in the aggregate? The very language which we are compelled to use when speaking of our political institutions, affords proof conclusive as to its real character. The terms union, federal, united, all imply a combination of sovereignties, a confederation of States. They are never applied to an association of individuals. Who ever heard of the United State of New York, of Massachusetts, or of Virginia? Who ever heard the term federal or union applied to the aggregation of individuals into one community? Nor is the other point less clear—that the sovereignty is in the several States, and that our system is a union of twenty-four sovereign powers, under a constitutional compact, and not of a divided sovereignty between the States severally and the United States. In spite of all that has been said, I maintain that sovereignty is in its nature indivisible. It is the supreme power in a State, and we might just as well speak of half a square, or half of a triangle, as of half a sovereignty. It is a gross error to confound tho *oxoroioo* of oovorcign powcr3 with *sovereignty* itself, or the *delegation* of such powers with the *surrender* of them. A sovereign may delegate his powers to be exercised by as many agents as he may think proper, under such conditions and with such limitations as he may impose; but to surrender any portion of his sovereignty to another is to annihilate the whole. The Senator from Delaware (Mr. Clayton) calls this metaphysical reasoning, which he says he cannot comprehend. If by metaphysics he means that scholastic refinement which makes distinctions without difference, no one can hold it in more utter contempt than I do; but if, on the contrary, he means the power of analysis and combination—that power which reduces the most complex idea into its elements, which traces causes to their first principle, and, by the power of generalization and combination, unites the whole in one harmonious system—then, so far from deserving contempt, it is the highest attribute of the human mind. It is the power which raises man above the brute—which distinguishes his faculties from mere sagacity, which he holds in common with inferior animals. It is this power which has raised the astronomer from being a mere gazer at the stars to the high intellectual eminence of a Newton or a La Place; and astronomy itself from a mere observation of insulated facts into that noble science which displays to our admiration the system of the universe. And shall this high power of the mind, which has effected such wonders when directed to the laws which control the material world, be forever prohibited, under a senseless cry of metaphysics, from being applied to the high purpose of political science and legislation? I hold them to be subject to laws as fixed as matter itself, and to be as fit a subject for the application of the highest intellectual power. Denunciation may, indeed, fall upon the philosophical inquirer into these first principles, as it did upon Galileo and Bacon when they first unfolded the great discoveries which have immortalized their names; but the time will come when truth will prevail in spite of prejudice and denunciation, and when politics and legislation will be considered as much a science as astronomy and chemistry.

In connection with this part of the subject, I understood the Senator from Virginia (Mr. Rives) to say that sovereignty was divided, and that a portion remained with the States severally, and that the residue was vested in the Union. By Union, I suppose the Senator meant the United States. If such be his meaning—if he intended to affirm that the sovereignty was in the twenty-four States, in whatever light he may view them, our opinions will not disagree; but, according to my conception, the whole sovereignty is in the several States, while the exercise of sovereign powers is divided—a part being exercised under compact, through this General Government, and the residue through the separate State Governments. But if the Senator from Virginia (Mr. Rives) means to assert that the twenty-four States form but one community, with a single sovereign power as to the objects of the Union, it will be but the revival of the old question, of whether the Union is a union between States, as distinct communities, or a mere aggregate of the American people, as a mass of individuals; and in this light his opinions would lead directly to consolidation.

But to return to the bill. It is said that the bill ought to pass, because the law must be enforced. The law must be enforced! The imperial edict must be executed! It is under such sophistry, couched in general terms, without looking to the limitations which must ever exist in the practical exercise of power, that the most cruel and despotic acts ever have been covered. It was such sophistry as this that cast Daniel into the lion's den, and the three Innocents into the fiery furnace. Under the same sophistry the bloody edicts of Nero and Caligula were executed. The law must be enforced. Yes, the act imposing the "tea-tax must be executed." This was the very argument which impelled Lord North and his administration to that mad career which forever separated us from the British crown. Under a similar sophistry, "that religion must be protected," how many massacres have been perpetrated? and how many martyrs have been tied to the stake? What! acting on this vague abstraction, are you prepared to enforce a law without considering whether it be just or unjust, constitutional or unconstitutional? Will you collect money when it is acknowledged that it is not wanted? He who earns the money, who digs it from the earth with the sweat of his

brow, has a just title to it against the universe. No one has a right to touch
it without his consent except his government, and this only to the extent of
its legitimate wants; to take more is robbery, and you propose by this bill to
enforce robbery by murder. Yes: to this result you must come, by this
miserable sophistry, this vague abstraction of enforcing the law, without a
regard to the fact whether the law be just or unjust, constitutional or
unconstitutional.

In the same spirit, we are told that the Union must be preserved, without
regard to the means. And how is it proposed to preserve the Union? By
force! Does any man in his senses believe that this beautiful structure—
this harmonious aggregate of States, produced by the joint consent of all—
can be preserved by force? Its very introduction will be certain destruction
to this Federal Union. No, no. You cannot keep the States united in their
constitutional and federal bonds by force. Force may, indeed, hold the
parts together, but such union would be the bond between master and
slave—a union of exaction on one side and of unqualified *obedience* on the
other. That *obedience* which, we are told by the Senator from Pennsylvania
(Mr. Wilkins), is the Union! Yes, exaction on the side of the master; for this
very bill is intended to collect what can be no longer called taxes—the
voluntary contribution of a free people—but tribute—tribute to be collected under the mouths of the cannon! Your custom-house is already
transferred to a garrison, and that garrison with its batteries turned, not
against the enemy of your country, but on subjects (I will not say citizens),
on whom you propose to levy contributions. Has reason fled from our
borders? Have we ceased to reflect? It is madness to suppose that the
Union can be preserved by force. I tell you plainly, that the bill, should it
pass, cannot be enforced. It will prove only a blot upon your statute-book,
a reproach to the year, and a disgrace to the American Senate. I repeat, it
will not be executed; it will rouse the dormant spirit of the people, and
open their eyes to the approach of despotism. The country has sunk into
avarice and political corruption, from which nothing can arouse it but some

measure, on the part of the Government, of folly and madness, such as that now under consideration.

Disguise it as you may, the controversy is one between power and liberty; and I tell the gentlemen who are opposed to me, that, as strong as may be the love of power on their side, the love of liberty is still stronger on ours. History furnishes may instances of similar struggles, where the love of liberty has prevailed against power under every disadvantage, and among them few more striking than that of our own Revolution; where, as strong as was the parent country, and feeble as were the colonies, yet, under the impulse of liberty, and the blessing of God, they gloriously triumphed in the contest. There are, indeed, many and striking analogies between that and the present controversy. They both originated substantially in the same cause—with this difference—in the present case, the power of taxation is converted into that of regulating industry; in the other, the power of regulating industry, by the regulation of commerce, was attempted to be converted into the power of taxation. Were I to trace the analogy further, we should find that the perversion of the taxing power, in the one case, has given precisely the same control to the Northern section over the industry of the Southern section of the Union, which the power to regulate commerce gave to Great Britain over the industry of the colonies in the other; and that the very articles in which the colonies were permitted to have a free trade, and those in which the mother-country had a monopoly, are almost identically the same as those in which the Southern States are permitted to have a free trade by the act of 1832, and in which the Northern States have, by the same act, secured a monopoly. The only difference is in the means. In the former, the colonies were permitted to have a free trade with all countries south of Cape Finisterre, a cape in the northern part of Spain; while north of that, the trade of the colonies was prohibited, except through the mother-country, by means of her commercial regulations. If we compare the products of the country north and south of Cape Finisterre, we shall find them almost identical with the list of the protected and unprotected articles contained in the act of last year. Nor does the analogy terminate here. The very arguments resorted to at the commencement of the American Revolution, and the measures adopted, and the motives assigned to bring on that contest (to enforce the law), are almost identically the same.

But to return from this digression to the consideration of the bill. Whatever difference of opinion may exist upon other points, there is one on which I should suppose there can be none: that this bill rests on principles which, if carried out, will ride over State sovereignties, and that it will be idle for any of its advocates hereafter to talk of State rights. The Senator from Virginia (Mr. Rives) says that he is the advocate of State rights; but he must permit me to tell him that, although he may differ in premises from the other gentlemen with whom he acts on this occasion, yet, in supporting this bill, he obliterates every vestige of distinction between him and them, saving only that, professing the principles of '98, his example will be more pernicious than that of the most open and bitter opponents of the rights of the States. I will also add, what I am compelled to say, that I must consider him (Mr. Rives) as less consistent than our old opponents, whose conclusions were fairly drawn from their premises, while his premises ought to have led him to opposite conclusions. The gentleman has told us that the new-fangled doctrines, as he chooses to call them, have brought State rights into disrepute. I must tell him, in reply, that what he calls new-fangled are but the doctrines of '98; and that it is he (Mr. Rives), and others with him, who, professing these doctrines, have degraded them by explaining away their meaning and efficacy. He (Mr. R.) has disclaimed, in behalf of Virginia, the authorship of nullification. I will not dispute that point. If Virginia chooses to throw away one of her brightest ornaments, she must not hereafter complain that it has become the property of another. But while I have, as a representative of Carolina, no right to complain of the disavowal of the Senator from Virginia, I must believe that he (Mr. R.) has done his native State great injustice by declaring on this floor, that when she gravely resolved, in '98, that "in cases of deliberate and dangerous infractions of the constitution, the States, as parties to the compact, have the right, and are in duty bound, to interpose to arrest the progress of the evil, and to maintain within their respective limits the authorities, rights, and liberties, appertaining to them," she meant no more than to ordain the right to protest and to remonstrate. To suppose that, in putting forth so solemn a declaration, which she afterwards sustained by so able and elaborate an argument, she meant no more than to assert what no one had ever denied, would be to suppose that the State had been guilty of the most egregious trifling that ever was exhibited on so solemn an occasion.

In reviewing the ground over which I have passed, it will be apparent that the question in controversy involves that most deeply important of all political questions, whether ours is a federal or a consolidated government—a question, on the decision of which depend, as I solemnly believe, the liberty of the people, their happiness, and the place which we are destined to hold in the moral and intellectual scale of nations. Never was there a controversy in which more important consequences were involved; not excepting that between Persia and Greece, decided by the battles of Marathon, Platea, and Salamis—which gave ascendency to the genius of Europe over that of Asia—which, in its consequences, has continued to affect the destiny of so large a portion of the world even to this day. There are often close analogies between events apparently very remote, which are strikingly illustrated in this case. In the great contest between Greece and Persia, between European and Asiatic polity and civilization, the very question between the federal and consolidated form of government was involved. The Asiatic governments, from the remotest time, with some exceptions on the eastern shore of the Mediterranean, have been based on the principle of consolidation, which considers the whole community as but a unit, and consolidates its powers in a central point. The opposite principle has prevailed in Europe—Greece, throughout all her states, was based on a federal system. All were united in one common but loose bond, and the governments of the several States partook, for the most part, of a complex organization, which distributed political power among different members of the community. The same principles prevailed in ancient Italy; and, if we turn to the Teutonic race, our great ancestors—the race which occupies the first place in power, civilization, and science, and which possesses the largest and the fairest part of Europe—we shall find that their governments were based on federal organization, as has been clearly illustrated by a recent and able writer on the British Constitution (Mr. Palgrave), from whose works I take the following extract:

In this manner the first establishment of the Teutonic States was effected. They were assemblages of septs, clans, and tribes; they were confederated hosts and armies, led on by princes, magistrates, and chieftains; each of whom was originally independent, and each of whom lost a portion of his pristine independence in proportion as he and his compeers became united under the supremacy of a sovereign, who was superinduced upon the state, first as a military commander and afterward as a king. Yet, notwithstanding this political connection, each member of the state continued to retain a considerable portion of the rights of sovereignty. Every ancient Teutonic monarchy must be considered as a federation; it is not a unit, of which the smaller bodies politic therein contained are the fractions, but they are the integers, and the state is the multiple which results from them. Dukedoms and counties, burghs and baronies, towns and townships, and shires, form the kingdom; all, in a certain degree, strangers to each other, and separate in jurisdiction, though all obedient to the supreme executive authority. This general description, though not always strictly applicable in terms, is always so substantially and in effect; and hence it becomes necessary to discard the language which has been very generally employed in treating on the English Constitution. It has been supposed that the kingdom was reduced into a regular and gradual subordination of government, and that the various legal districts of which it is composed, arose from the divisions and subdivisions of the country. But this hypothesis, which tends greatly to perplex our history, cannot be supported by fact; and, instead of viewing the constitution as a whole, and then proceeding to its parts, we must examine it synthetically, and assume that the supreme authorities of the state were created by the concentration of the powers originally belonging to the members and corporations of which it is composed.

[Here Mr. C. gave way for a motion to adjourn.]

On the next day Mr. Calhoun said: I have omitted at the proper place, in the course of my observations yesterday, two or three points, to which I will now advert, before I resume the discussion where I left off. I have stated that the ordinance and acts of South Carolina were directed, not against the revenue, but against the system of protection. But it may be asked, if such was her object, how happens it that she has declared the whole system void—revenue as well as protection, without discrimination? It is this question which I propose to answer. Her justification will be found in the necessity of the case; and if there be any blame, it cannot attach to her. The two are so blended, throughout the whole, as to make the entire revenue system subordinate to the protective, so as to constitute a complete system of protection, in which it is impossible to discriminate the two elements of which it is composed. South Carolina, at least, could not make the discrimination; and she was reduced to the alternative of acquiescing in a system which she believed to be unconstitutional, and which she felt to be oppressive and ruinous, or to consider the whole as one, equally contaminated through all its parts, by the unconstitutionality of the protective portion, and as such, to be resisted by the act of the State. I maintain that the State has a right to regard it in the latter character, and that, if a loss of revenue follow, the fault is not hers, but of this Government, which has improperly blended together, in a manner not to be separated by the State, two systems wholly dissimilar. If the sincerity of the State be doubted; if it be supposed that her action is against revenue as well as protection, let the two be separated—let so much of the duties as are intended for revenue be put in one bill, and the residue intended for protection be put in another, and I pledge myself that the ordinance and the acts of the State will cease as to the former, and be directed exclusively against the latter.

I also stated, in the course of my remarks yesterday, and I trust that I have conclusively shown, that the act of 1816, with the exception of a single item, to which I have alluded, was, in reality, a revenue measure, and that Carolina and the other States, in supporting it, have not incurred the slightest responsibility in relation to the system of protection which has since grown up, and which now so deeply distracts the country. Sir, I am willing, as one of the representatives of Carolina, and I believe I speak the sentiment of the State, to take that act as the basis of a permanent adjustment of the tariff, simply reducing the duties, in an average proportion, on all the items to the revenue point. I make that offer now to the advocates of the protective system; but I must, in candor, inform them that such an adjustment would distribute the revenue between the protected and unprotected articles more favorably to the State, and to the South, and less so to the manufacturing interest, than an average uniform *ad valorem*; and, accordingly, more so than that now proposed by Carolina through her convention. After such an offer, no man who values his candor will dare accuse the State, or those who have represented her here, with inconsistency in reference to the point under consideration.

I omitted, also, on yesterday, to notice a remark of the Senator from Virginia (Mr. Rives), that the only difficulty in adjusting the tariff grew out of the ordinance and the acts of South Carolina. I must attribute an assertion, so inconsistent with the facts, to an ignorance of the occurrences of the last few years in reference to this subject, occasioned by the absence of the gentleman from the United States, to which he himself has alluded in his remarks. If the Senator will take pains to inform himself, he will find that this protective system advanced with a continued and rapid step, in spite of petitions, remonstrances, and protests, of not only Carolina, but also of Virginia and of all the Southern States, until 1828, when Carolina, for the first time, changed the character of her resistance, by holding up her reserved rights as the shield of her defence against further encroachment. This attitude alone, unaided by a single State, arrested the further progress of the system, so that the question from that period to this, on the part of the manufacturers, has been, not how to acquire more, but to retain that which they have acquired. I will inform the gentleman that, if this attitude had not been taken on the part of the State, the question would not now be how duties ought to be repealed, but a question, as to the protected articles, between prohibition on one side and the duties established by the act of 1828 on the other. But a single remark will be sufficient in reply to, what I must consider, the invidious remark of the Senator from Virginia (Mr. Rives). The act of 1832, which has not yet gone into operation, and which was passed but a few months since, was declared by the supporters of the system to be a *permanent* adjustment, and the bill proposed by the Treasury Department, not essentially different from the act itself, was in like manner declared to be intended by the administration as a permanent arrangement. What has occurred since, except this ordinance, and these abused acts of the calumniated State, to produce this mighty revolution in reference to this odious system? Unless the Senator from Virginia can assign some other cause, he is bound, upon every principle of fairness, to retract this unjust aspersion upon the acts of South Carolina.

The Senator from Delaware (Mr. Clayton), as well as others, has relied with great emphasis on the fact that we are citizens of the United States. I do not object to the expression, nor shall I detract from the proud and elevated feelings with which it is associated; but I trust that I may be permitted to raise the inquiry, In what manner are we citizens of the United States? without weakening the patriotic feeling with which, I trust, it will ever be uttered. If by citizen of the United States he means a citizen at large, one whose citizenship extends to the entire geographical limits of the country, without having a local citizenship in some State or territory, a sort of citizen of the world, all I have to say is, that such a citizen would be a perfect nondescript; that not a single individual of this description can be found in the entire mass of our population. Notwithstanding all the pomp and display of eloquence on the occasion, every citizen is a citizen of some State or territory, and, as such, under an express provision of the constitution, is entitled to all privileges and immunities of citizens in the several States; and it is in this, and in no other sense, that we are citizens of the

United States. The Senator from Pennsylvania (Mr. Dallas), indeed, relies upon that provision in the constitution which gives Congress the power to establish an uniform rule of naturalization; and the operation of the rule actually established under this authority, to prove that naturalized citizens are citizens at large, without being citizens of any of the States. I do not deem it necessary to examine the law of Congress upon this subject, or to reply to the argument of the Senator, though I cannot doubt that he (Mr. D.) has taken an entirely erroneous view of the subject. It is sufficient that the power of Congress extends simply to the establishment of a uniform rule by which foreigners may be naturalized in the several States or territories, without infringing, in any other respect, in reference to naturalization, the rights of the States as they existed before the adoption of the constitution.

Having supplied the omissions of yesterday, I now resume the subject at the point where my remarks then terminated. The Senate will remember that I stated, at their close, that the great question at issue is, whether ours is a federal or a consolidated system of government; a system in which the parts, to use the emphatic language of Mr. Palgrave, are the integers, and the whole the multiple, or in which the whole is an unit and the parts the fractions. I stated, that on the decision of this question, I believed, depends not only the liberty and prosperity of this country, but the place which we are destined to hold in the intellectual and moral scale of nations. I stated, also, in my remarks on this point, that there is a striking analogy between this and the great struggle between Persia and Greece, which was decided by the battles of Marathon, Platea, and Salamis, and which immortalized the names of Miltiades and Themistocles. I illustrated this analogy by showing that centralism or consolidation, with the exception of a few nations along the eastern borders of the Mediterranean, has been the pervading principle in the Asiatic governments, while the federal system, or, what is the same in principle, that system which organizes a community in reference to its parts, has prevailed in Europe.

Among the few exceptions in the Asiatic nations, the government of the twelve tribes of Israel, in its early period, is the most striking. Their government, at first, was a mere confederation without any central power, till a military chieftain, with the title of king, was placed at its head, without, however, merging the original organization of the twelve distinct tribes. This was the commencement of that central action among that peculiar people which, in three generations, terminated in a permanent division of their tribes. It is impossible even for a careless reader to peruse the history of that event without being forcibly struck with the analogy in the causes which led to their separation, and those which now threaten us with a similar calamity. With the establishment of the central power in the king commenced a system of taxation, which, under King Solomon, was greatly increased, to defray the expenses of rearing the temple, of enlarging and embellishing Jerusalem, the seat of the central government, and the other profuse expenditures of his magnificent reign. Increased taxation was followed by its natural consequences—discontent and complaint, which, before his death, began to excite resistance. On the succession of his son, Rehoboam, the ten tribes, headed by Jeroboam, demanded a reduction of the taxes; the temple being finished, and the embellishment of Jerusalem completed, and the money which had been raised for that purpose being no longer required, or, in other words, the debt being paid, they demanded a reduction of the duties—a repeal of the tariff. The demand was taken under consideration, and after consulting the old men, the counsellors of '98, who advised a reduction, he then took the opinion of the younger politicians, who had since grown up, and knew not the doctrines of their fathers; he hearkened unto their counsel, and refused to make the reduction, and the secession of the ten tribes under Jeroboam followed. The tribes of Judah and Benjamin, which had received the disbursements, alone remained to the house of David.

But to return to the point immediately under consideration. I know that it is not only the opinion of a large majority of our country, but it may be said to be the opinion of the age, that the very beau ideal of a perfect government is the government of a majority, acting through a representative body, without check or limitation on its power; yet, if we may test this theory by experience and reason, we shall find that, so far from being perfect, the necessary tendency of all governments, based upon the will of an absolute majority, without constitutional check or limitation of power, is to faction, corruption, anarchy, and despotism; and this, whether the will of the majority be expressed directly through an assembly of the people themselves, or by their representatives. I know that, in venturing this assertion, I utter what is unpopular both within and without these walls; but where truth and liberty are concerned, such considerations should not be regarded. I will place the decision of this point on the fact that no government of the kind, among the many attempts which have been made, has ever endured for a single generation, but, on the contrary has invariably experienced the fate which I have assigned to it. Let a single instance be pointed out, and I will surrender my opinion. But, if we had not the aid of experience to direct our judgment, reason itself would be a certain guide. The view which considers the community as a unit, and all its parts as having a similar interest, is radically erroneous. However small the community may be, and however homogeneous its interests, the moment that government is put into operation, as soon as it begins to collect taxes and to make appropriations, the different portions of the community must, of necessity, bear different and opposing relations in reference to the action of the government. There must inevitably spring up two interests—a direction and a stock-holder interest—an interest profiting by the action of the government, and interested in increasing its powers and action; and another, at whose expense the political machine is kept in motion. I know how difficult it is to communicate distinct ideas on such a subject, through the medium of general propositions, without particular illustration; and in order that I may be distinctly understood, though at the hazard of being tedious, I will illustrate the important principle which I have ventured to advance, by examples.

Let us, then, suppose a small community of five persons, separated from the rest of the world; and, to make the example strong, let us suppose them all to be engaged in the same pursuit, and to be of equal wealth. Let us further suppose that they determine to govern the community by the will of a majority; and, to make the case as strong as possible, let us suppose that the majority, in order to meet the expenses of the government, lay an equal tax, say of one hundred dollars on each individual of this little community. Their treasury would contain five hundred dollars. Three are a majority; and they, by supposition, have contributed three hundred as their portion, and the other two (the minority), two hundred. The three have the right to make the appropriations as they may think proper. The question is, How would the principle of the absolute and unchecked majority operate, under these circumstances, in this little community? If the three be governed by a sense of justice—if they should appropriate the money to the objects for which it was raised, the common and equal benefit of the five, then the object of the association would be fairly and honestly effected, and each would have a common interest in the government. But, should the majority pursue an opposite course—should they appropriate the money in a manner to benefit their own particular interest, without regard to the interest of the two (and that they will so act, unless there be some efficient check, he who best knows human nature will least doubt), who does not see that the three and the two would have directly opposite interests in reference to the action of the government? The three who contribute to the common treasury but three hundred dollars, could, in fact, by appropriating the five hundred to their own use, convert the action of the government into the means of making money, and, of consequence, would have a direct interest in increasing the taxes. They put in three hundred and take out five; that is, they take back to themselves all that they put in, and, in addition, that which was put in by their associates; or, in other words, taking taxation and appropriation together, they have gained, and their associates have lost, two hundred dollars by the fiscal action of the government. Opposite interests, in reference to the action of the government, are thus created between them: the one having a interest in favor, and the other against the taxes; the one to increase, and the other to decrease the taxes; the one to retain the taxes when the money is no longer wanted, and the other to repeal them when the objects for which they were levied have been secured.

Let us now suppose this community of five to be raised to twenty-four individuals, to be governed, in like manner, by the will of a majority: it is obvious that the same principle would divide them into two interests—into a majority and a minority, thirteen against eleven, or in some other proportion; and that all the consequences which I have shown to be applicable to the small community of five would be equally applicable to the greater, the cause not depending upon the number, but resulting necessarily from the action of the government itself. Let us now suppose that, instead of governing themselves directly in an assembly of the whole, without the intervention of agents, they should adopt the representative principle; and that, instead of being governed by a majority of themselves, they should be governed by a majority of their representatives. It is obvious that the operation of the system would not be affected by the change: the representatives being responsible to those who chose them, would conform to the will of their constituents, and would act as they would do were they present and acting for themselves; and the same conflict of interest, which we have shown would exist in one case, would equally exist in the other. In either case, the inevitable result would be a system of hostile legislation on the part of the majority, or the stronger interest, against the minority, or the weaker interest; the object of which, on the part of the former, would be to exact as much as possible from the latter, which would necessarily be resisted by all the means in their power. Warfare, by legislation, would thus be commenced between the parties, with the same object, and not less hostile than that which is carried on between distinct and rival nations— the only distinction would be in the instruments and the mode. Enactments, in the one case, would supply what could only be effected by arms in the other; and the inevitable operation would be to engender the most hostile feelings between the parties, which would merge every feeling of patriotism—that feeling which embraces the whole—and substitute in its place the most violent party attachment; and instead of having one common centre of attachment, around which the affections of the community might rally, there would in fact be two—the interests of the majority, to which those who constitute that majority would be more attached than they would be to the whole—and that of the minority, to which they, in like manner, would also be more attached than to the interests of the whole. Faction would thus take the place of patriotism; and, with the loss of patriotism, corruption must necessarily follow, and in its train, anarchy, and, finally, despotism, or the establishment of absolute power in a single individual, as a means of arresting the conflict of hostile interests; on the principle that it is better to submit to the will of a single individual, who by being made lord and master of the whole community, would have an equal interest in the protection of all the parts.

Let us next suppose that, in order to avert the calamitous train of consequences, this little community should adopt a written constitution, with limitations restricting the will of the majority, in order to protect the minority against the oppression which I have shown would necessarily result without such restrictions. It is obvious that the case would not be in the slightest degree varied, if the majority be left in possession of the right of judging exclusively of the extent of its powers, without any right on the part of the minority to enforce the restrictions imposed by the constitution on the will of the majority. The point is almost too clear for illustration. Nothing can be more certain than that, when a constitution grants power, and imposes limitations on the exercise of that power, whatever interests may obtain possession of the government, will be in favor of extending the power at the expense of the limitation; and that, unless those in whose behalf the limitations were imposed have, in some form or mode, the right of enforcing them, the power will ultimately supersede the limitation, and the government must operate precisely in the same manner as if the will of the majority governed without constitution or limitation of power.

I have thus presented all possible modes in which a government founded upon the will of an absolute majority will be modified; and have demonstrated that, in all its forms, whether in a majority of the people, as in a mere Democracy, or in a majority of their representatives, without a constitution or with a constitution, to be interpreted as the will of the majority, the result will be the same: two hostile interests will inevitably be created by the action of the government, to be followed by hostile legislation, and that by faction, corruption, anarchy, and despotism.

The great and solemn question here presents itself, Is there any remedy for these evils? on the decision of which depends the question, whether the people can govern themselves, which has been so often asked with so much skepticism and doubt. There is a remedy, and but one—the effect of which, whatever may be the form, is to organize society in reference to this conflict of interests, which springs out of the action of government; and which can only be done by giving to each part the right of self-protection; which, in a word, instead of considering the community of twenty-four a single community, having a common interest, and to be governed by the single will of an entire majority, shall, upon all questions tending to bring the parts into conflict, the thirteen against the eleven, take the will, not of the twenty-four as a unit, but of the thirteen and of the eleven separately, the majority of each governing the parts; and where they concur, governing the whole—and where they disagree, arresting the action of the government. This I will call the concurring, as distinct from the absolute majority. It would not be, as was generally supposed, a minority governing the majority. In either way the number would be the same, whether taken as the absolute or as the concurring majority. Thus, the majority of the thirteen is seven, and of the eleven six; and the two together make thirteen, which is the majority of twenty-four. But, though the number is the same, the mode of counting is essentially different: the one representing the strongest interest, and the other, the entire interests of the community. The first mistake is, in supposing that the government of the absolute majority is the government of the people—that beau ideal of a perfect government which has been so enthusiastically entertained in every age by the generous and patriotic, where civilization and liberty have made the smallest progress. There can be no greater error: the government of the people is the government of the whole community—of the twenty-four—the self-government of all the parts—too perfect to be reduced to practice in the present, or any past stage of human society. The government of the absolute majority, instead of being the government of the people, is but the government of the strongest interests, and, when not efficiently checked, is the most tyrannical and oppressive that can be devised. Between this ideal perfection on the one side, and despotism on the other, no other system can be devised but that which considers society in reference to its parts, as differently affected by the action of the government, and which takes the sense of each part separately, and thereby the sense of the whole, in the manner already illustrated.

These principles, as I have already stated, are not affected by the number of which the community may be composed, but are just as applicable to one of thirteen millions, the number which composes ours, as of the small community of twenty-four, which I have supposed, for the purpose of illustration; and are not less applicable to the twenty-four States united in one community, than to the case of the twenty-four individuals. There is, indeed, a distinction between a large and a small community, not affecting the principle, but the violence of the action. In the former, the similarity of the interests of all the parts will limit the oppression from the hostile action of the parts, in a great degree, to the fiscal action of the government merely; but in the large community, spreading over a country of great extent, and having a great diversity of interests, with different kinds of labor, capital, and production, the conflict and oppression will extend only to a monopoly of the appropriations on the part of the stronger interests, but will end in unequal taxes, and a general conflict between the entire interests of conflicting sections, which, if not arrested by the most powerful checks, will terminate in the most oppressive tyranny that can be conceived, or in the destruction of the community itself.

If we turn our attention from these supposed cases, and direct it to our government and its actual operation, we shall find a practical confirmation of the truth of what has been stated, not only of the oppressive operation of the system of an absolute majority, but also a striking and beautiful illustration, in the formation of our system, of the principle of the concurring majority, as distinct from the absolute, which I have asserted to be the only means of efficiently checking the abuse of power, and, of course, the only solid foundation of constitutional liberty. That our government, for many years, has been gradually verging to consolidation; that the constitution has gradually become a dead letter; and that all restrictions upon the power of government have been virtually removed, so as practically to convert the General Government into a government of an absolute majority, without check or limitation, cannot be denied by any one who has impartially observed its operation.

It is not necessary to trace the commencement and gradual progress of the causes which have produced this change in our system; it is sufficient to state that the change has taken place within the last few years. What has been the result? Precisely that which might have been anticipated—the growth of faction, corruption, anarchy, and, if not despotism itself, its near approach, as witnessed in the provisions of this bill. And from what have these consequences sprung? We have been involved in no war. We have been at peace with all the world. We have been visited with no national calamity. Our people have been advancing in general intelligence, and, I will add, as great and alarming as has been the advance of political corruption among the mercenary corps who look to Government for support, the morals and virtue of the community at large have been advancing in improvement. What, I again repeat, is the cause? No other can be assigned but a departure from the fundamental principles of the constitution, which has converted the Government into the will of an absolute and irresponsible majority, and which, by the laws that must inevitably govern in all such majorities, has placed in conflict the great interests of the country, by a system of hostile legislation, by a oppressive and unequal imposition of taxes, by unequal and profuse appropriations, and by rendering the entire labor and capital of the weaker interest subordinate to the stronger.

This is the cause, and these the fruits, which have converted the Government into a mere instrument of taking money from one portion of the community, to be given to another; and which has rallied around it a great, a powerful, and mercenary corps of office-holders, office-seekers, and expectants, destitute of principle and patriotism, and who have no standard of morals or politics but the will of the Executive—the will of him who has the distribution of the loaves and the fishes. I hold it impossible for any one to look at the theoretical illustration of the principle of the absolute majority in the cases which I have supposed, and not be struck with the practical illustration in the actual operation of our Government. Under every circumstance, the absolute majority will ever have its American system (I mean nothing offensive to any Senator); but the real meaning of the American system is, that system of plunder which the strongest interest has ever waged, and will ever wage, against the weaker, where the latter is not armed with some efficient and constitutional check to arrest its action. Nothing but such check on the part of the weaker interest can arrest it: mere constitutional limitations are wholly insufficient. Whatever interest obtains possession of the Government, will, from the nature of things, be in favor of the powers, and against the limitations imposed by the constitution, and will resort to every device that can be imagined to remove those restraints. On the contrary, the opposite interest, that which I have designated as the stockholding interest, the tax-payers, those on whom the system operates, will resist the abuse of powers, and contend for the limitations. And it is on this point, then, that the contest between the delegated and the reserved powers will be waged; but in this contest, as the interests in possession of the Government are organized and armed by all its powers and patronage, the opposite interest, if not in like manner organized and possessed of a power to protect themselves under the provisions of the constitution, will be as inevitably crushed as would be a band of unorganized militia when opposed by a veteran and trained corps of regulars. Let it never be forgotten, that power can only be opposed by power, organization by organization; and on this theory stands our beautiful federal system of Government. No free system was ever further removed from the principle that the absolute majority, without check or limitation, ought to govern. To understand what our Government is, we must look to the constitution, which is the basis of the system. I do not intend to enter into any minute examination of the origin and the source of its powers: it is sufficient for my purpose to state, what I do fearlessly, that it derived its power from the people of the separate States, each ratifying by itself, each binding itself by its own separate majority, through its separate convention—the concurrence of the majorities of the several States forming the constitution—thus taking the sense of the whole by that of the several parts, representing the various interests of the entire community. It was this concurring and perfect majority which formed the constitution, and not that majority which would consider the American people as a single community, and which, instead of representing fairly and fully the interests of the whole, would but represent, as has been stated, the interests of the stronger section. No candid man can dispute that I have given a correct description of the constitution-making power: that power which created and organized the Government, which delegated to it, as a common agent, certain powers, in trust for the common good of all the States, and which imposed strict limitations and checks against abuses and usurpations. In administering the delegated powers, the constitution provides, very properly, in order to give promptitude and efficiency, that the Government shall be organized upon the principle of the absolute majority, or, rather, of two absolute majorities combined: a majority of the States considered as bodies politic, which prevails in this body; and a majority of the people of the States, estimated in federal numbers, in the other House of Congress. A combination of the two prevails in the choice of the President; and, of course, in the appointment of Judges, they being nominated by the President and confirmed by the Senate. It is thus that the concurring and the absolute majorities are combined in one complex system: the one in forming the constitution, and the other in making and executing the laws; thus beautifully blending the moderation, justice, and equity of the former, and more perfect majority, with the promptness and energy of the latter, but less perfect.

To maintain the ascendency of the constitution over the law-making majority is the great and essential point, on which the success of the system must depend. Unless that ascendency can be preserved, the necessary consequence must be, that the laws will supersede the constitution; and, finally, the will of the Executive, by the influence of his patronage, will supersede the laws—indications of which are already perceptible. This ascendency can only be preserved through the action of the States as organized bodies, having their own separate governments, and possessed of the right, under the structure of our system, of judging of the extent of their separate powers, and of interposing their authority to arrest the unauthorized enactments of the General Government within their respective limits. I will not enter, at this time, into the discussion of this important point, as it has been ably and fully presented by the Senator from Kentucky (Mr. Bibb), and others who preceded him in this debate on the same side, whose arguments not only remain unanswered, but are unanswerable. It is only by this power of interposition that the reserved rights of the States can be peacefully and efficiently protected against the encroachments of the General Government—that the limitations imposed upon its authority can be enforced, and its movements confined to the orbit allotted to it by the constitution.

It has, indeed, been said in debate, that this can be effected by the organization of the General Government itself, particularly by the action of this body, which represents the States—that the States themselves must look to the General Government for the preservation of many of the most important of their reserved rights. I do not underrate the value to be attached to the organic arrangement of the General Government, and the wise distribution of its powers between the several departments, and, in particular, the structure and the important functions of this body; but to suppose that the Senate, or any department of the Government, was intended to be the only guardian of the reserved rights, is a great and fundamental mistake. The Government, through all its departments, represents the delegated, and not the reserved powers; and it is a violation of the fundamental principle of free institutions to suppose that any but the responsible representative of any interest can be its guardian. The distribution of the powers of the General Government, and its organization, were arranged to prevent the abuse of power in fulfilling the important trusts confided to it, and not, as preposterously supposed, to protect the reserved powers, which are confided wholly to the guardianship of the several States.

Against the view of our system which I have presented, and the right of the States to interpose, it is objected that it would lead to anarchy and dissolution. I consider the objection as without the slightest foundation; and that, so far from tending to weakness or disunion, it is the source of the highest power and of the strongest cement. Nor is its tendency in this respect difficult of explanation. The government of an absolute majority, unchecked by efficient constitutional restraints, though apparently strong, is, in reality, an exceedingly feeble government. That tendency to conflict between the parts, which I have shown to be inevitable in such governments, wastes the powers of the state in the hostile action of contending factions, which leaves very little more power than the excess of the strength of the majority over the minority. But a government based upon the principle of the concurring majority, where each great interest possesses within itself the means of self-protection, which ultimately requires the mutual consent of all the parts, necessarily causes that unanimity in council, and ardent attachment of all the parts to the whole, which give an irresistible energy to a government so constituted.

I might appeal to history for the truth of these remarks, of which the Roman furnishes the most familiar and striking proofs. It is a well-known fact, that, from the expulsion of the Tarquins to the time of the establishment of the tribunitian power, the government fell into a state of the greatest disorder and distraction, and, I may add, corruption. How did this happen? The explanation will throw important light on the subject under consideration. The community was divided into two parts, the patricians and the plebeians, with the power of the state principally in the hands of the former, without adequate checks to protect the rights of the latter. The result was as might be expected. The patricians converted the powers of the government into the means of making money, to enrich themselves and their dependants. They, in a word, had their American system, growing out of the peculiar character of the government and condition of the country. This requires explanation. At that period, according to the laws of nations, when one nation conquered another, the lands of the vanquished belonged to the victor; and, according to the Roman law, the lands thus acquired were divided into two parts—one allotted to the poorer class of the people, and the other assigned to the use of the treasury—of which the patricians had the distribution and administration. The patricians abused their power by withholding from the plebeians that which ought to have been allotted to them, and by converting to their own use that which ought to have gone to the treasury. In a word, they took to themselves the entire spoils of victory—and had thus the most powerful motive to keep the state perpetually involved in war, to the utter impoverishment and oppression of the plebeians. After resisting the abuse of power by all peaceable means, and the oppression becoming intolerable, the plebeians, at last, withdrew from the city—they, in a word, seceded; and to induce them to reunite, the patricians conceded to the plebeians, as the means of protecting their separate interests, the very power, which I contend is necessary to protect the rights of the States, but which is now represented as necessarily leading to disunion. They granted to them the right of choosing three tribunes from among themselves, whose persons should be sacred, and who should have the right of interposing their veto, not only against the passage of laws, but even against their execution—a power which those, who take a shallow insight into human nature, would pronounce inconsistent with the strength and unity of the state, if not utterly impracticable; yet so far from this being the effect, from that day the genius of Rome became ascendant, and victory followed her steps till she had established an almost universal dominion.

How can a result so contrary to all anticipation be explained? The explanation appears to me to be simple. No measure or movement could be adopted without the concurring assent of both the patricians and plebeians, and each thus became dependent on the other; and, of consequence, the desire and objects of neither could be effected without the concurrence of the other. To obtain this concurrence, each was compelled to consult the goodwill of the other, and to elevate to office, not those only who might have the confidence of the order to which they belonged, but also that of the other. The result was, that men possessing those qualities which would naturally command confidence—moderation, wisdom, justice, and patriotism—were elevated to office; and these, by the weight of their authority and the prudence of their counsel, combined with that spirit of unanimity necessarily resulting from the concurring assent of the two orders, furnish the real explanation of the power of the Roman State, and of that extraordinary wisdom, moderation, and firmness which in so remarkable a degree characterized her public men. I might illustrate the truth of the position which I have laid down by a reference to the history of all free states, ancient and modern, distinguished for their power and patriotism, and conclusively show, not only that there was not one which had not some contrivance, under some form, by which the concurring assent of the different portions of the community was made necessary in the action of government, but also that the virtue, patriotism, and strength of the state were in direct proportion to the perfection of the means of securing such assent.

In estimating the operation of this principle in our system, which depends, as I have stated, on the right of interposition on the part of a State, we must not omit to take into consideration the amending power, by which new powers may be granted, or any derangement of the system corrected, by the concurring assent of three-fourths of the States; and thus, in the

same degree, strengthening the power of repairing any derangement occasioned by the eccentric action of a State. In fact, the power of interposition,
fairly understood, may be considered in the light of an appeal against the
usurpations of the General Government, the joint agent of all the States,
to the States themselves—to be decided under the amending power, by
the voice of three-fourths of the States, as the highest power known under
the system. I know the difficulty, in our country, of establishing the truth
of the principle for which I contend, though resting upon the clearest
reason, and tested by the universal experience of free nations. I know that
the governments of the several States, which, for the most part, are constructed on the principle of the absolute majority, will be cited as an
argument against the conclusion to which I have arrived; but, in my opinion, the satisfactory answer can be given—that the objects of expenditure
which fall within the sphere of a State Government are few and inconsiderable, so that be their action ever so irregular, it can occasion but little
derangement. If, instead of being members of this great confederacy, they
formed distinct communities, and were compelled to raise armies, and
incur other expenses necessary to their defence, the laws which I have laid
down as necessarily controlling the action of a State where the will of an
absolute and unchecked majority prevailed, would speedily disclose themselves in faction, anarchy, and corruption. Even as the case is, the operation of the causes to which I have referred is perceptible in some of the
larger and more populous members of the Union, whose governments have
a powerful central action, and which already show a strong moneyed tendency, the invariable forerunner of corruption and convulsion.

But, to return to the General Government. We have now sufficient experience to ascertain that the tendency to conflict in its action is between the
southern and other sections. The latter having a decided majority, must
habitually be possessed of the powers of the Government, both in this and
in the other House; and, being governed by that instinctive love of power
so natural to the human breast, they must become the advocates of the
power of Government, and in the same degree opposed to the limitations;

while the other and weaker section is as necessarily thrown on the side of the limitations. One section is the natural guardian of the delegated powers, and the other of the reserved; and the struggle on the side of the former will be to enlarge the powers, while that on the opposite side will be to restrain them within their constitutional limits. The contest will, in fact, be a contest between power and liberty, and such I consider the present— a contest in which the weaker section, with its peculiar labor, productions, and institutions, has at stake all that can be dear to freemen. Should we be able to maintain in their full vigor our reserved rights, liberty and prosperity will be our portion; but if we yield, and permit the stronger interest to concentrate within itself all the powers of the Government, then will our fate be more wretched than that of the aborigines whom we have expelled. In this great struggle between the delegated and reserved powers, so far from repining that my lot, and that of those whom I represent, is cast on the side of the latter, I rejoice that such is the fact; for, though we participate in but few of the advantages of the Government, we are compensated, and more than compensated, in not being so much exposed to its corruptions. Nor do I repine that the duty, so difficult to be discharged, of defending the reserved powers against apparently such fearful odds, has been assigned to us. To discharge successfully this high duty requires the highest qualities, moral and intellectual; and should we perform it with a zeal and ability proportioned to its magnitude, instead of being mere planters, our section will become distinguished for its patriots and statesmen. But, on the other hand, if we prove unworthy of this high destiny—if we yield to the steady encroachments of power, the severest calamity and most debasing corruption will overspread the land. Every Southern man, true to the interests of his section, and faithful to the duties which Providence has allotted him, will be forever excluded from the honors and emoluments of this Government, which will be reserved for those only who have qualified themselves, by political prostitution, for admission into the Magdalen Asylum.

SPEECH ON THE RECEPTION OF ABOLITION PETITIONS

[February 6, 1837]

———•—•·———

By the mid-1830s, the controversy concerning the tariff had shifted in large measure to the broader question of slavery and the general nature of federal-state relations. Congress was inundated with petitions calling for, in one form or another, the restriction or abolition of slavery, especially in the District of Columbia. Calhoun argued that Congress was not obligated to receive these petitions and should not do so, for their receipt implied congressional jurisdiction over this matter. Questions of slavery, argued Calhoun, had been left by the Constitution for the states to decide. Furthermore, Calhoun objected to the fact that these petitions were becoming increasingly hostile, not only to the institution of slavery, but to the whole way of Southern life and culture.

It was during this debate that Calhoun first articulated the idea that slavery, that "peculiar institution" of the South, was a positive good. He came under immediate criticism for both the content and intent of his speech. He, in turn, complained bitterly that his remarks had been taken out of context and that his views were being intentionally misrepresented.

This document is also important to consider because Calhoun formulated his defense of slavery within the broader context of his views of history, economics, and philosophy. Because of the sensitive nature of this issue, both the first report and the revised report have been reprinted here. While the general substance of the two versions does not differ, there is considerable variance in the language and tone used in the two reports.

FIRST REPORT

[On February 6, 1837, John Tipton of Indiana presented two petitions from his constituents, calling upon Congress to abolish slavery in the District of Columbia. Although Mr. Tipton acknowledged that he believed the petitions to be unwise, unconstitutional, and unrepresentative of his constituents in general, he thought their acceptance and referral to committee would quiet the public mind. Mr. Calhoun rose immediately and asked the Chair for a ruling on the procedures to be used in the Senate for addressing such petitions.][1]

Mr. Calhoun expressed the hope that a question would be made on the reception of the petitions. He insisted that, if an objection should be made to the reception of a petition, it was the rule, and for forty years had been the practice of the Senate, to take the vote of reception, without a motion not to receive. He read the rule on this point, which stated that, if there was a cry of the House to receive, and no objection should be made, or if the House were silent, the reception would take place of course. Otherwise, a vote must be taken on its reception. Mr. C. said he had in vain insisted on this at the last session. He hoped the Chair would now sustain the rule, before Mr. C. would be compelled to move a non-reception.

[The Chair ruled that whenever an objection is raised by a Senator rising

[1]In the First Report, the original reporter's commentary is in parentheses and the bracketed material is mine.—*R.M.L.*

in his place or objecting in his seat to the reception of a petition, the Senate itself shall judge whether the petition will be received.]

Mr. Calhoun expressed his satisfaction at the decision of the Chair. He hoped the old mode, which had been uniformly practiced till within five or six years, would now be pursued.

[Considerable discussion then ensued about the proper course to follow. Unanimous consent was given to consider all such petitions at the same time. Several petitions were introduced by a number of Senators, including Mr. Ewing and Mr. Morris of Ohio, Mr. Swift and Mr. Prentiss of Vermont, Mr. Buchanan of Pennsylvania, and Mr. Knight of Rhode Island. During the course of that discussion, Mr. Calhoun delivered the following remarks.]

Mr. Calhoun said he thought it very desirable that the Senate and the South should know in what manner these petitioners spoke of Southern people. For this purpose he had selected, from the numerous petitions on the table, two, indiscriminately, which he wished the Secretary to read.

(These two petitions were read, and proved to be rather more moderate in their language than usual.)

Such is the language (said Mr. C.) with which they characterize us and ours. That which was the basis of Southern institutions, and which could not be dispensed without blood and massacre, was denounced as sinful and outrageous on the rights of men. And all this was proclaimed, in the Senate of the United States, of States that were united together for the purpose of maintaining their institutions in a more perfect manner. Were Southern members to sit quietly and hear themselves denounced in this manner? And if they should speak at all under these circumstances, were they to be denounced as agitators? This institution existed when the constitution was formed; and yet Senators would not only sit and receive them, but were ready to throw blame on those who opposed them.

Mr. C. said he did not belong to the school of those who believed that agitations of this sort could be quieted by concessions; on the contrary, he maintained all usurpations should be resisted in the beginning; and those who would not do so were prepared to be slaves themselves. Mr. C. knew, and had predicted, that if the petitions were received, it would not avail in satisfying the petitioners; but they would then be prepared for the next step, to compel action upon the petitions. Mr. C. would ask Southern gentlemen if they did not see the second step prepared to be taken, not only that the petitions should be received, but referred.

Mr. C. had told Mr. Buchanan and his friends, last year, that they were taking an impossible position; and had said that these men would, at this session, press a reference. Were we now to be told that this second concession would satisfy this incendiary spirit? Such was the very position (a reference) at which the other House arrived at the last session. Had they at all quieted the spirit of abolition? On the contrary, it had caused it to spread wider and strike its roots still deeper. The next step would be to produce discussion and argument on the subject. Mr. C. insisted that the South had surrendered essentially by permitting the petitions to be received. He said it was time for the South to take her stand and reject the petitions. He conscientiously believed that Congress were as much under obligation to act on the subject as they were to receive the petitions; and that they had just as good a right to abolish slavery in the States as in this District.

Mr. C. said the decision of the Chair settled the question that the Senate had a right to refuse to receive the petitions; for, if they had a right to vote at all on the subject, they had the right to vote in the negative; and to yield this point was to yield it for the benefit of the abolitionists, at the expense of the Senate. But it was in vain to argue on the subject. Mr. C. would warn Southern members to take their stand on this point without concession. He had foreseen and predicted this state of things three years ago, as a legitimate result of the force bill. All this body were now opposed to the object of these petitions. Mr. C. saw where all originated—at the very bottom of society, among the lowest and most ignorant; but it would go on, and rise higher and higher, till it should ascend the pulpit and the schools, where it had, indeed, arrived already; thence it would mount up to this and the other House. The only way to resist was to close the doors; to open them was virtually to surrender the question. The spirit of the times (he said) was one of dollars and cents, the spirit of speculation, which had diffused itself from the North to the South. Nothing (he said) could resist the spirit of abolition but the united action of the South. The opinions of most people in the North and South were now sound on this subject; but the rising generation would be imbued by the spirit of fanaticism, and the North and South would become two people, with feelings diametrically opposite. The decided action of the South, within the limits of the constitution, was indispensable.

[Mr. Tipton expressed considerable surprise at Mr. Calhoun's remarks, saying that he thought there was nothing in the petitions before them that could produce such feelings. Mr. Bayard of Delaware moved to table the question of the reception of the petitions. A favorable vote on Mr. Bayard's motion did not end debate, however, as Mr. Davis of Massachusetts immediately introduced some forty additional petitions. Returning to the issue of the procedures of the Senate, Mr. King of Georgia announced that he thought Mr. Calhoun was in error in his interpretation of the differences between the current and the last session of the Senate.]

Mr. Calhoun said he, for one, was extremely pleased with the decision of the Chair (that a mere objection required a vote on the reception of the petitions). But he ought to go further, and put the question of reception, whether the petition were objected to or not. According to the rule, he said, the burden of making a motion to receive should fall on those presenting the petitions. Mr. C. had formerly pressed the Chair twice on this point, but was then overruled. The question was, whether we were bound to receive the petitions by the constitution. That question the Chair had now yielded, and had admitted that it was in the power of the body itself to say whether or not the petitions should be received.

Mr. C. again argued that, if Congress were bound to receive petitions, they were equally bound to refer and act upon them.

[Intense debate now ensued. In the course of that discussion, Mr. Rives of Virginia, who noted that he had observed the whole debate with pain and mortification, said that while he did not object to the presentation of the abolitionists' petitions, he did object to the gratuitous exhibition of those horrid pictures of misery that had no foundation in fact. He noted that he did not subscribe to slavery in the abstract—a point on which he differed with the gentleman from South Carolina.]

Mr. Calhoun explained, and denied having expressed any opinion in regard to slavery in the abstract. He had merely stated, what was a matter of fact, that it was an inevitable law of society that one portion of the community depended upon the labor of another portion, over which it must unavoidably exercise control. He had not spoken of slavery in the abstract, but of slavery as existing where two races of men, of different color, and striking dissimilarity in conformation, habits, and a thousand other particulars, were placed in immediate juxtaposition. Here the existence of slavery was a good to both. Did not the Senator from Virginia consider it as a good?

Mr. Rives said, no. He viewed it as a misfortune and an evil in all circumstances, though; in some, it might be the lesser evil.

Mr. Calhoun insisted on the opposite opinion, and declared it as his conviction that, in point of fact, the Central African race (he did not speak of the north or the east of Africa, but of its central regions) had never existed in so comfortable, so respectable, or so civilized a condition, as that which it now enjoyed in the Southern States. The population doubled in the same ratio with that of the whites—a proof of ease and plenty; while, with respect to civilization, it nearly kept pace with that of the owners; and as to the effect upon the whites, would it be affirmed that they were inferior to others, that they were less patriotic, less intelligent, less humane, less brave, than where slavery did not exist? He was not aware that any inferiority was pretended. Both races, therefore, appeared to thrive under the practical operation of this institution. The experiment was in progress, but had not been completed. The world had not seen modern society go through the entire process, and he claimed that its judgment should be postponed for another ten years. The social experiment was going on both at the North and the South—in the one with almost pure and unlimited democracy, and in the other with a mixed race. Thus far, the results of the experiment had been in favor of the South. Southern society had been far less agitated, and he would venture to predict that its condition would prove by far the most secure, and by far the most favorable to the preservation of liberty. In fact, the defence of human liberty against the aggressions of despotic power had been always the most efficient in States where domestic slavery was found to prevail. He did not admit it to be an evil. Not at all. It was a good—a great good. On that point, the Senator from Virginia and himself were directly at issue.

[Mr. Rives said that he had no desire to get into a family quarrel with Mr. Calhoun on this matter. He, for one, however, did not believe slavery was a good—morally, politically, or economically. And while he would defend the constitutional rights of the South to the end, that commitment would not cause him to return to the explored dogmas of Sir Robert Filmer in order to vindicate the institution of slavery in the abstract.]

Mr. Calhoun complained of having been misrepresented. Again [he] denied having pronounced slavery in the abstract a good. All he had said of it referred to existing circumstances; to slavery as a practical, not as an abstract thing. It was a good where a civilized race and a race of a different description were brought together. Wherever civilization existed, death too was found, and luxury; but did he hold that death and luxury were good in themselves? He believed slavery was good, where the two races co-existed. The gentleman from Virginia held it an evil. Yet he would defend it. Surely if it was an evil, moral, social, and political, the Senator, as a wise and virtuous man, was bound to exert himself to put it down. This position, that it was a moral evil, was the very root of the whole system of operations against it. That was the spring and well-head from which all these streams of abolition proceeded—the effects of which so deeply agitated the honorable Senator.

Mr. C. again adverted to the successful results of the experiment thus

far, and insisted that the slaveholders of the South had nothing in the case
to lament or to lay to their conscience. He utterly denied that his doctrines
had anything to do with the tenets of Sir Robert Filmer, which he abhorred.
So far from holding the dogmas of that writer, he had been the known and
open advocate of freedom from the beginning. Nor was there anything in
the doctrines he held in the slightest degree inconsistent with the highest
and purest principles of freedom.

REVISED REPORT

If the time of the Senate permitted, I would feel it to be my duty to call
for the reading of the mass of petitions on the table, in order that we might
know what language they hold towards the slaveholding States and their
institutions; but as it will not, I have selected, indiscriminately from the
pile, two; one from those in manuscript, and the other from the printed,
and without knowing their contents will call for the reading of them, so that
we may judge, by them, of the character of the whole.

[Here the Secretary, on the call of Mr. Calhoun, read the two petitions.]

Such, resumed Mr. C., is the language held towards us and ours. The
peculiar institution of the South—that, on the maintenance of which the
very existence of the slaveholding States depends, is pronounced to be
sinful and odious, in the sight of God and man; and this with a systematic
design of rendering us hateful in the eyes of the world—with a view to a
general crusade against us and our institutions. This, too, in the legislative
halls of the Union; created by these confederated States, for the better
protection of their peace, their safety, and their respective institutions—
and yet, we, the representatives of twelve of these sovereign States against
whom this deadly war is waged, are expected to sit here in silence, hearing
ourselves and our constituents day after day denounced, without uttering a
word; for if we but open our lips, the charge of agitation is resounded on
all sides, and we are held up as seeking to aggravate the evil which we

resist. Every reflecting mind must see in all this a state of things deeply and dangerously diseased.

I do not belong, said Mr. C., to the school which holds that aggression is to be met by concession. Mine is the opposite creed, which teaches that encroachments must be met at the beginning, and that those who act on the opposite principle are prepared to become slaves. In this case, in particular, I hold concession or compromise to be fatal. If we concede an inch, concession would follow concession—compromise would follow compromise, until our ranks would be so broken that effectual resistance would be impossible. We must meet the enemy on the frontier, with a fixed determination of maintaining our position at every hazard. Consent to receive these insulting petitions, and the next demand will be that they be referred to a committee in order that they may be deliberated and acted upon. At the last session we were modestly asked to receive them, simply to lay them on the table, without any view to ulterior action. I then told the Senator from Pennsylvania (Mr. Buchanan), who so strongly urged that course in the Senate, that it was a position that could not be maintained; as the argument in favor of acting on the petitions if we were bound to receive, could not be resisted. I then said, that the next step would be to refer the petition to a committee, and I already see indications that such is now the intention. If we yield, that will be followed by another, and we will thus proceed, step by step, to the final consummation of the object of these petitions. We are now told that the most effectual mode of arresting the progress of abolition is, to reason it down; and with this view it is urged that the petitions ought to be referred to a committee. That is the very ground which was taken at the last session in the other House, but instead of arresting its progress, it has since advanced more rapidly than ever. The most unquestionable right may be rendered doubtful if once admitted to be a subject of controversy, and that would be the case in the present instance. The subject is beyond the jurisdiction of Congress—they have no right to touch it in any shape or form, or to make it the subject of deliberation or discussion.

In opposition to this view it is urged that Congress is bound by the constitution to receive petitions in every case and on every subject, whether within its constitutional competency or not. I hold the doctrine to be absurd, and do solemnly believe, that it would be as easy to prove that it has the right to abolish slavery, as that it is bound to receive petitions for that purpose. The very existence of the rule that requires a question to be put on the reception of petitions, is conclusive to show that there is no such obligation. It has been a standing rule from the commencement of the Government, and clearly shows the sense of those who formed the constitution on this point. The question on the reception would be absurd, if, as is contended, we are bound to receive; but I do not intend to argue the question; I discussed it fully at the last session, and the arguments then advanced neither have been nor can be answered.

As widely as this incendiary spirit has spread, it has not yet infected this body, or the great mass of the intelligent and business portion of the North; but unless it be speedily stopped, it will spread and work upwards till it brings the two great sections of the Union into deadly conflict. This is not a new impression with me. Several years since, in a discussion with one of the Senators from Massachusetts (Mr. Webster), before this fell spirit had showed itself, I then predicted that the doctrine of the proclamation and the Force Bill—that this Government had a right, in the last resort, to determine the extent of its own powers, and enforce its decision at the point of the bayonet, which was so warmly maintained by that Senator, would at no distant day arouse the dormant spirit of abolitionism. I told him that the doctrine was tantamount to the assumption of unlimited power on the part of the Government, and that such would be the impression on the public mind in a large portion of the Union. The consequence would be inevitable—a large portion of the Northern States believed slavery to be a sin, and would believe it as an obligation of conscience to abolish it if they should feel themselves in any degree responsible for its continuance, and that this doctrine would necessarily lead to the belief of such responsibility. I then predicted that it would commence as it has with this fanatical portion of society, and that they would begin their operations on the ignorant, the weak, the young, and the thoughtless, and would gradually extend upwards till they would become strong enough to obtain political control, when he and others holding the highest stations in society, would, however reluctant, be compelled to yield to their doctrines, or be driven into obscurity. But four years have since elapsed, and all this is already in a course of regular fulfilment.

Standing at the point of time at which we have now arrived, it will not be more difficult to trace the course of future events now than it was then. They who imagine that the spirit now abroad in the North, will die away of itself without a shock or convulsion, have formed a very inadequate conception of its real character; it will continue to rise and spread, unless prompt and efficient measures to stay its progress be adopted. Already it has taken possession of the pulpit, of the schools, and, to a considerable extent, of the press; those great instruments by which the mind of the rising generation will be formed.

However sound the great body of the non-slaveholding States are at present, in the course of a few years they will be succeeded by those who will have been taught to hate the people and institutions of nearly one-half of this Union, with a hatred more deadly than one hostile nation ever entertained towards another. It is easy to see the end. By the necessary course of events, if left to themselves, we must become, finally, two people. It is impossible under the deadly hatred which must spring up between the two great sections, if the present causes are permitted to operate unchecked, that we should continue under the same political system. The conflicting elements would burst the Union asunder, as powerful as are the links which hold it together. Abolition and the Union cannot co-exist. As the friend of the Union I openly proclaim it, and the sooner it is known the better. The former may now be controlled, but in a short time it will be beyond the power of man to arrest the course of events. We of the South will not, cannot, surrender our institutions. To maintain the existing relations between the two races, inhabiting that section of the Union, is indispensable to the peace and happiness of both. It cannot be subverted without drenching the country in blood, and extirpating one or the other of the races. Be it good or bad, it has grown up with our society and institutions, and is so interwoven with them, that to destroy it would be to destroy us as a people. But let me not be understood as admitting, even by implication, that the existing relations between the two races in the slaveholding States is an evil—far otherwise; I hold it to be a good, as it has thus far proved itself to be to both, and will continue to prove so if not disturbed by the fell spirit of abolition. I appeal to facts. Never before has the black race of Central Africa, from the dawn of history to the present day, attained a condition so civilized and so improved, not only physically, but morally and intellectually. It came among us in a low, degraded, and savage condition, and in the course of a few generations it has grown up under the fostering care of our institutions, as reviled as they have been, to its present comparatively civilized condition. This, with the rapid increase of numbers, is conclusive proof of the general happiness of the race, in spite of all the exaggerated tales to the contrary.

In the mean time, the white or European race has not degenerated. It has kept pace with its brethren in other sections of the Union where slavery does not exist. It is odious to make comparison; but I appeal to all sides whether the South is not equal in virtue, intelligence, patriotism, courage, disinterestedness, and all the high qualities which adorn our nature. I ask whether we have not contributed our full share of talents and political wisdom in forming and sustaining this political fabric; and whether we have not constantly inclined most strongly to the side of liberty, and been the first to see and first to resist the encroachments of power. In one thing only are we inferior—the arts of gain; we acknowledge that we are less wealthy than the Northern section of this Union, but I trace this mainly to the fiscal action of this Government, which has extracted much from, and spent little among us. Had it been the reverse—if the exaction had been from the other section, and the expenditure with us, this point of superiority would not be against us now, as it was not at the formation of this Government.

But I take higher ground. I hold that in the present state of civilization, where two races of different origin, and distinguished by color, and other physical differences, as well as intellectual, are brought together, the relation now existing in the slaveholding States between the two, is, instead of an evil, a good—a positive good. I feel myself called upon to speak freely upon the subject where the honor and interests of those I represent are involved. I hold then, that there never has yet existed a wealthy and civilized society in which one portion of the community did not, in point of fact, live on the labor of the other. Broad and general as is this assertion, it is fully borne out by history. This is not the proper occasion, but if it were, it would not be difficult to trace the various devices by which the wealth of all civilized communities has been so unequally divided, and to show by what means so small a share has been allotted to those by whose labor it was produced, and so large a share given to the non-producing classes. The devices are almost innumerable, from the brute force and gross superstition of ancient times, to the subtle and artful fiscal contrivances of modern. I might well challenge a comparison between them and the more direct, simple, and patriarchal mode by which the labor of the African race is, among us, commanded by the European. I may say with truth, that in few countries so much is left to the share of the laborer, and so little exacted from him, or where there is more kind attention paid to him in sickness or infirmities of age. Compare his condition with the tenants of the poor houses in the more civilized portions of Europe—look at the sick, and the old and infirm slave, on one hand, in the midst of his family and friends, under the kind superintending care of his master and mistress, and compare it with the forlorn and wretched condition of the pauper in the poor house. But I will not dwell on this aspect of the question; I turn to the political; and here I fearlessly assert that the existing relation between the two races in the South, against which these blind fanatics are waging war, forms the most solid and durable foundation on which to rear free and stable political institutions. It is useless to disguise the fact. There is and always has been in an advanced stage of wealth and civilization, a conflict between labor and capital. The condition of society in the South exempts us from the disorders and dangers resulting from this conflict; and which explains why it is that the political condition of the slaveholding States has been so much more stable and quiet than that of the North. The advantages of the former, in this respect, will become more and more manifest if left undisturbed by interference from without, as the country advances in wealth and numbers. We have, in fact, but just entered that condition of society where the strength and durability of our political institutions are to be tested; and I venture nothing in predicting that the experience of the next generation will fully test how vastly more favorable our condition of society is to that of other sections for free and stable institutions, provided we are not disturbed by the interference of others, or shall have sufficient intelligence and spirit to resist promptly and successfully such interference. It rests with ourselves to meet and repel them. I look not for aid to this Government, or to the other States; not but there are kind feelings towards us on the part of the great body of the non-slaveholding States; but as kind as their feelings may be, we may rest assured that no political party in those States will risk their ascendency for our safety. If we do not defend ourselves none will defend us; if we yield we will be more and more pressed as we recede; and if we submit we will be trampled under foot. Be assured that emancipation itself would not satisfy these fanatics—that gained, the next step would be to raise the negroes to a social and political equality with the whites; and that being effected, we would soon find the present condition of the two races reversed. They and their northern allies would be the masters, and we the slaves; the condition of the white race in the British West India Islands, bad as it is, would be happiness to ours. There the mother country is interested in sustaining the supremacy of the European race. It is true that the authority of the former master is destroyed, but the African will there still be a slave, not to individuals but to the community—forced to labor, not by the authority of the overseer, but by the bayonet of the soldiery and the rod of the civil magistrate.

Surrounded as the slaveholding States are with such imminent perils, I

rejoice to think that our means of defence are ample, if we shall prove to
have the intelligence and spirit to see and apply them before it is too late.
All we want is concert, to lay aside all party differences, and unite with zeal
and energy in repelling approaching dangers. Let there be concert of
action, and we shall find ample means of security without resorting to
secession or disunion. I speak with full knowledge and a thorough examination of the subject, and for one, see my way clearly. One thing alarms
me—the eager pursuit of gain which overspreads the land, and which
absorbs every faculty of the mind and every feeling of the heart. Of all
passions, avarice is the most blind and compromising—the last to see and
the first to yield to danger. I dare not hope that any thing I can say will
arouse the South to a due sense of danger; I fear it is beyond the power of
mortal voice to awaken it in time from the fatal security into which it has
fallen.

PUBLIC LETTER
TO J[OHN] BAUSKETT
AND OTHERS,
EDGEFIELD DISTRICT, S.C.

[November 3, 1837]

Having successfully overthrown the protective tariff and having checked the dangerous tendencies toward usurpation on the part of both the legislative and executive branches of government, many Southerners believed that the dangers to liberty had abated. By 1837, however, it had become apparent to Calhoun that the relief the South had won for itself would only be temporary if the banking system were allowed to ally itself with the government—a combination of money and power that was certain to lead to a centralization of the currency, commerce, and capital of the country in a manner far more detrimental to the South than any other previous issue of public policy. In an effort to offset that concentration of power and to counteract the corruption and inefficiency of the league of state banks supported by General Jackson, Calhoun grudgingly argued in favor of the restoration of a national bank.

Frustrated by the charges of men such as Clay and Webster that his public position was inconsistent and driven by political expediency, Calhoun penned the Edgefield Letter to a number of influential constituents from his home state of South Carolina to explain his position on the question of a national bank. The Edgefield Letter, then, presents us with a synopsis of the complex nature of the bank within the context of sectional politics. It also allows us to understand both the reasons for Calhoun's decision to return to the ranks of the Democratic Party and for his enormous distrust of both the Jackson and the Van Buren administrations.

GENTLEMEN: It is with very great reluctance I decline your kind invitation to partake of a public dinner. From no quarter, and on no occasion, could an expression of approbation be more acceptable, but so short is the interval between this and the next regular session of Congress, and so indispensable is it, that I should devote it exclusively to my domestic concerns, preparatory to my long absence from home, that I am compelled to decline the honor intended.

In saying that on no occasion could the expression of your confidence be more welcome, I intend no unmeaning common place. During the long period of my public service, never have I seen a more important crisis, than the present, and in none have I ever been compelled, in the discharge of my duty, to assume a greater responsibility. I saw clearly on my arrival at Washington, at the commencement of the late extra session, that our affairs had reached the point, when, according to the course we might take, we should reap the full harvest of our long and arduous struggle against the encroachments and abuses of the general government, or lose the fruits of all our labour. I clearly saw, that our bold and vigorous attacks had made a deep and successful impression. State interposition had overthrown the protective tariff and with it the American system, and put a stop to congressional usurpation; and the joint attacks of our party and that of our old opponents, the national republicans, had effectually brought down the power of the executive, and arrested its encroachments for the present. It

479

was for that purpose, we had united. True to our principles of opposition to the encroachment of power, from whatever quarter it might come, we did not hesitate, after overthrowing the protective system and arresting legislative usurpation, to join the authors of that system, in order to arrest the encroachments of the executive, although we differed as widely as the poles on almost every other question, and regarded the usurpation of the executive, but as a necessary consequence of the principles and policy of our new allies. In joining them, we were not insensible to the embarrassment of our position. With such allies, success was difficult, and victory itself, without a change of principles and policy on their part, dangerous; and, accordingly, while we united with them against the executive, we refused all participation in the presidential contest. But, with all its embarrassments, it was the only practicable course left us, short of abandoning our principles, or the country, by retiring altogether from the field of contest. In this embarrassing position, we waited the development of events, with the fixed determination, that let what might come, we would inflexibly pursue the course, which a regard to our principles; and the success of our cause demanded.

Such was the position we occupied, from 1833, when our contest with the general government terminated, to the commencement of the late extra session, when it became manifest a great change had been effected, which could not but have a powerful influence over our future course. It soon became apparent after the meeting of Congress, that the joint resistance of ourselves and our late allies in conjunction with the course of events in reference to the currency, had brought down the lofty pretensions of the executive department. The union between the government and the money power, which had so greatly strengthened those in authority at first had not only ceased, but they were forced to take ground against the reunion of the two, and to make war against those very banks, which had been the instruments of their power and aggrandizement. Forced to take this position, and divested in a great measure of patronage and influence from the exhausted state of the treasury, they were compelled to fall back, as the only means of saving themselves, on the principles of 1827, by which we had ejected from office the national republican party, and to which our portion of the old party of '27 have inflexibly adhered, but from which, the other, adhering to the administration, had so greatly departed in practice. As soon as I saw this state of things, I clearly perceived, that a very important question was presented for our determination, which we were compelled to decide forthwith; shall we continue our joint attack, with the nationals, on those in power, in the new position, which they have been compelled to occupy? It was clear, with our joint forces, we could utterly overthrow and demolish them, but it was not less clear, that the victory would inure, not to us, but exclusively to the benefit of our allies and their cause. They were the most numerous and powerful, and the point of assault on the position, which the party to be assaulted had taken in relation to the banks, would have greatly strengthened the settled principles and policy of the national party, and weakened, in the same degree, ours. They are, and ever have been, the decided advocates of a national bank, and are now in favor of one, with a capital so ample, as to be sufficient to control the state institutions, and to regulate the currency and exchanges of the country. To join them, with their avowed object in the attack, to overthrow those in power, on the ground they occupied against a bank, would, of course, not only have placed the government and country in their hands without opposition, but would have committed us, beyond the possibility of extrication, for a bank, and absorbed our party in the ranks of the national republicans. The first fruits of the victory, would have been an overshadowing national bank, with an immense capital, not less than from fifty to an hundred millions, which would have centralized the currency and exchanges, and with them, the commerce and capital of the country, in whatever section the head of the institution might be placed. The next would be the indissoluble union of the political and money power in the hands of our old political opponents, whose principles and policy are so opposite to ours, and so dangerous to our institutions as well as oppressive to us.

Such clearly would have been the inevitable result if we had joined in the assault on those in power, in the position they had been constrained to occupy; and he must indeed be blind—all past experience must be lost to him, who does not see, that so infatuated a course would have been fatal to us and ours. The connection between the government and the bank would, by necessary consequence in the hands of that party, have led to a renewal of that system of unequal and oppressive legislation, which have impoverished the staple states, and from which we have escaped with such peril and difficulty. The bank, when united with the government, is the natural ally of high duties and extravagant expenditure. The greater the revenue and the more profuse the disbursements, the greater its circulation and the more ample its deposits. This tendency on the part of that institution, and the known principles and views of policy of the party, would have co-operated, with irresistible force, to renew the system we have pulled down with so much labour, with an aggravation of its oppression far beyond any thing we have ever yet experienced, and thus the fruits of all our exertions and struggles against the system, would have been lost—forever lost.

By taking the opposite course, the reverse of all this will follow, if our states rights party be but firmly united and true to their principles. Never was there before, and never, probably, will there be again, so fair an opportunity to carry out fully our principles and policy, and to reap the fruits of our long and arduous struggle. By keeping the banks and the government separated, we effectually prevent the centralization of the currency and exchanges of the country at any one point, and, of course, the commerce and the capital, leaving each to enjoy that portion which its natural advantages, with its industry and enterprise may command. By refusing to join our late allies in their attack on those in power, where they have sheltered themselves, we prevent the complete ascendency of the party and their principles, which must have followed, and gain the only opportunity we could have of rallying anew the old states rights party of 1827, on the ground they then occupied, as an opposing power, to hold in check their old opponents, the national republican party. It would also give us the chance of effecting, what is still more important to us, the union of the entire South. The southern division of the administration party must reoccupy the old state rights ground. They have no alternative; and unless we, who have so long and under so many difficulties adhered to it, shall now desert our stand, the South must be united. If once united, we will rally round the old state rights party all in every section, who are opposed to consolidation, or the overaction of the central government; and the political parties will again be formed on the old and natural division of state rights and national, which divided them at the commencement of the government, and which experience has shown is that division of party most congenial to our system, and most favorable to its successful operation.

As obvious as all this must appear, I felt, that I assumed a heavy responsibility in taking the course I did. It was impossible, that all the circumstances and motives, under which I acted, could at once be generally understood, and, of course, the part I was compelled to take was liable to be misconceived and grossly misrepresented. We had been so long contending against the abuses and encroachments of the executive power, as to forget that they originated in the prior abuses and encroachments of Congress, and were accordingly exclusively intent on expelling from office, those who had acquired and exercised their authority in a manner so dangerous, without reflecting into whose hands the power would go, and what principles and policy would gain the ascendency. With this state of feelings on the part of our friends, I saw it was impossible to take a position, which, by consequence, was calculated to cover those in power, however urgent the cause, without occasioning a shock, in the first instance, and the imputation of unworthy motives, to meet which, however transient the misapprehension might be, required some resolution and firmness. But there were other, and far greater causes of responsibility, to which this was as nothing. Of all the interests in the community, the banking is by far the most influential and formidable—the most active; and the most concentrating and pervading; and of all the points, within the immense circle of this interest, there is none, in relation to which the banks are more sensitive and tenacious, than their union with the political power of the country. This is the source of a vast amount of their profits, and of a still larger portion of their respectability and influence. To touch their interest on this tender point is to combine all in one united and zealous opposition, with some exceptions in our portion of the community, where the union of the two powers acts injuriously to the banking, as well as the commercial and other great interests of the section. To encounter so formidable an opposition, supported by a powerful political party with whom I had been acting for some years against entire power, and who regarded the union of the government and the banks as essential to the union of the states themselves, was to assume a heavy responsibility, under the most favorable circumstances; but to back and sustain those in such opposition, in whose wisdom, firmness and patriotism, I have no reason to confide, and over whom I have no control, is to double that responsibility. This responsibility, I have voluntarily assumed. Desiring neither office, nor power, and having nothing to hope personally from the movement, no motive, but the disastrous political consequences, which I clearly saw must follow from any other course, to the country, and its institutions generally, and our section in particular, and a deep sense of duty, could have induced me to take the step I did. That it has met the approbation of so respectable a portion of my old constituents and friends, to whose early and steadfast support, under every trial and difficulty I am so much indebted, is a source of deep gratification which I shall long remember and acknowledge. With great respect, I am, &c.

J. C. CALHOUN.

To Messrs. J. Bauskett, A. Wigfall, J. P. Carroll, M. Laborde, J. Jones, F. H. Wardlaw, J. W. Wimbish, committee.

SPEECH ON THE VETO POWER

[February 28, 1842]

———————

Calhoun's address was a direct response to a resolution by Henry Clay calling for a constitutional amendment to restrict the veto power of the president by requiring only a simple majority to override a presidential veto, and by eliminating the "pocket veto." The immediate object of Clay's amendment was to restrict the executive power of John Tyler, a Southerner who assumed the presidency after the early demise of William Henry Harrison. Tyler had frustrated the Whigs with his veto of the national bank (on both August 16 and September 9, 1841) and his general opposition to the tariff. By all accounts, Calhoun's critical remarks were brilliant. The Congressional Globe was particularly effusive in its praise:

> Mr. Calhoun's speech on this occasion is justly esteemed one of the ablest, most luminous, and unanswerable ever delivered on the nature of government. We noticed, at its conclusion, that he was warmly congratulated by both friends and opponents, indiscriminately; all concurring in eulogy on the profound, statesmanlike, and comprehensive knowledge displayed in his remarks, not only on the origin of the Constitution, but the genius and true theory of our institutions.*

In this speech, Calhoun returns to the theme of majority tyranny and the abuse of legislative authority. Against the assumption advanced by Clay and

---

*The Congressional Globe, 27th Congress, Second Session, p. 266.

others that a numerical majority of the whole people of the several states collectively has a right to rule, Calhoun argues that the very intention, object, and design of the Constitution was to provide checks and balances against the dangers of legislative usurpation, especially the usurpation of an overbearing majority in the House of Representatives. In that context, the veto power of the president is part of an elaborate scheme of government designed to assure the maintenance of self-government through concurring majorities. This speech proves to be one of the most succinct, precise essays on the origin and extent of the government of the United States ever written.

THE Senator from Kentucky (Mr. Clay), in support of his amendment, maintained that the people of these States constitute a nation; that the nation has a will of its own; that the numerical majority of the whole was the appropriate organ of its voice; and that whatever derogated from it, to that extent departed from the genius of the Government, and set up the will of the minority against the majority. We have thus presented, at the very threshold of the discussion, a question of the deepest import—not only as it regards the subject under consideration, but the nature and character of our Government; and this question is, Are these propositions of the Senator true?

[Mr. Clay here interrupted Mr. Calhoun and said that he meant a majority according to the forms of the constitution.

Mr. Calhoun, in return, said he had taken down the words of the Senator at the time, and would vouch for the correctness of his statement. The Senator not only laid down the propositions as stated, but he drew conclusions from them against the President's veto, which could only be sustained on the principle of the numerical majority. In fact, his course at the extra session, and the grounds assumed both by him and his colleague in this discussion, had their origin in the doctrines embraced in that proposition.]

If they be, then he admitted the argument against the veto would be conclusive; not, however, for the reason assigned by him—that it would make the voice of a single functionary of the Government (the President) equivalent to that of some six Senators and forty members of the other House—but, for the far more decisive reason, according to his theory, that the President is not chosen by the voice of numerical majority, and does not, therefore, according to his principle, represent truly the will of the nation.

It is a great mistake to suppose that he is elected simply on the principle of numbers. They constitute, it is true, the principal element in his election; but not the exclusive. Each State is, indeed, entitled to as many votes in his election, as it is to representatives in the other House—that is, to its federal population; but to these, two others are added, having no regard to numbers for their representation in the Senate; which greatly increases the relative influence of the small States compared with the large, in the Presidential election. What effect this latter element may have on the numbers necessary to elect a President, may be made apparent by a very short and simple calculation.

The population of the United States, in federal numbers, by the late census, is 15,908,376. Assuming that 68,000, the number reported by the committee of the other House, will be fixed on for the ratio of representation there, it will give, according to the calculation of the committee, two hundred and twenty-four members to the other House. Add fifty-two—the number of the Senators—and the electoral college will be found to consist of two hundred and seventy-six, of which one hundred and thirty-nine is a majority. If nineteen of the smaller States, excluding Maryland, be taken—beginning with Delaware and ending with Kentucky inclusive—they will be found to be entitled one hundred and forty votes—one more than a majority—with a federal population of only 7,227,869; while the seven other States, with a population of 8,680,507, would be entitled to but one hundred and thirty-six votes—three less than a majority—with a population of almost a million and a half greater than the others. Of the one hundred and forty electoral votes of the smaller States, thirty-eight would be on account of the addition of two to each State for their representation in this body; while of the larger there would be but fourteen on this account—making a difference of twenty-four votes—being two more than the entire electoral vote of Ohio, the third State, in point of numbers, in the Union.

The Senator from Kentucky, with these facts, but acts in strict conformity with his theory of government, in proposing the limitation he has on the veto power; but as much cannot be said in favor of the substitute he has offered. The argument is as conclusive against the one, as the other, or any other modification of the veto that could possibly be devised. It goes further—and is conclusive against the Executive Department itself, as elected; for there can be no good reason offered why the will of the nation, if there be one, should not be as fully and perfectly represented in that department as in the Legislative.

But it does not stop there. It would be still more conclusive, if possible, against this branch of the Government. In constituting the Senate, numbers are totally disregarded. The smallest State stands on a perfect equality with the largest—Delaware with her seventy-seven thousand, and New York with her two millions and a half. Here a majority of States control, without regard to population; and fourteen of the smallest States, with a federal population of but 4,064,457—little less than a fourth of the whole—can, if they unite, overrule the twelve others with a population of 11,844,919. Nay, more; they could virtually destroy the Government, and put a veto on the whole system, by refusing to elect Senators; and yet this equality among States, without regard to numbers, including the branch where it prevails, would seem to be the favorite with the constitution. It cannot be altered without the consent of every State; and this branch of the Government where it prevails, is the only one that participates in the powers of all the others. As a part of the Legislative Department, it has full participation with the other in all matters of legislation, except originating money bills; while it participates with the Executive in two of its highest functions— those of appointing to office and making treaties; and in that of the Judiciary, in being the high court before which all impeachments are tried.

But we have not yet got to the end of the consequences. The argument would be as conclusive against the Judiciary as against the Senate, or the Executive and his veto. The judges receive their appointments from the Executive and the Senate; the one nominating, and the other consenting to and advising the appointment; neither of which departments, as has been shown, is chosen by the numerical majority. In addition, they hold their office during good behavior, and can only be turned out by impeachment; and yet they have the power, in all cases in law and equity brought before them, in which an act of Congress is involved, to decide on its constitutionality—that is, in effect, to pronounce an absolute veto.

If, then, the Senator's theory be correct, its clear and certain result, if carried out in practice, would be to sweep away, not only the veto, but the Executive, the Senate, and the Judiciary, as now constituted; and to leave nothing standing in the midst of the ruins but the House of Representatives, where only, in the whole range of the Government, numbers exclusively prevail. But, as desolating as would be its sweep, in passing over the Government, it would be far more destructive in its whirl over the constitution. There it would not leave a fragment standing amidst the ruin in its rear.

In approaching this topic, let me premise, what all will really admit, that if the voice of the people may be sought for any where with confidence, it may be in the constitution, which is conceded by all to be the fundamental and paramount law of the land. If, then, the people of these States do really constitute a nation, as the Senator supposes; if the nation has a will of its own, and if the numerical majority of the whole is the only appropriate and true organ of that will, we may fairly expect to find that will, pronounced through the absolute majority, pervading every part of that instrument, and stamping its authority on the whole. Is such the fact? The very reverse. Throughout the whole—from first to last—from the beginning to the end—in its formation, adoption, and amendment, there is not the slightest evidence, trace, or vestige of the existence of the facts on which the Senator's theory rests; neither of the nation, nor its will, nor of the numerical majority of the whole, as its organ, as I shall next proceed to show.

The convention which formed it was called by a portion of the States; its members were all appointed by the States; received their authority from their separate States; voted by States in forming the constitution; agreed to it, when formed, by States; transmitted it to Congress to be submitted to the States for their ratification; it was ratified by the people of each State in convention, each ratifying by itself, for itself, and bound exclusively by its own ratification; and by express provision it was not to go into operation, unless nine out of the twelve States should ratify, and then to be binding only between the States ratifying. It was thus put in the power of any four States, large or small, without regard to numbers, to defeat its adoption; which might have been done by a very small proportion of the whole, as will appear by reference to the first census. That census was taken very shortly after the adoption of the constitution—at which time the federal population of the then twelve States was 3,462,279, of which the four smallest, Delaware, Rhode Island, Georgia, and New Hampshire, with a population of only 241,490, something more than the fourteenth part of the whole, could have defeated the ratification. Such was the total disregard of population in the adoption and formation of the constitution.

It may, however, be said, it is true, that the constitution is the work of the States, and that there was no nation prior to its adoption; but that its adoption fused the people of the States into one, so as to make a nation of what before constituted separate and independent sovereignties. Such an assertion would be directly in the teeth of the constitution, which says that, when ratified, "it should be binding" (not over the States ratifying, for that would imply that it was imposed by some higher authority; nor between the individuals composing the States, for that would imply that they were all merged in one; but) "between the States ratifying the same;" and thus, by the strongest implication, recognizing them as the parties to the instrument, and as maintaining their separate and independent existence as States, after its adoption. But let that pass. I need it not to rebut the Senator's theory—to test the truth of the assertion, that the constitution has formed a nation of the people of these States. I go back to the grounds already taken—that if such be the fact—if they really form a nation, since the adoption of the constitution, and the nation has a will, and the numerical majority is its only proper organ—in such case, the mode prescribed for the amendment of the constitution would furnish abundant and conclusive evidence of the fact. But here again, as in its formation and adoption, there is not the slightest trace or evidence that such is the fact; on the contrary, most conclusive to sustain the very opposite opinion.

There are two modes in which amendments to the constitution may be proposed. The one, such as that now proposed, by a resolution to be passed by two-thirds of both Houses; and the other, by a call of a convention, by Congress, to propose amendments, on the application of two-thirds of the States; neither of which gives the least countenance to the theory of the Senator. In both cases the mode of ratification, which is the material point, is the same—and requires the concurring assent of three-fourths of the States, regardless of population, to ratify an amendment. Let us now pause for a moment to trace the effects of this provision.

There are now twenty-six States, and the concurring assent, of course, of twenty States, is sufficient to ratify an amendment. It then results that twenty of the smaller States, of which Kentucky would be the largest, are sufficient for this purpose, with a population in federal numbers, of only 7,652,097—less by several hundred thousand than the numerical majority of the whole—against the united voice of the other six, with a population of 8,216,279—exceeding the former by more than half a million. And yet this minority, under the amending power, may change, alter, modify, or destroy every part of the constitution, except that which provides for an equality of representation of the States in the Senate: while, as if in mockery and derision of the Senator's theory, nineteen of the larger States, with a population, in federal numbers, of 14,526,073, cannot, even if united to a man, alter a letter in the constitution, against the seven others, with a population of only 1,382,303; and this, too, under the existing constitution, which is supposed to form the people of these States into a nation. Finally, Delaware, with a population of little more than 77,000, can put her veto on all the other States, on a proposition to destroy the equality of the States in the Senate. Can facts more clearly illustrate the total disregard of the numerical majority, as well in the process of amending, as in that of forming and adopting the constitution?

All this must appear anomalous, strange, and unaccountable, on the theory of the Senator; but harmonious and easily explained on the opposite; that ours is a union, not of individuals, united by what is called a social compact—for that would make it a nation; nor of governments—for that would have formed a mere confederacy, like the one superceded by the present constitution; but a union of States, founded on a written, positive compact, forming a Federal Republic, with the same equality of rights among the States composing the Union, as among the citizens composing the States themselves. Instead of a nation, we are in reality an assemblage of nations, or peoples (if the plural noun may be used where the language affords none), united in their sovereign character immediately and directly by their own act, but without losing their separate and independent existence.

It results from all that has been stated, that either the theory of the Senator is wrong, or that our political system is throughout a profound and radical error. If the latter be the case, then that complex system of ours, consisting of so many parts, but blended, as was supposed, into one harmonious and sublime whole, raising its front on high and challenging the admiration of the world, is but a misshapen and disproportionate structure, that ought to be demolished to the ground, with the single exception of the apartment allotted to the House of Representatives. Is the Senator prepared to commence the work of demolition? Does he believe that all other parts of this complex structure are irregular and deformed appendages; and that if they were taken down, and the Government erected exclusively on the will of the numerical majority, it would effect as well, or better, the great objects for which it was instituted· "to establish justice; ensure domestic tranquillity; provide for the common defence; promote the general welfare; and secure the blessings of liberty to ourselves and our posterity?" Will the Senator—will any one—can any one—venture to assert that? And if not, why not? This is the question, on the proper solution of which hangs not only the explanation of the veto, but that of the real nature and character of our complex, but beautiful and harmonious system of government. To give a full and systematic solution, it would be necessary to descend to the elements of political science, and discuss principles little suited to a discussion in a deliberative assembly. I waive the attempt, and shall content myself with giving a much more matter-of-fact solution.

It is sufficient, for that purpose, to point to the actual operation of the Government, through all the stages of its existence, and the many and important measures which have agitated it from the beginning; the success of which one portion of the people regarded as essential to their prosperity and happiness, while other portions have viewed them as destructive of both. What does this imply, but a deep conflict of interests, real or supposed, between the different portions of the community, on subjects of the first magnitude—the currency, the finances, including taxation and disbursements; the bank, the protective tariff, distribution, and many others; on all of which the most opposite and conflicting views have prevailed? And what would be the effect of placing the powers of the Government under the exclusive control of the numerical majority—of 8,000,000 over 7,900,000, of six States over all the rest—but to give the dominant interest, or combination of interests, an unlimited and despotic control over all others? What, but to vest it with the power to administer the Government for its exclusive benefit, regardless of all others, and indifferent to their oppression and wretchedness? And what, in a country of such vast extent and diversity of condition, institutions, industry, and productions, would that be, but to subject the rest to the most grinding despotism and oppression? But what is the remedy? It would be but to increase the evil, to transfer the power to a minority—to abolish the House of Representatives, and place the control exclusively in the hands of the Senate—in that of the four millions, instead of the eight. If one must be sacrificed to the other, it is better that the few should be to the many, than the many to the few.

What then is to be done, if neither the majority nor the minority, the greater nor less part, can be safely trusted with exclusive control? What but to vest the powers of the Government in the whole—the entire people—to make it, in truth and reality, the government of the people, instead of the government of a dominant over a subject part, be it the greater or less—of the whole people—self-government; and, if this should prove impossible in practice, then to make the nearest approach to it, by requiring the concurrence in the action of the Government, of the greatest possible number consistent with the great ends for which Government was instituted—justice and security, within and without. But how is this to be effected? Not, certainly, by considering the whole community as one, and taking its sense as a whole by a single process, which, instead of giving the voice of all, can but give that of a part. There is but one way by which it can possibly be accomplished; and that is by a judicious and wise division and organization of the Government and community, with reference to its different and conflicting interests, and by taking the sense of each part separately, and the concurrence of all as the voice of the whole. Each may be imperfect of itself; but if the construction be good, and all the keys skilfully touched, there will be given out, in one blended and harmonious whole, the true and perfect voice of the people.

But on what principle is such a division and organization to be made to effect this great object, without which it is impossible to preserve free and popular institutions? To this no general answer can be given. It is the work of the wise and experienced—having full and perfect knowledge of the country and the people, in every particular—for whom the Government is intended. It must be made to fit; and when it does, it will fit no other, and will be incapable of being imitated or borrowed. Without, then, attempting to do what cannot be done, I propose to point out how that which I have stated has been accomplished in our system of government, and the agency the veto is intended to have in effecting it.

I begin with the House of Representatives. There each State has a representation according to its federal numbers, and, when met, a majority of the whole number of members controls its proceedings; thus giving to the numerical majority the exclusive control throughout. The effect is to place its proceedings in the power of eight millions of people over all the rest, and six of the largest States, if united, over the other twenty; and the consequence, if the House were the exclusive organ of the voice of the people, would be the domination of the stronger over the weaker interests of the community, and the establishment of an intolerable and oppressive despotism, To find the remedy against what would be so great an evil, we must turn to this body. Here an entirely different process is adopted to take the sense of the community. Population is entirely disregarded, and States, without reference to the number of the people, are made the basis of representation; the effect of which is to place the control here in a majority of the States, which, had they the exclusive power, would exercise it as despotically and oppressively as would the House of Representatives.

Regarded, then, separately, neither truly represents the sense of the community, and each is imperfect of itself; but when united, and the concurring voice of each is made necessary to enact laws, the one corrects the defects of the other; and, instead of the less popular derogating from the more popular, as is supposed by the Senator, the two together give a more full and perfect utterance to the voice of the people than either could separately. Taken separately, six States might control the House; and a little upwards of four millions might control the Senate, by a combination of the fourteen smaller States; but by requiring the concurrent votes of the two, the six largest States must add eight others to have the control in both bodies. Suppose, for illustration, they should unite with the eight smallest (which would give the least number by which an act could pass both Houses), it will be found, by adding the population in federal numbers of the six largest to the eight smallest States, that the least number by which an act can pass both Houses, if the members should be true to those they represent, would be 9,788,570 against a minority of 6,119,797, instead of 8,000,000 against 7,900,000, if the assent of the most popular branch alone were required.

This more full and perfect expression of the voice of the people by the concurrence of the two, compared to either separately, is a great advance towards a full and perfect expression of their voice; but, great as it is, it falls far short, and the framers of the constitution were accordingly not satisfied with it. To render it still more perfect, their next step was to require the assent of the President, before an act of Congress could become a law; and, if he disapproved, to require two-thirds of both Houses to overrule his veto. We are thus brought to the point immediately under discussion, and which, on that account, claims a full and careful examination.

One of the leading motives for vesting the President with this high power, was, undoubtedly, to give him the means of protecting the portion of the powers allotted to him by the constitution, against the encroachment of Congress. To make a division of power effectual, a veto in one form or another is indispensable. The right of each to judge for itself of the extent of the power allotted to its share, and to protect itself in its exercise, is what in reality is meant by a division of power. Without it, the allotment to each department would be a mere partition, and no division at all. Acting under this impression, the framers of the constitution have carefully provided that his approval should be necessary, not only to the acts of Congress, but to every resolution, vote, or order, requiring the consent of the two Houses, so as to render it impossible to elude it by any conceivable device. This of itself, was an adequate motive for the provision, and, were there no other, ought to be a sufficient reason for the rejection of this resolution. Without it, the division of power between the Legislative and Executive Departments would have been merely nominal.

But it is not the only motive. There is another and deeper, to which the division itself of the Government into departments is subordinate—to enlarge the popular basis, by increasing the number of voices necessary to its action. As numerous as are the voices required to obtain the assent of the people through the Senate and the House to an act, it was not thought by the framers of the constitution sufficient for the action of the Government in all cases. 9,800,000—large as is the number—were regarded as still too few, and 6,100,000 too many, to remove all motives for oppression; the latter being not too few to be plundered, and the former not too large to divide the spoils of plunder among. Till the increase of numbers on one side, and the decrease on the other, reaches that point, there is no security for the weaker against the stronger, especially in so extensive a country as ours. Acting in the spirit of these remarks, the authors of the constitution, although they deemed the concurrence of the Senate and the House as sufficient, with the approval of the President, to the enactment of laws in ordinary cases; yet, when he dissented, they deemed it a sufficient presumption against the measure to require a still greater enlargement of the popular basis for its enactment. With this view, the assent of two-thirds of both Houses was required to overrule his veto; that is, eighteen States in the Senate, and a constituency of 10,600,000 in the other House.

But it may be said that nothing is gained towards enlarging the popular basis of the Government by the veto power; because the number necessary to elect a majority to the two Houses, without which the act could not pass, would be sufficient to elect him. This is true. But he may have been elected by a different portion of the people; or, if not, great changes may take place during his four years, both in the Senate and the House, which may change the majority that brought him into power, and with it the measures and policy to be pursued. In either case, he might find it necessary to interpose his veto to maintain his views of the constitution, or the policy of the party of which he is the head, and which elevated him to power.

But a still stronger consideration for vesting him with the power may be found in the difference in the manner of his election, compared with that of the members of either House. The Senators are elected by the vote of the Legislatures of the respective States; and the members of the House by the people, who, in almost all the States, elect by districts. In neither is there the least responsibility of the members of any one State, to the Legislature or people of any other State. They are, as far as their responsibility may be concerned, solely and exclusively under the influence of the States and people who respectively elect them. Not so the President. The votes of the whole are counted in his election, which makes him more or less responsible to every part—to those who voted against him, as well as those to whom he owes his election; which he must feel sensibly. If he should be an aspirant for a re-election, he will desire to gain the favorable opinion of States that opposed him, as well as to retain that of those which voted for him. Even if he should not be a candidate for re-election, the desire of having a favorite elected, or maintaining the ascendency of his party, may have, to a considerable extent, the same influence over him. The effect in either case, would be to make him look more to *the interest of the whole*— to soften sectional feelings and asperity—to be more of a patriot than the partisan of any particular interest; and, through the influence of these causes, to give a more general character to the politics of the country, and thereby render the collision between sectional interests less fierce than it would be if legislation depended solely on the members of the two Houses, who owe no responsibility but to those who elected them. The same influence acts even on the aspirants for the Presidency, and is followed to a very considerable extent by the same softening and generalizing effects. In the case of the President, it may lead to the interposing of his veto against oppressive and dangerous sectional measures, even when supported by those to whom he owes his election. But, be the cause of interposing his veto what it may, its effect in all cases is to require a greater body of constituency, through the legislative organs, to put the Government in action against it—to require another key to be struck, and to bring out a more full and perfect response from the voice of the people.

There is still another impediment, if not to the enactment of laws, to their execution, to be found in the Judiciary Department. I refer to the right of the courts, in all cases coming before them in law or equity, where an act of Congress comes in question, to decide on its unconstitutionality; which, if decided against the law in the Supreme Court, is, in effect, a permanent veto. But here a difference must be made between a decision against the constitutionality of a law of Congress and of a State. The former acts as a restriction on the powers of this Government, but the latter as an enlargement.

Such are the various processes of taking the sense of the people through the divisions and organization of the different departments of the Government; all of which, acting through their appropriate organs, are intended to widen its basis and render it more popular, instead of less, by increasing the number necessary to put it in action—and having for their object to prevent one portion of the community from aggrandizing or enriching itself at the expense of the other, and to restrict the whole to the sphere intended by the framers of the constitution. Has it effected these objects? Has it prevented oppression and usurpation on the part of the Government? Has it accomplished the objects for which the Government was ordained, as enumerated in the preamble to the constitution? Much, very much, certainly has been done, but not all. Many instances might be enumerated, in the history of the Government, of the violation of the constitution—of the assumption of powers not delegated to it—of the perversion of those delegated to uses never intended—and of their being wielded by the dominant interest, for the time, for its aggrandizement, at the expense of the rest of the community—instances that may be found in every period of its existence, from the earliest to the latest, beginning with the bank and bank connection at its outset, and ending with the Distribution Act at the late extraordinary session. How is this to be accounted for? What is the cause?

The explanation and cause will be found in the fact, that, as fully as the sense of the people is taken in the action of the Government, it is not taken fully enough. For, after all that has been accomplished in that respect, there are but two organs through which the voice of the community acts directly on the Government; and which, taken separately, or in combination, constitute the elements of which it is composed: the one is the majority of the States, regarded in their corporate character as bodies politic, which, in its simple form, constitutes the Senate; and the other is the

majority of the people of the States, of which, in its simple form, the House
of Representatives is composed. These combined, in the proportions already stated, constitute the Executive Department; and that department
and the Senate appoint the judges, who constitute the Judiciary. But it is
only in their simple form in the Senate and the other House that they have
a steady and habitual control over the legislative acts of the Government.
The veto of the Executive is rarely interposed—not more than about
twenty times during the period of more than fifty years that the Government has existed. Their effects have been beneficially felt—but only casu-
ally, at long intervals, and without steady and habitual influence over the
action of the Government. The same remarks are substantially applicable
to what, for the sake of brevity, may be called the veto of the Judiciary—
the right of negativing a law for the want of constitutionality, when it comes
in question, in a case before the courts.

The Government, then, of the Union, being under no other habitual and
steady control but of these two majorities, acting through this and the other
House, is, in fact, placed substantially under the control of the portion of
the community, which the united majorities of the two Houses represent
for the time, and which may consist of but fourteen States, with a federal
population of less than ten millions, against a little more than six, as has
been already explained. But, as large as is the former, and small as is the
latter, the one is not large enough, in proportion, to prevent it from plun-
dering, under the forms of law, nor the other small enough from being
plundered; and hence the many instances of violation of the constitution, of
usurpation, of powers perverted, and wielded for selfish purposes, which the
history of the Government affords. They furnish proof conclusive that the
principle of plunder, so deeply implanted in all governments, has not been
eradicated in ours, by all the precautions taken by its framers against it.

But, in estimating the number of the constituency necessary to control
the majority in the two Houses of Congress at something less than ten
millions, I have estimated it altogether too high, regarding the practical
operation of the Government. To form a correct conception of its practical

operation in this respect, another element, which has, in practice, an important influence, must be taken into the estimate, and which I shall next proceed to explain.

Of the two majorities, which, acting either separately or in combination, control the Government, the numerical majority is by far the most influential. It has the exclusive control in the House of Representatives, and preponderates more than five to one in the choice of the President—assuming that the ratio of representation will be fixed at sixty-eight thousand under the late census. It also greatly preponderates in the appointment of judges—the right of nominating having much greater influence in making appointments than that of advising and consenting. From these facts, it must be apparent that the leaning of the President will be to that element of power to which he mainly owes his elevation—and on which he must principally rely to secure his re-election, or maintain the ascendency of the party and its policy, of which he usually is the head. This leaning of his must have a powerful effect on the inclination and tendency of the whole Government. In his hands are placed, substantially, all the honors and emoluments of the Government; and these, when greatly increased, as they are and ever must be when the powers of the Government are greatly stretched and increased, must give the President a corresponding influence over, not only the members of both Houses, but also public opinion—and, through that, a still more powerful indirect influence over them; and thus they may be brought to sustain or oppose, through his influence, measures which otherwise they would not have opposed or sustained—and the whole Government be made to lean in the same direction with the Executive.

From these causes, the Government, in all its departments, gravitates steadily towards the numerical majority—and has been moving slowly towards it from the beginning; sometimes, indeed, retarded, or even stopped or thrown back—but, taking any considerable period of time, always advancing towards it. That it begins to make near approach to that fatal point, ample proof may be found in the oft-repeated declaration of the mover of this resolution, and of many of his supporters at the extraordinary session—that the late Presidential election decided all the great measures which he so ardently pressed through the Senate. Yes, even here—in this Chamber—in the Senate—which is composed of the opposing element— and on which the only effectual resistance to this fatal tendency exists that is to be found in the Government—we are told that the popular will, as expressed in the Presidential election, is to decide, not only the election, but every measure which may be agitated in the canvass in order to influence the result. When what was thus boldly insisted on comes to be an established principle of action, the end will be near.

As the Government approaches nearer and nearer to the one absolute and single power—the will of the greater number—its action will become more and more disturbed and irregular; faction, corruption, and anarchy, will more and more abound; patriotism will daily decay, and affection and reverence for the Government grow weaker and weaker—until the final shock occurs, when the system will rush into ruin; and the sword take the place of law and constitution.

Let me not be misunderstood. I object not to that structure of the Government which makes the numerical majority the predominant element: it is, perhaps, necessary that it should be so in all popular constitutional governments like ours, which excludes classes. It is necessarily the exponent of the strongest interest, or combination of interests, in the community; and it would seem to be necessary to give it the preponderance, in order to infuse into the Government the necessary energy to accomplish the ends for which it was instituted. The great question is—How is due preponderance to be given to it, without subjecting the whole, in time, to its unlimited sway? which brings up the inquiry, Is there anywhere, in our complex system of governments, a guard, check, or contrivance, sufficiently strong to arrest so fearful a tendency of the Government? Or, to express it in more direct and intelligible language—Is there anywhere in the system a more full and perfect expression of the voice of the people of the States; calculated to counteract this tendency to the concentration of all the powers of the Government in the will of the numerical majority, resulting from the partial and imperfect expression of their voice through its organs?

Yes, fortunately, doubly fortunately, there is; not only a more full and perfect, but a full and perfect expression to be found in the constitution, acknowledged by all to be the fundamental and supreme law of the land. It is full and perfect, because it is the expression of the voice of each State, adopted by the separate assent of each, by itself, and for itself; and is the voice of all by being that of each component part, united and blended into one harmonious whole. But it is not only full and perfect, but as just as it is full and perfect; for, combining the sense of each, and therefore all, there is nothing left on which injustice, or oppression, or usurpation can operate. And, finally, it is as supreme as it is just; because, comprehending the will of all, by uniting that of each of the parts, there is nothing within or above to control it. It is, indeed the *vox populi vox Dei;* the creating voice that called the system into existence—and of which the Government itself is but a creature, clothed with delegated powers to execute its high behests.

We are thus brought to a question of the deepest import, and on which the fate of the system depends. How can this full, perfect, just, and supreme voice of the people, embodied in the constitution, be brought to bear, habitually and steadily, in counteracting the fatal tendency of the Government to the absolute and despotic control of the numerical majority? Or—if I may be permitted to use so bold an expression—how is this, the Deity of our political system, to be successfully invoked, to interpose its all-powerful creating voice to save from perdition the creature of its will and the work of its hand? If it cannot be done, ours, like all free governments preceding it, must go the way of all flesh; but if it can be, its duration may be from generation to generation, to the latest posterity. To this all-important question I will not attempt a reply at this time. It would lead me far beyond the limits properly belonging to this discussion. I descend from the digression nearer to the subject immediately at issue, in order to reply to an objection to the veto power, taken by the Senator from Virginia on this side the chamber (Mr. Archer).

He rests his support of this resolution on the ground that the object intended to be effected by the veto has failed; that the framers of the constitution regarded the Legislative Department of the Government as the one most to be dreaded; and that their motive for vesting the Executive with the veto, was to check its encroachments on the other departments; but that the Executive, and not the Legislature had proved to be the most dangerous, and that the veto had become either useless or mischievous, by being converted into a sword to attack, instead of a shield to defend, as was originally intended.

I make no issue with the Senator, as to the correctness of his statement. I assume the facts to be as he supposes; not because I agree with him, but simply with the view of making my reply more brief.

Assuming, then, that the Executive Department has proved to be the more formidable, and that it requires to be checked, rather than to have the power of checking others—the first inquiry, on that assumption, should be into the cause of its increase of power, in order to ascertain the seat and the nature of the danger; and the next, whether the measure proposed— that of divesting it of the veto, or modifying it as proposed—would guard against the danger apprehended.

I begin with the first; and in entering on it, assert, with confidence, that if the Executive has become formidable to the liberty or safety of the country, or other departments of the Government, the cause is not in the constitution, but in the acts and omissions of Congress itself.

According to my conception, the powers vested in the President by the constitution are few and effectually guarded, and are not of themselves at all formidable. In order to have a just conception of the extent of his powers, it must be borne in mind that there are but two classes of powers known to the constitution; namely—powers that are expressly granted, and those that are necessary to carry the granted powers into execution. Now, by a positive provision of the constitution, all powers necessary to the execution of the granted powers are expressly delegated to Congress, be they powers granted to the Legislative, Executive, or Judicial Department;

and can only be exercised by the authority of Congress, and in the manner prescribed by law. This provision will be found in what is called the residuary clause, which declares that Congress shall have the power "to make all laws which shall be necessary and proper to carry into execution the foregoing powers" (those granted to Congress), "and all other powers vested by this constitution in the Government of the United States, or in any department or officer thereof." A more comprehensive provision cannot be imagined. It carries with it all powers necessary and proper to the execution of the granted powers, be they lodged where they may, and vests the whole, in terms not less explicit, in Congress. And here let me add, in passing, that the provision is as wise as it is comprehensive. It deposits the right of deciding what powers are necessary for the execution of the granted powers, where, and where only, it can be lodged with safety—in the hands of the law-making power; and forbids any department or officer of the Government from exercising any power not expressly authorized by the constitution or the laws—thus making ours emphatically a Government of *law and constitution.*

Having now shown that the President is restricted by the constitution to powers expressly granted to him, and that if any of his granted powers be such that they require other powers to execute them, he cannot exercise them without the authority of Congress, I shall now show that there is not one power vested in him that is in any way dangerous, unless made so by the acts or permission of Congress. I shall take them in the order in which they stand in the constitution.

He is, in the first place, made commander-in-chief of the army and navy of the United States, and the militia, when called into actual service. Large and expensive military and naval establishments, and numerous corps of militia, called into service, would no doubt increase very dangerously the power and patronage of the President; but neither can take place but by the action of Congress. Not a soldier can be enlisted, a ship of war built, nor a militiaman called into service, without its authority; and, very fortunately, our situation is such, that there is no necessity, and, probably, will be none, why his power and patronage should be dangerously increased by either of those means.

He is next vested with the power to make treaties, and to appoint officers, with the advice and consent of the Senate. And here again his power can only be made dangerous by the action of one or both Houses of Congress. In the formation of treaties, two-thirds of the Senate must concur; and it is difficult to conceive of a treaty that could materially enlarge his powers, which would not require an act of Congress to carry it into effect. The appointing power may, indeed, dangerously increase his patronage, if officers be uselessly multiplied and too highly paid; but if such should be the case, the fault would be in Congress, by whose authority, exclusively, they can be created or their compensation regulated.

But much is said, in this connection, of the power of removal, justly accompanied by severe condemnation of the many and abusive instances of the use of the power, and the dangerous influence it gives the President; in all of which I fully concur. It is, indeed, a corrupting and dangerous power, when officers are greatly multiplied, and highly paid—and when it is perverted from its legitimate object to the advancement of personal or party purposes. But I find no such power in the list of powers granted to the Executive, which is proof conclusive that it belongs to the class necessary and proper to execute some other power, if it exists at all, which none can doubt; and, for reasons already assigned, cannot be exercised without authority of law. If, then, it has been abused, it must be because Congress has not done its duty in permitting it to be exercised by the President without the sanction of law, and guarding against the abuses to which it is so liable.

The residue of the list are rather duties than rights—that of recommending to Congress such measures as he may deem expedient; of convening both Houses on extraordinary occasions; of adjourning them when they cannot agree on the time; of receiving ambassadors and other ministers; of taking care that the laws be faithfully executed, and commissioning the officers of the United States. Of all these, there is but one which claims particular notice, in connection with the point immediately under consideration; and that is, his power as the administrator of the laws. But whatever power he may have in that capacity depends on the action of Congress. If Congress should limit its legislation to the few great subjects confided to it; so frame its laws as to leave as little as possible to discretion, and take care to see that they are duly and faithfully executed, the administrative powers of the President would be proportionally limited, and divested of all danger. But if, on the contrary, it should extend its legislation in every direction; draw within its action subjects never contemplated by the constitution; multiply its acts, create numerous offices, and increase the revenue and expenditures proportionally—and, at the same time, frame its laws vaguely and loosely, and withdraw, in a great measure, its supervising care over their execution, his power would indeed become truly formidable and alarming. Now I appeal to the Senator and his friend, the author of this resolution, whether the growth of Executive power has not been the result of such a course on the part of Congress. I ask them whether this power has not, in fact, increased, or decreased, just in proportion to the increase or decrease of that system of legislation, such as has been described? What was the period of its maximum increase, but the very period which they have so frequently and loudly denounced as the one most distinguished for the prevalence of Executive power and usurpation? Much of that power certainly depended on the remarkable man then at the head of the department; but much—far more—on the system of legislation which the author of this resolution had built up with so much zeal and labor—and which carried the powers of the Government to a point far beyond that to which it had ever before attained—drawing many and important ones into its vortex, of which the framers of the constitution never dreamed. And here let me say to both of the Senators—and the party of which they are prominent members—that they labor in vain to bring down Executive power, while they support the system they so zealously advocate. The power they complain of is but its necessary fruit. Be assured, that as certain as Congress transcends its assigned limits, and usurps powers never conferred, or stretches those conferred beyond the proper limits; so surely will the fruits of its usurpation pass into the hands of the Executive. In seeking to become master, it but makes a master in the person of the President. It is only by confining itself to its allotted sphere, and a discreet use of its acknowledged powers, that it can retain that ascendency in the Government which the constitution intended to confer on it.

Having now pointed out the cause of the great increase of the Executive power on which the Senator rested his objection to the veto power; and having satisfactorily shown, as I trust I have, that, if it has proved dangerous in fact, the fault is not in the constitution, but in Congress—I would next ask him, in what possible way could the divesting the President of his veto, or modifying it as he proposes, limit his power? Is it not clear that, so far from the veto being the cause of the increase of his power, it would have acted as a limitation on it, if it had been more freely and frequently used? If the President had vetoed the original bank, the connection with the banking system, the tariffs of 1824 and 1828, and the numerous acts appropriating money for roads, canals, harbors, and a long list of other measures not less unconstitutional—would his power have been half as great as it now is? He has grown great and powerful, not because *he used* his veto, but because *he abstained* from using it. In fact, it is difficult to imagine a case in which its application can tend to enlarge his power, except it be the case of an act intended to repeal a law calculated to increase his power—or to restore the authority of one which, by a arbitrary construction of his power, he has set aside.

Now let me add, in conclusion, that this is a question, in its bearings, of vital importance to that wonderful and sublime system of governments which our patriotic ancestors established, not so much by their wisdom— wise and experienced as they were—as by the guidance of a kind Providence, who, in his divine dispensation, so disposed events as to lead to the establishment of a system of government wiser than those who framed it. The veto, of itself, as important as it is, sinks into nothing compared to the principle involved. It is but one, and that by no means the most consider-

able, of those many wise devices which I have attempted to explain, and
which were intended to strengthen the popular basis of our Government,
and resist its tendency to fall under the control of the dominant interest,
acting through the mere numerical majority. The introduction of this resolution may be regarded as one of the many symptoms of that fatal tendency—and of which we had such fearful indications in the bold attempt at
the late extraordinary session, of forcing through a whole system of measures of the most threatening and alarming character, in the space of a few
weeks, on the ground that they were all decided in the election of the late
President; thus attempting to substitute the will of a majority of the people,
in the choice of a Chief Magistrate, as the legislative authority of the Union,
in lieu of the beautiful and profound system established by the constitution.

SPEECH ON THE INTRODUCTION OF HIS RESOLUTIONS ON THE SLAVE QUESTION

[February 19, 1847]

———————

By the mid-1840s, tension over the issue of slavery had begun to consume the energies of the nation. Finding itself in the middle of a war with Mexico, the country could not long forestall the question of slavery in the new territories. The admission of Iowa threatened to tip the balance of power in the U.S. Senate between free and slave states. If that balance were lost, said Calhoun, the whole government would be turned over to the hands of the numerical majority—"a day that will not be far removed from political revolution, anarchy, civil war, and wide-spread disaster."

This speech contains more than a mere discussion of the pragmatic difficulties of maintaining the delicate balance between the free and slave states. In anticipation of several of the critical elements of A Disquisition on Government, *Calhoun offers a preliminary analysis of the tension between liberty of the community and individual liberty. He also advances his reasons for objecting to compromise founded upon the momentary whims of this or that majority in the Congress. Such compromise could no longer preserve the Union or offer any real security against an overbearing majority. What Calhoun saw as a pernicious form of compromise was quite different from his view of compromise within the framework of constitutional government argued for in the* Disquisition *and which forms the basis of his doctrine of the concurrent majority.*

In increasingly ominous language, Calhoun warns that if recourse to fundamental, constitutional principles cannot resolve the crisis between the two great sections, then the parties to the compact may well have to consider extra-constitutional means to preserve and protect themselves.

MR. CALHOUN rose and said: Mr. President, I rise to offer a set of resolutions in reference to the various resolutions from the State legislatures upon the subject of what they call the extension of slavery, and the proviso attached to the House bill, called the Three Million Bill. What I propose before I send my resolutions to the table, is to make a few explanatory remarks.

Mr. President, it was solemnly asserted on this floor, some time ago, that all parties in the non-slaveholding States had come to a fixed and solemn determination upon two propositions. One was—that there should be no further admission of any States into this Union which permitted, by their constitutions, the existence of slavery; and the other was—that slavery shall not hereafter exist in any of the territories of the United States; the effect of which would be to give to the non-slaveholding States the monopoly of the public domain, to the entire exclusion of the slaveholding States. Since that declaration was made, Mr. President, we have had abundant proof that there was a satisfactory foundation for it. We have received already solemn resolutions passed by seven of the non-slaveholding States—one-half of the number already in the Union, Iowa not being counted—using the strongest possible language to that effect; and no doubt, in a short space of time, similar resolutions will be received from all of the non-slaveholding States. But we need not go beyond the walls of Congress. The subject has been agitated in the other House, and they have sent up a bill "prohibiting the extension of slavery" (using their own language) "to any territory which may be acquired by the United States hereafter." At the same time, two resolutions which have been moved to extend the compromise line from the Rocky Mountains to the Pacific, during the present session, have been rejected by a decided majority.

Sir, there is no mistaking the signs of the times; and it is high time that the Southern States, the slaveholding States, should inquire what is now their relative strength in this Union, and what it will be if this determination should be carried into effect hereafter. Sir, already we are in a minority—I use the word "we" for brevity's sake—already we are in a minority in the other House, in the electoral college, and I may say, in every department of this Government, except at present in the Senate of the United States— there for the present we have an equality. Of the twenty-eight States, fourteen are non-slaveholding and fourteen are slaveholding, counting Delaware, which is doubtful, as one of the non-slaveholding States. But this equality of strength exists only in the Senate. One of the clerks, at my request, has furnished me with a statement of what is the relative strength of the two descriptions of States, in the other House of Congress and in the electoral college. There are two hundred and twenty-eight representatives, including Iowa, which is already represented there. Of these, one hundred and thirty-eight are from non-slaveholding States, and ninety are from what are called the slave States—giving a majority, in the aggregate, to the former of forty-eight. In the electoral college there are one hundred and sixty-eight votes belonging to the non-slaveholding States, and one hundred and eighteen to the slaveholding, giving a majority of fifty to the non-slaveholding.

We, Mr. President, have at present only one position in the Government, by which we may make any resistance to this aggressive policy which has been declared against the South, or any other that the non-slaveholding States may choose to adopt. And this equality in this body is one of the most transient character. Already Iowa is a State; but owing to some domestic difficulties, is not yet represented in this body. When she appears here, there will be a addition of two Senators to the representatives here of the non-slaveholding State. Already Wisconsin has passed the initiatory stage, and will be here the next session. This will add two more, making a clear majority of four in this body on the side of the non-slaveholding States, who will thus be enabled to sway every branch of this Government at their will and pleasure. But, Sir, if this aggressive policy be followed—if the determination of the non-slaveholding States is to be adhered to hereafter, and we are to be entirely excluded from the territories which we already possess, or may possess—if this is to be the fixed policy of the Government, I ask, what will be our situation hereafter?

Sir, there is ample space for twelve or fifteen of the largest description of States in the territories belonging to the United States. Already a law is in course of passage through the other House creating one north of Wisconsin. There is ample room for another north of Iowa; and another north of that; and then that large region extending on this side of the Rocky Mountains, from 49 degrees down to the Texan line, which may be set down fairly as an area of twelve and a half degrees of latitude. That extended region of itself is susceptible of having six, seven, or eight large States. To this, add Oregon which extends from 49 to 42 degrees, which will give four more; and I make a very moderate calculation when I say that, in addition to Iowa and Wisconsin, twelve more States upon the territory already ours—without reference to any acquisitions from Mexico—may be, and will be, shortly added to these United States. How will we then stand? There will be but fourteen on the part of the South—we are to be fixed, limited, and forever—and twenty-eight on the part of the non-slaveholding States! Twenty-eight! Double our number! And with the same disproportion in the House and in the electoral college! The Government, Sir, will be entirely in the hands of the non-slaveholding States—overwhelmingly.

Sir, if this state of things is to go on; if this determination, so solemnly made, is to be persisted in—where shall we stand, as far as this Federal Government of ours is concerned? We shall be at the entire mercy of the non-slaveholding States. Can we look to their justice and regard for our interests? Now, I ask, can we rely on that? Ought we to trust our safety and prosperity to their mercy and sense of justice? These are the solemn questions which I put to all—this and the other side of the Chamber.

Sir, can we find any hope by looking to the past? If we are to look to that—I will not go into the details—we will see from the beginning of this Government to the present day, as far a pecuniary resources are concerned—as far as the disbursement of revenue is involved, it will be found that we have been a portion of the community which has substantially supported this Government without receiving any thing like a proportionate return. But why should I go beyond this very measure itself? Why go beyond this determination on the part of the non-slaveholding States—that there shall be no further addition to the slaveholding States—to prove what our condition will be?

Sir, what is the entire amount of this policy? I will not say that it is so designed. I will not say from what cause it originated. I will not say whether blind fanaticism on one side—whether a hostile feeling to slavery entertained by many not fanatical on the other, has produced it; or whether it has been the work of men, who, looking to political power, have considered the agitation of this question as the most effectual mode of obtaining the spoils of this Government. I look to the fact itself. It is a policy now openly avowed as one to be persisted in. It is a scheme, Mr. President, which aims to monopolize the powers of this Government and to obtain sole possession of its territories.

Now, I ask, is there any remedy? Does the Constitution afford any remedy? And if not, is there any hope? These, Mr. President, are solemn questions—not only to us, but, let me say to gentlemen from the non-slaveholding States: to them. Sir, the day that the balance between the two sections of the country—the slaveholding States and the non-slaveholding States—is destroyed, is a day that will not be far removed from political revolution, anarchy, civil war, and widespread disaster. The balance of this system is in the slaveholding States. They are the conservative portion—

always have been the conservative portion—always will be the conservative portion; and with a due balance on their part may, for generations to come, uphold this glorious Union of ours. But if this scheme should be carried out—if we are to be reduced to a handful—if we are to become a mere ball to play the presidential game with—to count something in the Baltimore caucus—if this is to be the result—wo! wo! I say, to this Union!

Now, Sir, I put again the solemn question—Does the constitution afford any remedy? Is there any provision in it by which this aggressive policy (boldly avowed, as if perfectly consistent with our institutions and the safety and prosperity of the United States) may be confronted? Is this a policy consistent with the Constitution? No, Mr. President, no! It is, in all its features, daringly opposed to the constitution. What is it? Ours is a Federal Constitution. The States are its constituents, and not the people. The twenty-eight States—the twenty-nine States (including Iowa)—stand under this Government as twenty-nine individuals, or as twenty-nine millions of individuals would stand to a consolidated power! No, Sir; it was made for higher ends; it was so formed that every State, as a constituent member of this Union of ours, should enjoy all its advantages, natural and acquired, with greater security, and enjoy them more perfectly. The whole system is based on justice and equality—perfect equality between the members of this republic. Now, can that be consistent with equality which will make this public domain a monopoly on one side—which, in its consequences, would place the whole power in one section of the Union, to be wielded against the other sections? Is that equality?

How, then, do we stand in reference to this territorial question—this public domain of ours? Why, Sir, what is it? It is the common property of the States of this Union. They are called "the territories of the United States." And what are the "United States" but the States united? Sir, these territories are the property of the States united; held jointly for their common use. And is it consistent with justice—is it consistent with equality, that any portion of the partners, outnumbering another portion, shall oust them of this common property of theirs—shall pass any law which shall proscribe the citizens of other portions of the Union from emigrating with their property to the territories of the United States? Would that be consistent—can it be consistent with the idea of a common property, held jointly for the common benefit of all? Would it be so considered in private life? Would it not be considered the most flagrant outrage in the world, one which any court of equity would restrain by injunction—which any court of law in the world would overrule?

Mr. President, not only is that proposition grossly inconsistent with the constitution, but the other, which undertakes to say that no State shall be admitted into this Union, which shall not prohibit by its constitution the existence of slaves, is equally a great outrage against the constitution of the United States. Sir, I hold it to be a fundamental principle of our political system that the people have a right to establish what government they may think proper for themselves; that every State about to become a member of this Union has a right to form its government as it pleases; and that, in order to be admitted there is but one qualification, and that is, that the Government shall be republican. There is no express provision to that effect, but it results from that important section which guarantees to every State in this Union a republican form of government. Now, Sir, what is proposed? It is proposed, from a vague, indefinite, erroneous, and most dangerous conception of private individual liberty, to overrule this great common liberty which a people have of framing their own constitution! Sir, the right of framing self-government on the part of individuals is not near so easily to be established by any course of reasoning, as the right of a community or State to self-government. And yet, Sir, there are men of such delicate feeling on the subject of liberty—men who cannot possibly bear what they call slavery in one section of the country—although not so much slavery, as an institution indispensable for the good of both races— men so squeamish on this point, that they are ready to strike down the higher right of a community to govern themselves, in order to maintain the absolute right of individuals in every possible condition to govern themselves!

Mr. President, the resolutions that I intend to offer present, in general terms, these great truths. I propose to present them to the Senate; I propose to have a vote upon them; and I trust there is no gentleman here who will refuse it. It is manly—it is right, that such a vote be given. It is due to our constituents that we should insist upon it; and I, as one, will insist upon it that the sense of this body shall be taken; the body which represents the States in their capacity as communities, and the members of which are to be their special guardians. It is due to them, Sir, that there should be a fair expression of what is the sense of this body. Upon that expression much depends. It is the only position we can take, that will uphold us with any thing like independence—which will give us any chance at all to maintain an equality in this Union, on those great principles to which I have referred. Overrule these principles, and we are nothing! Preserve them, and we will ever be a respectable portion of the Union.

Sir, here let me say a word as to the compromise line. I have always considered it as a great error—highly injurious to the South, because it surrendered, for mere temporary purposes, those high principles of the constitution upon which I think we ought to stand. I am against any compromise line. Yet I would have been willing to acquiesce in a continuation of the Missouri compromise, in order to preserve, under the present trying circumstances, the peace of the Union. One of the resolutions in the House, to that effect, was offered at my suggestion. I said to a friend there, "Let us not be disturbers of this Union. Abhorrent to my feelings as is that compromise line, let it be adhered to in good faith; and if the other portions of the Union are willing to stand by it, let us not refuse to stand by it. It has kept peace for some time, and, in the present circumstances, perhaps, it would be better to be continued as it is." But it was voted down by a decided majority. It was renewed by a gentleman from a non-slaveholding State, and again voted down by a like majority.

I see my way in the constitution. I cannot in a compromise. A compromise is but an act of Congress. It may be overruled at any time. It gives us no security. But the constitution is stable. It is a rock. On it we can stand,

and on it we can meet our friends from the non-slaveholding States. It is a firm and stable ground, on which we can better stand in opposition to fanaticism, than on the shifting sands of compromise.

Let us be done with compromises. Let us go back and stand upon the constitution!

Well, Sir, what if the decision of this body shall deny to us this high constitutional right, not the less clear because deduced from the entire body of the instrument, and the nature of the subject to which it relates, instead of being specially provided for? What then? I will not undertake to decide. It is a question for our constituents, the slaveholding States—a solemn and a great question. If the decision should be adverse, I trust and do believe that they will take under solemn consideration what they ought to do. I give no advice. It would be hazardous and dangerous for me to do so. But I may speak as an individual member of that section of the Union. Here I drew my first breath; there are all my hopes. There is my family and connections. I am a planter—a cotton-planter. I am a Southern man and a slaveholder—a kind and a merciful one, I trust—and none the worse for being a slaveholder. I say, for one, I would rather meet any extremity upon earth than give up one inch of our equality—one inch of what belongs to us as members of this great republic! What acknowledge inferiority! The surrender of life is nothing to sinking down into acknowledged inferiority!

I have examined this subject largely—widely. I think I see the future if we do not stand up as we ought. In my humble opinion, in that case, the condition of Ireland is prosperous and happy—the condition of Hindostan is prosperous and happy—the condition of Jamaica is prosperous and happy, to what the Southern States will be if they should not now stand up manfully in defence of their rights.

Mr President, I desire that the resolutions which I now send to the table be read.

[The resolutions were read as follows:

Resolved, That the territories of the United States belong to the several States composing this Union, and are held by them as their joint and common property.

Resolved, That Congress, as the joint agent and representative of the States of this Union, has no right to make any law, or do any act whatever, that shall directly, or by its effects, make any discrimination between the States of this Union, by which any of them shall be deprived of its full and equal right in any territory of the United States, acquired or to be acquired.

Resolved, That the enactment of any law, which should directly, or by its effects, deprive the citizens of any of the States of this Union from emigrating, with their property, into any of the territories of the United States, will make such discrimination, and would, therefore, be a violation of the constitution and the rights of the States from which such citizens emigrated, and in derogation of that perfect equality which belongs to them as members of this Union—and would tend directly to subvert the Union itself.

Resolved, That it is a fundamental principle in our political creed, that a people, in forming a constitution, have the unconditional right to form and adopt the government which they may think best calculated to secure their liberty, prosperity, and happiness; and that, in conformity thereto, no other condition is imposed by the Federal Constitution on a State, in order to be admitted into this Union, except that its constitution shall be republican; and that the imposition of any other by Congress would not only be in violation of the constitution, but in direct conflict with the principle on which our political system rests."]

I move that the resolutions be printed. I shall move that they be taken up tomorrow; and I do trust that the Senate will give them early attention and an early vote upon the subject.

SPEECH AT THE MEETING
OF THE CITIZENS
OF CHARLESTON

[March 9, 1847]

———•——

Although the South had been successful in its efforts to block passage of the Wilmot Proviso (which would have prohibited slavery in any territory acquired in the Mexican War), there was a new sense of urgency when Calhoun returned to his native state of South Carolina. Arriving one week late due to ill health, Calhoun was greeted at the Charleston meeting house by an enthusiastic crowd so large that "hundreds had to retire for the impossibility of getting in."* Attacking those southerners who gave the appearance of indifference to the North's assault upon the Southern section, Calhoun argued that the time was at hand for the South to put forth a united front and to support a southern party to alter the direction of presidential elections. Only promptitude and unanimity could prevent the further corruption of the political arena and increased agitation of the slavery question.

In spite of his warning at the close of his speech on the Resolutions on the Slave Question (1847) that the time for constitutional, legal solution to the tensions between the Union and the states could be drawing to a close, Calhoun seemed still optimistic that a concerted effort on the part of Southerners could influence, if not control, the direction of the federal policies through the election of a president. It is in that context that Cal-

---

*Annual Report of the American Historical Association for the Year 1899, Vol. II, ed. J. E. Jameson, p. 720, "To Thomas G. Clemson, March 19, 1047."

houn calls upon the citizens of Charleston to pray to God that the South will have "the wisdom to adopt the best and most efficient course for our own security, and the peace and preservation of the Union."

FELLOW-CITIZENS: In complying with the request of your committee to address you on the general state of our affairs, in connection with the Federal Government, I shall restrict my remarks to the subject of our peculiar domestic institution, not only because it is by far the most important to us, but also because I have fully expressed my views, in my place in the Senate, on the only other important subject, the Mexican war.

I fully concur in the address of your committee, and the resolutions accompanying it. The facts stated are unquestionable, and the conclusions irresistible.

Indeed, after all that has occurred during the last twelve months, it would be almost idiotic to doubt that a large majority of both parties in the non-slaveholding States have come to a fixed determination to appropriate all the territories of the United States now possessed, or hereafter to be acquired, to themselves, to the entire exclusion of the slaveholding States. Assuming, then, that to be beyond doubt, the grave, and to us, vital question is presented for consideration: Have they the power to carry this determination into effect?

It will be proper to premise, before I undertake to answer this question, that it is my intention to place before you the danger with which we are threatened from this determination, plainly and fully, without exaggeration or extenuation, and, also, the advantages we have for repelling it, leaving it to you to determine what measures should be adopted for that purpose.

I now return to the question, and answer—Yes, they have the power, as far as mere numbers can give it. They will have a majority in the next Congress in every department of the Federal Government. The admission of Iowa and Wisconsin will give them two additional States, and a majority of four in the Senate, which heretofore has been our shield against this and other dangers of the kind. We are already in a minority in the House of Representatives and the Electoral College; so that with the loss of the Senate, we shall be in a minority in every department of the Federal Government; and ever must continue so, if the non-slaveholding States should carry into effect their scheme of appropriating to their exclusive use all the territories of the United States. But, fortunately, under our system of government, mere numbers are not the only element of power. There are others, which would give us ample means of defending ourselves against the threatened danger, if we should be true to ourselves.

We have, in the first place, the advantage of having the constitution on our side, clearly and unquestionably, and in its entire fabric; so much so, that the whole body of the instrument stands opposed to their scheme of appropriating the territories to themselves. To make good this assertion, it is only necessary to remind you, that ours is a federal, and not a national, or consolidated Government—a distinction essential to a correct understanding of the constitution, and our safety. It ought never to be forgotten or overlooked. As a federal Government, the States composing the Union are its constituents, and stand in the same relation to it, in that respect, as the individual citizens of a State do to its government. As constituent members of the Union, all the territories and other property of the Union belong to them as joint owners or partners, and not to the Government, as is erroneously supposed by some. The Government is but the agent intrusted with the management; and hence the constitution expressly declares the territory to be the property of the United States—that is, the States united, or the States of the Union, which are but synonymous expressions. And hence, also, Congress has no more right to appropriate the territories of the United States to the use of any portion of the States, to the exclusion of the others, than it has to appropriate in the same way, the forts, or other public buildings, or the navy, or any other property of the United States. That it has such a right, no one would venture to assert; and yet, the one is placed exactly on the same ground with the other by the constitution.

It was on this solid foundation that I placed the right of the slaveholding States to a full and equal participation in the territories of the United States, in opposition to the determination of the non-slaveholding States to appropriate them exclusively to themselves. It was my intention to urge them to a vote, but I was unable to do so, in consequence of the great pressure of business during the last few days of the session. It was felt by those opposed to us, that if the foundation on which I placed my resolutions be admitted, the conclusion could not be successfully assailed: and hence the bold but unsuccessful attempt to assail the foundation itself, by contending that ours is a national or consolidated Government, in which the States would stand to the Union, as the counties do to the States, and be equally destitute of all political rights. Such a conclusion, if it could be established, would, indeed, place us and our peculiar domestic institutions, at the mercy of the non-slaveholding States; but, fortunately, it cannot be maintained, without subverting the very foundation of our entire political system, and denying the most incontrovertible facts connected with the formation and adoption of the constitution.

But, it may be asked, what do we gain by having the constitution ever so clearly on our side when a majority in the non-slaveholding States stand prepared to deny it? Possibly such may be the case; still we cannot fail to gain much by the advantage it gives us. I speak from long experience—I have never known truth, promptly advocated in the spirit of truth, fail to succeed in the end. Already there are many highly enlightened and patriotic citizens in those States, who agree with us on this great and vital point. The effects of the discussion will not improbably greatly increase their number; and, what is of no little importance, induce a still greater number to hesitate and abate somewhat in their confidence in former opinions, and thereby prepare the way to give full effect to another advantage which we possess. To understand what it is, it will be necessary to explain what is the motive and object of this crusade on the part of the non-slaveholding States against our peculiar domestic institution.

It is clear that it does not originate in any hostility of interests. The labor of our slaves does not conflict with the profit of their capitalists or the wages of their operatives; or in any way injuriously affect the prosperity of those States, either as it relates to their population or wealth. On the contrary, it greatly increases both. It is its products, which mainly stimulate and render their capital and labor profitable; while our slaves furnish, at the same time, an extensive and profitable market for what they make. Annihilate the products of their labor—strike from the list the three great articles which are, most exclusively, the products of their labor—cotton, rice, and tobacco—and what would become of the great shipping, navigating, commercial, and manufacturing interests of the non-slaveholding States? What of their Lowell and Waltham, their New York and Boston, and other manufacturing and commercial cities? What, to enlarge the question, would become of the exports and imports of the Union itself; its shipping and tonnage; its immense revenue, on the disbursements of which, millions in those States, directly or indirectly, live and prosper? Fortunately, then, the crusade against our domestic institution does not originate in hostility of interests. If it did, the possibility of arresting the threatened danger, and saving ourselves, short of a disrupture of the Union, would be altogether hopeless; so predominant is the regard for interest in those States, over all other considerations.

Nor does it originate in any apprehension that the slave-holding States would acquire an undue preponderance in the Union, unless restricted to their present limits. If even a full share of the territories should fall to our lot, we could never hope to outweigh, by any increased number of slaveholding States the great preponderance which their population gives to the non-slaveholding States in the House of Representatives and the Electoral College. All we could hope for would be, to preserve an equality in the

Senate, or, at most, to acquire a preponderance in that branch of the Government.

But, if it originates neither in the one nor the other of these, what are the real motives and objects of their crusade against our institution? To answer this, it will be necessary to explain what are the feelings and views of the people of the non-slaveholding States in reference to it, with their effects on their party operations, especially in relation to the Presidential election.

They may, in reference to the subject under consideration, be divided into four classes. Of these, the abolitionists proper—the rabid fanatics, who regard slavery as a sin, and thus regarding it, deem it their highest duty to destroy it, even should it involve the destruction of the constitution and the Union—constitute one class. It is a small one, not probably exceeding five per cent of the population of those States. They voted, if I recollect correctly, about 15,000, or at most 20,000 votes in the last test of their strength in the State of New York, out of about 400,000 votes, which would give about five per cent. Their strength in that State, I would suppose, was fully equal to their average strength in the non-slaveholding States generally. Another class consists of the great body of the citizens of those States, constituting at least seven-tenths of the whole, and who, while they regard slavery as an evil, and as such are disposed to aid in restricting and extirpating it, when it can be done consistently with the constitution, and without endangering the peace or prosperity of the country, do not regard it as a sin, to be put down by all and every means.

Of the other two, one is a small class, perhaps not exceeding five per cent of the whole, who view slavery as we do, more as an institution, and the only one, by which two races, so dissimilar as those inhabiting the slaveholding States, can live together nearly in equal numbers, in peace and prosperity, and that its abolition would end in the extirpation of one or the other race. If they regard it as an evil, it is in the abstract; just as government with all of its burdens, labor with all its toils, punishment with all its inflictions, and thousands of other things, are evils, when viewed in the abstract, but far otherwise, when viewed in the concrete, because they prevent a greater amount of evil than they inflict, as is the case with slavery as it exists with us.

The remaining class is much larger, but still relatively a small one; less, perhaps, than twenty per cent of the whole, but possessing great activity and political influence in proportion to its numbers. It consists of the political leaders of the respective parties, and their partizans and followers. They, for the most part, are perfectly indifferent about abolition, and are ready to take either side, for or against, according to the calculation of political chances; their great and leading object being to carry the elections, especially the Presidential, and thereby receive the honors and emoluments incident to power, both in the Federal and State Governments.

Such are the views and feelings of the several classes in the non-slaveholding States in reference to slavery, as it exists with us. It is manifest, on a survey of the whole, that the first class—that is, the abolition party proper—is the centre which has given the impulse that has put in motion this crusade against our domestic institution. It is the only one that has any decidedly hostile feelings in reference to it, and which, in opposing it, is actuated by any strong desire to restrict or destroy it.

But it may be asked, how can so small a class rally a large majority of both parties in the non-slaveholding States to come to the determination they have, in reference to our domestic institution? To answer this question, it is necessary to go one step further and explain the habitual state of parties in those, and, indeed, in almost all the States of the Union.

There are few of the non-slaveholding States, perhaps not more than two or three, in which the parties are not so nicely balanced, as to make the result of elections, both State and Federal, so doubtful as to put it in the power of a small party, firmly linked together, to turn the elections, by throwing their weight into the scale of the party which may most favor its views. Such is the abolition party. They have, from the first, made their views paramount to the party struggles of the day, and thrown their weight where their views could be best promoted. By pursuing this course, their influence was soon felt in the elections; and, in consequence, to gain them soon became the object of party courtship: first by the Whigs; but for the last twelve months, more eagerly by the Democrats, as if to make up for lost time. They are now openly courted by both; each striving by their zeal to win their favor by expressing their earnest desire to exclude what they call slavery from all the territories of the United States, acquired or to be acquired. No doubt the Mexican war, and the apprehension of large acquisition of territory to the slaveholding States, has done much to produce this state of things, but of itself it would have been feeble. The main cause or motive, then, of this crusade against our domestic institution, is to be traced to the all-absorbing interest, which both parties take, in carrying the elections, especially the Presidential. Indeed, when we reflect that the expenditure of the Federal Government, at all times great, is now swelled probably to the rate of seventy million of dollars annually, and that the influence of its patronage gives it great sway, not only over its own, but over the State elections—which gives in addition a control over a vast amount of patronage—and the control of the Federal patronage, with all its emoluments and honors, centres in the President of the United States—it is not at all surprising, that both parties should take such absorbing interest in the Presidential election; acting, as both do, on the principle of turning opponents out of office, and bestowing the honors and emoluments of Government on their followers, as the reward of partizan services. In such a state of things, it is not a matter for wonder, that a course of policy, so well calculated to conciliate a party like the abolitionists, as that of excluding slavery from the territories, should be eagerly embraced by both parties in the non-slaveholding States; when by securing their support, each calculates on winning the rich and glittering prize of the Presidency. In this is to be found the motive and object of the present crusade against our domestic institution, on the part of political leaders and their partizans in those States.

It would be a great mistake to suppose that it is the less dangerous, because it originates mainly in mere party considerations in connection with elections. It will be on that account but the more so, unless, indeed, it should be met by us with promptitude and unanimity. The absorbing, overriding interest, felt by both parties to carry the elections—especially the Presidential—would give such an impulse to their efforts to conciliate the abolitionists, at our expense, if we should look on with apparent indifference, as would enlist in their favor the large portion of the non-slaveholding States, estimated at seven-tenths of the whole, which are, as yet, well affected towards us, and utterly dishearten the small but intelligent class, which, as yet, is perfectly sound. The former would conclude, in that case, that we ourselves were ready to yield and surrender our domestic institution, as indefensible; and that the non-slaveholding States might carry their determination into full effect, without hazard to the constitution or the Union, or even disturbing the harmony and peace of the country. Indeed, such has already been our apparent indifference, that these opinions have been expressed, even on the floor of Congress. But, if we should act as we ought—if we, by our promptitude, energy, and unanimity, prove that we stand ready to defend our rights, and to maintain our perfect equality, as members of the Union, be the consequences what they may; and that the immediate and necessary effect of courting abolition votes, by either party, would be to lose ours, a very different result would certainly follow. That large portion of the non-slaveholding States, who, although they consider slavery as an evil, are not disposed to violate the constitution, and much less to endanger its overthrow, and with it the Union itself, would take sides with us against our assailants; while the sound portion, who are already with us, would rally to the rescue. The necessary effect would be, that the party leaders and their followers, who expect to secure the Presidential election, by the aid of the abolitionists, seeing their hopes blasted by the loss of our votes, would drop their courtship, and leave the party, reduced to insignificance, with scorn. The end would be, should we act in the manner indicated, the rally of a new party in the non-slaveholding States, more powerful than either of the old, who, on this great question, would be faithful to all of the compromises and obligations of the constitution; and who by uniting with us, would put a final stop to the further agitation of this dangerous question. Such would be the certain effect of meeting, with promptitude and unanimity, the determination of the non-slaveholding States to appropriate all the territories to their own use—That it has not yet been so met is certain; and the next question is: Why has it not been, and what is the cause of this apparent indifference in reference to a danger so menacing, if not promptly and unitedly met on our part?

In answering this important question, I am happy to say, that I have seen no reason to attribute this want of promptitude and unanimity to any division of sentiment, or real indifference, on the part of the people of the slaveholding States, or their delegates in Congress. On the contrary, as far as my observation extends, there is not one of their members of Congress who has given any certain indication of either. On the trying questions connected with the Wilmot Proviso, the votes of the members from the slaveholding States, at the last and present sessions, were unanimous. To explain what is really the cause, I must again recur to what has already been stated; the absorbing interest felt in the elections—especially the Presidential—and the controlling influence which party leaders and their followers exercise over them. The great struggle between the parties is, which shall succeed in electing its candidate; in consequence of which the Presidential election has become the paramount question. All others are held subordinate to it by the leaders and their followers. It depends on them to determine whether any question shall be admitted into the issue between the parties, in the Presidential contest, or whether it shall be partially or entirely excluded. Whether it shall be one or the other, is decided entirely in reference to its favorable or unfavorable bearing on the contest, without looking to the higher considerations of its effects on the prosperity, the institutions, or safety of the country. Nothing can more strongly illustrate the truth of what I have asserted, than the course of the parties in relation to the question which now claims your attention. Although none can be more intimately connected with the peace and safety of the Union, it is kept out of the issue between the parties, because it is seen that the Presidential vote of New York, and many others of the non-slaveholding States, will, in all probability, depend on the votes of the abolitionists; and that the election of the President may, in like manner, depend on the votes of those States. And hence the leaders in them are tolerated by many of the leaders and their followers in the slaveholding States, in openly canvassing for the vote of the abolitionists, by acting in unison with them, in reference to a question, on the decision of which the safety of their own section, and that of the Union itself may depend. But while it is seen that the Presidential election may be secured by courting the abolition votes, it is at the same time seen, that it may be lost, if the consequence should be the loss of the vote of the slaveholding States; and hence the leaders are forced to attempt to secure the former without losing the latter. The game is a difficult one; but difficult as it is, they do not despair of success, with the powerful instruments which they have under their control. They have, in the first place, that of the party press, through which a mighty influence is exerted over public opinion. The line of policy adopted is for the party press to observe a profound silence on this great and vital question, or if they speak at all, so to speak as to give a false direction to public opinion. Acting in conformity to this policy, of the two leading organs at the seat of Government, one never alludes to the question; so that, as far as its remarks are concerned, no one could suppose that it was the cause of the least agitation or feeling in any portion of the Union. The other occasionally alludes to it, when it cannot well avoid doing so, but only to palliate the conduct of those who assail us, by confounding them with our defenders as agitators, and holding both up equally to the public censure. It is calculated by pursuing this course, that the people of the slaveholding States will be kept quiet, and in a state of indifference, until another and still more powerful instrument can be brought into play, by which it is hoped that slaveholders and abolitionists will be coerced to join in nominating and supporting the same candidate for the Presidency. I allude to what is called a National Convention, or Caucus, for nominating candidates for the Presidency and Vice-Presidency. Already the machinery

has been put in motion, in order to coerce the oldest and most populous of
the slaveholding States; and no doubt, will, in due season, be put in motion
to effect the same object in all of them. Should it succeed—should the
party machinery for President-making prove strong enough to force the
slaveholding States to join in a convention to nominate and support a
candidate who will be acceptable to the abolitionists, they will have committed the most suicidal act that a people ever perpetrated. I say acceptable; for it is clear that the non-slaveholding States will outnumber in
convention the slaveholding, and that no one who is not acceptable to the
abolitionists can receive their votes—and of course, the votes of the States
where they hold the balance; and that no other will be nominated, or, if
nominated, be elected. And yet, there are not a few in the slaveholding
States, men of standing and influence, so blinded by party feeling, or the
prospect of personal gain or advancement by the success of their party,
who advocate a step which must prove so fatal to their portion of the Union
under existing circumstances. Can party folly, or rather madness, go
further?

As to myself, I have ever been opposed to such conventions, because
they are irresponsible bodies, not known to the constitution; and because
they, in effect, set aside the constitution with its compromises, in reference
to so important a subject as the election of the Chief Magistrate of the
Union. I hold it far safer, and every way preferable, to leave the election
where the constitution has placed it—to the Electoral College to choose;
and if that fails to make a choice, to the House of Representatives, voting
by States, to elect the President from the three candidates having the
highest votes. But, if I had no objection to such conventions, under ordinary circumstances, I would regard the objection as fatal under the existing
state of things, when all parties of the non-slaveholding States stand united
against us on the most vital of all questions; and when to go into one would
be, in effect, a surrender on our part. As both parties there have united to
divest us of our just and equal rights in the public domain, it is time that
both parties with us should unite in resistance to so great an outrage. Let

us show at least as much spirit in defending our rights and honor, as they have evinced in assailing them. Let us, when our safety is concerned, show at least as firm a determination, and as much unanimity, as they do, with no other interest on their part but the temporary one of succeeding in the Presidential contest. Henceforward, let all party distinction among us cease, so long as this aggression on our rights and honor shall continue, on the part of the non-slaveholding States. Let us profit by the example of the abolition party, who, as small as they are, have acquired so much influence by the course they have pursued. As they make the destruction of our domestic institution the paramount question, so let us make, on our part, its safety the paramount question. Let us regard every man as of our party, who stands up in its defence; and every one as against us, who does not, until aggression ceases. It is thus, and thus only, that we can defend our rights, maintain our honor, ensure our safety, and command respect. The opposite course, which would merge them in the temporary and mercenary party struggles of the day, would inevitably degrade and ruin us.

If we should prove true to ourselves and our peculiar domestic institution, we shall be great and prosperous, let what will occur. There is no portion of the globe more abundant in resources—agricultural, manufacturing and commercial—than that possessed by us. We count among our productions the great staples of cotton, rice, tobacco and sugar, with the most efficient, well fed, well clad, and well trained body of laborers for their cultivation. In addition to furnishing abundant means for domestic exchanges among ourselves, and with the rest of the world, and building up flourishing commercial cities, they would furnish ample resources for revenue. But far be it from us to desire to be forced on our own resources for protection. Our object is to preserve the Union of these States, if it can be done consistently with our rights, safety, and perfect equality with other members of the Union. On this we have a right to insist. Less we cannot take. Looking at the same time to our safety and the preservation of the Union, I regard it as fortunate that the promptitude and unanimity, on our part, necessary to secure the one, are equally so to preserve the other.

Delay, indecision, and want of union among ourselves would in all probability, in the end, prove fatal to both—The danger is of a character, whether we regard our safety or the preservation of the Union, which cannot be safely tampered with. If not met promptly and decidedly, the two portions of the Union will gradually become thoroughly alienated, when no alternative will be left to us as the weaker of the two, but to sever all political ties, or sink down into abject submission. It is only by taking an early and decided stand, while the political ties are still strong, that a rally of the sound and patriotic of all portions of the Union can be successfully made to arrest so dire an alternative.

Having now pointed out the danger with which we are menaced, and the means by which it may be successfully met and resisted, it is for you and the people of the slaveholding States, to determine what shall be done, at a juncture so trying and eventful. In conclusion, it is my sincere prayer, that the Great Disposer of events may enlighten you and them to realize its full extent, and give the wisdom to adopt the best and most efficient course for our own security, and the peace and preservation of the Union.

SPEECH ON THE OREGON BILL

[June 27, 1848]

———•◆•———

*By 1848, both sides of the sectional controversy were becoming more
rigidly entrenched. Fewer and fewer men believed that dialogue could resolve the differences between the North and South. Calhoun, however,
would not be dissuaded from the powers of analysis. In his speech on the
status of the Oregon territory, he presents a point-by-point refutation of
arguments defending the exclusion of slavery from the territories on the
basis of the U.S. Constitution, the Ordinance of 1787, the Missouri Compromise, and the intentions and thoughts of Thomas Jefferson. Calhoun calls
upon the North to recognize its obligations under the Constitution and to
stop its policies of aggression, and he calls upon the South to take action to
defend itself before it is too late.*

*Ironically, by the end of his own speech, Calhoun himself seemed to have
abandoned hope that meaningful dialogue was possible. In his clearest
statement on the conflict between freedom and equality, Calhoun perceived
that the real source of conflict between the North and South was, in the
final analysis, based on fundamental beliefs about human nature, and not
upon principles of political practice. Beginning from a false premise, a vast
majority of people on both sides of the Atlantic have come to confuse the
three states of man: individual, political, and social. If, posits Calhoun, our
Union and government should perish, a historian writing about the dissolution of the American political system will find that the remote cause of the
crisis originated in the hypothetical proposition that "all men are born free*

and equal." This theoretical truism has been repeated so often that it is now taken as axiomatic. And from this small beginning, writes Calhoun, a pernicious teaching has won sway in the world that holds individual liberty in higher regard than the liberty of the community and the safety of the society. Developing the arguments and reasoning that characterize his Disquisition on Government, Calhoun argues that liberty is not a natural right of individual men—no matter how often the phrase is repeated—but a blessing bestowed on a people as a reward for their intelligence, virtue, and patriotism.

THERE is a very striking difference between the position on which the slaveholding and non-slaveholding States stand, in reference to the subject under consideration. The former desire no action of the Government; demand no law to give them any advantage in the territory about to be established; are willing to leave it, and other territories belonging to the United States, open to all their citizens, so long as they continue to be territories—and when they cease to be so, to leave it to their inhabitants to form such governments as may suit them, without restriction or condition, except that imposed by the constitution, as a prerequisite for admission into the Union. In short, they are willing to leave the whole subject where the constitution and the great and fundamental principles of self-government place it. On the contrary, the non-slaveholding States, instead of being willing to leave it on this broad and equal foundation, demand the interposition of the Government, and the passage of an act to exclude the citizens of the slaveholding States from emigrating with their property into the territory, in order to give their citizens and those they may permit, the exclusive right of settling it, while it remains in that condition, preparatory to subjecting it to like restrictions and conditions when it becomes a State. The 12th section of this bill is intended to assert and maintain this demand of the non-slaveholding States, while it remains a territory, not openly or directly, but indirectly, by extending the provisions of the bill for the establishment of the Iowa Territory to this, and by ratifying the acts of the

541

informal and self-constituted government of Oregon, which, among others, contains one prohibiting the introduction of slavery. It thus, in reality, adopts what is called the Wilmot Proviso, not only for Oregon, but, as the bill now stands, for New Mexico and California. The amendment, on the contrary, moved by the Senator from Mississippi, near me (Mr. Davis), is intended to assert and maintain the position of the slaveholding States. It leaves the territory free and open to all the citizens of the United States, and would overrule, if adopted, the act of the self-constituted Territory of Oregon and the 12th section, as far as it relates to the subject under consideration. We have thus fairly presented the grounds taken by the non-slaveholding and the slaveholding States, or, as I shall call them, for the sake of brevity, the Northern and Southern States, in their whole extent for discussion.

The first question which offers itself for consideration is—Have the Northern States the power which they claim, to prevent the Southern people from emigrating freely, with their property, into territories belonging to the United States, and to monopolize them for their exclusive benefit?

It is, indeed, a great question. I propose to discuss it calmly and dispassionately. I shall claim nothing which does not fairly and clearly belong to the Southern States, either as members of this Federal Union, or appertain to them in their separate and individual character; nor shall I yield any thing which belongs to them in either capacity. I am influenced neither by sectional nor party considerations. If I know myself, I would repel as promptly and decidedly any aggression of the South on the North, as I would any on the part of the latter on the former. And let me add, I hold the obligation to repel aggression to be not much less solemn than that of abstaining from making aggression; and the party which submits to it when it can be resisted, to be not much less guilty and responsible for consequences than that which makes it. Nor do I stand on party grounds. What I shall say in reference to this subject, I shall say entirely without reference to the Presidential election. I hold it to be infinitely higher than that and all other questions of the day. I shall direct my efforts to ascertain what is constitutional, right and just, under a thorough conviction that the best and only way of putting an end to this, the most dangerous of all questions to our Union and institutions, is to adhere rigidly to the constitution and the dictates of justice.

With these preliminary remarks, I recur to the question—Has the North the power which it claims under the 12th section of this bill? I ask at the outset, where is the power to be found? Not, certainly, in the relation in which the Northern and Southern States stand to each other. They are the constituent parts or members of a common Federal Union; and, as such, are equals in all respects, both in dignity and rights, as is declared by all writers on governments founded on such union, and as may be inferred from arguments deduced from their nature and character. Instead, then, of affording any countenance or authority in favor of the power, the relation in which they stand to each other furnishes a strong presumption against it. Nor can it be found in the fact that the South holds property in slaves. That, too, fairly considered, instead of affording any authority for the power, furnishes a strong presumption against it. Slavery existed in the South when the constitution was framed, fully to the extent, in proportion to the population, that it does at this time. It is the only property recognized by it; the only one that entered into its formation as a political element, both in the adjustment of the relative weight of the States in the Government, and the apportionment of direct taxes; and the only one that is put under the express guaranty of the constitution. It is well known to all conversant with the history of the formation and adoption of the constitution, that the South was very jealous in reference to this property; that it constituted one of the difficulties both to its formation and adoption; and that it would not have assented to either, had the convention refused to allow to it its due weight in the Government, or to place it under the guaranty of the constitution. Nor can it be found in the way that the territories have been acquired. I will not go into particulars, in this respect, at this stage of the discussion. Suffice it to say, the whole was acquired either by purchase, out of the common funds of all the States—the South as well as the North—or by arms and mutual sacrifice of men and money; which, instead of giving any countenance in favor of the power claimed by the North, on every principle of right and justice, furnishes strong additional presumption against it.

But, if it cannot be found in either, if it exists at all, the power must be looked for in the constitutional compact, which binds those States together in a Federal Union; and I now ask, can it be found there? Does that instrument contain any provision which gives the North the power to exclude the South from a free admission into the territories of the United States with its peculiar property, and to monopolize them for its own exclusive use? If it in fact contains such power, expressed or implied, it must be found in a specific grant, or be inferred by irresistible deduction, from some clear and acknowledged power. Nothing short of the one or the other can overcome the strong presumption against it.

That there is no such specific grant may be inferred, beyond doubt, from the fact that no one has ever attempted to designate it. Instead of that, it has been assumed—taken for granted without a particle of proof— that Congress has the absolute right to govern the territories. Now, I concede, if it does in reality possess such power, it may exclude from the territories whom or what it pleases, and admit into them whom or what it pleases; and of course may exercise the power claimed by the North to exclude the South from them. But I again repeat, where is this absolute power to be found? All admit that there is no such specific grant of power. If, then, it exists at all, it must be inferred from some such power. I ask where is that to be found? The Senator from New York, behind me (Mr. Dix), points to the clause in the constitution, which provides that "Congress shall have power to dispose of and make all needful rules and regulations respecting the territory and other property belonging to the United States." Now, I undertake to affirm and maintain, beyond the possibility of doubt, that, so far from conferring absolute power to govern the territories, it confers no governmental power whatever; no, not a particle. It refers exclusively to territory, regarded simply as public lands. Every word relates to it in that character, and is wholly inapplicable to it considered in any other character than property. Take the expression "dispose of" with which it begins. It is easily understood what it means when applied to lands; and is the proper and natural expression regarding the territory in that character, when the object is to confer the right to sell or make other disposition of it. But who ever heard the expression applied to government? And what possible meaning can it have when so applied? Take the next expression, "to make all needful rules and regulations." These, regarded separately, might, indeed, be applicable to government in a loose sense; but they are never so applied in the constitution. In every case where they are used in it, they refer to property, to things, or some process, such as the rules of Court, or of the Houses of Congress for the government of their proceedings; but never to government, which always implies persons to be governed. But if there should be any doubt in this case, the words immediately following, which restrict them to making "rules and regulations respecting the territory and other property of the United States," must effectually expel it. They restrict their meaning, beyond the possibility of doubt, to territory regarded as property.

But if it were possible for doubt still to exist, another and conclusive argument still remains to show that the framers of the constitution did not intend to confer by this clause governmental powers. I refer to the clause in the constitution which delegates the power of exclusive legislation to Congress over this District and "all places purchased by the consent of the legislature of the State in which the same may be for the erection of forts, magazines, arsenals, dockyards, and other needful buildings." The places therein referred to are clearly embraced by the expression, "other property belonging to the United States," contained in the clause I have just considered. But it is certain, that if it had been the intention of the framers of the constitution to confer governmental powers over such places by that clause, they never would have delegated it by this. They were incapable of doing a thing so absurd. But it is equally certain, if they did not intend to confer such power over them, they could not have intended it over territories. Whatever was conferred by the same words, in reference to one, must have been intended to be conferred in reference to the other, and the reverse. The opposite supposition would be absurd. But, it may be asked why the term—territory—was omitted in the delegation of exclusive legislation to Congress over the places enumerated? Very satisfactory reasons may, in my opinion, be assigned. The former were limited to places lying within the limits and jurisdiction of the States, and the latter to public land lying beyond both. The cession and purchase of the former, with the consent of the State within which they might be situated, did not oust the sovereignty or jurisdiction of the State. They still remained in the State, the United States acquiring only the title to the place. It, therefore, became necessary to confer on Congress, by express delegation, the exercise of exclusive power of legislation over this District and such places, in order to carry out the object of the purchase and session. It was simply intended to withdraw them from under the legislatures of the respective States within which they might lie, and substitute that of Congress in its place, subject to the restrictions of the constitution and the objects for which the places were acquired, leaving, as I have said, the sovereignty still in the State in which they are situated, but in abeyance, as far as it extends to legislation. Thus, in the case of this District, since the retrocession to Virginia of the part beyond the Potomac, the sovereignty still continues in Maryland in the manner stated. But the case is very different in reference to territories, lying as they do beyond the limits and jurisdictions of all the States. The United States possess not simply the right of ownership over them, but that of exclusive dominion and sovereignty; and hence it was not necessary to exclude the power of the States to legislate over them, by delegating the exercise of exclusive legislation to Congress. It would have been an act of supererogation. It may be proper to remark in this connection, that the power of exclusive legislation, conferred in these cases, must not be confounded with the power of absolute legislation. They are very different things. It is true that absolute power of legislation is always exclusive, but it by no means follows that exclusive power of legislation or of government is likewise always absolute. Congress has the exclusive power of legislation, as far as this Government is concerned, and the State legislatures as far as their respective governments are concerned—but we all know that both are subject to many and important restrictions and conditions which the nature of absolute power excludes.

I have now made good the assertion I ventured to make, that the clause in the constitution relied on by the Senator from New York, so far from conferring the absolute power of government over the territory claimed by him, and others who agree with him, confers not a particle of governmental power. Having conclusively established this, the long list of precedents, cited by the Senator to prop up the power which he sought in the clause, falls to the ground with the fabric which he raised; and I am thus exempted from the necessity of referring to them, and replying to them one by one.

But there is one precedent, referred to by the Senator, unconnected with the power, and on that account requiring particular notice. I refer to the ordinance of 1787, which was adopted by the old Congress of the Confederation while the convention that framed the constitution was in session, and about one year before its adoption—and of course on the very eve of the expiration of the old Confederation. Against its introduction, I might object that the act of the Congress of the Confederation cannot rightfully form precedents for this Government; but I waive that. I waive also the objection that the act was consummated when that Government was *in extremis*, and could hardly be considered *compos mentis*. I waive also the fact that the ordinance assumed the form of a compact, and was adopted when only eight States were present, while the articles of confederation required nine to form compacts. I waive also the fact, that Mr. Madison declared that the act was without shadow of constitutional authority, and shall proceed to show, from the history of its adoption, that it cannot justly be considered of any binding force.

Virginia made the cession of the territory north of the Ohio, and lying between it and the Mississippi and the lakes, in 1784. It now contains the States of Ohio, Indiana, Illinois, Michigan, Wisconsin, and a very considerable extent of territory lying north of the latter. Shortly after the cession, a committee of three was raised, of whom Mr. Jefferson was one. They reported an ordinance for the establishment of the territory, containing, among other provisions, one, of which Mr. Jefferson was the author, excluding slavery from the territory after the year 1800. It was reported to Congress, but this provision was struck out. On the question of striking out, every Southern State present voted in favor of it; and, what is more striking, every Southern delegate voted the same way, Mr. Jefferson alone excepted. The ordinance was adopted without the provision. At the next session, Rufus King, then a member of the old Congress, moved a proposition, very much in the same shape as the sixth article (that which excludes slavery) in the ordinance as it now stands, with the exception of its proviso. It was referred to a committee, but there was no action on it. A committee was moved the next or the subsequent year, which reported without including or noticing Mr. King's proposition. Mr. Dane was a member of that committee, and proposed a provision the same as that in the ordinance as it passed, but the committee reported without including it. Finally, another committee was raised, at the head of which was Mr. Carrington of Virginia, and of which Mr. Dane was also a member. That committee reported without including the amendment previously proposed by him. Mr. Dane moved his proposition, which was adopted, and the report of the committee thus amended became the ordinance of 1787.

It may be inferred from this brief historical sketch, that the ordinance was a compromise between the Southern and Northern States, of which the terms were, that slavery should be excluded from the territory upon condition that fugitive slaves, who might take refuge in the territory, should be delivered up to their owners, as stipulated in the proviso of the sixth article of the ordinance. It is manifest, from what has been stated, that the South was unitedly and obstinately opposed to the provision when first moved; that the proposition of Mr. King, without the proviso, was in like manner resisted by the South, as may be inferred from its entire want of success, and that it never could be brought to agree to it until the provision for the delivery up of fugitive slaves was incorporated in it. But it is well understood that a compromise involves not a surrender, but simply a waiver of the right or power; and hence in the case of individuals, it is a well-established legal principle, that an offer to settle by compromise a litigated claim, is no evidence against the justice of the claim on the side of the party making it. The South, to her honor, has observed with fidelity her engagements under this compromise; in proof of which, I appeal to the precedents cited by the Senator from New York, intended by him to establish the fact of her acquiescence in the ordinance. I admit that she has acquiesced in the several acts of Congress to carry it into effect; but the Senator is mistaken in supposing that it is proof of a surrender, on her part, of the power over the territories which he claims for Congress. No, she never has, and I trust never will, make such a surrender. Instead of that, it is conclusive proof of her fidelity to her engagements. She has never attempted to set aside the ordinance, or to deprive the territory, and the States erected within its limits, of any right or advantage it was intended to confer. But I regret that as much cannot be said in favor of the fidelity with which it has been observed on their part. With the single exception of the State of Illinois—be it said to her honor—every other State erected within its limits has pursued a course, and adopted measures, which have rendered the stipulations of the proviso to deliver up fugitive slaves nugatory. Wisconsin may, also, be an exception, as she has just entered the Union, and has hardly had time to act on the subject. They have gone further, and suffered individuals to form combinations, without an effort to suppress them, for the purpose of enticing and seducing the slaves to leave their masters, and to run them into Canada beyond the reach of our laws—in open violation, not only of the stipulations of the ordinance, but of the constitution itself. If I express myself strongly, it is not for the purpose of producing excitement, but to draw the attention of the Senate forcibly to the subject. My object is to lay bare the subject

under consideration, just as a surgeon probes to the bottom and lays open
a wound, not to cause pain to his patient, but for the purpose of healing it.

I come now to another precedent of a similar character, but differing in
this—that it took place under this Government, and not under that of the
old Confederation; I refer to what is known as the Missouri Compromise. It
is more recent and better known, and may be more readily despatched.

After an arduous struggle of more than a year, on the question whether
Missouri should come into the Union with or without restrictions prohibiting
slavery, a compromise line was adopted between the North and the South;
but it was done under circumstances which made it nowise obligatory on the
latter. It is true, it was moved by one of her distinguished citizens (Mr. Clay);
but it is equally so, that it was carried by the almost united vote of the North
against the almost united vote of the South; and was thus imposed on the
latter by superior numbers in opposition to her strenuous efforts. The South
has never given her sanction to it, or assented to the power it asserted. She
was voted down, and has simply acquiesced in an arrangement which she has
not had the power to reverse, and which she could not attempt to do without
disturbing the peace and harmony of the Union—to which she has ever been
averse. Acting on this principle, she permitted the Territory of Iowa to be
formed, and the State to be admitted into the Union, under the compromise,
without objection; and that is now quoted by the Senator from New York to
prove her surrender of the power he claims for Congress.

To add to the strength of this claim, the advocates of the power hold up
the name of Jefferson in its favor, and go so far as to call him the author of
the so-called Wilmot Proviso, which is but a general expression of a power
of which the Missouri compromise is a case of its application. If we may
judge by his opinion of that case, what his opinion was of the principle,
instead of being the author of the proviso, or being in its favor, no one
could be more deadly hostile to it. In a letter addressed to the elder Adams
in 1819, in answer to one from him, he uses these remarkable expressions
in reference to the Missouri question:

The banks, bankrupt law, manufactures, Spanish treaty, are nothing. These are occurrences, which, like waves in a storm, will pass under the ship. But the Missouri question is a breaker on which we lose the Missouri country by revolt, and what more, God only knows.

To understand the full force of these expressions, it must be borne in mind that the questions enumerated were the great and exciting political questions of the day, on which parties divided. The banks and bankrupt law had long been so. Manufactures, or what has since been called the protective tariff, was at the time a subject of great excitement, as was the Spanish treaty, that is, the treaty by which Florida was ceded to the Union, and by which the western boundary between Mexico and the United States was settled, from the Gulf of Mexico to the Pacific ocean. All these exciting party questions of the day Mr. Jefferson regarded as nothing, compared to the Missouri question. He looked on all of them as in their nature fugitive; and, to use his own forcible expression, "would pass off under the ship of State like waves in a storm." Not so that fatal question. It was a breaker on which it was destined to be stranded. And yet his name is quoted by the incendiaries of the present day in support of, and as the author of, a proviso which would give indefinite and universal extension of this fatal question to all the territories! It was compromised the next year by the adoption of the line to which I have referred. Mr. Holmes of Maine, long a member of this body, who voted for the measure, addressed a letter to Mr. Jefferson, inclosing a copy of his speech on the occasion. It drew out an answer from him which ought to be treasured up in the heart of every man who loves the country and its institutions. It is brief: I will send it to the Secretary to be read. The time of the Senate cannot be better occupied than in listening to it:

To John Holmes.

Monticello, April 22, 1820.

I thank you, dear sir, for the copy you have been so kind as to send me of the letter to your constituents on the Missouri question. It is a perfect justification to them. I had for a long time ceased to read newspapers, or pay any attention to public affairs, confident they were in good hands, and content to be a passenger in our bark to the shore from which I am not distant. But this momentous question, like a fire-bell in the night, awakened and filled me with terror. I considered it at once as the knell of the Union. It is hushed, indeed, for the moment; but this is a reprieve only, not the final sentence. A geographical line, coinciding with a marked principle, moral and political, once conceived and held up to the angry passions of men, will never be obliterated; and every new irritation will mark it deeper and deeper. I can say, with conscious truth, that there is not a man on earth who would sacrifice more than I would to relieve us from this heavy reproach, in any *practicable* way. The cession of that kind of property (for so it is misnamed) is a bagatelle, which would not cost me a second thought, if in that way a general emancipation and *expatriation* could be effected; and gradually, and with due sacrifices, I think it might be. But, as it is, we have the wolf by the ears, and we can neither hold him nor safely let him go. Justice is in one scale, and self-preservation in the other. Of one thing I am certain, that as the free passage of slaves from one State to another would not make a slave of a single human being who would not be so without it, so their diffusion over a greater surface would make them individually happier, and proportionally facilitate the accomplishment of their emancipation, by dividing the burden on a greater number of coadjutors. An abstinence, too, from this act of power, would remove the jealousy excited by the undertaking of Congress to regulate the condition of the different descriptions of men composing a State. This certainly is the exclusive right of every State, which nothing in the constitution has taken from them, and given to the General Government. Could Congress, for example, say that the non-freemen of Connecticut shall be freemen, or that they shall not emigrate into any other State?

I regret that I am now to die in the belief that the useless sacrifice of themselves by the generation of 1776, to acquire self-government and happiness to their country, is to be thrown away by the unwise and unworthy passions of their sons, and that my only consolation is to be, that I shall live not to weep over it. If they would but dispassionately weigh the blessings they will throw away against an abstract principle, more likely to be effected by union than by scission, they would pause before they would perpetrate this act of suicide on themselves, and of treason against the hopes of the world. To yourself, as the faithful advocate of the Union, I tender the offering of my high esteem and respect.

THOMAS JEFFERSON

Mark his prophetic words! Mark his profound reasoning!

It [the question] is hushed for *the moment*. But this is a *reprieve only*, not a *final sentence*. A geographical line coinciding with a marked principle, moral and political, *once conceived, and held up to the angry passions of men, will never be obliterated, and every new irritation will mark it deeper and deeper.*

Twenty-eight years have passed since these remarkable words were penned, and there is not a thought which time has not thus far verified, and, it is to be feared, continue to verify until the whole will be fulfilled. Certain it is, that he regarded the compromise line as utterly inadequate to arrest that fatal course of events, which his keen sagacity anticipated from the question. It was but a "reprieve." Mark the deeply melancholy impression which it made on his mind:

I regret that I am to die in the belief that the useless sacrifice of themselves by the generation of 1776, to acquire self-government and happiness for themselves, is to be thrown away by the unwise and unworthy passions of their sons, and that my only consolation is to be, that I shall live not to weep over it.

Can any one believe, after listening to this letter, that Jefferson is the author of the so-called Wilmot Proviso, or ever favored it? And yet there are at this time strenuous efforts making in the North to form a purely sectional party on it, and that, too, under the sanction of those who profess the highest veneration for his character and principles! But I must speak the truth: while I vindicate the memory of Jefferson from so foul a charge, I hold he is not blameless in reference to this subject. He committed a great error in inserting the provision he did in the plan he reported for the government of the territory, as much modified as it was. It was the first blow—the first essay "to draw a geographical line coinciding with a marked principle, moral and political." It originated with him in philanthropic, but mistaken views of the most dangerous character, as I shall show in the sequel. Others, with very different feelings and views, followed, and have given to it a direction and impetus, which, if not promptly and efficiently arrested, will end in the dissolution of the Union, and the destruction of our political institutions.

I have, I trust, established beyond controversy, that neither the ordinance of 1787, nor the Missouri compromise, nor the precedents growing out of them, nor the authority of Mr. Jefferson, furnishes any evidence whatever to prove that Congress possesses the power over the territory, claimed by those who advocate the 12th section of this bill. But admit, for the sake of argument, that I am mistaken, and that the objections I have urged against them are groundless—give them all the force which can be claimed for precedents—and they would not have the weight of a feather against the strong presumption which I, at the outset of my remarks, showed to be opposed to the existence of the power. Precedents, even in a court of justice, can have but little weight, except where the law is doubtful, and should have little in a deliberative body in any case on a constitutional question—and none, where the power to which it has been attempted to trace it does not exist, as I have shown, I trust, to be the case in this instance.

But, while I deny that the clause relating to the territory and other property of the United States, confers any governmental, or that Congress possesses absolute, power over the territories, I by no means deny that it has any power over them. Such a denial would be idle on any occasion, but much more so on this, when we are engaged in constituting a territorial government, without an objection being whispered from any quarter against our right to do so. If there be any Senator of that opinion, he ought at once to rise and move to lay the bill on the table, or to dispose of it in some other way, so as to prevent the waste of time on a subject upon which we have no right to act. Assuming, then, that we possess the power, the only questions that remain are—whence is it derived? and, what is its extent?

As to its origin, I concur in the opinion expressed by Chief Justice Marshall, in one of the cases read by the Senator from New York, that it is derived from the right of acquiring territory; and I am the more thoroughly confirmed in it from the fact that I entertained the opinion long before I knew it to be his. As to the right of acquiring territory, I agree with the Senator from New York, that it is embraced, without going further, both in the war and treaty powers. Admitting, then—what has never been denied, and what it would be idle to deny in a discussion which relates to territories acquired both by war and treaties—that the United States have the right to acquire territories, it would seem to follow, by necessary consequence, that they have the right to govern them. As they possess the entire right of soil, dominion, and sovereignty over them, they must necessarily carry with them the right to govern. But this Government, as the sole agent and representative of the United States—that is, the States of the Union in their federal character—must, as such, possess the sole right, if it exists at all. But, if there be any one disposed to take a different view of the origin of the power, I shall make no points with him—for whatever may be its origin, the conclusion would be the same, as I shall presently show.

But it would be a great error to conclude that Congress has the absolute power of governing the territories, because it has the sole or exclusive power. The reverse is the case. It is subject to many and important restrictions and conditions, of which some are expressed and others implied. Among the former may be classed all the general and absolute prohibitions of the constitution; that is, all those which prohibit the exercise of certain powers under any circumstance. In this class is included the prohibition of granting titles of nobility; passing *ex post facto* laws and bills of attainder; the suspension of the writ of *habeas corpus,* except in certain cases; making laws respecting the establishment of religion, or prohibiting its free exercise; and every other of like description, which conclusively shows that the power of Congress over the territories is not absolute. Indeed, it is a great error to suppose that either this or the State Governments possess, in any case, absolute power. Such power can belong only to the supreme ultimate power, called sovereignty, and that, in our system, resides in the people of the several States of the Union. With us, governments, both federal and State, are but agents, or, more properly, trustees, and, as such, possess, not absolute, but subordinate and limited powers; for all powers possessed by such governments must, from their nature, be trust powers, and subject to all the restrictions to which that class of powers are.

Among them, they are restricted to the nature and the objects of the trust; and hence no government under our system, federal or State, has the right to do any thing inconsistent with the nature of the powers intrusted to it, or the objects for which it was intrusted; or to express it in more usual language, for which it was delegated. To do either would be to pervert the power to purposes never intended, and would be a violation of the constitution—and that in the most dangerous way it could be made, because more easily done and less easily detected. But there is another and important class of restrictions which more directly relate to the subject under discussion. I refer to those imposed on the trustees by the nature and character of the party, who constituted the trustees and invested them with the trust powers to be exercised for its benefit. In this case it is the United States, that is, the several States of the Union. It was they who constituted the Government as their representative or trustee, and intrusted it with powers to be exercised for their common and joint benefit. To them in their united character the territories belong, as is expressly declared by the constitution. They are their joint and common owners, regarded as property or land; and in them, severally, reside the dominion and sovereignty over them. They are as much the territories of one State as another—of Virginia as of New York, of the Southern as the Northern States. They are the territories of all, because they are the territories of each; and not of each, because they are the territories of the whole. Add to this the perfect equality of dignity, as well as of rights, which appertain to them as members of a common federal Union, which all writers on the subject admit to be a fundamental and essential relation between States so united; and it must be manifest that Congress, in governing the territories, can give no preference or advantage to one State over another, or to one portion or section of the union over another, without depriving the State or section over which the preference is given, or from which the advantage is withheld, of their clear and unquestionable right, and subverting the very foundation on which the Union and Government rest. It has no more power to do so than to subvert the constitution itself. Indeed, the act itself would be subversion. It would destroy the relation of equality on the part of the Southern States, and sink them to mere dependants of the Northern, to the total destruction of the federal Union.

I have now shown, I trust, beyond controversy, that Congress has no power whatever to exclude the citizens of the Southern States from emigrating with their property into the territories of the United States, or to give an exclusive monopoly of them to the North. I now propose to go one step further, and show that neither the inhabitants of the territories nor their legislatures have any such right. A very few words will be sufficient for the purpose; for of all the positions ever taken, I hold that which claims the power for them to be the most absurd. If the territories belong to the United States—if the ownership, dominion and sovereignty over them be in the States of this Union, then neither the inhabitants of the territories, nor their legislatures, can exercise any power but what is subordinate to them: but if the contrary could be shown, which I hold to be impossible, it would be subject to all the restrictions, to which I have shown the power of Congress is; and for the same reason, whatever power they might hold, would, in the case supposed, be subordinate to the constitution, and controlled by the nature and character of our political institutions. But if the reverse be true—if the dominion and sovereignty over the territories be in their inhabitants, instead of the United States—they would indeed, in that case, have the exclusive and absolute power of governing them, and might exclude whom they pleased, or what they pleased. But, in that case, they would cease to be the territories of the United States the moment we acquired them and permitted them to be inhabited. The first half-dozen of squatters would become the sovereigns, with full dominion and sovereignty over them; and the conquered people of New Mexico and California would become the sovereigns of the country as soon as they became the territories of the United States, vested with the full right of excluding even their conquerors. There is no escaping from the alternative, but by resorting to the greatest of all absurdities, that of a divided sovereignty—a sovereignty, a part of which would reside in the United States, and a part in the inhabitants of the territory. How can sovereignty—the ultimate and supreme power of a State—be divided? The exercise of the powers of sovereignty may be divided, but how can there be two supreme powers?

We are next told that the laws of Mexico preclude slavery; and assuming that they will remain in force until repealed, it is contended that, until Congress passes an act for their repeal, the citizens of the South cannot emigrate with their property into the territory acquired from her. I admit the laws of Mexico prohibit, not slavery, but slavery in the form it exists with us. The Puros are as much slaves as our negroes, and are less intelligent and well treated. But, I deny that the laws of Mexico can have the effect attributed to them. As soon as the treaty between the two countries is ratified, the sovereignty and authority of Mexico in the territory acquired by it becomes extinct, and that of the United States is substituted in its place, carrying with it the constitution, with its overriding control, over all the laws and institutions of Mexico inconsistent with it. It is true, the municipal laws of the territory not inconsistent with the condition and the nature of our political system would, according to the writers on the laws of nations, remain, until changed, not as a matter of right, but merely of sufferance, and as between the inhabitants of territory, in order to avoid a state of anarchy, before they can be brought under our laws. This is the utmost limit to which sufferance goes. Under it the peon system would continue; but not to the exclusion of such of our citizens as may choose to emigrate with their slaves or other property, that may be excluded by the laws of Mexico. The humane provisions of the laws of nations go no further than to protect the inhabitants in their property and civil rights, under their former laws, until others can be substituted. To extend them further and give them the force of excluding emigrants from the United States, because their property or religion are such as are prohibited from being introduced by the laws of Mexico, would not only prevent a great majority of the people of the United States from emigrating into the acquired territory, but would give a higher authority to the extinct power of Mexico over the territory than to our actual authority over it. I say the great majority, for the laws of Mexico not only prohibit the introduction of slaves, but of many other descriptions of property, and also the Protestant religion, which Congress itself cannot prohibit. To such absurdity would the supposition lead.

I have now concluded the discussion, so far as it relates to the power; and have, I trust, established beyond controversy, that the territories are free and open to all of the citizens of the United States, and that there is no power, under any aspect the subject can be viewed in, by which the citizens of the South can be excluded from emigrating with their property into any of them. I have advanced no argument which I do not believe to be true, nor pushed any one beyond what truth would strictly warrant. But, if mistaken—if my arguments, instead of being sound and true, as I hold them beyond controversy to be, should turn out to be a mere mass of sophisms—and if in consequence, the barrier opposed by the want of power, should be surmounted, there is another still in the way, that cannot be. The mere possession of power is not, of itself, sufficient to justify its exercise. It must be, in addition, shown that, in the given case, it can be rightfully and justly exercised. Under our system, the first inquiry is: Does the constitution authorize the exercise of the power? If that be decided in the affirmative, the next is: Can it be rightfully and justly exercised under the circumstances? And it is not, until this, too, is decided in the affirmative, that the question of the expediency of exercising it, is presented for consideration.

Now, I put the question solemnly to the Senators from the North: Can you rightly and justly exclude the South from territories of the United States, and monopolize them for yourselves, even if, in your opinion, you should have the power? It is this question I wish to press on your attention with all due solemnity and decorum. The North and the South stand in the relation of partners in a common Union, with equal dignity and equal rights. We of the South have contributed our full share of funds, and shed our full share of blood for the acquisition of our territories. Can you, then, on any principle of equity and justice, deprive us of our full share in their benefit and advantage? Are you ready to affirm that a majority of the partners in a joint concern have the right to monopolize its benefits to the exclusion of the minority, even in cases where they have contributed their full share to the concern? But, to present the case more strongly and vividly, I shall descend from generals to particulars, and shall begin with the Oregon Territory. Our title to it is founded first, and in my opinion, mainly on our purchase of Louisiana; that was strengthened by the Florida treaty, which transferred to us the title also of Spain; and both by the discovery of the mouth of the Columbia river by Capt. Gray, and the exploration of the entire stream, from its source down to its mouth, by Lewis and Clark. The purchase of Louisiana cost fifteen millions of dollars; and we paid Spain five millions for the Florida treaty; making twenty in all. This large sum was advanced out of the common funds of the Union, the South, to say the least, contributing her full share. The discovery was made, it is true, by a citizen of Massachusetts; but he sailed under the flag and protection of the Union, and of course, whatever title was derived from his discovery, accrued to the benefit of the Union. The exploration of Lewis and Clark was at the expense of the Union. We are now about to form it into a territory; the expense of governing which, while it remains so, must be met out of the common fund, and towards which the South must contribute her full share. The expense will not be small. Already there is an Indian war to be put down, and a regiment for that purpose, and to protect the territory, has been ordered there. To what extent the expense may extend we know not, but it will, not improbably, involve millions before the territory becomes a State. I now ask, Is it right, is it just, after having contributed our full share for the acquisition of the territory, with the liability of contributing, in addition, our full share of the expense for its government, that we should be shut out of the territory, and be excluded from participating in its benefits? What would be thought of such conduct in the case of individuals? And can that be right and just in Government, which any right-minded man would cry out to be base and dishonest in private life? If it would be so pronounced in a partnership of thirty individuals, how can it be pronounced otherwise in one of thirty States?

The case of our recently acquired territory from Mexico is, if possible, more marked. The events connected with the acquisition are too well known to require a long narrative. It was won by arms, and a great sacrifice of men and money. The South, in the contest, performed her full share of military duty, and earned a full share of military honor; has poured out her full share of blood freely, and has and will bear a full share of the expense; has evinced a full share of skill and bravery, and if I were to say even more than her full share of both, I would not go beyond the truth; to be attributed, however, to no superiority in either respect, but to accidental circumstances, which gave both its officers and soldiers more favorable opportunities for their display. All have done their duty nobly, and high courage and gallantry are but common attributes of our people. Would it be right and just to close a territory thus won against the South, and leave it open exclusively to the North? Would it deserve the name of free soil, if one-half of the Union should be excluded and the other half should monopolize it, when it was won by the joint expense and joint efforts of all? Is the great law to be reversed—that which is won by all should be equally enjoyed by all? These are questions which address themselves more to the heart than the head. Feeble must be the intellect which does not see what is right and just, and bad must be the heart, unless unconsciously under the control of deep and abiding prejudice, which hesitates in pronouncing on which side they are to be found. Now, I put the question to the Senators from the North: What are you prepared to do? Are you prepared to prostrate the barriers of the constitution, and in open defiance of the dictates of equity and justice, to exclude the South from the territories and monopolize them for the North? If so, vote against the amendment offered by the Senator from Mississippi (Mr. Davis); and if that should fail, vote against striking out the 12th section. We shall then know what to expect. If not, place us on some ground where we can stand as equals in rights and dignity, and where we shall not be excluded from what has been acquired at the common expense, and won by common skill and gallantry. All we demand is to stand on the same level with yourselves, and to participate equally in what belongs to all. Less we cannot take.

I turn now to my friends of the South, and ask: What are you prepared to do? If neither the barriers of the constitution nor the high sense of right and justice should prove sufficient to protect you, are you prepared to sink down into a state of acknowledged inferiority; to be stripped of your dignity of equals among equals, and be deprived of your equality of rights in this federal partnership of States? If so, you are wofully degenerated from your sires, and will well deserve to change condition with your slaves; but if not, prepare to meet the issue. The time is at hand, if the question should not be speedily settled, when the South must rise up, and bravely defend herself, or sink down into base and acknowledged inferiority; and it is because I clearly perceive that this period is favorable for settling it, if it is ever to be settled, that I am in favor of pressing the question now to a decision—not because I have any desire whatever to embarrass either party in reference to the Presidential election. At no other period could the two great parties into which the country is divided be made to see and feel so clearly and intensely the embarrassment and danger caused by the question. Indeed, they must be blind not to perceive that there is a power in action that must burst asunder the ties that bind them together, strong as they are, unless it should be speedily settled. Now is the time, if ever. Cast your eyes to the North, and mark what is going on there; reflect on the tendency of events for the last three years in reference to this the most vital of all questions, and you must see that no time should be lost.

I am thus brought to the question, How can the question be settled? It can, in my opinion, be finally and permanently adjusted but one way, and that is on the high principles of justice and the constitution. Fear not to leave it to them. The less you do the better. If the North and South cannot stand together on their broad and solid foundation, there is none other on which they can. If the obligations of the constitution and justice be too feeble to command the respect of the North, how can the South expect that she will regard the far more feeble obligations of an act of Congress? Nor should the North fear that, by leaving it where justice and the constitution leave it, she would be excluded from her full share of the territories. In my opinion, if it be left there, climate, soil and other circumstances would fix the line between the slaveholding and non-slaveholding States in about 36° 30′. It may zigzag a little, to accommodate itself to circumstances— sometimes passing to the north, and at others passing to the south of it; but that would matter little, and would be more satisfactory to all, and tend less to alienation between the two great sections, than a rigid, straight, artificial line, prescribed by an act of Congress.

And here, let me say to Senators from the North—you make a great mistake in supposing that the portion which might fall to the south of whatever line might be drawn, if left to soil, and climate, and circumstances to determine, would be closed to the white labor of the North, because it could not mingle with slave labor without degradation. The fact is not so. There is no part of the world where agricultural, mechanical, and other descriptions of labor are more respected than in the South, with the exception of two descriptions of employment, that of menial and body servants. No Southern man—not the poorest or the lowest—will, under any circumstance, submit to perform either of them. He has too much pride for that, and I rejoice that he has. They are unsuited to the spirit of a freeman. But the man who would spurn them feels not the least degradation to work in the same field with his slave, or to be employed to work with them in the same field or in any mechanical operation; and, when so employed, they claim the right, and are admitted, in the country portion of the South, of sitting at the table of their employers. Can as much, on the score of equality, be said for the North? With us the two great divisions of society are not the rich and poor, but white and black; and all the former, the poor as well as the rich, belong to the upper class, and are respected and treated as equals, if honest and industrious, and hence have a position and pride of character of which neither poverty nor misfortune can deprive them.

But I go further, and hold that justice and the constitution are the easiest and safest guard on which the question can be settled, regarded in reference to party. It may be settled on that ground simply by non-action—by leaving the territories free and open to the emigration of all the world, so long as they continue so; and when they become States, to adopt whatever constitution they please, with the single restriction, to be republican, in order to * their admission into the Union. If a party cannot safely take this broad and solid position and successfully maintain it, what other can it take and maintain? If it cannot maintain itself by an appeal to the great principles of justice, the constitution, and self-government, to what other, sufficiently strong to uphold them in public opinion, can they appeal? I greatly mistake the character of the people of this Union, if such an appeal would not prove successful, if either party should have the magnanimity to step forward and boldly make it. It would, in my opinion, be received with shouts of approbation by the patriotic and intelligent in every quarter. There is a deep feeling pervading the country that the Union and our political institutions are in danger, which such a course would dispel.

Now is the time to take the step, and bring about a result so devoutly to be wished. I have believed, from the beginning, that this was the only question sufficiently potent to dissolve the Union, and subvert our system of government; and that the sooner it was met and settled, the safer and better for all. I have never doubted but that, if permitted to progress beyond a certain point, its settlement would become impossible, and am

*Word missing.—R.M.L.

under deep conviction that it is now rapidly approaching it—and that if it is ever to be averted, it must be done speedily. In uttering these opinions I look to the whole. If I speak earnestly, it is to save and protect all. As deep as is the stake of the South in the Union and our political institutions, it is not deeper than that of the North. We shall be as well prepared and as capable of meeting whatever may come, as you.

Now, let me say, Senators, if our Union and system of government are doomed to perish, and we to share the fate of so many great people who have gone before us, the historian, who, in some future day, may record the events ending in so calamitous a result, will devote his first chapter to the ordinance of 1787, lauded as it and its authors have been, as the first of that series which led to it. His next chapter will be devoted to the Missouri compromise, and the next to the present agitation. Whether there will be another beyond, I know not. It will depend on what we may do.

If he should possess a philosophical turn of mind, and be disposed to look to more remote and recondite causes, he will trace it to a proposition which originated in a hypothetical truism, but which, as now expressed and now understood, is the most false and dangerous of all political errors. The proposition to which I allude, has become an axiom in the minds of a vast majority on both sides of the Atlantic, and is repeated daily from tongue to tongue, as an established and incontrovertible truth; it is, that "all men are born free and equal." I am not afraid to attack error, however deeply it may be intrenched, or however widely extended, whenever it becomes my duty to do so, as I believe it to be on this subject and occasion.

Taking the proposition literally (it is in that sense it is understood), there is not a word of truth in it. It begins with "all men are born," which is utterly untrue. Men are not born. Infants are born. They grow to be men. And concludes with asserting that they are born "free and equal," which is not less false. They are not born free. While infants they are incapable of freedom, being destitute alike of the capacity of thinking and acting, without which there can be no freedom. Besides, they are necessarily born subject to their parents, and remain so among all people, savage and civilized, until the development of their intellect and physical capacity enables them to take care of themselves. They grow to all the freedom of which the condition in which they were born permits, by growing to be men. Nor is it less false that they are born "equal." They are not so in any sense in which it can be regarded; and thus, as I have asserted, there is not a word of truth in the whole proposition, as expressed and generally understood.

If we trace it back, we shall find the proposition differently expressed in the Declaration of Independence. That asserts that "all men are created equal." The form of expression, though less dangerous, is not less erroneous. All men are not created. According to the Bible, only two, a man and a woman, ever were, and of these one was pronounced subordinate to the other. All others have come into the world by being born, and in no sense, as I have shown, either free or equal. But this form of expression being less striking and popular, has given way to the present, and under the authority of a document put forth on so great an occasion, and leading to such important consequences, has spread far and wide, and fixed itself deeply in the public mind. It was inserted in our Declaration of Independence without any necessity. It made no necessary part of our justification in separating from the parent country, and declaring ourselves independent. Breach of our chartered privileges, and lawless encroachment on our acknowledged and well-established rights by the parent country, were the real causes, and of themselves sufficient, without resorting to any other, to justify the step. Nor had it any weight in constructing the governments which were substituted in the place of the colonial. They were formed of the old materials and on practical and well-established principles, borrowed for the most part from our own experience and that of the country from which we sprang.

If the proposition be traced still further back, it will be found to have been adopted from certain writers on government who had attained much celebrity in the early settlement of these States, and with whose writings all the prominent actors in our revolution were familiar. Among these, Locke and Sydney were prominent. But they expressed it very differently. According to their expression, "all men in the state of nature were free and equal." From this the others were derived; and it was this to which I referred when I called it a hypothetical truism. To understand why, will require some explanation.

Man, for the purpose of reasoning, may be regarded in three different states: in a state of individuality; that is, living by himself apart from the rest of his species. In the social; that is, living in society, associated with others of his species. And in the political; that is, being under government. We may reason as to what would be his rights and duties in either, without taking into consideration whether he could exist in it or not. It is certain, that in the first, the very supposition that he lived apart and separated from all others, would make him free and equal. No one in such a state could have the right to command or control another. Every man would be his own master, and might do just as he pleased. But it is equally clear, that man cannot exist in such a state; that he is by nature social, and that society is necessary, not only to the proper development of all his faculties, moral and intellectual, but to the very existence of his race. Such being the case, the state is a purely hypothetical one; and when we say all men are free and equal in it, we announce a mere hypothetical truism; that is, a truism resting on a mere supposition that cannot exist, and of course one of little or no practical value.

But to call it a state of nature was a great misnomer, and has led to dangerous errors; for that cannot justly be called a state of nature which is so opposed to the constitution of man as to be inconsistent with the existence of his race and the development of the high faculties, mental and moral, with which he is endowed by his Creator.

Nor is the social state of itself his natural state; for society can no more exist without government, in one form or another, than man without society. It is the political, then, which includes the social, that is his natural state. It is the one for which his Creator formed him, into which he is impelled irresistibly, and in which only his race can exist and all its faculties be fully developed.

Such being the case, it follows that any, the worst form of government, is better than anarchy; and that individual liberty, or freedom, must be subordinate to whatever power may be necessary to protect society against anarchy within or destruction from without; for the safety and well-being of society is as paramount to individual liberty, as the safety and well-being of the race is to that of individuals; and in the same proportion, the power necessary for the safety of society is paramount to individual liberty. On the contrary, government has no right to control individual liberty beyond what is necessary to the safety and well-being of society. Such is the boundary which separates the power of government and the liberty of the citizen or subject in the political state, which, as I have shown, is the natural state of man—the only one in which his race can exist, and the one in which he is born, lives, and dies.

It follows from all this that the quantum of power on the part of the government, and of liberty on that of individuals, instead of being equal in all cases, must necessarily be very unequal among different people, according to their different conditions. For just in proportion as a people are ignorant, stupid, debased, corrupt, exposed to violence within and danger from without, the power necessary for government to possess, in order to preserve society against anarchy and destruction becomes greater and greater, and individual liberty less and less, until the lowest condition is reached, when absolute and despotic power becomes necessary on the part of the government, and individual liberty extinct. So, on the contrary, just as a people rise in the scale of intelligence, virtue, and patriotism, and the more perfectly they become acquainted with the nature of government, the ends for which it was ordered, and how it ought to be administered, and the less the tendency to violence and disorder within, and danger from abroad, the power necessary for government becomes less and less, and individual liberty greater and greater. Instead, then, of all men having the same right to liberty and equality, as is claimed by those who hold that they are all born free and equal, liberty is the noble and highest reward bestowed on mental and moral development, combined with favorable circumstances. Instead, then, of liberty and equality being born with man; instead of all men and all classes and descriptions being equally entitled to them, they are high prizes to be won, and are in their most perfect state, not only the highest reward that can be bestowed on our race, but the most difficult to be won—and when won, the most difficult to be preserved.

They have been made vastly more so by the dangerous error I have attempted to expose, that all men are born free and equal, as if those high qualities belonged to man without effort to acquire them, and to all equally alike, regardless of their intellectual and moral condition. The attempt to carry into practice this, the most dangerous of all political error, and to bestow on all, without regard to their fitness either to acquire or maintain liberty, that unbounded and individual liberty supposed to belong to man in the hypothetical and misnamed state of nature, has done more to retard the cause of liberty and civilization, and is doing more at present, than all other causes combined. While it is powerful to pull down governments, it is still more powerful to prevent their construction on proper principles. It is the leading cause among those which have placed Europe in its present anarchical condition, and which mainly stands in the way of reconstructing good governments in the place of those which have been overthrown, threatening thereby the quarter of the globe most advanced in progress and civilization with hopeless anarchy, to be followed by military despotism. Nor are we exempt from its disorganizing effects. We now begin to experience the danger of admitting so great an error to have a place in the declaration of our independence. For a long time it lay dormant; but in the process of time it began to germinate, and produce its poisonous fruits. It had strong hold on the mind of Mr. Jefferson, the author of that document, which caused him to take an utterly false view of the subordinate relation of the black to the white race in the South; and to hold, in consequence, that the former, though utterly unqualified to possess liberty, were as fully entitled to both liberty and equality as the latter; and that to deprive them of it was unjust and immoral. To this error, his proposition to exclude slavery from the territory northwest of the Ohio may be traced, and to that the ordinance of '87, and through it the deep and dangerous agitation which now threatens to ingulf, and will certainly ingulf, if not speedily settled, our political institutions, and involve the country in countless woes.

SPEECH ON THE ADMISSION OF CALIFORNIA—AND THE GENERAL STATE OF THE UNION

[March 4, 1850]

By 1850, the entire country had become virtually deadlocked over the question of slavery. On March 4, Calhoun, weakened by pneumonia, appeared in the Senate and asked that his remarks be read for him by his friend and colleague, Mr. Mason of Virginia. In a last desperate effort to avoid the necessity of choosing between the abolition of slavery and secession, Calhoun raised the question of how the Union had come to this critical juncture. The general discontent of the South, argued Calhoun, was not a consequence of the natural course of time and events, but rather, of active interference on the part of the federal government. If there had been any doubt about the intentions of the North, it had been dispelled by Congress's willingness to entertain the question of the statehood for California, in spite of all the irregularities and inconsistencies of her petition. The exclusion of slavery from the territories had become the paramount issue in the eyes of Congress. All other considerations—variously principles of justice, the Constitution, or consistency—were to be sacrificed in the struggle to destroy slavery.

Here was Calhoun's final assessment of the nature of the Union and the requisites for its preservation. The cords of Union have been ripped asunder, he argues, and all power rests in the hands of the Northern majority. The South "has no compromise to offer but the Constitution, and no concession or surrender to make . . . The responsibility for saving the Union rests on the North, and not on the South. The South cannot save it by any act of hers, and the North may save it without any sacrifice whatever. . . . "

With that, Calhoun left the Senate chambers. This would be his last major address: On March 31, 1850, he died in Washington, D.C., leaving the nation his two posthumous works, A Disquisition on Government *and* A Discourse on the Constitution and Government of the United States.

As much indisposed as I have been, Mr. President and Senators, I have felt it to be my duty to express to you my sentiments upon the great question which has agitated the country and occupied your attention. And I am under peculiar obligations to the Senate for the very courteous manner in which they have afforded me an opportunity of being heard today.

I had hoped that it would have been in my power during the last week to have delivered my views in relation to this all-engrossing subject, but I was prevented from doing so by being attacked by a cold which is at this time so prevalent, and which has retarded the recovery of my strength.

Acting under the advice of my friends, and apprehending that it might not be in my power to deliver my sentiments before the termination of the debate, I have reduced to writing what I intended to say. And, without further remark, I will ask the favor of my friend, the Senator behind me to read it.

Mr. Mason: It affords me great pleasure to comply with the request of the honorable Senator, and to read his remarks.

The honorable gentleman then read Mr. Calhoun's remarks as follows:

I have, Senators, believed from the first that the agitation of the subject of slavery would, if not prevented by some timely and effective measure, end in disunion. Entertaining this opinion, I have, on all proper occasions, endeavored to call the attention of both the two great parties which divide the country to adopt some measure to prevent so great a disaster, but without success. The agitation has been permitted to proceed, with almost no attempt to resist it, until it has reached a point when it can no longer be disguised or denied that the Union is in danger. You have thus had forced upon you the greatest and the gravest question that can ever come under your consideration—How can the Union be preserved?

To give a satisfactory answer to this mighty question, it is indispensable to have an accurate and thorough knowledge of the nature and the character of the cause by which the Union is endangered. Without such knowledge it is impossible to pronounce, with any certainty, by what measure it can be saved; just as it would be impossible for a physician to pronounce, in the case of some dangerous disease, with any certainty, by what remedy the patient could be saved, without familiar knowledge of the nature and character of the cause of the disease. The first question, then, presented for consideration, in the investigation I propose to make, in order to obtain such knowledge, is—What is it that has endangered the Union?

To this question there can be but one answer—that the immediate cause is the almost universal discontent which pervades all the States composing the Southern section of the Union. This widely extended discontent is not of recent origin. It commenced with the agitation of the slavery question, and has been increasing ever since. The next question, going one step further back, is—What has caused this widely diffused and almost universal discontent?

It is a great mistake to suppose, as is by some, that it originated with demagogues, who excited the discontent with the intention of aiding their personal advancement, or with the disappointed ambition of certain politicians, who resorted to it as the means of retrieving their fortunes. On the contrary, all the great political influences of the section were arrayed against excitement, and exerted to the utmost to keep the people quiet. The great mass of the people of the South were divided, as in the other section, into Whigs and Democrats. The leaders and the presses of both parties in the South were very solicitous to prevent excitement and to preserve quiet; because it was seen that the effects of the former would necessarily tend to weaken, if not destroy, the political ties which united them with their respective parties in the other section. Those who know the strength of party ties will readily appreciate the immense force which this cause exerted against agitation, and in favor of preserving quiet. But, great as it was, it was not sufficiently so to prevent the widespread discontent which now pervades the section. No; some cause, far deeper and more powerful than the one supposed, must exist, to account for discontent so wide and deep. The question then recurs—What is the cause of this discontent? It will be found in the belief of the people of the Southern States, as prevalent as the discontent itself, that they cannot remain, as things now are, consistently with honor and safety, in the Union. The next question to be considered is—What has caused this belief?

One of the causes is, undoubtedly, to be traced to the long-continued agitation of the slave question on the part of the North, and the many aggressions which they have made on the rights of the South during the time. I will not enumerate them at present, as it will be done hereafter in its proper place.

There is another lying back of it, with which this is intimately connected, that may be regarded as the great and primary cause. This is to be found in the fact that the equilibrium between the two sections in the Government, as it stood when the constitution was ratified and the Government put in action, has been destroyed. At that time there was nearly a perfect equilibrium between the two, which afforded ample means to each to protect itself against the aggression of the other; but, as it now stands, one section has the exclusive power of controlling the Government, which leaves the other without any adequate means of protecting itself against its encroachment and oppression. To place this subject distinctly before you, I have, Senators, prepared a brief statistical statement, showing the relative weight of the two sections in the Government under the first census of 1790 and the last census of 1840.

According to the former, the population of the United States, including Vermont, Kentucky, and Tennessee, which then were in their incipient condition of becoming States, but were not actually admitted, amounted to 3,929,827. Of this number the Northern States had 1,977,899, and the Southern 1,952,072, making a difference of only 25,827 in favor of the former States. The number of States, including Vermont, Kentucky, and Tennessee, were sixteen; of which eight, including Vermont, belonged to the Northern section, and eight, including Kentucky and Tennessee, to the Southern—making an equal division of the States between the two sections under the first census. There was a small preponderance in the House of Representatives, and in the Electoral College, in favor of the Northern, owing to the fact that, according to the provisions of the constitution, in estimating federal numbers, five slaves count but three; but it was too small to affect sensibly the perfect equilibrium which, with that exception, existed at the time. Such was the equality of the two sections when the States composing them agreed to enter into a Federal Union. Since then the equilibrium between them has been greatly disturbed.

According to the last census the aggregate population of the United States amounted to 17,063,357, of which the Northern section contained 9,728,920, and the Southern 7,334,437, making a difference, in round numbers, of 2,400,000. The number of States had increased from sixteen to twenty-six, making an addition of ten States. In the mean time the position of Delaware had become doubtful as to which section she properly belonged. Considering her as neutral, the Northern States will have thirteen and the Southern States twelve, making a difference in the Senate of two Senators in favor of the former. According to the apportionment under the census of 1840, there were two hundred and twenty-three members of the House of Representatives, of which the Northern States had one hundred and thirty-five, and the Southern States (considering Delaware as neutral) eighty-seven, making a difference in favor of the former in the House of Representatives of forty-eight. The difference in the Senate of two members, added to this, gives to the North, in the electoral college, a majority of fifty. Since the census of 1840, four States have been added to the Union—Iowa, Wisconsin, Florida, and Texas. They leave the difference in the Senate as it stood when the census was taken; but add two to the side of the North in the House, making the present majority in the House in its favor fifty, and in the electoral college fifty-two.

The result of the whole is to give the Northern section a predominance in every part of the Government, and thereby concentrate in it the two elements which constitute the Federal Government—majority of States, and a majority of their population, estimated in federal numbers. Whatever section concentrates the two in itself possesses the control of the entire Government.

But we are just at the close of the sixth decade, and the commencement of the seventh. The census is to be taken this year, which must add greatly to the decided preponderance of the North in the House of Representatives and in the electoral college. The prospect is, also, that a great increase will be added to its present preponderance in the Senate, during the period of the decade, by the addition of new States. Two territories, Oregon and Minnesota, are already in progress, and strenuous efforts are making to bring in three additional States from the territory recently conquered from Mexico; which, if successful, will add three other States in a short time to the Northern section, making five States; and increasing the present number of its States from fifteen to twenty, and of its Senators from thirty to forty. On the contrary, there is not a single territory in progress in the Southern section, and no certainty that any additional State will be added to it during the decade. The prospect then is, that the two sections in the Senate, should the efforts now made to exclude the South from the newly acquired territories succeed, will stand, before the end of the decade, twenty Northern States to fourteen Southern (considering Delaware as neutral), and forty Northern Senators to twenty-eight Southern. This great increase of Senators, added to the great increase of members of the House of Representatives and the electoral college on the part of the North, which must take place under the next decade, will effectually and irretrievably destroy the equilibrium which existed when the Government commenced.

Had this destruction been the operation of time, without the interference of Government, the South would have had no reason to complain; but such was not the fact. It was caused by the legislation of this Government, which was appointed, as the common agent of all, and charged with the protection of the interests and security of all. The legislation by which it has been effected, may be classed under three heads. The first is, that series of acts by which the South has been excluded from the common territory belonging to all the States as members of the Federal Union—which have had the effect of extending vastly the portion allotted to the Northern section, and restricting within narrow limits the portion left the South; the next consists in adopting a system of revenue and disbursements, by which an undue proportion of the burden of taxation has been imposed upon the South, and an undue proportion of its proceeds appropriated to the North; and the last is a system of political measures, by which the original character of the Government has been radically changed. I propose to bestow upon each of these, in the order they stand, a few remarks, with the view of showing that it is owing to the action of this Government, that the equilibrium between the two sections has been destroyed, and the whole powers of the system centered in a sectional majority.

The first of the series of acts by which the South was deprived of its due share of the territories, originated with the confederacy, which preceded the existence of this Government. It is to be found in the provision of the ordinance of 1787. Its effect was to exclude the South entirely from that vast and fertile region which lies between the Ohio and the Mississippi rivers, now embracing five States and one territory. The next of the series is the Missouri compromise, which excluded the South from that large portion of Louisiana which lies north of 36° 30′, excepting what is included in the State of Missouri. The last of the series excluded the South from the whole of the Oregon Territory. All these, in the slang of the day, were what are called slave territories, and not free soil; that is, territories belonging to slaveholding powers and open to the emigration of masters with their slaves. By these several acts, the South was excluded from

1,238,025 square miles—an extent of country considerably exceeding the entire valley of the Mississippi. To the South was left the portion of the Territory of Louisiana lying south of 36° 30′, and the portion north of it included in the State of Missouri; with the portion lying south of 36° 30′, including the States of Louisiana and Arkansas; and the territory lying west of the latter, and south of 36° 30′, called the Indian country. These, with the Territory of Florida, now the State, makes in the whole 283,503 square miles. To this must be added the territory acquired with Texas. If the whole should be added to the Southern section, it would make an increase of 325,520, which would make the whole left to the South 609,023. But a large part of Texas is still in contest between the two sections, which leaves it uncertain what will be the real extent of the portion of territory that may be left to the South.

I have not included the territory recently acquired by the treaty with Mexico. The North is making the most strenuous efforts to appropriate the whole to herself, by excluding the South from every foot of it. If she should succeed, it will add to that from which the South has already been excluded 526,078 square miles, and would increase the whole which the North has appropriated to herself to 1,764,023, not including the portion that she may succeed in excluding us from in Texas. To sum up the whole, the United States, since they declared their independence, have acquired 2,373,046 square miles of territory, from which the North will have excluded the South, if she should succeed in monopolizing the newly acquired territories, about three-fourths of the whole, leaving to the South but about one-fourth.

Such is the first and great cause that has destroyed the equilibrium between the two sections in the Government.

The next is the system of revenue and disbursements which has been adopted by the Government. It is well known that the Government has derived its revenue mainly from duties on imports. I shall not undertake to show that such duties must necessarily fall mainly on the exporting States, and that the South, as the great exporting portion of the Union, has in reality paid vastly more than her due proportion of the revenue; because I deem it unnecessary, as the subject has on so many occasions been fully discussed. Nor shall I, for the same reason, undertake to show that a far greater portion of the revenue has been disbursed at the North than its due share; and that the joint effect of these causes has been to transfer a vast amount from South to North, which, under an equal system of revenue and disbursements, would not have been lost to her. If to this be added, that many of the duties were imposed, not for revenue, but for protection—that is, intended to put money, not in the treasury, but directly into the pocket of the manufacturers—some conception may be formed of the immense amount which, in the long course of sixty years, has been transferred from South to North. There are no data by which it can be estimated with any certainty; but it is safe to say, that it amounts to hundreds of millions of dollars. Under the most moderate estimate, it would be sufficient to add greatly to the wealth of the North, and thus greatly increase her population by attracting emigration from all quarters to that section.

This, combined with the great primary cause, amply explains why the North has acquired a preponderance in every department of the Government by its disproportionate increase of population and States. The former, as has been shown, has increased, in fifty years, 2,400,000 over that of the South. This increase of population, during so long a period, is satisfactorily accounted for by the number of emigrants, and the increase of their descendants, which have been attracted to the Northern section from Europe and the South, in consequence of the advantages derived from the causes assigned. If they had not existed—if the South had retained all the capital which has been extracted from her by the fiscal action of the Government; and, if it had not been excluded by the ordinance of 1787 and the Missouri compromise, from the region lying between the Ohio and the Mississippi rivers, and between the Mississippi and the Rocky Mountains north of 36° 30′, it scarcely admits of a doubt that it would have divided the emigration with the North, and by retaining her own people, would have at least equalled the North in population under the census of 1840, and probably under that about to be taken. She would also, if she had retained her equal rights in those territories, have maintained an equality in the number of States with the North, and have preserved the equilibrium between the two sections that existed at the commencement of the Government. The loss, then, of the equilibrium is to be attributed to the action of this Government.

But while these measures were destroying the equilibrium between the two sections, the action of the Government was leading to a radical change in its character, by concentrating all the power of the system in itself. The occasion will not permit me to trace the measures by which this great change has been consummated. If it did, it would not be difficult to show that the process commenced at an early period of the Government; and that it proceeded, almost without interruption, step by step, until it absorbed virtually its entire powers. But without going through the whole process to establish the fact, it may be done satisfactorily by a very short statement.

That the Government claims, and practically maintains the right to decide in the last resort, as to the extent of its powers, will scarcely be denied by any one conversant with the political history of the country. That it also claims the right to resort to force to maintain whatever power she claims, against all opposition, is equally certain. Indeed it is apparent, from what we daily hear, that this has become the prevailing and fixed opinion of a great majority of the community. Now, I ask, what limitation can possibly be placed upon the powers of a government claiming and exercising such rights? And, if none can be, how can the separate governments of the States maintain and protect the powers reserved to them by the constitution—or the people of the several States maintain those which are reserved to them, and among others, the sovereign powers by which they ordained and established, not only their separate State Constitutions and Governments, but also the Constitution and Government of the United States? But, if they have no constitutional means of maintaining them against the right claimed by this Government, it necessarily follows, that they hold them at

its pleasure and discretion, and that all the powers of the system are in
reality concentrated in it. It also follows, that the character of the Government has been changed, in consequence, from a federal republic, as it
originally came from the hands of its framers, and that it has been changed
into a great national consolidated democracy. It has indeed, at present, all
the characteristics of the latter, and not one of the former, although it still
retains its outward form.

The result of the whole of these causes combined is, that the North has
acquired a decided ascendency over every department of this Government,
and through it a control over all the powers of the system. A single section,
governed by the will of the numerical majority, has now, in fact, the control
of the Government and the entire powers of the system. What was once a
constitutional federal republic, is now converted, in reality, into one as
absolute as that of the Autocrat of Russia, and as despotic in its tendency
as any absolute government that ever existed.

As, then, the North has the absolute control over the Government, it is
manifest, that on all questions between it and the South, where there is a
diversity of interests, the interest of the latter will be sacrificed to the
former, however oppressive the effects may be, as the South possesses no
means by which it can resist through the action of the Government. But if
there was no question of vital importance to the South, in reference to
which there was a diversity of views between the two sections, this state of
things might be endured, without the hazard of destruction to the South.
But such is not the fact. There is a question of vital importance to the
Southern section, in reference to which the views and feelings of the two
sections are as opposite and hostile as they can possibly be.

I refer to the relation between the two races in the Southern section,
which constitutes a vital portion of her social organization. Every portion of
the North entertains views and feelings more or less hostile to it. Those
most opposed and hostile, regard it as a sin, and consider themselves
under the most sacred obligation to use every effort to destroy it. Indeed,
to the extent that they conceive they have power, they regard themselves as

implicated in the sin, and responsible for not suppressing it by the use of all and every means. Those less opposed and hostile, regard it as a crime—an offence against humanity, as they call it; and, although not so fanatical, feel themselves bound to use all efforts to effect the same object; while those who are least opposed and hostile, regard it as a blot and a stain on the character of what they call the Nation, and feel themselves accordingly bound to give it no countenance or support. On the contrary, the Southern section regards the relation as one which cannot be destroyed without subjecting the two races to the greatest calamity, and the section to poverty, desolation, and wretchedness; and accordingly they feel bound, by every consideration of interest and safety, to defend it.

This hostile feeling on the part of the North towards the social organization of the South long lay dormant, but it only required some cause to act on those who felt most intensely that they were responsible for its continuance, to call it into action. The increasing power of this Government, and of the control of the Northern section over all its departments, furnished the cause. It was this which made an impression on the minds of many, that there was little or no restraint to prevent the Government from doing whatever it might choose to do. This was sufficient of itself to put the most fanatical portion of the North in action, for the purpose of destroying the existing relation between the two races in the South.

The first organized movement towards it commenced in 1835. Then, for the first time, societies were organized, presses established, lecturers sent forth to excite the people of the North, and incendiary publications scattered over the whole South, through the mail. The South was thoroughly aroused. Meetings were held every where, and resolutions adopted, calling upon the North to apply a remedy to arrest the threatened evil, and pledging themselves to adopt measures for their own protection, if it was not arrested. At the meeting of Congress, petitions poured in from the North, calling upon Congress to abolish slavery in the District of Columbia, and to prohibit, what they called, the internal slave trade between the States— announcing at the same time, that their ultimate object was to abolish slavery, not only in the District, but in the States and throughout the Union. At this period, the number engaged in the agitation was small, and possessed little or no personal influence.

Neither party in Congress had, at that time, any sympathy with them or their cause. The members of each party presented their petitions with great reluctance. Nevertheless, small and contemptible as the party then was, both of the great parties of the North dreaded them. They felt, that though small, they were organized in reference to a subject which had a great and a commanding influence over the Northern mind. Each party, on that account, feared to oppose their petitions, lest the opposite party should take advantage of the one who might do so, by favoring their petitions. The effect was, that both united in insisting that the petitions should be received, and that Congress should take jurisdiction of the subject for which they prayed. To justify their course, they took the extraordinary ground, that Congress was bound to receive petitions on every subject, however objectionable they might be, and whether they had, or had not, jurisdiction over the subject. These views prevailed in the House of Representatives, and partially in the Senate; and thus the party succeeded in their first movements, in gaining what they proposed—a position in Congress, from which agitation could be extended over the whole Union. This was the commencement of the agitation, which has ever since continued, and which, as is now acknowledged, has endangered the Union itself.

As for myself, I believed, at that early period, if the party who got up the petitions should succeed in getting Congress to take jurisdiction, that agitation would follow, and that it would, in the end, if not arrested, destroy the Union. I then so expressed myself in debate, and called upon both parties to take grounds against assuming jurisdiction; but in vain. Had my voice been heeded, and had Congress refused to take jurisdiction, by the united votes of all parties, the agitation which followed would have been prevented, and the fanatical zeal that gives impulse to the agitation, and which has brought us to our present perilous condition, would have become extinguished, from the want of something to feed the flame. *That* was the time for the North to have shown her devotion to the Union; but, unfortunately, both of the great parties of that section were so intent on obtaining or retaining party ascendency, that all other considerations were overlooked or forgotten.

What has since followed are but natural consequences. With the success of their first movement, this small fanatical party began to acquire strength; and with that, to become an object of courtship to both the great parties. The necessary consequence was, a further increase of power, and a gradual tainting of the opinions of both of the other parties with their doctrines, until the infection has extended over both; and the great mass of the population of the North, who, whatever may be their opinion of the original abolition party, which still preserves its distinctive organization, hardly ever fail, when it comes to acting, to co-operate in carrying out their measures. With the increase of their influence, they extended the sphere of their action. In a short time after the commencement of their first movement, they had acquired sufficient influence to induce the legislatures of most of the Northern States to pass acts, which in effect abrogated the provision of the constitution that provides for the delivery up of fugitive slaves. Not long after, petitions followed to abolish slavery in forts, magazines, and dockyards, and all other places where Congress had exclusive power of legislation. This was followed by petitions and resolutions of legislatures of the Northern States, and popular meetings, to exclude the Southern States from all territories acquired, or to be acquired, and to prevent the admission of any State hereafter into the Union, which, by its constitution, does not prohibit slavery. And Congress is invoked to do all this, expressly with the view to the final abolition of slavery in the States. That has been avowed to be the ultimate object from the beginning of the agitation until the present time; and yet the great body of both parties of the North, with the full knowledge of the fact, although disavowing the abolitionists, have co-operated with them in almost all their measures.

Such is a brief history of the agitation, as far as it has yet advanced. Now, I ask, Senators, what is there to prevent its further progress, until it fulfils the ultimate end proposed, unless some decisive measure should be adopted to prevent it? Has any one of the causes, which has added to its increase from its original small and contemptible beginning until it has attained its present magnitude, diminished in force? Is the original cause of the movement—that slavery is a sin, and ought to be suppressed—weaker now than at the commencement? Or is the abolition party less numerous or influential, or have they less influence over, or control over the two great parties of the North in elections? Or has the South greater means of influencing or controlling the movements of this Government now, than it had when the agitation commenced? To all these questions but one answer can be given: no, no, no! The very reverse is true. Instead of being weaker, all the elements in favor of agitation are stronger now than they were in 1835, when it first commenced, while all the elements of influence on the part of the South are weaker. Unless something decisive is done, I again ask, what is to stop this agitation, before the great and final object at which it aims—the abolition of slavery in the States—is consummated? Is it, then, not certain, that if something decisive is not done to arrest it, the South will be forced to choose between abolition and secession? Indeed, as events are now moving, it will not require the South to secede, in order to dissolve the Union. Agitation will of itself effect it, of which its past history furnishes abundant proof—as I shall next proceed to show.

It is a great mistake to suppose that disunion can be effected by a single blow. The cords which bind these States together in one common Union, are far too numerous and powerful for that. Disunion must be the work of time. It is only through a long process, and successively, that the cords can be snapped, until the whole fabric falls asunder. Already the agitation of the slavery question has snapped some of the most important, and has greatly weakened all the others, as I shall proceed to show.

The cords that bind the States together are not only many, but various in character. Some are spiritual or ecclesiastical; some political; others social. Some appertain to the benefit conferred by the Union, and others to the feeling of duty and obligation.

The strongest of those of a spiritual and ecclesiastical nature, consisted in the unity of the great religious denominations, all of which originally embraced the whole Union. All these denominations, with the exception, perhaps, of the Catholics, were organized very much upon the principle of our political institutions. Beginning with smaller meetings, corresponding with the political divisions of the country, their organization terminated in one great central assemblage, corresponding very much with the character of Congress. At these meetings the principal clergymen and lay members of the respective denominations, from all parts of the Union, met to transact business relating to their common concerns. It was not confined to what appertained to the doctrines and discipline of the respective denominations, but extended to plans for disseminating the Bible, establishing missionaries, distributing tracts, and of establishing presses for the publication of tracts, newspapers, and periodicals, with a view of diffusing religious information, and for the support of the doctrines and creeds of the denomination. All this combined contributed greatly to strengthen the bonds of the Union. The strong ties which held each denomination together formed a strong cord to hold the whole Union together; but, powerful as they were, they have not been able to resist the explosive effect of slavery agitation.

The first of these cords which snapped, under its explosive force, was that of the powerful Methodist Episcopal Church. The numerous and strong ties which held it together are all broken, and its unity gone. They now form separate churches; and, instead of that feeling of attachment and devotion to the interests of the whole church which was formerly felt, they are now arrayed into two hostile bodies, engaged in litigation about what was formerly their common property.

The next cord that snapped was that of the Baptists, one of the largest and most respectable of the denominations. That of the Presbyterian is not entirely snapped, but some of its strands have given way. That of the Episcopal Church is the only one of the four great Protestant denominations which remains unbroken and entire.

The strongest cord, of a political character, consists of the many and strong ties that have held together the two great parties, which have, with some modifications, existed from the beginning of the Government. They both extended to every portion of the Union, and strongly contributed to hold all its parts together. But this powerful cord has fared no better than the spiritual. It resisted, for a long time, the explosive tendency of the agitation, but has finally snapped under its force—if not entirely, in a great measure. Nor is there one of the remaining cords which has not been greatly weakened. To this extent the Union has already been destroyed by agitation, in the only way it can be, by snapping asunder and weakening the cords which bind it together.

If the agitation goes on, the same force, acting with increased intensity, as has been shown, will finally snap every cord, when nothing will be left to hold the States together except force. But, surely, that can, with no propriety of language, be called a Union, when the only means by which the weaker is held connected with the stronger portion is *force*. It may, indeed, keep them connected; but the connection will partake much more of the character of subjugation, on the part of the weaker to the stronger, than the union of free, independent, and sovereign States, in one confederation, as they stood in the early stages of the Government, and which only is worthy of the sacred name of Union.

Having now, Senators, explained what it is that endangers the Union, and traced it to its cause, and explained its nature and character, the question again recurs—How can the Union be saved? To this I answer, there is but one way by which it can be, and that is, by adopting such measures as will satisfy the States belonging to the Southern section, that they can remain in the Union consistently with their honor and their safety. There is, again, only one way by which that can be effected, and that is— by removing the causes by which this belief has been produced. Do *that*, and discontent will cease, harmony and kind feelings between the sections be restored, and every apprehension of danger to the Union removed. The question, then, is—How can this be done? But, before I undertake to answer this question, I propose to show by what the Union cannot be saved.

It cannot, then, be saved by eulogies on the Union, however splendid or numerous. The cry of "Union, Union, the glorious Union!" can no more prevent disunion than the cry of "Health, health, glorious health!" on the part of the physician, can save a patient lying dangerously ill. So long as the Union, instead of being regarded as a protector, is regarded in the opposite character, by not much less than a majority of the States, it will be in vain to attempt to conciliate them by pronouncing eulogies on it.

Besides, this cry of Union comes commonly from those whom we cannot believe to be sincere. It usually comes from our assailants. But we cannot believe them to be sincere; for, if they loved the Union, they would necessarily be devoted to the constitution. It made the Union, and to destroy the constitution would be to destroy the Union. But the only reliable and certain evidence of devotion to the constitution is, to abstain, on the one hand, from violating it, and to repel, on the other, all attempts to violate it. It is only by faithfully performing these high duties that the constitution can be preserved, and with it the Union.

But how stands the profession of devotion to the Union by our assailants, when brought to this test? Have they abstained from violating the constitution? Let the many acts passed by the Northern States to set aside and annul the clause of the constitution providing for the delivery up of fugitive slaves answer. I cite this, not that it is the only instance (for there are many others), but because the violation in this particular is too notorious and palpable to be denied. Again, have they stood forth faithfully to repel violations of the constitution? Let their course in reference to the agitation of the slavery question, which was commenced and has been carried on for fifteen years, avowedly for the purpose of abolishing slavery in the States—an object all acknowledged to be unconstitutional—answer. Let them show a single instance, during this long period, in which they have denounced the agitators or their attempts to effect what is admitted to be unconstitutional, or a single measure which they have brought forward for that purpose. How can we, with all these facts before us, believe that they are sincere in their profession of devotion to the Union, or avoid believing their profession is but intended to increase the vigor of their assaults and to weaken the force of our resistance?

Nor can we regard the profession of devotion to the Union, on the part of those who are not our assailants, as sincere, when they pronounce eulogies upon the Union, evidently with the intent of charging us with disunion, without uttering one word of denunciation against our assailants. If friends of the Union, their course should be to unite with us in repelling these assaults, and denouncing the authors as enemies of the Union. Why they avoid this, and pursue the course they do, it is for them to explain.

Nor can the Union be saved by invoking the name of the illustrious Southerner whose mortal remains repose on the western bank of the Potomac. He was one of us—a slaveholder and a planter. We have studied his history, and find nothing in it to justify submission to wrong. On the contrary, his great fame rests on the solid foundation, that, while he was careful to avoid doing wrong to others, he was prompt and decided in repelling wrong. I trust that, in this respect, we profited by his example.

Nor can we find any thing in his history to deter us from seceding from the Union, should it fail to fulfil the objects for which it was instituted, by being permanently and hopelessly converted into the means of oppressing instead of protecting us. On the contrary, we find much in his example to encourage us, should we be forced to the extremity of deciding between submission and disunion.

There existed then, as well as now, a Union—that between the parent country and her then colonies. It was a union that had much to endear it to the people of the colonies. Under its protecting and superintending care, the colonies were planted and grew up and prospered, through a long course of years, until they became populous and wealthy. Its benefits were not limited to them. Their extensive agricultural and other productions, gave birth to a flourishing commerce, which richly rewarded the parent country for the trouble and expense of establishing and protecting them. Washington was born and grew up to manhood under that Union. He acquired his early distinction in its service, and there is every reason to believe that he was devotedly attached to it. But his devotion was a rational one. He was attached to it, not as an end, but as a means to an end. When it failed to fulfil its end, and, instead of affording protection, was converted into the means of oppressing the colonies, he did not hesitate to draw his sword, and head the great movement by which that union was forever severed, and the independence of these States established. This was the great and crowning glory of his life, which has spread his fame over the whole globe, and will transmit it to the latest posterity.

Nor can the plan proposed by the distinguished Senator from Kentucky, nor that of the administration, save the Union. I shall pass by, without remark, the plan proposed by the Senator, and proceed directly to the consideration of that of the administration. I, however, assure the distinguished and able Senator, that, in taking this course, no disrespect whatever is intended to him or his plan. I have adopted it, because so many Senators of distinguished abilities, who were present when he delivered his speech, and explained his plan, and who were fully capable to do justice to the side they support, have replied to him.

The plan of the administration cannot save the Union, because it can have no effect whatever, towards satisfying the States composing the southern section of the Union, that they can, consistently with safety and honor, remain in the Union. It is, in fact, but a modification of the Wilmot Proviso. It proposes to effect the same object—to exclude the South from all territory acquired by the Mexican treaty. It is well known that the South is united against the Wilmot Proviso, and has committed itself, by solemn resolutions, to resist, should it be adopted. Its opposition *is not to the name*, but that which it *proposes to effect*. That, the Southern States hold to be unconstitutional, unjust, inconsistent with their equality as members of the common Union, and calculated to destroy irretrievably the equilibrium between the two sections. These objections equally apply to what, for brevity, I will call the Executive Proviso. There is no difference between it and the Wilmot, except in the mode of effecting the object; and in that respect, I must say, that the latter is much the least objectionable. It goes to its object openly, boldly, and distinctly. It claims for Congress unlimited power over the territories, and proposes to assert it over the territories acquired from Mexico, by a positive prohibition of slavery. Not so the Executive Proviso. It takes an indirect course, and in order to elude the Wilmot Proviso, and thereby avoid encountering the united and determined resistance of the South, it denies, by implication, the authority of Congress to legislate for the territories, and claims the right as belonging exclusively to the inhabitants of the territories. But to effect the object of excluding the South, it takes care, in the mean time, to let in emigrants freely from the Northern States and all other quarters, except from the South, which it takes special care to exclude by holding up to them the danger of having their slaves liberated under the Mexican laws. The necessary consequence is to exclude the South from the territory, just as effectually as would the Wilmot Proviso. The only difference in this respect is, that what one proposes to effect directly and openly, the other proposes to effect indirectly and covertly.

But the Executive Proviso is more objectionable than the Wilmot, in another and more important particular. The latter, to effect its object, inflicts a dangerous wound upon the constitution, by depriving the Southern States, as joint partners and owners of the territories, of their rights in them; but it inflicts no greater wound than is absolutely necessary to effect its object. The former, on the contrary, while it inflicts the same wound, inflicts others equally great, and, if possible, greater, as I shall next proceed to explain.

In claiming the right for the inhabitants, instead of Congress, to legislate for the territories, the Executive Proviso, assumes that the sovereignty over the territories is vested in the former: or to express it in the language used in a resolution offered by one of the Senators from Texas (General Houston, now absent), they have "the same inherent right of self-government as the people in the States." The assumption is utterly unfounded, unconstitutional, without example, and contrary to the entire practice of the Government, from its commencement to the present time, as I shall proceed to show.

The recent movement of individuals in California to form a constitution and a State government, and to appoint Senators and Representatives, is the first fruit of this monstrous assumption. If the individuals who made this movement had gone into California as adventurers, and if, as such, they had conquered the territory and established their independence, the sovereignty of the country would have been vested in them, as a separate and independent community. In that case, they would have had the right to form a constitution, and to establish a government for themselves; and if, afterwards, they thought proper to apply to Congress for admission into the Union as a sovereign and independent State, all this would have been regular, and according to established principles. But such is not the case. It was the United States who conquered California and finally acquired it by treaty. The sovereignty, of course, is vested in them, and not in the individuals who have attempted to form a constitution and a State without their consent. All this is clear, beyond controversy, unless it can be shown that they have since lost or been divested of their sovereignty.

Nor is it less clear, that the power of legislating over the acquired territory is vested in Congress, and not, as is assumed, in the inhabitants of the territories. None can deny that the Government of the United States has the power to acquire territories, either by war or treaty; but if the power to acquire exists, it belongs to Congress to carry it into execution. On this point there can be no doubt, for the constitution expressly provides, that Congress shall have power "to make all laws which shall be necessary and proper to carry into execution the foregoing powers" (those vested in Congress), "and all other powers vested by this constitution in *the Government* of the United States, or in *any department* or *officer* thereof." It matters not, then, where the power is vested; for, if vested at all in the Government of the United States, or any of its departments, or officers, the power of carrying it into execution is clearly vested in Congress. But this important provision, while it gives to Congress the power of legislating over territories, imposes important restrictions on its exercise, by restricting Congress to passing laws necessary and proper for carrying the power into execution. The prohibition extends, not only to all laws not suitable or appropriate to the object of the power, but also to all that are unjust, unequal, or unfair—for all such laws would be unnecessary and improper, and, therefore, unconstitutional.

Having now established, beyond controversy, that the sovereignty over the territories is vested in the United States—that is, in the several States composing the Union—and that the power of legislating over them is expressly vested in Congress, it follows, that the individuals in California who have undertaken to form a constitution and a State, and to exercise the power of legislating without the consent of Congress, have usurped the sovereignty of the State and the authority of Congress, and have acted in open defiance of them both. In other words, what they have done, is revolutionary and rebellious in its character, anarchical in its tendency, and calculated to lead to the most dangerous consequences. Had they acted from premeditation and design, it would have been, in fact, actual rebellion; but such is not the case. The blame lies much less upon them than upon those who have induced them to take a course so unconstitutional and dangerous. They have been led into it by language held here, and the course pursued by the Executive branch of the Government.

I have not seen the answer of the Executive to the calls made by the two Houses of Congress for information as to the course which it took, or the part which it acted, in reference to what was done in California. I understand the answers have not yet been printed. But there is enough known to justify the assertion, that those who profess to represent and act under the authority of the Executive, have advised, aided, and encouraged the movement, which terminated in forming, what they call a constitution and a State. General Riley, who professed to act as civil Governor, called the convention, determined on the number and distribution of the delegates, appointed the time and place of its meeting, was present during the session, and gave its proceedings his approbation and sanction. If he acted without authority, he ought to have been tried, or at least reprimanded, and his course disavowed. Neither having been done, the presumption is, that his course has been approved. This, of itself, is sufficient to identify the Executive with his acts, and to make it responsible for them. I touch not the question, whether General Riley was appointed, or received the instructions under which he professed to act from the present Executive, or its predecessor. If from the former, it would implicate the preceding, as well as the present administration. If not, the responsibility rests exclusively on the present.

It is manifest from this statement, that the Executive Department has undertaken to perform acts preparatory to the meeting of the individuals to form their so-called constitution and government, which appertain exclusively to Congress. Indeed, they are identical, in many respects, with the provisions adopted by Congress, when it gives permission to a territory to form a constitution and government, in order to be admitted as a State into the Union.

Having now shown that the assumption upon which the Executive and the individuals in California acted throughout this whole affair is unfounded, unconstitutional, and dangerous, it remains to make a few remarks, in order to show that what has been done, is contrary to the entire practice of the Government, from commencement to the present time.

From its commencement until the time that Michigan was admitted, the practice was uniform. Territorial governments were first organized by Congress. The Government of the United States appointed the governors, judges, secretaries, marshals, and other officers; and the inhabitants of the territory were represented by legislative bodies, whose acts were subject to the revision of Congress. This state of things continued until the government of a territory applied to Congress to permit its inhabitants to form a constitution and government, preparatory to admission into the Union. The preliminary act to giving permission was, to ascertain whether the inhabitants were sufficiently numerous to authorize them to be formed into a State. This was done by taking a census. That being done, and the number proving sufficient, permission was granted. The act granting it fixed all the preliminaries—the time and place of holding the convention; the qualification of the voters; establishment of its boundaries, and all other measures necessary to be settled previous to admission. The act giving permission necessarily withdraws the sovereignty of the United States, and leaves the inhabitants of the incipient State as free to form their constitution and government as were the original States of the Union after they had declared their independence. At this stage, the inhabitants of the territory became, for the first time, a people, in legal and constitutional language. Prior to this, they were, by the old acts of Congress, called inhabitants, and not people. All this is perfectly consistent with the sovereignty of the United States, with the powers of Congress, and with the right of a people to self-government.

Michigan was the first case in which there was any departure from the uniform rule of acting. Hers was a very slight departure from established usage. The ordinance of 1787 secured to her the right of becoming a State when she should have 60,000 inhabitants. Owing to some neglect, Congress delayed taking the census. In the mean time her population increased, until it clearly exceeded more than twice the number which entitled her to admission. At this stage, she formed a constitution and government, without a census being taken by the United States, and Congress waived the omission, as there was no doubt she had more than a sufficient number to entitle her to admission. She was not admitted at the first session she applied, owing to some difficulty respecting the boundary between her and Ohio. The great irregularity, as to her admission, took place at the next session—but on a point which can have no possible connection with the ease of California.

The irregularities in all other cases that have since occurred, are of a similar nature. In all, there existed territorial governments established by Congress, with officers appointed by the United States. In all, the territorial government took the lead in calling conventions, and fixing the preliminaries preparatory to the formation of a constitution and admission into the Union. They all recognized the sovereignty of the United States, and the authority of Congress over the territories; and wherever there was any departure from established usage, it was done on the presumed consent of Congress, and not in defiance of its authority, or the sovereignty of the United States over the territories. In this respect California stands alone, without usage, or a single example to cover her case.

It belongs now, Senators, for you to decide what part you will act in reference to this unprecedented transaction. The Executive has laid the paper purporting to be the Constitution of California before you, and asks you to admit her into the Union as a State; and the question is, will you or will you not admit her? It is a grave question, and there rests upon you a heavy responsibility. Much, very much, will depend upon your decision. If you admit her, you indorse and give your sanction to all that has been done. Are you prepared to do so? Are you prepared to surrender your power of legislation for the territories—a power expressly vested in Congress by the constitution, as has been fully established? Can you, consistently with your oath to support the constitution, surrender the power? Are you prepared to admit that the inhabitants of the territories possess the sovereignty over them, and that any number, more or less, may claim any extent of territory they please; may form a constitution and government, and erect it into a State, without asking your permission? Are you prepared to surrender the sovereignty of the United States over whatever territory may be hereafter acquired to the first adventurers who may rush into it? Are you prepared to surrender virtually to the Executive Department all the powers which you have heretofore exercised over the territories? If not, how can you, consistently with your duty and your oaths to support the constitution, give your assent to the admission of California as a State, under a pretended constitution and government? Again, can you believe that the project of a constitution which they have adopted has the least validity? Can you believe that there is such a State in reality as the State of

California? No; there is no such State. It has no legal or constitutional existence. It has no validity, and can have none, without your sanction. How, then, can you admit it as a *State*, when, according to the provision of the constitution, your power is limited to admitting new *States*? To be admitted, it must be a State—and an existing State, independent of your sanction, before you can admit it. When you give your permission to the inhabitants of a territory to form a constitution and a State, the constitution and State they form, derive their authority from the people, and not from you. The State before it is admitted is actually a State, and does not become so by the *act of admission*, as would be the case with California, should you admit her contrary to the constitutional provisions and established usage heretofore.

The Senators on the other side of the Chamber must permit me to make a few remarks in this connection particularly applicable to them, with the exception of a few Senators from the South, sitting on the other side of the Chamber. When the Oregon question was before this body, not two years since, you took (if I mistake not) universally the ground, that Congress had the sole and absolute power of legislating for the territories. How, then, can you now, after the short interval which has elapsed, abandon the ground which you took, and thereby virtually admit that the power of legislating, instead of being in Congress, is in the inhabitants of the territories? How can you justify and sanction by your votes the acts of the Executive, which are in direct derogation of what you then contended for? But to approach still nearer to the present time, how can you, after condemning, little more than a year since, the grounds taken by the party which you defeated at the last election, wheel round and support by your votes the grounds which, as explained recently on this floor by the candidate of the party in the last election, are identical with those on which the Executive has acted in reference to California? What are we to understand by all this? Must we conclude that there is no sincerity, no faith in the acts and declarations of public men, and that all is mere acting or hollow profession? Or are we to conclude that the exclusion of the South from the territory acquired from Mexico is an object of so paramount a character in your estimation, that right, justice, constitution and consistency must all yield, when they stand in the way of our exclusion?

But, it may be asked, what is to be done with California, should she not be admitted? I answer, remand her back to the territorial condition, as was done in the case of Tennessee, in the early stage of the Government. Congress, in her case, had established a territorial government in the usual form, with a governor, judges, and other officers, appointed by the United States. She was entitled, under the deed of cession, to be admitted into the Union as a State as soon as she had sixty thousand inhabitants. The territorial government, believing it had that number, took a census, by which it appeared it exceeded it. She then formed a constitution, and applied for admission. Congress refused to admit her, on the ground that the census should be taken by the United States, and that Congress had not determined whether the territory should be formed into one or two States, as it was authorized to do under the cession. She returned quietly to her territorial condition. An act was passed to take a census by the United States, containing a provision that the territory should form one State. All afterwards was regularly conducted, and the territory admitted as a State in due form. The irregularities in the case of California are immeasurably greater, and offer much stronger reasons for pursuing the same course. But, it may be said, California may not submit. That is not probable; but if she should not, when she refuses it will then be time for us to decide what is to be done.

Having now shown what cannot save the Union, I return to the question with which I commenced, How can the Union be saved? There is but one way by which it can with any certainty; and that is, by a full and final settlement, on the principle of justice, of all the questions at issue between the two sections. The South asks for justice, simple justice, and less she ought not to take. She has no compromise to offer but the constitution, and no concession or surrender to make. She has already surrendered so much that she has little left to surrender. Such a settlement would go to the root of the evil, and remove all cause of discontent, by satisfying the South she could remain honorably and safely in the Union, and thereby restore the harmony and fraternal feelings between the sections which existed anterior to the Missouri agitation. Nothing else can, with any certainty, finally and for ever settle the questions at issue, terminate agitation, and save the Union.

But can this be done? Yes, easily; not by the weaker party, for it can of itself do nothing—not even protect itself—but by the stronger. The North has only to will it to accomplish it—to do justice by conceding to the South an equal right in the acquired territory, and to do her duty by causing the stipulations relative to fugitive slaves to be faithfully fulfilled—to cease the agitation of the slave question, and to provide for the insertion of a provision in the constitution, by an amendment, which will restore to the South, in substance, the power she possessed of protecting herself, before the equilibrium between the sections was destroyed by the action of this Government. There will be no difficulty in devising such a provision—one that will protect the South, and which, at the same time, will improve and strengthen the Government, instead of impairing and weakening it.

But will the North agree to do this? It is for her to answer the question. But, I will say, she cannot refuse, if she has half the love of the Union which she professes to have, or without justly exposing herself to the charge that her love of power and aggrandizement is far greater than her love of the Union. At all events, the responsibility of saving the Union rests on the North, and not on the South. The South cannot save it by any act of hers, and the North may save it without any sacrifice whatever, unless to do justice, and to perform her duties under the constitution, should be regarded by her as a sacrifice.

It is time, Senators, that there should be an open and manly avowal on all sides, as to what is intended to be done. If the question is not now settled, it is uncertain whether it ever can hereafter be; and we, as the representatives of the States of this Union, regarded as governments, should come to a distinct understanding as to our respective views, in order to ascertain whether the great questions at issue can be settled or not. If you, who represent the stronger portion, cannot agree to settle them on the broad principle of justice and duty, say so; and let the States we both represent agree to separate and part in peace. If you are unwilling we should part in peace, tell us so, and we shall know what to do, when you reduce the question to submission or resistance. If you remain silent, you will compel us to infer by your acts what you intend. In that case, California will become the test question. If you admit her, under all the difficulties that oppose her admission, you compel us to infer that you intend to exclude us from the whole of the acquired territories, with the intention of destroying, irretrievably, the equilibrium between the two sections. We would be blind not to perceive in that case, that your real objects are power and aggrandizement, and infatuated not to act accordingly.

I have now, Senators, done my duty in expressing my opinions fully, freely, and candidly, on this solemn occasion. In doing so, I have been governed by the motives which have governed me in all the stages of the agitation of the slavery question since its commencement. I have exerted myself, during the whole period, to arrest it, with the intention of saving the Union, if it could be done; and if it could not, to save the section where it has pleased Providence to cast my lot, and which I sincerely believe has justice and the constitution on its side. Having faithfully done my duty to the best of my ability, both to the Union and my section, throughout this agitation, I shall have the consolation, let what will come, that I am free from all responsibility.

INDEX

The typefaces used in this book are Bodoni and Bodoni Book, contemporary renderings derived from eighteenth-century faces cut by the Italian typefounder, designer, and printer Giambattista Bodoni.

This book is printed on paper that is acid-free and meets the requirements of the American National Standard for Permanence of Paper for Printed Library Materials, Z39.48-1992. ⊗

Editorial services by Custom Editorial Productions, Inc., Cincinnati, Ohio
Book design by Madelaine Cooke, Athens, Georgia
Composition by Shepard Poorman Communications Corporation, Indianapolis, Indiana
Printed and bound by Edwards Brothers, Inc., Ann Arbor, Michigan